Lecture Notes in Computer Science   8048

Commenced Publication in 1973
Founding and Former Series Editors:
Gerhard Goos, Juris Hartmanis, and Jan van Leeuwen

Richard Wilson   Edwin Hancock
Adrian Bors   William Smith (Eds.)

Computer Analysis of Images and Patterns

15th International Conference, CAIP 2013
York, UK, August 27-29, 2013
Proceedings, Part II

 Springer

Volume Editors

Richard Wilson
Edwin Hancock
Adrian Bors
William Smith
University of York
Department of Computer Science
Deramore Lane
York YO10 5GH, UK
E-mail:{wilson, erh, adrain, wsmith} @cs.york.ac.uk

ISSN 0302-9743   e-ISSN 1611-3349
ISBN 978-3-642-40245-6   e-ISBN 978-3-642-40246-3
DOI 10.1007/978-3-642-40246-3
Springer Heidelberg Dordrecht London New York

Library of Congress Control Number: 2013944666

CR Subject Classification (1998): I.5, I.4, I.2, H.2.8, I.3, H.3

LNCS Sublibrary: SL 6 – Image Processing, Computer Vision, Pattern Recognition, and Graphics

Typesetting: Camera-ready by author, data conversion by Scientific Publishing Services, Chennai, India

Printed on acid-free paper

Springer is part of Springer Science+Business Media (www.springer.com)

Preface

This volume contains the papers presented at the 15th International Conference on Computer Analysis of Images and Patterns (CAIP 2013) held in York during August 27–29, 2013.

CAIP was first held in 1985 in Berlin, and since then has been organized biennially in Wismar, Leipzig, Dresden, Budapest, Prague, Kiel, Ljubljana, Warsaw, Groningen, Versailles, Vienna, Münster, and Seville.

We received 243 full papers, from authors in 48 countries. Of these 142 were accepted, 39 oral presentation and 103 posters. There were three invited speakers, Rama Chellappa from the University of Maryland, Xiaoyi Jiang from the University of Münster, and Tim Weyrich from University College London.

We hope that participants benefitted scientifically from the meeting, but also got a flavor of York's rich history and saw something of the region too. To this end, we organized a reception at the York Castle Museum, and the conference dinner at the Yorkshire Sculpture Park. The latter gave participants the chance to view large-scale works by the Yorkshire artists Henry Moore and Barbara Hepworth.

We would like to thank a number of people for their help in organising this event. Firstly, we would to thank the IAPR for sponsorship. Furqan Aziz managed the production of the proceedings, and Bob French co-ordinated local arrangements.

June 2013

Edwin Hancock
William Smith
Richard Wilson
Adrian Bors

Organization

Program Committee

Ceyhun Burak Akgül	Vistek ISRA Vision, Turkey
Madjid Allili	Bishop's University, Canada
Nigel Allinson	University of Lincoln, UK
Apostolos Antonacopoulos	University of Salford, UK
Helder Araujo	University of Coimbra, Portugal
Nicole M. Artner	PRIP, Vienna University of Technology, Austria
Furqan Aziz	University of York, UK
Andrew Bagdanov	Media Integration and Communication Center University of Florence, Italy
Antonio Bandera	University of Malaga, Spain
Elisa H. Barney Smith	Boise State University, USA
Ardhendu Behera	University of Leeds, UK
Abdel Belaid	Université de Lorraine - LORIA, France
Gunilla Borgefors	Centre for Image Analysis, Swedish University of Agricultural Sciences, Sweden
Adrian Bors	University of York, UK
Luc Brun	GREYC, ENS, France
Lorenzo Bruzzone	University of Trento, Italy
Horst Bunke	University of Bern, Switzerland
Martin Burger	WWU Münster, Germany
Gustavo Carneiro	University of Adelaide, Australia
Andrea Cerri	University of Bologna, Italy
Kwok-Ping Chan	The University of Hong Kong, SAR China
Rama Chellappa	University of Maryland, USA
Sei-Wang Chen	National Taiwan Normal University, Taiwan
Dmitry Chetverikov	Hungarian Academy of Sciences, Hungary
John Collomosse	University of Surrey, UK
Bertrand Coüasnon	Irisa/Insa, France
Marco Cristani	University of Verona, Italy
Guillaume Damiand	LIRIS/Université de Lyon, France
Justin Dauwels	M.I.T., USA
Mohammad Dawood	University of Münster, Germany
Joachim Denzler	University Jena, Germany
Cecilia Di Ruberto	Università di Cagliari, Italy
Junyu Dong	Ocean University of China, China

Hazim Kemal Ekenel	InterACT Research, Universität Karlsruhe, Germany
Hakan Erdogan	Sabanci University, Turkey
Francisco Escolano	University of Alicante, Spain
M. Taner Eskil	ISIK University, Turkey
Alexandre Falcão	Institute of Computing - University of Campinas (Unicamp), Brazil
Chiung-Yao Fang	National Taiwan Normal University, Taiwan
Massimo Ferri	University of Bologna, Italy
Gernot Fink	TU Dortmund University, Germany
Ana Fred	Instituto Superior Tecnico, Portugal
Patrizio Frosini	University of Bologna, Italy
Laurent Fuchs	XLIM-SIC, UMR CNRS 7252, Université de Poitiers, France
Xinbo Gao	Xidian University, China
Dr. Anarta Ghosh	Research Fellow, Ireland
Georgy Gimelfarb	The University of Auckland, New Zealand
Daniela Giorgi	IMATI Genova, Italy
Dmitry Goldgof	University of South Florida, USA
Rocio Gonzalez-Diaz	University of Seville, Spain
Cosmin Grigorescu	European Patent Office, Brussels
Miguel A Gutiérrez-Naranjo	University of Seville, Italy
Michal Haindl	Institute of Information Theory and Automation, Czech Republic
Edwin Hancock	University of York, UK
Yll Haxhimusa	Vienna University of Technology, Austria
Vaclav Hlavac	Czech Technical University in Prague, Czech Republic
Zha Hongbin	Peking University, China
Yo-Ping Huang	National Taipei University of Technology, Taiwan
Yung-Fa Huang	Chaoyang University of Technology, Taiwan
Atsushi Imiya	IMIT Chiba University, Japan
Xiaoyi Jiang	Universität Münster, Germany
Maria Jose Jimenez	University of Seville, Spain
Martin Kampel	Vienna University of Technology, Computer Vision Lab, Austria
Nahum Kiryati	Tel Aviv University, Israel
Reinhard Klette	University of Auckland, New Zealand
Andreas Koschan	University of Tennessee, USA
Walter Kropatsch	Vienna University of Technology, Austria
Xuelong Li	University of London, UK
Pascal Lienhardt	SIC Laboratory, France
Guo-Shiang Lin	Da-Yeh University, Taiwan
Agnieszka Lisowska	University of Silesia, Poland

Josep Llados	Computer Vision Center, Universitat Autonoma de Barcelona, Spain
Jean-Luc Mari	Faculté des Sciences de Luminy, Université Aix-Marseille 2, LSIS Laboratory, UMR CNRS 6168, France
Eckart Michaelsen	FGAN-FOM, Germany
Majid Mirmehdi	University of Bristol, UK
Radu Nicolescu	The University of Auckland, New Zealand
Mark Nixon	University of Southampton, UK
Darian Onchis	University of Vienna, Austria
Ioannis Patras	Queen Mary College London, UK
Petra Perner	Institute of Computer Vision and Applied Computer Sciences, Germany
Nicolai Petkov	University of Groningen, The Netherlands
Ioannis Pitas	Aristotle University of Thessaloniki, Greece
Eugene Popov	Nizhegorodsky Architectural and Civil Engineering State University (NNACESU), Russia
Mario J. Pérez Jiménez	University of Seville, Spain
Petia Radeva	Computer Vision Center, Universitat Autònoma de Barcelona, Spain
Pedro Real	University of Seville, Spain
Bodo Rosenhahn	University of Hannover, Germany
Paul Rosin	Cardiff University, UK
Samuel Rota Bulo	Università Ca' Foscari, Italy
Jose Ruiz-Shulcloper	Advanced Technologies Applications Center (CENATAV) MINBAS, Cuba
Robert Sablatnig	Vienna University of Technology, Austria
Hideo Saito	Keio University, Japan
Albert Salah	Bogazici University, Turkey
Gabriella Sanniti Di Baja	Institute of Cybernetics "E. Caianiello", CNR, Italy
Sudeep Sarkar	University of South Florida, USA
Oliver Schreer	Fraunhofer Heinrich Hertz Institute, Germany
Francesc Serratosa	Universitat Rovira i Virgili, Spain
Luciano Silva	Universidade Federal do Parana, Brazil
William Smith	University of York, UK
Mingli Song	Zhejiang University, China
K.G. Subramanian	Universiti Sains Malaysia, Malaysia
Akihiro Sugimoto	National Institute of Informatics, Japan
Dacheng Tao	The Hong Kong Polytechnic University, SAR China
Bernie Tiddeman	University of Wales, Wales
Klaus Toennies	Otto-von-Guericke-Universität, Germany
Javier Toro	Desarrollo para la Ciencia y la Tecnologia, C.A., Venezuela

Table of Contents – Part II

Table of Contents – Part I

Classified-Distance Based Shape Descriptor for Application to Image Retrieval*

Jinhee Chun, Natsuda Kaothanthong**, and Takeshi Tokuyama

Graduate School of Information Sciences, Tohoku University, Japan
{jinhee,natsuda,tokuyama}@dais.is.tohoku.ac.jp

Abstract. We propose a method to improve the quality and the query time of shape-based image retrieval. We define a novel and an accurate shape descriptor named *Distance Interior Ratio (DIR)* that is invariant to rigid motion and scaling. The DIR of shapes can also be stored in an efficient search structure. Our experimental result shows a higher retrieval rate and efficient query time.

Keywords: 2D Shape Description, Image Retrieval, Shape Recognition.

1 Introduction

Image retrieval is the process of identifying images (objects) in a large database that are similar to a given image [14]. Shape is an important feature used for describing image content. Computing similarity of two shapes is a fundamental task in a shape-based image retrieval. Assume that image segmentation has been done and each object in the database is a simple polygon with n vertices. The aim is to find a set of objects whose shape is similar to a query.

We can consider a shape distance such as Hausdorff distance as the similarity measurement of two objects. In naive method, a linear scan of the database would require computing the shape distance for each database member against the given query object [11]. Therefore, the time complexity would be linear in the database size and also polynomial time for the shape distance computation ($O(n^2)$ for the Hausdorff distance). The linear search method is never used in a commercial retrieval system. Unfortunately, the search space of shapes based on the shape distance is not easy to organize to support fast query.

A shape descriptor is used to describe a shape in a compact fashion. The shape descriptor should be invariant to rigid motion, scaling, and noise. It is also desired that we can organize and store a set of the descriptors in an efficient search structure to avoid the linear retrieval time in the database size. On the other hand, the shape descriptor should accurately capture the important features of a shape and give a good classification of the shapes. Finding a good shape

---

* This work was supported by Grand-in-Aid for Scientific Reserch (C) 25330002, Grants-in-Aid for JSPS fellows 247851, and Scientific Research on Innovative Areas 24106007.
** Corresponding author.

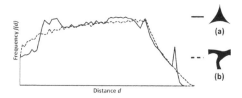

Fig. 1. The distance distributions of the boundary of (a) Triangle and (b) T

descriptor is a central issue in object retrieval. Moreover, it is a grand challenge to attain two trade-off requirements of efficiency and accuracy.

Two families of shape representations have been proposed: region-based and contour-based methods [13,14]. The first method considers the global information of the pixels within the shape, while the second one considers the information obtained from the shape contour. In this research, we focus on the contour-based shape descriptor that is invariant to rigid motion, scaling, and noise. Moreover, it can be integrated in an efficient search structure such as a Locality Sensitive Hashing (LSH) [2]. Examples of the established method include centroid distance [16], shape context [1], and distance distribution. Osada *et al.*[8] proposed a pairwise distance descriptor called *D2*. One problem of D2 is the existence of *homometric pairs* [12], which are pairs of objects with different shape but similar distance distribution. For illustration purpose, see Figure 1.

Consider the pairwise distances from a point p to points on the boundary of a convex shape (a) and a non-convex shape (b) as in Figure 2. Both shapes have the same distance distribution. This is because the pairwise distance distribution does not take into account whether or not the line segment crosses the boundary.

Ip *et al.*[6] describes a three dimensional object using three pairwise distance histograms of the classified line segments. The line segments are classified according to its position on the shape boundary: *interior*, *exterior*, and *mixed* as shown in Figure 3.

Inspired by the line segment classification, we propose a histogram-based shape descriptor called *Distance Interior Ratio* (DIR). The DIR is the distribution of the fraction of the line segments lying in the polygon and the length of the line segments on the contour points. Using the DIR descriptor, the two shapes in Figure 2 are different. The DIR of all line segments of shape (a) equals 1, while it is strictly less than 1 for some line segments in shape (b). Note that, in this research, we are only interested in the efficiency of the descriptor. In other words, no shape matching procedure is conducted on our proposed method.

2   Descriptor

2.1   Distance Features

Given a set $P = \{p_1, \ldots, p_n\}$ of n arbitrary points on the boundary of a simple polygon which is extracted from a binary image. Let $[pq]$ be the line segment connecting the two points $p, q \in P$.

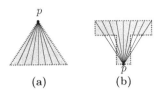

Fig. 2. The distance interior of shapes: (a) Triangle and (b) T

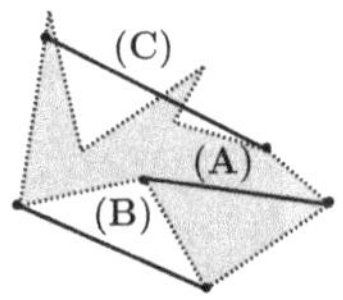

Fig. 3. Classified distances [6] (A) Interior, (B) Exterior, and (C) Mixed

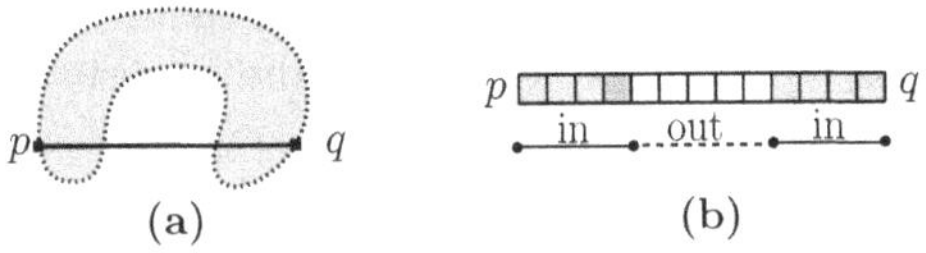

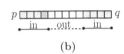

(a)   (b)

Fig. 4. (a) A line segment $[pq]$. (b) The digital line segment extracted from point p to q. "in" represents the portion of a line within the shape boundary while "out" represents the outside portion.

Let d_{pq} denote the Euclidean distance of $[pq]$. The Euclidean distance can be computed as $d_{pq} = \sqrt{(p_x - q_x)^2 + (p_y - q_y)^2}$. Let d_{pq}^{ir} be the DIR, i.e., the fraction of the line segment lying in the polygon and the length of the line segment. To calculate d_{pq}^{ir}, let $L(p,q) = \{l_1, \ldots, l_k\}$ be a digital line segment from a point p and q where l_i for $1 \leq i \leq k$ is a pixel on the $L(p,q)$ and k is $|L(p,q)|$. In this research, we use Bressenham's Algorithm [3] for approximating a digital line segment. An example of a digital line segment $L(p,q)$ is shown in Figure 4(b). As we only consider binary images, we assume that the intensity $f(l_i)$ of every pixel l_i is either 1 or 0. See Figure 4(b). Let d_{pq}^{in} be the number of pixels l_i with $f(l_i) = 1$. For the DIR, we have $d_{pq}^{ir} = d_{pq}^{in}/k$.

The shape information is transformed to a feature space F, where each line segment $[pq]$ is represented by the point (d_{pq}, d_{pq}^{ir}). More precisely, the x-axis represents the Euclidean distances between the vertices of P and the y-axis corresponds the DIR of P. The ranges of the x-axis and the y-axis are $[d_{min}, d_{max}]$ and $[d_{min}^{ir}, d_{max}^{ir}]$ respectively, where d_{min} is the minimum Euclidean distance between points in P and d_{max}, d_{min}^{ir}, and d_{max}^{ir} are defined analogously.

2.2   Structural Histogram

Given two positive integers c and r, the feature space F is equally divided into $c \times r$ blocks. The x-axis and the y-axis are divided into c and r blocks respectively. The interval of each block on the x-axis is $\lfloor (d_{max} - d_{min})/c \rfloor$ and the y-axis is $\lfloor (d_{max}^{ir} - d_{min}^{ir})/r \rfloor$.

Let (u, v) denote a block in F where u and v are the index on the x-axis and the y-axis respectively. The interval of each block is denoted by $[x_u, x_{u+1}], [y_v, y_{v+1}]$. Let $h(u, v)$ be the number of points that fall into $[x_u, x_{u+1}], [y_v, y_{v+1}]$. To avoid scaling problem, $h(u, v)$ is normalized by dividing the total number of points in the feature space. We have

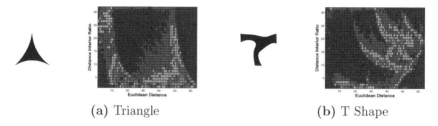

(a) Triangle   (b) T Shape

Fig. 5. The DIR of the homometric pair in Figure 1. The intensity of each pixel represent the number of points in the block. The higher the intensity represents the higher number of points.

$$h(u,v) = \frac{2}{n(n-1)} \sum_{i=0}^{n} \sum_{j=1}^{n-1} g(d_{ij}, d_{ij}^{ir}, x_u, x_{u+1}, y_v, y_{v+1}),$$

where,

$$g(d_{ij}, d_{ij}^{ir}, x_u, x_{u+1}, y_v, y_{v+1}) = \begin{cases} 1, \text{ if } d_{ij} \in [x_u, x_{u+1}] \text{ and } d_{ij}^{ir} \in [y_v, y_{v+1}], \\ 0, \text{ otherwise.} \end{cases}$$

The distribution of the classified distances of P, denoted by $H(\text{P})$, is a $c \times r$ histogram matrix of $h(u,v)$, where $0 \leq u \leq c-1$ and $0 \leq v \leq r-1$. The histogram of the homometric pair objects in Figure 1 are shown in Figure 5.

The similarity of the two descriptions is measured using L_1 norm. Given the two descriptors of shapes P and Q, let $D(P,Q)$ be the distance between the descriptors. It is computed as $D(P,Q) = \sum_{i=0}^{r-1} \sum_{j=0}^{c-1} |h_P(i,j) - h_Q(i,j)|$.

3   Shape Classification Using Convexity and Concavity

To avoid a linear scan of the database when using the shape distance, we find a set of candidate objects according to the shape property that shares among the members and the query, for instance convexity [9,18]. Then, we compute the shape distance for each candidate member against the query.

Two shape properties obtained from the DIR descriptor, the convexity and the concavity, are used for classifying the objects according to the simplicity of the shape boundary. The shape is simple if its boundary is convex or almost convex. On the other hand, it is complicated if its boundary have many concavity portions. Let C_i be the convexity value and let V_i be the concavity value of an object i.

Definition 1. *For a given boundary points P of a shape, its convexity value is the probability that for any $p, q \in \text{P}$ picked uniformly at random, all points from the line segment $L(p,q)$ also belong to P.*

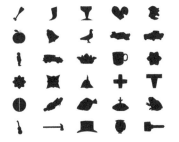

Fig. 6. Examples of convex shapes which are assigned to the same class

Fig. 7. Examples of concave shapes which are assigned to the same class

In other words, the convexity value is the fraction of the line segments that map into blocks in $r - 1$ row of $H(P)$. It is $C = \sum_{j=0}^{c-1} h(r - 1, j)$.

Definition 2. *For a given shape boundary points* P, *its concavity value is the probability that for any* $p, q \in$ P *picked uniformly at random, some points from the line segment* $L(p, q)$ *belong to* P *and some do not.*

The concavity of the shape is the fraction of exterior and mixed line segments. It is $V = \sum_{i=0}^{r-2} \sum_{j=0}^{c-1} h(i, j)$.

Given a positive even integer b, the objects in the database are classified into b classes. The mean of the convexity and the concavity values of the database are employed to distribute the objects into classes based on the standard deviation.

Let μ_C and μ_V be the mean convexity and mean concavity, respectively. We have $\mu_C = \frac{1}{N} \sum_{i=1}^{N} C_i$ and $\mu_V = \frac{1}{N} \sum_{i=1}^{N} V_i$, where N is the database size. Let σ_C and σ_V be the corresponding standard deviations, i.e., we have $\sigma_C = \sqrt{\frac{1}{N} \sum_{i=1}^{N} (C_i - \mu_C)^2}$ and $\sigma_V = \sqrt{\frac{1}{N} \sum_{i=1}^{N} (V_i - \mu_V)^2}$.

Consider the convexity value, let $B(C_i)$ be the class number of an object i with respect to the convexity value. $B(C_i)$ is the variation from the mean value. We have $B(C_i) = \lceil (C_i - \mu_C)/\sigma_C \rceil$. If $C_i < \mu_C$ then $B(C_i)$ is negative. We limit the number of classes using the following procedure. If $B(C_i) < -b/2$ then $B(C_i) = -b/2$. On the other hand, if $B(C_i) > b/2$ then $B(C_i) = b/2$. The class number of the concavity value, denoted by $B(V_i)$, is computed analogously by using $g_i = \lceil (V_i - \mu_V)/\sigma_V \rceil$ and applying the same condition.

Collections of objects from the MPEG7 CE-Shape-1 [7] dataset which are classified into the same class according our proposed convexity and concavity values are depicted in Figure 6 and 7 respectively. From the two figures we can clearly see the differences of the shape of objects from the two classes.

4 Computational Complexity

The DIR descriptor of any given P can be computed in $O(n^2)$ time, where n is the number of vertices on the shape contour. The time complexity for computing the distance between the two descriptors is $O(rc)$, where rc is the descriptor size.

Given a query object Q, the time complexity for retrieving the similar objects using a naive method is $O(Nrc)$ where N is the database size.

We can avoid a linear scan of the database by applying an efficient search structure. In this work, we apply the Locality Sensitive Hashing method proposed by Gionis et al.[2] which employs the L_1 norm. Using the LSH, we retrieve a set of candidate objects and compare the descriptor for each candidate against the query. In theory, the candidate size is $O(\sqrt{N})$. Therefore, the retrieval time complexity is sublinear in N which is $O(\sqrt{N}rc)$.

5   Experimental Result

The performance of DIR descriptor is evaluated using the MPEG7 CE-Shape-1 [7] and Kimia's 99 [10] datasets. For the distance interior ratio histogram matrix, we choose $c = 64$ and $r = 32$. The boundary pixels of each object are extracted and then 1000 points randomly selected. The experiments are conducted on a desktop machine with the Intel Core i7 3.4 GHz CPU and 16 GB of memory.

Recognition: We compare the recognition accuracy of DIR to the following established method: Shape Context (SC) [1], Inner Distance Shape Description (IDSC) [4], D2 Distance Distribution (D2) [8], and Structural Feature Histogram Matrix (SFHM) [17]. The recognition is done on the Kimia's 99 shape dataset consisting of 9 classes, and each containing 11 objects. For each shape, we check whether the 10 closest matches are in the same class as the query object.

The comparison of the recognition rates is summarized in Table 1. Our shape descriptor achieves a higher recognition rate than SC, even though DIR does not use any shape matching. On the other hand, the recognition rate of our descriptor is lower than the one of the IDSC descriptor which applies shape matching after obtaining a set of the best corresponding feature points.

Retrieval: The retrieval rate of our method is compared to the following methods: $D2$, SC, IDSC, and Contour Point Distribution Histogram (CPDH). We use the MPEG7 CE-Shape [7] dataset which consists of 1400 images from 70 classes and each class containing 20 shapes. The efficiency of the description is measured using Bull's Eye Percentage (BEP). Every image in the dataset is matched with every other image and among the top 40 most similar images from the same class are counted. So, at most 20 out of 40 candidates are correct hits.

To measure the efficiency of the description, we use a shape context distance (D_{sc}) [1] for SC and IDSC. The result in Table 2 shows that our proposed method achieves a retrieval rate of 73.72% which is higher than SC and IDSC achieved [4]: even if the size of DIR descriptor is much smaller.

Retrieving using Locality Sensitive Hash: We retrieve similar objects via a Locality Sensitive Hash (LSH). In this experiment, we store the DIR descriptor of each object from the MPEG7 CE-Shape [7] dataset in the LSH. The LSH framework being applied is the one proposed by Gionis et al.[2] and an implementation can be found in [5]. The parameters being used in this experiment are as follow: the number of hash tables L is 35, the key size k is 69, and the size of each bucket B is $\sqrt{N}$.

Table 1. Recognition Result

Top	D2	SFHM [17]	SC [4]	**DIR**	IDSC +DP[4]
1st	95	96	97	**97**	99
2nd	88	96	91	**98**	99
3rd	82	91	88	**90**	99
4th	77	89	85	**91**	98
5th	76	84	84	**81**	98
6th	70	84	77	**74**	97
7th	65	75	75	**79**	97
8th	55	77	66	**70**	98
9th	58	56	56	**61**	94
10th	35	55	37	**49**	79

Table 2. Comparison of the retrieval rate. For SC, IDSC, and CPDH, shape context distance (D_{sc}) [1] is used.

Descriptor	BEP
D2	50.18%
SC[4]	64.59%
IDSC[4]	68.83%
CPDH[15]	71.89%
DIR	**73.72%**

Given a query object Q, a set of objects that are in the same bucket as Q is retrieved from each table and stored in a set X. Let K be a candidate set of objects such that $K \subset X$ and K does not contain any duplicate objects. Every object in K is compared to Q and the 40 most similar objects in K are counted.

The retrieval rate is 71.87%. The average size of a candidate set is 573 which is very small as compared to the database size. The average retrieval time is 0.957 seconds. Comparing to the naive method which averagely takes 2.975 seconds, applying LSH is much faster.

Classification: In this experiment, we measure the classification efficiency of the proposed shape values, i.e., the convexity and the concavity values, as presented in Section 3 using the MPEG7 CE-Shape [7] dataset.

Given a query object Q, the class numbers $B(C_Q)$ and $B(V_Q)$ are computed. The objects whose class number equals $B(C_Q)$ and $B(V_Q)$ are retrieved. Precision and recall are applied to measure the efficiency of the proposed method. Precision is defined as the ratio of the number of retrieved relevant shapes to the total number of retrieved shapes. Recall is defined as the ratio of the number of retrieved relevant shapes to the number of relevant shapes in the whole dataset. The average precision is 4.54% and the average recall is 73.34%. The average number of retrieved relevant shapes is 364. By classifying the shapes according to the proposed values, we can ignore half of the irrelevant objects in the database.

6 Conclusion

We proposed a descriptor called *Distance Interior Ratio* (DIR), which is a distance-based descriptor. The proposed descriptor is easy to compute and requires less space than other methods, such as SC and IDSC. Moreover, the experimental result shows the efficiency of the proposed descriptor and the capability to be integrated in a Locality Sensitive Hashing (LSH). Moreover, the proposed descriptor achieves the highest retrieval rate even if shape matching is not applied. The convexity and the concavity values can be employed to classify the objects efficiently.

References

1. Belongie, S., Malik, J., Puzicha, J.: Shape Matching and Object Recognition Using Shape Contexts. IEEE Transactions on Pattern Analysis and Machine Intelligence 24(24), 509–522 (2002)
2. Gionis, A., Indyk, P., Motwani, R.: Similarity Search in High Dimensions via Hashing. In: Proceedings of the 25th International Conference on Very Large Data Basess, pp. 518–529 (1999)
3. Bresenham, J.E.: Algorithm for computer control of a digital plotter. IBM Systems Journal 4(1), 25–30 (1965)
4. Ling, H., Jacobs, D.W.: Shape Classification Using Inner-Distance. IEEE Trans. Pattern Analysis and Machine Intelligence 29(2), 286–299 (2007)
5. LSH package, http://ttic.uchicago.edu/gregory/download.html
6. Ip, C.Y., Lapadat, D., Sieger, L., Regil, W.C.: Using Shape Distributions to Compare Solid Models. In: Symposium on Solid Modeling and Applications, pp. 273–280 (2002)
7. Latecki, L.J., Lakamper, R., Eckhardt, U.: Shape Descriptors for Non-rigid Shapes with a Single Closed Controur. In: IEE Conf. on Computer Vision and Pattern Recognition, pp. 424–429 (2000)
8. Osada, R., Funkhouser, T., Chazelle, B., Dobkin, D.: Shape Distributions. ACM Transctions on Graphics 21, 807–832 (2002)
9. Rosin, P.L., Mumford, C.L.: A Symmetric Convexity Measure. Computer Vision and Image Understanding 103, 101–111 (2006)
10. Sebastian, T.B., Klein, P.N., Kimia, B.B.: Recognition of Shapes by Editing Their Shock Graphs. IEEE Trans. Pattern anal. Mach. Intell. 26(5), 550–571 (2004)
11. Shakhnarovich, G., Darrel, T., Indyk, P.: Nearest-Neighbor Methods in Learning and Vision Theory and Practise. MIT Press (March 2006)
12. Skiena, S.S., Smith, W.D., Lemke, P.: Reconstructing Sets From Interpoint Distances (extended abstract). In: The 6th Annual Symposium on Computational Geometry, pp. 332–339 (1990)
13. Mingqiang, Y., Idiyo, K.K., Joseph, R.: A Survey of Shape Feature Extraction Techniques. Pattern Recognition Techniques 24(2), 626–664 (2008)
14. Zhang, D., Lu, G.: Review of Shape Representation and Description Techniques. Pattern Recognition, 1–19 (2003)
15. Shu, X., Wu, X.J.: A Novel Contour Descriptor for 2D Shape Matching and Its Application to Image Retrieval. Image and Vision Computing 29, 286–294 (2011)
16. Zhang, D., Lu, G.: A Comparative Study of Fourier Descriptors for Shape Representation and Retrieval. In: The 5th Asian Conference on Computer Vision, pp. 646–651 (2002)
17. Zhang, J., Wenyin, L.: A Pixel-level Statistical Structural Descriptor for Shape Measure and Recognition. In: The 10th International Conference on Document Analysis and Recognition, pp. 386–390 (2009)
18. Zunic, J., Rosin, P.L.: A Convexity Measurement for Polygons. IEEE Trans. Pattern Anal. Mach. Intell. 26, 173–182 (2002)

A Shape Descriptor
Based on Trainable COSFIRE Filters
for the Recognition of Handwritten Digits

George Azzopardi and Nicolai Petkov

Johann Bernoulli Institute for Mathematics and Computer Science
University of Groningen, The Netherlands
{g.azzopardi,n.petkov}@rug.nl

Abstract. The recognition of handwritten digits is an application which has been used as a benchmark for comparing shape recognition methods. We train COSFIRE filters to be selective for different parts of handwritten digits. In analogy with the neurophysiological concept of population coding we use the responses of multiple COSFIRE filters as a shape descriptor of a handwritten digit. We demonstrate the effectiveness of the proposed approach on two data sets of handwritten digits: Western Arabic (MNIST) and Farsi for which we achieve high recognition rates of 99.52% and 99.33%, respectively. COSFIRE filters are conceptually simple, easy to implement and they are versatile trainable feature detectors. The shape descriptor that we propose is highly effective to the automatic recognition of handwritten digits.

Keywords: COSFIRE, feature, descriptor, trainable, recognition, shape.

1 Introduction

Handwritten digit recognition is a challenging task with various applications, such as bank cheque processing [23] and postal mail sorting [2]. Feature extraction plays an important role in the effectiveness of such systems. A number of methods have been proposed, including Zernike moments [3], direct matching [9], Fourier descriptors [12], geometric moment invariants [21], shape context [4], zoning [8] and biologically motivated features [10]. For a thorough overview of recent advances in the recognition of Western Arabic and Farsi handwritten digits we refer the reader to [16,22] and [20,5], respectively.

We use trainable COSFIRE feature detectors of the type introduced in [1]. They are automatically configured to be selective for parts of given training digit images. The automatic configuration process extracts information about the local geometric arrangement of contour segments. COSFIRE filters are inspired by the properties of a specific type of shape-selective neuron in area V4 of visual cortex, which exhibit selectivity for parts of (curved) contours or for combinations of line segments [18].

R. Wilson et al. (Eds.): CAIP 2013, Part II, LNCS 8048, pp. 9–16, 2013.

The response of a COSFIRE filter in a given point is computed as a function of the shifted responses of simpler (in this case orientation-selective) filters. Using shifted responses of simpler filters, such as Gabor filters that we use in this study, corresponds to combining their respective supports at different locations to obtain a more sophisticated filter with a bigger support. The specific function that we use here to combine the responses of Gabor filters is geoemetric mean, essentially multiplication, which has specific advantages regarding shape recognition and robustness to contrast variations. One consequence is that a COSFIRE filter produces a non-zero response only when all constituent parts of a pattern of interest are present.

The rest of the paper is organized as follows: in Section 2 we present the COS-FIRE filter and demonstrate how it can be configured and used to detect features of handwritten digits. We also show how the responses of multiple COSFIRE filters can be used to form a shape descriptor of a handwritten digit. In Section 3, we evaluate the effectiveness of our method on two data sets of handwritten digits: Western Arabic (MNIST) [15] and Farsi [13]. We provide a discussion in Section 4 and draw conclusions in Section 5.

2   Proposed Method

2.1   Overview

Fig. 1a illustrates a handwritten digit with an encircled feature. We use this local pattern (shown enlarged in Fig.1b) to automatically configure a COSFIRE filter that will respond (with certain tolerance) to the same and similar patterns.

Fig. 1. (a) The circle indicates a feature that is selected from a given training digit image. (b) Enlargement of the selected feature. The ellipses represent the dominant orientations around the specified point of interest that is marked by a '+' marker.

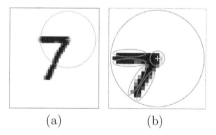

(a)   (b)

The four ellipses shown in Fig.1b illustrate the dominant orientations of edges in the surroundings of the point of interest. We use 2D Gabor filters to detect these orientations. The small central circle represents the overlapping supports of a group of such Gabor filters. The response of a COSFIRE filter is computed by combining the responses of the concerned Gabor filters by geometric mean.

The preferred orientations of these Gabor filters and the locations at which we take their responses are determined by a configuration process which automatically analyses the specified pattern. Taking the responses of Gabor filters at different locations around a point can be implemented by shifting the responses of these Gabor filters by different vectors before using them for the pixel-wise evaluation of a (geometric mean) function that gives the COSFIRE filter output.

In the following, we explain the automatic configuration process of a COSFIRE filter that determines which responses of which Gabor filters in which locations need to be multiplied in order to obtain the output of the filter. Subsequently, we introduce a feature vector as a shape descriptor of a handwritten digit that is formed by the responses of multiple COSFIRE filters. Finally, we apply support vector machines (SVM) to such feature vectors to achieve handwritten digit recognition.

2.2   Detection of Dominant Orientations by 2D Gabor Filters

We use 2D antisymmetric Gabor filters to detect the edges of the pen strokes in the handwritten digit images. We denote by $g_{\lambda,\theta}(x,y)$ the half-wave rectified response of a Gabor filter of preferred wavelength λ and orientation θ to a given input image. Such a filter has a number of other parameters, including spatial aspect ratio, bandwidth and phase offset, which we set as proposed in [19].

We apply a bank of Gabor filters with one wavelength $\lambda = 2\sqrt{2}$ and 16 orientations ($\theta \in \{0, \frac{\pi}{16}, \ldots, \frac{15\pi}{8}\}$) on handwritten digit images of width 28 pixels.

We threshold the responses of Gabor filters at a given fraction $t_1 = 0.1$ of the maximum response of $g_{\lambda,\theta}(x,y)$ across all combinations of values (λ, θ) used and all positions (x, y) in the image. The threshold value $t_1 = 0.1$ is sufficient to suppress the undesirable responses of Gabor filters to background noise.

2.3   Detection of Digit Parts by COSFIRE Filters

We use COSFIRE filters of the type proposed in [1] to detect digit parts. The automatic configuration process of a COSFIRE filter results in a set of four-tuples: $S_f = \{(\lambda_i, \theta_i, \rho_i, \phi_i) \mid i = 1 \ldots n_f\}$ where n_f stands for the number of dominant contour parts in a given pattern f. Each tuple of four parameter values $(\lambda_i, \theta_i, \rho_i, \phi_i)$ characterizes the properties of a given orientation of a contour part that is present in the specified pattern of interest: the parameters (λ_i, θ_i) represent a Gabor filter that is selective for the concerned contour part and (ρ_i, ϕ_i) are the polar coordinates of the location where that contour part lies with respect to the center of the COSFIRE filter.

We compute the response of a COSFIRE filter as follows. For each tuple with index i we first apply the Gabor filter with parameters (λ_i, θ_i). Then, we blur the Gabor responses with a Gaussian function in order to allow for some tolerance in the position of the involved contour part. The standard deviation σ_i of such a blurring function grows linearly with the parameter ρ_i:

$$\sigma_i = \sigma_0 + \alpha\rho_i \tag{1}$$

where σ_0 and α are constant values. Finally, we shift the blurred Gabor responses with ρ_i pixels in the direction opposite to ϕ_i such that the responses of different Gabor filters meet at a point which we consider the center of the concerned COSFIRE filter. The output of a COSFIRE filter $r_{S_f}(x,y)$ is computed as the geometric mean of the blurred and shifted responses of the involved Gabor filters.

Rotation invariance is achieved by manipulating the set of parameter values in S_f, rather than by computing them from the responses to rotated versions of the original pattern. Using the set S_f that defines the concerned filter, we first form a new set $\Re_\psi(S_f) = \{(\lambda_i, \theta_i + \psi, \rho_i, \phi_i + \psi) \mid \forall\, (\lambda_i, \theta_i, \rho_i, \phi_i) \in S_f\}$. Then, we define the rotation-invariant response as $\widehat{r}_{S_f}(x, y) = \max_{\psi \in \Psi}(r_{\Re_\psi(S_f)}(x, y))$ for a given set Ψ of rotation increments.

2.4 Formation of a Shape Descriptor

We use the collective responses of multiple COSFIRE filters as a shape descriptor of a given handwritten digit. Such a description is inspired by the neurophysiological concept of population coding [18] where a given stimulus can be described by the pattern of neuronal activity that it invokes in a given cortical area. One can speculate that the response of a COSFIRE filter in a given point corresponds to the activity of a shape-selective V4 neuron. The responses of many different COSFIRE filters, possibly at different positions, to an input digit image would represent the collective activity of a group of shape-selective V4 neurons.

For a given training set of digit images, we first configure a number of COSFIRE filters for different parts of the handwritten digits. In the configuration step, we choose a random subset of training digit images from each digit class. We configure one COSFIRE filter for every selected digit with a local pattern that is randomly selected in the input image. For a randomly selected pattern to be valid and used for configuration it should result in the configuration of a filter that combines at least four Gabor filter responses, otherwise we choose a different location. Such a restriction is required in order to avoid the selection of small patterns which may consequently result in filters with low discriminative power. The configuration of the COSFIRE filters is determined by four values of ρ ($\rho \in \{0, 3, 7, 12\}$).

Every training digit is then described by a feature vector where each element corresponds to the maximum response of a COSFIRE filter across all locations in the input image. For instance, with k filters, a digit is described by a vector of k elements. A value of zero means that the corresponding filter is not activated for the presented digit image, while a non-zero response corresponds to the activation strength of the filter. We then use the resulting feature vectors of the training set to train an all-pairs multi-class (with majority vote) SVM classifier[1] with a linear kernel.

3 Experimental Results

In the following, we evaluate the effectiveness of the proposed approach on two data sets of handwritten digits: MNIST data set of Western Arabic digits[2] [15] that comprises 60000 training digits and 10000 test digits, and a data set of Farsi digits[3] [13] which includes 60000 training digits and 20000 test digits. The digits in the MNIST data set are given as grayscale images of size 28×28 pixels. The Farsi digits are given as binary images of varying sizes. We use bicubic interpolation to resize the images of the Farsi digits to a width of 28 pixels.

For each data set, we perform a number of experiments with different values of the threshold parameter t_1 ($t_1 \in \{0.05, 0.1, 0.15\}$). The values of the other two

---

[1] We use the SVM^{light} implementation: http://svmlight.joachims.org/

[2] The MNIST data set can be downloaded from http://yann.lecun.com/exdb/mnist

[3] The Farsi data set can be downloaded from http://www.modares.ac.ir/eng/kabir

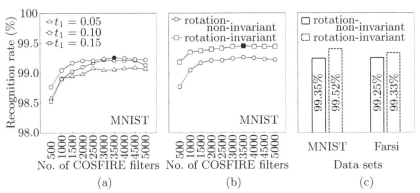

Fig. 2. Experimental results. (a) The three plots show the recognition rates for the MNIST data set achieved for different values of the threshold t_1 as a function of the number of COSFIRE filters used. Here, we use $\sigma_0 = 0.05$ and $\alpha = 0.80$. The filled-in circle represents the maximum recognition rate of 99.26% achieved for $t_1 = 0.1$ with 3500 filters. In these experiments the COSFIRE filters are used in rotation-non-invariant mode. (b) Performance comparison between a set of COSFIRE filters and $t_1 = 0.1$ that are first applied in rotation-non-invariant mode and then in a partially rotation-invariant mode with the best parameters $\sigma_0 = 0.07$ and $\alpha = 0.85$. Here, partial rotation-invariance is based on five values of the rotation tolerance angle ψ ($\psi \in \{-\frac{\pi}{4}, -\frac{\pi}{8}, 0, \frac{\pi}{8}, \frac{\pi}{4}\}$). The performance improves with partial rotation-invariant filters that achieve a recognition rate of 99.52% (shown as a filled-in square). (c) The best recognition rates achieved for the MNIST and Farsi data sets with 3500 rotation-non-invariant and partially rotation-invariant COSFIRE filters with parameters $\sigma_0 = 0.07$ and $\alpha = 0.85$.

parameters are kept fixed for all experiments: $\sigma_0 = 0.05$ and $\alpha = 0.80$. For every value of t_1 we run an experiment by configuring up to 5000 COSFIRE filters. We repeat such an experiment five times and report the average recognition rate. Repetition of experiments is required in order to compensate for the random selection of digits and the random selection of locations that are used to configure the concerned filters. In Fig. 2a we plot the recognition rates that we achieve for the MNIST data set for different values of the threshold t_1 and for different number of COSFIRE filters used. We achieve a maximum recognition rate of 99.26% with 3500 COSFIRE filters for $t_1 = 0.1$, $\sigma_0 = 0.05$ and $\alpha = 0.80$.

Then, we run another set of experiments with different values of the parameters σ_0 ($\sigma_0 \in \{0.01, 0.03, \ldots, 0.15\}$ and α ($\alpha \in \{0.70, 0.75, \ldots, 1\}$). For the new set of experiments we use the value of the threshold parameter $t_1 = 0.1$, the one which performed best in the previous experiments. We achieve a maximum recognition rate of 99.35% for $\sigma_0 = 0.07$ and $\alpha = 0.85$ with 3500 COSFIRE filters.

For this set of experiments we apply the COSFIRE filters in rotation-non-invariant mode. One can observe, however, that some of the digits given in the two data sets differ slightly in orientation. We consider this fact and repeat the five experiments for the threshold $t_1 = 0.1$, $\sigma_0 = 0.07$ and $\alpha = 0.85$ (that contributed to the best performance so far), but this time applying the same COSFIRE filters in a partially rotation-invariant mode with five values of the rotation tolerance angle ψ ($\psi \in \{-\frac{\pi}{4}, -\frac{\pi}{8}, 0, \frac{\pi}{8}, \frac{\pi}{4}\}$). The plots in Fig. 2b show that the performance that is achieved with the partially rotation-invariant filters is improved to a maximum recognition rate of 99.52% with 3500 filters. This means that the error rate is decreased by 26.15%.

We run similar experiments on the Farsi data set and achieve the best average recognition rate of 99.25% for $t_1 = 0.1$, $\sigma_0 = 0.07$ and $\alpha = 0.85$ with rotation-non-invariant COSFIRE filters and an average recognition rate of 99.33% with the same filters applied in a partially rotation-invariant mode. Fig. 2c illustrates these results next to the best results that we obtain for the MNIST data set.

4   Discussion

The high recognition rates that we achieve demonstrate the effectiveness of the proposed COSFIRE filters for the application at hand. The recognition rate of 99.52% that we achieve for the MNIST data set is comparable to the best existing approaches[4]. In particular, our method outperforms the shape context approach (99.37% in [4]), and three other approaches (94.20% in [17], 97.62% in [5] and 98.73% in [10]) that use biologically inspired feature detectors combined with a multi-layer perceptron (MLP) [17] and a linear SVM classifier [5,10]. The highest recognition rate achieved to date is 99.73% [7]. The approach used to achieve such a result extends the original training data set by elastically distorting the training images. For the Farsi data set, the recognition rate of 99.33% that we achieve is better than the best results ever reported in the literature. The COSFIRE filters outperform other biologically inspired feature detectors (96% in [5] and 99.1% in [10]) combined with a linear SVM classifier and also outperform the modified gradient technique which resulted in a recognition rate of 98.8% when combined with a multiple classifier system based on MLP classifiers [13].

Notable is the fact that we achieve the above results without performing any pre- and/or post-processing operations, neither do we use an extended training data set with elastic distortion. We apply the same methodology for both data sets, even though the corresponding numerals have different characteristics. This versatility is attributable to the fact that the COSFIRE filters are trainable, in that they can be automatically configured to any given patterns. This is in contrast to the best methods applied on the MNIST data set in which elaborate application-specific techniques have resulted from long-lasting research effort.

The proposed method contains an interesting aspect from a machine learning point of view. In traditional machine learning, the features to be used are fixed in advance and the machine learning aspect concerns the classification of observed feature vectors. If traditional machine learning is concerned with features at all, this is typically limited to the selection of predefined features or using them to derive 'new' features as (linear) combinations of the original ones. Examples are principle component analysis and generalized matrix learning vector quantization [6]. Traditional machine learning is typically not concerned with the question of how the features are defined. This aspect of the problem is, however,

---

[4] A list of results obtained by state-of-the-art approaches is maintained at http://yann.lecun.com/exdb/mnist/

crucial for the success: almost any machine learning method will perform well with good features. The interesting aspect we would like to point out is that in the proposed approach the appropriate features are learned in the filter configuration process when a digit part is presented. We configure COSFIRE filters to be selective for local contour patterns that are randomly selected (with few restrictions) from given training images. In our experiments, we do not analyse the discriminative ability of the configured filters. This might cause the generation of filters that are selective to correlated patterns or to patterns with low distinctiveness. A feature selection method can therefore be incorporated in a machine learning algorithm, such as relevance learning vector quantization [11] or a support feature machine [14], in order to identify the most relevant filters.

It is worth noting that we do not use information about the mutual arrangement of the features obtained with different COSFIRE filters - a high value of the response of a given COSFIRE filter signals the presence of a given feature, but does not specify where this feature is in the image.

5 Conclusion

We demonstrated that the versatile COSFIRE filters are very effective feature detectors of handwritten digits. We achieved recognition rates of 99.52% and 99.33% for the MNIST and Farsi data sets, respectively. These results outperform other techniques that are based on biologically inspired features.

The proposed approach of combining the responses of a collection of COSFIRE filters to form a shape descriptor can be thought of as a general framework for many pattern recognition and machine vision problems.

References

1. Azzopardi, G., Petkov, N.: Trainable COSFIRE Filters for Keypoint Detection and Pattern Recognition. IEEE Transactions on Pattern Analysis and Machine Intelligence 35(2), 490–503 (2013)
2. Basu, S., Das, N., Sarkar, R., Kundu, M., Nasipuri, M., Basu, D.K.: Recognition of Numeric Postal Codes from Multi-script Postal Address Blocks. In: Chaudhury, S., Mitra, S., Murthy, C.A., Sastry, P.S., Pal, S.K. (eds.) PReMI 2009. LNCS, vol. 5909, pp. 381–386. Springer, Heidelberg (2009)
3. Belkasim, S.O., Shridhar, M., Ahmadi, M.: Shape recognition using Zernike moment invariants. In: Chen, R.R. (ed.) Conference Record. Twenty-Third Asilomar Conference on Signals, Systems ands Computers (IEEE Cat. No.89-CH2836-5), vol. 1, pp. 167–171. IEEE, Naval Postgraduate Sch., San Jose State Univ. Conference Record. Twenty-Third Asilomar Conference on Signals, Systems ands Computers (IEEE Cat. No.89-CH2836-5), Pacific Grove, CA, USA, October 30–November 1 (1989)
4. Belongie, S., Malik, J., Puzicha, J.: Shape matching and object recognition using shape contexts. IEEE Transactions on Pattern Analysis and Machine Intelligence 24(4), 509–522 (2002)
5. Borji, A., Hamidi, M., Mahmoudi, F.: Robust handwritten character recognition with features inspired by visual ventral stream. Neural Processing Letters 28(2), 97–111 (2008)

6. Bunte, K., Biehl, M., Jonkman, M.F., Petkov, N.: Learning effective color features for content based image retrieval in dermatology. Pattern Recognition 44(9), 1892–1902 (2011)
7. Ciresan, D.C., Meier, U., Gambardella, L.M., Schmidhuber, J.: Convolutional Neural Network Committees for Handwritten Character Classification. In: 11th International Conference on Document Analysis and Recognition, Beijing, China, pp. 1135–1139 (2011)
8. Freitas, C.O.A., Oliveira, L.S., Aires, S.B.K., Bortolozzi, F.: Metaclasses and zoning mechanism applied to handwriting recognition. Journal of Universal Computer Science 14(2), 211–223 (2008)
9. Gader, P., Forester, B., Ganzberger, M., Gillies, A., Mitchell, B., Whalen, M., Yocum, T.: Recognition of handwritten using template and model-matching. Pattern Recognition 24(5), 421–431 (1991)
10. Hamidi, M., Borji, A.: Invariance analysis of modified C2 features: case study-handwritten digit recognition. Machine Vision and Applications 21(6), 969–979 (2010)
11. Hammer, B., Villmann, T.: Generalized relevance learning vector quantization. Neural Networks 15(8-9), 1059–1068 (2002)
12. Kauppinen, H., Seppanen, T., Pietikainen, M.: An experimental comparison of autoregressive and fourier-based descriptors in 2D shape classification. IEEE Transactions on Pattern Analysis and Machine Intelligence 17(2), 201–207 (1995)
13. Khosravi, H., Kabir, E.: Introducing a very large dataset of handwritten Farsi digits and a study on their varieties. Pattern Recognition Letters 28(10), 1133–1141 (2007)
14. Klement, S., Martinetz, T.: The support feature machine for classifying with the least number of features. In: Diamantaras, K., Duch, W., Iliadis, L.S. (eds.) ICANN 2010, Part II. LNCS, vol. 6353, pp. 88–93. Springer, Heidelberg (2010)
15. LeCun, Y., Bottou, L., Bengio, Y., Haffner, P.: Gradient-based learning applied to document recognition. Proceedings of the IEEE 86(11), 2278–2324 (1998)
16. Liu, C.L., Nakashima, K., Sako, H., Fujisawa, H.: Handwritten digit recognition: benchmarking of state-of-the-art techniques. Pattern Recognition 36(10), 2271–2285 (2003)
17. Oberhoff, D., Kolesnik, M.: Unsupervised shape learning in a neuromorphic hierarchy. Pattern Recognition and Image Analysis, 314–322 (2008)
18. Pasupathy, A., Connor, C.E.: Population coding of shape in area v4. Nature Neuroscience 5, 1332–1338 (2002)
19. Petkov, N.: Biologically motivated computationally intensive approaches to image pattern-recognition. Future Generation Computer Systems 11, 451–465 (1995)
20. Soltanzadeh, H., Rahmati, M.: Recognition of Persian handwritten digits using image profiles of multiple orientations. Pattern Recognition Letters 25(14), 1569–1576 (2004)
21. Wang, D., Xie, W.: Invariant image recognition by a neural networks and modified moment invariants. In: Proceedings of the SPIE - The International Society for Optical Engineering, SPIE; China Opt. & Optoelectron, Manuf. Assoc.; Chinese Opt. Soc. Electronic Imaging and Multimedia Systems, Beijing, China, November 4-5, pp. 217–223 (1996)
22. Wang, X.W., Ding, X.Q., Liu, C.S.: Gabor filters-based feature extraction for character recognition. Pattern Recognition 38(3), 369–379 (2005)
23. Chuang, Z., Zhiqing, L., Bo, X., Jun, G.: The segmentation algorithm for handwritten numeral strings in bank-check recognition. Frontiers of Electrical and Electronic Engineering in China, 39–44 (2007)

Supporting Ancient Coin Classification by Image-Based Reverse Side Symbol Recognition

Hafeez Anwar, Sebastian Zambanini, and Martin Kampel

Computer Vision Lab., Vienna University of Technology, Vienna, Austria
{hafeez,zamba,kampel}@caa.tuwien.ac.at

Abstract. Coins and currency are studied in the field of Numismatics. Our aim in this article is to use the knowledge of Numismatics for the development of part of a framework for the visual classification of ancient coins. Symbols minted on the reverse side of these coins vary greatly in their shapes and visual structures. Due to this property of symbols, we propose to use them as a discriminative feature for the visual classification of ancient coins. We use dense sampling based bag of visual words (BoVWs) approach for our problem. Due to the fact that BoVWs lack the spatial information, we evaluate three types of schemes to incorporate spatial information. Other parameters of BoVWs such as the size of visual vocabulary, level of detail of the dense sampling grid and number of features per image to construct the visual vocabulary are also investigated.

Keywords: Bag of visual words (BoVWs), spatial tiling, visual vocabulary.

1 Introduction

This paper aims at the problem of visual classification of ancient coins. Our research is focused on the Roman Republican coins. The knowledge about these coins can be found in the expert sources of Numismatics [2] and are indexed by a standard reference book [1].We use the embossed symbols on the coins for classification. These symbols are usually found on the reverse side of ancient coins while the obverse side of coins depicts the portraits of emperors or gods. The description of an ancient coin type given by a reference book contains, amongst others, the information about the symbol on the reverse side and thus it provides a strong and natural feature to classify the coin. Reverse side symbols can be shared by different defined coin types [1], but their recognition provides a coarse classification in the first place which can be refined by exploiting other information sources like the coin legend [3].

A framework for the visual classification of ancient coins can efficiently support the manual classification. Classifying a newly discovered coin into one of the existing classes is a task that needs an expert level knowledge of Numismatics. Apart from expert knowledge, the correct classification of coins is time-consuming as well because one has to search through the standard books where

R. Wilson et al. (Eds.): CAIP 2013, Part II, LNCS 8048, pp. 17–25, 2013.

| Curule | She-wolf | Dolphin | Griffin | Two Bulls | Galloping Rider | Caduceus | Rider |

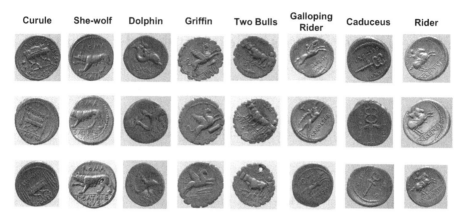

Fig. 1. Symbols used for classification

ancient coins are indexed [1]. Therefore a visual classification framework that incorporates the knowledge from Numismatics can prove superior to manual classification in terms of time. Such a framework can also be used for sorting large collections of ancient coins owned by museums and individuals as well as newly found hoards of coins.

In current research, we consider eight symbols for classification which are shown in Fig. 1 while their details are given in Table. 1. There are significant variations in these symbols due to several reasons. First reason is the lack of technology at the time when coins were produced. The dies used for minting symbols on the coins were not as much precise as the modern coins minting machines. Therefore various parts coins of the same type are depicted at different places. Usually ancient coins are discovered in ruins and fields where they are buried in soil. This preserving condition causes wear and tear leading to the absence of visually vital parts of the ancient coins. The variations also come from the fact that the symbols are possibly present on different coin types minted at different places and times. Consequently, other parts of the coin like the legend or the motive on the obverse side can be substantially different. Due to these reasons, there is significant similarity among the coins of different classes whereas coins of the same class have significant dissimilarities. These dissimilarities can be seen in Fig. 1 among the coins of the same class.

Related Work. The problem of modern coins classification involves fewer challenges than ancient coins classification due to several reasons. Firstly, their manufacturing process is much improved compared to that of ancient coins. Secondly, they do not suffer wear and tear like ancient coins. Therefore Zaharieva et al.[4] have shown that the techniques developed for modern coins classification [5–7] are not sufficient for ancient coins classification. As a first attempt, Kampel and Zaharieva [8] used SIFT [9] for ancient coins recognition. They used the sparse SIFT features matching technique where the images having the greatest number of matches are assigned to the same class. 90% accuracy is reported on a

Table 1. Number of visual examples and classes in dataset for each symbol

	Curule	She Wolf	Dolphin	Griffin	Two Bulls	Galloping Rider	Caduceus	Rider
Classes per Symbol	9	1	2	1	2	3	9	1
Images per Symbol	51	37	22	101	63	78	30	52

dataset of 390 images belonging to only 3 classes. Dense correspondence search is used by [10] to derive visual similarity among the coins. This visual similarity is then used in a coarse-to-fine search to retrieve the most similar image from the database. Accuracy rate of 82.8% is reported on a test set that contains 60 classes of Roman Republican coins. In the method of Arandjelovic [11], directional histograms are calculated at the positions of the SIFT keypoints leading to the incorporation of geometry to SIFT features. The method achieved 52.7% classification accuracy which is far superior to 2.5% achieved with BoVWs; however, the spatial information is not incorporated in these BoVWs.

We propose to use symbol recognition as a feature for ancient coins classification. Our proposed method integrates semantic knowledge from expert sources of Numismatics and therefore can be extended to a comprehensive classification framework. We take an approach that is very close to the human intuition as humans would rely on the symbols minted on the reverse side of coins for classification. This is due to the fact that symbols vary significantly in their visual structures and therefore can easily be distinguished from one another. On the other hand, the portraits of emperors on the obverse side show a higher similarity [1]. We propose to use the dense SIFT based BoVWs representation for the visual classification of ancient coins. We evaluate various schemes to incorporate spatial information to BoVWs representation. An evaluation of various parameters of BoVWs is also done. These parameters include the size of vocabulary and the number of features per image used to construct the visual vocabulary.

The remainder of the paper is organized as follows. In Section 2, we give an overview of the BoVWs approach. Section 3 discusses the schemes used to incorporate spatial information to BoVWs representation and Section 4 reports the results. Finally Section 5 concludes the paper and gives an overview of the future directions for the current research.

2 Bag of Visual Words (BoVWs)

The concept of BoVWs is drawn from text analysis. A text document can compactly be represented as a distribution of words. In a similar way, an image can be represented as a distribution of *'visual words'* [12]. Interest points or keypoints in an image contain important visual information and are used for

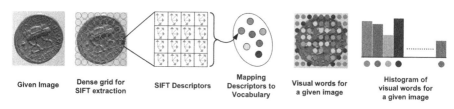

Fig. 2. Visual vocabulary generation and BoVWs image representation

image representation. We use Lowe's SIFT keypoints [9] for image representation. A dense sampling approach is used in which SIFT features are extracted throughout the image on a regular grid with constant pixel stride. Due to their high dimensionality, SIFT descriptors are not appropriate to be used as visual words. Therefore a vocabulary of visual words is built by imposing a quantization scheme on the feature space of the SIFT descriptors. The visual vocabulary is built by performing the following steps.

1. Dense features are extracted from an image set.
2. The extracted features are quantized to build a visual vocabulary of size M. The most common method used for quantization is k-means clustering where k is number of cluster centers equal to M.
3. To represent a novel image using the visual vocabulary, dense features are extracted from it and mapped to the visual vocabulary. The mapping is based on Euclidean distance between a word and a given descriptor.
4. Finally, a histogram of visual words is built to represent the novel image.

The procedure for BoVWs image representation is visually summarized in Fig. 2.

3   Incorporating Spatial Information to BoVWs Representation

An important issue that is worth investigation in our problem is the incorporation of spatial information to BoVWs image representation. BoVWs do not consider the spatial layout of the image. On one hand it is an advantage because this property of BoVWs makes them flexible to viewpoint and pose changes. On the other hand lack of spatial information can cause low performance at places where the spatial information is an important discriminating factor. Since we take a symbol based approach to ancient coins classification and these symbols have specific geometric structures, incorporating spatial information to BoVWs becomes necessary to get a higher performance rate. We investigate three schemes to add spatial information to BoVWs and report the results in Section 4. Here we will give a brief overview of the three types of schemes.

3.1   Rectangular Tiling

A given image is partitioned into 2×2 subregions. For each partition, a histogram of M visual words is generated resulting in 4 histograms of M words. These histograms are then concatenated into a single feature vector of size $M \times 4$. Fig. 3 shows the rectangular spatial tiling of 2×2.

3.2   Log-Polar Tiling

The log-polar binning scheme was used by Belongie et al.[13] for the first time to develop their shape matching descriptor. Zhang and Mayo [14] used log-polar binning to incorporate spatial information to BoVWs. In their reported results, they showed that their proposed scheme outperformed Spatial Pyramid Matching (SPM) of Lazebnik et al.[15] on three benchmark datasets. When log-polar tiling is applied on a given image, this image is partitioned into sectors of various scales and orientation. Such sectoring helps to capture the distribution of image features both in distance and orientation. A log-polar spatial scheme of r scales and θ orientations is imposed on the image resulting in $r \times \theta$ sectors. For each sector, a histogram of size M is generated and a total of $r \times \theta$ histograms are calculated for the whole image. These histograms are then concatenated in a single feature vector of size $M \times r \times \theta$. Fig. 3 shows the log-polar tiling. It can be seen that the sectors near the center of the image are smaller than those far from the center. This results in a spatial configuration where the sectors near the center of the image contain less visual words that those far from the center.

3.3   Circular Tiling

As coins are circular, we also propose to use the circular tiling. In this scheme as shown in Fig. 3, concentric circular binning is imposed on the BoVWs

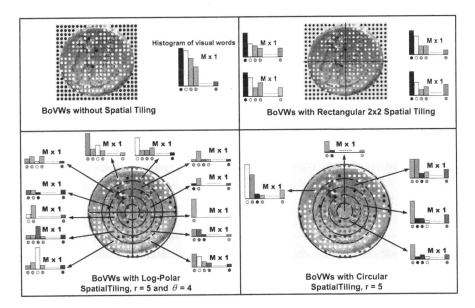

Fig. 3. BoVWs representation of an image with various spatial tilings and without spatial tiling

representation of an image. For a vocabulary size of M, a histogram of M visual words is generated for each circular bin. If the number of concentric circles is r, then r number of M sized histograms are calculated for the whole image. These histograms are then concatenated in a single feature vector of size $M \times r$. Here it is worth mentioning that the radii of the concentric circles are calculated based on the smaller dimension of a rectangular image. For instance, if the width of the image is smaller than the height, it is utilized to calculate the radii. Doing so keeps the outermost circle well inside the boundaries of the image.

4   Experiments and Results

We carried out experiments on the 434 images of eight different symbols minted on reverse sides of ancient coins. The image dataset is divided into two disjoint sets. The training set consists of 70% of the images while the rest 30% images form the validation set. Dense sampling based BoVWs representation is computationally expensive both in terms of memory and time. Therefore in our experiments, we evaluate the following parameters for the BoVWs representation of ancient coins and report results in Fig. 4.

1. **Size of pixels stride on dense grid:** This is an important parameter as we use a dense grid approach to collect features from each image at 4 different scales. The stride parameter controls the degree of detail of the grid. A smaller value of pixel stride results in a finer grid while a larger value makes a grid coarse. We evaluate a number of pixels strides for dense grid which are $\{5, 15, 25\}$. For instance, for the pixels stride of 15, we consider every 15th pixel as a feature and calculate its SIFT descriptor.

2. **Number of features per image to construct visual vocabulary:** As shown by [16], increasing the number of features per image increase the accuracy rate in dense sampling based BoVWs. We evaluate certain values of features per image in our experiments which are $\{7, 14, 28, 42, 56\}$. For each of the three settings of dense grid, these features are collected from each image of the training set to construct the visual vocabulary.

3. **Size of visual vocabulary:** The size of vocabulary is a major parameter as evaluated by [16, 17]. They report an increase in performance with the increase of vocabulary size however, larger sizes of vocabulary tend to overfit. We evaluate a number vocabulary sizes for each spatial scheme. The vocabulary sizes that we evaluate in our experiments are $\{10, 50, 100, 200, 400, 800, 1600\}$.

For classification, we use one-vs-all approach of SVM. An RBF kernel is used for which the best values of C and γ are determined using n-fold cross validation on the training set. Fig. 4 shows the performance of each spatial scheme on the BoVWs representation of test set for the predefined ranges of vocabulary sizes and number of features per image. Here the pixel stride for the dense grid is 5. In order to calculate the mean performance of spatial schemes for each vocabulary size, we take the row mean of each matrix of Fig. 4. Similarly, to calculate the mean performance of spatial schemes for each feature size, we take

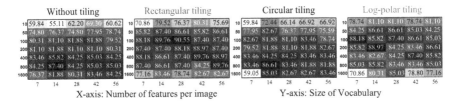

Fig. 4. Classification accuracy as a function of vocabulary size and features per image for pixel stride $= 5$

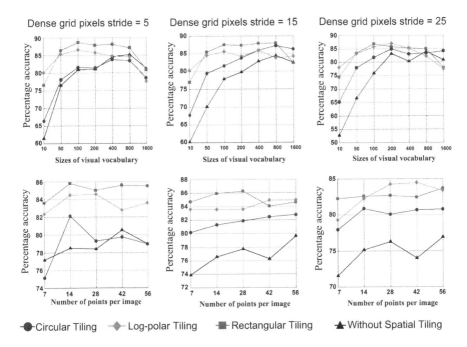

Fig. 5. Mean classification accuracies as function of vocabulary sizes and features per image for all the grids

the column mean of each matrix of Fig. 4. Fig. 5 shows these mean performances for all the predefined pixels strides from which it can be concluded that the rectangular tiling dominates the other two schemes. This is due to the fact that our test set lacks a challenging variation in rotations. Intuitively, circular tiling is a natural choice for challenging rotations. It can be observed from Fig. 5 that the performance of circular tiling is very low as compared to rectangular tiling on finer grid i.e. pixels stride of 5, however; the difference in performance of all the three spatial schemes decreases on coarser grids i.e. pixel strides of 15 and 25. Both the rectangular and log-polar binning are not robust to severe coins image rotations . For instance in case of log-polar binning, if a coin image is rotated then it is more likely that the visual words of one sector will fall into the adjacent sector resulting in change of histograms of both the sectors. Lastly, increasing the number of features per image for the construction of visual vocabulary tends to increase the performance in BoVWs image representation as shown in Fig. 5. Therefore we conclude from the results that for our problem, to add spatial information to BoVWs, circular tiling is the most suitable choice subject to the condition that a coarser grid is used for dense sampling. Challenging coin image rotations are likely to have influence on the current results which will be studied in future by generating severely rotated synthetic coin images.

5 Conclusion and Future Work

A dense sampling based BoVWs approach is proposed for the visual classification of ancient coins. The classification is done on eight symbols minted on the reverse side of the ancient coins. Since all the symbols have proper structure, three schemes are evaluated to incorporate the spatial information to BoVWs representations. Other parameters of BoVWs like size of visual vocabulary and number of features per image to construct vocabulary, are also evaluated. In future we plan to consider saliency to suppress the homogeneous patches on the reverse side of coins. Apart from that we plan to validate the proposed framework on more challenging symbols from our coins dataset in order to extend it to a large-scale system.

Acknowledgments. This research was supported by the Austrian Science Fund (FWF) under the grant TRP140-N23-2010 (ILAC) and the Vienna PhD School of Informatics (http://www.informatik.tuwien.ac.at/teaching/phdschool).

References

1. Crawford, M.H.: Roman Republican Coinage, vol. 2. Cambridge University Press (1974)
2. Grierson, P.: Numismatics. Oxford University Press (1975)
3. Kavelar, A., Zambanini, S., Kampel, M.: Word Detection Applied to Images of Ancient Roman Coins. In: VSMM, pp. 577–580 (2012)
4. Zaharieva, M., Kampel, M., Zambanini, S.: Image based recognition of ancient coins. In: Kropatsch, W.G., Kampel, M., Hanbury, A. (eds.) CAIP 2007. LNCS, vol. 4673, pp. 547–554. Springer, Heidelberg (2007)
5. Van Der Maaten, L., Boon, P.: COIN - O - MATIC: A fast system for reliable coin classification. In: MUSCLE CIS Coin Competition Workshop, pp. 7–18 (2006)
6. Nölle, M., Penz, H., Rubik, M., Mayer, K., Holländer, I., Granec, R.: Dagobert - A new Coin Recognition and Sorting System. In: DICTA, pp. 329–338 (2003)
7. Reinhold, H., Herbert, R., Konrad, M., Harald, P., Michael, R.: classification of coins using an eigenspace approach. Pattern Recognition Letters 26(1), 61–75 (2005)
8. Kampel, M., Zaharieva, M.: Recognizing ancient coins based on local features. In: Bebis, G., et al. (eds.) ISVC 2008, Part I. LNCS, vol. 5358, pp. 11–22. Springer, Heidelberg (2008)

9. Lowe, D.G.: Distinctive Image Features from Scale-Invariant Keypoints. Int. J. Comput. Vision 60, 91–110 (2004)

10. Zambanini, S., Kampel, M.: Coarse-to-Fine Correspondence Search for Classifying Ancient Coins. In: Park, J.-I., Kim, J. (eds.) ACCV Workshops 2012, Part II. LNCS, vol. 7729, pp. 25–36. Springer, Heidelberg (2013)

11. Arandjelović, O.: Automatic attribution of ancient Roman imperial coins. In: CVPR, pp. 1728–1734 (2010)

12. Sivic, J., Zisserman, A.: Video Google: A text retrieval approach to object matching in videos. In: ICCV, pp. 1470–1477 (2003)

13. Belongie, S., Malik, J., Puzicha, J.: Shape matching and object recognition using shape contexts. TPAMI 24, 509–522 (2001)

14. Zhang, E., Mayo, M.: Enhanced spatial pyramid matching using log-polar-based image subdivision and representation. In: DICTA, pp. 208–213 (2010)

15. Lazebnik, S., Schmid, C., Ponce, J.: Beyond bags of features: spatial pyramid matching for recognizing natural scene categories

16. Nowak, E., Jurie, F., Triggs, B.: Sampling strategies for bag-of-features image classification. In: Leonardis, A., Bischof, H., Pinz, A. (eds.) ECCV 2006. LNCS, vol. 3954, pp. 490–503. Springer, Heidelberg (2006)

17. Csurka, G., Dance, C.R., Fan, L., Willamowski, J., Bray, C.: Visual categorization with bags of keypoints. In: Workshop on Statistical Learning in Computer Vision, ECCV, pp. 1–22 (2004)

Eyewitness Face Sketch Recognition
Based on Two-Step Bias Modeling

Hossein Nejati, Li Zhang, and Terence Sim

National University of Singapore
nejati@nus.edu.sg

Abstract. Over 30 years of psychological studies on eyewitness testimonies procedures show severe flaws including ignoring human face perception biases that render these procedures unreliable. In addition, recent studies show that current automatic face sketch recognition methods are only tested on over simplified databases, and therefore cannot address the real cases. We here present a face sketch recognition method based on non-artistic sketches in which we firstly estimate and remove personal face perception biases from face sketches, and then recognize them based on a psychologically inspired matching technique. In addition, we use a general-specific modeling that only needs a few training samples for each individual for an accurate and robust performance. In our experiments, we tested accuracy and robustness against previous works, and the effect of number of training samples on the accuracy of our method.

Keywords: Face Sketch Recognition, Image Processing, Biometrics, Biologically Inspired.

1 Introduction

Contradictory to common beliefs, over 30 years pf psychological studies have shown that eyewitness face sketches (forensic sketches) are highly susceptible to error and their use should be avoided in courts [1]. The unreliability of the forensic sketches is mainly caused by the bias (perceptual, descriptive, and drawing) added by both the eyewitness and the police artist [1]. The problem is worsened by numerous memory distorting properties of current testimony methods, including verbal overshadowing, implanted ideas, piecewise reconstruction of the face, and viewing similar faces (refer to [2,1,3]). With the forensic sketches being unreliable, any application based on these sketches (such as an automatic face sketch recognizer) is doomed to be unreliable - simply put, garbage in garbage out.

Despite that the unreliability of the forensic sketches and the applications based on these sketches are shown in several works including [2,8,4,9,10], as we discuss in the next section, currently proposed automatic face sketch recognizers (FSRs) have not only ignored unreliability of forensic sketches, but also tested their approaches on over simplified test beds, which cannot represent the real cases of forensic sketch recognition (Figure 1). Several proposed FSRs have considered that the amount of information in face photos is larger than in face

R. Wilson et al. (Eds.): CAIP 2013, Part II, LNCS 8048, pp. 26–33, 2013.
© Springer-Verlag Berlin Heidelberg 2013

Fig. 1. Left: Forensic sketches (the real face sketches [4,5]) vs. Middle: exact artistic sketches used to test previous works [6,7,8] vs. Right: non-artistic sketches used in our method.

sketches, and therfore tried to transform photos to sketch-like images, to prevent information loss. Among the first is the work by Tang et al. (2004) [7] in which an eigenface transformation is proposed to project a face photo to the face sketch space, resulting in a sketch-like image. This work reported recognition accuracy of 89%, tested on CUHK face sketch dataset [6]. This work was followed by [11] in which a sketch-photo pair image is concatenated into a single vector to learn the PCA classifier with correlation to both the sketch and the real face. A non-linear transformation was also presented in [12] to replace photo patches with the most similar patch from the sketch gallery (using a PCA-based scoring). The result of this patch replacement classified by non-linear discriminant analysis reported of recognition accuracy of 92% on the CUHK dataset. This method was further improved using multi-scale Markov random field [6], to synthesize a smooth sketch that marginally improved the accuracy. Xiao et al. [13] proposed a sketch-to-photo transformation in order to transform the problem into a photo-to-photo matching problem. They used an embedded hidden Markov model for patch replacement to synthesize a photo-like image, and then classification using PCA. The experimental results on CUHK dataset reported to have up to 89.1% accuracy in recognition. More recently, FSR methods have been proposed based on Partial Least Squares (PLS) [14], random forests [15], support vector regressors [16], combination of local binary pattern and histogram of Gabors [17], and combination of multiscale LBP and SIFT features [4].

Regardless of reported accuracy of the above algorithms, they are proposed to address the forensic sketch recognition problem, but all of them have been tested on *exact artistic sketches* (Figure 1), that have significant similarities to their target faces (including exactly similar facial component shape, illumination and shading, skin texture, and even hairstyle). A recent study [10] showed an astonishing recognition rate of 85.22% only using hair regions, as well as that the accuracy of an off-the-shelf face photo matcher (merely using shape and edges), even without training, can outperform the currently proposed FSRs [10].

In contrast, a real forensic sketch is very likely to be significantly different from its respective target face (see Figure 1 for some examples). Thus, we argue that although the test results of the previous FSRs show almost perfect performances for exact artistic sketches, these FSRs cannot be used for recognizing forensic sketches. This argument is tested in [4], showing that while LBP+SIFT algorithm can achieve 99.47% accuracy in matching exact artistic sketches, when it is tested on forensic sketches, the accuracy dramatically decreased to 16.33% (with a state-of-art face recognition software [18] performing as low as 2.04%). We can therefore conclude two main gaps from the literature. First that current eyewitness testimony procedures are unreliable (based on psychological studies); second that current FSRs cannot reliably recognize forensic sketches (based on several tests by [4,10]). Therefore we also conclude that there is a need for realistic automatic face sketch recognition.

There are 3 sources of disturbance in creating a forensic sketch: eyewitness's face perception bias, interactive verbal description, and the police artist's perceptual bias (for details, refer to [1]). Instead of analyzing the three-fold distorted forensic sketches (like previous works), we propose to bypass 2nd and 3rd distortion sources by asking the eyewitness to draw the target face by himself. The resulting non-artistic sketch (Figure 1) then only contain distortions from eyewitness' perceptual and drawing style biases (sketching bias).

Our contributions here is a realistic face sketch recognition based on non-artistic sketches, to avoid many psychological problems, with general-specific modeling that only requires few training samples for reliable performance. In our approach, we estimate the sketching bias based on samples of eyewitness' face drawings, and then match the debiased sketch to the photo database, using weighted dynamic time warping. We can reach an accurate bias estimation from a few number of training samples, using general-specific modeling, that utilizes general information embedded in the dataset for better estimation. We use a set of 710 sketches to test our approach on general recognition performance, effect of number of training samples, and comparison with previous methods (including [4], reported the highest accuracy on CUHK).

2   Proposed Face Sketch Recognition Method

The eyewitness' non-artistic sketch (Main Sketch) is a crude representation of the target face (Figure 1, more examples in the supplementary documents), and therefore, we need to estimate and remove eyewitness' sketching bias. In addition, we should define point correspondence and point difference functions between sketch outline and photo outline. Finally, because not all parts of the sketch contains the same amount of information (e.g. ignorantly drawn parts vs. parts representing specific appearance of the target face), we need a point weighting strategy.

We define the sketching bias as a point-to-point transformation function τ, mapping the facial outlines of photo ϕ, to the facial outlines in it respective sketch φ. For the sake of simplicity, we model τ only as a function of face perception

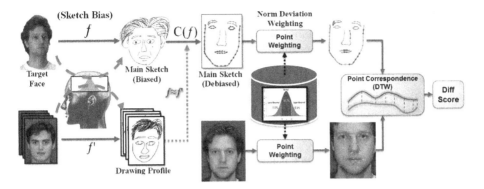

Fig. 2. Symbolic representation of our approach for sketching bias estimation and removal, by assuming that the Main sketch and the drawing profile are created using the same mental and motor processes

p, and drawing styles, with noise e: $\varphi = \tau(\phi) = s(p(\phi)) + e$. We estimate the sketching bias for each eyewitness based on his/her *drawing profile*: a set of sketch-photo pairs, drawn by the eyewitness from known faces.

We firstly detect points of all sketch and photo face outlines using a simple active shape model and WASM [19] respectively. After scale and rotation normalization based on the center of eyes, we fit 16 Piecewise Cubic Hermite Interpolating Polynomial splines [20] to the outlines of 7 facial components, namely, eyes, eyebrows, nose, mouth, and jaw-line (2 splines each eye, 2 each eyebrow, 2 mouth, 3 nose, and 3 jaw-line). Note that we do not use unreliable parts of the face image such as hair section, and we focus on these 7 components. Each of these 16 splines are then divided into four parts (quarter splines), and each part is sampled in 25 equally distributed data points. We now find corresponding points for these 25 points in each sketch-photo pair of drawing profile, and then learn 5 transformation functions. These learned functions represent the local sketching bias τ that we use to estimate the photo outlines, from the Main Sketch, to deduce what the eyewitness meant by the Main Sketch.

Based on psychological suggestions for face perception in humans in Exception Report Model (ERM) [21] and information theory, we assign higher weights to sketch parts with larger deviations from norm, assuming these parts represent visually interesting areas in the face photo. Thus, weight of a vector $\sigma \in \varphi$ is defined as the normalized distance of σ from its respective mean, i.e. the inverse of the probability of σ ($\omega(\sigma) = 1 - P(\sigma|g)$), where g is the associated distribution of σ. While we assume normal distributions for all points, the normal distribution for two parts of the sketch may be different (e.g. eyes vs. jaw-line distributions). Therefore, we account for distribution differences between two points σ and ς:

$$W(\sigma, \varsigma) = \frac{\omega(\sigma) \times \omega(\varsigma)}{D_{RAD}^2(g_\sigma, g_\varsigma) \times Euc^2(\sigma, \varsigma)^2} \tag{1}$$

$$D_{RAD}(p, q) = [D_{KL}(p \parallel q)^{-1} + D_{KL}(p \parallel q)^{-1}]^{-1} \tag{2}$$

The Kullback-Leibler Divergence (KL) [22] is well known to measure the distance between probability density functions (PDFs) and it follows an information theory approach to quantify how well PDF $q(x)$ describes samples from PDF $p(x)$. KL is non-negative and equal to zero iff $p(x) \equiv q(x)$, but KL is asymmetric. Therefore, we use an symmetrical extension of KL, Resistor-Average Distance (RAD) [22] as (Eq 2) that has the same properties as KL. It is also notable that when classes C_p and C_q are distributed according to $p(x)$ and $q(x)$, respectively, $D_{RAD}(p, q)$ reflects the error rate of the Bayes-optimal classifier between C_p and C_q .

We find point correspondence using weighted dynamic time warping, with the weights of each point σ being $\omega(\sigma)$. Given two outlines from photo ϕ and sketch φ, with points $\varsigma_i \in \phi$ and $\varsigma'_j \in \varphi$ to be matched, we find the corresponding points in the two outlines with the temporal order constraint, which can be formulated as maximizing of the total matching score, $\Upsilon(\phi, \varphi)$ with constraint Eq. 3:

$$\Upsilon(\phi, \varphi) = \{\varsigma_{i1} : \varsigma'_{j1}, \varsigma_{i2} : \varsigma'_{j2}, ...\varsigma_{ik} : \varsigma'_{jk}\}$$
$$s.t. \; \forall \; \varsigma_i : \varsigma'_j \; \& \; \varsigma_s : \varsigma'_t \; i > j \Leftrightarrow s > t \qquad (3)$$

The constraint in Eq. 3 forces a temporal order for matching points, i.e., given four points which are matched as $\varsigma_i : \varsigma'_j$ and $\varsigma_s : \varsigma'_t$, if ς_i is located before ς_j, then ς'_s should be located before ς'_t (See pseudo algorithm in the supplementary documents). Thus, given two outlines, ϕ, φ, we find the correspondence with the maximum similarity between the outlines of 7 facial components (eyes, nose, mouth, eyebrows, and jawline) and the relative locations of these 7 components. We use these similarity scores to learn to label a new pair of sketch-photo (drawn by the same person) as match/non-match by minimizing the estimation error $E = \sum_{\sigma \in \phi, \varsigma \in \varphi} \| W(\sigma_i, \tilde{f}(\varsigma_i) \|$ (see Figure 2).

General-Specific Modeling. The size of the drawing profile for each eyewitness is small (10 pairs) and relying merely on the drawing profile results in poor estimation of the sketching bias τ. We therefore propose to also utilize the general information embedded in the entire dataset of sketches (710 sketch-photo pairs). We divide the estimation into two steps of General and Specific modeling: using the entire dataset (excluding sketches from the eyewitness i) we learn a general transformation τ_i^G, and then fine-tune this transformation into a Specific model τ_i^{GS}, using the eyewitness' drawing profiles. Intuitively, the General model accounts for general way of sketching a face by non-artists, and the Specific model accounts for individual differences in sketching style and mental biases. We can formulate these two transformations as:

$$\{\bar{\varphi}_i = \tau_i^G(\varphi_i, \{\bar{\chi}_i, \bar{\mathbf{A}}_i\}) \qquad (4)$$
$$\bar{\phi}_i^{GS} = \tau_i^S(\bar{\varphi}_i, \bar{\mathbf{A}}_i) \qquad (5)$$

where $\bar{\chi}_i$ and $\bar{\mathbf{A}}_i$ are all training pairs which exclude samples from the ith eyewitness; χ_i and $\mathbf{A}_i$ are the training pairs from the drawing profile.

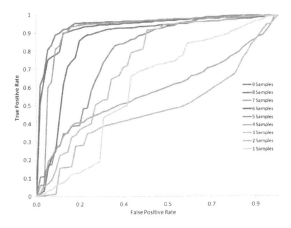

Fig. 3. The effect of number of training samples on the general-specific model performance

Table 1. Performance of direct, general, specific, and general-specific models

	Original	General	Specific	Gen-Spec
T. Sum	**0.7296**	0.7165	0.6442	0.6807
Comp.	0.6549	0.8602	0.8599	**0.9396**
Splines	0.6577	0.8648	0.8196	**0.942**

3   Experimental Results

We compare our method with the closest previously proposed algorithm [9], and [4] (reported the best performance on CUHK database), as well as [7], on both of artistic (CUHK) and non-artistic sketches. Our non-artistic sketch database contains 710 sketches, drawn from 249 face images (from Multi-PIE database [23]), by 71 subjects (24 female, age $\mu = 27.4, \sigma = 3.9$, from Caucasian, Indian, East Asian, and Middle Eastern races).

Table 1 illustrates the improvement due to the use general-specific modeling compared with direct comparison (original), specific, and general models. We also show that better results can be achieved by piecewise rather than holistic comparison (total sum of differences). Figure 3-right also shows the effect of number of samples in the drawing profile on the performance of our general-specific modeling. These results indicate that although the model behaves almost randomly with small number of training samples (< 4), as the number of samples grows we achieve better performances with very good recognition performances using only 7 to 9 samples. Figure 4 illustrates our comparison with previous works on recognizing both artistic sketches of CUHK database [6] (right) and non-artistic sketches (left). As the performances on the two sketch types show, each of these algorithms (ours vs. [4,7] are optimized to analyze specific types of sketches and cannot perform well on the other type, while our method has the advantages of avoiding psychological pitfalls and realistic similarity assumptions.

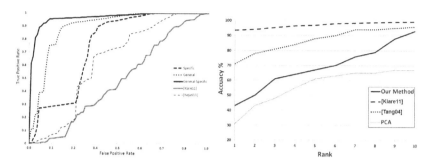

Fig. 4. Results of direct, general, specific, and general-specific modeling, compared with previous works on artistic (right) and non-artistic sketches (left)

4   Summary and Conclusion

A large body of psychological studies indicate severe problems in forensic sketches such as verbal overshadowing, implanted ideas, and piecewise reconstruction, that distort forensic sketches, and therefore render automatic methods (FSRs) that use these sketches, unreliable. In addition, previous FSRs can only recognize exact sketches and not forensic sketches. In this work we introduced a realistic FSR based on sketches directly drawn by eyewitnesses. Our FSR not only avoids the psychological problems, but also estimates and removes distortions due to personal sketching bias before attempting to recognize the the sketch. The introduced general-specific bias estimation can use only a few (7-9) training samples to reach an accurate bias estimation. In our experiments we showed the reliability of our method in comparison with previous methods, as well as on the number of training samples.

In conclusion, our method brings forth a new option to address the eyewitness face sketch recognition by avoiding distortions and accounting for individual differences between humans, that requires less time and effort (between 30 minutes to 1 hour), is far less than traditional eyewitness testimony procedures that may take up to days [1]. However, the accuracy in our approach deteriorates relative to the eyewitness' drawing skills and for subjects that have absolutely no drawing skills, we should fall back to traditional methods. Therefore, new techniques should be investigated to facilitate face drawings for non-artists, without causing psychological distortions to their mental image of the target face.

References

1. Toglia, M.P., Read, J.D., Ross, D.F., Lindsay, R.: Handbook of Eyewitness Psychology: Memory for events. Lawrence Erlbaum Associates (2007)
2. Sinha, P., Balas, B., Ostrovsky, Y., Russell, R.: Face recognition by humans: Nineteen results all computer vision researchers should know about. Proc. IEEE 94(11), 1948–1962 (2006)
3. Carlson, C., Gronlund, S., Clark, S.: Lineup composition, suspect position, and the sequential lineup advantage. J. Exp. Psychol. Appl. 14(2), 118–128 (2008)

4. Klare, B., Li, Z., Jain, A.: Matching forensic sketches to mug shot photos. IEEE Transactions on Pattern Analysis and Machine Intelligence 33, 639–646 (2011)
5. Sinha, P., Balas, B.J., Ostrovsky, Y., Russell, R.: Face recognition by humans. Face Recognition: Models and Mechanisms (2006)
6. Wang, X., Tang, X.: Face photo-sketch synthesis and recognition. IEEE Transactions on Pattern Analysis and Machine Intelligence 31, 1955–1967 (2009)
7. Tang, X., Wang, X.: Face sketch recognition. T-CSVT 14, 50–57 (2004)
8. Zhang, Y., McCullough, C., Sullins, J., Ross, C.: Hand-drawn face sketch recognition by humans and a pca-based algorithm for forensic applications. SMC-A 40, 475–485 (2010)
9. Nejati, H., Sim, T., Martinez-Marroquin, E.: Do you see what i see?: A more realistic eyewitness sketch recognition. IJCB (2011)
10. Choi, J., Sharma, A., Jacobs, D., Davis, L.: Data insufficiency in sketch versus photo face recognition. In: 2012 IEEE Computer Society Conference on Computer Vision and Pattern Recognition Workshops (CVPRW), pp. 1–8 (2012)
11. Li, Y.H., Savvides, M., Bhagavatula, V.: Illumination tolerant face recognition using a novel face from sketch synthesis approach and advanced correlation filters. In: ICASSP 2006, vol. 2, pp. II –II, 14-19 (2006)
12. Liu, Q., Tang, X., Jin, H., Lu, H., Ma, S.: A nonlinear approach for face sketch synthesis and recognition. In: CVPR 2005, vol. 1, pp. 1005–1010, 20-25 (2005)
13. Xiao, B., Gao, X., Tao, D., Li, X.: A new approach for face recognition by sketches in photos. Signal Process 89(8), 1576–1588 (2009)
14. Sharma, A., Jacobs, D.: Bypassing synthesis: Pls for face recognition with pose, low-resolution and sketch. In: 2011 IEEE Conference on Computer Vision and Pattern Recognition (CVPR), pp. 593–600 (2011)
15. Zhang, W., Wang, X., Tang, X.: Coupled information-theoretic encoding for face photo-sketch recognition. In: 2011 IEEE Conference on Computer Vision and Pattern Recognition (CVPR), pp. 513–520 (2011)
16. Zhang, J., Wang, N., Gao, X., Tao, D., Li, X.: Face sketch-photo synthesis based on support vector regression. In: 2011 18th IEEE International Conference on Image Processing (ICIP), pp. 1125–1128 (2011)
17. Galoogahi, H., Sim, T.: Inter-modality face sketch recognition. In: 2012 IEEE International Conference on Multimedia and Expo (ICME), pp. 224–229 (2012)
18. Facevacs software developer kit, cognitec systems gmbh(2010), http://www.cognitec-systems.de
19. Milborrow, S., Nicolls, F.: Locating facial features with an extended active shape model. In: Forsyth, D., Torr, P., Zisserman, A. (eds.) ECCV 2008, Part IV. LNCS, vol. 5305, pp. 504–513. Springer, Heidelberg (2008)
20. Fritsch, F.N., Carlson, R.E.: Monotone piecewise cubic interpolation. S-INUM 17, 238–246 (1980)
21. Unnikrishnan, M.: How is the individuality of a face recognized? J. Theor. Biol. 261(3), 469–474 (2009)
22. Arandjelovic, O., Cipolla, R.: An information-theoretic approach to face recognition from face motion manifolds. Image and Vision Computing 24(6), 639–647 (2006); Face Processing in Video Sequences
23. Gross, R., Matthews, I., Cohn, J., Kanade, T., Baker, S.: Multi-pie. In: FG 2008, pp. 1–8 (September 2008)

Weighted Semi-Global Matching and Center-Symmetric Census Transform for Robust Driver Assistance

Robert Spangenberg, Tobias Langner, and Raúl Rojas

Freie Universität Berlin, Institut für Informatik,
Arnimallee 7, 14195 Berlin, Germany
robert.spangenberg@fu-berlin.de

Abstract. Automotive applications based on stereo vision require robust and fast matching algorithms, which makes semi-global matching (SGM) a popular method in this field. Typically the Census transform is used as a cost function, since it is advantageous for outdoor scenes. We propose an extension based on center-symmetric local binary patterns, which allows better efficiency and higher matching quality. Our second contribution exploits knowledge about the three-dimensional structure of the scene to selectively enforce the smoothness constraints of SGM. It is shown that information about surface normals can be easily integrated by weighing the paths according to the gradient of the disparity. The different approaches are evaluated on the KITTI benchmark, which provides real imagery with LIDAR ground truth. The results indicate improved performance compared to state-of-the-art SGM based algorithms.

Keywords: stereo vision, matching costs, census transform, local binary pattern, semi-global matching.

1 Introduction

In recent years, driver assistance systems based on vision systems have become popular. Typical outdoor scenarios contain large scene depth, many detailed structures and high dynamic illumination, and thus complicate the stereo correspondence problem. Local matching methods usually fail on ambiguous low-texture areas and sharp depth discontinuities, while global methods are too slow for practical applications. Thus, semi-global matching (SGM) has become a popular choice [1–3], providing a good compromise between complexity and robustness. Many research efforts have been put on creating efficient implementations either by taking advantage of specific hardware, e.g FPGAs [4], GPUs [5] and CPUs [6], or by reducing the search space [2]. Geiger [7] achieves the latter for a local method by building a generative model on robust features on a sub-sampled grid, which is used to guide the search in the disparity space and reduce computational complexity. Lately, Hermann [2] used the consistency of the paths to decide where to restrict the search space and how to integrate the paths in order to get more robust matches. Disadvantages of the method are the

R. Wilson et al. (Eds.): CAIP 2013, Part II, LNCS 8048, pp. 34–41, 2013.

inherent priority order for the paths and the need to serialize several parts of the algorithm, which can be run in parallel in the original SGM formulation.

We propose a weighted integration based on the region's normal of the surface each pixel belongs to. This structure could be known a priori, or as in our case is computed approximately beforehand. We tested the preprocessing step of Geiger [7] and a coarse-to-fine step using a scaled down image for SGM.

Another crucial part of stereo matching algorithms is the matching cost function. It has been shown that the Census transform [8] is favorable for outdoor environments with uncontrolled lighting [9] and/or calibration errors [10]. To improve efficiency, a sparse version of it has been proposed [11]. For face recognition, histograms of local binary patterns (LBP) have been extremely popular to provide reliable features. In this context Heikkilä introduced Center-Symmetric LBPs (CS-LBPs, [12]) to gain speed and robustness to illumination. They have been proven to be superior to LBPs and several of its variants in this field [13].

Although having a formulation in parts similar to the Census transform, LBP-based descriptors are too costly for stereo matching. Therefore, we propose to use the idea of CS-LBPs to construct a likewise Census transform. Furthermore, we investigate the effect of weighing the pixels in the distance measure.

The rest of the paper is organized as follows. In Section 2 we briefly describe the Census transform, (CS-)LBPs and introduce the proposed transforms in detail. Section 3 recaptures the basic SGM formulation and presents our modifications. We furthermore explain the creation of the surface model. The experimental results are presented in Section 4. Finally, we conclude the paper in Section 5.

2   Center-Symmetric Census Transform

The LBP operator [14] describes each pixel using the relative intensity values of its surrounding neighbors. If the neighbor pixel is of equal or higher intensity, the value is set to one, otherwise to zero. The results for all neighbors are connected in a single number coded as a binary pattern (using the sign function $s(x) = 1$ for $x \geq 0$, $s(x) = 0$ otherwise):

$$LBP_{R,N}(x,y) = \sum_{i=0}^{N-1} s(n_i - n_c)2^i \qquad (1)$$

where n_j corresponds to the intensity of a pixel j of N equally spaced pixels on a circle of radius R around (x,y) and c is the index of the center pixel. Intensities of neighbors not lying exactly on a pixel are obtained by bilinear interpolation.

Center-Symmetric LBPs [12] provide a more compact representation, comparing only center-symmetric pairs of pixels. In addition, an intensity threshold T is introduced:

$$CS\text{-}LBP_{R,N,T}(x,y) = \sum_{i=0}^{(N/2)-1} s(n_i - n_{i+N/2} - T)2^i \qquad (2)$$

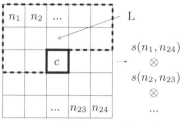

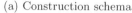

1	1	2	1	1
1	1	2	1	1
2	2	c	2	2
1	1	2	1	1
1	1	2	1	1

(a) Construction schema

(b) Additional pixel weights along central rows and columns

Fig. 1. Center-Symmetric Census Transform for a 5x5 patch

The Census transform [8] shares the idea of LBPs, but applies it to an image patch of $n \times m$ pixels instead of a circular region (now $s(u,v) = 0$, if $u \leq v$, $s(u,v) = 1$ otherwise):

$$CT_{m,n}(x,y) = \bigotimes_{i=-n'}^{n'} \bigotimes_{j=-m'}^{m'} s(I(x,y), I(x+i, y+j)) \qquad (3)$$

with $\otimes$ being a bit-wise concatenation and $n' = \lfloor n/2 \rfloor$, $m' = \lfloor m/2 \rfloor$. The matching cost of two pixels is the Hamming distance of the results of the Census transform for those two. Typical window sizes are 3×3, 5×5 or 9×7 as their results fit into 8, 32 and 64 bit. Real-time implementations often use 5×5 giving the best compromise between speed and quality [6].

We now introduce the Center-Symmetric Census Transform (CS-CT) as

$$CS\text{-}CT_{m,n}(x,y) = \bigotimes_{(i,j)\in L} s(I(x-i, y-j), I(x+i, y+j)) \qquad (4)$$

with $L = L_1 \cup L_2$, $L_1 = R_{-n',0} \times R_{-m',0} \setminus \{(0,0)\}$, $L_2 = R_{1,n'} \times R_{-m',1}$ and $R_{a,b} = \{x \in \mathbb{Z} | a \leq x \leq b\}$. As in CS-LBPs, only center-symmetric pairs of pixels are compared, but over an image patch of $n \times m$ (Figure 1a). Like the Sparse Census transform, CS-CT only needs 31 bits to describe a patch of 9×7 pixels, but takes all pixels into account.

The gained bits may be used to encode a weighted Hamming Distance (Figure 1b) through bit duplication. This fits well to implementations using hardware bit count instructions for the Hamming Distance. Alternatively, weighting can be achieved without additional bits by using lookup tables.

3   Weighted Semi-Global Matching

The SGM method by Hirschmüller[1] seeks to approximate a global MRF regularized cost function by following one dimensional paths L in several directions

r through the image. According to him it is sufficient to use 8 or 16 paths to cover the structure of the image (Figure 2a). Along each path, the minimum cost is calculated by means of dynamic programming

$$L_{\mathbf{r}}(\mathbf{p}, d) = C(\mathbf{p}, d) + \min(L_{\mathbf{r}}(\mathbf{p} - \mathbf{r}, d), L_{\mathbf{r}}(\mathbf{p} - \mathbf{r}, d - 1) + P_1$$
$$, L_{\mathbf{r}}(\mathbf{p} - \mathbf{r}, d + 1) + P_1, \min_i L_{\mathbf{r}}(\mathbf{p} - \mathbf{r}, i) + P_2) \tag{5}$$

For every pixel **p** and disparity d, the cost is calculated as the sum of the matching cost $C(\mathbf{p}, d)$ and the minimum path cost to the previous pixel, with the penalties P_1 and P_2. P_1 penalizes slanted surfaces and P_2 discontinuities.

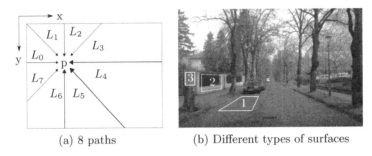

(a) 8 paths   (b) Different types of surfaces

Fig. 2. Path directions in Semi-Global matching and surface dependent weights

The information from all paths is summed for all pixels and disparities giving the accumulated costs

$$S(\mathbf{p}, d) = \sum_{\mathbf{r}} L_{\mathbf{r}}(\mathbf{p}, d). \tag{6}$$

The disparity for each pixel is now simply chosen by a winner-takes-all strategy on S. In contrast to other dynamic programming solutions, explicit occlusion handling is not possible. So a left-right consistency check is applied, either using the disparities of the right image D_R calculated by the same process or by diagonal search in S [1].

We propose a method called Weighted Semi-Global matching (wSGM) which weighs the cost of each path according to its compliance with the associated surface normal

$$S(\mathbf{p}, d) = \sum_{\mathbf{r}} W(\mathbf{r}, \mathbf{p}) L_{\mathbf{r}}(\mathbf{p}, d). \tag{7}$$

Assume we have a plane P which approximates a surface patch. Under central projection the vanishing line of P will coincide with the direction along which disparity values of points on this plane are constant. Hence disparities should be propagated preferably along paths close to this direction. We achieve this by increasing the weight of SGM paths according to the angle between the path and the vanishing line. If we imagine a road scene (Figure 2b), the pixels on the road surface (area 1) should have nearly constant disparity for the horizontal paths

Fig. 3. Support points with Delaunay triangulation (KITTI test set frame 112)

L_0 and L_4. Thus we can safely increase the weight for these paths, whereas vertical structures parallel to the road should benefit from increased weights for the vertical paths (area 2). Frontal-parallel structures should integrate the paths evenly (area 3). However, in many applications surface normals are unknown and as we try to recover the surface by the matching, we encounter a chicken-egg problem.

We tested two different approaches to resolve this. The first one applies SGM on a scaled-down image in a coarse-to-fine fashion, while the second is derived from the method by Geiger [7]. He reduces the search space for stereo matching by creating a generative model based on support points, which are selected from a set of image points sampled on a regular grid and matched for stereo correspondence. Robustly matched points which have sufficient texture, a high uniqueness and are consistent in a left/right-check qualify as support points. They have to be similar to their surrounding support points as well to ensure they are good representatives. The generative model constitutes a Delaunay triangulated mesh with valid disparities which approximates the surface (Figure 3). The weight adaption can be performed for all image points inside the mesh.

4   Experimental Results and Discussion

To evaluate our approach quantitatively we use the KITTI stereo data set [15], providing ground-truth obtained by a laser-scanner. The scenes are rather complex, with large regions of poor contrast, lighting differences among stereo pairs and a large disparity range ($d_{max} = 255$). It is separated in a training and testing data set of around 200 images each (Figure 4). Ground truth is provided freely accessible for the training data set only, results for the testing data set are obtained by an on-line service.

We implemented our own baseline SGM algorithm using a Census window of 9×7 pixels (SGM $CT_{9,7}$). It integrates over 16 paths and uses diagonal search for the left-right check. We use a linear penalty function for the adaption of P_2 depending on the image gradients along the path as in [16] and apply the gravitational constraint [3] to disambiguate regions like sky and improve consistency in vertical regions. Parameters are $P_1 = 7, P_{2_{min}} = 17, \alpha = 0.5, \gamma = 100, P_G = 3$. Results are ahead of the OpenCV implementation (Table 1, parameters equal to KITTI website), which can be attributed to the SAD matching costs. To evaluate the benefit of the two sparse encodings, a 5×5 Census transform was tested

Fig. 4. KITTI training data example, left image, ground truth and baseline SGM results (top to bottom)

Table 1. Comparing different variants with the KITTI training data set: baseline algorithms, modifications to the Census transform and weighted SGM (Out-Noc: outliers non-occluded pixels, Out-All: outliers all pixels)

Method	2px		3px		
	Out-Noc	Out-All	Out-Noc	Out-All	Density
OpenCV SGM	11.40 %	12.92 %	8.39 %	9.81 %	85.50 %
SGM $CT_{5,5}$	10.90 %	12.28 %	7.34 %	8.54 %	88.74 %
SGM $CT_{9,7}$	9.39 %	10.80 %	6.23 %	7.44 %	91.53 %
SGM $Sparse\text{-}CT_{9,7}$	9.70 %	11.15 %	6.61 %	7.87 %	91.49 %
SGM $CS\text{-}CT_{9,7}$	9.59 %	11.06 %	6.51 %	7.76 %	91.97 %
SGM $WCS\text{-}CT_{9,7}$	9.12 %	10.47 %	6.03 %	7.17 %	92.12 %
SGM $HWCS\text{-}CT_{9,7}$	9.09 %	10.44 %	6.05 %	7.20 %	92.18 %
wSGM $WCS\text{-}CT_{9,7}$	8.99 %	10.35 %	5.90 %	7.04 %	91.99 %
wSGM $HWCS\text{-}CT_{9,7}$	8.89 %	10.25 %	5.89 %	7.04 %	92.17 %

as well (SGM $CT_{5,5}$, adapted parameters, tuned to be optimal). Both sparse encodings expose a gain in matching quality, CS-CT being slightly better than Sparse-CT.

For the weighted CS-CT, we tested two variants, one with only additional horizontal weights (HWCS) and a fully weighted one (WCS), each weighted region being 3 pixels wide. Both variants perform better than the classic Census transform, providing a higher matching density and reduced outliers.

wSGM was tested with those two as well and gives additional improvements (weight factor 3 for preferred paths). Only the results using the generative model are reported. The scaled down SGM version did not provide any improvements. Limiting the weight adaption to the vertical and horizontal paths gave a slightly better result. In urban scenarios, the other surface types are not that prominent and harder to estimate with a sub-sampling approach due to their smaller size. Looking at the changes in detail (Figure 5a), one can see that the weighted Census transform reduces the number of outliers in general, whereas wSGM leads to large improvements at specific frames (Figure 5c). The poor contrast

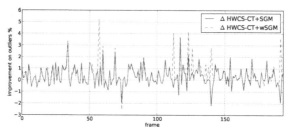

(a) Improvements per frame to SGM $CT_{9,7}$ on KITTI training set (% outlier pixels $> 2px$)

(b) Frame 112: SGM $CT_{9,7}$ (c) Frame 112: wSGM $HWCS\text{-}CT_{9,7}$

Fig. 5. KITTI training set: changes in detail

Table 2. Evaluation on KITTI test set: error threshold 3px

Rank	Method	Out-Noc	Out-All	Avg-Noc	Avg-All	Density	Runtime
1	PCBP-SS	3.49 %	4.79 %	0.8 px	1.0 px	100.00 %	5 min
2	StereoSLIC	3.99 %	5.17 %	0.9 px	1.0 px	99.89 %	2.3 s
3	PR-Sf+E	4.09 %	4.95 %	0.9 px	1.0 px	100.00 %	200 s
4	PCBP	4.13 %	5.45 %	0.9 px	1.2 px	100.00 %	5 min
5	PR-Sceneflow	4.46 %	5.32 %	1.0 px	1.1 px	100.00 %	150 s
6	wSGM	5.03 %	6.24 %	1.3 px	1.6 px	97.03 %	6 s
7	ATGV	5.05 %	6.91 %	1.0 px	1.6 px	100.00 %	6 min
8	iSGM	5.16 %	7.19 %	1.2 px	2.1 px	94.70 %	8 s
9	AABM	5.50 %	6.60 %	1.1 px	1.3 px	100.00 %	0.43 s
10	SGM	5.83 %	7.08 %	1.2 px	1.3 px	85.80 %	3.7 s

in the example frame leads to mis-propagations on the road surface with SGM. wSGM increases the weights for the horizontal paths and is able to recover the real surface.

The results of wSGM + WCS on the KITTI test set (Table 2, with additional interpolation) show a comparable performance to iSGM and a significant improvement to the baseline SGM method. Its runtime is similar or better to the closest competitors (C++ implementation, no SSE/multi-threading). Optimizations for speed should offer gains as in [6], enabling real-time performance.

5   Conclusion

We presented a new variant of the Census transform providing higher efficiency and quality. The robustness of SGM was improved by introducing surface normal based weights in the path integration step. For both we could show better performance on the KITTI stereo dataset. The estimation of the correct surface normals seems to be the crux of wSGM. Calculating a better approximation using stereo reconstructions from previous frames and optical flow looks promising. Further future work includes the integration of symbolic map knowledge.

References

1. Hirschmüller, H.: Stereo processing by semiglobal matching and mutual information. IEEE Trans. Pattern Anal. Mach. Intell. 30(2), 328–341 (2008)
2. Hermann, S., Klette, R.: Iterative semi-global matching for robust driver assistance systems. In: Lee, K.M., Matsushita, Y., Rehg, J.M., Hu, Z. (eds.) ACCV 2012, Part III. LNCS, vol. 7726, pp. 465–478. Springer, Heidelberg (2013)
3. Gehrig, S.K., Franke, U.: Improving stereo sub-pixel accuracy for long range stereo. In: ICCV, pp. 1–7. IEEE (2007)
4. Gehrig, S.K., Eberli, F., Meyer, T.: A real-time low-power stereo vision engine using semi-global matching. In: Fritz, M., Schiele, B., Piater, J.H. (eds.) ICVS 2009. LNCS, vol. 5815, pp. 134–143. Springer, Heidelberg (2009)
5. Ernst, I., Hirschmüller, H.: Mutual information based semi-global stereo matching on the GPU. In: Bebis, G., et al. (eds.) ISVC 2008, Part I. LNCS, vol. 5358, pp. 228–239. Springer, Heidelberg (2008)
6. Gehrig, S.K., Rabe, C.: Real-Time Semi-Global Matching on the CPU. In: CVPR Workshops, San Francisco, CA, USA, pp. 85–92 (June 2010)
7. Geiger, A., Roser, M., Urtasun, R.: Efficient large-scale stereo matching. In: Kimmel, R., Klette, R., Sugimoto, A. (eds.) ACCV 2010, Part I. LNCS, vol. 6492, pp. 25–38. Springer, Heidelberg (2011)
8. Cremers, D., Kohlberger, T., Schnörr, C.: Nonlinear shape statistics in mumford-shah based segmentation. In: Heyden, A., Sparr, G., Nielsen, M., Johansen, P. (eds.) ECCV 2002, Part II. LNCS, vol. 2351, pp. 93–108. Springer, Heidelberg (2002)
9. Hirschmüller, H., Scharstein, D.: Evaluation of stereo matching costs on images with radiometric differences. IEEE Trans. Pattern Anal. Mach. Intell. 31(9), 1582–1599 (2009)
10. Hirschmüller, H., Gehrig, S.K.: Stereo matching in the presence of sub-pixel calibration errors. In: CVPR, pp. 437–444. IEEE (2009)
11. Zinner, C., Humenberger, M., Ambrosch, K., Kubinger, W.: An optimized software-based implementation of a census-based stereo matching algorithm. In: Bebis, G., et al. (eds.) ISVC 2008, Part I. LNCS, vol. 5358, pp. 216–227. Springer, Heidelberg (2008)
12. Heikkilä, M., Pietikäinen, M., Schmid, C.: Description of interest regions with local binary patterns. Pattern Recogn. 42(3), 425–436 (2009)
13. Meena, K., Suruliandi, A.: Local binary patterns and its variants for face recognition. In: 2011 International Conference on Recent Trends in Information Technology (ICRTIT), pp. 782–786 (June 2011)
14. Ojala, T., Pietikainen, M., Maenpaa, T.: Multiresolution gray-scale and rotation invariant texture classification with local binary patterns. IEEE Transactions on Pattern Analysis and Machine Intelligence 24(7), 971–987 (July)
15. Geiger, A., Lenz, P., Urtasun, R.: Are we ready for autonomous driving? the kitti vision benchmark suite. In: CVPR, pp. 3354–3361. IEEE (2012)
16. Banz, C., Pirsch, P., Blume, H.: Evaluation of penalty functions for semi-global matching cost aggregation. ISPRS XXXIX-B3, 1–6 (2012)

Handwritten Word Image Matching
Based on Heat Kernel Signature

Xi Zhang and Chew Lim Tan

School of Computing, National University of Singapore
{xizhang,tancl}@comp.nus.edu.sg

Abstract. Keyword Spotting is an alternative method for retrieving query words, without Optical Character Recognition (OCR), by calculating the similarity between features of word images rather than ASCII content. However, because of unconstrained writing styles with large variations, the retrieving results are always not very satisfactory.

In this paper, we propose a novel method, which is based on Heat Kernel Signature (HKS) and Triangular Mesh Structure to achieve handwritten word image matching. HKS can tolerate large variations in handwritten word images and capture local features. On the other hand, the triangular mesh structure is used to present global characteristics. Moreover, our method does not need pre-processing steps.

Keywords: word image matching, heat kernel signature, triangular mesh structure.

1 Introduction

Most of valuable handwritten documents, such as historical manuscripts, business contracts, application forms, diagnosis reports, and envelops, have been scanned into databases and public access services are provided for information retrieval. In order to achieve efficient and reliable retrieving services, OCR is first used to convert image-based documents into ASCII format. However, degradation, noise and various unconstrained writing styles always prevent OCR providing satisfactory results. Keyword spotting [1] becomes an alternative way of OCR to spot query words. Only features extracted from the query images are needed, without knowing the ASCII content.

A very common used method to achieve handwritten word image matching is extracting geometrical features in each column of the word images from left to right [2] and applying Dynamic Time Warping (DTW) [3] to calculate the distance between two sequences of feature vectors. However, pre-processing steps are needed and crucial, including binarization, skew or slant correction, and normalization, so that the accuracy highly depends on the pre-processing results. Moreover, column features only take the current column into account and ignore the context information. Therefor, DTW based on column feature sequences may not deal with word images with large variations. In order to consider context

R. Wilson et al. (Eds.): CAIP 2013, Part II, LNCS 8048, pp. 42–49, 2013.

information of the handwritten text, [4] extracted features from a sliding window instead of only one column.

Scale Invariant Feature Transform (SIFT) [5] has been successfully used in computer vision and object recognition, and also shows its robust and reliability to be invariant to image scale and rotation. Some variations of SIFT feature are gradually used for document analysis. In [6], a new feature sequence is proposed based on the local gradient histogram based on the idea of SIFT, which is extracted from each cell of a sliding window.

In handwritten documents, infinite writing styles may occur, so that different writers, or even the same writer, may write the same word in large variant styles, just like the same word image is deformed by non-rigid deformations in every part of the word. [7] shows that SIFT can deal with affine-invariant situations quite well, but cannot handle non-rigid deformations. On the other hand, Heat Kernel Signature (HKS) [8] is proved to be invariant to non-rigid deformations. Motivated by this observation, we propose a new method for handwritten word image matching based on HKS. We also propose a new similarity measurement approach to calculate the distance between two sets of descriptors, based on triangular mesh structure, which can capture global spatial relations of keypoints. Moreover, our method do not need pre-processing steps, such as binarization, normalization, and skew or slant correction.

2 Descriptor Based on Heat Kernel Signature

2.1 Heat Kernel Signature

In order to apply HKS to our tasks, we should first embed a patch in a 2D word image into a 3D surface. We assume that P is a patch, with the size of $N \times N$, extracted from an word image I and centered at a keypoint. The 3D Riemannian manifold M is the 3D surface embedding from P, satisfying the condition that if (x, y) is a point in P, then there is a point (x, y, z) on M, where z is the intensity value of (x, y) in P [7]. The heat diffusion geometry of patch P is obtained by using the Laplace-Beltrami operator over the manifold M [9]:

$$(\Delta_M + \frac{\partial}{\partial t})u(\mathbf{x}, t) = 0, \tag{1}$$

where $\mathbf{x}$ is a point on M, Δ_M is the Laplace-Beltrami operator, and the solution $k(\mathbf{x}, \mathbf{x}', t)$ is named as the heat kernel, presenting how the heat between two points on one surface diffusing from one to the other at time t. When M is a compact manifold, $k(\mathbf{x}, \mathbf{x}', t)$ can be expressed compactly by the eigenvalues $\{\phi_i\}$ and eigenvectors $\{\lambda_i\}$ of Δ_M [9]:

$$k(\mathbf{x}, \mathbf{x}', t) = \sum_{i=0}^{\infty} e^{-\lambda_i t} \phi_i(\mathbf{x}) \phi_i(\mathbf{x}'). \tag{2}$$

Based on Eq. 2, HKS is proposed in [10] to present local and global characteristics around a point $\mathbf{p}$ on M as follows:

$$\mathrm{HKS}(\mathbf{p}, t) = k(\mathbf{p}, \mathbf{p}, t) = \sum_{i=0}^{\infty} e^{-\lambda_i t} \phi_i^2(\mathbf{p}). \qquad (3)$$

In order to tolerate 2D noise around keypoints [7], the descriptor of $\mathbf{p}$ is constructed from all the points in P, weighted by a Gaussian kernel considering their distances to the center. This descriptor is called Deformation Invariant (DI) descriptor [7]:

$$\mathrm{DI}(\mathbf{p}, t) = [\mathrm{HKS}(\mathbf{x}, t). * G(\mathbf{x}; \mathbf{p}, \sigma)]_{\forall \mathbf{x} \in \mathbf{P}}, \qquad (4)$$

where G is a 2D Gaussian filter centered at p with standard deviation σ.

2.2   Scale Invariant HKS

Because we extract features directly from word images, without any pre-processing steps, word images may have different intensity values along strokes, namely, the manifold M maybe scaled along the intensity axis, we use SI-HKS proposed in [11] to remove the dependence of HKS to scaling in the intensity dimension. Therefore, replacing HKS by SI-HKS in Eq. 4, the final descriptor of each point $\mathbf{p}$ is shown as below [7]:

$$\mathrm{DaLI}(\mathbf{p}, \omega) = [\mathrm{SI\text{-}HKS}(\mathbf{x}, \omega). * G(\mathbf{x}; \mathbf{p}, \sigma)]_{\forall \mathbf{x} \in \mathbf{P}} \qquad (5)$$

where $\mathrm{DaLI}(\mathbf{p}, \omega)$ will be denoted as $\mathrm{DaLI}(\mathbf{p})$ for short in the rest of the paper.

3   Word Image Matching

3.1   Keypoints Detection and Selection

When HKS is used for shape segmentation or recognition, all the points on the surfaces are used to measure the distances between two shapes, however, for our task, generating descriptors for all the points in the word images and finding the optimal matching between two sets of DaLI descriptors are very time consuming and unnecessary. Because there is no keypoint detection algorithm proposed specially for HKS, we use the keypoint detector for SIFT proposed by D. G. Lowe [5] in our experiments.

In our task, we focus on the keypoints located on the strokes, namely, we remove the keypoints in the background or near the contour of strokes. Word images are first smoothed by a Gaussian kernel, and keypoints of each word image are located, shown as the red points in Fig. 1(a). Then, the keypoints with the intensity value smaller than a threshold are removed. Fig. 1(b) shows the final selected keypoints, DaLI descriptors of which will be generated.

(a) Keypoints detected by SIFT detector.   (b) Removing uninteresting points.

(c) The triangular mesh structure of keypoints.

Fig. 1. Keypoints selection and the corresponding triangular mesh structure

3.2   Structure of Keypoints

Because keypoints may appear in any part of the word images and two keypoints may be located in the same column, we can not concatenate all descriptors, sorted by their vertical locations from left to right, therefore DTW or other methods measuring distance between two feature sequences are not applicable.

As illustrated in Fig. 1, the selected keypoints are mostly located at the start or end of strokes, intersection of two strokes or the locations strokes tending to change orientations. The local patches around these points can capture local characteristics of word images very well, and the spatial relations among them can be used to present the global structure of word images. Due to cursive handwritten styles, some keypoints belonging to different characters may have similar descriptors, but they have different spatial relations with respect to their neighboring keypoints. We use the structure based on triangular mesh to connect spatial related keypoints together, as shown in Fig. 1(c), in which two keypoints connected by a blue line are treated as neighbors.

Assume that we find n unique keypoints $\{kp_i\}$ in I, each of which with a coordinate $(x_i, y_i), i \in [1, n]$, sorting by y_i in ascending order, presenting the location of each keypoint. By applying Delaunay Triangulation algorithm to coordinates of all $\{kp_i\}$, we can get a triangular mesh for all keypoints, aiming at connecting neighboring keypoints together, and constructing a triangular mesh structure (TMS) to present I. From TMS, we generate two functions, one is $neighors(kp_i)$, which returns all neighbors of kp_i, and the other one is $Adj(kp_i, kp_j)$, which returns whether kp_i and kp_j is neighbors, if so returns 1, 0 otherwise.

3.3   Score Matrix

Assuming Q is a query image having n_q keypoints, denoted by kp_j, with coordinates $(x_j, y_j), j \in [1, n_q]$, and C is a candidate image in the collection, having n_c keypoints, denoted by kp'_i, with coordinates $(x'_i, y'_i), i \in [1, n_c]$. Our task is given a sequence of keypoints in Q, we should find the optimal matching sequence of keypoints in C and calculate the matching score. In order to present the triangular mesh structure of the query image, we first reorder all kp_i in a new sequence, by from the first keypoint, choosing one neighbor of the previous keypoint until all the keypoints are in the sequence and no one is reduplicated, consequently every two consecutive keypoints kp_i and kp_{i+1} are neighbors in the new sequence. So that, in the corresponding sequence of keypoints we will find in each candidate image, two consecutive keypoints should be also neighbors.

SM is a score matrix with the size of $n_c \times n_q$, each component of which contains two types of information, the optimal matching score $SM_s(i,j)$ and the optimal matching history $SM_h(i,j)$ from kp_1 to kp_{j-1}, if kp'_i is matched to kp_j. SM is constructed as described in Algorithm 1, and the aim is to find a matching sequence including the keypoints in C, each component of which can be matched to the corresponding keypoint in the query image optimally. In a local area of the query image, matched keypoints in the candidate image should have similar spatial relations to those in the query image, because at each matching step, we only considering neighbors according to the triangular mesh structure, as shown in *Line* 9 in the algorithm. One advantages of our algorithm is that it can remove dissimilar images more effectively, because in such situations, similar triangular mesh structure cannot be found, most of the entries of SM_s will be Inf, especially the last half of columns. We can discard these images quickly by only finding the matching score in the right-bottom part of SM_s, controlled by the thresholds T_c and T_r.

4 Experiments

4.1 Experiments Setup

The dataset we use is IAM public handwritten database [12], with very large variations, and we choose 4000 common used handwritten word images written by different writers as the searching collection and 69 query word images, which appear more than 10 times in the collection. For comparison, we also carry out the experiments by following methods: DTW with column features and local gradient histogram features [6], keypoints matching based on SIFT descriptor with BBF, and SIFT descriptor with SM. Assuming the width of one query image is w, in the pruning step, all the methods will discard the images with the width smaller than $0.5 * w$, or larger than $2w$.

After preprocessing steps, column features (LF) and local gradient histogram features (LGH) are extracted based on the methods in [13] and [6] respectively, and the similarity measurement is calculated by DTW. SIFT features are extracted by the matlab codes provided by D. G. Lowe online. Keypoints are matched by BBF, and word images in which the query image cannot find matches for more than 30% of its keypoints are discarded. The matching score for each candidate image is the sum of all the distances between matching keypoints.

Parameters needed for DaLI descriptors are set according to the experiment results shown in [7]. All other thresholds are chosen to give the best performance.

Algorithm 1. Construct SM and find the optimal matching score

---

1: $D(i, j) = \|\text{DaLI}(\mathbf{kp}'_i)) - \text{DaLI}(\mathbf{kp_j})\|$, for all $i \in [1, n_c]$, $j \in [1, n_q]$, $\|\cdot\|$ is the L2-norm
2: Initialize SM_s to Inf and SM_h to $NULL$ for all components
3: **for** $i = 1 \to n_c$ **do**
4: $\quad SM_s(i, 1) \leftarrow D(i, 1)$
5: $\quad SM_h(i, 1) \leftarrow i$
6: **end for**
7: **for** $j = 2 \to n_q$ **do**
8: $\quad$ **for** $i = 1 \to n_c$ **do**
9: $\quad\quad Adj \leftarrow \{z | z \in neighbors'(kp'_i) \text{ and } kp'_i \notin SM_h(z, j - 1)\}$
10: $\quad\quad z^* \leftarrow argmax_{z \in Adj}SM_s(z, j - 1)$
11: $\quad\quad$ **if** Adj is not an empty set and $SM_s(ne, j - 1) \neq Inf$ **then**
12: $\quad\quad\quad SM_s(i, j) \leftarrow SM_s(z^*, j - 1) + D(i, j)$
13: $\quad\quad\quad SM_h \leftarrow SM_h(z^*, j - 1) \bigcup kp'_i$
14: $\quad\quad\quad$ %comment: kp'_i is added to the last position
15: $\quad\quad$ **end if**
16: $\quad$ **end for**
17: **end for**
18:
19: $score \leftarrow Inf$
20: $j \leftarrow n_q$
21: **while** $j \leq T_c$ and $score == Inf$ **do**
22: $\quad$ **for** $i = T_r \to n_c$ **do**
23: $\quad\quad$ **if** $SM_s(i, j)/j < score$ **then**
24: $\quad\quad\quad score \leftarrow SM_s(i, j)/j$
25: $\quad\quad$ **end if**
26: $\quad$ **end for**
27: $\quad j \leftarrow j - 1$
28: **end while**
29: **return** $score$

4.2 Results and Discussion

Given a query image, all the distances or matching scores are sorted in the ascending order, and top n candidate images are returned, where n is the number of the matching images in the ground truth. The percentage of the number of correct matching candidate images in the final return list is used to compare different methods, named Matching Rate (MR) in Table 1.

Table 1. Experiment Results

Methods	CF + DTW	LGH + DTW	SIFT + BBF	SIFT + SM	Our Method
MR(%)	28.598	22.996	8.126	21.584	**37.827**

As shown in Table 1, our proposed method outperforms other methods. In Fig. 2, the top 15 candidate images returned by different methods for the query word image in Fig. 1(c), our method can return correct matches much better, even for two images with large variations and different illumination values, however, column features and local gradient histogram features with DTW can only spot very similar word images shown in Fig. 2(a) and Fig. 2(b), and fails when some word images can not be de-skewed or de-slanted correctly. Between two word images, if we only apply BBF to find matching keypoints based on their SIFT features, many correct matching pairs are discarded or keypoints are matched incorrectly. As shown in Fig. 2(c), some very dissimilar word images are returned. If combining SIFT with SM, instead of finding matching pairs throughout the whole word image, which always brings in errors, the searching range is limited to a local area and global consistency is taken into account, therefore, the matching results is improved, however, both methods with SIFT can not provide more satisfactory results than others.

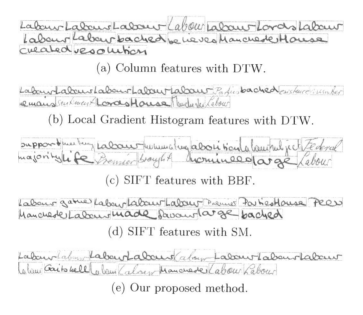

(a) Column features with DTW.

(b) Local Gradient Histogram features with DTW.

(c) SIFT features with BBF.

(d) SIFT features with SM.

(e) Our proposed method.

Fig. 2. Top 15 candidate images returned by different methods

5 Conclusion

We extract HKS descriptor for every keypoint in the query and candidate images and propose a new similarity measurement method based on a triangular mesh structure, in order to keep global structure consistency. As shown in our experiments, our new method can capture local and global features more robustly and reliably and outperforms other commonly used methods.

In the further, efforts should be put on how to find stable keypoints, so that HKS and triangular mesh structure can be made full use of. Moreover, more sophistic method should be proposed to find optimal alignment of two sets of DaLI descriptors for rotated images.

References

1. Manmatha, R., Han, C., Riseman, E.M.: Word spotting: A new approach to indexing handwriting. In: Proceedings of IEEE Computer Society Conference on Computer Vision and Pattern Recognition, pp. 631–637 (1996)
2. Rath, T.M., Manmatha, R.: Features for word spotting in historical manuscripts. In: Proceedings of the Seventh International Conference on Document Analysis and Recognition, pp. 218–222. IEEE (2003)
3. Rath, T.M., Manmatha, R.: Word spotting for historical documents. International Journal on Document Analysis and Recognition 9(2), 139–152 (2007)
4. Bunke, H., Bengio, S., Vinciarelli, A.: Offline recognition of unconstrained handwritten texts using hmms and statistical language models. IEEE Transactions on Pattern Analysis and Machine Intelligence 26(6), 709–720 (2004)
5. Lowe, D.G.: Distinctive image features from scale-invariant keypoints. International Journal of Computer Vision 60(2), 91–110 (2004)
6. Rodrıguez, J.A., Perronnin, F.: Local gradient histogram features for word spotting in unconstrained handwritten documents. In: Int. Conf. on Frontiers in Handwriting Recognition (2008)
7. Moreno-Noguer, F.: Deformation and illumination invariant feature point descriptor. In: 2011 IEEE Conference on Computer Vision and Pattern Recognition (CVPR), pp. 1593–1600. IEEE (2011)
8. Rustamov, R.M.: Laplace-beltrami eigenfunctions for deformation invariant shape representation. In: Proceedings of the Fifth Eurographics Symposium on Geometry Processing, pp. 225–233. Eurographics Association (2007)
9. Reuter, M., Wolter, F.E., Peinecke, N.: Laplace–beltrami spectra as shape-dnaof surfaces and solids. Computer-Aided Design 38(4), 342–366 (2006)
10. Sun, J., Ovsjanikov, M., Guibas, L.: A concise and provably informative multi-scale signature based on heat diffusion. In: Computer Graphics Forum, vol. 28, pp. 1383–1392. Wiley Online Library (2009)
11. Bronstein, M.M., Kokkinos, I.: Scale-invariant heat kernel signatures for non-rigid shape recognition. In: 2010 IEEE Conference on Computer Vision and Pattern Recognition (CVPR), pp. 1704–1711. IEEE (2010)
12. Marti, U.V., Bunke, H.: The iam-database: an english sentence database for offline handwriting recognition. International Journal on Document Analysis and Recognition 5(1), 39–46 (2002)
13. Fischer, A., Keller, A., Frinken, V., Bunke, H.: Hmm-based word spotting in handwritten documents using subword models. In: 2010 20th International Conference on Pattern Recognition (ICPR), pp. 3416–3419. IEEE (2010)

Wrong Roadway Detection for Multi-lane Roads

Junli Tao, Bok-Suk Shin, and Reinhard Klette

The .enpeda.. Project, Department of Computer Science
The University of Auckland, New Zealand

Abstract. The paper contributes to the detection of driving on the wrong side of the road by addressing in particular multi-lane road situations. We suggest a solution using video data of a single camera only for identifying the current lane of the ego-vehicle. GPS data are used for knowing defined constraints on driving directions for the current road.

1 Introduction

According to the report [1] by the *World Health Organization* (WHO), road accidents rank as one of the top ten killers worldwide. Enormous research is carried out for creating an *intelligent vehicle* (IV), or, at least, a *driver assistance system* (DAS). Detecting or tracking a roadway or carriageway, called a *lane* in the following, is a major subject in IV or DAS research [3,19].

The number of wrong-roadway related accidents is relatively small but these are high-risk accidents due to their heads-on crash nature. Countries with 33.6 percent of the world population drive on the left-hand side, and the remaining countries on the right-hand side. For example, tourists crossing this divide are at high risk for driving on the wrong side. In January 2013, Daimler reported about a first assistance system for the detection of driving on the wrong side of the road by reading no-entry signs of motorways [2]. Motion patterns in highway traffic are analysed in [13] for understanding wrong-lane driving. To our best knowledge, there is no further paper published so far addressing explicitly computer-vision-based prevention from driving on the wrong lane.

Lane level positioning is a related area of research, with proposed algorithms based on enhanced digital maps and a *global positioning system* (GPS) [5,14,16,17,18]. The performance of those algorithms relies significantly on the accuracy of the used GPS. In 2005, common GPS systems had a typical accuracy defined by maximum errors (after local stabilization) of 5-10 m [12]. When using an *inertial measurement unit* (IMU), a 2008 solution [15] provided an accuracy improvement to about 1 m. However, commonly used GPS systems are still not yet at this accuracy level (see next section for references). Identifying the currently driven-on road is a realistic assumption, but not yet the lane due to the given variance in GPS data and publicly available digital maps.

This paper proposes a system, operated in the *ego-vehicle*, to identify the driven lane using monocular vision, publicly available digital maps, and standard GPS data. The location, provided by GPS, is matched to the available

R. Wilson et al. (Eds.): CAIP 2013, Part II, LNCS 8048, pp. 50–58, 2013.

digital map, thus obtaining the number of lanes and lane direction(s) at the current location. A monocular camera mounted behind the ego-vehicle's windscreen records road images. Multiple-lane detection is conducted to detect candidate lanes visible in the recorded frames. Lane detection results are then embedded into the derived map information for positioning the current lane and for deciding whether the ego-vehicle is driving in correct lane direction or on the wrong lane. The rest of this paper is structured as follows. Section 2 reviews related research. The proposed system is outlined in Section 3. Section 4 defines experiments and informs about results. Section 5 concludes.

2 Related Work

We briefly review work on enhanced digital maps, and on lane detection and lane tracking, which is closely related to the subject of wrong-lane detection.

GPS and digital maps are currently adopted to identify the driven lane. In [8], a lane determination algorithm is proposed using a differential GPS (DGPS, with an accuracy of 1-2 m) and roadway network data (a *digital map*) at lane-level accuracy. The sequence of the ego-vehicle's locations is obtained via the onboard DGPS, mapped into a trajectory, and this curve is then matched with the network data to determine the driven lane. In [16], a smart-phone GPS and GoogleEarth are employed to locate the car by measuring the azimuth angle of a sequence of GPS responses and their distances to the lane's centre. In [18], apart from using GPS and a digital map, onboard odometer and gyroscope information is also used to define a particle filter to conduct positioning at lane-level accuracy.

Lane detection methods typically only detect the driven lane, and not, for example, also adjacent lanes. In [10], a particle filter and an oriented distance transform are adopted to detect both straight or curved lane borders using a road model defined by 5 individual parameters for each image row. Further single-lane detection algorithms are discussed in [3,19]. However, there are also a few papers which deal with multiple-lane detection. In [11] it is suggested to do camera pitch-angle calibration online while the ego-vehicle is driving on a straight road by analysing an available digital map. Triggered by the digital map information, straight roads and curved roads are handled with different methods. Accumulator voting (in parameter space) for paired lines is used in [9] for generating lane parameters for autonomous vehicle navigation tasks. This algorithm mainly focuses on detecting the driven lane for calculating control parameters for the ego-vehicle (e.g. turning angle, speed). The use of a Catmull-Rom spline model is proposed in [21] for detecting lane mark segments, and then to fuse those segments with an extended Kalman filter. In [7], a modified particle filter defines a method for lane detection. Initial position values are replaced by a random finite set (the particles); the number of elements in the set depends on the number of lanes in the image. This method detect in some experiments up to four lanes, due to the used expansion of the search space. These methods can potentially be used to detect multiple lanes, but none of them considers the robustness of detection results for positioning with lane-level accuracy [7,9,21]. This paper proposes (1) a low-cost system for reducing wrong-lane related accidents, (2) a solution for wrong-lane driving detection, and (3) a new multiple-lane detection method.

3   A Wrong-Lane Warning System

The proposed system takes the current road images and the corresponding (possibly erroneous) GPS coordinates as inputs, and outputs a warning if the ego-vehicle is identified as being currently in the wrong lane.

Recorded monocular road images are preprocessed to obtain at first bird's-eye view images, followed by an oriented distance transform (ODT), being a variant of the Euclidean distance transform [20]. The ODT map is then processed for multiple-lane detection. Next we apply a lane confidence measure to eliminate false lane detections, and assign weights for the remaining candidate lanes. Separately, the GPS coordinates are used to request map location information from a digital map, including the number of lanes, and lane directions. (The current country is also known.) Then we combine the output from the image processing module with the map information routine to conclude whether the currently driven lane is possible or a wrong lane.

Preprocessing. Each single input image I is warped into a bird's-eye view image I^b. In I^b, lane borders are expected to be roughly parallel, which benefits the lane-detection procedure. To obtain I^b, some methods [4,22] require camera focal length and external parameters (mounting angle) information, others [10,6] use

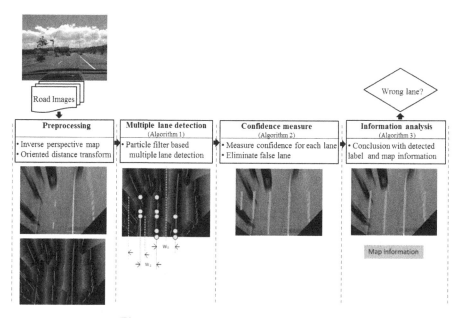

Fig. 1. Overview of the proposed system

simply a rectangular planar pattern to calculate the required homography. We adopt the four-points warp-perspective mapping method [10].

The ODT image I^o is calculated from I^b and used for initializing a particle filter. Figure 1 shows in the upper-left a colour-coded I^o where magnitude of colour saturation represents distance, and blue pixels denote cases $I^o(i,j) = 0$, for pixel coordinates (i,j).

Multiple Lane Detection. Different to lane departure applications, which only require to detect the driven lane, the wrong-lane detection task requires to detect all the lanes visible in the image. We modified the single-lane detection algorithm of [10] for this purpose, now able to detect multiple lanes.

When initializing the detection process for an image, in the chosen initial row, left and right lane borders are located by searching the first blue pixel from the middle column towards both sides. A state vector $s = \{c, \alpha, \beta_1, \beta_2\}$ is initialized, corresponding to the initial borders, representing lane centre point (c), width of the lane (α), and tangential slopes (β_1, β_2) at lane borders in this row. Then the state vector is updated upward in the given image from the initial row, row by row. Details are given in [10].

With the driven lane partially detected, denoted by $L_0 = \{s_0, s_1, \ldots, s_n\}$, the lane width is employed as a prior for initializing the adjacent left L_{l1} and right L_{r1} lanes. Furthermore, lane L_{l2} (if it exists) adjacent on the left of the detected adjacent left lane is detected with prior width of L_{l1}. Iterative initialization and detection is conducted until we reach the image border. The same procedure is used to detect lanes on right-hand side, illustrated in Fig. 1. The yellow dots denotes state vectors, the dashed line is the start-column for searching the initial lane borders. w_0 and w_{l1} are the width of the driven lane, and the lane adjacent on the left, respectively. See Algorithm 1 for details.

Lane Confidence Measure. As false-positives and false-negatives affect this application significantly, detected lanes are weighted to produce more stable candidate lanes. The colour within a detected lane and the chosen particles' confidence are used to generate a lane confidence value P_i, defined by

$$P_i = \exp^{-S(c^0, c^i)} + \sum_{n=1}^{N_i} f_{s_n} \qquad (1)$$

where c denotes (in general) the main colour of a lane, with, for example, c^0 as the main colour of the currently driven lane. f_{s_n} is the particle confidence for the control point (state vector) s_n. $S(\cdot)$ is a colour similarity function (defined in HSV colour space).

Lanes with $P_i < \tau$ are eliminated, where τ is a chosen constant. Due to the limitation of the viewing angle of the camera, not all of the lanes are possibly visible in the image. Thus, a confidence A is measured for detecting the farthest lanes on the left $L_{l|L_l|}$ or on the right $L_{r|L_r|}$. For instance, for regions adjacent to $L_{l|L_l|}$, A^l is defined by

$$A^l = \exp^{-S(c^0, c^{|L_l|+1})} \qquad (2)$$

and encodes information about from which side to count from. See Algorithm 2.

Algorithm 1. (Particle-filter-based algorithm for multiple lane detection)
Input: ODT image I°, image size $W \times H$.
Output: Detected lanes $L_0, L_l = \{L_{l1}, \ldots, L_{l|L_l|}\}, L_r = \{L_{r1}, \ldots, L_{r|L_r|}\}$

1: Let r_0 be the start row, *interval* $= N \cdot 0.2$, and the current lane control point
    number $n_0 = N$, $L_0 = \emptyset$, $L_l = \emptyset$, $L_r = \emptyset$, out-of-border-symbol $flag = FALSE$,
    control point row distance d, birds'-eye view height h
2: **for** $i = W/2, \ldots, 0$ **do**
3:    **if** $I^\circ(r_0, i) == 0$ **then**
4:       left border $lb^0 = i$; **break;**
5:    **end if**
6: **end for**
7: **for** $i = W/2, \ldots, W - 1$ **do**
8:    **if** $I^\circ(r_0, i) == 0$ **then**
9:       right border $rb^0 = i$; **break;**
10:    **end if**
11: **end for**
12: $L_0 = L_0 \cup (lb^0, rb^0)$;
13: $\alpha = \text{atan}((rb^0 - lb^0)/2h)$, $\beta_1 = \beta_2 = 0, c = (rb^0 + lb^0)/2$;
14: $s_0 = \{\alpha, \beta_1, \beta_2, c\}$;
15: **for** $i = 1, \ldots, N$ **do**
16:    update s_{i-1} to s_i with particle filter;
17:    $L_0 = L_0 \cup (lb_i^0, rb_i^0)$;
18:    **if** $i > interval$ **then**
19:       **if** $L_l \neq \emptyset$ **then**
20:          **for** each $L_{lk} \in L_l$ **do**
21:             update s_{i-1}^{lk} to s_i^{lk} with particle filter;
22:             $L_{lk} = L_{lk} \cup (lb_i^{lk}, rb_i^{lk})$;
23:          **end for**
24:          lane width $w_l = \frac{1}{|L_l|} \sum_m^{|L_l|} (lb_m^{l|L_l|} - rb_m^{l|L_l|})$;
25:          $rb^l = \frac{1}{|L_l|} \sum_m^{|L_l|} lb_m^{l|L_l|}$;
26:       **else**
27:          lane width $w_l = \frac{1}{|L_0|} \sum_m^{|L_0|} (lb_m^0 - rb_m^0)$;
28:          $rb^l = \frac{1}{|L_0|} \sum_m^{|L_0|} lb_m^0$;
29:       **end if**
30:       **if** $i - interval * |L_l| > interval \,\&\, flag$ **then**
31:          **if** $rb^l - \gamma * w_l < 0$ **then**
32:             $flag = TRUE$; **continue;**
33:          **end if**
34:          **for** $j = rb^l - \gamma * w_l, \ldots, 0$ **do**
35:             **if** $I^\circ(r_0 + i * d, j) == 0$ **then**
36:                $lb^l = i$; **break;**
37:             **end if**
38:          **end for**
39:          $L_{l(|L_l|+1)} = L_{l(|L_l|+1)} \cup (lb^l, rb^l)$;
40:          $L_l = L_l \cup L_{l(|L_l|+1)}$;
41:       **end if**
42:       process right lanes in the same way;
43:    **end if**
44: **end for**
45: Return L_0, L_l, and L_r.

Algorithm 2. (Lane confidence measure)
Input: L_0, L_l, and L_r.
Output: Lane confidence P_l, P_r, pruned detection results L_l, and L_r
1: Let $P_l = \emptyset$, $P_r = \emptyset$, $A^l = 1$, $A^r = 1$.
2: **for** $i = 0, \ldots, |L_l|$ **do**
3:　　calculate confidence p^{li} for lane L_{li};
4:　　**if** $p^{li} < \tau$ **then**
5:　　　　remove lanes $L_{li}, \ldots, L_{l|L_l|}$ from L_l;
6:　　　　set adjacent lane confidence $A^l = 0$, for L_l; break;
7:　　**else**
8:　　　　$P_l = P_l \cup p_{li}$;
9:　　**end if**
10: **end for**
11: **if** $A^l \neq 0$ **then**
12:　　calculate A^l with Equ. (2);
13: **end if**
14: L_r, P_r, A^r obtained in the same way;
15: Return P_l, P_r, A^l, A^r L_l, and L_r.

Information Analysis. Having standard GPS, the coordinates (longitude and latitude) are used to map the driving location onto a publicly available digital map, for instance, an *openstreet map*. We obtain the corresponding number of lanes and lane directions with tags (e.g. *lanes, lanes:forward, lane:backward*). Detected results L_r, L_l, P_l, P_r, A^l, and A^r, aligned with map information, are analysed to conclude whether the ego-vehicle is currently driving in a wrong lane. First, A^l and A^r are adopted to decide which side (left or right) to count from. We are able to decide by utilizing the number of directed lanes l_r, l_w and L_r, L_l. For details, see Algorithm 3.

4   Experiments

We tested the proposed system on three sequences recorded with a smart phone mounted behind the ego-vehicle's windscreen. The total length of the sequences is 1,239 frames, with a resolution of 640×480 $(30Hz)$. Two sequences are recorded while driving on a two-lane road, denoted as 2-lane (1) and 2-lane (2). One sequence is obtained on a four-lane road, denoted by 4-lane. All sequences are recorded in a left-hand side driving country.

Sequences are processed with the same set of parameters, except the parameters used to calculate bird's-eye view images. The performance is measured by (1) number of false-positive lane detection per frame (FP), (2) number of false-negative lane detection per frame (FN), (3) number of false alarms (FA), (4) number of ignored frames as only the driven lane is detected (Ignored). The obtained results are given in the following table:

Sequences	FP	FN	FA	Ignored
4-lane	0	0.047	0	14
2-lane (1)	0	0.035	0	2
2-lane (2)	0.207	0.117	28	75

For "simple road situations" [2-lane (1) and 4-lane], the proposed system works fine. The false-positives and false-negatives do not necessarily lead to false alarm, due to the process of the confidence measure aligned with the information analysis. However, if there are complicated road markings or other driving cars, blocking the camera view [as in 2-lane (2)], the single-frame process is not robust (see $FA = 28$). Considering temporal information from previous frames improves the performance, but this paper is not discussing this extension.

Algorithm 3. (Information analysis)
Input: L_r, L_l, P_l, P_r, A^l, and A^r.
Output: Wrong-lane-driving $flagWarning$
 1: Let $flagWarning = FALSE$, and l_r, l_w are numbers of correct and incorrect
     direction lanes.
 2: **if** $A^l == 0$ **then**
 3:    **if** $|L_l| + 1 > l_r$ **then**
 4:       $flagWarning = TRUE$;
 5:    **end if**
 6: **else**
 7:    **if** $A^r == 0$ **then**
 8:       **if** $|L_r| + 1 \leq l_w$ **then**
 9:          $flagWarning = TRUE$;
10:       **end if**
11:    **else**
12:       **if** $A^l > \tau_1$ **then**
13:          **if** $A^r \leq \tau_1 \& |L_r| + 1 \leq l_w$ **then**
14:             $flagWarning = TRUE$;
15:          **end if**
16:       **else**
17:          **if** $|L_l| + 1 > l_r$ **then**
18:             $flagWarning = TRUE$;
19:          **end if**
20:       **end if**
21:    **end if**
22: **end if**
23: Return $flagWarning$.

5   Conclusions

This paper proposed to adopt a monocular camera to detect multiple lanes, and then to analyse the detected lanes aligned with GPS information to located the car more accurately at lane-level. The proposed system proved to be valid for the detection of wrong-lane driving if road marking is "fairly" visible and not occluded by other cars. The system could be modified to handle GPS temporally occlusion situation, as the GPS information is not needed for each frame.

References

1. Anonymous. Global status report on road safety (2009), http://www.who.int/violence_injury_prevention/road_traffic/global_status_report/en/
2. Anonymous. First assistance system in the fight against vehicles driving on the wrong side of the road (January 21, 2013), http://www.daimler.com/dccom/
3. Bar Hillel, A., Lerner, R., Levi, D., Raz, G.: Recent progress in road and lane detection: a survey. Machine Vision Applications 23, 1–19 (2012)
4. Bertozzi, M., Broggi, A.: GOLD: A parallel real-time stereo vision system for generic obstacle and lane detection. In: Proc. IEEE Conf. Image Processing, vol. 7, pp. 62–81 (1998)
5. Bétaille, D., Toledo-Moreo, R., Laneurit, J.: Making an enhanced map for lane location based services. In: Proc. IEEE Conf. Intelligent Transportation Systems, pp. 711–716 (2008)
6. Broggi, A., Bertozzi, M., Fascioli, A.: Self-calibration of a stereo vision system for automotive applications. In: Proc. IEEE Conf. Robotics Automation, vol. 4, pp. 3698–3703 (2001)
7. Deusch, H., Wiest, J., Reuter, S., Szczot, M., Konrad, M., Dietmayer, K.: A random finite set approach to multiple lane detection. Proc. Intelligent Transportation Systems, 270–275 (2012)
8. Du, J., Barth, M.J.: Next-generation automated vehicle location systems: Positioning at the lane level. IEEE Trans. Intelligent Transportation Systems 9, 48–57 (2008)
9. Gupta, R.A., Snyder, W., Pitts, W.S.: Concurrent visual multiple lane detection for autonomous vehicles. In: Proc. IEEE Conf. Robotics Automation, pp. 2416–2422 (2010)
10. Jiang, R., Terauchi, M., Klette, R., Wang, S., Vaudrey, T.: Low-level image processing for lane detection and tracking. In: Proc. Arts and Technology. LNICST, vol. 30, pp. 190–197 (2010)
11. Jiang, Y., Gao, F., Xu, G.: Self-calibrated multiple-lane detection system. In: Proc. IEEE Position Location Navigation Symposium, pp. 1052–1056 (2010)
12. Michael, W., Aaron, E., Loren, K.: Consumer-grade global positioning system (GPS) accuracy and reliability. J. Forestry 103, 169–173 (2005)
13. Monteiro, G., Ribeiro, M., Marcos, J., Batista, J.: Wrongway drivers detection based on optical flow. In: Proc. IEEE Int. Conf. Image Processing, vol. 5, pp. 141–144 (2007)
14. Peyret, F., Laneurit, J., Bétaille, D.: A novel system using enhanced digital maps and WAAS for a lane-level positioning. Proc. World Congress Intelligent Transport Systems, 12 pages (2008)
15. Urmson, C., et al.: Autonomous driving in urban environments: Boss and the urban challenge. J. Field Robotics 25, 425–466 (2008)
16. Sekimoto, Y., Matsubayashi, Y., Yamada, H., Imai, R., Usui, T., Kanasugi, H.: Light weight lane positioning of vehicles using a smartphone GPS by monitoring the distance from the center line. In: Proc. IEEE Conf. Intelligent Transportation Systems, pp. 1561–1565 (2012)

17. Selloum, A., Bétaille, D., Le Carpentier, E., Peyret, F.: Lane level positioning using particle filtering. In: Proc. IEEE Conf. Intelligent Transportation Systems, pp. 1–6 (2009)
18. Selloum, A., Bétaille, D., Le Carpentier, E., Peyret, F.: Robustification of a map aided location process using road direction. In: Proc. IEEE Conf. Intelligent Transportation Systems, pp. 1504–1510 (2010)
19. Shin, B.-S., Klette, R.: Visual lane analysis - a concise review. Multimedia Imaging, MItech-TR-85. The University of Auckland (2013)
20. Wu, T., Ding, X.Q., Wang, S.J., Wang, K.Q.: Video object tracking using improved chamfer matching and condensation particle filter. In: SPIE Proc. Machine Vision Applications, vol. 6813, 4 pages (2008)
21. Zhao, K., Meuter, M., Nunn, C., Muller, D., Muller-Schneiders, S., Pauli, J.: A novel multi-lane detection and tracking system. In: Proc. IEEE Intelligent Vehicles Symposium, pp. 1084–1089 (2012)
22. Zhaoxue, C., Pengfei, S.: Efficient method for camera calibration in traffic scenes. Electronics Letters 40, 368–369 (2004)

Blind Deconvolution
Using Alternating Maximum a Posteriori
Estimation with Heavy-Tailed Priors*

Jan Kotera[1,2], Filip Šroubek[1], and Peyman Milanfar[3]

[1] Institue of Information Theory and Automation,
Academy of Sciences of the Czech Republic, Prague, Czech Republic
{kotera,sroubekf}@utia.cas.cz
[2] Charles University in Prague, Faculty of Mathematics and Physics, Czech Republic
[3] University of California Santa Cruz, Electrical Engineering Department,
Santa Cruz CA 95064 USA
milanfar@ee.ucsc.edu

Abstract. Single image blind deconvolution aims to estimate the unknown blur from a single observed blurred image and recover the original sharp image. Such task is severely ill-posed and typical approaches involve some heuristic or other steps without clear mathematical explanation to arrive at an acceptable solution. We show that a straightforward maximum a posteriory estimation combined with very sparse priors and an efficient numerical method can produce results, which compete with much more complicated state-of-the-art methods.

Keywords: image blind deconvolution, blur estimation, heavy-tailed priors, augmented Lagrangian method.

1   Introduction

Single channel blind deconvolution amounts to estimating an image u from a single observed image g satisfying a convolutional degradation model

$$g = u * h + n, \tag{1}$$

where h, called point spread function (PSF), is unknown and n is random additive noise. Since we have only one observation (Single-Channel) and no knowledge of the PSF, the problem is extremely ill-posed. One way to tackle this problem is to assume a parametric model of the PSF and search in the space of parameters and not in the full space of PSFs. Chang *et al.* in [2] investigated zero patterns in the Fourier transform or in the cepstrum, and assumed only parametric motion or out-of-focus blurs. More low-level parametric methods for estimating general motion blurs were proposed in [14,16]. Unfortunately

---

* This work was supported by GA UK under grant 938213, by GACR under grant 13-29225S, and by AVCR under grant M100751201.

R. Wilson et al. (Eds.): CAIP 2013, Part II, LNCS 8048, pp. 59–66, 2013.

real PSFs seldom follow parametric models and this prevents the parametric methods from finding the exact solution.

There has been a considerable effort in the image processing community in the last three decades to find a reliable algorithm for SC blind deconvolution with general (non-parametric) PSFs. First algorithms appeared in telecommunication and signal processing in early 80's [6]. For a long time, the problem seemed too difficult to be solvable for arbitrary blur kernels. Proposed algorithms usually worked only for special cases, such as symmetric PSFs or astronomical images with uniform black background, see [1].

Over the last few years, SC blind deconvolution based on the Bayesian paradigm experiences a renaissance. In probabilistic point of view, simultaneous recovery of u and h amounts to solving standard MAP (Maximum A Posteriori) estimation

$$P(u, h|g) \propto P(g|u, h)P(u, h) = P(g|u, h)P(u)P(h)$$

where $P(g|u, h) \propto \exp(-\frac{\gamma}{2}\|u * h - g\|^2)$ is the noise distribution (in this case assumed Gaussian) and $P(u)$, $P(h)$ are the prior distributions on the latent image and blur kernel, respectively. The key idea of new algorithms is to address the ill-posedness of blind deconvolution by characterizing the prior $P(u)$ using natural image statistics and by a better choice of estimators.

Levin *et al.* in [10,9] claim that a proper estimator matters more than the shape of priors. They showed that marginalizing the posterior with respect to the latent image u leads to the correct solution of the PSF h. The marginalized probability $P(h|g)$ can be expressed in a closed form only for simple priors that are, e.g., Gaussian. Otherwise approximation methods such as variational Bayes [11] or the Laplace approximation [5] must be used. A frantic activity in this area started with the work of Fergus *et al.* [4], who applied variational Bayes to approximate the posterior $P(u, h|g)$ by a simpler distribution $q(u, h) = q(u)q(h)$. Other authors [7,8,13,15] stick to the "good old" alternating MAP approach, but by using ad hoc steps, which often lack rigorous explanation, they converge to the correct solution.

The main contribution of our paper is to show that a simple alternating MAP approach without any ad hoc steps results in an efficient blind deconvolution algorithm that outperforms sophisticated state-of-the-art methods. The novelty is to use image priors $P(u)$ that are more heavy-tailed than Laplace distribution and apply a method of augmented Lagrangian to tackle this non-convex optimization problem.

In the next section we define the energy function of u and h that we want to minimize. Sec. 3 provides a detailed description of the optimization algorithm and the final experimental section illustrates algorithm's performance.

2   Mathematical Model

Let us assume that the variables in (1) are discrete quantities (vectors) with indexing denoted as u_i or $[u]_i$. Maximization of the posterior $P(u, h|g)$ is equivalent to minimization of its negative logarithm, i.e.,

$$L(u,h) = -\log(P(u,h|g)) + const = \frac{\gamma}{2}\|u*h - g\|_2^2 + Q(u) + R(h) + const, \quad (2)$$

where $Q(u) = -\log P(u)$ and $R(h) = -\log P(h)$ can be regarded as regularizers that steer the optimization to the right solution and away from infinite number of trivial or other unwanted solutions. A typical prior on u allows only few nonzero resulting coefficients of some linear or nonlinear image transform. The most popular choice is probably the l_1 norm of the image derivatives, either directionally separable $Q(u) = \sum_i |[D_x u]_i| + |[D_y u]_i|$ (this corresponds to the Laplace distribution of image derivatives) or isotropic (in terms of image gradient) $Q(u) = \sum_i \sqrt{[D_x u]_i^2 + [D_y u]_i^2}$, where D_x and D_y are partial derivative operators. The prior on h depends on the task at hand, for motion blurs it again favors sparsity and, in addition, disallows negative values.

It has been reported (e.g. [10]) that the distribution of gradients of natural images is even more heavy-tailed than Laplace distribution, we therefore use a generalized version of $Q(u)$ defined as

$$Q(u) = \Phi(D_x u, D_y u) = \sum_i \left([D_x u]_i^2 + [D_y u]_i^2\right)^{\frac{p}{2}}, \quad 0 \le p \le 1.$$

For the blur kernel we use Laplace distribution on the positive kernel values to force sparsity and zero on the negative values. This results in the following regularizer R:

$$R(h) = \sum_i \Psi(h_i), \quad \Psi(h_i) = \begin{cases} h_i & h_i \ge 0 \\ +\infty & h_i < 0. \end{cases}$$

3   Optimization Algorithm

In order to numerically find the solution u, h, we alternately minimize the functional L in (2) with respect to either u or h while keeping the other constant, this allows for easy minimization of the joint data fitting term. In each minimization subproblem we use the augmented Lagrangian method (ALM) (see e.g. [12, Chap. 17]), let us describe the procedure in detail.

3.1   Minimization with Respect to u

We wish to solve

$$\min_u \frac{\gamma}{2}\|Hu - g\|^2 + \Phi(D_x u, D_y u),$$

where H denotes a (fixed) convolution operator constructed from the h estimate from the previous iteration. This problem is equivalent to introducing new variables $v_x = D_x u$, $v_y = D_y u$ and solving

$$\min_{u,v} \frac{\gamma}{2}\|Hu - g\|^2 + \Phi(v_x, v_y) \quad \text{s.t. } v_x = D_x u, \; v_y = D_y u.$$

ALM adds quadratic penalty term for each constraint to the traditional Lagrangian, which (after some reshuffling) results in the functional

$$L_u(u, v_x, v_y) = \frac{\gamma}{2}\|Hu - g\|^2 + \Phi(v_x, v_y) + \frac{\alpha}{2}\|D_x u - v_x - a_x\|^2 + \frac{\alpha}{2}\|D_y u - v_y - a_y\|^2,$$

where the new variables a_x, a_y are proportional to the estimates of the Lagrange
multipliers of the corresponding constraints. After such reformulation, the data
term $\|Hu - g\|^2$ and the regularizer $\Phi(v_x, v_y)$ can be minimized separately since
they depend on different variables. By introducing penalty terms, ALM allows us
to treat the constrained variables $D_x u$ and v_x (similarly $D_y u$ and v_y) as though
they were unrelated and by keeping the penalty weight α sufficiently large, we
will obtain the solution to the original problem [3, Thm. 8].

We solve the minimization of L_u via coordinate descent in the u, v_x, v_y "direction" alternately. That is, we compute derivative with respect to one variable
while keeping others fixed, solve it for minimum and update that variable accordingly, then move on to the next variable and so on for sufficiently many
iterations. Let us state the whole process at once and explain the individual
steps afterwards.

1: Set $v_x^0 := 0, v_y^0 := 0, a_x^0 := 0, a_y^0 := 0$, and $j := 0$
2: **repeat**
3:      Solve $(H^T H + \frac{\alpha}{\gamma}(D_x^T D_x + D_y^T D_y))u^{j+1} = H^T g + \frac{\alpha}{\gamma}(D_x^T(v_x^j + a_x^j) + D_y^T(v_y^j + a_y^j))$ for u^{j+1}
4:      $\{[v_x^{j+1}]_i, [v_y^{j+1}]_i\} := \mathrm{LUT}_p([D_x u^{j+1} - a_x^j]_i, [D_y u^{j+1} - a_y^j]_i), \quad \forall i$
5:      $a_x^{j+1} := a_x^j - D_x u^{j+1} + v_x^{j+1}$
6:      $a_y^{j+1} := a_y^j - D_y u^{j+1} + v_y^{j+1}$
7:      $j := j + 1$
8: **until** stopping criterion is satisfied
9: **return** u^j

After differentiating L_u w.r.t. u and setting the derivative to zero, we must
solve the linear system on line 3 for u. If we treat the $u * h$ convolution as circular,
then H and consequently the whole matrix on the left-hand side is block-circulant
and can be dignolized by 2D Fourier transform. Thus, the solution u can be
computed directly and only at the cost of Fourier transform.

Minimization of L_u w.r.t. v_x, v_y on line 4 is trickier. If we disregard terms
not depending on v_x, v_y, we get $\Phi(v_x, v_y) + \frac{\alpha}{2}\|D_x u - v_x - a_x\|^2 + \frac{\alpha}{2}\|D_y u - v_y - a_y\|^2$, where all three terms are summations of simpler terms over all image
pixels. Derivatives and minimzation can be therefore carried out pixel by pixel
independently. Let i be fixed pixel index. Let $t = ([v_x]_i, [v_y]_i)$ and $r = (D_x u_i - [a_x]_i, D_y u_i - [a_y]_i)$, then the problem of minimizing L_u w.r.t. $[v_x]_i, [v_y]_i$ can be
rewritten as

$$\min_t \|t\|^p + \frac{\alpha}{2}\|t - r\|^2. \tag{3}$$

For some p a closed form solution can be computed. After simple calculation it
can be seen that for the common choice of $p = 1$, minimization of (3) results

in vector soft thresholding $t = \frac{r}{\|r\|} \max\left(\|r\| - \frac{1}{\alpha}, 0\right)$. Similarly, for the binary penalty $p = 0$ we get hard thresholding with threshold $\sqrt{2/\alpha}$. For the general case $0 < p < 1$, no closed form solution exists, but becasue p is known beforehand and (3) is basically 1D minimization, it can be precomputed numerically and used in the minimization of L_u w.r.t. v_x, v_y in the form of lookup table (LUT), which is then used independently for each ith component of v_x, v_y.

Update equations for a_x, a_y on lines 5 and 6 are reminiscent of simple gradient descent but actually originate from the ALM theory, [12].

3.2   Minimization with Respect to h

Minimizing with respect to h can be done in similar fashion. To separate the minimization of data term and regularizer, we again make the substitution $v_h = h$, which yields the following optimization problem

$$\min_{h, v_h} \frac{\gamma}{2}\|Uh - g\|^2 + R(v_h) \quad \text{s.t. } h = v_h,$$

where U is (fixed) convolutional operator constructed from u. Applying ALM again results in the functional

$$L_h(h, v_h) = \frac{\gamma}{2}\|Uh - g\|^2 + R(v_h) + \frac{\beta}{2}\|h - v_h - a_h\|^2,$$

where a_h is again related to ALM method and is proportional to the Lagrange multiplier of the prescribed constraint. This functional can be minimized by the following coordinate descent algorithm:

1: Set $v_h^0 := 0, a_h^0 := 0$, and $j := 0$
2: **repeat**
3:     Solve $(U^T U + \frac{\beta}{\gamma}I)h^{j+1} = U^T g + \frac{\beta}{\gamma}(v_h^j + a_h^j)$ for h^{j+1}
4:     $[v_h^{j+1}]_i := \max([h^{j+1} - a^j]_i - \frac{1}{\beta}, 0), \quad \forall i$
5:     $a_h^{j+1} := a_h^j - h^{j+1} + v_h^{j+1}$
6:     $j := j + 1$
7: **until** stopping criterion is satisfied
8: **return** h^j

As in the previous case, the linear system on line 3, originating from differentiating L_h w.r.t. h, can be diagonalized by 2D Fourier transform and therefore solved directly. I denotes identity matrix.

Minimization w.r.t. v_h can be again done component-wise. Let i be a pixel index, $t = [v_h]_i$, $r = [h - a_h]_i$, then the problem on line 4 can be rewritten as $\min_t \frac{\beta}{2}(r - t)^2 + \psi(t)$, which is basically scalar version of (3) for $p = 1$ with the additional constraint that only positive values of t are allowed. The solution is thus component-wise soft thresholding as specified on line 4. Line 5 originates again from the ALM theory.

3.3   Implementation Details

To avoid getting trapped in a local minimum, we estimate the PSF in the multiscale fashion. The input image g is downsampled such that the estimated PSF at this scale is small (3×3 pixels or similar), then we upsample such estimated PSF (with factor 2) and use this as the initial point of the next level estimation. This procedure is repeated until the target PSF size is reached.

The no-blur solution is favored by blind deconvolution algorithms based on MAP. It is thus advantageous to exaggerate some parameters to push the optimization away from this trivial solution. We have discovered that setting the parametr γ lower than its correct value (as it corresponds to the observed image noise level) and slowly increasing it during the optimization helps the PSF estimation. Also, we set the sparsity parameter p to much lower value than would be expected for natural images and only after estimating the PSF we run the u estimation one last time with p and γ set to realistic values.

For our experiments we use for the PSF estimation $\gamma = 1$, $\alpha = 1$, $\beta = 10^4$, $p = 0.3$ and we multiply the γ by 1.5 after each pass of the u-estimation and h-estimation pair. For the final nonblind deconvolution, we use $\gamma = 10, p = 1$.

4   Experimental Results

We tested our algorithm on the dataset provided by [10] consisting of four grayscale images and eight PSFs of true motion blur, resulting in 32 test images. We compare our method to the method of [15], which is arguably currently the best performing single-channel blind deconvolution method, and the method of [4], which frequently appears in comparisons of blind deconvolution methods. In our comparison, we focus on the accuracy assesment of the estimated PSF, which we measure by the MSE of the (registered) estimated PSF to the ground truth.

Fig. 2 shows the result of kernel estimation measured as MSE from the ground truth kernel. We see that in most cases our method is superior. Fig. 3 shows the estimeted PSFs for the first input image. The remaining 24 estimates look

Fig. 1. The dataset of [10]. First row contains sharp images, second row measured motion blur PSFs.

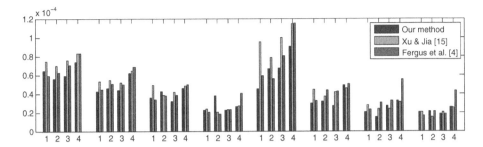

Fig. 2. MSE of estimated kernels (low values mean better performance) in the 32 test examples, grouped by PSFs. Numbers on x-axis indicate image index.

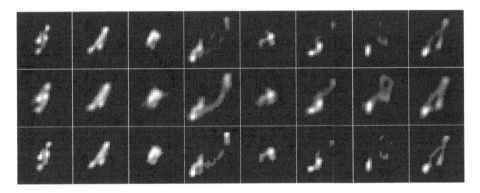

Fig. 3. Estimated PSFs, image 1. Rows from top to bottom: our method, method of [15], method of [4]. Compare with ground truth in Fig. 1.

Fig. 4. Deconvolution of true motion blur. Left: captured image, right: deconvolved result (estimated PSF superimposed).

similar. All methods perform very well but it can be seen that our method produces slightly more accurate results. The last experiment in Fig. 4 shows the deconvolution result of severely motion-blurred photo captured by handheld camera, the improvement in quality is evident.

References

1. Chan, T.F., Wong, C.K.: Total variation blind deconvolution. IEEE Trans. Image Processing 7(3), 370–375 (1998)
2. Chang, M.M., Tekalp, A.M., Erdem, A.T.: Blur identification using the bispectrum. IEEE Trans. Signal Processing 39(10), 2323–2325 (1991)
3. Eckstein, J., Bertsekas, D.P.: On the Douglas-Rachford splitting method and the proximal point algorithm for maximal monotone operators. Math. Program. 55(3), 293–318 (1992)
4. Fergus, R., Singh, B., Hertzmann, A., Roweis, S.T., Freeman, W.T.: Removing camera shake from a single photograph. In: SIGGRAPH 2006: ACM SIGGRAPH 2006 Papers, pp. 787–794. ACM, New York (2006)
5. Galatsanos, N.P., Mesarovic, V.Z., Molina, R., Katsaggelos, A.K.: Hierarchical Bayesian image restoration from partially known blurs. IEEE Transactions on Image Processing 9(10), 1784–1797 (2000)
6. Godard, D.: Self-recovering equalization and carrier tracking in two-dimensional data communication systems. IEEE Transactions on Communications 28(11), 1867–1875 (1980)
7. Jia, J.: Single image motion deblurring using transparency. In: Proc. IEEE Conference on Computer Vision and Pattern Recognition CVPR 2007, June 17–22, pp. 1–8 (2007)
8. Joshi, N., Szeliski, R., Kriegman, D.J.: PSF estimation using sharp edge prediction. In: Proc. IEEE Conference on Computer Vision and Pattern Recognition CVPR 2008, June 23–28, pp. 1–8 (2008)
9. Levin, A., Weiss, Y., Durand, F., Freeman, W.T.: Understanding blind deconvolution algorithms. IEEE Transactions on Pattern Analysis and Machine Intelligence 33(12), 2354–2367 (2011)
10. Levin, A., Weiss, Y., Durand, F., Freeman, W.T.: Understanding and evaluating blind deconvolution algorithms. In: Proc. IEEE Conference on Computer Vision and Pattern Recognition, CVPR 2009, pp. 1964–1971 (2009)
11. Miskin, J., MacKay, D.J.C.: Ensemble learning for blind image separation and deconvolution. In: Girolani, M. (ed.) Advances in Independent Component Analysis, pp. 123–142. Springer (2000)
12. Nocedal, J., Wright, S.: Numerical Optimization. Springer Series in Operations Research. Springer (2006)
13. Shan, Q., Jia, J., Agarwala, A.: High-quality motion deblurring from a single image. In: SIGGRAPH 2008: ACM SIGGRAPH 2008 Papers, pp. 1–10. ACM, New York (2008)
14. Shan, Q., Xiong, W., Jia, J.: Rotational motion deblurring of a rigid object from a single image. In: Proc. IEEE 11th International Conference on Computer Vision ICCV 2007, October 14–21, pp. 1–8 (2007)
15. Xu, L., Jia, J.: Two-phase kernel estimation for robust motion deblurring. In: Daniilidis, K., Maragos, P., Paragios, N. (eds.) ECCV 2010, Part I. LNCS, vol. 6311, pp. 157–170. Springer, Heidelberg (2010)
16. Yitzhaky, Y., Kopeika, N.S.: Identification of blur parameters from motion blurred images. Graphical Models and Image Processing 59(5), 310–320 (1997)

Focus Fusion
with Anisotropic Depth Map Smoothing

Madina Boshtayeva, David Hafner, and Joachim Weickert

Mathematical Image Analysis Group,
Faculty of Mathematics and Computer Science,
Campus E1.7, Saarland University, 66041 Saarbrücken, Germany
{boshtayeva,hafner,weickert}@mia.uni-saarland.de

Abstract. Focus fusion methods combine a set of images focused at different depths into a single image where all parts are in focus. The quality of the fusion result strongly depends on a decision map that determines the in-focus areas. Most approaches in the literature achieve this by local decisions without explicitly enforcing smoothness of the depth map. The goal of our paper is to introduce a modern regularisation strategy where we assume that neighbouring pixels in the resulting image have a similar depth. To this end, we consider a partial differential equation (PDE) for the depth map. It combines a robustified data fidelity term with an anisotropic diffusion strategy that involves a matrix-valued diffusion tensor. Experiments with synthetic and real-world data show that this depth map regularisation can improve existing fusion methods substantially. Our methodology is general and can be applied to improve many existing fusion methods.

Keywords: focus fusion, depth map, anisotropic diffusion.

1 Introduction

Certain applications such as microscopy and macro photography create images with a very limited depth of field. To overcome this problem, a common approach is to acquire a set of images with focal planes at different depths, and to fuse these data into a single image that is in focus everywhere. This is called *focus fusion*.

We categorise the focus fusion techniques into two main groups: The first group of methods performs a multiresolution decomposition of the input images. This is done by transforming the image set into a particular domain, e.g. a pyramid domain [1, 2] or a wavelet domain [3, 4]. Then they identify the in-focus areas and combine them into a single composite image. In the last step, this composite is transformed back into the original image domain. These methods suffer from the drawback that fusion in the transformed domain may result in undesirable artefacts in the original domain.

The second group of algorithms operates in the image domain directly. In contrast to the decomposition approaches, they rely on the original intensities and,

R. Wilson et al. (Eds.): CAIP 2013, Part II, LNCS 8048, pp. 67–74, 2013.

hence, reproduce the image structures without any modification. An intuitive idea is to select for each pixel the input frame that is in focus according to some sharpness criterion [5]. Then these pixels are directly combined within a single composite image. However, this direct pixel fusion is prone to unpleasant seams in the final result.

The following approaches have been proposed to deal with this drawback. Wang *et al.* [6] and Pop *et al.* [7] explicitly model a smoothness assumption of the fused image by formulating an appropriate energy or partial differential equation (PDE), respectively. However, in this case the resulting image may loose important structures due to the inherent smoothing. Another way is to apply the smoothness constraint not on the final image itself, but on the per-pixel decision. In this regard, a common approach is to first construct an initial noisy map using a simple criterion, and segment it afterwards with a segmentation-based algorithm [8–10].

Our Contributions. The goal of our paper is to address these problems of direct pixel fusion methods. We avoid unpleasant seams by introducing a modern regularisation strategy of the depth map such that neighbouring pixels correspond to similar depth values. In contrast to the segmentation approaches in [8–10] that create *piecewise constant* depth maps, our method aims a *piecewise smooth* results. Thus, it is able to handle pixels that are in focus between two frames. This causes not only more realistic depth maps, but also allows smooth transitions in the fused image.

Our method is based on a PDE model that features a robust data term in conjunction with a sophisticated anisotropic diffusion term. It relies on a diffusion tensor that allows *joint image- and depth-driven* regularisation: Image edges determine the direction of depth map discontinuities, while the smoothing across these discontinuities is steered by the magnitude of the depth map gradient. We show that this novel strategy leads to substantially better fusion results than methods that do not incorporate smoothness assumptions on the depth field.

In contrast to decomposition methods that may change the underlying images structures by transforming them into another domain, our method relies on the unmodified intensity values and, hence, is able to reproduce the sharp image structures accurately.

Organisation. Our paper is organised as follows: Sec. 2 introduces our new approach for focus fusion. In Sec. 3, we show experimental results of the method on a synthetic as well as on a real–world image set. The paper is concluded with a summary in Sec. 4.

2   Our Focus Fusion Method

Let $f(\boldsymbol{x}, z)$ be a 3-D volume, where $\boldsymbol{x} := (x, y)^{\top} \in \Omega$ denotes the location within a rectangular image domain $\Omega \subset \mathbb{R}^2$ and $z \in \mathbb{R}$ denotes the depth. Consequently, the n input images $f(\boldsymbol{x}, z_k)$ with $k = 1, \ldots, n$ represent slices of this volume, where we assume z_k to be distributed equidistantly. To remove noise, we presmooth each image via a convolution with a Gaussian of standard deviation σ. This results in f_σ. Our goal is to find a depth map $d : \Omega \to [1, n]$ that selects for each location $\boldsymbol{x}$ the frame that is in focus. To this end, we formulate a PDE that models the similarity to a precomputed depth map d_{init}, combined with an anisotropic smoothness constraint.

2.1 Initial Depth Map

Let us now construct the initial depth map that is later embedded in the similarity assumption of our PDE. We exploit the fact that the sharp regions most probably correspond to the locations where the gradient has the largest magnitude. Since each frame corresponds to a certain depth, selecting a gradient at each location can be understood as deciding for the corresponding depth. Thus, it is possible to estimate a depth map of the resulting image.

Two types of locations cause a problem while estimating the initial depth map: homogeneous regions that hardly have any texture, and regions that are never in focus, such as the background. Here the gradients have approximately the same magnitude in all frames, and thus, the final decision is highly influenced by noise. Accordingly, the initial depth map appears noisy within these locations. An example of such a noisy initial depth map obtained from the real-world image set is shown in Fig. 2d. Here, black pixels correspond to the closest frame and white pixels refer to the farthest frame.

Confidence Function. To separate reliable pixels from noisy ones in the initial depth map, we use a confidence function as proposed in [11]. It is defined as

$$c(\boldsymbol{x}) = \begin{cases} 1 & \text{if } \ |\boldsymbol{\nabla} f_\sigma(\boldsymbol{x}, d_{\text{init}}(\boldsymbol{x}))| > T \\ 0 & \text{else} \end{cases} \tag{1}$$

where $\boldsymbol{\nabla} := (\partial_x, \partial_y)^\top$ denotes the spatial gradient operator, and T is a threshold. (In the case of colour images, we define the combined gradient magnitude as the square root of the sum over all squared gradient entries.) An example of the previously shown initial depth map after gradient thresholding ($\sigma = 1.0, T = 13$) is presented in Fig. 2e. Here, red colour denotes unreliable pixels that have been eliminated. The proposed confidence function leaves only reliable locations in the initial depth map and thus allows a better modelling. We see that the depth map may become very sparse, but the filling-in effect of the smoothness term of our new model will allow to reconstruct a dense depth map from these sparse data.

2.2 Our PDE-Based Approach

Let us now discuss our PDE-based approach that allows to find the desired depth map. The underlying idea is that there is a spatial continuity between the parts selected from different frames. This means that for each pixel the neighbouring pixels most probably should be chosen from a similar depth level. Thus, we apply a smoothness constraint on the resulting depth map.

We are searching for the depth map $d(\boldsymbol{x})$ which minimises an energy functional of the form

$$E(d) := \frac{1}{2} \int_{\Omega} \left(c(\boldsymbol{x}) \cdot M(d(\boldsymbol{x})) + \alpha\, S(\boldsymbol{\nabla} d(\boldsymbol{x})) \right) d\boldsymbol{x}, \qquad (2)$$

where $c(\boldsymbol{x})$ is the proposed confidence function, and $\alpha > 0$ is the smoothness parameter. The data term $M(d(\boldsymbol{x}))$ assumes that $d(\boldsymbol{x})$ should be similar to the initial depth map $d_{\text{init}}(\boldsymbol{x})$. Furthermore, to reduce the influence of outliers we use the regularised L^1-norm $\Psi(s^2):=\sqrt{s^2+\varepsilon^2}$ as a penalisation function, where s denotes the data constraint and $\varepsilon > 0$ is a small constant. The data term is finally given by

$$M(d(\boldsymbol{x})) := \Psi\left((d(\boldsymbol{x}) - d_{\text{init}}(\boldsymbol{x}))^2 \right). \qquad (3)$$

A simple smoothness term enforcing $d(\boldsymbol{x})$ to vary smoothly in space is given by

$$S(\boldsymbol{\nabla} d(\boldsymbol{x})) := |\boldsymbol{\nabla} d(\boldsymbol{x})|^2 . \qquad (4)$$

Minimisation by Gradient Descent. Applying gradient descent to minimise the energy (2) with data term (3) and smoothness term (4) yields the following evolution for $d(\boldsymbol{x}, t)$:

$$\partial_t d = \alpha\, \Delta d - c \cdot \Psi'\left((d - d_{\text{init}})^2 \right) \cdot (d - d_{\text{init}}). \qquad (5)$$

The desired minimiser is obtained as the steady state for $t \to \infty$.

Anisotropic Modification. The smoothness term (4) leads to the homogeneous diffusion operator Δd in (5). It smooths in all directions without respecting image structures. To overcome this problem, we replace it by an anisotropic diffusion term that is inspired by the optic flow approach of Zimmer $et\ al.$ [12]. It allows an adaptation of the diffusion process to the image edges, which are characterised by the eigenvectors $\boldsymbol{v}_1, \boldsymbol{v}_2$ of the structure tensor [13]

$$\boldsymbol{J}_{\rho,\sigma} := K_\rho * \left(\boldsymbol{\nabla} f_\sigma(\boldsymbol{x}, d)\, \boldsymbol{\nabla} f_\sigma^\top(\boldsymbol{x}, d) \right). \qquad (6)$$

Here K_ρ is a Gaussian of standard deviation ρ, and $*$ denotes the convolution operator. We assume that $\boldsymbol{v}_1$ belongs to the larger eigenvalue of $\boldsymbol{J}_{\rho,\sigma}$.

To steer the diffusion process by the directions $\boldsymbol{v}_1, \boldsymbol{v}_2$ that point across and along the image edges respectively, we construct a diffusion tensor

$$\boldsymbol{D} := (\boldsymbol{v}_1 \boldsymbol{v}_2) \begin{pmatrix} g\left((\boldsymbol{v}_1^\top \boldsymbol{\nabla} d)^2 \right) & 0 \\ 0 & 1 \end{pmatrix} \begin{pmatrix} \boldsymbol{v}_1^\top \\ \boldsymbol{v}_2^\top \end{pmatrix}, \qquad (7)$$

where g is the Perona-Malik diffusivity [14]

$$g(s^2) := \frac{1}{1 + s^2/\lambda^2} \qquad (8)$$

with contrast parameter $\lambda > 0$. It allows to smooth strongly along edges, while reducing the diffusion across edges. We obtain the desired anisotropic evolution by replacing Δd in (5) by its anisotropic counterpart div $(D\,\nabla d)$:

$$\partial_t d \;=\; \alpha \operatorname{div}\left(D\left(v_1, v_2, \nabla d\right)\nabla d\right) \;-\; c\cdot\Psi'\left((d-d_{\mathrm{init}})^2\right)\cdot(d-d_{\mathrm{init}}). \tag{9}$$

The steady state of this evolution depends on the initialisation. Based on our experiments we recommend to initialise it with the depth of the middle frame.

This is our final model for anisotropic depth map smoothing with a robustified fidelity term. It performs a joint image- and depth-driven diffusion in adaptive directions.

Implementation. We implement the anisotropic evolution equation (9) with an explicit finite difference scheme, where the space discretisation of the divergence expression uses the stencil from [15]. In order to avoid any stability deteriorations by the data term, we approximate the expression $(d-d_{\mathrm{init}})$ outside the argument of Ψ' in an implicit way. This still allows an explicit update of d without any need to solve linear or nonlinear systems of equations.

Colour Images. It is easy to extend our model to colour images. We exchange the structure tensor $J_{\rho,\sigma}$ in (6) by the combined structure tensor [16, 17]

$$K_\rho * \sum_i \nabla f_\sigma^i(x, d)\,\nabla f_\sigma^{i\;\top}(x, d), \tag{10}$$

where $f^i(x, d)$ represents colour channel i.

2.3   Image Fusion

After computing the optimal depth map by means of our PDE, we can easily construct the fused image by combining the colour values directly from the source images. However, our approach computes the continuous depth map that represents the corresponding depth for every pixel, while we have a discrete number of images. Therefore, results at non-integer depth values are obtained by linear interpolation. For colour images, the fusion is performed channelwise.

3   Experimental Results

We test our model with two image sets. For the first experiment we use two synthetically generated images where the ground truth is known (Fig. 1a, 1b). For the second experiment we used a commonly available[1] real-world image set Fig. 2a, 2b).

---

[1] http://grail.cs.washington.edu/projects/photomontage/

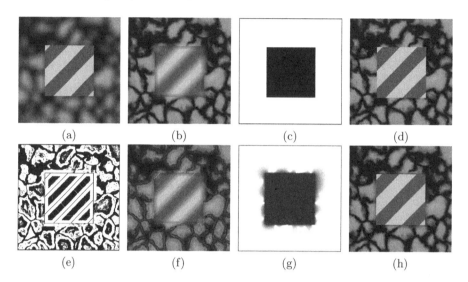

Fig. 1. Results for the synthetic data set. (**a**) Frame 1 with small focal length. (**b**) Frame 2 with large focal length. (**c**) Ground truth depth map. Brighter grey tones describe larger depth values. (**d**) Ground truth image (all-in-focus). (**e**) Initial depth map. (**f**) Fused image obtained with initial depth map. (**g**) Depth map of our approach. (**h**) Our fused image.

Synthetic Data Set. The image set consists of two frames of size 400×400. In the first frame the foreground is in focus, in the second frame the background is in focus. For this synthetic images *ground truth* data is available, thus it is possible to rate the quality of our result in terms of an error measure. Figure 1 depicts the ground truth depth map and the *all-in-focus* image (Fig. 1c, 1d), the initial depth map and the corresponding image (Fig. 1e, 1f), as well as the final smoothed depth map and the resulting image (Fig. 1g, 1h). The initial depth map is not reliable, thus it produces an unsharp result with a mean squared error (MSE) 535.42. The final depth map obtained with our approach is very close to the ground truth depth map, and the fused image is sharp with an MSE of 45.88.

Real–World Data Set. The image set consists of 13 images of size 1344×1021 pixels with increasing focal length. Figure 2 demonstrates the results: In the middle row we observe the depth maps corresponding to the different stages of our algorithm (the initial, the thresholded, and the final depth map). We can see that the final depth map is nicely segmented, the noise is removed, and we obtain the desired piecewise smooth result. In the bottom row we observe the magnified details of the fused image obtained with the initial depth map (Fig. 2g), the details of the fused image obtained with our approach (Fig. 2h) as well as the fused image itself (Fig. 2i). Comparing the details we see that the result of our approach is sharper, the fine details are well-preserved, and it contains much less noise.

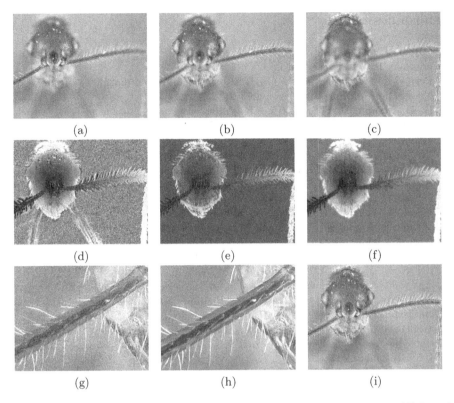

Fig. 2. Results for the real-world data set. **(a)-(c)** Input frames 3, 7, and 13. **(d)** Initial depth map. Brighter pixels correspond to farther frames. **(e)** Thresholded depth map. Red colour denotes unreliable pixels that have been removed. **(f)** Final depth map. **(g)** Zoom into the fused images obtained with initial depth map. **(h)** Zoom with final depth map. **(i)** Fused image.

4   Conclusions and Outlook

We have identified depth map regularisation as an important aspect of focus fusion that has hardly been explored in the literature so far. Applying concepts of modern PDE-based smoothing methods such as robustified fidelity terms and anisotropic smoothness terms, it was possible to improve the quality of the fusion result substantially.

This approach is very general since it can be combined with many fusion criteria. The fact that we have chosen a gradient-based depth map initialisation and direct pixel fusion was for didactic reasons only, since we wanted to keep the method as simple as possible.

Last but not least, focus fusion is only one special application of image fusion. Our approach can also be extended to other fusion tasks such as exposure fusion or superresolution. This is part of our ongoing research.

References

1. Ogden, J.M., Adelson, E.H., Bergen, J.R., Burt, P.J.: Pyramid-based computer graphics. RCA Engineer 30(5), 4–15 (1985)
2. Petrovic, V.S., Xydeas, C.S.: Gradient-based multiresolution image fusion. IEEE Transactions on Image Processing 13(2), 228–237 (2004)
3. Li, H., Manjunath, B.S., Mitra, S.K.: Multisensor image fusion using the wavelet transform. Computer Vision, Graphics, and Image Processing 57(3), 235–245 (1995)
4. Valdecasas, A.G., Marshall, D., Becerra, J.M., Terrero, J.J.: On the extended depth of focus algorithms for bright field microscopy. Micron 32(6), 559–569 (2001)
5. Aslantas, V., Kurban, R.: A comparison of criterion functions for fusion of multi-focus noisy images. Optics Communications 282(16), 3231–3242 (2009)
6. Wang, W.-W., Shui, P.-L., Feng, X.-C.: Variational models for fusion and denoising of multifocus images. IEEE Signal Processing Letters 15, 65–68 (2008)
7. Pop, S., Lavialle, O., Terebes, R., Borda, M.: A PDE-based approach for image fusion. In: Blanc-Talon, J., Philips, W., Popescu, D., Scheunders, P. (eds.) ACIVS 2007. LNCS, vol. 4678, pp. 121–131. Springer, Heidelberg (2007)
8. Agarwala, A., Dontcheva, M., Agrawala, M., Drucker, S.M., Colburn, A., Curless, B., Salesin, D., Cohen, M.F.: Interactive digital photomontage. ACM Transactions on Graphics 23(3), 294–302 (2004)
9. Šroubek, F., Cristóbal, G., Flusser, J.: Image fusion based on level set segmentation. In: Proc. 14th European Signal Processing Conference, Florence, Italy, pp. 1–5 (September 2006)
10. Li, S., Bin, Y.: Multifocus image fusion using region segmentation and spatial frequency. Image and Vision Computing 26(7), 971–979 (2008)
11. Barth, O., Osthof, M.: "Focal stack photography" project. "Computational photography" lecture. Saarland University, Germany (2010),
   http://www.mpi-inf.mpg.de/departments/d4/teaching/ss2010/
   ComputationalPhotography/projects/focalstack/
12. Zimmer, H., Bruhn, A., Weickert, J.: Optic flow in harmony. International Journal of Computer Vision 93(3), 368–388 (2011)
13. Förstner, W., Gülch, E.: A fast operator for detection and precise location of distinct points, corners and centres of circular features. In: Proc. ISPRS Intercommission Conference on Fast Processing of Photogrammetric Data, pp. 281–305 (1987)
14. Perona, P., Malik, J.: Scale space and edge detection using anisotropic diffusion. IEEE Transactions on Pattern Analysis and Machine Intelligence 12, 629–639 (1990)
15. Weickert, J., Welk, M., Wickert, M.: L^2-stable nonstandard finite differences for anisotropic diffusion. In: Kuijper, A., Pock, T., Bredies, K., Bischof, H. (eds.) SSVM 2013. LNCS, vol. 7893, pp. 380–391. Springer, Heidelberg (2013)
16. Di Zenzo, S.: A note on the gradient of multi-image. Computer Vision, Graphics, and Image Processing 33, 116–125 (1986)
17. Weickert, J.: Coherence-enhancing diffusion of colour images. Image and Vision Computing 17, 201–212 (1999)

Accurate Fibre Orientation Measurement for Carbon Fibre Surfaces*

Stefan Thumfart, Werner Palfinger, Matthias Stöger, and Christian Eitzinger

Profactor GmbH,
Im Stadtgut A2, 4407 Steyr-Gleink, Austria
stefan.thumfart@profactor.at

Abstract. Carbon- and glass fibre materials exhibit challenging optical properties, in particular highly specular reflectivity. State of the art vision-based sensor systems use diffuse light setups to suppress the specific reflectivity and texture analysis methods to obtain the fibre orientation for surface patches.

We propose a different sensor that is based on a fibre reflection model and directly measures fibre orientation, diffuse and specular reflectivity for each surface pixel. The proposed sensor is robust to changes of the fibre material and capable to deliver fast and accurate information about fibre direction without requiring time consuming texture analysis. We show that the root mean squared measurement error is around $0.4°$ for dry carbon fibre and $1.2°$ for pre-preg materials.

Keywords: quality control, fibre-angle measurement, carbon fibre inspection, photometric stereo, texture analysis.

1 Introduction

The automatic inspection of woven material and fabric has been investigated from the early days of machine vision [3]. Texture analysis is the main tool used for segmentation, classification and defect detection on such materials [8]. Recently the topic has gained more attention due the increase of carbon fibre and glass fibre parts in industrial manufacturing [10]. These materials, however, have very difficult optical properties due to their specular reflection and - in case of carbon fibres - high absorbtion of light. Traditional machine vision methods try to deal with these effects by using diffuse lighting to suppress the specular reflection and to generate homogeneous images [11]. However, at the same time also the contrast of important textural characteristics is reduced, which makes the analysis sensitive to noise, small material variations or illumination.

Of particular relevance in carbon and glass fibre parts production is the measurement of the fibre orientation relative to the part. The parts have highly anisotropic mechanical properties and the fibres are aligned to fit to the particular forces that are expected to act on the part [6]. It is thus of high importance

---

* This work was funded by the Austrian Research Agency (FFG) under grant no. 498817 (ProFIT) and grant no. 830376 (SelTec). It reflects only the authors' view.

R. Wilson et al. (Eds.): CAIP 2013, Part II, LNCS 8048, pp. 75–82, 2013.

to ensure that fibres are oriented as has been planned, which requires automatic methods for quality control [7].

In this paper we propose a vision-based approach for fibre-angle measurement that uses a new method for analysing the images in order to obtain precise fibre orientation measurements. We will first review the state of the art of different methods for determining dominant orientations in textures and then proceed with a description of the reflection model, sensor system and algorithms that we used for performing fibre-angle measurements on carbon fibre materials. Furthermore we present a detailed investigation of the measurement accuracy that we achieved using this method.

2   Texture Orientation Estimation

The basic approach to determining principal orientations in textured images is to use the covariance matrix of the gradient vectors [5] in a local neighbourhood. The assumption is that the texture has significant contrast and a "line-like" structure, so that the gradients can be assumed to be perpendicular to the main direction of the texture. A similar approach is based on the directional evidence accumulation [2]. After converting the original image to an edge image the local dominant orientations are computed for non-overlapping subwindows and used to increment a histogram of orientations. The maximum peaks are chosen from the histogram, assuming that the highest peak defines the orientation of the texture. A similar approach is used by Miene et al. [7].

In the field of texture analysis scale and orientation are often jointly evaluated in order to obtain algorithms that are invariant to changes in scale and orientation. Chang and Fisher [1] propose texture analysis based on Gabor filters and steerable pyramids. Their approach builds upon the assumption that features change smoothly in order to interpolate between the discrete results of the single filters.

With respect to measuring fibre directions in carbon fibre parts, there are two main challenges that have not yet been adequately addressed. Firstly, the line-like structure of the fibres has very low contrast and requires high resolution in order to be visible in the image. The visibility of these structures is also sensitive to the illumination and to the type of material. This makes it difficult to apply edge- or gradient-based methods. Secondly, woven material consists of a dense grid of regions with different orientations, which causes problems whenever larger neighbourhoods are used for the analysis as the neighbourhood will often contain regions with multiple fibre orientations. Computational effort is also a problem with these methods in real world applications.

What would be preferable is to have a method that provides an orientation per pixel, that requires low computational effort and works well for different kinds of materials. In the following section we present a method based on photometric stereo that provides a solution to these issues.

3   New Approach to Fibre Orientation Measurement

The common idea of Photometric Stereo (PS) is to compute surface orientation and reflectance values from multiple images, captured from the same viewpoint. For each of these raw images the surface is lighted from a different, well known, light source. PS must not be confused with Shape from Shading [14] that aims to derive the surface orientation from shading variations of a single image.

Initially PS was introduced by Woodham [13] who used three different point light sources. The reconstruction was done under the assumption that the surface exhibits Lambertian reflectivity. Later PS was extended towards distributed light sources [4] and non-Lambertian reflectance models [12].

PS has been applied successfully to a wide range of objects with different geometry and reflectivity. However the specific properties of carbon fibre surfaces require a novel reflection model that serves as theoretical basis for sensor design and the "fibre reflection analysis". The fibre reflection analysis computes four feature images: diffuse reflectivity, specular reflectivity, azimuth (in-plane) orientation and polar (out-of-plane) orientation of the fibres. These feature images can be directly used for fibre orientation measurements, segmentation and defect detection. Details on the reflection model and the fibre reflection analysis are also given in [9].

For fibre reflection analysis we approximate the optical properties of a carbon fibre by an infinitesimal cylindrical perfect mirror. A ray r that reaches a point O on the carbon fibre surface hits several microscopic parallel fibres. As shown in Fig. 1, the ray forms a reflection cone around the fibre direction at O.

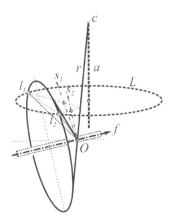

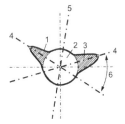

Fig. 1. Illustration of the fibre reflection model. The camera c looks down to a surface point O. The light source positions l_1 and l_2 are used to calculate the fibre orientation f.

Fig. 2. The sensor consists of a CMOS camera and a light ring L built from 96 LEDs that are used to generate different light patterns

Fig. 3. Circular reflection diagram that shows the intensity of the observed light (1) that consists of diffuse (2) and specular parts (3)

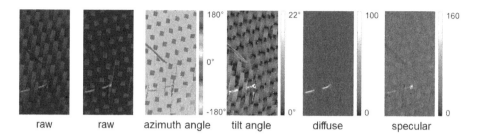

raw   raw   azimuth angle   tilt angle   diffuse   specular

Fig. 4. Eight raw images (only two are shown here) are used to calculate four feature images for a carbon fibre fabric. The azimuth angle encodes the in-plane angle, while we can see the curvature of the fabric segments in the tilt angle image. A misplaced yarn can be identified best in the diffuse reflectivity image.

Let us assume that r represents a ray from a single camera pixel c through the lens to the surface. Without loss of generality we assume that r reaches the surface in the origin O and hits fibres characterized by the direction vector $\boldsymbol{f}$. Every light source, directed towards O, that intersects with the inverse reflection cone of r would be mapped on the camera pixel c. To ensure that such an intersection is present for different $\boldsymbol{f}$, we employ a circular light ring L, centered around and orthogonal to the optical axis a of the camera (Fig. 1). Given the intersections l_1 and l_2 between L and the inverse reflection cone, the vector $\boldsymbol{f}$ can be calculated as

$$s_i \propto \frac{c}{\|c\|} + \frac{l_i}{\|l_i\|}, i = 1, 2 \tag{1}$$

$$\boldsymbol{f} = s_1 \times s_2 \tag{2}$$

with c and l_i representing the vectors from O to the camera pixel and the light ring intersection points respectively. Figure 3 illustrates how the reflected light for a single surface point is interpreted. The reflected light is typically a superposition of a diffuse part (2) and two peaks of specular reflected light (3). As we know the position of light sources and camera, we can compute the fibre orientation $\boldsymbol{f}$ from the specular peak positions (4) using Eq. 1 and Eq. 2. The fibre reflection analysis typically relies on eight raw images obtained for different light patterns. The eight gray values per surface pixel are sufficient to calculate $\boldsymbol{f}$ as well as diffuse and specular reflectivity. For further processing we split the information $\boldsymbol{f}$ into an in-plane azimuth angle and an out-of-plane (tilt) polar angle. Thus we obtain four feature images depicted, together with two raw images, in Fig. 4.

4   Experimental Evaluation

The image analysis and fibre-angle measurement described in the previous section depends on a complex interaction between the mechanical setup of the sensor (Fig. 2), the optical properties of the materials and the algorithms used. For the

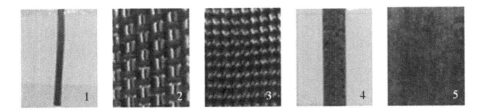

Fig. 5. Samples used in the experiment include dry unidirectional material (1), dry carbon fibre fabric (2,3), a pre-preg unidirectional tow (4) and a unidirectional pre-preg tape (5)

evaluation we use a setup consisting of a rotation module with a repeatability of $0.03°$ and an X/Y-table with a repeatability of $0.3\mu m$ and an absolute accuracy of $3\mu m$. This 3-axis system was used to position the sensor system and to rotate the sample. Five samples (Fig. 5) which cover the typical range of materials used for the production of carbon fibre parts have been chosen for the experiment.

The evaluation of the experimental results is focused on the azimuth measurement accuracy, as this measure is most critical for the majority of application scenarios. In the following we use the *Root Mean Squared Error* given as

$$\sigma_\phi = \sqrt{\frac{1}{n-1} \sum_{i=0}^{n-1} \delta_\phi^2},$$
(3)

calculated from the differences between measured angle α_i and expected angle $\overline{\alpha_i}$ given as $\delta_\phi = \alpha_i - \overline{\alpha_i}$.

For a single measurement position P_j, the angle measurements α_i are obtained for $n = 18$ rotation steps $r_i = \{0°, 10°, ..., 170°\}$. To increase robustness to local noise, α_i is computed as average angle from a square patch of 5×5 pixels (corresponding to $300 \times 300 \mu m^2$) centred at P_j. As the real fibre angle is unknown for the measured surface patch, we fit a reference line $\overline{\alpha_i} = k \cdot r_i + d$ to obtain the expected angles $\overline{\alpha_i}$. As the steepness $k = 1$ of the line is fixed, we only have to compute $d = \frac{1}{n} \sum_{i=0}^{n-1} \alpha_i - k \cdot \frac{1}{n} \sum_{i=0}^{n-1} r_i$.

We conducted three measurement experiments to evaluate (1) if the measurement accuracy differs for different measurement positions in the sensor's field of view, (2) the measurement accuracy for different materials and (3) the influence of patch size on σ_ϕ. Depending on the experiment all or a subset of the measurement positions shown in Fig. 6 have been chosen for evaluation.

4.1 Experiment 1: Measurement Accuracy within Field of View

The first experiment was done to investigate the accuracy of the angle measurement at different positions in the field of view of the sensor system. All nine measurement positions shown in Fig. 6 were used. In a manual procedure the measurement position was placed exactly (within appr. $150\mu m$) over the sample

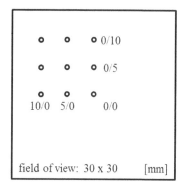

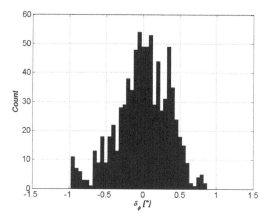

Fig. 6. Positions chosen relative to the field of view of the sensor

Fig. 7. δ_ϕ histogram for all measurements in experiment 1

rotation axis, to ensure that the same material patch is used for evaluation. Material (2) was chosen for the experiment, because a microscopic analysis revealed that this material is very homogeneous in terms of fibre directions in local neighbourhoods. The measurement process was repeated five times for each position $P_1, ..., P_9$, resulting in $5 \cdot 9 \cdot 18$ measurements.

Figure 7 shows the δ_ϕ histogram of all measurements. The histogram corresponds to a normal distribution with errors being in the range of $+/-1°$. Position-wise σ_ϕ was smallest in the centre position $(0/0)$ with $0.23°$ and largest close to the field of view border at $(0/10)$ with $0.42°$. The average σ_ϕ for the nine positions is $0.35°$. A reason for an increase of σ_ϕ close to the field of view borders is the absence of calibration for lens distortion during the experiments. Also the inaccuracy in positioning the senor's measurement position over the rotation axis of the sample is a source of error, as slightly different patches of the sample might be used for angle measurement. As there are no real world samples with perfectly parallel neighbouring fibres, the reported σ_ϕ values can be considered as an upper bound of the sensor's actual measurement error.

4.2   Experiment 2: Measurement Error for Different Materials

This experiment was done to evaluate the sensitivity of the sensor to deviations from the ideal reflection model originating from material properties. All five samples (Fig. 5) were evaluated for four positions $P_j \in \{0/0, 10/0, 0/10, 10/10\}$. Measurements have been repeated ten times per position resulting in $18 \cdot 4 \cdot 10$ values per sample. The resulting σ_ϕ values are reported in Table 1.

We observe that the reflection model fits better to dry materials (1-3), where errors are within the range observed in the first experiment. We thus conclude that there is not a strong dependence between the material and the average error for dry materials. Pre-pregs (4, 5) show significantly higher errors. This is clearly

Table 1. Measurement error σ_ϕ per sample

sample no.	1	2	3	4	5
σ_ϕ [°]	0.55	0.37	0.49	0.96	1.54

due to the fact that the actual reflection properties differ from the ideal model of an infinitely small, cylindrical mirror because of the resin between the fibres.

4.3   Experiment 3: Influence of Patch Size on Measurement Error

As the results for experiment 1 and 2 were obtained for a surface patch of 5×5 pixels, corresponding to an area of $300 \times 300 \mu m^2$ the influence of the patch size on σ_ϕ should be investigated. As reported in Table 2 for material (2), even the highest resolution results in an σ_ϕ of only $0.42°$ which level off to σ_ϕ around $0.22°$ for patch sizes larger than 5×5.

Table 2. Measurement error σ_ϕ vs. patch size

patch size [pixel]	1×1	3×3	5×5	7×7	9×9	11×11	13×13	15×15	17×17	19×19
σ_ϕ [°]	0.42	0.29	0.23	0.22	0.22	0.22	0.22	0.23	0.24	0.24

As the highest sensor resolution of $60 \times 60 \mu m^2$ is typically not required if precise angle measurements should be acquired the evaluation patch size can be set to 5×5 or 7×7. Segmentation or defect detection on the other hand typically require higher resolutions to deliver precise segment borders or smallest defects. For these applications however, a small reduction in angle measurement accuracy (for single pixel measurements) can be accepted.

5   Conclusions

We proposed a new method for determining fibre orientations for unidirectional and woven material, applicable to carbon and glass fibres. Image analysis is based on photometric stereo and uses different illumination patterns in combination with a fibre reflection model. The analysis delivers four image modalities that provide independent measurements for each pixel. Among these modalities is the in-plane fibre orientation. To assess the suitability of the method for measuring fibre-angles, three experiments were conducted. The key advantage of the method is its robustness with respect to materials and its capability of dealing with black and shiny surfaces structures. It could be shown that the fibre-angle can be determined with a root mean squared error around $0.4°$ for dry carbon fibre materials up to $1.5°$ for pre-pregs. Assuming a normal distribution of the error, we can interpret these results such that 95% of the measurements lie within an error bound of $\pm 0.8°$ for dry materials and $\pm 3°$ for pre-pregs.

From a practical point of the reported accuracies are sufficient to realize multiple interesting applications. For a majority of fibre materials an angle deviation of up to 5° with respect to the layup design is still sufficient to preserve most of the mechanical stability. Schmitt et al. [10] have recently shown to reach a measurement uncertainty of 0.4° at a confidence level of 95%. They analyse the power density spectrum for a image patch of 128 × 128 pixel acquired under diffuse lighting for dry materials.

References

1. Chang, J., Fisher, J.: Analysis of orientation and scale in smoothly varying textures. In: IEEE 12th International Conference on Computer Vision, pp. 881–888 (2009)
2. Chaudhuri, B., Kundu, P., Sarkar, N.: Detection and gradation of oriented texture. Pattern Recognition Letters 14(2), 147–153 (1993)
3. Cohen, F.S., Fan, Z., Attali, S.: Automated inspection of textile fabrics using textural models. IEEE Transactions on Pattern Analysis and Machine Intelligence 13(8), 803–808 (1991)
4. Ikeuchi, K.: Determining surface orientations of specular surfaces by using the photometric stereo method. IEEE Transactions on Pattern Analysis and Machine Intelligence PAMI-3(6), 661–669 (1981)
5. Kass, M., Witkin, A.: Analyzing oriented patterns. Computer Vision, Graphics, and Image Processing 37(3), 362–385 (1987)
6. Kim, J.W., Lee, D.G.: Effect of fiber orientation and fiber contents on the tensile strength in fiber-reinforced composites. Journal of Nanoscience and Nanotechnology 10(5), 3650–3653 (2010)
7. Miene, A., Herrmann, A.S., Göttinger, M.: Quality assurance by digital image analysis for the preforming and draping process of dry carbon fibre material. In: SAMPE Europe Conference, Paris, April 1-3 (2008)
8. Özdemir, S., Baykut, A., Meylani, R., Erçil, A., Ertüzün, A.: Comparative evaluation of texture analysis algorithms for defect inspection of textile products. In: Proceedings of the 14th International Conference on Pattern Recognition, vol. 2, pp. 1738–1740 (1998)
9. Palfinger, W., Thumfart, S., Eitzinger, C.: Photometric stereo on carbon fiber surfaces. Presented at the 35th Workshop of the Austrian Association for Pattern Recognition, Graz, May 26-27 (2011), http://oagm2011.joanneum.at/papers/27.pdf
10. Schmitt, R., Mersmann, C., Schoenberg, A.: Machine vision industrialising the textile-based FRP production. In: Proceedings of 6th International Symposium on Image and Signal Processing and Analysis, pp. 260–264 (2009)
11. Shi, L., Wu, S.: Automatic fiber orientation detection for sewed carbon fibers. Tsinghua Science & Technology 12(4), 447–452 (2007)
12. Vogiatzis, G., Hernández, C.: Practical 3d reconstruction based on photometric stereo. In: Cipolla, R., Battiato, S., Farinella, G. (eds.) Computer Vision. SCI, vol. 285, pp. 313–345. Springer, Heidlberg (2010)
13. Woodham, R.J.: Photometric method for determining surface orientation from multiple images. Optical Engineering 19(1), 139–144 (1980)
14. Zhang, R., Tsai, P.S., Cryer, J., Shah, M.: Shape-from-shading: a survey. IEEE Transactions on Pattern Analysis and Machine Intelligence 21(8), 690–706 (1999)

Benchmarking GPU-Based Phase Correlation for Homography-Based Registration of Aerial Imagery

Falk Schubert[1] and Krystian Mikolajczyk[2]

[1] EADS Innovations Works, Germany
falk.schubert@eads.net
[2] University of Surrey
k.mikolajczyk@surrey.ac.uk

Abstract. Many multi-image fusion applications require fast registration methods in order to allow real-time processing. Although the most popular approaches, local-feature-based methods, have proven efficient enough for registering image pairs at real-time, some applications like multi-frame background subtraction, super-resolution or high-dynamic-range imaging benefit from even faster algorithms. A common trend to speed up registration is to implement the algorithms on graphic cards (GPUs). However not all algorithms are specially suited for massive parallelization via GPUs. In this paper we evaluate the speed of a well-known global registration method, i.e. phase correlation, for computing 8-DOF homographies. We propose a benchmark to compare a CPU- and GPU-based implementation using different systems and a dataset of aerial imagery. We demonstrate that phase correlation benefits from GPU-based implementations much more than local methods, significantly increasing the processing speed.

Keywords: Registration, Phase Correlation, GPU, Hardware Acceleration.

1 Introduction

Fast registration algorithms are a key component of real-time image fusion applications like mosaicing, motion detection and superresolution. For registering image pairs using 8-DOF homographies, local-feature-based methods have proven flexible, robust and fast enough for aligning them at real-time. However in some applications even faster registration methods are required to increase the performance. For instance background-subtraction[18] or multi-frame, reconstruction-based superresolution[4] typically use image stacks containing about 10-20 images. In order to avoid accumulation of pairwise homography errors, all images in the stack are registered to the reference image for every final resulting frame [12]. Therefore image registration methods need to be much faster than the current state-of-the-art to allow these applications to run at real-time as well.

R. Wilson et al. (Eds.): CAIP 2013, Part II, LNCS 8048, pp. 83–90, 2013.
© Springer-Verlag Berlin Heidelberg 2013

With the increasing ease of programming field programmable gate arrays (FPGA) and graphic cards (GPU) a common way to speed up the registration algorithms is to implement them on such parallel platforms. However not all algorithms benefit from hardware-accelerated implementations. In this paper we show that the less frequently used method of phase correlation is slower on CPU but significantly faster on GPU when compared to the results reported in the literature for the efficient local feature-based registration on both platforms. In some applications the computational platform is constraint by regulatory limitations. For instance certified CPUs used in aircrafts are often not powerful enough, leaving FPGAs or GPUs as the only alternative to speed up algorithms. The registration methods such as phase correlation which benefit from FPGA- or GPU-implementations are therefore much more preferred.

In the following section we discuss existing GPU implementations for registration. In section 3 we briefly introduce the phase correlation and explain how it benefits from parallel implementations. The registration scheme used for benchmarking the GPU implementations is discussed in section 4. Finally, in section 5 we present the benchmarking results followed by the conclusions.

2   Related Work

Current local feature-based methods are by far the most popular ones for image registration [17] and all of them share a similar processing chain. First, sparse local features are detected in the two images to be registered. Second, corresponding features are matched using descriptors computed at the feature locations. Third, a transformation (i.e. 8-DOF homography) is computed. The most time consuming parts are the detection of feature locations and the computation of the descriptors. Although very efficient algorithms exist [3,14] which already allow real-time processing for small image sizes, some applications require even faster algorithms. Moreover, not all algorithms including efficient ones are easily parallelizable and hence benefit less from an implementation on a GPU or FPGA. In [16] SIFT and KLT features achieved speed-up factors of 10 and 20 respectively compared to CPU implementations. FPGA implementations of SIFT features show similar speed-up factors around 10 as presented in [15]. In [6] the efficient SURF features have shown to speed up by a factor of around 26 compared to the original CPU implementation by [3]. Because many local features (e.g. around 1000) are typically computed for robust homography estimation and each one can be computed independently, feature detection is an inherent parallel problem and benefits from GPU and FPGA implementations as shown by the work referenced above. However, depending on the complexity of the feature, different speed-up factors can be achieved, e.g. simple KLT features (speed-up by 20) vs. complex SIFT features (speed-up by 10). The feature matching is also parallel in nature and speed-up factors between 10-30 are achieved when implementing it using GPUs [5].

However, even with those speed-up factors, the overall frame rates achieved for typical videos i.e. 640×480 are close to $100\,\text{fps}$ [6]. Although direct image registration methods which use all pixels of the image for alignment are much slower on CPUs than feature-based methods, their GPU-implementations such as the one presented in [11] achieve similar frame rates. Registering 10 images per processed frame is therefore bound to around 10 fps. To achieve faster processing or to allow the registration of more images (e.g. 20 images to compute a background image), a faster registration method is needed. In this paper we present such a registration approach which is based on phase correlation. The core components of phase correlation are fourier transforms which are highly parallelizable [9]. This results in very fast processing (i.e. up to 200 fps) when implementing this registration method on a fast GPU.

3   Phase Correlation

Registration methods based on the Fourier transform have been studied since [13] and many extensions and applications have been proposed to date [1]. In Fig. 1 the computation scheme of standard phase correlation is illustrated. Consider two images I_1, I_2 that are related by simple translation Δx

$$I_1(x) = I_2(x - \Delta x) \tag{1}$$

According to the Fourier shift theorem, their Fourier transforms $\hat{I}_1, \hat{I}_2$ are related such that

$$\hat{I}_2(u) = \exp\left[-2\pi i(u_1 \Delta x_1 + u_2 \Delta x_2)\right] \hat{I}_1(u) \tag{2}$$

To find the shift in phase, the correlation of them is computed

$$\frac{\hat{I}_1(u)\hat{I}_2^*(u)}{\|\hat{I}_1(u)\hat{I}_2^*(u)\|} = \exp\left[-2\pi i(u_1 \Delta x_1 + u_2 \Delta x_2)\right] \tag{3}$$

where $\hat{I}_2^*$ is the complex conjugate. The term is also called cross-power spectrum of I_1 and I_2. Its phase is equivalent to the phase shift between both images. Hence transforming the cross-power spectrum back into spatial domain, results in a Dirac impulse at the position of the displacement. The sub-pixel location is estimated by fitting a quadratic to a data triplet around the maximal peak at location x and y respectively. The refinement offsets Δx and Δy are given by

$$\Delta x = \frac{\log(v(x+1,y)) - \log(v(x-1,y))}{4\log(v(x,y)) - 2\log(v(x-1,y)) - 2\log(v(x+1,y))} \tag{4}$$

and analogous for Δy where $v(x,y)$ denotes the value of the cross correlation peak in the spatial domain at location (x,y). Strong signal changes at image boundaries can seriously affect the correlation surface. Therefore, peaks are well enhanced if the image is filtered prior to applying phase correlation. This is typically handled by using windowing methods, i.e. by multiplying the image with a Blackman window function. In theory different types of windowing functions such as Cosine, Gaussian and Tukey can be applied. In section 5 we evaluate their impact on the registration accuracy.

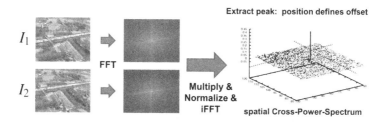

Fig. 1. Phase correlation scheme

The greatest advantages of phase correlation are its simplicity and robustness. It can handle narrow and larger baselines (given the images overlap) at the same computational cost, it is robust to noise, has the ability to register less textured images (where usually not enough features can be detected) and requires considerably less parameter tuning than feature-based and intensity-based methods. Since standard phase correlation only computes a translational offset between two images, an extension is presented in the section 4 which allows the computation of a full 8-DOF homography. Furthermore, because the computational core consists of 3 fast fourier transforms, the speed of phase correlation can be significantly increased by implementations on parallel platforms. In section 5 we evaluate the speed-up factors achieved when registering images using CPU and GPU.

4   Registration Scheme

The image is subdivided into a fixed grid of regions. For each pair of regions the translational offset is computed using phase correlation as explained in section 3. The region centers from the first frame are then projected into the second frame to generate matching point pairs. Finally, a homography is estimated using the discrete linear transform (DLT) algorithm [10] and RANSAC for outlier detection. More accurate homography estimation algorithms which are based on minimizing special cost-functions exist [10] and can be used as well. The overall workflow of the algorithm is illustrated in Fig. 2.

A good trade-off has to be found between computing many offsets, which increases the accuracy of the homography estimation and computational costs. We therefore consider 12 different grid layouts with an increasing number of regions (i.e. 4, 5, 8, 9, 16, 25, 36, 64, 100, 225, 400, 625) which we will evaluate in section 5. Using only 4 regions results in 4 phase correlation operations each using image patches of the size 360×288 for in input image of 720×576px. Splitting the image in 625 regions results in 625 independent phase correlation operations on image patches of the size 38×33.

5   Evaluation

In the following we present a benchmark demonstrating the speed-up of the phase correlation by using GPU-implementations instead of a CPU one. In order to

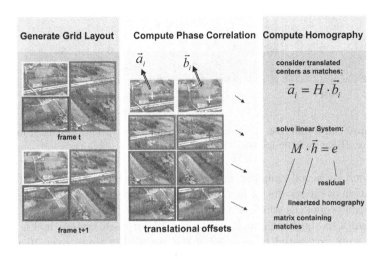

Fig. 2. Registration scheme using phase correlation

allow a fair comparison with the results for local feature-based methods reported in the literature, we use the registration scheme (see section 4) which also outputs 8-DOF homographies. We benchmark the implementations using 4 different systems with increasingly powerful CPUs and GPUs (see Tab. 1). The CPU implementation is based on the FFTW library [8] whereas the GPU implementation employs the CUFFT library [7] from the CUDA framework. In the latter all steps (i.e. extraction of regions along grid, forward/backward FFTs, computing the pixel-wise correlation and fitting of the quadratic to detect the offset at sub-pixel level) except the DLT are carried out on the GPU minimizing transfers between GPU and CPU memory.

Table 1. CPU and GPU configurations used for benchmarking

System 1 – slow GPU and medium CPU

GPU:	NVIDIA GeForce 8600M GT, 128MB RAM, 32 Cores, 475 MHz
CPU:	Intel Core2 Duo 2.2GHz, 2GB RAM, 2 Cores

System 2 – medium GPU and slow CPU

GPU:	NVIDIA Quadro FX 4600, 768MB RAM, 128 Cores, 500 MHz
CPU:	Intel Core2 Duo 1.86GHz, 2GB RAM, 2 Cores

System 3 – fast GPU and fast CPU

GPU:	NVIDIA Quadro FX 5800, 2GB RAM, 240 Cores, 650 MHz
CPU:	Intel Xeon 3.2GHz, 12GB RAM, 4 Cores

System 4 – fast GPU and fast CPU

GPU:	NVIDIA Tesla C1060, 4GB RAM, 240 Cores, 1.3 Ghz
CPU:	Intel Xeon 3.2GHz, 12GB RAM, 4 Cores

Although the registration algorithm is independent of the image content it does depend on the image size. We therefore use two typical image sizes that

Fig. 3. Dataset of 4 different aerial images used for registration. Left two: image size 640×480px. Right two: image size 720×576px.

are produced by aerial cameras: 640×480 and 720×576. To demonstrate the generalization of the results we use two different image sets per size configuration, resulting in 4 sequences which are depicted in Fig. 3.

The results of the benchmark are presented for each system in Fig. 4. The run-times were computed by averaging the processing times over 10 runs per sequence. These average times were further summarized by averaging across all 4 sequences of the dataset. The final average run-times in milli-seconds are then plotted for each grid-layout. The speed-up factors from CPU to GPU achieved are around 3 for layouts with many phase correlation operations (e.g. 625) and up to 30 for smaller layouts (e.g. 4). As FFTs greatly benefit from input sizes of power-of-two, the same images were padded with zeros to the nearest power-of-two dimension. The run-times were computed in the same way as before and are referenced with "P2" in the figures. It can be seen that the GPU implementations in all systems are much faster with this padding. Although slow GPUs can not keep up with the 100fps as reported in [6], due to the much weaker hardware (our GPU NVIDIA Geforce 8600M GT has 32 stream processors with 475MHz, whereas [6] use a NVIDIA Geforce 8800 GTX with 128 stream processors and 575 MHz). Medium and fast GPUs however accelerate the computation to around 200fps. Interestingly the FFTW-library chooses between different internal optimization schemes depending on the input size. This leads to higher computation times for small variations in image size (e.g. see the peak at tile configuration 36 in Fig. 4). Hence the choice of the grid-layout is critical depending on the type of implementation and FFT-library used.

The fast algorithms are only useful if their accuracy is high enough for a given application. We therefore compared the registration accuracy of the implementation used for benchmarking to the results of the dual-inverse compositional method [2] combined with a local feature-based pre-registration which is considered as a very accurate but slow method. In Tab. 2 the root-means-square error (RMS)[4] is presented for each sequence using a grid-layout with 64 regions. All homographies are close to the reference ones as indicated by RMS pixel errors below sub-pixel level.

Table 2. RMS errors for each sequence using 64 regions

	Sequence 1	Sequence 2	Sequence 3	Sequence 4
RMS error in pixels	0.21	0.62	0.4	0.37

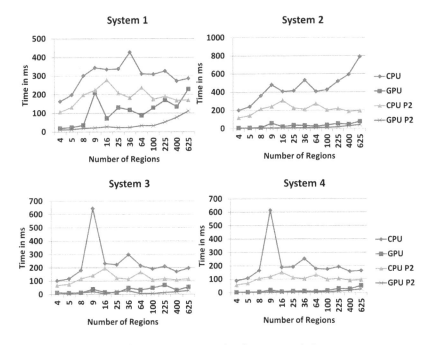

Fig. 4. Timing results for system 1-4

Furthermore we investigate the impact of different windowing functions. In Tab. 3 the RMS errors for different window functions and parameter settings are listed which were computed using sequence 4. It is clear that windowing produces better results than not using any window function and the choice of the function or settings is not critical.

Table 3. Comparison of RMS errors for different windowing functions and parameters

no window	Blackman $(\alpha = 0.0001)$	Blackman $(\alpha = 0.16)$	Cosine	Gaussian $(\alpha = 0.3)$	Gaussian $(\alpha = 0.1)$	Tukey $(\alpha = 0.9)$	Tukey $(\alpha = 0.6)$
0.358	0.234	0.23	0.266	0.288	0.25	0.318	0.245

6   Conclusions

In this paper we demonstrate that the computational speed of a well-known registration method can greatly benefit from a GPU implementation making it the preferred choice in some applications (e.g. aerial platforms with limitations on the computing power) over current state-of-the-art methods based on local features. We presented benchmark results for comparing GPU-based implementations (i.e. achieving 200 fps) which favorably compare to the results reported in the literature for more widely used local feature-based approaches (i.e. achieving 100 fps). In addition, for the application of registering aerial imagery the phase correlation was shown to produce accurate homographies (i.e. down to sub-pixel accuracy) comparable to state-of-the-art approaches such as a combination of the dual-inverse-compositional and feature-based methods. In the future we would like to investigate the computational benefits on certifiable hardware. These are typically much less powerful and only provide FPGAs to speed up computation. Therefore algorithms that can benefit from such hardware-accelerated implementations are more favored for these applications.

References

1. Argyriou, V.: Advanced Motion Estimation Algorithms in the Frequency Domain for Digital Video Applications. PhD thesis, University of Surrey (2006)
2. Bartoli, A.E.: Groupwise geometric and photometric direct image registration. PAMI (2008)
3. Bay, H., Ess, A., Tuytelaars, T., Van Gool, L.: Surf: Speeded up robust features. In: CVIU (2008)
4. Capel, D.P.: Image Mosaicing and Super-resolution. PhD thesis, University of Oxford (2001)
5. Chariot, A., Keriven, R.: GPU-boosted online image matching. In: ICPR (2008)
6. Cornelis, N., Van Gool, L.: Fast scale invariant feature detection and matching on programmable graphics hardware. In: CVPRW (2008)
7. NVIDIA Corporation. CUDA CUFFT library (2007)
8. Frigo, M., Johnson, S.G.: The design and implementation of FFTW3. In: Proceedings of the IEEE, Special Issue on Program Generation, Optimization, and Platform Adaptation (2005)
9. Garland, M., Le Grand, S., Nickolls, J., Anderson, J., Hardwick, J., Morton, S., Phillips, E., Zhang, Y., Volkov, V.: Parallel computing experiences with cuda. IEEE Micro (2008)
10. Hartley, R.I., Zisserman, A.: Multiple View Geometry in Computer Vision. Cambridge University Press (2004)
11. Ito, E., Saga, S., Okatani, T., Deguchi, K.: GPU-based high-speed and high-precision visual tracking. In: SICE (2010)
12. Kang, J., Cohen, I., Medioni, G.: Continuous tracking within and across camera streams. In: CVPR (2003)
13. Kuglin, C.D., Hines, D.C.: The phase correlation image alignment method. In: IEEE International Conference of Cybernetic Society (1975)
14. Rosten, E., Porter, R., Drummond, T.: Faster and better: A machine learning approach to corner detection. PAMI (2010)
15. Se, S., Ng, H.K., Jasiobedzki, P., Moyung, T.J.: Vision based modeling and localization for planetary exploration rovers. In: 55th International Astronautical Congress (2004)
16. Sinha, S.N., Frahm, J.M., Pollefeys, M., Genc, Y.: GPU-based video feature tracking and matching. Technical report. In: Workshop on Edge Computing Using New Commodity Architectures (2006)
17. Szeliski, R.: Computer Vision: Algorithms and Applications. Springer (2010)
18. Yu, Q., Medioni, G.: A GPU-based implementation of motion detection from a moving platform. In: CVGPU (2008)

Robustness of Point Feature Detection

Zijiang Song and Reinhard Klette

The .enpeda.. Project, Department of Computer Science
The University of Auckland, New Zealand

Abstract. This paper evaluates 2D feature detection methods with respect to invariance and efficiency properties. The studied feature detection methods are as follows: Speeded Up Robust Features, Scale Invariant Feature Transform, Binary Robust Invariant Scalable Keypoints, Oriented Binary Robust Independent Elementary Features, Features from Accelerated Segment Test, Maximally Stable Extremal Regions, Binary Robust Independent Elementary Features, and Fast Retina Keypoint. A long video sequence of traffic scenes is used for testing these feature detection methods. A brute-force matcher and Random Sample Consensus are used in order to analyse how robust these feature detection methods are with respect to scale, rotation, blurring, or brightness changes. After identifying matches in subsequent frames, RANSAC is used for removing inconsistent matches; remaining matches are taken as correct matches. This is the essence of our proposed evaluation technique. All the experiments use a proposed repeatability measure, defined as the ratio of the numbers of correct matches, and of all keypoints.

1   Introduction

A diversity of 2D or 3D feature or keypoint detection methods has been proposed in computer vision in recent years. For a 2008 review on 2D feature detectors, see [15], and for current evaluations of 3D keypoint detectors, see [14,16].

The different methods have their own advantages and disadvantages. This paper focuses on 2D feature detection methods which are implemented in OpenCV (Version 2.4.4) [11]. We test the robustness of these feature detection methods with respect to rotation, Illumination changes, scaling, shearing and blur.

Our motivation for this test arose when we had to decide for 2D or 3D feature detectors for accurate ego-motion analysis in a driver-assistance context, and for unifications of partially 3D-reconstructed surfaces (during different runs) obtained from recorded stereo street views. Because of the existence of the above cited 3D evaluations, we only focus on the 2D case in this paper.

Figure 1 illustrates video data as recorded in a driver-assistance context. Due to the limited length of this paper, we only use the illustrated video sequence (of 400 stereo frames, recorded at 25 Hz) for the reported tests in this paper. Due to actually occurring changes in recorded videos (with respect to brightness or blurring), and due to changes in pose of recorded objects (mainly with respect to scale, but also with respect to rotation), we are interested in 2D keypoints which

R. Wilson et al. (Eds.): CAIP 2013, Part II, LNCS 8048, pp. 91–99, 2013.

Fig. 1. Sample of an image of the discussed video sequence (*top left*, the black pixels at the border are due to rectification of the stereo frames), with five images after processing, illustrating blurring (*top, middle*), scaling (*top, right*), brightness changes (*bottom, left*), rotation (*bottom, middle*), and shearing (*bottom, right*). The used sequence of 400 stereo frames is in Set 4 of EISATS [5], and called "Cyclist"; 640 × 480 images are recorded with 10 bit per pixel.

can be robustly tracked in the presence of variations in brightness, blurring, scaling, shearing, or rotation. Basically, the provided features for those keypoints should allow to do such a robust tracking.

The rest of the paper is structured as follows: Section 2 gives a brief introduction for the used feature detectors. Section 3 discusses the design of our experiments. Section 4 informs about our experimental results. Section 5 concludes the paper.

2   Used Feature Detectors

We briefly introduce the used keypoint detectors, together with features for those keypoints.

SIFT. The *scale-invariant feature detector* (SIFT) was published in 1999; see [7]. It consists of four major stages: scale-space extrema detection, keypoint localization, orientation assignment, and keypoint description. The first stage uses difference-of-Gaussians (DoG) to identify potential interest points, which were invariant to scale and orientation. DoG is used instead of the Laplacian to improve computation speed. In the keypoint localization step, the operator rejects low contrast points and eliminates edge response. The Hessian matrix is used to compute the principal curvatures and to eliminate keypoints that have a ratio between both principal curvatures that is greater than a threshold. An orientation histogram is formed from gradient orientations of sample points within a region around the keypoint (defined by the scale of the keypoint) in order to get an orientation assignment. It was suggested that best results are achieved with an 4×4 array of histograms, with eight orientation bins in each. Thus, the SIFT descriptor is a vector of $4 \cdot 4 \cdot 8 = 128$ dimensions.

MSER. The detection of *maximally stable extremal regions* (MSER) was published in 2002; see [10]. It is used as a method of blob detection in images, for example to find correspondences between image elements from two images with different viewpoints. A new set of image elements, that are put into correspondence, are called *extremal regions* that have two important properties. The set is closed under (1) continuous transformations of image coordinates (i.e. affine transformations, warping, or skewing), and (2) monotonic transformations of image intensities. However, the approach is known to be sensitive to natural lighting effects such as change of day light, or moving shadows.

SURF. The detector of *speeded up robust features* (SURF) was presented in 2006; see [2]. SIFT and SURF algorithms employ slightly different ways for detecting features. SIFT builds an image pyramid, filters each layer with Gaussians of increasing sigma values, and takes the differences. SURF is inspired by the SIFT detector, but designed with emphasis on speed, being SIFT's main weakness. SURF is often said to be "a few times faster than SIFT with no performance drop". The detector uses a Haar-wavelet approximation of the blob detector based on the Hessian determinant. Haar-wavelet approximations can be efficiently computed at different scales using integral images. Due to the use of integral images, SURF filters the stack using a box-filter approximation of second-order Gaussian partial derivatives, since integral images allow the computation of rectangular box filters in near-constant time. Accurate localization of features requires interpolation.

FAST. The detection of *features from accelerated segment test* FAST was also published in 2006; see [12]. It performs two tests. At first, candidate points are being detected by applying a segment test to every image pixel. Let I_p denote the brightness of the investigated pixel p. The test is passed, if n pixels on a Bresenham circle, with the radius r around the pixel p, are darker than $I_p - t$ (*dark pixels*), or brighter than $I_p + t$ (*bright pixels*), where t is a threshold value. The authors use a circle with $r = 3$, and $r = 9$ for best results. The ordering of questions used to classify a pixel is learned by using the ID3 algorithm, which speeds this step up significantly. As the first test produces many adjacent responses around the interest point, an additional criterion is applied to perform a non-maximum suppression. Because the second test is only performed for a fraction of image points that passed the first test, the processing time remains short.

BRIEF. Binary robust independent elementary features (BRIEF) have been suggested in 2010; see [3]. This is is a general-purpose feature point descriptor that can be combined with arbitrary detectors. It uses binary strings for efficiency reasons. The descriptor is highly discriminative even when using relatively few bits and can be computed using simple intensity difference tests. It is robust to typical classes of photometric and geometric image transformations. Similarity between descriptions can be evaluated using the Hamming distance, which is very efficient to compute, instead of using the usual L_2-norm. BRIEF is targeting real-time applications leaving them with a large portion of available CPU power for subsequent tasks but also allows running feature point matching algorithms on computationally weak devices such as mobile phones.

BRISK. The detector of *binary robust invariant scalable keypoints* (BRISK) is a method for keypoint detection, description and matching, published in 2011; see [6]. In this paper, a comprehensive evaluation on benchmark datasets reveals BRISK's adaptive, high-quality performance compared to state-of-the-art algorithms, albeit at a dramatically lower computational cost (an order of magnitude faster than SURF in many cases). The key to speed lies in the application of a novel scale-space FAST-based detector in combination with the assembly of a bit-string descriptor from intensity comparisons retrieved by dedicated sampling of each keypoint neighbourhood.

ORB. The detection of *oriented binary robust independent elementary features* (ORB) was also published in 2011; see [13]. It is a standard for oriented FAST and rotated BRIEF. The algorithm uses FAST in pyramids to detect stable keypoints, selects the strongest features using FAST or a Harris response, finds their orientation using first-order moments, and computes the descriptors using BRIEF (where the coordinates of random-point pairs (or k-tuples) are rotated according to the measured direction).

FREAK. The *fast retina keypoint* (FREAK) detection was published in 2012; see [1]. The algorithm proposes a novel keypoint descriptor inspired by the human visual system, and, more precisely, the retina. A cascade of binary strings is computed by efficiently comparing image intensities over a retinal sampling pattern. It is commonly stated that FREAKs are in general faster to compute with lower memory load and also "more robust" than SIFT, SURF, or BRISK, and that they are competitive alternatives to existing keypoints, in particular for embedded applications.

In the brief descriptions above we also mentioned "common believe" about the performance of those detectors, and we are now aiming at quantifying such statements by experiments on extensive data. For providing repeatable data, we use a data set available online on [5].

3   Experiment Design

We are interested in comparative evaluations of efficiency (the time used for a measurement of feature points and description extraction time), rotation invariance (how the feature detection method depends on feature direction), scaling invariance (how the feature detection method depends on feature size), blur invariance (how the feature detection method is robust against blur), illumination invariance (how the feature detection method is robust against illumination changes), and shearing invariance (how the feature detection method is robust against shearing).

All the reported quality tests work in a similar way: For a given sequence (our set of source images), we apply the defined workflow identically on each image, and take finally the average of calculated data for the whole image sequence. Here we report for experiments on the sequence "Cyclist", see Fig 1, which is a "typical" day-time sequence with respect to occurring diversities in shown objects and lighting variations.

For any image in the sequence, the following steps are done for each of the tested ten feature detectors:

1. Read the source image I_s as a greyscale image.
2. Use the feature detector to detect the keypoints and extract descriptors D_s from I_s; get the number K_s of keypoints.
3. Transform the source image for the different invariance test scenarios:
   - For testing rotation invariance, rotate I_s around its centre in steps of 1 degree; we obtain 360 transformed images.
   - For testing scaling invariance, resize I_s in scaling steps of 0.01, from $0.25\times$ size to $2 \times size$, thus calculating 175 scaled images.
   - For testing illumination invariance, we change the overall image brightness by adding a scalar to every pixel value of I_s; the scalar changes from -127 to 127 in stepsize 1, thus generating 255 transformed images.
   - For testing blurring invariance, we Gaussian blur I_s by using 20 different kernel sizes between 3 to 41, thus calculating 20 blurred versions of I_s.
   - For test shearing invariance, shear I_s in shearing steps of 0.01, from 0 to 0.5, thus calculating 50 sheared images.
4. For each of those transformed images I_t, we use the feature detector again to detect the keypoints and extract descriptors D_t; in particular we note the number K_t of keypoints.
5. We use the two sets of descriptors D_s and D_t and a brute-force descriptor matcher to find matching image keypoints between source image and transformed image.
6. There are inconsistent matches. We use *Random Sample Consensus* (RANSAC) to remove those; all the remaining are considered to be *correct matches*. We note the number K_{cm} of correct matches.

The *repeatability measure* $r(I_s, I_t)$ is defined as being the ratio between the number of correct matches between the two sets of image keypoints (for source and transformed image) and the number of keypoints detected in the source image:

$$r(I_s, I_t) = \frac{K_{cm}}{K_s}$$

Obtained measure values are then averaged for all the selected frames of the used test sequence. Here we report about results for 90 randomly selected images from this sequence. For the feature detectors we used the default parameters implemented in OpenCV.

4 Experimental Results

The following four graphs in Figs. 2 to 6 summarize our experimental results. The y-axis is always for values $r_{(I_s, I_t)}$. The x-axis for the blur graph is a number

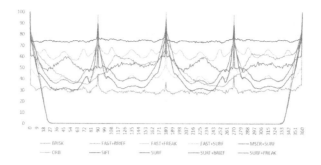

Fig. 2. Repeatability values for the tested 360 rotations

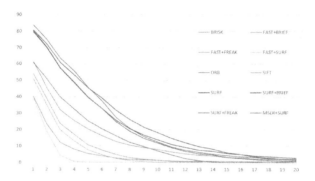

Fig. 3. Repeatability values for the tested 20 blurrings

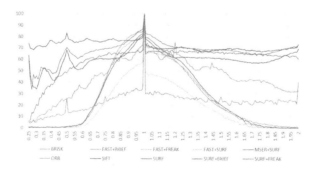

Fig. 4. Repeatability values for the tested 175 scalings

which indicates the kernel size ($2\times$ number $+1$) of the used Gauss function. When naming a feature detection method 'A+B' then this means that we use feature detector 'A' and feature descriptor 'B'. For the brightness variations note that the brightness mean for all the used 90 source images equals 108.

Table 1 summarizes time measurements on original images, and illustrates numbers of detected keypoints for the image shown in Fig. 1. The measured

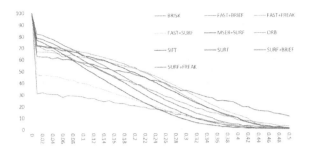

Fig. 5. Repeatability values for the tested 50 shearings

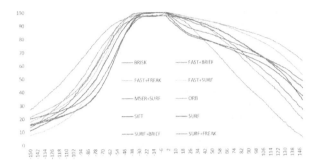

Fig. 6. Repeatability values for the tested 255 brightness variations

Table 1. Averages are for the detectors on all the 90 source images, and the numbers of keypoints are for the image shown in Fig. 1

Method	Ave. time per frame	Ave. time per keypoint	No. of keypoints
SIFT	320	0.441	728
SURF	508	0.381	1,332
ORB	13	0.026	500
BRISK	12	0.048	258
SURF+BRIEF	128	0.100	1,273
SURF+FREAK	126	0.148	851
FAST+SURF	86	0.056	1,522
FAST+BRIEF	7	0.005	1,404
FAST+FREAK	6	0.004	1,423
MSER+SURF	113	0.744	151

computation times per keypoint in all the generated test images are summarized in Fig. 7.

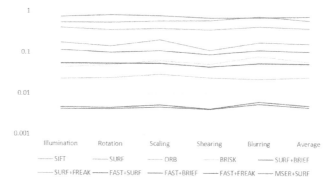

Fig. 7. Averaged time per keypoint for the five generated sets of transformed images, over all the selected 90 frames. The up-axis shows the time used in milliseconds.

5   Conclusions

This paper compared the performance of ten feature detection methods. The performed tests show that SIFT has the best robustness with respect to rotation and scale changes, but its time issue has been confirmed again. FAST and BRIEF provide better results for increased brightness, and ORB better for decreased brightness. ORB also shows good performance on blurred images. Many more comments are possible for the given graphs, but the reader may see for himself. The results also show that claimed invariances are only valid to some limited degree, and further research on improving invariance properties appears to be justified.

References

1. Alahi, A., Ortiz, R., Vandergheynst, P.: FREAK: Fast retina keypoint. In: Proc. CVPR, pp. 510–517 (2012)
2. Bay, H., Tuytelaars, T., Van Gool, L.: SURF: Speeded up robust features. In: Leonardis, A., Bischof, H., Pinz, A. (eds.) ECCV 2006, Part I. LNCS, vol. 3951, pp. 404–417. Springer, Heidelberg (2006)
3. Calonder, M., Lepetit, V., Strecha, C., Fua, P.: BRIEF: Binary robust independent elementary features. In: Daniilidis, K., Maragos, P., Paragios, N. (eds.) ECCV 2010, Part IV. LNCS, vol. 6314, pp. 778–792. Springer, Heidelberg (2010)
4. Donoser, M., Bischof, H.: Efficient maximally stable extremal region (MSER) tracking. In: Proc. CVPR, pp. 553–560 (2006)
5. EISATS Website, http://www.mi.auckland.ac.nz/index.php (last visited in April 2013)
6. Leutenegger, S., Chli, M., Siegwart, R.Y.: BRISK: Binary robust invariant scalable keypoints. In: IEEE Int. Conf. ICCV, pp. 2548–2555 (2011)
7. Lowe, D.G.: Distinctive image features from scale-invariant keypoints. Int. J. Computer Vision 60, 91–110 (2004)

8. Luo, J., Oubong, G.: A comparison of SIFT, PCA-SIFT and SURF. Int. J. Image Processing, 143–152 (2009)
9. Martin, A.F., Robert, C.B.: Random sample consensus: A paradigm for model fitting with applications to image analysis and automated cartography. Comm. ACM 24, 381–395 (1981)
10. Matas, J., Chum, O., Urban, M., Pajdla, T.: Robust wide baseline stereo from maximally stable extremal regions. In: Proc. BMVC, pp. 384–396 (2002)
11. OpenCV Documentation, http://www.docs.opencv.org/index.html (last visited in April 2013)
12. Rosten, E., Drummond, T.: Machine learning for high-speed corner detection. In: Leonardis, A., Bischof, H., Pinz, A. (eds.) ECCV 2006, Part I. LNCS, vol. 3951, pp. 430–443. Springer, Heidelberg (2006)
13. Rublee, E., Rabaud, V., Konolige, K., Bradski, G.: ORB: An efficient alternative to SIFT or SURF. In: Proc. ICCV, pp. 2564–2571 (2011)
14. Tombari, F., Salti, S., Di Stefano, L.: Performance evaluation of 3D keypoint detectors. Int. J. Computer Vision 102, 198–220 (2013)
15. Tuytelaars, T., Mikolajczyk, K.: Local invariant feature detectors: A survey. Foundations Trends Computer Graphics Vision 3, 177–280 (2008)
16. Yu, T.-H., Woodford, O.J., Cipolla, R.: A performance evaluation of volumetric interest point detectors. Int. J. Computer Vision 102, 180–197 (2013)

Depth Super-Resolution by Enhanced Shift and Add[*]

Kassem Al Ismaeil[1], Djamila Aouada[1], Bruno Mirbach[2], and Björn Ottersten[1]

[1] Interdisciplinary Centre for Security, Reliability and Trust
Universtity of Luxembourg
{kassem.alismaeil,djamila.aouada,bjorn.ottersten}@uni.lu
[2] Advanced Engineering Department, IEE S.A.
bruno.mirbach@iee.lu

Abstract. We use multi-frame super-resolution, specifically, *Shift & Add*, to increase the resolution of depth data. In order to be able to deploy such a framework in practice, without requiring a very high number of observed low resolution frames, we improve the initial estimation of the high resolution frame. To that end, we propose a new data model that leads to a median estimation from densely upsampled low resolution frames. We show that this new formulation solves the problem of undefined pixels and further allows to improve the performance of pyramidal motion estimation in the context of super-resolution without additional computational cost. As a consequence, it increases the motion diversity within a small number of observed frames, making the enhancement of depth data more practical. Quantitative experiments run on the Middlebury dataset show that our method outperforms state-of-the-art techniques in terms of accuracy and robustness to the number of frames and to the noise level.

Keywords: Time-of-flight depth data, Super-resolution, Dense upsampling, Pyramidal optical flow, Motion diversity.

1 Introduction

The usage of depth data captured by time-of-flight (ToF) cameras is often limited because of its low resolution (LR). Most of the work proposed to enhance the resolution of this data has been based on fusion with high resolution (HR) images acquired with a second camera, e.g., 2D camera [1,2], stereo camera [3], or both 2D and stereo cameras [4]. These multi-modality methods provide solutions with undesired texture copying artifacts in addition to being highly dependent on parameter tuning. Moreover, using an additional camera requires dealing with data mapping and synchronization issues.

The super-resolution (SR) framework offers an alternative solution where an HR image is to be recovered from a set of LR images captured with the same

---

[*] This work was supported by the National Research Fund, Luxembourg, under the CORE project C11/BM/1204105/FAVE/Ottersten.

R. Wilson et al. (Eds.): CAIP 2013, Part II, LNCS 8048, pp. 100–107, 2013.

camera. The key idea is to explore the deviation between these LR images and a reference frame. SR techniques have been largely explored in the 2D case. The extension of these algorithms to depth data is not straightforward as presented in [5] where a dedicated preprocessing has been proposed to achieve depth SR from a single image, hence calling upon a heavy training. Earlier, the classical *Shift & Add* (*S&A*) was applied on depth data [6] in a multi-frame setup. While this work showed that SR may be used successfully on depth data without any training, it is still not a practical solution as it requires a large number of frames to ensure sufficient depth discontinuities between frames. An extended version has been proposed by the same authors in [7] by defining a new cost function dedicated to depth data. Both approaches in [6] and [7] do not solve the limitation on the number of frames inherent to classical *S&A*; thus, they remain unpractical solutions. In what follows, we show that this limitation goes back to the initialization step even before reaching to the iterative optimization step. Indeed, estimating the initial HR frame relies on LR frames only. In the case where the motion diversity within these frames is not sufficient, the initial estimate ends up with undefined pixels that affect the result of any iterative optimization. Therefore, we propose to estimate the initial HR frame from upsampled LR frames. By doing so, we ensure that no undefined pixels are present; moreover, we prove that, in the SR context, a more accurate motion estimation using pyramidal optical flow may be achieved resulting in an increased motion diversity within a smaller number of frames. In contrast to [13], this work is dedicated to depth data, where the upsampling has to be a dense one.

The remainder of the paper is organized as follows: Section 2 gives the classical SR formulation and a description of *S&A*. In Section 3, a new data model is provided leading to our proposed algorithm. Experimental results on the Middlebury dataset and on real ToF data are given in Section 4.

2   Motivation and Background

Let $\mathbf{X}$ be an HR depth image of size $(m \times n)$ and $\mathbf{Y}_k$, $k = 0, ..., (N-1)$, N observed LR images, where each LR image is of size $(\acute{m} \times \acute{n})$ pixels, such that $n = r \cdot \acute{n}$ and $m = r \cdot \acute{m}$, where r is the SR factor. Every frame $\mathbf{Y}_k$ may be viewed as a LR noisy and deformed realization of $\mathbf{X}$ caused by the ToF imaging system at the kth acquisition. Considering $\mathbf{Y}_k$'s and $\mathbf{X}$'s respective lexicographic vector forms $\mathbf{y}_k$ and $\mathbf{x}$, the SR data model may be defined as follows:

$$\mathbf{y}_k = \mathbf{DHW}_k\mathbf{x} + \mathbf{n}_k, \qquad k = 0, ..., (N-1), \qquad (1)$$

where $\mathbf{W}_k$ is an $(mn \times mn)$ matrix corresponding to the geometric motion between $\mathbf{x}$ and $\mathbf{y}_k$. In this framework, this motion is assumed to be global translational; hence, $\mathbf{W}_k$ represents a global shifting operator by u_k in x direction, and by v_k in y direction. The point spread function (PSF) of the ToF camera is modelled by the $(mn \times mn)$ space and time invariant blurring matrix $\mathbf{H}$. The matrix $\mathbf{D}$ of dimension $(\acute{m}\acute{n} \times mn)$ represents the downsampling operator, and the vector $\mathbf{n}_k$ is the additive noise at k. Using the same approach as in [8], we consider that $\mathbf{H}$ and $\mathbf{W}_k$ are block circulant matrices. Therefore:

$$\mathbf{H}\mathbf{W}_k = \mathbf{W}_k\mathbf{H}. \tag{2}$$

Estimating $\mathbf{x}$ may thus be decomposed into two main steps: estimation of a blurred HR image $\mathbf{z}_0 = \mathbf{H}\mathbf{x}_0$, where $\mathbf{x}_0$ is an initial guess for $\mathbf{x}$, followed by a deblurring step by an iterative optimization. The classical $S\&A$ approach [8] defines $\mathbf{z}_0$ by first setting its corresponding full HR image grid $\mathbf{Z}_0$ to zeros, i.e., $\mathbf{Z}_0 = \mathbf{0}_{m \times n}$. Then, all LR images $\mathbf{Y}_k$ are used to update the pixel values in $\mathbf{Z}_0$. To that end, given a reference LR image $\mathbf{Y}_0$ chosen as the closest one to the target HR image $\mathbf{X}$, the global translational motions $\mathbf{w}_k = (u_k, v_k)$ between each image $\mathbf{Y}_k$ and $\mathbf{Y}_0$ are computed for $k = 1, \cdots, (N-1)$. These motions are used to register all LR images $\mathbf{Y}_k$ with respect to the reference image $\mathbf{Y}_0$. The resulting registered images $\overline{\mathbf{Y}}_k$ are simply defined at each pixel position $\mathbf{p} = (x, y)$ as follows:

$$\overline{\mathbf{Y}}_k(\mathbf{p}) = \mathbf{Y}_k(\mathbf{p} + \mathbf{w}_k). \tag{3}$$

These images are then grouped into M sets based on their relative motions $\mathbf{w}_k$. Note that to avoid aliasing problems, the range of this motion is forced to be within the SR factor r by a simple modulo function, i.e., $u_k = u_k\mathrm{mod}(r)$ and $v_k = v_k\mathrm{mod}(r)$. The frames in one set are fused by median filtering resulting in one LR image $\overline{\overline{\mathbf{Y}}}_i$ per motion $\mathbf{w}_i$, with $1 \leq i \leq M \leq N$. Each frame is then used to update the pixels of $\mathbf{Z}_0$ as follows:

$$\mathbf{Z}_0\left(r \cdot \mathbf{p} + \mathbf{w}_i\right) = \overline{\overline{\mathbf{Y}}}_i(\mathbf{p}). \tag{4}$$

This operation is known as zero filling in the $S\&A$ approach. We note that for a successful filling, there should be enough motion diversity in the considered LR frames. Indeed, in order to further update the zero pixels in $\mathbf{Z}_0$, an additional $(r \times r)$ median filtering is applied. Given that the median filter's breakdown point is $\frac{1}{2}$, a meaningful filling that does not leave pixels undefined should be achieved if the following condition is satisfied:

$$\mathrm{round}\left(\frac{r^2}{2}\right) \leq M. \tag{5}$$

As a second step, the estimation of $\mathbf{x}$ follows a maximum likelihood approach that, by assuming $\mathbf{n}_k$ as a Laplacian white noise, leads to the following minimization:

$$\hat{\mathbf{x}} = \underset{\mathbf{x}}{\mathrm{argmin}}\left(\|\mathbf{H}\mathbf{x} - \mathbf{z}_0\|_1 + \lambda\Gamma(\mathbf{x})\right), \tag{6}$$

where $\Gamma(\mathbf{x})$ is a regularization term added to compensate undetermined cases by enforcing prior information about $\mathbf{x}$, and λ being the regularization parameter.

Starting with an accurate initial guess $\mathbf{z}_0$ has a strong impact on the final solution of (6). We show the effect of undefined pixels in $\mathbf{Z}_0$ caused by classical $S\&A$ in Fig. 1(b). A similar phenomenon is observed using interpolation-based

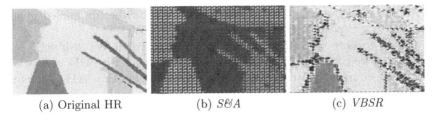

(a) Original HR   (b) *S&A*   (c) *VBSR*

Fig. 1. Undefined pixels using state-of-the-art SR methods (Red colors are the closest objects and green colors are the furthest ones.)

initialization such as variational Bayesian SR (*VBSR*) [9] as seen in Fig. 1(c), suggesting that interpolation is not a sufficient solution to remove undefined pixels. Moreover, it creates additional artifacts on depth data such as jagged values on edges. It is common to face this serious problem of undefined pixels in practice. It is dealt with by restricting the SR factor to low values, e.g., $r = 2$, and by taking a relatively large number of frames, e.g., $N > 30$, thus indirectly attempting to satisfy inequality (5), which, in turn, limits the practical usage of SR algorithms on depth data. In what follows, our aim is to increase motion diversity M to give more freedom in the choice of r without having to increase N. We propose to tackle the aforementioned problem by a new non-zero initialization of $\mathbf{Z}_0$ as detailed in Section 3.

3   Proposed Algorithm

Estimating the motions $\mathbf{w}_k$ with high sub-pixel accuracy is crucial in capturing the full diversity in motion as contained in the observed LR depth frames; hence, important in increasing M. Indeed, for two frames $\mathbf{Y}_i$ and $\mathbf{Y}_j$ with respective relative motions $\mathbf{w}_i$ and $\mathbf{w}_j$, such that $\|\mathbf{w}_i - \mathbf{w}_j\|_2 = \epsilon$; if the motion estimation approach has an accuracy that is smaller than ϵ, the two frames will be wrongly fused and labeled under the same motion. Classical *S&A* uses pyramidal motion estimation (*PyrME*) [10,11]. This method represents state-of-art in motion estimation increasing both accuracy and robustness by a gain $\mathcal{G}(L) = 2^{(L+1)} - 1$, where L is the number of pyramidal levels [10]. In the case of SR, we note that the target resolution at which we want to land is the HR ($m \times n$). This gives us a natural way to further improve the performance of *PyrME*. We thus propose to start by upsampling the LR depth frames up to the SR factor r prior to any motion estimation such that $\mathbf{y}_k \uparrow = \mathbf{U} \cdot \mathbf{y}_k$, where $\mathbf{U}$ is a dense upsampling matrix of size ($mn \times \acute{m}\acute{n}$). By doing so, we increase the size of the basis of the pyramid by a factor r. Changing the starting point in *PyrME* leads to an increased pyramid height $L \uparrow$ by $\log_2(r)$ which results in a new increased gain $\mathcal{G}(L \uparrow) = r \cdot \mathcal{G}(L) + (r - 1)$. This demonstrates that, in the SR context, the performance of *PyrME*, in terms of accuracy and robustness, may further be enhanced. Therefore, to estimate $\mathbf{w}_k$ more accurately, we now work with $\mathbf{Y}_k \uparrow$, $k = 0, \cdots, (N - 1)$, the N upsampled LR frames corresponding to the vectors

$\mathbf{y}_k \uparrow$. Performing the registration process as in (3) on the upsampled images $\mathbf{Y}_k \uparrow$ gives: $\overline{\mathbf{Y}}_k \uparrow (\mathbf{p}) = \mathbf{Y}_k \uparrow (\mathbf{p} \mid \mathbf{w}_k)$ $\Leftrightarrow$ $\mathbf{y}_k \uparrow = \mathbf{W}_k \overline{\mathbf{y}}_k \uparrow$.

It is easy to note that the new corresponding matrices $\mathbf{W}_k$ still verify (2). Furthermore, we choose $\mathbf{U}$ to be the transpose of $\mathbf{D}$, such that $\mathbf{UD} = \mathbf{A}$, where $\mathbf{A}$ is a block circulant matrix that defines a new blurring $\mathbf{B} = \mathbf{AH}$. Therefore, we redefine $\mathbf{z}_0$ as $\mathbf{z}_0 = \mathbf{Bx}_0$, and by left multiplying (1) by $\mathbf{U}$ we find:

$$\mathbf{y}_k \uparrow = \mathbf{W}_k \mathbf{Bx} + \mathbf{Un}_k, \qquad k = 0, ..., (N-1). \tag{7}$$

In addition, similarly to [12], for analytical convenience, we assume that all pixels in $\mathbf{y}_k \uparrow$ originate from pixels in $\mathbf{x}$ in a one to one mapping. Therefore, each row in $\mathbf{W}_k$ contains 1 for each position corresponding to the address of the source pixel in $\mathbf{x}$. This bijective property implies that the matrix $\mathbf{W}_k$ is an invertible permutation. By left multiplying (7) by $\mathbf{W}_k^{-1}$, we define the following new data model from upsampled registered observed LR frames:

$$\overline{\mathbf{y}}_k \uparrow = \mathbf{Bx} + \boldsymbol{\nu}_k, \qquad k = 0, ..., (N-1), \tag{8}$$

where $\boldsymbol{\nu}_k$ is an upsampled additive white Laplacian noise at k, leading to the following estimation of the initial guess:

$$\hat{\mathbf{z}}_0 = \arg\min_{\mathbf{z}_0} \sum_{k=0}^{(N-1)} \|\mathbf{z}_0 - \overline{\mathbf{y}}_k \uparrow \|_1. \tag{9}$$

The non-zero initialization in (9) releases the condition in (5), thus solving the problem of undefined pixels. In order not to fall under the same artifacts as those present with interpolation-based SR approaches, e.g., *VBSR* (Fig. 1(c)), it is necessary to perform the filling operation from registered and clustered LR images as in (4). Indeed, the values from LR frames remain more reliable sources of information than the ones due to upsampling. They are further processed by a (3×3) median filtering to smooth out noisy depth pixels. We point out that the higher accuracy in the estimation of $\mathbf{w}_k$ leads to a higher discrimination between motions, resulting in a higher diversity M and a better update of the pixel values in $\mathbf{z}_0$ as compared to the case of classical *S&A*. In our algorithm, it is more accurate to refer to this operation as initialization update rather than filling. After the new initialization and update step described above, a last deblurring step is performed to recover $\hat{\mathbf{x}}$ from $\hat{\mathbf{z}}_0$ using (6).

4   Experimental Results

To evaluate the performance of the proposed algorithm, we tested its robustness on synthetic and real depth images against two parameters: number of considered LR images N, and image contamination with noise measured by signal to noise ratio (SNR). Each time we compare with two state-of-the-art SR methods, namely, classical *S&A* [8], and *VBSR* [9]. First, we ran Monte-Carlo simulations on synthetic sequences of a static scene subjected to a randomly

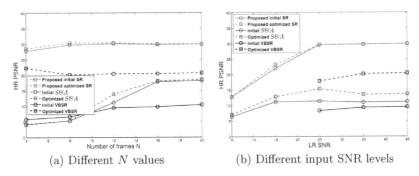

(a) Different N values   (b) Different input SNR levels

Fig. 2. Mean PSNR values for different SR methods applied to a (75×75) LR sequence of a static depth scene with $r = 4$

generated global frame motion. These sequences were created by downsampling the HR image "ART" from the Middlebury dataset [10] with a factor $r = 4$, and PSF of $\sigma = 0.4$, and further degrading them by additive white Gaussian noise (AWGN). For a fixed noise level corresponding to SNR = 45dB, and 100 different realizations, Fig. 2(a) shows the average PSNR for N progressively increasing from 4 to 20 frames. It is clear that the proposed method outperforms both $S\&A$ and $VBSR$ across different numbers of LR frames. This difference is even more noticeable for very low values of N, which illustrates the practicality of the proposed method. Next, we ran another round of experiments to evaluate the performance across different noise levels. In this experiment, a sequence of 12 (75×75) LR depth images was used. It was generated in the same way as in the previous experiment, and further degraded by AWGN with SNR of 5, 15, 25, 35 and 45dB. Fig. 2(b) shows that the proposed method is consistently more robust to noise. Furthermore, the textureless property of depth images combined with dense upsampling boost the performance of the proposed initial HR frame estimation, even for a very high noise level, e.g., SNR = 5dB, leading to comparable results before and after optimization with (6) as shown, respectively, with the dashed and continuous red lines in Fig. 2(a) and Fig. 2(b). This result suggests that the non-zero initialization may be considered as a standalone approach in the case of depth data as it does not deviate much from the assumptions related to the data model in (8). We give, in Fig. 3, an example of an HR estimated image of "ART" using 8 and 12 LR images in the first and second rows, respectively. Due to the condition (5), it is not surprising to see the artifacts caused by undefined pixels where the number of images is not sufficient to cover the motion range. Moreover, as seen in Fig. 3(d),(h), it is clear that our method provides the best visually enhanced HR depth images with sharper edges as compared to the results of $S\&A$ and $VBSR$. Finally, we tested the proposed algorithm on two real short depth sequences. The first sequence contains 8 LR depth images acquired using an IEE MLI ToF camera of resolution (56×61) pixels. The second sequence contains 5 LR frames acquired using a PMD CamBoard nano of resolution (120×165) pixels. Considering an SR factor of 4, the final results are given in Fig. 4, clearly showing that for these practical cases with a small N,

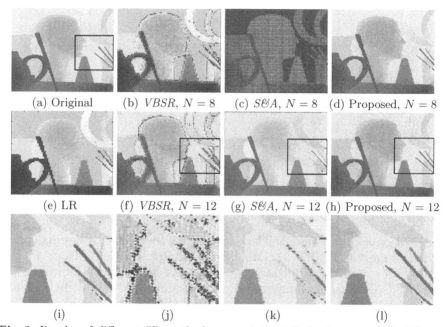

(a) Original   (b) *VBSR*, $N = 8$ (c) *S&A*, $N = 8$ (d) Proposed, $N = 8$

(e) LR   (f) *VBSR*, $N = 12$ (g) *S&A*, $N = 12$ (h) Proposed, $N = 12$

(i)   (j)   (k)   (l)

Fig. 3. Results of different SR methods on a static ToF depth scene with different frame numbers ($N = 8, N = 12$) and SR factor of $r = 4$.)

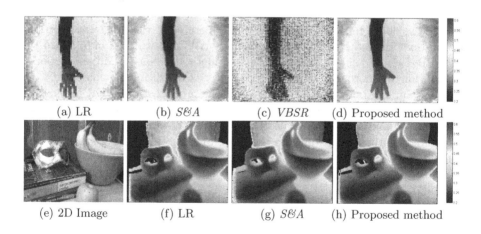

(a) LR   (b) *S&A*   (c) *VBSR*   (d) Proposed method

(e) 2D Image   (f) LR   (g) *S&A*   (h) Proposed method

Fig. 4. Results of different SR methods on real LR ToF short sequences

the proposed method nicely super-resolves the LR frames by preserving edges and details while *S&A* and *VBSR* fail due to undefined pixels. Note that for the sake of practical deployment, to avoid any additional computal cost in the proposed method, the motion estimation from upsampled LR frames may be approximated by upscaling the corresponding LR motion vectors.

5 Conclusion

We proposed a practical SR solution for LR depth data acquired by ToF cameras. Our algorithm is based on a new SR data model that uses the upsampled and registered versions of the observed LR images. The benefits of this new formulation are twofold: It leads to a non-zero initialization of the estimate of the HR depth frame which solves the problem of undefined pixels inherent to classical SR techniques. Furthermore, it increases the accuracy and robustness of pyramidal motion estimation, which contributes in increasing the motion diversity within the observed frames. Both results help to reach good SR performances even in the challenging case of a relatively small number of LR frames, hence making the proposed algorithm usable in practice. While this method may be applied to 2D data, it is specifically designed to improve depth data thanks to a dense upsampling. Moreover, the textureless nature of depth data allows to use the proposed initialization step as a standalone algorithm where additional optimization is only required in the presence of high level non Laplacian noise.

References

1. Garcia, F., Aouada, D., Mirbach, B., Solignac, T., Ottersten, B.: Real-time Hybrid ToF Multi-Camera Rig Fusion System for Depth Map Enhancement. In: IEEE CVPRW 2011 (2011)
2. Yang, Q., Yang, R., Davis, J., Nister, D.: Spatial-Depth Super Resolution for Range Images. In: IEEE CVPR 2007 (2007)
3. Zhu, J., Wang, L., Yang, R., Davis, J.: Fusion of Time-of-Flight Depth and Stereo for High Accuracy Depth Maps. In: IEEE CVPR 2008 (2008)
4. Yang, Q., Tan, K., Culbertson, B., Apostolopoulos, J.: Fusion of Active and Passive Sensors for fast 3D Capture. In: MMSP 2010 (2010)
5. Mac Aodha, O., Campbell, N.D.F., Nair, A., Brostow, G.J.: Patch Based Synthesis for Single Depth Image Super-Resolution. In: Fitzgibbon, A., Lazebnik, S., Perona, P., Sato, Y., Schmid, C. (eds.) ECCV 2012, Part III. LNCS, vol. 7574, pp. 71–84. Springer, Heidelberg (2012)
6. Schuon, S., Theobalt, C., Davis, J., Thrun, S.: High-Quality Scanning Using Time-of-Flight Depth Superresolution. In: IEEE CVPRW 2008 (2008)
7. Schuon, S., Theobalt, C., Davis, J., Thrun, S.: LidarBoost: Depth Superresolution for ToF 3D Shape Scanning. In: IEEE CVPR (2009)
8. Farsiu, S., Robinson, D., Elad, M., Milanfar, P.: Fast and Robust Multi-Frame Super-Resolution. In: IEEE TIP 2003 (2003)
9. Babacan, S.D., Molina, R., Katsaggelos, A.K.: Variational Bayesian Super Resolution. In: IEEE TIP 2011 (2011)
10. Bouguet, J.Y.: Pyramidal Implementation of the Lukas Kanade Feature Tracker. Description of the Algorithm,
http://robots.stanford.edu/cs223b04/algo_tracking
11. Bergen, J.R., Anandan, P., Hanna, K.J., Hingorani, R.: Hierarchical Model-Based Motion Estimation. In: Sandini, G. (ed.) ECCV 1992. LNCS, vol. 588, pp. 237–252. Springer, Heidelberg (1992)
12. Elad, M., Feuer, A.: Super-Resolution Reconstruction of Continuous Image Sequence. In: IEEE PAMI 1999 (1999)
13. Al Ismaeil, K., Aouada, D., Mirbach, B., Ottersten, B.: Multi-Frame Super-Resolution by Enhanced Shift & Add. In: IEEE ISPA 2013 (2013)

Using Region-Based Saliency for 3D Interest Points Detection

Yitian Zhao[1], Yonghuai Liu[1], and Ziming Zeng[1,2]

[1] Department of Computer Science, Aberystwyth University, UK
[2] Information and Control Engineering Faculty, Shenyang Jianzhu University, China
yyz10@aber.ac.uk

Abstract. The detection of interest points is an important pre-processing step for the analysis of mesh surfaces. This paper proposes a new method for the detection of the interest points for 3D surfaces. We first use a smoothing process, then estimate the saliency employing a region-based detection method and select the interest points in terms of the entropy in due voxel. The evaluation is carried out by studying the repeatability of the detected interest points under different perceptual conditions, such as different viewpoints and noise corruption. The results show that the proposed method achieves better performance than competitors.

Keywords: salient, surface, bilateral, region, repeatability.

1 Introduction

3D interest points detection is helpful in capturing the property of a point or region on a surface. Interest points, also referred to as feature points, salient points, or keypoints, are those points that are distinctive in their locality and stable at all instances of an object, or of its category of objects [1]. Therefore, interest points detection has a wide range of applications in the fields of computer vision and graphics, such as mesh simplification, view point selection, point cloud matching, and object recognition. Use of interest points has the advantage of providing local features that are semantically significant and also invariant to rotation, scaling, noise, deformation, and articulation.

Recent years have witnessed the rapid development of methods for saliency and interest points detection on 3D surfaces. Most of the current 3D interest point detection methods have been developed over the last decade, as have defined functions summarizing the geometrical content of localities on a 3D model in multiple scales, and selected local extrema of those functions as interest points. Gelfand et al. [2] proposed a method that is related to the surface curvature, and which is invariant to rotation and translation. Lee et al. [3] produced an approach that used a center-surround operator on the local curvature as the discriminative feature and generated the mesh saliency. Castellani et al. [4] applied Difference-of-Gaussian (DoG) on various scales, and vertices that are highly displaced after the filtering are marked as interest points. Sun et al.al [5] proposed a Heat Kernel

R. Wilson et al. (Eds.): CAIP 2013, Part II, LNCS 8048, pp. 108–116, 2013.
© Springer-Verlag Berlin Heidelberg 2013

Signature (HKS) feature point detection and the maxima of the kernel were chosen as keypoints. Mian et al. [6] proposed a keypoint detection algorithm along with an automatic scale selection technique for subsequent feature extraction. The keypoints are detected by calculating the ratio of the covariance matrices. A 3D-Harris approach [7] calculated the derivatives via fitting a quadratic surface to a neighborhood of the vertex, then the interest point were located by the first order derivatives along two orthogonal directions on the 3D surface. A 3D-SIFT technique was proposed which constructed a scale space by applying 3D Gaussian filters with increasingly large scales to the voxelized model [8]. The extreme points are detected by searching the DoG space in both spatial and scale dimensions.

Some techniques were inspired by corresponding 2D approaches. However, such extensions are not always straightforward: for example, the keypoints represent interesting information at fine scales and thus, may be sensitive to noise and other transformations. Therefore, it is necessary to find larger and interesting structures to overcome the problems at fine scales. In this paper, we propose an algorithm to select interest points from salient regions. It consists of bilateral normal filtering, region-based saliency detection and interest points selection. As we mentioned above, the sensitivity to noise affects the accuracy of the interest points detection, thus, in order to overcome this problem, we take the following three measures:

1. A **Relative distance-based** bilateral normal filter is used in the smoothing step. The relative distance has the capacity to characterize the local details of the geometry, since the local scale changes of features will not affect its value: thus it is able to capture both large and small scale features.
2. **Retinex** is a theory of color constancy that is usually applied for purposes of image enhancement. This method has been adapted for estimation of viewpoint invariant information in the saliency detection stage, so that the same salient regions will be independent of viewpoints.
3. **Region-based saliency** detection is proposed for stability and continuity, while vertex-based the saliency detection[10] is affected by occlusion and holes.

2   Bilateral Normal Filtering

Lee et al. [3] proposed mesh saliency as a measure of regional importance for graphics meshes. The basic idea is to filter the curvature of vertices in meshes using a center-surround operator on Gaussian-weighted average curvatures. The disadvantage of Gaussian-weighted average is that it might make two opposite and symmetric vertices have the same value. Compared with the Gaussian operation, the output of the bilateral operation on a vertex is a weighted average of the surrounding vertices, and the weight depends not only on the spatial distance, but also on the scalar function difference.

Moreover, the bilateral filter has been extended to filter the normals of meshes due to its nonlinear, feature-preserving characteristics. However, the standard

Gaussian function in terms of the normal vector decreases as the normal vector difference of two neighboring faces increases, suggesting that a higher level of noise has less effect on the filtering result. Consequently, this method is sensitive to high levels of noise. Hence, we propose a new bilateral normal filtering method. Given a face with an unit normal n_i and a centroid c_i, the bilateral filtered normal $\overline{n}_i$ of the face is defined as:

$$\overline{n}_i = \frac{\sum\limits_{j \in N_i} W_c(\|c_i - c_j\|)W_s(n_i, n_j)n_j}{\sum\limits_{j \in N_i} W_c(\|c_i - c_j\|)W_s(n_i, n_j)} \tag{1}$$

where N_i is the neighborhood of i. W_c is the closeness spatial smoothing function, which is the standard Gaussian filter with the standard deviation σ_c. W_s is the standard Gaussian function in terms of the normal vector:

$$W_s(n_i, n_j) = \begin{cases} 0 & \text{if } (n_i, n_j) \cdot n_j \geq R(n_i, n_j) \\ \frac{1}{\sqrt{4\pi}}exp\{-\frac{R(n_i,n_j)^2}{2}\} & \text{otherwise} \end{cases} \tag{2}$$

We use relative distance R rather than the absolute distance, the relative average distance of n_i and n_j is defined as:

$$R(n_i, n_j) = \frac{\|n_i - n_j\|^2}{ave_{n_k \subset N_i}(\|n_i - n_k\|^2)} \tag{3}$$

where $ave_{n_k \subset N}(\|n_i - n_k\|_2)$ is the average Euclidean distance between n_i and other neighboring normals. k is the number of neighboring normals.

The relative distance is used in case the distribution of the data is not uniform, as the distance metric mainly focuses on the representation of neighboring relationship between points. For two sets of points with a similar neighboring relationship but different densities, the Euclidean distances between corresponding points differ dramatically from each other, but the relative distances are in general similar. This is an advantage of the relative distance over the absolute distance in reflecting the relative density. We truncate the normal vectors if the differences between them and n_i are greater than the relative average distance of the normal vector. Thus, large noise aspects are ignored by this filter and it

Noised surface   Smoothed surface

Fig. 1. Comparison of noise added model *buddha* before and after our smoothing method. The surfaces are illustrated by the mean curvature and surface normal.

is less sensitive to a high level of noises. Fig. 1 shows initial and smoothed surfaces. The quality of the surfaces is validated by the mean curvature and surface normal.

3 Saliency Detection and Interest Points Selection

Initially, we employ *Retinex* [9] for estimation of the viewpoint invariant properties of the given surfaces. Normally, human perception and objective information with respect to vision are not in agreement, especially in the case of regions that have been captured by camera or scanner but are showing a lack of sensitivity to human eyes. The human brain interprets a 3D shape image differently from how photo-sensors or scanners may sense them by consciously correcting brightness, removing noise, shadows, glare, or reflections. After the application of *Retinex*, the 3D shape, component or surface can be represented more faithfully to the original one, thereby simulating the human visual systems. *Retinex* algorithm for 3D surfaces has been proposed in our previous papers [10] [11] for surface details enhancement. It significantly improved the quality of the surface presentation, especially enhancing the local details.

The second step is surface segmentation. A large number of 3D mesh segmentation methods have been developed: an overview of mesh segmentation can be found in survey [12,13]. We use our previous segmentation method [10] in this work.

Finally, for a segment r_k, we define the region-based saliency as:

$$Saliency(r_k) = \sum_{r_k \neq r_i} exp(\frac{-D_s(r_k, r_i)}{\sigma_s^2}) w(r_i) D_r(r_k, r_i) \tag{4}$$

where $D_s(r_k, r_i)$ is the spatial distance between segments r_k and r_i, in order to increase the effects of closer segments and decrease the effects of segments which are farther away. The spatial distance between two segments is defined as the Euclidean distance between the centroids of the respective segments. σ_s controls the strength of spatial weighting. Larger values of σ_s reduce the effect of spatial weighting, so farther segments would contribute more to the saliency of the current segment. In our implementation, we use $\sigma_s^2 = 0.4$. The average *Retinex* value of the vertices in the segment r_i is defined as the weight $w(r_i)$. $D_r(r_k, r_i)$ is the relative importance distance between two regions r_i and r_j:

$$D_r(r_i, r_j) = \sum_{i=1}^{t_1} \sum_{j=1}^{t_2} f(c_{1,i}) f(c_{2,j}) d(c_{1,i}, c_{2,j}) \tag{5}$$

where t_k denotes the number of different *Retinex* values of the vertices in the kth region r_k, $f(c_{k,i})$ is the frequency of the *Retinex* values in r_k, where $c_{k,i}$ indicates the ith *Retinex* values among all n_k values in the r_k with $k = 1, 2$. $d(c_{k,i}, c_{k,j})$ is the Euclidean distance between the ith and j^{th} *Retinex* values.

Fig. 2(a) shows the detected salient region on the *buddha* and *rick-face* surfaces, the non-blue colors denote visually important regions. The regions with

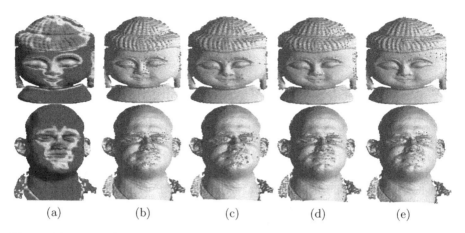

(a)   (b)   (c)   (d)   (e)

Fig. 2. (a) Proposed detected salient region. (b)-(e) interest points detection based on different methods. (b) Our method. (c) 3D-SIFT. (d) 3D-Harris. (e) MBO.

more geometrical information and larger curvature values have been located: for example, the eyes, nose and mouth of the *buddha*.

Interest Points Selection. The first step is the voxelization of the saliency mapped model. Voxels without saliency content will be removed. The entropy of saliency values of points in a voxel is calculated based on the saliency of the histogram map as $H(X) = \sum_{i=1}^{t} - P(S_i) * log_2(P(S_i))$, where $P(S_i)$ is the probability of saliency value S_i at a local voxel, n denotes the total number of the saliency values. The entropy measures how the saliency of vertices for a voxel varies. The larger the variation, the larger the entropy, the more detail the voxel contains. Thus the entropy can be used to guide the points sampling. Normally, the maximum entropy will be chosen by default. The minimum distances between the samples are used to address the possibility that the generated samples are close to the boundary between two or more adjacent voxels which might be too close to each other. Fig. 2(b) shows the detected interest points on the *buddha* and *rick-face*.

4   Experimental Evaluation and Discussion

In this section we perform a comprehensive evaluation of our interest point detector, investigating its performance under different variations of input data: viewpoints changed and noise corrupted. The performance of the proposed method is also compared with existing state-of-art 3D surface point detectors: 3D-Harris [7], 3D-SIFT [8] , and MBO [6], respectively. Fig. 2(c)-(d) show the outcomes of the different 3D interest point detectors on model *buddha* and *rick-face*.

To evaluate the proposed and other interest point detectors, we study their repeatability of interest points. This characteristic accounts for the ability of the detector to find the same set of keypoints on different instances of a given model, where the differences may vary under conditions of changed viewpoint

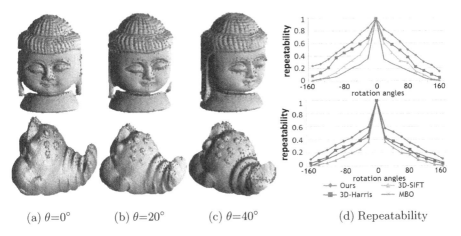

(a) $\theta=0°$ (b) $\theta=20°$ (c) $\theta=40°$ (d) Repeatability

Fig. 3. (a)-(c) Model *buddha* and *lobster* subject to a rotation of θ at intervals of $20°$ around an unknown rotation axis are used to test the robustness of the proposed method. (d) Repeatability of interest points on the *buddha* and *lobster* with different detectors under different rotation of θ from $0°$ to $\pm160°$.

or noise corruption. Once the correspondence of the points under these different conditions has been obtained, we define the repeatability rate of interest points:

$$rep = \frac{|np_i \cap np_r|}{|np_r|} \tag{6}$$

where np_i is the number of interest points found under one of the instances and np_r is the number of interest points detected from the original given model (reference model). For a perfect detector, it detects the same interest points in the first and last frame, i.e. $rep = 1$. In this paper, we only select 1% of total number of the vertices as interest points, as too few keypoints may not be enough to represent the global shape or supply further geometrical verification, while too many points leads to unnecessary waste of computational resources.

4.1 Viewpoints Changing

This experiment evaluates the susceptibility of the proposed detector and its competitors under changing viewpoints. We set the models *buddha* and *lobster* at rotation angle $0°$ as the reference viewpoint and calculated the repeatability of interest points from 16 alternative viewpoints, of which 8 viewpoints were anti-clockwise rotated ($20°,40°...160°$) and 8 viewpoints were clockwise rotated ($-20°,-40°...-160°$).

The effect of such rotations is shown in Fig. 3(a)-(c). Fig. 3(d) shows the repeatabilities under such transformation. Most detectors show excellent tolerance with small rotation, such as $\pm20°$. Our method achieves repeatability rates above 0.8, 3D-Harris achieves a 0.7 repeatability rates and 3D-SIFT gives a repeatability rate around 0.6, while only 0.38 with MBO. With increasing rotation

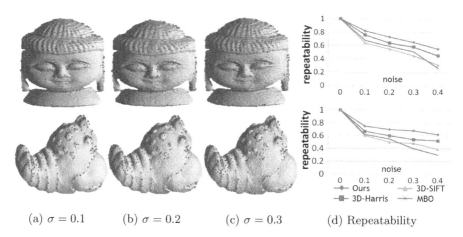

(a) $\sigma = 0.1$ (b) $\sigma = 0.2$ (c) $\sigma = 0.3$ (d) Repeatability

Fig. 4. Interest points detected with different noise levels.(a) $\sigma = 0.1$. (b) $\sigma = 0.2$.(c) $\sigma = 0.3$. (d) Repeatability of interest points on the *buddha* and *lobster* with different detectors applied under different noise levels.

angles, repeatability rates fall, since the larger the rotation angles the larger the difference of the point distribution. In summary, the proposed method achieves the best performance. For instance, our detector is able to find approximately 60% of the overlapping points in the image with a rotation angle difference of $20°$ on model *lobster*. The second best performer is 3D-Harris, which achieves an accuracy of 42%, as much as 18% lower than our method. The worst approach in this case is 3D-SIFT, which detected only 34% of overlapping points a reduction of almost 50% compared with our detector.

4.2   Noise Corruption

To demonstrate the robustness of our method and others, we also added different levels of random Gaussian white noise with a standard deviation of σ to the original data. However, the distribution of detected interest points on the surface remains, as shown in Fig 4(a)-(c). These outcomes show the adaptive neighborhood estimation of the proposed method. After the surface was noise corrupted, the local tessellations around a vertex changed considerably. In this case, our proposal estimated good neighborhoods to mitigate the noise.

The resulting interest points repeatability rates of model *lobster* and *buddha* before and after noise addition are shown by Fig. 4. The results were obtained by adding different levels of Gaussian noise. As Gaussian noise is generated randomly, accordingly, we ran experiments multiple times at each noise level and report the average repeatability rate.

As we expected, the noise affects the calculation of repeatability: as the σ increases, the repeatability rates decrease for all the detectors. Fig. 4(d) illustrates the repeatability of interest points under different levels of noise. 3D-Harris achieves a high repeatability rate. 3D-SIFT presents a relatively stronger tolerance than MBO, since MBO is based upon the principal curvature to measure the keypoints and the curvature is known to be sensitive to noise. The proposed method demonstrates the highest robustness. By contrast with the alternative methods, the proposed method has the most stable repeatability results under noise corruption.

5 Conclusions

In this paper, we proposed and demonstrated a novel interest points detection method for 3D surfaces. We defined a relative distance rather than the absolute distance on the bilateral filtering, in order that the local details should not be over-smoothed, as the relative distance metric in the algorithm focuses primarily on the representation of neighboring relationship between points. The interest points were detected by the region-based saliency detection, since it generates spatially consistent high quality saliency maps rather than vertex-based. In addition, we tested the repeatability of interest points of our and three other state-of-art detectors. The results show that the proposed method yielded the best scores in response to viewpoints changing and noise corruption. Future research will include applying the detected saliency for segmentation and automatically fine-tuning parameters in the proposed method.

References

1. Dutagaci, H., Cheung, C., Godil, A.: Evaluation of 3D interest point detection techniques via human-generated ground truth. Vis. Comput. 28(9), 901–917 (2012)
2. Gelfand, N., Ikemoto, L.: Geometrically Stable Sampling for the ICP Algorithm. In: Proc. of 3D Digital Imaging and Modeling (2003)
3. Lee, C., Varshney, A., Jacobs, D.: Mesh saliency. In: ACM Transactions on Graphics, vol. 24(3), pp. 659–666 (2005)
4. Castellani, U., Cristani, M., Fantoni, A., Murino, V.: Sparse points matching by combining 3D mesh saliency with statistical descriptors. Comput. Graph. Forum 27(2), 643–652 (2008)
5. Sun, J., Ovsjanikov, M., Guibas, L.: A Concise and Provably Informative Multi-Scale Signature Based on Heat Diffusion. Comput. Graph. Forum 28(5), 1383–1392 (2009)
6. Mian, A., Bennamoun, M., Owens, R.: On the repeatability and quality of keypoints for local feature-based 3D object retrieval from cluttered scenes. Int. J. Comput. Vis. 89(2-3), 348–361 (2010)
7. Sipiran, I., Bustos, B.: Harris 3D: A robust extension of the Harris operator for interest point detection on 3D meshes. Vis. Comput. 27(11), 963–976 (2010)
8. Godil, A., Wagan, A.I.: Salient local 3D features for 3D shape retrieval. In: Proc. of 3DIP (2011)
9. Land, E., McCann, J.: Lightness and Retinex Theory. JOSA 61(1), 1–11 (1971)
10. Zhao, Y., Liu, Y., Song, R., Zhang, M.: Extended non-local means filter for surface saliency detection. In: Proc. of ICIP, pp. 633–636 (2012)

11. Zhao, Y., Liu, Y., Song, R.: A Retinex theory based points sampling method for mesh simplification. In: Proc. of ISPA, pp. 230–235 (2011)
12. Attene, M., Katz, S., Mortara, M., Patane, G., Spagnulo, M., Tal, A.: Mesh segmentation-comparative study. In: Proc. of SMI, pp. 14–25 (2006)
13. Shamir, A.: A survey on Mesh Segmentation Techniques. Comput. Graph. Forum 27(6), 1539–1556 (2008)
14. Felzenszwalab, P.: Efficient graph-based image segmentation. Int. J. Comput. Vis. 59(2), 167–181 (2004)

Accurate 3D Multi-marker Tracking in X-ray Cardiac Sequences Using a Two-Stage Graph Modeling Approach

Xiaoyan Jiang[1], Daniel Haase[1], Marco Körner[1],
Wolfgang Bothe[2], and Joachim Denzler[1]

[1] Computer Vision Group, Friedrich Schiller University of Jena
{xiaoyan.jiang,daniel.haase,marco.koerner,joachim.denzler}@uni-jena.de
[2] Department of Cardiothoracic Surgery, University Hospital Jena
bothe@med.uni-jena.de

Abstract. The in-depth analysis of heart movements under varying conditions is an important problem of cardiac surgery. To reveal the movement of relevant muscular parts, biplanar X-ray recordings of implanted radio-opaque markers are acquired. As manually locating these markers in the images is a very time-consuming task, our goal is to automate this process. Taking into account the difficulties in the recorded data such as missing detections or 2D occlusions, we propose a two-stage graph-based approach for both 3D tracklet and 3D track generation. In the first stage of our approach, we construct a directed acyclic graph of 3D observations to obtain tracklets via shortest path optimization. Afterwards, full tracks are extracted from a tracklet graph in a similar manner. This results in a globally optimal linking of detections and tracklets, while providing a flexible framework which can easily be adapted to various tracking scenarios based on the edge cost functions. We validate our approach on an X-ray sequence of a beating sheep heart based on manually labeled ground-truth marker positions. The results show that the performance of our method is comparable to human experts, while standard 3D tracking approaches such as particle filters are outperformed.

Keywords: Multiple object tracking, Directed acyclic graph, Min-cost optimization.

1 Introduction

A fully automated system capable of analyzing cardiac movements could significantly help doctors to gain a highly detailed insight into muscular movements under various conditions and to refine surgical strategies for treating heart-related diseases. To analyze heart movements, X-ray recordings are employed in which implanted radio-opaque markers reveal the movement of all relevant cardiac muscles. Fig. 1a shows the biplanar acquisition setup. However, as can be seen in Fig. 1b, X-ray videos of the beating heart containing implanted markers usually have low contrast due to contiguous anatomical structures, and inevitably contain numerous occlusions of the markers. As manually locating these markers is a tedious and time-consuming task, the automatic and accurate tracking

R. Wilson et al. (Eds.): CAIP 2013, Part II, LNCS 8048, pp. 117–125, 2013.

 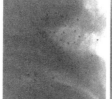 

(a) Acquisition system   (b) Example images

Fig. 1. (a) Biplanar high-speed X-ray acquisition system (Neurostar®, Siemens AG), (b) X-ray images of both camera views showing a sheep heart with implanted markers

and identification of divergently moving markers under severe occlusions is an important, practically relevant, and challenging task.

Previous works dealing with heart motion tracking [14,13] involve a lot of manual interactions, yet only sparse marker configurations can be processed. In the computer vision community, multi-object tracking algorithms mainly assume appearance or motion affinity [5,8,19]. However, as is the case in this application, targets are not always distinguishable. Simple online object tracking approaches such as the Kalman [17] or particle filter [5,11] typically fail in such settings due to improper predictions that cause wrong matches between tracks and detections. Local optimization schemes such as the Hungarian algorithm [10], bipartite graph matching [4], or energy minimization [1] consider the best assignment between tracks and detections or detections and detections.

Recently, several global tracking methods based on flow networks have been proposed to avoid local optima and to prevent linking of non-stationary false positive detections [20,2,18,12]. For these approaches, multi-object tracking is solved by conversion into a combinatorial optimization problem which can be solved in polynomial time [6,20]. Generally, for graph-based tracking, observations are represented by vertices, while costs are assigned to edges to denote various levels of support for associations between observations. Solutions of the multi-object tracking problem are then returned as paths with minimum or maximum costs. The popular mass-flow approach presented in [2], however, is not applicable in our scenario, as the graph topology is based on a discrete spatial subdivision which leads to impractically large graphs to achieve sub-pixel accuracy.

Current work on tracklet-based multi-object tracking has shown promising results [19,15,9,16]. Possible approaches are based on tracklet assignment in an iterative [19,10] or non-iterative way [15]. In [16], a sliding window that shifts with every frame is used and tracklets are found via inference from a set of Bayesian networks. Similarly, in [19] particle filters are used to locally generate tracklets from a temporal sliding window. However, the general drawback of extracting tracklets by considering only observations over a short period of time is that useful global information might be lost.

We tackle the dense multiple 3D object tracking problem by a two-stage *Directed Acyclic Graph* (DAG) formulation. Motivated by our medical application scenario, we do not use any appearance consistency or common assumptions such as the homography constraint [1]. In the first stage of our approach,

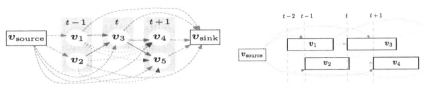

(a) The landmark graph $\mathcal{G}$ includes vertices for all 3D point hypotheses and edges between vertices of succeeding frames.

(b) The tracklet graph $\mathcal{G}'$ contains vertices for all tracklets and edges between all vertices in a temporally consistent order.

Fig. 2. Exemplary graph topologies used in our approach. Additional edges from source and to sink vertex (dotted and dashed lines) allow initiation and termination of tracklets or tracks at any time.

tracklets are generated by finding the shortest path in the graph of all 3D detections. Afterwards, final tracks are found in a similar way by finding the shortest path in the graph of all tracklets. This results in a globally optimal linking of detections and tracklets, while providing a flexible framework which can easily be adapted to various tracking scenarios based on the edge cost functions.

The structure of the paper is as follows: Section 2 will in detail present our two-stage graph-based method for multi-object tracking. Experimental results on real X-ray recordings of a beating sheep heart are presented in Sect. 3, including qualitative results and a quantitative comparison to ground-truth data provided by human experts. Section 4 concludes this work and discusses further plans.

2 Two-Stage Graph-Based Tracking

In this section we present our approaches for both extraction and linking of tracklets. We assume to have access to calibration data and detections for the individual views. The application of this approach to our medical scenario of 3D marker tracking in X-ray sequences is described in detail in Sect. 3.

2.1 Tracklet Generation

In order to overcome the problem of trajectory occlusions and interactions, we designed our tracking approach to directly operate on 3D data. We assume to have access to 3D point hypotheses $\boldsymbol{P}_0^t, \boldsymbol{P}_1^t, \ldots \in \mathbb{R}^3$ reconstructed from 2D marker detections $\boldsymbol{p}_0^{t,I_l}, \boldsymbol{p}_0^{t,I_r}, \boldsymbol{p}_1^{t,I_l}, \boldsymbol{p}_1^{t,I_r}, \ldots \in \mathbb{R}^2$ obtained from left and right images I_l, I_r. Using these observations, we construct a landmark graph $\mathcal{G} = (\boldsymbol{V}, \boldsymbol{E}, \boldsymbol{w})$, where each node $\boldsymbol{v}_i^t \in \boldsymbol{V}$ represents one 3D point $\boldsymbol{P}_i^t$ hypothesis. These nodes are connected across neighboring frames $t, t+1$ by directed edges $\boldsymbol{e}_{i,j} = (\boldsymbol{v}_i^t, \boldsymbol{v}_j^{t+1}) \in \boldsymbol{E}$, and we obtain a bipartite graph topology as outlined in Fig. 2a. Framewise misdetections are handled by creating additional edges $\boldsymbol{e}_{i,j}^{t,t+\Delta t} = (\boldsymbol{v}_i^t, \boldsymbol{v}_j^{t+\Delta t})$ across further time steps, which allows skipping certain frames without appropriate detections. The assigned edge weights

$$w_{i,j} = w(\boldsymbol{v}_i^t, \boldsymbol{v}_j^{t+\Delta t}) = \begin{cases} d_{\text{spat}}\left(\boldsymbol{v}_i^t, \boldsymbol{v}_j^{t+\Delta t}\right) \cdot d_{\text{temp}}\left(\boldsymbol{v}_i^t, \boldsymbol{v}_j^{t+\Delta t}\right) & \Delta t > 0 \\ \infty & \text{else} \end{cases} \in \boldsymbol{w} \quad (1)$$

are proportional to the product of the Euclidean distance $d_{\text{spat}}(\boldsymbol{v}_i^t, \boldsymbol{v}_j^{t+\Delta t}) = \|\boldsymbol{P}_i^t - \boldsymbol{P}_j^{t+\Delta t}\|_2$ between the two represented 3D points and the number Δt of skipped frames. Additionally, we connect each vertex $\boldsymbol{v}_i^t$ with the source $\boldsymbol{v}_{\text{source}}$ and the sink $\boldsymbol{v}_{\text{sink}}$ in order to obtain shorter tracklets when a marker was not detected for longer times. The associated edge weights

$$w_{\text{source}}(\boldsymbol{v}_i^t) = (t+1) \cdot d_{\text{penalty}} \qquad \text{and} \qquad w_{\text{sink}}(\boldsymbol{v}_i^t) = (t_{\max} - t) \cdot d_{\text{penalty}} \quad (2)$$

are proportional to the product of the number of skipped frames and the average linking distance to discourage unnecessary shortcuts.

Having such a graph $\mathcal{G}$ as exemplary outlined in Fig. 2a, a consistent tracklet $\tau = (\wp, t_{\tau,0}, t_{\tau,1})$ from frame $t_{\tau,0}$ to frame $t_{\tau,1}$ can be obtained by finding a path $\wp = (\boldsymbol{v}_{\text{source}}, \boldsymbol{v}^{t_{\tau,0}}, \dots, \boldsymbol{v}^{t_{\tau,1}}, \boldsymbol{v}_{\text{sink}})$ from the source to the sink with minimal cumulated weight. For this purpose we iteratively employ Dijkstra's *shortest path* algorithm [7] until a specified number of iterations is reached or no more optimal paths can be extracted from the graph. Found paths are invalidated by setting the weights of all outgoing edges to infinity for each node of the path. In a post-processing step, missing observations between linked tracklets are interpolated linearly. Furthermore, duplicate tracklets, *i.e.* tracklets with almost identical spatial and temporal extents are merged.

2.2   Tracklet Linking

To fuse individual tracklets into complete tracks, we again formulate this problem in a graph-based way. Each vertex $\boldsymbol{v}_i' \in \boldsymbol{V}'$ in the new tracklet graph $\mathcal{G}' = (\boldsymbol{V}', \boldsymbol{E}', \boldsymbol{w}')$ represents a tracklet $\tau_i = (\wp_i, t_{\tau_i,0}, t_{\tau_i,1})$ from frame $t_{\tau_i,0}$ to frame $t_{\tau_i,1}$. All vertices are connected by directed edges $\boldsymbol{e}_{i,j}' \in \boldsymbol{E}'$, which results in a linear graph structure. The associated weights

$$w_{i,j}' = w'(\boldsymbol{v}_i', \boldsymbol{v}_j') = \begin{cases} d_{\text{spat}}'(\boldsymbol{v}_i', \boldsymbol{v}_j') \cdot d_{\text{temp}}'(\boldsymbol{v}_i', \boldsymbol{v}_j') & t_{\tau_j,0} - t_{\tau_i,1} > 0 \\ \infty & \text{else} \end{cases} \in \boldsymbol{w}' \quad (3)$$

are proportional to the product of spatial distances $d_{\text{spat}}'(\boldsymbol{v}_i, \boldsymbol{v}_j) = \|\boldsymbol{P}_i^{t_{\tau_j,1}} - \boldsymbol{P}_j^{t_{\tau_i,0}}\|_2$ and temporal distance $d_{\text{temp}}'(\boldsymbol{v}_i', \boldsymbol{v}_j') = t_{\tau_j,0} - t_{\tau_i,1}$ between two represented tracklets. If two tracklets have a conflicting temporal order or overlap in time, the edge is weighted with infinite costs. Again, each vertex $\boldsymbol{v}_i' \in \boldsymbol{V}'$ is directly connected to $\boldsymbol{v}_{\text{source}}'$ and $\boldsymbol{v}_{\text{sink}}'$ with associated weights similar to those of Eq. 2. In this case, paths $\wp' = (\boldsymbol{v}_{\text{source}}', \boldsymbol{v}_1', \boldsymbol{v}_2', \dots, \boldsymbol{v}_{\text{sink}}')$ with minimal cumulated weights within this tracklet graph $\mathcal{G}'$ represent consistent sequences of tracklets $\mathcal{T} = (\wp', t_{\tau,0}, t_{\tau,1})$. The extraction of tracks is performed iteratively until no optimal path can be found or a certain number of paths are found. In a further post-processing step, gaps between linked tracklets are interpolated.

3   Experiments and Results

To assess the general performance and practical applicability of our proposed 3D tracking approach, we conducted experiments on real-world X-ray recordings of a beating sheep heart. Specifically, our goal was to analyze the following questions: (i) Is our proposed method generally able to deal with the difficulties in this application (*e.g.* 2D marker occlusions, non-distinguishable marker appearance, inhomogeneous marker movement)? (ii) How does our method perform compared to standard 3D tracking approaches such as particle filter based tracking for the scenario at hand? (iii) Is the tracking accuracy of our approach comparable to human experts, and are the results sufficient for medical analyses? In the following, the experimental setup and the according results are presented.

3.1   Experimental Setup

The data used in our experiments was acquired by cardiac surgeons using the biplanar X-ray system shown in Fig. 1a. It shows the beating heart of a sheep, including 42 radio-opaque markers. The markers have a diameter of 2 mm and a spherical (30 times) or cylindrical (12 times) shape. The recorded images have a spatial resolution of 1024×768 pixels and a temporal resolution of 500 Hz. The total length of the sequence is 3,001 frames and covers 8 complete cardiac cycles.

For the calibration of the camera setup, we used a custom-built 140 mm × 60 mm × 0.5 mm radio-opaque steel plate containing 18 circular holes of diameter 5 mm. The holes can automatically be detected and identified in the resulting X-ray images. We performed the calibration based on Zhang [21], yielding an average backprojection error of 1.3 pixels. The angle between both cameras was 115°, while the distance between each camera and the heart was about 825 mm.

For each camera, 2D detections were obtained by firstly finding discontinuities in the images, *e.g.* using the Laplace operator. Afterwards, initial detections were extracted using simple blob detection. To reduce the number of false positives, saliency maps were built based on temporal variations throughout the whole sequence. By triangulating all detection pairs of the two camera views which were supported by the estimated epipolar geometry, we obtained 3D marker hypotheses which were then used as input for our proposed tracking approach.

To evaluate the quality of the tracking results, we performed a comparison to ground-truth data provided by human experts, which is available for every 10th frame and all uniquely identifiable markers (37 out of 42). We employ the *multiple object tracking precision* (MOTP) and *multiple object tracking accuracy* (MOTA) metrics [3], which have become the *de facto* standard in the field of multi-object tracking evaluation. The former allows to assess the precision of the tracker independently of correct object matches, while the latter provides information about object misses, mismatches, and false positive tracks.

3.2   Tracking Results

We extracted 3,000 tracklets using the first stage of our algorithm. In the second stage, we extracted all tracks whose length was at least 50% of the total sequence length, resulting in 39 tracks. In order to assess the quality of our results with respect to standard 3D tracking approaches, we performed a comparison to the particle filter based tracking approach presented in [11]. To ensure a fair comparison, we extended the method of [11] to 3D in a straightforward way

Table 1. Multiple object tracking accuracy (MOTA) for the sheep heart sequence of our approach and the 3D extension of the particle filter approach presented in [11]. While the mismatch rate is equally low for both methods, our approach clearly outperforms [11] in terms of false positives, misses, and MOTA.

Method	Miss Rate	False Pos. Rate	Mismatch Rate	MOTA
Our Approach	**26.02%**	**6.23%**	1.26%	**66.49%**
3D Extension of [11]	43.78%	16.22%	**0.37%**	39.64%

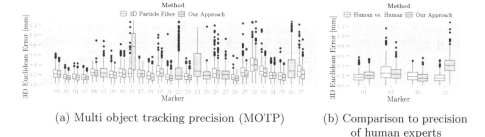

(a) Multi object tracking precision (MOTP)   (b) Comparison to precision of human experts

Fig. 3. Quantitative results for the sheep heart sequence. (a) Multi object tracking precision (MOTP) in comparison to the 3D extension of the particle filter approach of [11]. While the precision is comparable for both methods, in six cases our approach reliably tracks markers which can not be tracked by [11]. (b) Comparison to precision of human experts for four markers having ground-truth data provided by multiple persons.

(3D state vectors and updates instead of 2D). Furthermore, we used identical 3D detections and selected the same amount of best tracks as for our algorithm.

The MOTA results of both approaches are shown in Tab. 1. It can be seen that our approach has a moderate miss rate, while the false positive rate and the mismatch rate are relatively low. This behavior can be explained by the fact that the tracklet association step of our approach favors long and reliable tracks, while short and unreliable tracks are discarded at the expense of *full misses*, *i.e.* markers for which no track is present throughout the whole sequence. In the medical scenario at hand, this property is to be favored, as it is more reliable to have no tracks instead of wrong tracks for certain markers. While the mismatch rate of the approach of [11] is even lower than for the proposed method, it is clearly outperformed by our approach in terms of false positives and misses.

The results of MOTP evaluation are presented in Fig. 3a, separately for each marker. Only results are included for markers whose ground-truth data could be obtained and no full misses occurred. We can state that the average 3D precision of our approach is about 0.2 mm, with only minor differences between markers. A notable exception is marker 16, which is located at the end of a cardiac valve and suffers from the very abrupt movements. The particle filter approach of [11] gives comparable results on many markers. However, in six cases our approach is able to reliably track markers which can not be tracked using [11]. Qualitative results,

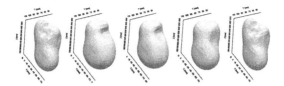

Fig. 4. 3D surface reconstruction of the sheep heart sequence based on our marker tracking results for one cardiac cycle (approximately 350 frames)

namely 3D surface reconstructions for one cardiac cycle based on tracking results of our algorithm are shown in Fig. 4.

Given the qualitative and quantitative evaluations, it can be stated that our approach is able to deal with the difficulties in the data and provides promising results while outperforming standard 3D tracking approaches.

3.3 Comparison to Human Experts

In order to relate the tracking precision of our approach to human experts, for four representative markers ground-truth data was provided by more than one person. The results of the comparison are presented in Fig. 3b. In three out of four cases, our approach is able to compete with the precision of human experts. Only for marker 32, the human results are more precise, which might be caused by the fact that the marker is partly occluded by an anatomical structure in one camera view. All in all, however, we can state that the results are very promising and indeed comparable to human experts. Thus, our approach is clearly suited for practical applications. The fact that it can be used fully automatically supports above argumentation, and shows its applicability for medical marker tracking.

3.4 Complexity and Runtime

The entire system was implemented in C++. Our method has a complexity of $\mathcal{O}(k \cdot (n \log n + m))$, where n is the number of nodes, m is the number of edges, and k the number paths to be found in the respective graph. For the extraction of 3,000 tracklets from a 1.16×10^6 node 3D detection graph, our algorithm needs approximately 78 minutes, while the extraction of 39 final tracks from the tracklet graph takes about 31 seconds. All measurements were conducted on a standard desktop computer with an Intel® Core™ i5-760 CPU (2.80 GHz).

4 Conclusions

In this work, we presented a two-stage graph based approach for multiple marker tracking in X-ray recordings of beating hearts. The first stage of our approach consists of constructing a 3D observation graph, from which tracklets are extracted via shortest path optimization. Similarly, in the second stage, full tracks are found by constructing a tracklet graph. This process allows for a global linking of detections and tracklets and can easily be adaptapted based on the edge cost functions. We evaluate our approach on a sequence of a beating sheep heart and achieve a results which are comparable to human experts.

As next steps, we would like to incorporate efficient motion models. Also, adapting the edge cost functions based on additional knowledge such as occupancy maps or geometric information could improve the tracking performance.

Acknowledgements. Animal experiments adhered to relevant regulations and were approved by the federal state of Thuringia, Germany. We thank Christoph Bettag for his valuable comments and Rommy Petersohn for technical support during the experiments.

References

1. Andriyenko, A., Schindler, K.: Multi-target tracking by continuous energy minimization. In: CVPR, pp. 1265–1272 (2011)
2. Berclaz, J., Fleuret, F., Turetken, E., Fua, P.: Multiple object tracking using k-shortest paths optimization. TPAMI 33, 1806–1819 (2011)
3. Bernardin, K., Stiefelhagen, R.: Evaluating multiple object tracking performance: The clear mot metrics. EJIVP 246–309 (2008)
4. Bredereck, M., Jiang, X., Körner, M., Denzler, J.: Data association for multi-object tracking-by-detection in multi-camera networks. In: ICDSC (2012)
5. Breitenstein, M., Reichlin, F., Leibe, B., Koller-Meier, E., Gool, L.: Online muti-person tracking-by-detection from a single, uncalibrated camera. TPAMI 33(9), 1820–1833 (2011)
6. Collins, R.T.: Multitarget data association with higher-order motion models. In: CVPR, pp. 744–751 (2012)
7. Dijkstra, E.W.: A note on two problems in connexion with graphs. Numerische Mathematik 1, 269–271 (1959)
8. Fleuret, F., Berclaz, J., Lengagne, R., Fua, P.: Multi-camera people tracking with a probabilistic occupancy map. TPAMI 30, 267–282 (2008)
9. Ge, W., Collins, R.T.: Multi-target data association by tracklets with unsupervised parameter estimation. In: BMVC (2008)
10. Huang, C., Wu, B., Nevatia, R.: Robust object tracking by hierarchical association of detection responses. In: Forsyth, D., Torr, P., Zisserman, A. (eds.) ECCV 2008, Part II. LNCS, vol. 5303, pp. 788–801. Springer, Heidelberg (2008)
11. Jiang, X., Rodner, E., Denzler, J.: Multi-person tracking-by-detection based on calibrated multi-camera systems. In: ICCVG, pp. 743–751 (2012)
12. Leal-Taixé, L., Pons-Moll, G., Rosenhahn, B.: Branch-and-price global optimization for multi-view multi-target tracking. In: CVPR, pp. 1987–1994 (2012)
13. Malassiotis, S., Strintzis, M.G.: Tracking the left ventricle in echocardiographic images by learning heart dynamics. IEEE Trans. on Med. Imag. 18, 282–290 (1999)
14. Muijtjens, A., Roos, J., Arts, T., Hasman, A., Reneman, R.: Tracking markers with missing data by lower rank approximation. J. Biomech. 30, 95–98 (1997)
15. Nillius, P., Sullivan, J., Carlsson, S.: Multi-target tracking - linking identities using bayesian network inference. In: CVPR, pp. 2187–2194 (2006)
16. Prokaj, J., Duchaineau, M., Medioni, G.: Inferring tracklets for multi-object tracking. In: CVPR Workshops, pp. 37–44 (2011)
17. Satoh, Y., Okatani, T., Deguchi, K.: A color-based tracking by kalman particle filter. In: ICPR, pp. 502–505 (2004)

18. Wu, Z., Kunz, T.H., Betke, M.: Efficient track linking methods for track graphs using network-flow and set-cover techniques. In: CVPR, pp. 1185–1192 (2011)
19. Xing, J., Ai, H., Lao, S.: Multi-object tracking through occlusions by local tracklets filtering and global tracklets association with detection responses. In: CVPR, pp. 1200–1207 (2009)
20. Zhang, L., Li, Y., Nevatia, R.: Global data association for multi-object tracking using network flows. In: CVPR (2008)
21. Zhang, Z.: A flexible new technique for camera calibration. TPAMI 22(11), 1330–1334 (2000)

3D Mesh Decomposition
Using Protrusion and Boundary Part Detection

Fattah Alizadeh and Alistair Sutherland

School of Computing, Dublin City University, Dublin, Ireland
fattah.alizadeh2@mail.dcu.ie

Abstract. The number of 3D models is growing every day and the segmentation of such models has recently attracted a lot of attention. In this paper we propose a two-phase approach for segmentation of 3D models. We leverage a well-known fact from electrical physics about charge distribution for both initial protruding part extraction and boundary detection. The first phase tries to locate the initial protruding parts, which have higher charge density, while the second phase utilizes the minima rule and an area-based approach to find the boundary in the concave regions. The proposed approach has a great advantage over the similar approach proposed by Wu and Levine [1]; our approach can find boundaries for some joining parts not entirely located in the concave region which is not the case in the work of Wu and Levine. The experimental result on the McGill and SHREC 2007 datasets show promising results for partial matching in 3D model retrieval.

Keywords: 3D Model Segmentation, Charge Density, Minima Rule, Model Retrieval.

1   Introduction

After recent developments in 3D modelling technology, enormous attention has been paid to certain 3D model fields viz. 3D indexing, 3D understanding, 3D retrieval and 3D segmentation. 3D Model segmentation has a lot of applications in computer graphics such as texture mapping [3], 3D shape retrieval [4] and etc.

In this paper we propose an algorithm for segmentation of 3D models using a well-known fact from electrical physics about the tendency of charge density to accumulate at sharp convex areas and to diminish at sharp concavities on the surface of a solid. Fig. 1 shows three different coloured model samples based on their charge density distribution.

The algorithm is based on two main concepts:

— The premise that a 3D model can be considered as a core body and some parts connected to that in the protrusion areas [5].
— A particular regularity in nature-transversality (minima rule) which states that, "when two arbitrarily shaped surfaces are made to interpenetrate, they always meet at a contour of concave discontinuity of their tangent planes" [6].

R. Wilson et al. (Eds.): CAIP 2013, Part II, LNCS 8048, pp. 126–134, 2013.
© Springer-Verlag Berlin Heidelberg 2013

These two concepts enable us to locate the segments in protruding parts having higher charge density and the boundary sections in concave areas possessing lower charge density. The original idea for this work is borrowed from the work of Wu and Levine [1] in which they used the same electrical physics fact for boundary detection, but as will be shown later, their approach requires a challenging prerequisite which cannot be satisfied in the real available 3D models. We employed an area-based algorithm coupled with the minima-rule to detect the boundary parts for models whose joint parts are not fully located on the concave regions.

Fig. 1. Coloured models based on the distribution of charge density on the surface; the redder parts specify the denser faces

After finding the sharp points of models in the protruding parts, a region-growing algorithm is leveraged to extend the protrusions toward the core body until they reach the boundaries.

2   Related Works

After recent developments in 3D domain modelling technology, a lot of attention has been paid to 3D model understanding and segmentation [5][11]. For complete details about available approaches and their categories we refer the reader to the survey paper by Shamir [9]. Due to their connection to our work, we focus on the part-based approaches here.

One of the main concepts employed in the segmentation process is the minima rule introduced by Hoffman and Richards [6]. It is mainly realized by measuring the surface properties such as curvature or dihedral angles. Some approaches utilize the minima rule to find the segment boundaries of models [1] [11]. In order to find distinct parts of a model, a watershed-based approach along with the normal curvature was proposed by Page *et al.* [11]. In this work, the boundaries are located in the areas in which the flooded regions meet. Similar to our work, Wu and Levine leverage the charge density distribution for locating the concave areas [1]. The dual graph of a model is employed to decompose the model into segments at the concave areas. The main drawback of the aforementioned approaches is the questionable assumption, which they all make; viz. all of the boundary faces must satisfy the concavity conditions, which is not usually the case for the available models in the standard datasets.

Recently, Agthos *et al.* [5] uses a geodesic-oriented approach to find and group the salient points on the surface of models. After approximating the core body of the model and finding the boundaries between segments, they refined the boundaries to perform more precise segmentation. Another well-known geodesic-based segmentation algorithm is introduced based on the work of Hilaga *et al.* [13]. They define the Average Geodesic Distance (AGD) or the Centricity on each vertex as the average geodesic distance from each vertex to all other vertices on the mesh. The weak point of the AGD approach is how to identify the exact threshold value to detect the real boundaries between neighbour segments.

In [14] the authors used pre-defined primitives and fit them to the mesh parts to specify the partitions. In a different manner in the work of Katz *et al.* [15] the multi-dimensional scaling algorithm is leveraged to calculate the canonical form of the models. Then, after prominent feature point extraction on the tips of components, images of models in a spherical mirror are extracted. Finally, the convex hull of the image is utilized in a hierarchical approach to perform segmentation following core extraction.

Generally speaking, although the performance of segmentation approaches are mainly depends on the application used, they can be evaluated via comparison to human's insight. Therefore, some approaches such as SDF-based [7] and [15] are outperforming other approaches in terms of similarity to human's perception.

3   Proposed Approach

The protrusion-oriented approach proposed in this work focuses on the nature of charge density distribution over the model surfaces during the entire process of meaningful parts decomposition. It can be divided mainly into two phases, namely: protrusion parts extraction and boundary detection for both of which the electrical charge density plays a central role.

In the sequel, first we briefly introduce the background of charge distribution, which is the cornerstone of our work and then its application in 3D model segmentation will be presented.

3.1   Background

When a pre-defined electrical charge Q is placed on the surface of an arbitrary surface, it is spread over the surface so that its distribution follows a well-known fact in physics of electricity which says: "the electric charges on the surface of a conductor tend to accumulate at the sharp convex areas and diminish at the sharp concave areas".

Inspired by this fact, each triangular face has its own scalar charge density value which will be used in the segmentation process. To this end, 3D models are treated as conductors which are placed in a free space (a space without any electric charge) and the electrical charge Q is distributed on the surface of them. We should note that since the 3D models have arbitrary surfaces, it is not possible to calculate the charge density on the surface using an analytical approach. Thus, a Finite-Element-Method (FEM) is utilized to this end. We used the approach proposed by Wu and Levine to calculate the charge density. More details on the above equations can be found in [1]. As depicted in Fig. 1, the convex parts possess more charge density than the concave areas.

3.2   Segmentation Process

Having the simulated charge density distributed on the surface of mesh models, we are able to the perform segmentation process through the following two main phases: Protruding parts extraction and Boundary detection.

Fig. 2. Examples of protruding parts along with the corresponding representative faces indicated by red points

Fig. 3. The canonical representation of ant model in Fig. 2 and the representative faces of each extracted protrusion

Protrusion Parts Extraction. As stated before, based on a premise in [5], segments can be considered as protruding areas connected to the main part of the model. So, we need to extract the protruding parts as the first step of segmentation.

In order to extract the protruding parts, we identify Π connected faces having a charge density higher than other faces on the model surface. Where $\Pi=1/3*$(number of faces for the model). Each disjoint set of identified faces creates a protruding part, which is an initial extracted segment.

For each defined protruding part k, we select a representative face r_k, which is the face which possessing the highest charge density among the faces creating protrusion part k.

Fig. 2 shows some examples of protruding parts connected to the main body in different colours along with their representative faces.

In the proposed algorithm we expect to see the representative faces on the very end of segments, which have most convexity. But for some of initial segments having bending regions, it is possible to locate some faces, which have the most charge density at the bending region. Two representative faces of the ant model identified by rectangles in Fig. 2, are examples of representative faces which are not located on the very end of protruding parts. To avoid this discrepancy we utilize the canonical form representation of models to locate the representative faces. As presented in Fig. 3, in the canonical form presentation, all of representative faces are located at the very end parts of each segment.

Boundary Detection. Based on the minima rule, Wu and Levine [1] use the charge density distribution to locate the boundary parts of models at the concave areas having local minimum charge density. The concave face in their work is defined as a face possessing charge density lower than a predefined threshold as well as lower than all of its neighbours. To specify boundary parts, starting from the concave face, they proceed to the neighbours with the lowest charge density until they return to the initial concave face. Although their approach is applicable for some parts of specific models, it suffers from two main challenging issues. Firstly, the entire boundary must lie in a concavity to be detected accurately, which is not the case for lot of models. And secondly, for some boundary parts, there is no face meeting their requirement to be considered as a concave face (see Fig.7).

To overcome these issues, we base our boundary detection algorithm on the semi-concave faces, which is defined as follows:

Definition1: Semi-concave face: a face is semi-concave if its charge density is less than the density of 75% of its neighbours.

The detected semi-concave faces are candidate boundary faces in the process of segmentation. Based on the minima rule, all models have at least one semi-concave face located in the boundary areas. Due to noise or the presence of some bumps on the surface of the models, there are some spurious semi-concave faces which are not boundary faces (see Fig. 4). In order to remove these outliers, we employ a simple and efficient area-based fact as follows:

All of the boundaries will be closed loops. If we draw an annular region of constant width on both sides of the boundary, then the region on the core side will have a significantly greater area than the region on the protruded side. Fig. 5 demonstrates the regions located on either side of a boundary by different colours, the region which belongs to the core occupies a bigger area by far compared to the region placed on the protruded part. This is the case for all of the models in our tested datasets.

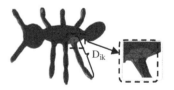

Fig. 4. The canonical form representation of Human and Hand models with detected semi-concave faces. Green circles specify correctly detected faces and red circle indicates extra detected faces.

Fig. 5. Protruded_annular_region (purple colour) and the Core_annular_region (green colour) on either side of a boundary

We utilize the mentioned fact to remove the spurious semi-concave faces. Firstly, all of the candidate semi-concave faces are sorted in ascending order of their geodesic distance to the representative face of the protruded segment. Then, starting from the top of the list for each semi-concave face k two different regions are specified; the Protruded_annular_region and the Core_annular_region. These two regions can be defined as follows (see Fig. 5):

Definition 2: Protruded_annular_region: The set of triangular faces whose geodesic distance from the representative faces are in the range $[D_{ik} - w, D_{ik})$.

Definition 3: Core_annular_region: The set of triangular faces whose geodesic distance from the representative faces are in the range $[D_{ik}, D_{ik} + w)$.

Here w is the average length of edges on the model surface considered as the annular width and D_{ik} is the geodesic distance between representative face i and the candidate semi-concave face k. If face k is located in a boundary part, a big difference should be observed in the surface area of the two regions. So, if the difference between these two areas for face k is greater than a threshold τ, the face is considered as a boundary face, otherwise the procedure is repeated for the next semi-concave face in the list. We experimentally set the threshold τ as 1% of surface area of the model. By repeating the above approach for all the representative faces, a set of 3-tuples will be created to define the protruded parts $\{(s_1, r_1, d_1), (s_2, r_2, d_2), ..., (s_N, r_N, d_N)\}$. Here N is the number of protruded parts and s_i and r_i are semi-concave boundary face and representative face for the protruded part i, respectively and d_i indicates the geodesic distance between faces s_i and r_i.

To identify the whole boundary part of any segment k, all of the faces have the geodesic distance d_k to the representative face r_k are marked as boundary faces (see Fig. 6). Finally, the initial protruded parts are growing until reaching the detected boundaries.

The boundary faces detected on the surface of canonical form representation of models, are finally mapped into the original models to find the boundary parts.

4 Experimental Results

We applied our algorithm to the models available in the standard McGill and SHREC2007 datasets and some other known models namely Dinopet, Crab and Spider. Fig. 8 shows the final segmentation results performed by our approach on some of the models. We compare our approach with the similar approach introduced by Wu and Levine [1] and some other popular approaches.

It should be noted that the current algorithm, like other protrusion-oriented approaches, has limitations in decomposing models containing small protrusions such as Bust model shown in the right hand end of the Fig. 8.

4.1 Comparing with the Similar Work of Wu and Levine [1]

As discussed before in the section 3.2, the charge density distribution has been utilized for model decomposition in the work of Wu and Levine [1]. Their approach only focuses on concavity of the mesh for detecting the boundary parts, that is, the boundary parts must fully contain concavities to be detected accurately, which is not the case for lots of models. As Fig. 7 demonstrates that the algorithm introduced by Wu and Levine cannot extract the boundary parts due to unavailability of concavity in the boundaries. Comparing these results to those of ours shown in Fig. 8 reveals the superiority of our approach in boundary detection and then in model decomposition.

4.2   Comparison with Other Part-Based Approaches

To evaluate the proposed approach we compare our approach with 4 other popular part-based segmentation approaches, applied to some models whose segmentation results are available for us. These approaches are: Protrusion-oriented segmentation approach by Agathos *et al.* [5] (**PO**), Visual salience-guided decomposition algorithm by Lin *et al.* [12] (**VSG**), Protrusion conquest mesh partitioning algorithm by Valette *et al.* [10] (**PC**) and Graph-based shape decomposition algorithm by Kim *et al.* [8] (**GB**).

Based on the comparison results shown in Fig. 10, the following conclusions for the segmented models can be drawn: in terms of correctness of extracted segments in comparison to human perception, our results and those of **PO** and **VSG** coincide with that based on human insight, which is not the case for the segments extracted by the **PC** and **GB** approaches. Of course, the **PO** approach could not detect the main part of the plier models precisely.

Fig. 6. The boundary faces extracted using proposed algorithm on the surface of canonical form models

Fig. 7. Detected wrong boundaries (green parts) by the approach of Wu and Levine [1] for a concave face (specified by arrow lines)

And with respect to insensitivity to an object's parts deformation, it can be seen that our approach and **PO** and **VSG** offer the same segments for different poses of the human models in Fig. 10, while other approaches do not.

It is important to state that since our ultimate objective is to apply the extracted segments to part-based matching in 3D model retrieval, it is crucial for the segmentation algorithm to be insensitive against model deformations and perturbations. Additionally, due to robustness of charge density to noise [2], our algorithm shows good ability in decomposing noisy models into meaningful parts for different noise levels *nl* (*nl* is the ratio of largest displacement to the longest edge of the object's bounding box) see Fig. 9.

Fig. 8. Experimental results

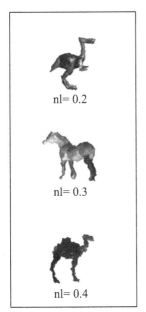

Model Name	Proposed Approach	PO	VSG	PC	GB
ANT					
CAMEL					
HAND					
HUMAN					
HUMAN					
PLIER					

Fig. 9. Segmentation results for noisy models

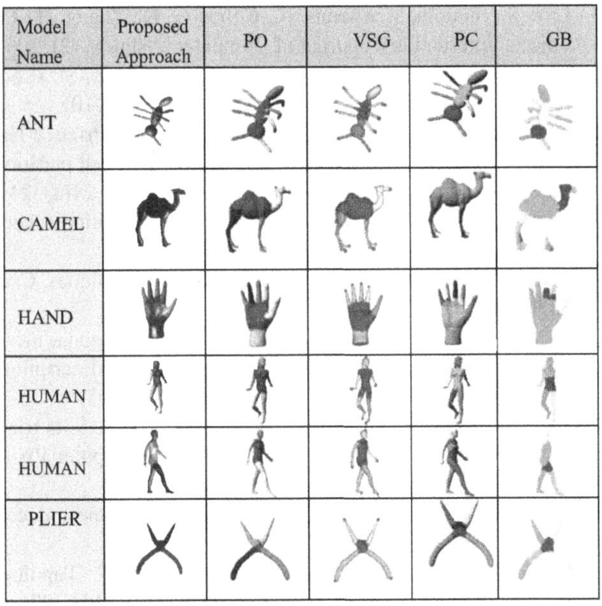

Fig. 10. Comparison table of different segmentation approaches

5   Conclusion

In this paper we have introduced a two-phase approach for 3D model segmentation. A famous fact from electrical physics is leveraged in both phases. During the first phase the protruding parts joined to the core body of models are detected using faces possessing higher charge density. An area-based approach along with the minima rule is utilized in the second phase for detecting the boundary parts. The reasonable segmentation results for the models available in McGill and SHREC 2007 datasets as well as its robustness to noise and deformation show acceptable results for our future work directions.

References

1. Wu, K., Levine, M.: 3D part segmentation using simulated electrical charge distribu-tions. IEEE Transactions on Pattern Analysis and Machine Intelligence 19(11), 1223–1235 (1997)
2. Alizadeh, F., Sutherland, A.: A Robust 3D Shape Descriptor Based on the Electrical Charge Distribution. In: Proc. Intl. Conf. on computer vision theory and application, VISAPP 2013, Barcelona, pp. 213–218 (2013)
3. Levy, B., Petitjean, S., Ray, N., Maillot, J.: Least squares conformal maps for automatic tex-ture atlas generation. ACM Trans. Graph. 21(3), 362–371 (2002)

4. Lior, S., Shalom, S., Shamir, A., Cohen-or, D., Zhang, H.: Contextual part analogies in 3D objects. International Journal of Computer Vision 89(2), 309–326 (2010)
5. Agathos, A., Pratikakis, I., Perantonis, S., Sapidis, S.: Protrusion-oriented 3D mesh seg-men-tation. The Visual Computer 26(1), 63–81 (2010)
6. Guillemin, V., Pollack, A.: Differential topology. Printice-Hall, Englewood Cliffs (1974)
7. Lior, S., Shamir, A., Cohen-Or, D.: Consistent mesh partitioning and skeletonisation using the shape diameter function. The Visual Computer 24(4), 249–259 (2008)
8. Kim, D., Yun, I., Lee, S.: A new shape decomposition scheme for graph-based representation. Pattern Recognition 38(5), 673–689 (2005)
9. Shamir, A.: A survey on mesh segmentation techniques. Computer Graphics Forum 27(6), 1539–1556 (2008)
10. Valette, S., Kompatsiaris, I., Strintzis, M.: A polygonal mesh partitioning algorithm based on protrusion conquest for perceptual 3D shape description. In: Workshop Towards Semantic Virtual Environments SVE, pp. 68–76 (2005)
11. Page, D., Koschan, A., Abidi, M.: Perception-based 3D triangle mesh segmentation using fast marching watersheds. In: Proc. Conf. on Computer Vision and Pattern Rec., pp. 27–32 (2003)
12. Lin, H., Liao, H., Lin, J.: Visual salience-guided mesh decomposition. IEEE Transactions on Multimedia 9(1), 46–57 (2007)
13. Hilaga, M., Shinagawa, Y., Kohmura, T., Kunii, T.: Topology matching for fully automatic similarity estimation of 3D shapes. In: SIGGRAPH 2001, pp. 203–212 (2001)
14. Mortara, M., Patanè, G., Spagnuolo, M., Falcidieno, B., Rossignac, J.: Blowing bubbles for multi-scale analysis and decomposition of triangle meshes. Algorithmica 38(1) (2003)
15. Sagi, K., Leifman, G., Tal, A.: Mesh segmentation using feature point and core extrac-tion. The Visual Computer 21(8), 649–658 (2005)

Isometrically Invariant Description of Deformable Objects Based on the Fractional Heat Equation

Eric Paquet[1,2] and Herna Lydia Viktor[2]

[1] National Research Council, 1200 Montreal Road, Ottawa, Canada
[2] University of Ottawa, 800 King Edward Road, Ottawa, Canada

Abstract. Recently, a number of researchers have turned their attention to the creation of isometrically invariant shape descriptors based on the heat equation. The reason for this surge in interest is that the Laplace-Beltrami operator, associated with the heat equation, is highly dependent on the topology of the underlying manifold, which may lead to the creation of highly accurate descriptors. In this paper, we propose a generalisation based on the fractional heat equation. While the heat equation enables one to explore the shape with a Markovian Gaussian random walk, the fractional heat equation explores the manifold with a non-Markovian Lévy random walk. This generalisation provides two advantages. These are, first, that the process has a memory of the previously explored geometry and, second, that it is possible to correlate points or vertices which are not part of the same neighbourhood. Consequently, a highly accurate, contextual shape descriptor may be obtained.

Keywords: Fractional, Heat Equation, Isometry, Kernel, Lévy distribution, Path Integral.

1 Introduction

The development of novel techniques that allow for the invariant description of deformable objects is an active research area. To this end, a number of approaches to obtain invariance under isometry have been proposed [1,2]. Given an object, an isometric transformation, also known as a non-elastic deformation, is a deformation that preserves the geodesic distance in between all pair of points. Here, the geodesic distance refers to the length of the shortest path connecting a pair of points and, for which the path is entirely contains within the manifold associated with the object. Most procedures for the isometrically invariant description of objects rely either on the geodesic distance or on physics-based modelling. When using physics-based modelling, the object under consideration is assimilated to a manifold on which some physical entity, (such as heat), is propagated according to a physical process (such as heat propagation) [1,2]. The analysis of the distribution of this entity, at various time intervals, allows for the definition of invariants, multiresolution quantities which, after dimensional reduction, constitute an invariant descriptor (or index) associated with the deformable object. The objective is to obtain a descriptor that characterises the shape of the object in an informative and discriminative manner. In this paper, we propose a further generalisation of this approach based on the fractional heat equation.

R. Wilson et al. (Eds.): CAIP 2013, Part II, LNCS 8048, pp. 135–143, 2013.

The heat equation may be formulated in terms of a Markovian-Gaussian random walk which means that the underlying shape is explored, analysed and understood with such a walk. In turn, that implies that only small steps are permitted (large steps are exponentially suppressed by the Gaussian) and that the walk is memoryless. Consequently, the exploration is intrinsically local (small steps) and non-contextual (small steps and memorylessness). Our objective is to perform a contextual analysis of a shape in order to overcome these limitations. In our analysis, distant points may be put into relation by large steps and part of the motion is remembered. This is done in order to establish a relation or context [3] in between nearby points. We will illustrate that such an objective may be attained by replacing the Gaussian transition probability with a Lévy distribution and by introducing fractional temporal derivatives which shall lead us to the fractional heat equation.

This paper is organised as follows. In Section 2, we formulate the Laplacian in terms of discrete differential geometry. Next, in Section 3, we review some important properties of the heat equation. This is followed, in Section 4, by a formulation of the heat equation in terms of path integral. This allows us to introduce the fractional heat or Fokker-Planck equation, which is analysed in terms of the spectral decomposition of the fractional heat kernel from which isometrically invariant quantities are defined. Finally, some initial experimental results are presented in order to illustrate our approach. This is followed by a Conclusion.

2   Discrete Differential Geometry

In this section, we present a discrete version of the de Rham operator (Laplacian), the spatial operator associated with the heat equation, based on discrete differential geometry [4,5]. Our objective is to construct the Laplacian from, and only from, the discrete vertices forming the underlying shape or object. Our method differs from other approaches in which some kind of interpolation is required, either through the finite difference equations or through the interpolation function as for the finite element method [6]. The main advantage of our procedure is that most topological properties are preserved, contrarily to the two previous schemes in which they may not be [4,5]. Indeed, it is possible to formulate the Laplacian in such a way that these properties and theorems are enforced at all times. This may be done by using only the discrete points and their associated topology, without any attempt to interpolate in between them like in finite difference and finite element methods [6]. In order to introduce this approach, certain notions of differential geometry [4,5] are required. In differential geometry, the Laplacian or the de Rham operator [4,5] is defined as $\Delta f = \left(dd^* + d^*d \right)f$ where d is the exterior derivative , f a differential k -form and $\wedge$ is the exterior product while d^* is the codifferential [4,5]. For a scalar function or 0-form, the de Rham operator reduces to $\Delta = d^*d$. The discrete formulation of differential geometry [4,5] is based on the incidence matrix. Let σ_j^p be a p -simplex or cell. For instance, a 0-simplex is a vertex or node, a 1-simplex is an edge and a 2-simplex is a triangle. The incidence matrix $\mathbf{N}_p^T$ encodes the relationships in between the p -cells and the $\left(p-1 \right)$ -cells.

Consequently, N_p is equal to zero if the $(p-1)$-simplex j is not in the neighbourhood of the p-simplex i, is equal to +1 if the orientation of the $(p-1)$-simplex j is compatible with the one of the p-simplex i and -1 if their respective orientations are not compatible. In the particular case of an edge and a vertex, the incidence matrix is equal to 1 if the edge is entering the vertex and -1 otherwise.

In discrete differential geometry, the discrete exterior derivative and the discrete codifferential [4,5] are given by

$$d_p \sim N_p^T \qquad d_p^* \sim \left(N_{p+1}^T\right)^* = *N_p^T* = G_{n-p+1}^* N_p^T G_p^{-1} \tag{1}$$

where G_p is the metric associated with the p-simplices. If we replace, in the definition of the de Rham operator, the external derivatives and the codifferentials in terms of their discrete operator equivalences we obtain [4,5]:

$$L_p = N_p N_p^* + N_{p+1}^* N_{p+1} \sim \Delta \equiv dd^* + d^*d \tag{2}$$

where L_0 is the Laplacian associated with the nodes or vertices, L_1 is the Laplacian associated with the edges and L_2 is the Laplacian associated with the triangles or simplices. The Laplacian associated with the nodes has a particularly simple form: $L_0 = N_0 N_0^* + N_1^* N_1 = G_0 A^T G_1^{-1} A$.

Depending on the specific application, the metrics associated with the various simplices may be defined in diverse ways [4,5]. For instance, one may choose G_1, the metric associated with the edges, as the affinity of the vertices associated with a particular edge [4,5]. The metric associated with the vertices, G_0, is a diagonal matrix of the areas of the neighbourhood associated with each vertex [4,5]. The neighbourhood may be defined either as the 1-ring neighbourhood (the total area of all the triangles connected to vertex i) or from the dual cell associated with a particular vertex. It may be constructed, for instance, by joining the barycentres of all the triangles connected to vertex i through their respective common edge.

3   Heat Equation and Heat Kernel

It follows that that physics-based modelling implies that objects are governed and described using the laws of physics. In this section, we introduce one such modelling, based on the heat equation and the heat kernel [1,2]. The heat equation describes how heat propagates through an object. The study of the heat distribution on an object is isomorphic to the characterisation of the manifold associated with the object itself, since the heat distribution is strongly dependent on the geometry and on the topology associated with the object [1,2]. The heat equation is defined as $\dfrac{\partial u(x,t)}{\partial t} = \Delta u(x,t)$.

The heat kernel is the solution of the heat equation with the initial conditions $u(x,0) = \delta(x_i - x_j)$. Now, if we expand the Laplacian in terms of its spectral decomposition $\quad \Delta \phi_i = \lambda_i \phi_i \quad$ we   may   express   the   heat   kernel   as

$K_{ij}(t) = \sum_{l=1}^{L} \exp(-\lambda_l t) \phi_l(x_i) \phi_l(x_j)$ where $\{\lambda_l\}$ are the Eigen values associated with the Laplacian and where $\{\phi_l\}$ are the corresponding Eigen vectors. Consequently, the heat equation, which describes the propagation of heat on an object, may be entirely characterised in terms of its heat kernel [1,2]. From the heat kernel, one may define isometrically invariant descriptors. That is, descriptors that remain invariant if the geodesic distances in between the vertices are preserved. One common descriptor associated with the heat kernel is the heat kernel signature [2] which is defined as

$\kappa_i = [K_{ii}(t_1), ..., K_{ii}(t_n)]^T / \sqrt{\sum_{k=1}^{n} K_{ii}(t_k)}$. One may demonstrate that the heat kernel is a

metric and a propagator [2]. This implies that the heat kernel may relate two heat kernel signatures (descriptors) at two different locations. Consequently, one may define a spatially sensitive descriptor [2]. Another possible descriptor is the generalised heat signature [1] which is formed by the concatenation of the histograms of the diagonal elements of the heat kernel at various times or resolutions. Such a descriptor is also invariant under isometry.

4   Fractional Heat Equation and Fractional Heat Kernel

In this section, we establish that the heat equation may be assimilated to a stochastic Markovian process with a Gaussian transition probability. Also, we demonstrate that the heat kernel may be formulated in terms of a path or Feynman integral. Then, we introduce the Lévy random walk [7], the fractional heat equation [8], the fractional heat kernel as well as its formulation in terms of path integrals.

In order to proceed further in our analysis, we must introduce the concept of a random walk or random process. According to the Kolmogorov-Chapman formula, which applies to stochastic Markovian processes, the transition probability in between two points (x_0, t_0) and (x, t) may be obtained by marginalising or integrating the conditional   or   transition   probabilities   on   the   intermediate   positions:

$P(x, t | x_0, t_0) = \prod_{j=0}^{N-1} \int P(x_{j+1}, t_{j+1} | x_j, t_j) \, dx_{j+1}$. Then, if we apply the Kolmogorov-

Chapman formula to a Gaussian transition probability we obtain for the transition probability in between two arbitrary points

$$P(x, t | x_0, t_0) = (4\pi \mathfrak{D} \, \Delta t)^{-(N+1)/2} \int_{(x_0, t_0)}^{(x, t)} \lim_{\substack{N \to \infty \\ \Delta t \to \infty}} \prod_{j=0}^{N-1} dx_j \, \exp\left(-\frac{(x_{j+1} - x_j)^2}{2\mathfrak{D} \, \Delta t}\right) \tag{3}$$

Such transition probability is the solution to the inhomogeneous heat equation, with a point source:

$$\left(\frac{\partial}{\partial t} - \mathfrak{D} \frac{\partial^2}{\partial x^2}\right) P(x, t | x_0, t_0) = \delta(x - x_0) \delta(t - t_0) \tag{4}$$

which corresponds to the definition of the heat kernel that was introduced earlier. Consequently, the heat kernel may be assimilated to the transition probability in between a pair of points on the manifold associated with a shape.

The Gaussian transition probability, introduced in the previous section, exponentially suppresses large transitions or steps in between two consecutive positions [7]. In order to allow large transitions, one may replace the Gaussian transition probability by a Lévy transition probability which, for large transitions, decays as a power law and not exponentially as for a Gaussian transition [7]. The Lévy distribution is defined in terms of its Fourier transform or characteristic function [7]. As in the Gaussian case, we may apply the Kolmogorov-Chapman formula in order to obtain the transition probability in between two arbitrary points

$$P_L\left(x,t\middle|x_0,t_0\right) = \frac{1}{2\pi} \lim_{\substack{N\to\infty \\ \Delta t\to\infty}} \int_{(x_0,t_0)}^{(x,t)} \prod_{j=0}^{N-1} dx_j \int_{-\infty}^{\infty} dk \, \exp\left(ik\left(x_{j+1} - x_j\right)\right) \exp\left(-\Delta t \, \gamma^\alpha \left|k\right|^\alpha\right) \quad (5)$$

where γ is the scale parameter and α is the stability exponent. Once more, the transition probability is obtained by a weighted summation over all paths in between these points. If one takes the temporal derivative of this formula one obtains, after a tedious calculation [9]:

$$\frac{\partial P_L\left(x,t\middle|x_0,t_0\right)}{\partial t} = \frac{b}{\pi}\Gamma\left(\alpha + 1\right)\sin\left(\frac{\pi\alpha}{2}\right) \int_{-\infty}^{\infty} \frac{P_L\left(x',t\middle|x_0,t_0\right)}{\left|x' - x\right|^{1+\alpha}} \, dx' \triangleq R_x^\alpha \, P_L\left(x,t\middle|x_0,t_0\right) \quad (6)$$

where R_x^α is the Riesz fractional derivative [9] of the conditional probability. The main difference in between the Riesz fractional derivative and the Riemann-Liouville fractional derivative is that the denominator of the former involves the absolute value while the other does not. Indeed, the fractional derivative may be defined as the inverse of the Riemann-Liouville integral formula. Therefore, the conditional Lévy distribution is a solution of an inhomogeneous fractional heat equation, with a point source or delta function at the initial time and position: $\left[\frac{\partial}{\partial t} - R_x^\alpha - V\left(x\right)\right]P_L\left(x,t\middle|x_0,t_0\right) = \delta\left(x - x_0\right)\delta\left(t - t_0\right)$. If the standard time derivative is substituted by a fractional time derivative, one may define a fractional heat equation. It has been demonstrated that such a substitution is consistent with the initial conditions if the heat equation is reformulated as [8]: $D_t^\beta\left(u\left(x,t\right)\right) - u\left(x,0\right)\frac{t^{-\beta}}{\Gamma\left(1 - \beta\right)} = \Delta u\left(x,t\right)$. Then, it is possible to demonstrate that the variance of u is indeed time dependent [8]: $\left\langle\left(u\left(t\right) - u\left(0\right)\right)^2\right\rangle \propto t^{2\beta-1}$. This equation means that when $\beta > \frac{1}{2}$, the correlation tends to increase with time: then, the stochastic process is said to be persistent. Otherwise, when $\beta < \frac{1}{2}$, the correlation tends to decrease with time and the stochastic process is said to be anti-persistent. Consequently, the outcome of the stochastic process depends on its history which means that it is non-Markovian (temporally). Therefore, one of the main consequences of the fractional temporal derivative is to replace the Markovian stochastic process associated with the ordinary derivative with a non-Markovian process (a process with memory).

If we choose $u(x,0) = \delta(x - x_0)$ as the initial condition, the solution of the fractional heat equations becomes

$$u_\beta(x,t|x_0) = K_\beta(x,x_0;t) = \sum_{n=0}^{\infty} \phi_{n,\beta}(x)\,\phi_{n,\beta}(x_0)\,E_\beta(-t^\beta\,\lambda_{n,\beta}) \qquad (7)$$

where $E_\beta(x) \triangleq \sum_{k=0}^{\infty} \dfrac{x^{\beta k}}{\Gamma(\beta k + 1)}$ is the Mittag-Leffler function [8].

It is possible to write down a discrete version of the fractional heat equation which is fractional both in space and time. Indeed, the discrete de Rham operator is a matrix which means that the discrete fractional de Rham operator may be obtained by taking the fractional power of the corresponding non-fractional matrix [10]. As was outlined in a previous section, the ordinary time derivative must be substituted by the fractional time derivative plus an additional term in order to take into account the initial conditions consistently. Therefore, the discrete fractional counterpart of the heat equation becomes:

$$D_t^\beta \mathbf{u} - \mathbf{u}_0\,\frac{t^{-\beta}}{\Gamma(1-\beta)} - (\mathbf{L}_0)^\alpha\,\mathbf{u} = 0 \qquad (8)$$

Once more, the fractional kernel $K_{\alpha,\beta}(t)$ is the solution of fractional heat equation when the initial conditions are $\mathbf{u}_0 = \mathbf{e}\,\delta(t - t_0)$ where $\mathbf{e} = [1,...,1]^T$. As outlined earlier, it may be obtained by the method of separation of variables and it is equal to $K_{\alpha,\beta}(t) = \sum_{n=1}^{N} \Phi_{n,\alpha,\beta}^T\,\Phi_{n,\alpha,\beta}\,E_\beta(-\kappa\,t^\beta\,\lambda_{n,\alpha,\beta})$ where $\{\phi_{n,\alpha,\beta}\}$ and $\{\lambda_{n,\alpha,\beta}\}$ are the Eigen vectors and the corresponding Eigen values of the fractional de Rham operator $(\mathbf{L}_0)^\alpha$:

$(\mathbf{L}_0)^\alpha\,\Phi_{n,\alpha,\beta} = -\lambda_{n,\alpha,\beta}\,\Phi_{n,\alpha,\beta}$ and where $E_\beta(x)$ is the Mittag-Leffler function which was defined earlier. In order to solve the Eigen equation, we must first calculate the fractional power of the non-fractional discrete de Rham operator $\mathbf{L}_0$. Since the non-fractional de Rham operator is symmetrical (as defined in section 2), its fractional power may be obtained from its spectral decomposition as follow [10]:

$(\mathbf{L}_0)^\alpha = \Phi_{\mathbf{L}_0}^T\,\Lambda_{\mathbf{L}_0}^\alpha\,\Phi_{\mathbf{L}_0}$ where $\Lambda_{\mathbf{L}_0}$ is the diagonal matrix of the Eigen values of $\mathbf{L}_0$ while $\Phi_{\mathbf{L}_0}$ is the matrix of the corresponding Eigen vectors (one column per Eigen vector).

Subsequently, the calculation of the fractional power becomes trivial since the power of a diagonal matrix is equal to the power of its individual diagonal elements. From the previous equation, it follows that the fractional de Rham operator is also symmetrical which means its Eigen values are real and that the corresponding Eigen vectors are mutually orthogonal. Most heat kernel-based descriptors may be generalised by simply replacing the original heat kernel with the fractional one. For instance, one may substitute the heat kernel by the fractional heat kernel in order to obtain the fractional heat kernel signature, the fractional integrated heat kernel signature and the spatially sensitive fractional heat kernel signature. In the next section, we shall describe the shapes in terms of fractional generalised kernel signature $\mathcal{K}_{\alpha,\beta}$ on a manifold $\mathcal{M}$ which is a generalisation, to the fractional case, of the generalised kernel signature: $\mathcal{K}_{\alpha,\beta}(\mathcal{M}) = \bigcup_{t=t_0}^{t_n} \mathfrak{H}\left(\mathrm{diag}\left(\mathbf{K}_{\alpha,\beta}(t)\right)\right)$ where $\mathfrak{H}$ is the histogram function.

Finally, we present some initial examples to illustrate the efficiency of our approach. Our dataset consists of a subset of the benchmarking TOSCA database [11] and our code was implemented using Mathematica 8. We considered six poses (0-5) for the centaur, the cat, the dog, the gorilla, the lioness, the seahorse, Michael and Victoria. Due to a lack of space, only the results for the centaur are shown. The six poses of the centaur are illustrated in Fig. 1.

Fig. 1. The six poses of the centaur from the TOSCA database

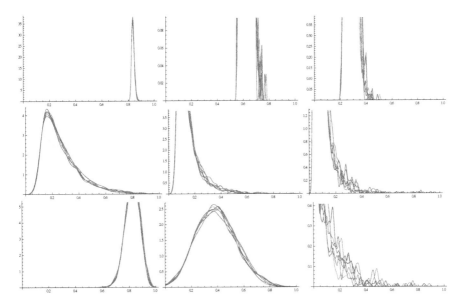

Fig. 2. Last three histograms (from left to right) associated with the fractional generalised heat kernel signature for various order of the fractional derivatives

The last three histograms associated with the fractional generalised heat kernel signature are shown below with all the poses superimposed, for the fractional derivatives $\alpha = 1, \beta = 0.2$, $\alpha = 1, \beta = 1.8$ and $\alpha = 1.5, \beta = 1$ respectively (from top to bottom).

The superimposed histograms clearly show that the fractional generalised heat kernel signature is robust against a wide range of deformations, since the shape of corresponding histograms remains relatively unaffected by the various poses.

5   Conclusions

We introduced a new approach for creating an isometrically invariant description of shapes based on the fractional heat equation. We performed a study both in terms of fractional heat kernel and path integrals. Our analysis indicates that the temporal fractional derivative allows one to explore a shape locally, while keeping track of the previous exploration (memory process). This provides one with the ability to position the shape analysis into local context. On the other hand, the spatial fractional de Rham operator or Laplacian allows one to place points or vertices that do not belong to the same neighbourhood into relation. This is due to the fact that the underlying Lévy distribution associated with the underlying fractional random process allows large random steps. The fractional heat equation thus favours a contextual analysis of the manifold associated with the shape, but this time with a non-local context. In future work, we intend to present an extensive experimental analysis of our algorithm, to determine the types of objects for which our approach is the most adapted and to generalise the fractional heat equation in terms of edges and simplices by replacing the de Rham operator $\mathbf{L}_0$ by $\mathbf{L}_1$ and $\mathbf{L}_2$ as defined by Eq. (2).

References

1. Castellani, U., Mirtuono, P., Murino, V., Bellani, M., Rambaldelli, G., Tansella, M., Brambilla, P.: A new shape diffusion descriptor for brain classification. In: Fichtinger, G., Martel, A., Peters, T. (eds.) MICCAI 2011, Part II. LNCS, vol. 6892, pp. 426–433. Springer, Heidelberg (2011)
2. Bronstein, A.M., et al.: Shape Google: geometric words and expression for invariant shape retrieval. ACM Transactions on Graphics 30(1), 20 (2011)
3. Shapira, L., et al.: Contextual part analogies in 3D objects. Int. J. Comput. Vis. 89, 309–326 (2010)
4. Desbrun, M., Kanso, E., Tong, Y.: Discrete differential forms for computational modeling. ACM SIGGRAPH, 39–54 (2006)
5. Hirani, A.N.: Discrete exterior calculus. Ph. D. Thesis, California Institute of Technology. p. 103 (2003)
6. Reuter, M., et al.: Discrete Laplace-Beltrami operators for shape analysis and segmentation. Computers & Graphics 33, 381–390 (2009)

7. Chaves, A.S.: A fractional diffusion equation to describe Lévy flights. Physics Letters A **239**, 13–16 (1998)
8. Metzler, R., Barkai, E., Klafter, J.: Anomalous diffusion and relaxation close to thermal equilibrium: a fractional Fokker-Planck equation approach. Physical Review **82**(18), 3563–3567 (1999)
9. West, B.J.: Quantum Lévy propagators. J. Phys. Chem. B **104**, 3830–3832 (2000)
10. Higham, N.J., Lin, L.: A Schur-Padé algorithm for fractional power of a matrix. SIAM J. Matrix Anal. & Appl. **32**(3), 1056–1078 (2011)
11. Project Tosca, `http://tosca.cs.technion.ac.il/` (last accessed June 4, 2013)

Discriminant Analysis Based
Level Set Segmentation for Ultrasound Imaging

Daniel Tenbrinck[1,2] and Xiaoyi Jiang[1,2,3]

[1] Department of Mathematics and Computer Science,
University of Münster, Germany
[2] European Institute for Molecular Imaging, University of Münster, Germany
[3] Cluster of Excellence EXC 1003, Cells in Motion, CiM, Münster, Germany
{d_tenb01,xjiang}@uni-muenster.de

Abstract. Segmentation is one of the fundamental tasks in computer vision applications. The nature of ultrasound images, which are subject to multiplicative noise instead of the widely used additive noise modeling, leads to problems of standard segmentation algorithms. In this paper we propose a new level set approach for the segmentation of medical ultrasound data. The advantage of this approach is both its simpleness and robustness: the noise inherent in ultrasound images does not have to be modeled explicitly but is rather estimated by means of discriminant analysis. In particular, we determine an optimal threshold, which enables us to separate two signal distributions in the intensity histogram and incorporate this information in the evolution of the level set contour. The superiority of our approach over the popular Chan-Vese formulation is demonstrated on real 2D patient data from echocardiography.

1 Introduction

Segmentation of ultrasound (US) images is a fundamental task for computer aided diagnosis. In the field of echocardiography segmentation is used to assess medical parameters of the cardiovascular system. Information like left ventricular (LV) volume or the ejection fraction can be calculated by segmenting datasets from US examinations of a patient's myocardium [3].

Segmentation of US data is a hard task due to low contrast, shadowing effects, and speckle noise. In order to tackle these problems a variety of approaches has been proposed, e.g., [4] and references therein. Naturally, most segmentation algorithms for US images can be categorized as *region-based* approaches, since the physical effects in US data often lead to wrong gradient-information, hence making most *edge-based* methods unapplicable. Recently, we investigated the impact of explicit physical noise modeling for *low-level* segmentation formulations [7] and also *high-level* segmentation formulations [8] in US imaging. We observed a significant increase in both segmentation *accuracy* and *robustness*. Many segmentation methods implicitly assume an additive noise model and thus are inherently not suitable for US. However, the explicit modeling of physical noise leads to additional parameters and high computational effort for

R. Wilson et al. (Eds.): CAIP 2013, Part II, LNCS 8048, pp. 144–151, 2013.

the proposed algorithms in [7,8]. Thus, it is desirable to account for the effects in US images while maintaining *efficiency* of the used segmentation algorithm.

In Section 2 we investigate the characteristics of multiplicative speckle noise and discuss the fundamental weakness of standard methods in presence of this noise. This motivates our work on level set segmentation of US images incorporating information about multiplicative noise (Section 3). The experimental results of this approach on real patient data from echocardiography are presented in Section 4. Finally, this paper is ended by discussion in Section 5.

Note that the proposed methodology in this paper is motivated by applications from medical ultrasound imaging, but its use is not limited to this special field and can be applied more generally.

2   Motivation

2.1   Speckle Noise in Ultrasound Data

Speckle noise is a known phenomenon, e.g., in synthetic aperture radar (SAR) and medical ultrasound imaging, and has a signal-dependent form. One possibility to model the image degradation process [8] is given by,

$$f(x) = u(x) + s_\sigma(x) \cdot u(x)^{\frac{\gamma}{2}} . \tag{1}$$

Here, u is the unbiased image, s is a normally distributed random variable with mean 0 and variance σ^2, and f is the observed image. The parameter γ characterizes the signal-dependency of the noise term. Assumed values in the literature are $\gamma \in \{1,2\}$ (cf. [8] and references therein). This multiplicative noise leads to significant distortions in the image, especially in regions with high intensities.

With respect to typical segmentation tasks from medical image analysis, we assume *two signal sources* in US data: reflecting tissue with high intensities and a background signal with low intensities. The effect of speckle noise modeled in Eq. (1) on an intensity histogram is illustrated in Fig. 1. As can be seen, the *noise variance* is comparably higher for high signal values. Thus, it is more difficult to separate the two signal distributions compared to additive Gaussian noise. Our goal is to incorporate this a-priori knowledge about the signal distribution effectively and efficiently for a robust segmentation of US images.

2.2   Restrictions of the Chan-Vese Model

The two-phase segmentation task is to partition an image domain Ω into two subregions $\Omega_1, \Omega_2 \subset \Omega$, e.g., region-of-interest and background. In the following we discuss the level set formulation of the *Chan-Vese (CV)* model and analyze its behavior in the presence of multiplicative noise discussed in Section 2.1.

The popular CV approach [1], which is a special case of the Mumford-Shah formulation, uses a closed contour $\Gamma \subset \Omega$ to separate the two regions Ω_1, Ω_2. In particular, the authors in [1] represent the segmentation contour Γ implicitly by the level sets of a Lipschitz function $\Phi \colon \Omega \to \mathbb{R}$, i.e., $\Phi(x) < 0$ for $x \in \Omega_1$,

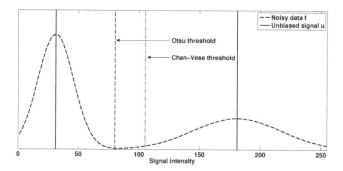

Fig. 1. Effect of multiplicative speckle noise on the intensity distribution in an image histogram and comparison of the Chan-Vese threshold t_{CV} and the Otsu threshold t_O

$\Phi(x) = 0$ for $x \in \Gamma$, and $\Phi(x) > 0$ for $x \in \Omega_2$. Disregarding regularization of the segmentation area, the CV energy functional in [1] is given as,

$$
\begin{aligned}
E_{CV}(c_1, c_2, \Phi) &= \beta \int_\Omega \delta_0(\Phi(x)) |\nabla \Phi(x)| \, dx \\
&+ \lambda_1 \int_\Omega (c_1 - f(x))^2 H(\Phi) \, dx + \lambda_2 \int_\Omega (c_2 - f(x))^2 (1 - H(\Phi(x))) \, dx .
\end{aligned}
\tag{2}
$$

Here f is the perturbed image to be segmented and c_1 and c_2 are *constant approximations* of f in Ω_1 and Ω_2, respectively. The Heaviside function H is used in Eq. (2) as indicator function for Ω_1, while δ_0 denotes the one-dimensional δ-Dirac measure. To obtain a segmentation result one has to iteratively minimize Eq. (2) using an *alternating minimization scheme*, since a simultaneous minimization for (c_1, c_2, Φ) is not feasible.

Data Fidelity. For a fixed Φ and assuming a standard image formation process with additive noise, it can be shown that the optimal constant approximations for f are computed as the *mean values* of the respective regions [7]. Disregarding the smoothness term for Φ, it gets obvious that the data fidelity terms in Eq. (2) get minimal if all intensity values are clustered according to these mean values. Thus, for fixed c_1, c_2 the energy in Eq. (2) gets minimal if Φ partitions the data according to a natural *threshold* $t_{CV} = (c_1 + c_2) / 2$ (cf. Fig. 1). For the case $\lambda_1 = \lambda_2$ (standard parameter choice in [1]) the associated Euler-Lagrange equation with respect to the level set function Φ is given by,

$$
\begin{aligned}
0 &= \delta_\epsilon(\Phi(x)) \left(\mu \operatorname{div} \left(\frac{\nabla \Phi(x)}{|\nabla \Phi(x)|} \right) - (f(x) - c_1)^2 + (f(x) - c_2)^2 \right) \\
&= \delta_\epsilon(\Phi(x)) \left(\mu \operatorname{div} \left(\frac{\nabla \Phi(x)}{|\nabla \Phi(x)|} \right) - 2(c_2 - c_1) \left(f(x) - \underbrace{\frac{c_1 + c_2}{2}}_{= t_{CV}} \right) \right) .
\end{aligned}
\tag{3}
$$

Here, μ is the rescaled parameter β in Eq. (2) and δ_ϵ denotes a regularized version of the one-dimensional δ-Dirac measure. Obviously, the optimality condition in Eq. (3) holds, if the data are partitioned by the threshold t_{CV}. Naturally, the situation in presence of multiplicative noise is different. It is clear that the optimal threshold cannot be t_{CV} in this case (see [7] for details). Instead, the wider distribution of the high intensity signal in Fig. 1 enforces a shift of the optimal threshold to the left side of the histogram as illustrated.

Local Minima. Another drawback of the CV functional in Eq. (2) is the existence of many local minima due to two facts. First, the parameter space has a relatively high dimension, i.e., effectively three parameters in [1]. Second, the estimation of optimal constants c_1, c_2 depends on the current state of Φ and vice versa. As indicated above, the energy functional (2) has to be minimized using an alternating minimization scheme with two subproblems, i.e., computation of the mean values for c_1, c_2 and the subsequent *minimal partition problem* for fixed c_1, c_2, which can be done, e.g., by using a gradient descent approach [1] or level set methods [5]. This alternating minimization frequently converges to a local minimum, depending on the parameter set for λ_1, λ_2, and β. Moreover, the success of the CV segmentation crucially depends on the chosen initialization of the segmentation contour Γ as illustrated in Fig. 2.

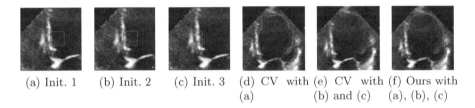

(a) Init. 1   (b) Init. 2   (c) Init. 3   (d) CV with (a)   (e) CV with (b) and (c)   (f) Ours with (a), (b), (c)

Fig. 2. Different initializations of Γ and the respective segmentation results of the Chan-Vese (CV) model in Eq. (2) and the proposed model (Ours) in Eq. (6)

3   Discriminant Analysis Based Level Set Segmentation

To tackle the problem of misclassification of pixels due to multiplicative noise we propose to use an established statistical approach to find an optimal threshold t_O. In this context, *optimal* refers to determining a threshold that minimizes the within-class and maximizes the between-class variance between the two classes of pixels simultaneously. This is done by a *discriminant analysis* as we show in the following.

3.1   Optimal Threshold by Discriminant Analysis

The proposed discriminant analysis in the following corresponds to the popular Otsu thresholding method [6] and hence is presented only shortly. Let us denote with N the number of pixels of a given grayscale image f and let $h(f)$ be the normalized histogram of this image. Then, h can be seen as a probability distribution with $h(i) = p_i$ being the probability of intensity value i. Naturally, a threshold $t \in \mathbb{N}$, $0 < t < 255$, induces two intensity classes C_1 and C_2. We denote the mean value of f by m and we use $m_1(t)$ and $m_2(t)$ as the mean values of C_1 and C_2 (induced by threshold t), respectively. Then, the intraclass variances are simply given by,

$$\sigma_1^2(t) = \sum_{i=0}^{t} p_i(i - m_1(t))^2 , \quad \sigma_2^2(t) = \sum_{i=t+1}^{255} p_i(i - m_2(t))^2 .$$

Based on this, the within-class variance σ_W and the between-class variance σ_B are defined by,

$$\sigma_W(t) = P_1\sigma_1^2(t) + P_2\sigma_2^2(t), \quad \sigma_B(t) = P_1(m_1(t) - m)^2 + P_2(m_2(t) - m)^2 , \quad (4)$$

where $P_1 = \sum_{i=0}^{t} p_i$ and $P_2 = \sum_{i=t+1}^{255} p_i$ represent the relative portion of each class. Finally, the *optimal threshold* t_O can be computed by maximizing,

$$t_O = \operatorname*{argmax}_{0<t<255} \frac{\sigma_B(t)}{\sigma_W(t)} . \qquad (5)$$

Fig. 1 illustrates how the threshold t_O adapts itself to multiplicative noise in contrast to the threshold t_{CV}, which is only based on the intensity mean values. Since this leads to misclassification of intensity values, we incorporate the optimal threshold t_O into a segmentation formulation in the next section.

3.2   Proposed Segmentation Model

In order to overcome the drawbacks of the popular CV segmentation model discussed in Section 2.2 we propose a novel variational segmentation formulation using level set methods. For the same notation and with the optimal threshold t_O in (5) the proposed segmentation model reads as,

$$E(\Phi) = \frac{1}{2} \int_{\Omega} \operatorname{sgn}(\Phi(x))\,(f(x) - t_O)\,dx + \beta \int_{\Omega} \delta_0(\Phi(x))\,|\nabla\Phi(x)|\,dx . \qquad (6)$$

The idea of the model in Eq. (6) is to partition the given data according to the optimal threshold t_O from Section 3.1 using a *linear distance measure* while following the regularity condition on Φ. Note that the linear distance measure penalizes outliers less severely compared to the quadratic data fidelity terms in (2) and hence corresponds to *robust distance measures* known from statistics, e.g., L^1 distance. Since the threshold t_O is fixed throughout the segmentation process, one only has to minimize with respect to Φ (*minimal partition problem*).

3.3   Numerical Realization

For minimization of (6) we use level set methods analogously to [1] (cf. [5] for technical details). Approximating the sign function by $\operatorname{sgn}(x) \approx 2H(x) - 1$, the respective Euler-Lagrange equation combined with a gradient descent approach leads to the following iteration scheme,

$$\Phi^{n+1}(x) = \Phi^n(x) + \Delta t\,\delta_\epsilon(\Phi(x)) \left(\beta \operatorname{div} \left(\frac{\nabla\Phi^n(x)}{|\nabla\Phi^n(x)|} \right) - (f(x) - t_O) \right). \quad (7)$$

Replacing δ_ϵ in Eq. (7) by $|\nabla\Phi|$ this method can be extended to all level sets of Φ, which is desirable in some situations. It gets clear that the segmentation contour Γ evolves in normal direction according to the data fidelity induced by t_O and the *mean curvature* of Φ controlled by the regularization parameter β. Note that the iteration scheme (7) corresponds to an Euler forward time discretization of a *convection-diffusion* partial differential equation (cf. [5] for details). Thus, using second-order *finite central differences* for the parabolic term (mean curvature term) and *upwind differencing* for the (optional) hyperbolic term $|\nabla\Phi|$ one has to fulfill the following Courant-Friedrich-Lewy (CFL) condition for stability of this method,

$$\Delta t < \frac{1}{d} \min_{x \in \Omega} \left\{ \frac{(\Delta x)^2}{2\beta} + \frac{\Delta x}{|\nabla\Phi(x)|\,|f(x) - t_O|} \right\}. \quad (8)$$

Here, d denotes the dimension of the image domain Ω (typically $d \in \{2,3\}$). Naturally, we choose the spatial discretization step width $\Delta x = 1$ for this image processing task. In the literature it has proven to be advantageous to initialize Φ^0 as *signed distance function* and reinitialize it after a fixed number of iterations [1,5]. To control if the segmentation contour *contracts* or *expands* one can invert the sign of Φ^0 accordingly during initialization. We terminate the iterative scheme in Eq. (7) if the relative change of the zero-level set Γ of Φ is smaller than $\epsilon = 10^{-5}$.

4   Results

In the following we validate the proposed method by using real 2D B-mode US images showing patient data from echocardiographic examinations of the human heart in an apical four-chamber view using a Philips iE33 ultrasound system. In this case the segmentation task is to indicate the inner contour of the left ventricle (LV) during the end-diastolic phase. To quantify the segmentation results we asked two experienced echocardiographers to manually segment images from eight different data sets. We use the Dice measure $D(A,B) = \frac{2|A \cap B|}{|A|+|B|}$ to compare two segmentations A and B. We optimized the parameters of the two segmentation models in Eq. (2) (i.e., $\lambda_1 = 1, \lambda_2 = 0.7, \beta = 500$) and Eq. (6) (i.e., $\beta = 95$) globally on all eight images by maximizing the average Dice index with respect to the two respective expert delineations.

In Fig. 3(c) and 3(g) one can see two segmentation results (data set 2 and 4 of Table 1) using the Chan-Vese algorithm. Naturally, the evolution of the contour stops in regions perturbed by speckle noise in the lumen of LV due to misclassification of pixel intensities as discussed in Section 2.2 and hence

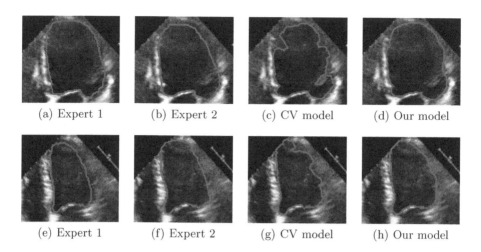

(a) Expert 1   (b) Expert 2   (c) CV model   (d) Our model

(e) Expert 1   (f) Expert 2   (g) CV model   (h) Our model

Fig. 3. Segmentation results for two 2D B-mode US images of the LV (row-wise) using the Chan-Vese (CV) model in Eq. (2) and the proposed model in Eq. (6) compared to manual delineations by two echocardiographic experts

Table 1. Dice index values for comparison with manual segmentation

Dataset	1	2	3	4	5	6	7	8
Observer variability	0.9217	0.9265	0.8906	0.8954	0.9083	0.9348	0.9201	0.9414
Chan-Vese	0.8731	0.9075	0.7551	**0.9278**	0.8229	0.7551	0.8674	0.8942
Proposed model	**0.8803**	**0.9443**	**0.8132**	0.9254	**0.8401**	**0.8172**	**0.8934**	**0.9192**

this method produces erroneous segmentation results compared to the manual delineations of the experts. On the other side, the proposed model from Section 3.2 overcomes these problems and turns out to be significantly more *robust* in the presence of speckle noise as can be seen in Fig. 3(d) and 3(h). This observation could be confirmed for all eight data sets as indicated by Table 1. The average segmentation performance of the CV method with respect to the Dice index is 0.8503, while the proposed method reaches 0.8791.

In addition, we observed that the CV algorithm (50s) needs less time for performing segmentation compared to the proposed methods (110s) using the optimized parameters indicated above for images of size 240×180 pixels on a 2.26GHz Intel Core 2 processor with 4GB RAM and Mathworks Matlab (2010a). However, if one chooses $\lambda_1 = \lambda_2$ in Eq. (2) the regularization parameter β has to be chosen accordingly higher and one gets very strict CFL conditions (8) for the temporal time discretization of the CV method and thus a slower convergence of the iteration scheme (120s). Hence, it is difficult to give a general statement on the performance of both methods since the runtime directly depends on the chosen parameters. When reinitializing the signed distance function more frequently and simultaneously violating the CFL conditions (8), we were able to speed up both methods by a factor of ~ 4 and perform segmentation in 12s−18s without numerical errors. However, note that in general one must obey the CFL conditions to guarantee stability of the iteration scheme. One possibility to decrease the runtime even further is to update the signed distance function Φ not globally on Ω but only in a narrow band around the contour Γ (see [5]).

5 Discussion

In this paper we proposed a novel segmentation formulation based on the choice of an optimal threshold by means of discriminant analysis. The proposed method considers the influence of multiplicative speckle noise in US data in a simple way and shows higher segmentation accuracy than the related CV method. The proposed model has only one parameter to be specified by the user in contrast to three parameters for the CV model. Since the optimal threshold for image partition t_O is computed only once on a global level, our method solves only a minimal partition problem and hence shows less local minima and a high robustness for different initializations. Note that the proposed method can also be easily extended to multiphase segmentation problems [2,6]. Finally, we note that the proposed method is not restricted on ultrasound data and will be tested on other imaging modalities in the near future.

Acknowledgment. We gratefully thank Jörg Stypmann from the University Hospital of Münster for his expertise in echocardiography, the provided US B-mode images, and the manual segmentations. This study was supported by the Deutsche Forschungsgemeinschaft (DFG), SFB 656 MoBil, Münster, Germany (project B3, C3).

References

1. Chan, T.F., Vese, L.A.: Active Contours Without Edges. IEEE-TIP 10(2), 266–277 (2001)
2. Chan, T.F., Vese, L.A.: A Multiphase Level Set Framework for Image Segmentation Using the Mumford and Shah Model. IJCV 50(3), 271–293 (2002)
3. Ma, M., et al.: Model Driven Quantification of Left Ventricular Function from Sparse Single-Beat 3D Echocardiography. Med. Img. Anal. 14, 582–593 (2010)
4. Noble, J.A., Boukerroui, D.: Ultrasound Image Segmentation: A Survey. IEEE-TMI 25(8), 987–1010 (2006)
5. Osher, S., Fedkiw, R.P.: Level Set Methods and Dynamic Implicit Surfaces. Springer, New York (2003)
6. Otsu, N.: A Threshold Selection Method from Gray-Level Histograms. IEEE-TSMC 9(1), 62–66 (1979)
7. Sawatzky, A., Tenbrinck, D., Jiang, X., Burger, M.: A Variational Framework for Region-Based Segmentation Incorporating Physical Noise Models. J. Math. Imaging and Vision (2013), doi:10.1007/s10851-013-0419-6
8. Tenbrinck, D., Sawatzky, A., Jiang, X., Burger, M., Haffner, W., Willems, P., Paul, M., Stypmann, J.: Impact of Physical Noise Modeling on Image Segmentation in Echocardiography. Eurographics Workshop on Vis. Comp. for Bio. and Med., 33–40 (2012)

Region Based Contour Detection
by Dynamic Programming

Xiaoyi Jiang[1,2,3] and Daniel Tenbrinck[1,2]

[1] Department of Mathematics and Computer Science,
University of Münster, Germany
[2] European Institute for Molecular Imaging, University of Münster, Germany
[3] Cluster of Excellence EXC 1003, Cells in Motion, CiM, Münster, Germany

Abstract. Dynamic programming (DP) is a popular technique for contour detection, particularly in biomedical image analysis. Although gradient information is typically used in such methods, it is not always a reliable measure to work with and there is a strong need of non-gradient based methods. In this paper we present a general framework for region based contour detection by dynamic programming. It is based on a global energy function which is approximated by a radial ray-wise summation to enable dynamic programming. Its simple algorithmic structure allows to use arbitrarily complex region models and model testing functions, in particular by means of techniques from robust statistics. The proposed framework was tested on synthetic data and real microscopic images. A performance comparison with the standard gradient-based DP and a recent non-gradient DP-based contour detection algorithm clearly demonstrates the superiority of our approach.

1 Introduction

Dynamic programming is a popular technique for contour detection due to its simpleness, efficiency, and guarantee of optimality. One class of detectable contours starts from the left, passes each image column exactly once, and ends in the last column, as exemplified by detecting arterial walls in sonographic artery images [2]. Another, even more important, application class deals with closed contours. Based on a point p in the interior of the contour, a polar transformation with p being the central point brings the original image into a matrix, in which a closed contour becomes one from left to right afterwards. Finally, the detected contour has to be transformed back to the original image space. This technique works well for star-shaped contours, particularly including convex contours. Note that special care must be taken in order to guarantee the closedness of the detected contour [8]. In the following we use the case of closed contours for our discussion, but it applies to the first class of contours as well.

Typically, DP-based contour detection assumes strong edges along the contour and is thus based on gradient computation. In the simplest case the contour measure is defined by the sum of gradient magnitudes. More sophisticated formulations can be found for instance in [5], where the object contour is expected

R. Wilson et al. (Eds.): CAIP 2013, Part II, LNCS 8048, pp. 152–159, 2013.

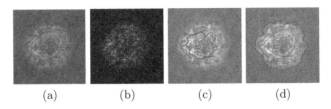

(a)   (b)   (c)   (d)

Fig. 1. (a) Tumor cell ROI; (b) gradient; (c) gradient-based optimal contour; (d) region-based optimal contour from our approach (with L_1 norm, see Section 3)

to have approximately uniform edge strength, leading to an alternative contour measure by ratio of the mean and the standard deviation of image gradients.

In practice, however, gradient is not always a reliable measure to work with, in particular in biomedical image analysis, due to limiting factors like low contrast, high noise level, etc. Generally, objects may have very smooth or even discontinuous boundaries. One such example is the region-of-interest (ROI) of a tumor cell from microscopic imaging shown in Figure 1. Based on the gradient alone, the contour in (c) is rather suboptimal in the application situation, but maximizes the sum of gradient magnitude (6428 in this case). On the other hand, the contour in (d) is much more reasonable although having a lower sum of gradient magnitude (1917). Looking at the gradient in (b), it indeed can be expected that a small change of intensity values may lead to substantially different contours when maximizing the sum of gradient magnitude. This example clearly demonstrates the need of alternate, *non-gradient* approaches.

There are only very few works on DP-based contour detection using non-gradient information. The approach from [9] considers two circular areas, one on each side of a point along the radial ray. The squared difference of their mean intensity values is interpreted as a measure of separability and used as cost for dynamic programming. The circular form for evaluation, however, leads to severe contamination by samples of other distributions, even for many convex shapes, thus substantially limiting the applicability. The authors of [4] present a homogeneity splitting cost for dynamic programming. This method will be further detailed and experimentally compared to our method in Section 4.

In the next section we start with a discussion of the fundamental idea of region-based segmentation. Then, Section 3 presents our framework of DP-based contour detection. Our experimental results and comparison with other methods are given in Section 4. Finally, a brief discussion concludes this paper.

2   Fundamentals of Region-Based Segmentation

Given an image $f(x, y)$, a contour C partitions the image into two regions, $inside(C)$ and $outside(C)$. We assume each region is well represented by some model, which can be validated by a model testing function F_i and F_o, respectively. Then, the segmentation task can be generally formulated as one of optimizing the following energy function:

$$E(C) = \int_{inside(C)} F_i(x,y)dxdy + \int_{outside(C)} F_o(x,y)dxdy \qquad (1)$$

If needed, the two terms can be further weighted.

The seminal work by Chan and Vese [1] is a prominent example of this region-based segmentation scheme with the assumption of two regions with approximately piecewise-constant intensities. Let c_1 and c_2 denote the average intensity of $inside(C)$ and $outside(C)$, respectively. The energy function in [1] is defined by (additional regularizing terms are ignored):

$$E(C) = \int_{inside(C)} |f(x,y) - c_1|^2 dxdy + \int_{outside(C)} |f(x,y) - c_2|^2 dxdy \qquad (2)$$

In [1] the optimization is done iteratively by means of a level set solution.

Such global optimization schemes suffer from several potential problems: Dependence of the final contour on the initialization, danger of falling into local optima, and high computational burden. For star-shaped contours, which are of interest in many real applications, they are not necessarily the best choice. In this case dynamic programming is applicable and its simpleness, efficiency, and guarantee of optimality make it an attractive option. In this work we explore the potential of region-based dynamic programming for contour detection.

3   Region Based Segmentation by Dynamic Programming

A star-shaped contour C can be represented in polar form $r(\theta)$, $\theta \in [0, 2\pi)$. Given the image boundary $B(\theta)$, $\theta \in [0, 2\pi)$, the energy function in (1) becomes:

$$E(C) = \int_{inside(C)} F_i(x,y)dxdy + \int_{outside(C)} F_o(x,y)dxdy$$

$$= \int_0^{2\pi} \int_0^{r(\theta)} F_i(\theta,r)drd\theta + \int_0^{2\pi} \int_{r(\theta)}^{B(\theta)} F_o(\theta,r)drd\theta$$

$$= \int_0^{2\pi} \underbrace{\left[\int_0^{r(\theta)} F_i(\theta,r)dr + \int_{r(\theta)}^{B(\theta)} F_o(\theta,r)dr \right]}_{E_\theta(C)} d\theta$$

$$= \int_0^{2\pi} E_\theta(C)d\theta \qquad (3)$$

The term $E_\theta(C)$ is simply a model testing function applied to one particular radial ray corresponding to angle θ. Note that the model parameters have to be estimated by the entirety of $inside(C)$ and $outside(C)$, respectively.

In this formulation the Chan-Vese energy function (2) becomes:

$$E_\theta(C) = \int_0^{r(\theta)} |f(\theta,r) - c_1|^2 dr + \int_{r(\theta)}^{B(\theta)} |f(\theta,r) - c_2|^2 dr \qquad (4)$$

$$c_1 = \frac{\int_0^{2\pi} \int_0^{r(\theta)} f(\theta,r)dr}{\int_0^{2\pi} \int_0^{r(\theta)} dr}, \qquad c_2 = \frac{\int_0^{2\pi} \int_{r(\theta)}^{B(\theta)} f(\theta,r)dr}{\int_0^{2\pi} \int_{r(\theta)}^{B(\theta)} dr}$$

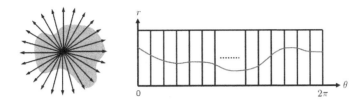

Fig. 2. Image in polar space. A star-shaped contour in the original image corresponds to a continuous contour from left to right in polar space.

Note that the two average intensities c_1 and c_2 depend on the entire $inside(C)$ and $outside(C)$, respectively, even when evaluating $E_\theta(C)$ for a single radial ray.

If the two average intensity c_1 and c_2 were known and thus not needed to be estimated, then $E_\theta(C)$ in (4) can be easily computed for each candidate r of a given θ. That is, we obtain a cost matrix $c(\theta, r) := E_\theta(C)$ for all image points in polar space, see Figure 2. A star-shaped contour in original image corresponds to a continuous contour from left to right in this polar space, which can be detected by means of dynamic programming [4] in a time linear to the size of polar space, thus also linear to the original image size.

Unfortunately, the two average intensities c_1 and c_2 are unknown before the contour is completely detected. Therefore, we cannot compute the cost matrix $c(\theta, r)$ beforehand and consequently cannot apply dynamic programming to solve the optimization problem (4). The same is true for general $E_\theta(C)$ since both model testing functions $F_i(\theta, r)$ and $F_o(\theta, r)$ depend on global model parameters of $inside(C)$ and $outside(C)$, respectively.

The optimization problem (4), however, does have a dynamic programming solution if *we model each radial ray separately*. Then, a radial ray is partitioned into an inside part $r \in [0, r(\theta)]$ with the average intensity $c_{\theta,1}$ and an outside part $r \in [r(\theta), B(\theta)]$ with the average intensity $c_{\theta,2}$. Here both average intensities are *locally* determined within a specific radial ray. Consequently, Eq.(4) becomes:

$$E_\theta(C) = \int_0^{r(\theta)} |f(\theta, r) - c_{\theta,1}|^2 dr + \int_{r(\theta)}^{B(\theta)} |f(\theta, r) - c_{\theta,2}|^2 dr \qquad (5)$$

It can be computed for each $r(\theta)$ of a given θ to obtain a cost matrix $c(\theta, r) := E_\theta(C)$ as follows. For a given θ, each potential value for $r(\theta)$ partitions the radial ray into an inside part $r \in [0, r(\theta)]$ and an outside part $r \in [r(\theta), B(\theta)]$. This partitioning immediately gives us the respective average intensity $c_{\theta,1}$ and $c_{\theta,2}$, thus enabling the evaluation of the model testing function $\int |f(\theta, r) - c_{\theta,k}|^2$, $k = 1, 2$. Given the computed cost matrix $c(\theta, r)$, dynamic programming can be applied to detect the optimal contour.

In general we can formulate:

$$E_\theta(C) = \int_0^{r(\theta)} F_i^*(\theta, r) dr + \int_{r(\theta)}^{B(\theta)} F_o^*(\theta, r) dr$$

In contrast to (3), the representation models and the resulting model testing functions $F_i^*(\theta, r)$ and $F_o^*(\theta, r)$ are bounded to a particular radial ray θ instead of the whole image. Also in this general case we have no trouble to compute a cost matrix $c(\theta, r)$ and then to apply dynamic programming for detecting an optimal contour in polar space.

This general approach can be flexibly concretized in many different ways:

- Any variant of average estimation can be used for the L_2^2 model testing function in (5). In particular, robust statistical estimation methods [6] provide more reliable results for noisy data.
- Any model testing function $T(f(\theta, r), c_{\theta,k})$, $k = 1, 2$, can be used, e.g. variants of L_p norm. The special case in (5) is the squared L_2 norm. Of particular interest is the L_1 norm, which is provably more robust than L_2.
- Also variance-based model testing is possible, e.g. $E(C) = \sigma_{\theta,1}^2 + \sigma_{\theta,2}^2$, where $\sigma_{\theta,1}^2$ and $\sigma_{\theta,2}^2$ are variance of $inside(C)$ and $outside(C)$, respectively.

So far, the inside and outside part are tested separately. We can go a step further and use combined testing. One example is:

$$E_\theta(C) = \frac{|c_{\theta,1} - c_{\theta,2}|^2}{\sigma_{\theta,1}^2 + \sigma_{\theta,2}^2}$$

in accordance with the Fisher linear discriminant. In this most general form the term $E_\theta(C)$ cannot be reformulated as a sum of inside and outside term.

In summary, the original optimization task (3) cannot be solved by dynamic programming in general. But by modeling each radial ray separately a dynamic programming solution is possible for *any representation model and model testing function independent of their form and complexity*. This universality gives the rather simple scheme of dynamic programming considerable power for real-world applications. For instance, robust estimation methods such as median-based approaches and L_1 norm are highly desired for improved robustness. Also, sophisticated testing criteria like Fisher linear discriminant and others from machine learning theory provides extra useful options for measuring the separability of two distributions. While all such variants are straightforward in our DP-based framework, they are rather complex to implement in calculus, e.g., in the context of level set methods.

The proposed approach of modeling each radial ray separately can be interpreted in two ways. First, it can be seen as an approximate solution of the optimization problem. We assume *all radial rays are approximately subject to the representation model of the whole image*. Taking the example of (5), it means $c_{\theta,1} \approx c_1$, $c_{\theta,2} \approx c_2$, $\theta \in [0, 2\pi)$. This assumption may be violated by some of the radial rays. Even in such a case the dynamic programming algorithm still has a good chance of finding a globally optimal solution due to the forced continuity. On the other hand, the dynamic programming solution can also been seen as an extension of the original optimization problem with extra power. The separate modeling of the radial rays allows to deal with inhomogeneous inside and outside regions. As soon as a separation in the individual radial rays can be assumed, an overall segmentation is still possible despite of the inhomogeneity.

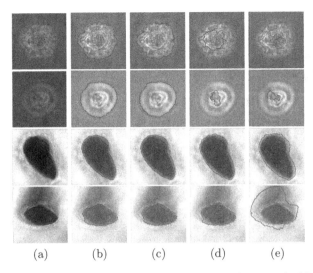

(a)   (b)   (c)   (d)   (e)

Fig. 3. (a) Tumor cell ROI; (b) contour by our approach (L_1 norm); (c) our approach (L_2^2); (d) gradient-based approach; (e) method from [4]. The first two rows are early stage and the last two are late stage cells.

4   Experimental Results

We have tested our approach on a series of tumor cell images from microscopic imaging. Given an image, cells of interest are marked by a biologist. Then, the approximate cell center and a ROI around the center point are manually selected. Note that we currently refrain to use an automatic detection of cell positions because the microscopic cell images have been acquired with a series of focus levels and the biologists are only interested in well focused cells. Thus, an automatic cell detection must contain a focus assessment which turns out to be not easy, even for an untrained person.

The following four algorithm variants have been tested and compared.

– Our approach with $T(f(\theta, r), c_{\theta,k}) = L_1$, $k = 1, 2$.
– Our approach with $T(f(\theta, r), c_{\theta,k}) = L_2^2$, $k = 1, 2$, see Eq. (5). In both variants of our approach $c_{\theta,k}$ is determined by a simple mean computation.
– Gradient-based contour detection, i.e., $E_\theta(C) := \text{GradientMagnitude}(\theta, r(\theta))$. In this case the dynamic programming is applied to maximize the sum of gradient magnitudes (computed by the Sobel operator) along the contour.
– The homogeneity splitting method from [4]: $E_\theta(C) = \sigma_\theta(r(\theta)) - \sigma_\theta(r(\theta) + \delta) + 1$. Here $\sigma_\theta(r)$ represents the standard deviation of inner segment $[0, r]$ on the radial ray θ and δ is a smoothing parameter. In our experiments this parameter was optimized manually.

The performance of the four algorithm variants is exemplarily demonstrated on the four images in Figure 3. Our segmentation results appear very convincing to the biologists, in particular using the L_1 norm. In contrast, both the standard

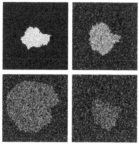

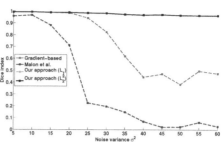

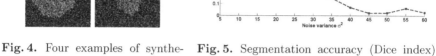

Fig. 4. Four examples of synthesized cell images

Fig. 5. Segmentation accuracy (Dice index) with increasing noise variance levels

gradient-based approach and the method from [4] fail in case of early stage cells with complex inner-cell textures which produce substantial "misleading" gradient hints. Similar reason explains the failure of [4]. The textures induce severe variations of standard deviations along a radial ray, thus leading to a deficient homogeneity splitting measure. On the other hand, late stage cells cause less problems. These images are typically of high contrast to the background and do not have complex inner-cell textures. Even the standard gradient-based approach works well. However, the method from [4] fails in some cases.

We have also conducted a study on synthetic data to quantitatively evaluate and compare the performance of the four algorithm variants. Random star-shaped objects (similar to cells from microscopic images) were generated with constant intensity value of 60 in a homogeneous background with intensity 0. We added additive Gaussian noise with mean 0 and different variance levels $\sigma^2 \in \{5, 10, \ldots, 55, 60\}$ (see Figure 4 for four examples with increasing level of noise 5, 20, 45, and 60 from top left to bottom right) and evaluated the four discussed methods on 10 arbitrary shapes per noise level. For quantification we compare the computed segmentation result with the (unperturbed) ground truth images using the Dice index $D(A, B) = 2|A \cap B|/(|A| + |B|)$, see Figure 5. This study indicates that the proposed region-based models are significantly more robust under the impact of noise and give good segmentation results even for very noisy data. In contrast, the gradient-based method cannot cope with the noisy edge information induced by the perturbations. The approach from [4] is very sensitive to inhomogeneities, since its homogeneity criterion is solely based on the inside region and ignores the outside region. These quantitative results are consistent with our observations on real microscopic images as discussed above.

5   Conclusion

In this paper we have presented a general framework of region based dynamic programming technique for contour detection. This non-gradient approach is efficient (linear to the image size) and allows to use arbitrarily complex region model and model testing functions. In particular, techniques from robust statistics and machine learning theory are helpful when dealing with noisy data. A performance comparison has clearly demonstrated the superiority of our approach.

An extension to simultaneously detecting multiple contours is straightforward [7]. The principle behind this work can also be applied to 3D surface detection [3]. The current formulation is based on the fundamental assumption that all the radial rays are approximately subject to the representation model of the whole image. This assumption is always violated to some extent. Although this fact may not effect the contour detection due to the forced continuity, multiple radial rays together as higher-level processing unit instead of single rays will reduce this modeling uncertainty. All these extensions will be studied in future.

Acknowledgments. The authors thank Kristen Mills at Max Planck Institute for Intelligent Systems, Stuttgart, for providing the microscopic images.

References

1. Chan, T.F., Vese, L.A.: Active contours without edges. IEEE Trans. on Image Processing 10(2), 266–277 (2001)
2. Cheng, D.C., Jiang, X.: Detections of arterial wall in sonographic artery images using dual dynamic programming. IEEE Trans. on Information Technology in Biomedicine 12(6), 792–799 (2008)
3. Li, K., Wu, X., Chen, D., Sonka, M.: Optimal surface segmentation in volumetric images - a graph-theoretic approach. IEEE Trans. on PAMI 28(1), 119–134 (2006)
4. Malon, C., Cosatto, E.: Dynamic radial contour extraction by splitting homogeneous areas. In: Real, P., Diaz-Pernil, D., Molina-Abril, H., Berciano, A., Kropatsch, W. (eds.) CAIP 2011, Part I. LNCS, vol. 6854, pp. 269–277. Springer, Heidelberg (2011)
5. Ray, N., Acton, S.T., Zhang, H.: Seeing through clutter: Snake computation with dynamic programming for particle segmentation. In: Proc. of ICPR, pp. 801–804 (2012)
6. Stewart, C.: Robust parameter estimation in computer vision. SIAM Reviews 41(3), 513–537 (1999)
7. Sun, C., Appleton, B.: Multiple paths extraction in images using a constrained expanded trellis. IEEE Trans. on PAMI 27(12), 1923–1933 (2005)
8. Sun, C., Pallottino, S.: Circular shortest path in images. Pattern Recognition 36(3), 709–719 (2003)
9. Yu, M., Huang, Q., Jin, R., Song, E., Liu, H., Hung, C.C.: A novel segmentation method for convex lesions based on dynamic programming with local intra-class variance. In: Proc. of ACM Symposium on Applied Computing, pp. 39–44 (2012)

Sparse Coding and Mid-Level Superpixel-Feature for ℓ_0-Graph Based Unsupervised Image Segmentation

Xiaofang Wang[1], Huibin Li[1], Simon Masnou[2], and Liming Chen[1,⋆]

[1] Ecole Centrale de Lyon, LIRIS UMR5205, F-69134, France
{xiaofang.wang,huibin.li,liming.chen}@ec-lyon.fr
[2] Université de Lyon, CNRS UMR 5208, Université Lyon 1, Institut Camille Jordan,
43 bd du 11 novembre 1918, F-69622 Villeurbanne cedex, France
masnou@math.univ-lyon1.fr

Abstract. We propose in this paper a graph-based unsupervised segmentation approach that combines superpixels, sparse representation, and a new mid-level feature to describe superpixels. Given an input image, we first extract a set of interest points either by sampling or using a local feature detector, and we compute a set of low-level features associated with the patches centered at the interest points. We define a low-level dictionary as the collection of all these low-level features. We call superpixel a region of an oversegmented image obtained from the input image, and we compute the low-level features associated with it. Then we compute for each superpixel a mid-level feature defined as the sparse coding of its low-level features in the aforementioned dictionary. These mid-level features not only carry the same information as the initial low-level features, but also carry additional contextual cue. We use the superpixels at several segmentation scales, their associated mid-level features, and the sparse representation coefficients to build graphs at several scales. Merging these graphs leads to a bipartite graph that can be partitioned using the Transfer Cut algorithm. We validate the proposed mid-level feature framework on the MSRC dataset, and the segmented results show improvements from both qualitative and quantitative viewpoints compared with other state-of-the-art methods.

Keywords: image segmentation, sparse coding, superpixels, mid-level features, ℓ_0-graph.

1 Introduction

Most unsupervised image segmentation methods, which are frequently used for high-level vision tasks like object recognition or image annotation, involve low level features such as color, boundary or texture. In particular, several methods using graphs and spectral clustering have been proposed in recent years [13] [8], however it remains challenging for those methods to provide desirable visually semantic partitions.

Generally, for those methods, building a faithful graph is critical to the final quality. The graph nodes can be pixels or regions, and the graph affinity matrix encodes the

⋆ Thanks to Chinese Scholarship Council (CSC) for funding. This work is supported in part by the French research agency, l'Agence Nationale de Recherche (ANR), through the Visen project within the ERA-NET CHIST-ERA program, under the grant ANR-12-CHRI-0002-04.

R. Wilson et al. (Eds.): CAIP 2013, Part II, LNCS 8048, pp. 160–168, 2013.
© Springer-Verlag Berlin Heidelberg 2013

similarity between either low level features or top down features associated with the nodes. Low level features capture object basic properties and they can be obtained with various descriptors or operators, such as color histograms, histogram of oriented gradients (HOG), scale invariant feature transform (SIFT), local binary patterns (LBP), etc. Despite progresses in the design of more informative low-level features, performances remain limited. Top down features usually convey semantic or prior knowledge about the segmented regions or objects. Many works treat the output of trained classifiers and object detectors [7], or semantic segmentation algorithm [5] as top down information to guide the low level unsupervised segmentation. However, all these top-down semantic methods require non-trivial amounts of human-labeled training data, which is unrealistic in practical situation.

In recent years, successful applications of mid-level features (e.g., bag of features) to content-based image retrieval and object categorization have motivated their introduction for other computer vision tasks such as image segmentation. Yu et al.[17] proposed bag of textons combined with clustering for image segmentation. The baseline of a mid-level feature mainly involves low-level feature extraction, representation (using hard assignments with k-means, or soft assignments via sparse coding) and pooling. In this paper, we focus on mid-level features based on sparse coding, as in [18] where first a dictionary is built by learning or human labeling, then the coefficients of the sparse representation in this dictionary are used to define mid-level features for classification or grouping. In contrast to [18], we build the dictionary from informative patches centered at interest points detected without any supervision, and each mid-level feature is the sparse coding in the dictionary of the low level feature associated with a superpixel. This way, the contextual information, which has been proved an efficient cue to discriminate two objects or images [6], is added to the original low-level features to improve the robustness of the similarity coefficient between two superpixels in the graph construction, whose quality plays a critical role to the segmentation result.

More precisely, the whole segmentation model starts by extracting interest points from the image, associating with them a set of low-level features whose collection forms a dictionary, and over-segmenting the input image into multi-layer superpixels. Then, each superpixel is associated with a sparse representation of its low level feature in the previously built dictionary. This proposed feature inherits of the original descriptors' property and covers also adaptive contextual information. Compared with related works and other benchmark algorithms on the MSRC dataset [14], the key contribution of this paper is that our new mid-level feature is able to describe better the superpixels. The similarities between superpixels are then computed based on ℓ_0 graph construction in the spirit of [16] (where only low-level features were used). Finally, the constructed graph is plugged into a robust unsupervised segmentation framework introduced in [8]. The proposed method can segment visually semantic regions, and can be used in many high-level computer vision tasks.

The organization of the paper is as follows: in Section 2 we introduce the proposed mid-level features based on the sparse coding and the segmentation framework, and in Section 3 we present and comment a few segmentation results on the MSRC dataset. We conclude in Section 4.

2   Superpixels, Mid-Level Features, and Sparse Representation

Our approach consists of three steps: 1) interest points extraction, low-level features computation, and dictionary building; 2) over-segmentation of the original image, extraction of superpixels (defined as the over-segmented regions), computation of a low-level feature for each superpixel, and sparse representation in the dictionary of step 1; 3) graph construction and partitioning.

2.1   Low-Level Features Detection and Extraction

We use low-level features extraction to build a meaningful dictionary to represent a given image. First, we extract a set of key points from the image. The meaningfulness of the low-level dictionary is highly dependent on the choice of the key points. If they capture the main structural information of the input image, then the derived dictionary will be highly meaningful. In practice, we have tested various approaches, see Fig. 1: either the interest points are randomly or densely sampled, or they are obtained using a feature descriptor, e.g., the Harris detector, the Difference of Gaussians (DoG), or the Hessian detector. The respective performances are discussed in Section 3.

(a) Hessian detector   (b) DoG detector   (c) Harris detector

(d) Random sampling   (e) Dense sampling   (d) Zooming

Fig. 1. Illustration of different types of interest points

Once interest points have been extracted, we consider the local image patches around them, from which low-level features can be computed (we use in this paper RGB color histograms for its strong discriminative skill, but other features as LBP histogram or SIFT may be used). Finally, our low-level dictionary is defined as the collection of all these low-level features, see Fig. 2.

2.2   Mid-Level Features Extraction over Superpixels

We call superpixel a region of an over-segmentation of the original image. In practice, we compute several over-segmentations, and we associate with each superpixel a low-level feature (in our experiments, we used RGB color histograms for its strong discriminative skill). Then we define the mid-level feature associated with a superpixel as the sparse representation of its low-level feature in the dictionary built previously, see Fig. 3 for an illustration of the whole process. More precisely, given a superpixel,

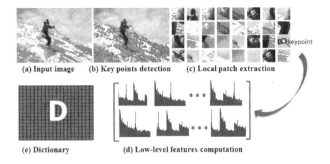

Fig. 2. Illustration of low-level features computation

suppose $x \in \mathbb{R}^m$ is the low-level feature associated with it, and let $D = [d_1 \cdots d_n] \in \mathbb{R}^{m \times n}$ be the low-level dictionary built in section 2.1. The sparse representation of x in D is obtained by solving the following optimization problem:

$$\min_{\alpha} ||x - D\alpha||_2^2 \quad s.t. \quad ||\alpha||_0 \leq L, \tag{1}$$

where $\alpha \in \mathbb{R}^n$, and $||\alpha||_0 := ||\alpha||_{\ell_0}$ is the number of its non-zero coefficients. Suppose $\hat{\alpha}$ is a solution of the problem and $\Lambda_{\hat{\alpha}} = \{j | \hat{\alpha}(j) \neq 0\}$ is the index set of non-zero coefficients of $\hat{\alpha}$, then the mid-level feature associated with the low-level feature x is defined as

$$\hat{x} = D\hat{\alpha} = \sum_{j \in \Lambda_{\hat{\alpha}}} d_j \hat{\alpha}(j). \tag{2}$$

Therefore, the mid-level feature $\hat{x}$ is a linear combination of several low-level features, thus not only carries the same information as the original low-level features, but also carries additional contextual cue.

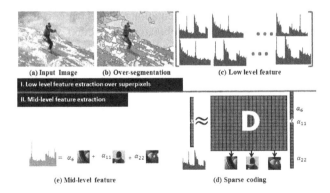

Fig. 3. Illustration of mid-level features computation

2.3   Graph Construction and Partitioning

Once mid-level features have been computed, we build the graph that will be plugged into a spectral clustering algorithm to perform image segmentation. This is done as follows: For each scale of over-segmentation (i.e. for each instance of over-segmentation), we construct a graph whose nodes are the superpixels at that scale, and whose graph edges and weights are computed using ℓ_0-sparse representation. More precisely, we consider as dictionary the mid-level features associated with the superpixels. Then, as in Equation (2), each mid-level feature $\hat{x}_i$ can be represented as a sparse linear combination $\hat{x}_i = \sum_j \alpha_j^i \hat{x}_j$ of the other mid-level features. The similarity coefficient of any pair $\hat{x}_i, \hat{x}_j$ of superpixels is defined as $w_{ij} = \begin{cases} 1 & \text{if } i = j \\ 1 - (r_{ij} + r_{ji})/2 & \text{if } i \neq j. \end{cases}$ where r_{ij} is the sparse representation error of $\hat{x}_i$ and $\hat{x}_j$, i.e. $r_{ij} = \|\hat{x}_i - \alpha_j^i \hat{x}_j\|_2^2$.

We collect all ℓ_0 affinity matrices obtained from all over-segmented images, and we concatenate them diagonally into a unique matrix denoted as W_{SS}, together with the pixel-superpixels affinity matrix W_{IS}. Then we consider the bipartite graph associated with the matrix $B = \begin{bmatrix} W_{IS} \\ W_{SS} \end{bmatrix}$ and the Transfer Cut algorithm [8] is applied to partition the bipartite graph into K clusters by solving the following generalized eigenvalue problem over superpixels only $L_V \mathbf{f} = \lambda D_V \mathbf{f}$, where $L_V = D_V - W_V$, $D_V = diag(B^\top \mathbf{1})$, and $W_V = B^\top D_U^{-1} B$, $D_U = diag(B\mathbf{1})$, see [8] for more details.

3   Experimental Results

3.1   Database and Parameter Settings

We evaluate our approach on the Microsoft Research Cambridge (MSRC) database, which contains 591 images from 23 object classes, and we use for the evaluation the accurate ground-truth segmentations of [9]. To quantitatively evaluate the performance, we apply four popular measurements : 1) Probabilistic Rand Index (PRI) [15]; 2) Variation of Information (VOI) [11]; 3) Global Consistency Error (GCE) [10]; and 4) Boundary Displacement Error (BDE) [4]. A segmentation result is better if PRI is higher and the other three ones are lower. For low-level features extraction, we only use the color feature in RGB space, and the feature dimension is reduced from 256×3 to 64 by PCA. For mid-level dictionary building via sparse coding, we use the Orthogonal Matching Pursuit (OMP) algorithm [12] to solve Eqn. 1 and set the sparsity number $L = 4$ according to the experimental results.

On the step of graph construction and partitioning, we proceed as in our previous work [16], i.e. we derive from the original image 5 or 6 oversegmented images (this number of scales being experimentally satisfactory) obtained by the Mean Shift (MS) method [2] and by the FH method [3]. More precisely, we derive three images by the MS method using the sets of parameters $(hs, hr, M) = \{(7,7,100), (7,9,100),$ and $(7,11,100)\}$, respectively, where hs and hr are bandwidth parameters in the spatial and range domains, and M is the minimum size of each segment. Either two of three oversegmented images are provided by the FH method using as parameters (σ, c, M) either $\{(0.5,100,50),(0.8,200,100)\}$,   or $\{(0.8,150,50),(0.8,200,100),(0.8,300,100)\}$.

Table 1. Comparison of different feature detectors on the whole MSRC database (red color indicates the best result)

Detector	PRI↑	Vol↓	GCE↓	BDE↓
Harris detector	0.8195	1.4214	0.1694	9.4530
Hessian detector	0.8177	1.4366	0.1691	9.9951
DoG detector	0.8226	1.3900	0.1670	9.3955
Random sampling	0.8069	1.5578	0.1781	10.1746
Dense sampling	0.8280	1.3452	0.1633	9.4403

To build the ℓ_0 graph, the sparsity number $L = 3$ is used for all the experiments, see [16] for more details. We organize our experimental results as follows: first, we compare the performances of the five different kinds of low-level feature detectors introduced in section 2.1; then, we list the quantitative results of our proposed method on different subsets of MSRC database and compare it with several state-of-the-art methods; finally, we show some visual examples of our method.

Table 2. Performances of our method on MSRC and comparison with state-of-the-art methods

Metric	PRI↑		Vol↓		GCE↓		BDE↓	
Object class	baseline	new	baseline	new	baseline	new	baseline	new
1. grass, cow	0.8889	0.8978	0.7927	0.8417	0.1006	0.1059	4.8316	4.9181
2. tree, grass, sky	0.7865	0.7963	1.2569	1.3664	0.1727	0.1990	18.6141	13.6065
3. building, sky	0.8429	0.8697	1.2660	1.3768	0.1670	0.1755	8.0268	8.3904
4. aeroplane, grass, sky	0.9083	0.9202	1.3133	1.2662	0.1463	0.1649	4.1802	4.3369
5. cow, grass, mount	0.9038	0.8647	0.5641	0.7804	0.0752	0.0889	4.2286	4.8817
6. face, body	0.7176	0.7277	2.2429	2.3892	0.2601	0.2669	16.1357	15.2383
7. car, building	0.7423	0.7624	2.2676	2.1879	0.2044	0.2546	12.3907	12.3268
8. bike, building	0.7037	0.7196	2.0662	2.1575	0.2729	0.2854	10.7725	10.9580
9. sheep, grass	0.8837	0.8867	0.7287	0.7166	0.0853	0.0874	4.7323	4.9983
10. flower	0.8712	0.8766	0.6368	0.7172	0.0836	0.0927	6.8501	5.7331
11. sign	0.8581	0.8839	0.7668	0.7591	0.0929	0.0940	6.4911	6.3972
12. bird, sky, grass, water	0.8820	0.8932	0.6977	0.7215	0.0963	0.0831	5.6918	5.9985
13. book	0.6714	0.6613	1.7574	1.9669	0.1596	0.1633	18.9275	17.7393
14. chair	0.7395	0.7806	1.3144	1.6839	0.1862	0.1807	11.7096	7.7027
15. cat	0.7532	0.7483	1.3479	1.2819	0.1272	0.1240	12.0134	11.8589
16. dog	0.8030	0.8029	1.2856	1.2436	0.1394	0.1613	9.7475	9.5381
17. road, building	0.8439	0.8610	1.6346	1.7412	0.2002	0.2025	9.0031	8.4299
18. water, boat	0.8548	0.8424	1.0310	1.0947	0.0935	0.1088	9.1329	12.4533
19. body, face	0.8376	0.8275	1.6961	1.9347	0.1931	0.2124	7.4399	8.8790
20. water, boat, sky, mount	0.8884	0.9154	1.1942	1.0002	0.1602	0.1279	6.3682	5.6792
Average performance								
Method	PRI↑		Vol↓		GCE↓		BDE↓	
Our new method	0.8269		1.3614		0.1590		9.0032	
Baseline [16]	0.8190		1.2930		0.1508		9.3644	
NCut [13]	0.8052		1.2516		-		-	
LRR(CH)[1]	0.7912		1.3002		-		-	
MS[2]	0.7307		1.7472		-		-	

3.2 Experimental Results

As mentioned in section 2.1, the property of the low-level dictionary is highly dependent on the selection of the key points. Therefore, we compared the Harris detector, Difference of Gaussian (DoG), Hessian detector, random sampling, and the dense sampling (see Fig. 1). The results are shown in Tab. 1, from which we can deduce that dense sampling is the most efficient way to extract interest points. The main reason is that dense sampling can capture almost all information of the image and is well-suited for sparse coding that requires an over-complete dictionary.

We compare in Table 2 the performances of our method on the MSRC database and the performances of the method we proposed in [16] (limiting to RGB histogram as superpixel feature, and calling *baseline* this reference algorithm). Obviously, our new method can achieve excellent performances on segmenting object classes such as *cow*, *building*, *sheep*, *flower*, *sign*, *bird*, *road*, and *boat*, but is less efficient for *tree*, *face*, *cat*, *dog*, *bike*, etc. The visual results are also shown in Fig.4. The reasons for the

Fig. 4. Examples of segmented results on the MRSC dataset (for each experiment, we show the segmentation result, and the segmentation superimposed with the original image)

difference performances are various: **1)** objects like *face*, *cat*, and *dog* usually have complex backgrounds mainly associated with indoor scene which makes the evaluation unfair for the machine algorithms since the ground-truth does not label the indoor objects. On the other side, in the case of objects without complex backgrounds, our method can segment them correctly even if the object itself presents obvious color variations like on *cow*, *building* and *flower*; **2)** objects like *face* or *bike* can be subject to strong illumination changes which prevent the machine algorithms from grouping object correctly if only color is used as low level descriptor. Results should be improved if other descriptors as LBP were used, and this is the purpose of future work. **3)** the quality of segmentation can also be influenced greatly by the way superpixels are extracted.

We compare the performances of our approach with other state-of-the-arts algorithms in Tab. 2. We used the scores given in [1], observing that GCE and BDE were not reported. Our method ranks first according to PRI and BDE, which makes it one of the most competitive algorithms.

4   Conclusion

We introduced a new unsupervised image segmentation method based on ℓ_0-graph, superpixels, mid-level features, and sparse coding. An nice property of the mid-level feature we propose is that it can capture adaptive contextual information and carries as well the original low level feature information. Quantitative comparison with the state-of-art methods, as well as visual results, indicate that our new algorithm is a competitive image segmentation method.

References

1. Cheng, B., Liu, G., Wang, J., Huang, Z., Yan, S.: Multi-task low-rank affinity pursuit for image segmentation. In: ICCV, pp. 2439–2446 (2011)
2. Comaniciu, D., Meer, P.: Mean shift: A robust approach toward feature space analysis. PAMI 24(5), 603–619 (2002)
3. Felzenszwalb, P.F., Huttenlocher, D.P.: Efficient graph-based image segmentation. IJCV 59(2), 167–181 (2004)
4. Freixenet, J., Muñoz, X., Raba, D., Martí, J., Cufí, X.: Yet another survey on image segmentation: Region and boundary information integration. In: Heyden, A., Sparr, G., Nielsen, M., Johansen, P. (eds.) ECCV 2002, Part III. LNCS, vol. 2352, pp. 408–422. Springer, Heidelberg (2002)
5. Fu, H., Qiu, G.: Integrating low-level and semantic features for object consistent segmentation. In: Int. Conf. on Image and Graphics (ICIG), pp. 39–44 (2011)
6. Lee, Y.J., Grauman, K.: Object-graphs for context-aware visual category discovery. PAMI 34(2), 346–358 (2012)
7. Li, L.J., Su, H., Xing, E.P., Fei-Fei, L.: Object bank: A high-level image representation for scene classification and semantic feature sparsification. Advances in Neural Information Processing Systems (2010)
8. Li, Z., Wu, X.M., Chang, S.F.: Segmentation using superpixels: A bipartite graph partitioning approach. In: CVPR, pp. 789–796 (2012)
9. Malisiewicz, T., Efros, A.A.: Improving spatial support for objects via multiple segmentations. In: BMVC (2007)

10. Martin, D.R., Fowlkes, C., Tal, D., Malik, J.: A database of human segmented natural images and its application to evaluating segmentation algorithms and measuring ecological statistics. In: ICCV, pp. 416–425 (2001)
11. Meila, M.: Comparing clusterings: an axiomatic view. In: ICML, pp. 577–584 (2005)
12. Pati, Y., Rezaiifar, R., Krishnaprasad, P.: Orthogonal matching pursuit: recursive function approximation with applications to wavelet decomposition. In: 27th Asilomar Conference on Signals, Systems and Computers, pp. 40–44 (1993)
13. Shi, J., Malik, J.: Normalized cuts and image segmentation. PAMI 22(8), 888–905 (2000)
14. Shotton, J., Winn, J.M., Rother, C., Criminisi, A.: Textonboost: Joint appearance, shape and context modeling for multi-class object recognition and segmentation. In: Leonardis, A., Bischof, H., Pinz, A. (eds.) ECCV 2006, Part I. LNCS, vol. 3951, pp. 1–15. Springer, Heidelberg (2006)
15. Unnikrishnan, R., Pantofaru, C., Hebert, M.: Toward objective evaluation of image segmentation algorithms. IEEE Trans. Pattern Anal. Mach. Intell. 29(6), 929–944 (2007)
16. Wang, X., Li, H., Masnou, S., Chen, L.: A graph-cut approach to image segmentation using an affinity graph based on ℓ_0- sparse representation of features. In: IEEE Int. Conf. on Image Proc. (2013) (accepted)
17. Yu, Z., Li, A., Au, O., Xu, C.: Bag of textons for image segmentation via soft clustering and convex shift. In: CVPR, pp. 781–788 (2012)
18. Zou, W., Kpalma, K., Ronsin, J.: Semantic segmentation via sparse coding over hierarchical regions. In: ICIP, pp. 2577–2580 (2012)

Intuitive Large Image Database Browsing Using Perceptual Similarity Enriched by Crowds

Stefano Padilla, Fraser Halley, David A. Robb, and Mike J. Chantler

The Texture Lab.,
School of Mathematical & Computer Sciences,
Heriot-Watt University,
Edinburgh, UK
{S.Padilla,M.J.Chantler}@hw.ac.uk

Abstract. The main objective of image browsers is to empower users to find a desired image with ease, speed and accuracy from a large database. In this paper we present a novel approach at creating an image browsing environment based on human perception with the aim of providing intuitive image navigation. In our approach, similarity judgments form the basic structural organization for the images in our browser. To enrich this we have developed a scalable crowd sourced method of augmenting a database with a large number of additional samples by capturing human judgments from members of a crowd. Experiments were conducted involving two databases that demonstrate the effectiveness of our method as an intuitive, fast browsing environment for large image databases.

Keywords: Databases, Images, Navigation, Browsers, Perception, Crowd Sourcing, Similarity, Retrieval, Indexing, Clustering, Abstracts, and Textures.

1 Introduction

Traditional image retrieval systems use keywords or textual metadata to retrieve samples. This approach is acceptable for images that are simple and easy to describe. However, complex images are intrinsically more difficult to express with textual descriptors as discussed by Faria et al [4]. Browsing environments offer an alternative to conventional search-by-query methods, as users can retrieve samples even when they don't have the actual sample in mind, or are unable to describe the desired sample. For example, an analogy is a shopper unable to think or describe a product that he or she requires, until they actually see it in the store.

Combs et al [3] offer the following distinction between *Image Retrieval* (*IR*) Systems and *Image Browsers*. *IR* systems return one or more images given some descriptive information. This information can be in the form of an image, keyword or natural language. In contrast, *Image Browsers* allow users to select one or more images from a set of multiple images displayed at one time. Our work concentrates on image browsers as such environments are crucial for online shopping, libraries and digital media. In addition, it is worth noting that browsing environments have received much less attention as described by Chen et al [2].

R. Wilson et al. (Eds.): CAIP 2013, Part II, LNCS 8048, pp. 169–176, 2013.

Often, image searches (or the basic underlying technique of image browsers) rely on the use of Content-Based Image Retrieval (CBIR) systems. In essence, a query image is given to the system with the aim of retrieving the most similar images in a database, taking into account certain visual features including colour, shape and texture. Previously contextual information has been used with the aim of mimicking human behaviour when judging the similarity among images [10, 11, 19]. However, the computational features used in this kind of system do not model human perception well as discussed by Clarke [1] and Plant [13].

In this paper, we present a fast and intuitive browsing environment using perceptual information obtained from human similarity judgements. Moreover, in this work we propose and evaluate a new innovative crowd-source method that easily and efficiently extends samples from a database.

2   Browsing Environments

For databases with a large number of images, it is not feasible to browse linearly through the images in the database. A desirable characteristic is to let the user navigate through the database in a structured manner as noted by Krishnamachari et al [7]. Furthermore, Rodden et al [15, 16] found that arranging a set of thumbnail images according to their similarity does indeed seem to be useful to designers.

Various authors have proposed different methods for browsing images. Chen et al [2] proposed a technique of browsing using similarity pyramids on distance measures from colour, edge and texture features. Pang [12] proposed a texture picker using Gabor wavelets to quantify image characteristics. Holmquist et al [6] developed a hierarchical browsing environment using meta data were images are grouped into folders which can be brought in or out of focus. Martinez et al [9] proposed the use of concept Lattices to access databases of image browsing. Strong et al [20] proposed an approach that generates a feature vector for each image in the collection, which is then used to train a Self-Organizing Map (SOM). A next generation browsing environment was proposed by Shaefer [18], his approach involved mapping thumbnails onto the surface of a sphere according to hue. Finally, a survey of browsing models for CBIR by Heesh [5] gives an alternative discussion of browsing environments.

In summary, all the previous browsing environments made use of computational distance measurements like hue, features or shape. In contrast, Rogowitz et al [17] compared similarity matrices built from two different psychophysical scaling experiments and two different algorithm approaches in an attempt to gain insight into how the dimensions that human observers use for judging similarity differ from the algorithmic methods. For our browsing method we exploit human judgments of similarity instead of computational features to create a fast and intuitive environment.

3   Capturing Human Judgements

In order to develop perceptually relevant browsing environments, we must resolve to involve human subjects in the process of acquiring perceptual descriptions of any database we utilize. Cognitive scientists through psychophysical experiments have successfully recorded human perception of similarity between objects, but a range of different approaches are available for capturing these judgements.

Pairwise comparison involves the presentation of two stimuli to an observer who is asked to compare some characteristics and offer their measure of the characteristic. The amount of observations required for this method makes it impracticable for large databases. *Perceptual ordering* interest is in how the human-mind orders the perceptual environment with respect of a visual stimulus [8]. In CBIR this human ability has been used to inform and improve the performance of Query-by-Example (QBE) retrieval engines. Although this approach may be useful in ordering, it is unlikely to prove useful in obtaining basic perceptual descriptions.

Perceptual grouping is the most suitable method to capture human judgements. It represents the ability of humans to group similar structural elements within images [8]. Lowe explained that perceptually groupings refer to the human visual ability to derive groupings or structures from images without a priori knowledge of the image content [8]. Rao el al [14] employed the approach as a technique for grouping together images that are visually similar in an attempt to identify the high-level features of texture perception.

In our method, we use a simple bootstrap experiment to collect *perceptual grouping* information from various observers. In the experiment, observers are asked to group a small number of images (100) into groups of similar samples following *Algorithm 1*.

Algorithm 1: Initial bootstrapping grouping

```
 1: Make groups from images you perceive to be similar.
 2: There are no restrictions on the # of images in a group.
 3: However, do not group singletons or outliers together.
 4: You may split, merge groups or move images between groups.
 5: If more images are available then
 9:    return to 1
10: else
11:    Make sure you are happy with the groups and stop.
10: end
```

The groups made by each observer were recorded in a *similarity matrix*, normalized to the number of observers giving values in the range 0-1. The base similarity matrix featured similarity coefficients representing the similarity distances between the subset images (100). Unfortunately, sorting longer sets of images exponentially increases the time needed to complete the task. Furthermore, the mental and physical fatigue which results for the observers reduces the quality of the results. Hence, we improved the method so it would be less time consuming and would allow us to expand the image database with ease.

4   Enriching Similarity Information Using Crowds

Until now we have asked observers to group images, but there is no reason why the task cannot be replaced by one of browsing for similar images given a new image (query). An algorithm was developed to translate the similarity information we hold concerning the selected images into similarity information about the new image.

The solution we propose to add a new texture to the database is to assign it a similarity vector, which represents the mean similarity values of the images selected by a user as those most similar to the new image. If, for example, a user is presented with new images numbered 101 and they selected images 1, 2, and 3 as the most similar existing images in the database, then image 101 would be assigned the similarity vector shown in *Equation 1*. Observe that each time a new image is added, the length of all similarity vectors increase by 1 and the added image is assigned a similarity with itself of 1.

$$sv = \left[d_{(101,1)}, d_{(101,2)}, d_{(101,3)}, d_{(101,4)}, \dots, d_{(101,100)}, 1 \right]$$

$$= \left[\frac{1 + s_{(2,1)} + s_{(3,1)}}{3}, \frac{1 + s_{(1,2)} + 1 + s_{(3,2)}}{3}, \frac{s_{(1,3)} + s_{(2,3)} + 1}{3}, \frac{s_{(1,4)} + s_{(2,4)} + s_{(3,4)}}{3}, \dots, \frac{s_{(1,100)} + s_{(2,100)} + s_{(3,100)}}{3}, 1 \right] \qquad (1)$$

Our data augmentation technique has a relatively low time overhead for each new image presented to the users; the key to make this scalable approach is to find a large pool of observers who would willingly analyse a relatively small number of images. These already exist in a variety of web-based communities. As a result, a crowd-source experiment was developed to collect information from this source.

For each new image, volunteers are asked to use a SOM (self-organizing map) browser to select images that they consider to be most similar to the stimuli. They must select two to four images before continuing to the next trial. In total volunteers contributed with 20 similar images for each new image. *Figure 1* shows the augmentation interface used by volunteers using textures from one of our databases. It is

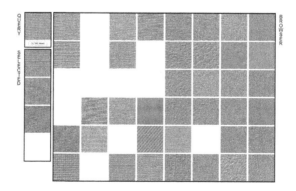

Fig. 1. An example of the interface used to expand the database using a crowd

possible to enrich and scale our database with new similarity information applying the similarity vector formula to each new sample from our crowd-source interface. In the next section we evaluate our browsing environments including our augmentation method.

5   Experimental Evaluation

To evaluate our browser we used *retrieval speed* and *accuracy* as our evaluation metrics. To fully evaluate our method we used two databases: *abstracts* and *texture* images. Both databases have samples that are intrinsically difficult to describe. In addition, abstract images provide the whole range of hue features whilst textures are dense in structural features.

To obtain perceptual similarity information for our databases, we first used our bootstrap method to group 100 samples from each of our two databases (*abstracts* and *textures*). Each database was then extended to 500 samples using our augmentation method with volunteers from the Amazon Mechanical Turk online crowd-source tool.

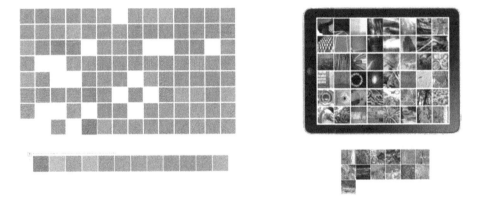

Fig. 2. Stacked SOM browser showing below a node extended. On the right the browser is shown with a different grid size and using abstract images. One example 'stack' of images is shown below each SOM browser.

Three different environments were created to evaluate our databases (a) a *random list* of images as the base benchmark, (b) a flat *SOM list* representing simple similarity browsing, and (c) a *stacked SOM* browser showcasing our navigation browsing environment. The SOM uses a vector quantization method [21] consisting of neurons organised on a regular low-dimensional grid. An N-dimensional weight vector represents each neuron where N is equal to the dimension of the input vectors. The most appealing feature of the SOM is that a neighbourhood relation which dictates the map's topology, connects the neurons to adjacent neurons. This relationship allows us to develop an intuitive method of navigation for our images.

Figure 2 shows the stacked SOM browser resulting from our perceptual similarity data. On clicking one of the thumbnails, the user is taken to the detail level where they can see all member samples of the selected neuron, in distance order from the centroid image whose thumbnail image they clicked on. The grid is also ordered by similarity distance, allowing similar samples to be near each other, facilitating the retrieval of samples. The interface is intuitive to users as it mimics the human organization of the samples.

In our study, 10 observers were asked to find 54 images using the three browsing environments (random, SOM list and Stacked SOM) at three different resolutions sizes (small, medium and large). The sizes represent different display sizes matching mobile, tablet and desktop devices. The samples were randomly chosen from both databases and from different areas of the image space. Each observer had to match images for each combination of environment, database and size.

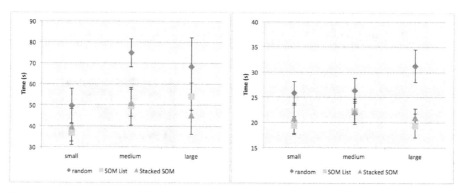

Fig. 3. On the left are shown the average time for each environment using the abstract images database, whilst the results from the texture database are shown on the right

Repeated measures ANOVAs were used to measure the statistical significance of the results (see *Figure 3*). For each database we found that the SOM list and stacked SOM browser outperformed the random list. The results can be summarized as follows for each database:

- *Abstract images*, there is a statistical mean effect of the browsing environment ($p = 0.001$); however, neither size ($p = 0.577$) nor interaction between environment and size ($p = 0.517$) were found to have a significant statistical effect. In addition, contrast revealed that there is no significant statistical difference between the SOM list and the stacked SOM browser ($p = 0.007$) for abstract images.
- *Texture images*, there is a statistical mean effect of the browsing environment ($p = 0.010$) and the size ($p = 0.007$). However, interaction ($p = 0.200$) had no significant statistical effect. In addition, contrast revealed that there is no significant statistical difference between the SOM list and the stacked SOM browser ($p = 0.038$).

As for the accuracy, the repeated measures ANOVA statistical method found that there is no statistical effect between browsing environments and the random lists ($p > 0.05$) as shown on *Figure 4*.

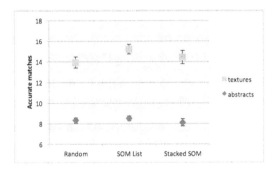

Fig. 4. Accuracy is shown for each browser environment in both databases

6   Conclusions

Our method for intuitive browsing of large image databases revealed that perceptual similarity information is an efficient method of organizing images for human-centric retrieval tasks. Moreover, the database augmentation technique using crowds, instead of lengthy group sessions, enables us to capture perceptual information for large databases with ease. In our evaluation, both of our test environments (SOM list and SOM stacks browser) were more efficient in terms of speed than a continuous list of random images. Subjects were also able to retrieve images with the same accuracy at various display sizes in both our test databases (abstracts and textures).

The flexibility of our proposed method allows it to be extended to any type of database. Furthermore, the grid environment works well with the various different resolutions on devices such as mobiles, tablets or desktop machines. We believe that with the rise of crowd-sourcing tools, online shopping and Internet communities that our browser and augmentation methods can be incorporated into websites, community games and be used with various devices and environments.

References

1. Clarke, A.D.F., Halley, F., Newell, A., Griffin, L., Chantler, M.J.: Perceptual similarity: a texture challenge. In: The 22nd British Machine Vision Conference, Dundee (2011)
2. Chen, J., Bouman, C.A., Dalton, J.: Hirachical Browsing and Search of Large Image Databases. IEEE Transactions on Image Processing, 442–455 (2000)
3. Combs, T.T.A., Bederson, B.B.: Does zooming improve image browsing? In: Proceedings of the Fourth ACM International Conference on Digital Libraries (1999)

4. Faria, F.F., Veloso, A., Almeida, H.M., Valle, E., da Torres, R.S., Gonzales, M.A., Meira Jr., W.: Learning to rank for content-based image retrieval. In: MIR 2010, pp. 285–294 (2010)

5. Heesch, D.: A survey of browsing models for content-based image retrieval. In: Multimedia Tools and Applications, vol. 40, pp. 261–284 (2008)

6. Holmquist, L.E.: Focus+context visualization with flip zooming and the zoom browser. In: CHI 1997 Extended Abstracts on Human Factors in Computer Systems, CHI EA 1997, pp. 263–264. ACM, New York (1997)

7. Krishnamachari, S., Abdel-Mottaleb, M.: Image browsing using hierarchical clustering. In: Proceedings IEEE International Symposium on Computers and Communications, pp. 301–307 (1999)

8. Lowe, D.G.: Perceptual Organization and Visual Recognition. Kluwer Acedemic Publishers, Norwell (1985)

9. Martinez, J., Loisant, E.: Browsing image databases with galois' lattices. In: Proceedings of the 2002 ACM Symposium on Applied Computing, SAC 2002, pp. 791–795. ACM, New York (2002)

10. Pedronette, D.C.G., da Torres, R.S.: Exploring contextual information for image re-ranking. In: CIARP, pp. 514–548 (2010)

11. Perronmin, F., Liu, Y., Renders, J.M.: A family of contextual measures of similarity between distributions with application to image retrieval. In: CVPR, pp. 2358–2365 (2009)

12. Pang, W.: An intuitive texture picker. In: Proceedings of the 14th International Conference on Intelligent User Interfaces, UIU 2010, pp. 365–368. ACM, New York (2010)

13. Plant, W., Schaefer, G.: Visualisation and browsing of image databases. In: Lin, W., Tao, D., Kacprzyk, J., Li, Z., Izquierdo, E., Wang, H. (eds.) Multimedia Analysis, Processing and Communications. SCI, vol. 346, pp. 3–57. Springer, Heidelberg (2011)

14. Rao, A.R., Lohse, G.L.: Identifying high level features of texture perception. CVGIP. Graph. Models Image Processing 55, 218–233 (1993)

15. Rodden, K.: How do people organize their photographs? In: Proceedings of the BCS IRSG Colloquium (1999)

16. Rodden, K., Basalaj, W., Sinclair, D., Wood, K.: Does organization by similarity assist image browsing? In: CHI 2001: Proceedings of the SIGCHI Conference on Human Factors in Computing Systems, pp. 190–197. ACM, New York (2001)

17. Rogowiz, B.E., Frese, T., Smith, J.R., Bouman, C.E., Kalin, E.: Perceptual image similarity experiments. In: SPIE Conference on Human Vision and Electronic Imaging (1998)

18. Schaefer, G.: A next generation browsing environment for large image repositories. In: Multimedia Tools Applications, vol. 47, pp. 105–120 (2010)

19. Schwander, O., Nielsen, F.: Reranking with contextual dissimilarity measures from representational Bregman K-means. In: VISAPP, vol. 1, pp. 118–122 (2010)

20. Strong, G., Gong, M.: Browsing a large collection of community photos based on similarity on GPU. In: Bebis, G., et al. (eds.) ISVC 2008, Part II. LNCS, vol. 5359, pp. 390–399. Springer, Heidelberg (2008)

21. Vesanto, J., Himberg, J., Alhoniemi, E., Parhankangas, J.: Self-organizing map in Matlab: the som toolbox. In: Proceeding of the Matlab DSP Conference, pp. 35–40 (2000)

Irreversibility Analysis of Feature Transform-Based Cancelable Biometrics

Christian Rathgeb and Christoph Busch

da/sec Biometrics and Internet Security Research Group
Hochschule Darmstadt, Darmstadt, Germany
{christian.rathgeb,christoph.busch}@h-da.de

Abstract. Technologies of cancelable biometrics protect biometric data by applying transforms to biometric signals which enable a comparison of biometric templates in the transformed domain. Thereby biometric data is permanently protected, preventing identity fraud and privacy violation. The inversion of transformed biometric signals must not be feasible for potential attackers, i.e. irreversibility must be guaranteed.

In this work we propose a theoretical estimation of the irreversibility of generic cancelable biometric systems. Based on a general formalization of cancelable feature transforms the complexity of reverse engineering is evaluated, quantifying the security provided by the respective approach. In addition, examples are presented which clearly point at the security provided by existing approaches.

Keywords: Biometrics, template protection, cancelable biometrics, irreversibility analysis, feature transforms.

1 Introduction

Most concerns against the common use of biometrics arise from the storage and misuse of biometric data. Cancelable biometrics represent emerging technologies of biometric template protection addressing these concerns and improving public confidence and acceptance of biometrics [1,2]. Cancelable biometrics consist of intentional, repeatable distortions of biometric signals based on transforms which provide a comparison of biometric templates in the transformed domain [3]. In contrast to templates protected by standard encryption algorithms, transformed templates are never decrypted since the comparison of biometric templates is performed in transformed space, which is the very essence of cancelable biometrics. Technologies of cancelable biometrics aim at meeting the two major requirements of biometric information protection (ISO/IEC IS 24745), irreversibility and unlinkability [1]: (1) Irreversibility: knowledge of the protected template can not be used to determine any information about the original biometric sample, while it should be easy to generate the protected template; (2) Unlinkability: different versions of protected biometric templates can be generated based on the same biometric data (renewability), while protected templates should not allow cross-matching (diversity). Focusing on existing approaches two main categories of

R. Wilson et al. (Eds.): CAIP 2013, Part II, LNCS 8048, pp. 177–184, 2013.

cancelable biometrics are distinguished, non-invertible transforms and biometric salting.

Within approaches to non-invertible transforms biometric data is obscured applying non-invertible functions. In order to provide updateable templates parameters of the applied transforms are modified. The advantage of applying non-invertible transforms is that potential impostors are not able to reconstruct the entire biometric data even if transforms are compromised. However, applying non-invertible transforms mostly implies a loss of accuracy. Performance decrease is caused by the fact that transformed biometric templates are difficult to align in order to perform a proper comparison and, in addition, information is reduced. For several approaches these effects have been observed (e.g. in [3,4]). Biometric salting usually denotes transforms of biometric templates which are selected to be invertible. Any invertible transform of biometric feature vector elements represents an approach to biometric salting even if biometric templates have been extracted in a way that it is not feasible to reconstruct the original biometric signal (e.g. in [5]). As a consequence, the parameters of the transform have to be kept secret. In case user-specific transforms are applied, the parameters of the transform (which can be seen as a secret seed [6]) have to be presented at each authentication. Impostors may be able to recover the original biometric template in case transform parameters are compromised. While approaches to biometric salting may maintain the recognition performance of biometric systems non-invertible transforms provide higher security [1].

The contribution of this work which focuses on non-invertible transforms, is the proposal of a generic theoretical analysis of irreversibility provided by cancelable biometric systems. From a general formalization of cancelable biometric transforms we derive the effort of re-constructing biometric data that matches the original biometric data, from the protected template. Proposed estimations can be easily applied in order to quantify the security provided by cancelable biometric systems. Furthermore, theoretical examples are presented which allow conclusions to be drawn about existing approaches.

This paper is organized as follows: Sect. 2 reviews related works on cancelable biometrics. In Sect. 3 cancelable biometrics are analyzed with respect to the provided irreversibility and the resulting performance/security trade-off, and theoretical evaluations are presented. Conclusions are drawn in Sect. 4.

2   Related Work

Ratha *et al.* [3] were the first to introduce the concept of cancelable biometrics applying non-invertible transforms. Several types of transforms for constructing multiple cancelable biometrics from pre-aligned fingerprints and face biometrics have been introduced [3,7] including cartesian transform and functional transform. In further work [4] different techniques to create cancelable iris biometrics have been proposed. The authors suggest four different transforms applied in image and feature domain where only small performance drops are reported. Hämmerle-Uhl *et al.* [8] applied classic transformations suggested in [3] to iris

Table 1. Experimental results of key concepts to cancelable biometric systems

Authors	Characteristic	Performance (in %)
Ratha *et al.* [12]	Fingerprints	FRR 15/ FAR 10^{-4}
Boult *et al.* [11]	Fingerprints	EER $\sim$0.08
Hämmerle-Uhl *et al.* [8]	Iris	EER 1.3
Zuo *et al.* [4]	Iris	FRR 0.005/ FAR 0
Maiorana *et al.* [10]	Online Signatures	EER 10.81

biometrics. Similar to [4] Rathgeb and Uhl [9] suggest to apply row-wise permutations to iris-codes. Maiorana *et al.* [10] apply non-invertible transforms to obtain cancelable templates from online signatures based on linear convolution of sequences. Boult *et al.* [11] proposed cryptographically secure biotokens which they applied to face and fingerprints. Each measured biometric feature is transformed via scaling and translation resulting in a stable and unstable part. Subsequently, the stable part is encrypted and the unstable part is transformed.

Approaches to cancelable biometrics can be classified further with respect to the biometric subsystem, in which transforms are applied. In the signal domain, transformations are either applied to the captured biometric sample (e.g. face image [3]) or to preprocessed biometric signals (e.g. iris texture [8]). Results of key concepts of are summarized in Table 1 and examples of cancelable biometric transforms applied to iris textures are depicted in Fig. 1.

3   Feature Transform-Based Cancelable Biometrics

In this section we provide a generic formalization of cancelable biometric transforms. A biometric input $x \in X^n$, be it a captured biometric sample or a biometric feature vector, consisting of n feature elements (e.g. gray scale values or binary features), is a vector $x = (x_1, x_2, ..., x_n)$ where X is the set of all possible values which a feature element x_i can attain. A cancelable transform T which maps biometric data to another domain is defined as,

$$T : X^n \to X^n. \tag{1}$$

For reasons of simplification we assume a fixed-length representation of biometric data, i.e. the application of T is length-preserving and, thus, does not reduce the size of the biometric input. Based on previous definitions, without loss of generality, a transformed feature vector $T(x)$ is of same size $T(x) = (x'_1, x'_2, ..., x'_n)$, $|x| = |T(x)| = n$ and, again, any x'_i can attain all values of X.

The biometric comparator which is defined as a distance function D estimates the dissimilarity between two feature vectors,

$$D : X^n \times X^n \to [0, 1], \tag{2}$$

that is, two given inputs are mapped to a dissimilarity score in the range $[0, 1]$ where low scores indicate high similarity and vice versa. In order to maintain biometric performance a comparison of two different biometric inputs $x \in X^n$

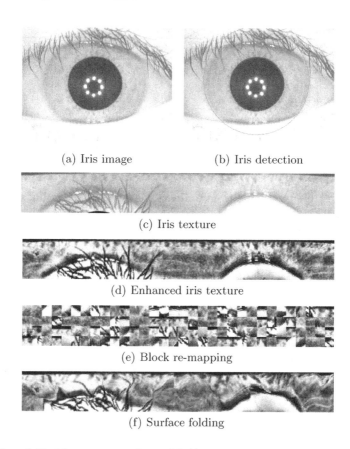

(a) Iris image   (b) Iris detection

(c) Iris texture

(d) Enhanced iris texture

(e) Block re-mapping

(f) Surface folding

Fig. 1. Cancelable biometric transforms (e)-(f) in image domain applied to (d); (a) is taken from the CASIAv3-Interval iris database, http://www.idealtest.org

and $y \in X^n$, should yield the same result in the transformed domain with respect to a predefined decision threshold t, i.e. the following formulas have to apply,

$$D(x,y) > t \Rightarrow D\big(T(x), T(y)\big) > t, \qquad D(x,y) < t \Rightarrow D\big(T(x), T(y)\big) < t. \quad (3)$$

In addition, the comparison of any biometric input $x \in X^n$ shall not be matched with its transformed representation,

$$D\big(x, T(x)\big) > t. \qquad (4)$$

Finally, in order to provide unlinkability of transformed templates (prevent from cross-matching) a comparison of a single biometric input $x \in X^n$, transformed by applying two different cancelable transforms T_1 and T_2, $T_1 \neq T_2$, must not yield successful authentication,

$$D\big(T_1(x), T_2(x)\big) > t. \qquad (5)$$

These generic definitions, which can be derived from previously mentioned requirements on template protection, define the basic properties of any cancelable biometric system. In the following subsections the irreversibility property of a generic cancelable biometric system is analyzed, the resulting trade-off between performance and security is discussed, and according examples are given.

3.1   Irreversibility Analysis

The vast majority of approaches to cancelable biometrics obscure biometric signals in a non-invertible manner, i.e. by definition it is not feasible to reconstruct the original biometric input,

$$\neg \exists\, T^{-1} : X^n \to X^n : T^{-1}\big(T(x)\big) = x. \tag{6}$$

For instance, while a simple permutation of texture blocks is invertible, a remapping of texture blocks (as shown in Fig. 1 (e)) is non-invertible since the transformed image does not contain the entire information of the original image. Based on the fact that a cancelable biometric system can only be operated in case Eq. 3 applies, any transformed biometric input $T(x)$ has to contain enough information to maintain biometric performance which implies,

$$\exists\, T^{-1} : X^n \to X^n : D\Big(x, T^{-1}\big(T(x)\big)\Big) < t. \tag{7}$$

In other words $T(x)$ contains at least $(1-t)\cdot 100$ percent of re-constructable information of x, otherwise $D\big(T(x), T(y)\big) > t$ could apply even though $D(x, y) < t$, violating conditions set in Eq. 3, e.g. $t = 0.35$ defines the Hamming distance-based decision threshold for an iris recognition system, any cancelable iris biometric transform is required to preserve at least 65% of information contained in the enrollment sample.

From an impostor's perspective it is desirable to estimate T^{-1}. Based on Eq. 3 the knowledge of T^{-1} and $T(x)$ can be applied in order to infiltrate any cancelable biometric system. Assume that a potential attacker has stolen $T_1(x)$ of a cancelable biometric database and has calculated T_1^{-1}, the attacker is capable of gaining access to any conventional biometric system or cancelable biometric system utilizing another transform T_2 since,

$$D(x, y) < t \Rightarrow D\Big(T_1^{-1}\big(T_1(x)\big), y\Big) < t \Rightarrow D\Big(T_2\Big(T_1^{-1}\big(T_1(x)\big)\Big), T_2(y)\Big) < t. \tag{8}$$

The security of a cancelable biometric system can be quantified by the effort required to estimate T^{-1} given a transformed biometric input $T(x)$. We assume that a potential impostor does not have any knowledge of the structure of the original biometric input x (which is rather unlikely, but defines an upper bound for the required effort), i.e. T^{-1} has to be guessed. In case $|X|$ is rather small (e.g. for a transformation of a binary feature vector $|X| = 2$) the number of correct inverse transforms increases, i.e. a large feature space aggravates guessing an inverse transform.

In addition, the total number of all possible inverse transforms depends on the amount of different feature elements. The set of different feature elements $\hat{X}$ is

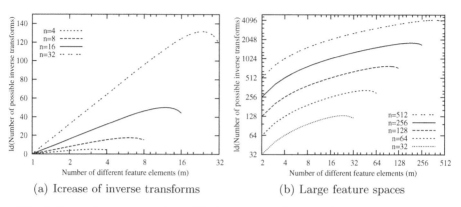

(a) Icrease of inverse transforms   (b) Large feature spaces

Fig. 2. Increasing amount of possible inverse transforms with respect to m and n

defined as, $\hat{X} = \{x_i | x_i \neq x_j : \forall j \neq i\}$ where $j \in \{1, ..., n\}$. The number of elements in $\hat{X}$ is denoted by $|\hat{X}| = m$, where $m \leq n$. In the most likely case $m \ll n$ applies, such that the amount of possible inverse transforms drastically decreases.

More precisely, the theoretical amount of inverse transforms, m^n is decreased by all transforms which take less than m different values into account. The number of possible transforms in which only $m - k$ different values appear, $k < m$ is $\binom{m}{k} = m! / k! \cdot (m - k)!$, such that the function f used to estimated the actual number of inverse transforms is defined recursively,

$$f(m,n) = m^n - \sum_{i=1}^{m-1} \binom{m}{i} \cdot f(i,n) \tag{9}$$

where $f(n,n) = n!$ and, obviously, $f(1,n) = 1$. For instance, for $n = 4$ and $m = 2$ we get $f(2,4) = 2^4 - \binom{2}{1} \cdot f(1,4) = 16 - 2 \cdot 1 = 14$ possible transforms, for $n = 4$ and $m = 3$ we get $f(3,4) = 3^4 - \binom{3}{1} \cdot f(1,4) - \binom{3}{2} \cdot f(2,4) = 81 - 3 \cdot 1 - 3 \cdot 14 = 36$ possible transforms and for $n = 4$ and $m = 4$ we get $f(4,4) = 4! = 24$ possible transforms and so forth. This estimation emphasises on the actual information loss l which is defined as, $l = (n - m)/n$.

3.2   Performance/Security Trade-Off

Based on the implications derived from the previously stated formalizations and estimations a natural trade-off between biometric performance and system security is yielded for generic cancelable biometric systems. On the one hand, in case, transforms turn out to be highly non-invertible information loss is inevitable. On the other hand, information loss implies a degradation of biometric performance. The proposed estimation provides an adequate indicator for the effort of transforming protected biometric data such that the resulting data achieves successful authentication when compared to the original input.

3.3   Evaluations

In addition to the previous mentioned examples, the rapidly increasing number of inverse transforms (calculated based on Eq. 9) is shown in Fig. 2 (a) according to different values of m and n. Fig. 2 (a) depicts that the increasing number of transforms a potential attacker has to try in order to guess a correct inverse transform, clearly security decreases for small values of m, i.e. information loss is high. In Fig. 2 (b) the amount of possible transforms an impostor has to test is evaluated for large values of n (note the logarithmic scales on both axis). For all different values of m and n peaks occur around $m = 3n/4$ (cf. example in 3.1), a further increase of n decreases the number of possible inverse transform. E.g., with respect to the vector $(1, 3, 2, z)$, $m = 4$ would yield $z = 4$, while $m = 3$ would yield $z \in \{1, 2, 3\}$, i.e. three possible combinations, such that $f(3, 4) = 36 > f(4, 4) = 24$. Focusing on existing approaches, m (which highly interrelates with the provided entropy) has to be calculated in order to apply the proposed estimation.

4   Conclusion

In contrast to the vast majorty of existing approaches to cancelable biometrics, in this work emphasis is put on a theoretical analysis of the irreversibility of cancelable biometric transforms. Based on definitions of constituent requirements on template protection basic properties of cancelable biometric systems are formulated and a detailed analysis of irreversibility is proposed.

The presented approach is rather generic and can be adapted to the vast majority of existing approaches. In addition, theoretical examples are presented which give a pointer to the security provided by cancelable biometric systems.

Acknowledgements. This work has been partially supported by the European FP7 FIDELITY project (SEC-2011-284862) and the Center of Applied Security Research Darmstadt.

References

1. Rathgeb, C., Uhl, A.: A survey on biometric cryptosystems and cancelable biometrics. EURASIP Journal on Information Security 2011, 3 (2011)
2. Breebaart, J., Busch, C., Grave, J., Kindt, E.: A reference architecture for biometric template protection based on pseudo identities. In: Proc. Biometrics and Electronic Signatures, Ges. Informatik, pp. 25–38 (2008)
3. Ratha, N., Connell, J., Bolle, R.: Enhancing security and privacy in biometrics-based authentication systems. IBM Systems Journal 40(3), 614–634 (2001)
4. Zuo, J., Ratha, N.K., Connel, J.H.: Cancelable iris biometric. In: Proc. 19th Int'l Conf. on Pattern Recognition, pp. 1–4 (2008)
5. Savvides, M., Kumar, B., Khosla, P.: Cancelable biometric filters for face recognition. In: Proc. 17th Int'l Conf. on Pattern Recognition, vol. 3, pp. 922–925 (2004)
6. Teoh, A.B.J., Kuan, Y.W., Lee, S.: Cancellable biometrics and annotations on biohash. Pattern Recognition 41(6), 2034–2044 (2008)

7. Ratha, N.K., Connell, J.H., Bolle, R.M., Chikkerur, S.: Cancelable biometrics: A case study in fingerprints. In: IEEE Proc. 18th Int'l Conf. on Pattern Recognition, pp. 370–373 (2006)
8. Hämmerle-Uhl, J., Pschernig, E., Uhl, A.: Cancelable iris biometrics using block remapping and image warping. In: Samarati, P., Yung, M., Martinelli, F., Ardagna, C.A. (eds.) ISC 2009. LNCS, vol. 5735, pp. 135–142. Springer, Heidelberg (2009)
9. Rathgeb, C., Uhl, A.: Secure iris recognition based on local intensity variations. In: Campilho, A., Kamel, M. (eds.) ICIAR 2010, Part II. LNCS, vol. 6112, pp. 266–275. Springer, Heidelberg (2010)
10. Maiorana, E., Campisi, P., Fierrez, J., Ortega-Garcia, J., Neri, A.: Cancelable templates for sequence-based biometrics with application to on-line signature recognition. IEEE Transactions on System, Man, and Cybernetics-Part A: Systems and Humans 40(3), 525–538 (2010)
11. Boult, T.: Robust distance measures for face-recognition supporting revocable biometric tokens. In: IEEE Proc. 7th Int'l Conf. on Automatic Face and Gesture Recognition, pp. 560–566 (2006)
12. Ratha, N.K., Connell, J.H., Chikkerur, S.: Generating cancelable fingerprint templates. IEEE Transactions on Pattern Analysis and Machine Intelligence 29(4), 561–572 (2007)

Appendix

Proof (by induction). For all $m, n \in \mathbb{N}$, $n \geq m > 1$, the theoretical amount of possible sequences is defined by $f(m, n)$, where each of the m codewords have to appear at least once within n columns,

$$f(m,n) = m^n - \sum_{i=1}^{m-1} \binom{m}{i} \cdot f(i,n). \tag{10}$$

Base case: $f(1, n) = 1$, and for $m = 2$, the number of possible sequences is $2^n - 2$, i.e. all sequences minus the two sequences where only one codeword occurs,

$$f(2,n) = 2^n - \sum_{i=1}^{1} \binom{2}{i} \cdot f(i,n) = 2^n - \binom{2}{1} \cdot f(1,n) = 2^n - 2.$$

Induction step: $m \to m + 1$, for $m + 1$ the number of all sequences is $(m + 1)^n$, the subtracted number of possible i-element subsets are now of a set containing $m + 1$ elements, and sequences comprising m codewords are subtracted. We get,

$$\begin{aligned}
f(m+1,n) &= (m+1)^n - \binom{m+1}{m} \cdot f(m,n) - \sum_{i=1}^{m-1} \binom{m+1}{i} \cdot f(i,n) \\
&= (m+1)^n - \binom{m+1}{m+1-m} \cdot f(m,n) - \sum_{i=1}^{m-1} \binom{m+1}{i} \cdot f(i,n) \\
&= (m+1)^n - (m+1) \cdot f(m,n) - \sum_{i=1}^{m-1} \binom{m+1}{i} \cdot f(i,n) \\
&= (m+1)^n - \sum_{i=1}^{m} \binom{m+1}{i} \cdot f(i,n)
\end{aligned}$$

Conclusion: (10) is true for all $m, n \in \mathbb{N}$, $n \geq m > 1$.

L∞ Norm Based Solution for Visual Odometry

Mohammed Boulekchour and Nabil Aouf

Department of Informatics and Systems Engineering
Cranfield University, Shrivenham SN6 8LA, United Kingdom
{m.boulekchour,n.aouf}@cranfield.ac.uk

Abstract. In the present work, a novel approach to the monocular visual odometry problem is detailed. More powerful and robust techniques such as convex optimisation with the L∞ norm and the H∞ Filter are adopted. Using monocular systems makes the motion estimation challenging due to the absolute scale ambiguity caused by projective effects. For this, we propose robust tools to estimate both the trajectory of a moving object and the unknown absolute scale ratio between consecutive image pairs. The proposed solution uses as input only images provided by a single camera mounted on the roof of a ground vehicle. Experimental evaluations showed that convex optimisation with the L∞ norm and the robust H∞ Filter clearly outperforms classical methods based on least squares and Levenberg-Marquardt algorithms.

Keywords: L∞ Norm, Monocular Visual Odometry, Triangulation, Convex optimisation, H∞ Filter.

1 Introduction

n vision systems, the camera pose is recovered from the available corresponding points between two views and the camera calibration parameters via the essential matrix which is commonly estimated through the eight-point algorithm [1]. One of the fundamental issues of the monocular visual odometry solution is related to the scale ambiguity due to the projective effects. In [2], I. Estiban et al, presented a successful algorithm relying on a linear computation of the scale ratio between frame pairs. In [3] an algorithm based on minimising the L∞ norm of re-projection error is proposed. For the optimisation task in motion estimation, the traditional bundle adjustment is frequently formulated as a non-linear least squares problem and the 3D point positions are recovered using triangulation via a numerical optimisation method such as Levenberg-Marquardt (LM) [1]. Alternatively, the L∞ norm optimisation, and on contrary to iterative optimisation methods like LM, ensures the global optimum of the error function. Indeed this function, which is geometrically meaningful, is of quasi-convex type that can be efficiently minimised by the bi-section method [4] [5] as a sequence of Second Order Cone Programs (SOCP).

Consequently, we propose to use more robust norms such as the L∞ norm. Our method uses convex optimisation based on an L∞ norm formulation for

R. Wilson et al. (Eds.): CAIP 2013, Part II, LNCS 8048, pp. 185–192, 2013.

the triangulation. Our scenario deals with a calibrated camera taking sequence of images as it moves along an unknown trajectory. The navigation solution proposed in this work can be summarised in the following steps:

- Computing image point tracks (using Harris corner detector and RANSAC).
- Estimating the essential matrix using the normalized 8-point algorithm [1].
- Estimating relative rotations R_i and the translations T_i.
- Optimising the estimated parameters using L$_\infty$ norm-based bundle adjust-
  ment with convex optimisation for the triangulation problem.
- Computing the unknown absolute scale ratio using robust H$_\infty$ filter for the
  motion estimation [2].

2   The L$_\infty$ Motion Estimation

In order to provide a good solution to subsequent bundle adjustment, a need for an efficient optimal triangulation algorithm will be crucial.

2.1   Triangulation with L$_\infty$ Norm

Assume we have m views of a 3D point $\hat{X}$ which maps to image points $x_i = [u_i, v_i]$ via camera matrices P_i, triangulation is to recover the 3D space position of points $\hat{X} = [X, 1]$ such that $x_i = P_i\hat{X}$ for $i = 1, ..., m$. These quantities are related by the projection equations:

$$u_i = \frac{p_i^1 X}{p_i^3 X}; v_i = \frac{p_i^2 X}{p_i^3 X} \tag{1}$$

Where p_i^j denotes the jth row vector of P_i and $X \in \mathbb{R}^3$. Then, the ith error residual may be rewritten as:

$$\varepsilon_i = d(x_i, P_i\hat{X}) \tag{2}$$

Where d denotes image-space Euclidean distances between the measured and the projected points. Our aim is then to recover X which minimises the maximum of this re-projection error across all images. Given the camera matrices $P_i = [R_i|t_i]$ where $R_i = [r_{i1}, r_{i2}, r_{i3}]$, $t_i = [t_{i1}, t_{i2}, t_{i3}]$, $\hat{X} = [X, 1]$ and their corresponding images $x_i = [u_i, v_i]$; the L$_2$ norm of this re-projection error function is given by:

$$f(x) = \left\| u_i - \frac{r_{i1}^\top X + t_{i1}}{r_{i3}^\top X + t_{i3}}, u_i - \frac{r_{i2}^\top X + t_{i2}}{r_{i3}^\top X + t_{i3}} \right\|_2 \tag{3}$$

This problem has been formulated within a quasi-convex optimisation framework in [6]. The optimisation function in (3) is of convex-over-concave and can be shown to be a quasi-convex function in the convex domain $D = \{X | r_{i3}^\top X + t_{i3} > $

0} [6] [7]. By using the L_∞ norm as an alternative, the projection error will be given by:

$$G(X) = \max_i f_i(X) \qquad (4)$$

The function $G(X)$ is still quasi-convex since the point-wise maximum of quasi-convex functions is also quasi-convex [7]. Now our optimisation problem is given by:

$$\min_X \quad \max_{i=1,\ldots,m} \left\| u_i - \frac{r_{i1}^\top X + t_{i1}}{r_{i3}^\top X + t_{i3}}, u_i - \frac{r_{i2}^\top X + t_{i2}}{r_{i3}^\top X + t_{i3}} \right\| \qquad (5)$$
$$\text{subject to} \quad r_{i3}^\top X + t_{i3} > 0, \forall i=1,\ldots,m$$

The residual errors in (2) give the error vector $\varepsilon = (\varepsilon_1, \ldots, \varepsilon_m)^\top$. The estimated scene point is then the vector X that minimises the norm of this error vector. Given an upper bound γ, the inequality $\varepsilon_i \leq \gamma$ defines a set representing a second order cone represented by the first equation in (5). Note that each projection defines a conical surface where the bound is the radius of this cone and the camera centre is its apex. It is worthy as well to mention here that each image measurement adds one conical constraint to (5).

2.2 Solving the Optimisation Problem

For a given value of $\gamma \in \mathbb{R}$ our optimisation problem has become a sequence of SOCP feasibility problems [8]. Therefore, each iteration of the bisection algorithm can be solved by checking its feasibility. If the SOCP problem is feasible then it must be a more optimal solution $\gamma^* \leq \gamma$. However, if the SOCP is infeasible, then the optimal solution must be greater than γ ($\gamma^* > \gamma$). This leads toward using a bisection search to find the minimum value of γ^* for which the optimisation problem is feasible [6]. As a result, the L_∞ norm of ε is defined to be the maximum of $(\varepsilon_1, \ldots, \varepsilon_m)$. The recovered 3D points using convex optimisation are then used in the subsequent bundle adjustment algorithm for exclusively recovering the motion parameters.

3 Robust H_∞ Filter for Scale Estimation

After having robustly estimated the motion of the camera using L_∞ norm-based bundle adjustment, ambiguities in the translation scale still occur. Unlike in the stereo scheme, the monocular visual odometry estimates both the relative motion and the 3D structure up to an unknown scale. Inspired from the work in [2], we assume we have i 3D points $\hat{X}_i$ which maps to image points $\hat{x}_i = [u_i, v_i, 1]^\top$ via the normalized camera matrix $P = [R|T]$ then [1]:

$$n\hat{x}_i = P\hat{X}_i \qquad (6)$$

Where n is the depth factor that takes into account the projection plan ambiguity. This should be chosen to obtain image points and not image plane points [2]. Hence:

$$n\hat{x}_i = [R|T]\hat{X}_i \qquad (7)$$

By introducing the unknown scale S we get:

$$n \begin{bmatrix} u_i \\ v_i \\ 1 \end{bmatrix} = \begin{bmatrix} R_{11} & R_{12} & R_{13} & St_x \\ R_{21} & R_{22} & R_{23} & St_y \\ R_{31} & R_{32} & R_{33} & St_z \end{bmatrix} \hat{X}_i \qquad (8)$$

Hence:

$$nu_i = r^1 X_i + St_x \qquad (9)$$

$$nv_i = r^2 X_i + St_y \qquad (10)$$

$$n = r^3 X_i + St_z \qquad (11)$$

Where r^i denotes the ith row vector of R_i and $\hat{X}_i = [X_i, 1]$. By substituting (11) in (9) to remove the image scale factor n, we get:

$$(r^3 X_i + St_z)u_i = r^1 X_i + St_x \qquad (12)$$

$$(t_z u_i - t_x)S = (r^1 - r^3 u_i)X_i \qquad (13)$$

$$AS = b \qquad (14)$$

Where $A = (t_z u_i - t_x)$ and $b = (r^1 - r^3 u_i)X_i$. In [2], this problem is solved in the least squares sense, by minimising $\|AS - b\|^2$. Here, we propose two new methods such as the Recursive Least Squares (RLS) and more robust one such as the H_∞. To formulate the unknown scale estimation problem in mathematical way, suppose x is the unknown constant, and y is a vector containing noisy measurements. Our aim is to find the best estimation $\hat{x}$ of x. Measurements y must be related to the unknown vector x in a certain combination with the accumulation of some measurement noise; hence we can write [9]:

$$y = Hx + v \qquad (15)$$

Where H is a known observation matrix and v is some additional noise. Thus, for a given estimate $\hat{x}$, the error related is given by:

$$\varepsilon = y - H\hat{x} \qquad (16)$$

Solving this problem in a Least Squares form leads to minimise the sum of squared errors between the elements of the measurements vector and those of the vector given by $H\hat{x}$. Suppose we have k measurements, the cost function is given by:

$$J = \varepsilon_1^2 + \ldots + \varepsilon_k^2$$

$$J = \varepsilon^\top \varepsilon$$

$$J = (y - H\hat{x})^\top (y - H\hat{x})$$

$$J = y^\top y - \hat{x}^\top H^\top y - y^\top H\hat{x} + \hat{x}^\top H^\top H\hat{x} \qquad (17)$$

Minimising J with respect to $\hat{x}$ means computing its partial derivative and setting it to zero:

$$\frac{\partial J}{\partial \hat{x}} = y^{\top}y - H^{\top}y - y^{\top}H + 2\hat{x}^{\top}H^{\top}H = 0 \tag{18}$$

$$\hat{x} = (H^{\top}H)^{-1}H^{\top}y \tag{19}$$

Therefore, the best estimate of $\hat{x}$ in least squares form is given in (19). Note that when H is equal to 1 this solution is simply computing the average of all measurements.

3.1   Recursive Least Squares (RLS) Method

We propose to solve the best value of $\hat{x}$ in a recursive manner. The first method to do this is using Recursive Least Squares (RLS) which is based on continuously estimating $\hat{x}$ while relying on its previous estimate. Thus:

$$y_k = H_k x + v_k \tag{20}$$
$$\hat{x}_k = \hat{x}_{k-1} + K_k(y_k - H_k\hat{x}_{k-1}) \tag{21}$$
$$K_k = P_k H_k^{\top} R_k^{-1} \tag{22}$$

Here K_k is the estimator gain matrix, R_k is the covariance of the noise vector v_k and P_k is the estimation error covariance given by:

$$P_k = (I - K_k H_k)P_{k-1} \tag{23}$$

The initial value of P_0 is depending on our knowledge of $\hat{x}$. The best our knowledge of $\hat{x}$ is, the smallest value for P_0 will be.

3.2   H∞ Filter Method

Least Squares algorithm assumes that the measurements noise is zero-mean and white with known variance. Unfortunately, these assumptions are not always valid. Therefore thinking about using more robust estimator, such as H∞ filter would be a valid option to investigate. The H∞ filter is based on a min-max estimation problem leading to an important difference from Kalman filter where the former is optimal in terms of minimising the L∞-norm between ranges of disturbances. In H∞ filter framework, our model is given by:

$$x_{k+1} = x_k + w_k \tag{24}$$
$$y_k = H x_k + v_k \tag{25}$$

Where w_k and v_k are noise terms with unknown distribution law. We aim, as designed in the filter, to estimate a linear combination of the states given by:

$$z_k = L x_k \tag{26}$$

Where L is a used defined matrix (assumed to be full rank), If we want to directly estimate x_k (as in Kalman filter) then we set $L = I$. The estimate $\hat{z}_k$ is found after minimising the cost function J_1 as $J_1 < \dfrac{1}{\theta}$ where θ is the performance bound defined as:

$$J_1 = \frac{\sum_{k=0}^{N-1} \|z_k - \hat{z}_k\|_{S_k}^2}{\|x_0 - \hat{x}_0\|_{P_0^{-1}}^2 + \sum_{k=0}^{N-1} \left(\|w_k\|_{Q_k^{-1}}^2 - \|v_k\|_{R_k^{-1}}^2 \right)} \tag{27}$$

Where P_0, Q_k, R_k and S_k are chosen matrices with the condition of being symmetric, positive definite. Hence, the min-max problem is finally defined as: $J^* = \min_{\hat{z}_k} \max_{w_k, v_k, x_0} J$. The worst-case is obtained when w_k, v_k and x_0 are chosen to maximize J. The solution then is to find an estimate $\hat{z}_k$ which minimises this maximum. This leads to the filter description below:

$$\begin{aligned}
\overline{S}_k &= L_k^\top S_k L_k \\
K_k &= P_k[I - \theta S_k P_k + H_k^\top R_k^{-1} H_k P_k]^{-1} H_k^\top R_k^{-1} \\
\hat{x}_{k+1} &= \hat{x}_k + K_k(y_k - H_k \hat{x}_{k-1}) \\
P_{k+1} &= P_k[I - \theta S_k P_k + H_k^\top R_k^{-1} H_k P_k]^{-1} + Q_k
\end{aligned} \tag{28}$$

Note that the output and the input of our system are gathered from the vectors A and b in (14) which are constructed using 3D points and their corresponding image projections. Using this, error calculation is given by:

$$e_k = y_k - H x_k \tag{29}$$

Note that vectors A and b in (14) can be built in four different ways to solve the system for S [2]. Choosing the best way depends on the used reference system and where most motion occurs whether in the x-axis direction, the y-axis direction or a combination between them.

4   Experimental Evaluation

The data we employed to test and validate our solution consists of a series of real outdoor datasets collected from a vehicle travelling in urban environment in the city of Karlsruhe [10]. In our experiment we used SeDuMi toolbox for optimisation [11].

4.1   Motion Estimation

Figure 1 shows the estimated trajectories corresponding to more than 200 meters. It is clearly seen here that convex optimisation is able to accurately estimate the motion in comparison with traditional methods based on LM algorithm. This is in accordance with the theory as the estimates should be globally optimal.

By analysing these results, we can confirm that convex optimisation with min-max error scheme is performing better for all the experimental set. This also shows that our approach is very much suitable for estimating the motion in urban environment where high levels of noises of unknown nature are likely to be presented. Clearer comparison is shown in figure 1b. Indeed, the Euclidian distances errors of camera motion estimation demonstrate better accuracy results with convex optimisation approach.

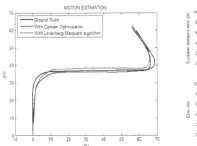 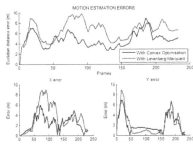

(a) The resulted motion estimates.   (b) Euclidian distance errors.

Fig. 1. Comparison between convex optimisation and LM algorithms for triangulation

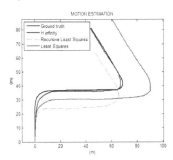 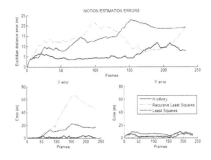

(a) The resulted motion estimates.   (b) Euclidian distance errors.

Fig. 2. Motion estimation after convex optimisation and absolute scale computation using three methods: H_∞, RLS and LS

4.2   Absolute Scale Estimation

Now we show the capability of our H_∞ filter to robustly estimate the frame-to-frame absolute scale in the presence of high level of noise. After having estimated the scale free motion, we now apply our filter on the resulted motion estimates. Figure 2a compares the obtained motion estimates using three methods for absolute scale estimation. The first method is linear using batch least squares (LS) as described in [2] and the two others are using recursive schemes: the H_∞ filter and the Recursive Least Square (RLS). Obtained results show that recursive methods perform well better in comparison with batch least squares method. Figure 2b depicts the comparison of camera motion estimation errors at each successive frame pair. These represent the Euclidian distance errors and errors over the x-axis and y-axis. Results illustrate here that H_∞ filter remarkably outperforms the RLS as well. This is due to its nature of minimising the worst case.

5   Conclusions

We have proposed in this work two novel contributions used to efficiently solve the monocular visual odometry problem. The first of which pertains using convex optimisation with the L_∞ norm in motion estimation for the triangulation part. Our second contribution, which follows on nicely from the first one, is to use an H_∞ filter capable of dealing with system uncertainties for frame to frame absolute scale estimation. Although solutions to the motion estimation problem based on least squares are eligible to provide accurate results, they present limitations that a system based on H_∞ filter is able to overcome. Through several experimental results, we show that our technique clearly outperforms these classical techniques which use the bundle adjustment based on Levenberg-Marquardt algorithm for motion and Least Squares for absolute scale estimations.

References

1. Hartley, R., Zisserman, A.: Multiple View Geometry in Computer Vision, 2nd edn. Cambridge University Press (2004) ISBN: 0521540518
2. Esteban, I., Dorst, L., Dijk, J.: Closed form solution for the scale ambiguity problem in monocular visual odometry. In: Liu, H., Ding, H., Xiong, Z., Zhu, X. (eds.) ICIRA 2010, Part I. LNCS, vol. 6424, pp. 665–679. Springer, Heidelberg (2010)
3. Mitra, K., Chellappa, R.: A Scalable Projective Bundle Adjustment Algorithm using the L_∞ Norm. In: ICVGIP 2008, Washington, DC, USA (2008)
4. Seo, Y., Hartley, R.: Sequential L_∞ norm minimization for triangulation. In: Yagi, Y., Kang, S.B., Kweon, I.S., Zha, H. (eds.) ACCV 2007, Part II. LNCS, vol. 4844, pp. 322–331. Springer, Heidelberg (2007)
5. Hartley, R., Schaffalitzky, F.: L_∞ minimization in geometric reconstruction problems. In: Computer Vision and Pattern Recognition (2004)
6. Hartley, R., Kahl, F.: Optimal algorithms in multiview geometry. In: Yagi, Y., Kang, S.B., Kweon, I.S., Zha, H. (eds.) ACCV 2007, Part I. LNCS, vol. 4843, pp. 13–34. Springer, Heidelberg (2007)
7. Kahl, F.: Multiple view geometry and the L_∞. In: Computer Vision, ICCV 2005, vol. 2, pp. 1002–1009 (2005)
8. Boyd, S., Vandenberghe, L.: Convex Optimization. Cambridge University Press, New York (2004)
9. Simon, D.: Optimal State Estimation: Kalman, H∞, and Non-linear Approaches. Wiley (2006)
10. Geiger, A., Roser, M., Urtasun, R.: Efficient large-scale stereo matching. In: Kimmel, R., Klette, R., Sugimoto, A. (eds.) ACCV 2010, Part I. LNCS, vol. 6492, pp. 25–38. Springer, Heidelberg (2011)
11. Sturm, J.F.: Using SeDuMi 1.02, a MATLAB toolbox for optimization over symmetric cones (1998)

Matching Folded Garments to Unfolded Templates Using Robust Shape Analysis Techniques

Ioannis Mariolis and Sotiris Malassiotis

Information Techologies Institute, Centre for Research & Technology Hellas,
Thessaloniki, Greece
{ymariolis,malasiot}@iti.gr

Abstract. This work presents a novel method performing shape matching of folded garments to unfolded templates, aiming to facilitate unfolding by robotic manipulators. The proposed method incorporates robust shape analysis techniques, estimating point correspondences between contours of folded garments and unfolded templates. The analysis results are also used for estimating the location of the folding axis on the templates and discriminating between different types of garments. The method has been experimentally evaluated using both synthetic and real datasets of folded garments and the produced results indicate the usefulness of the proposed approach.

Keywords: fold detection, partial matching, shape analysis, unfolding.

1 Introduction

Garment unfolding by robotic manipulators is becoming a very active research topic. Perhaps the most challenging aspect of such manipulation is the related vision tasks regarding modeling, reconstruction and recognition of the folded garments. A limited number of existing studies address such tasks, employing different approaches to their realization.

A template matching approach has been adopted in Osawa et al. [1], which focuses on the unfolding of massive laundry. The degree of similarity between templates is calculated by evaluating covariance between images. In Hamajima et al. [2], unfolding is facilitated by the detection of hemlines, which was based on the appearance of shadows. Maitin et al. [3] address robotic handling of towels using stereo cameras for searching geometric cues. A system handling different types of garments by comparing observed contours to simulated ones is presented in Cusumano et al. [4]. In Willimon et al. [5], features such as corners, peak region and continuity of the cloth are used to determine a location and orientation in order to interact with the cloth and unfold or flatten it. The presented studies are aiming to unfold hung garments by locating suitable regrasping points. In a different direction, in Triantafyllou et al. [6], edges and corners of a piece of fabric lying on a table are extracted and classified according to an estimated

R. Wilson et al. (Eds.): CAIP 2013, Part II, LNCS 8048, pp. 193–200, 2013.

topology. The classified corners are used to detect folds and facilitate unfolding by a single manipulator. However, that study addresses folds on convex pieces of fabric instead of real garments.

In this work, in order to facilitate unfolding of real garments lying on a table, matching their contours to unfolded templates is proposed. To the authors' knowledge, this is the first study addressing the problem of matching folded shapes to unfolded templates in general. However, additional challenges are presented to the matching task in case garments are considered, since non-rigid deformations can also be introduced to the folded shapes. The proposed approach considers zero-curvature folds yielding approximately planar configurations for the folded garments. The key assumption of the approach is that the folding axis becomes part of the contour of the folded garment. This assumption is always valid when only a single zero-curvature fold exists. Although the presented method mainly addresses single folds, it can be recursively applied in case of multiple folds.

This paper is organized as follows. In Section 2 the proposed method performing matching of folded shapes is presented, whereas in Section 3 the experimental results are demonstrated. The paper concludes in Section 4.

2   Matching Folded Shapes to Unfolded Templates

According to the proposed method, an image of a folded garment is acquired and its contour is extracted and approximated by a polygon [7]. Then, each side of the simplified polygon is examined as potential folding axis. The examined side is removed from the folded contour and partial matches between the resulted open contour and an unfolded template are detected. Each partial match defines an affine transformation, which is applied to the examined side generating a hypothesis about the folding axis location on the template. In order to test the hypothesis, the template is virtually folded and the resulted polygon is matched to the folded garment using Inner Distance Shape Contexts (IDSC) algorithm [8]. Based on the hypothesis producing the best match, point correspondences between the matched polygons are established, whereas the location of the folding axis on the template is estimated. An overview of the method is depicted in the block diagram of Figure 1.

2.1   Partial Matching

Matching the folded contour to the template is extremely challenging, since the original contour can be fragmented over several pieces after folding. Moreover, some fragments can be missing due to overlaps, whereas fragments belonging to different parts of the original contour can be wrongly connected after folding. The existence of fragmented correspondences indicates that only partial contour matching can be achieved. In order to tackle the above challenges, the approach proposed in Riemenschneider et al. [9], has been adopted.

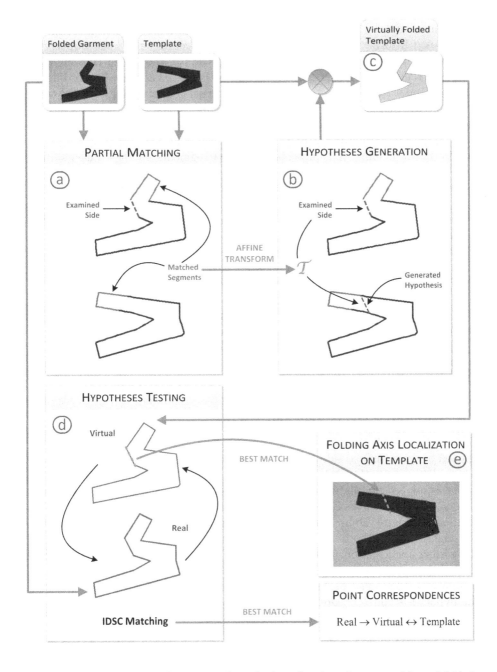

Fig. 1. Block diagram of the proposed method performing shape matching of folded garments

A significant advantage of the adopted matching technique is that it enables efficient aggregation of partial matches, whereas it is also translation and rotation invariant. In this work, a novel strategy for extracting the descriptors is proposed in order to achieve reflection invariance, as well. This property is very useful in case of folding, since some segments of the folded contour may represent reflections of segments belonging to the initial contour. According to the proposed strategy an initial contour orientation is selected for both the template and the folded contour and the descriptors are extracted, whereas a second set of descriptors is extracted by the folded contour after inverting its orientation. Then, partial matching is performed twice. The first time the initial set of descriptors is employed, matching unfolded segments on the contours. The second time the other set of descriptors is employed, matching segments on the template's contour to reflected segments on the folded contour. Each match is assigned with an affinity score As and after thresholding only strong matches remain. As described in [9] similar overlapping contours are merged and the remaining matches are aggregated.

The described matching procedure is repeated for every side of the folded contour. In each repetition, the template contour is matched to the open contour that results after removing the examined side. In Figure 1a the simplified contours of a folded pair of pants and an unfolded template are illustrated. The examined side is denoted by a red dashed line, whereas matched segments are denoted by magenta lines. The proposed method examines all sides and produces a large number of matches, which are not always correct. Each match is used to generate a hypothesis about the location of the folding axis on the template and the validity of the hypothesis is tested.

2.2   Hypothesis Generation and Testing

Each partial match is used to estimate a local affine transformation, which is then applied to the examined side. The new location of the transformed side generates a hypothesis about the position and orientation of the folding axis, with respect to the employed template. A significant advantage of using partial matches to generate the hypotheses is that the method presents insensitivity to local deformations. In Figure 1b an example of a generated hypothesis is illustrated. The red dashed line on the template corresponds to the generated hypothesis about the folding axis location. In this example the presented hypothesis is valid.

Each generated hypothesis is assigned with a confidence score Cs, which is computed as a product of the affinity score As of the match used for generating the hypothesis and Rs score, which is given by:

$$Rs = \begin{cases} e^{-\frac{Lout}{Lin}}, & \text{if } Lin \neq 0 \\ 0, & \text{if } Lin = 0 \end{cases} \tag{1}$$

where $Lout$ denotes the axis length that is predicted to be outside the template and Lin denotes the axis length that is predicted to be inside the template. Both As and Rs, take values in the $[0, 1)$ interval. The higher their values, the greater is the confidence on the validity of a certain hypothesis. In case $Rs = 0$, the hypothesis is automatically rejected.

Different partial matches can result in very similar hypotheses, in case the matches are correct. Therefore, an approach similar to the one used for merging the matched segments is proposed for aggregating the surviving hypotheses. Aggregation is based on a binary image, where each pixel represents a hypothesis. The horizontal image axis corresponds to angles, the vertical axis corresponds to distances and each pixel represents the folding axis of each hypothesis in polar form. Similar hypotheses are expected to create connected regions in this binary image, which can be extracted by connected component analysis. After extracting a component, the associated confidence scores are summed and the result is thresholded. The hypotheses of each component that survives thresholding are merged by calculating a weighted average of the corresponding folding axes. The assigned confidence scores are used as weights for the calculation. By thresholding and aggregating, only a small number of hypotheses proceed to the final testing stage, which is the most computationally intensive.

Each hypothesis determines a folding axis on the template contour. The predicted axis is used to virtually fold the template and a predicted folded contour is generated (Figure 1c). The predicted contour is matched to the folded contour using IDSC and a matching cost is estimated (Figure 1d). IDSC has been selected due to its insensitivity to articulations [8]. The hypothesis resulting to the minimum matching cost is selected as the most probable one. The selected hypothesis is accepted only if the associated matching cost is lower than the one produced when the unfolded template is employed. The IDSC correspondences between the folded garment and the virtual contour of the selected hypothesis are used for matching the folded garment to the unfolded template. The selected hypothesis provides also the location of the folding axis on the template.

In case multiple templates belonging to different garment types are employed, the selected hypothesis can be also used to predict the actual type of the folded garment. Thus, the garments can be recognized while they are folded and the estimated configuration can be exploited for planning the unfolding strategy.

In order to deal with garments presenting multiple folds the presented method can be applied recursively. The method is initially applied and the folding axis resulting to the most severe deformation is detected. Then, the corresponding virtually folded template is employed as new template and the method is reapplied. This procedure can be repeated until the configuration that presents the lowest matching cost is reached.

3   Experimental Evaluation

A series of experiments has been designed in order to assess the effectiveness of the proposed approach. In the first part of the experiments a synthetic dataset is created consisting of virtually folded templates, whereas for the second part of the experiments images of folded garments are employed.

3.1 Synthetic Dataset

The synthetic dataset consists of virtually folded polygons that were extracted from images of real garments. Five different types of garment shapes have been considered: shirts, t-shirts, pants, shorts and skirts. The extracted polygons were sampled by roughly 120 points and for each polygon 60 different folding axes have been randomly selected using pairs of contour points. Then, the polygons have been virtually folded using the selected axes. The original polygons before folding were used as templates.

Matching results are strongly dependent on the accuracy of the folding axis localization. Therefore, the main measure used for the evaluation of the method is the difference between the predicted location of the folding axis and the ground truth. A summary of the results is presented in Table 1, where the mean differences in the polar form parameters $(d\rho, d\theta)$ of the axis location over the 60 folds and the corresponding standard deviations are provided (Table 1, columns 2 and 3). A 0.1 difference in the normalized distances[1] and a 5 degrees difference in the angles have been selected as reasonable thresholds for measuring the rate of correct axis localization (Table 1, column 4). However, there are a few cases where localization failure is not a matter of accuracy, but is caused by accepting erroneous hypotheses that are based on wrong matches. However, as shown in the last column of Table 1, in the total of 300 folding scenarios only 4 such cases occur.

Table 1. Folding axis localization results for 5 garments, using 60 folding scenarios

Type	$d\rho$	$d\theta°$	Localization Rate	Mismatches
Pants	0.019 ± 0.020	1.75 ± 1.82	96.7%	2
Shorts	0.014 ± 0.019	0.96 ± 1.01	96.7%	1
Shirt	0.017 ± 0.018	1.17 ± 1.04	95%	1
T-shirt	0.016 ± 0.022	0.90 ± 1.12	98.3%	0
Skirt	0.014 ± 0.015	1.04 ± 0.91	98.3%	0

3.2 Real Dataset

In the second part of the experiments the method's performance in case of actual folds has been evaluated. Apart from the garment types used in the first part of the experiment, towels were also considered. Two different garments were employed for each type and an image database of 12 garments folded by 4 or 5 different axes has been acquired. In Figure 2 example images of the created database are presented. At first, the garments used for folding were also used as templates and a correct localization rate of 96.7%, with no mismatches, has been achieved for the entire database. Then, different templates have been employed

---

[1] The distance is normalized by dividing with the length of the major axis of the ellipse presenting the same second central moments with the template.

and the correct localization rate dropped to 88.5%, with two mismatches. However, in this case due to the lack of ground truth for the folding axis location on the template, localization failure has been determined subjectively through manual inspection.

In case multiple templates of different garment types were employed, the method was always able to discriminate between them based on the template that generates the hypothesis with the minimum matching cost.

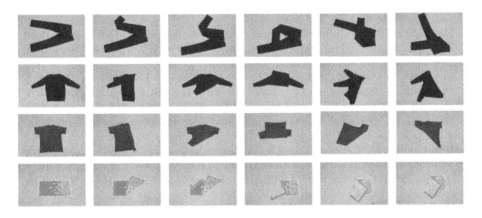

Fig. 2. Example images of the folded garments in the real dataset

4   Conclusion

In this work a method for matching contours of folded garments to unfolded templates in order to facilitate unfolding has been proposed. The method is based on the simple but reasonable assumption that the folding axis becomes part of the outer boundary of the folded garment. Hence, each side of the folded contour is considered to be potential folding axis. Using unfolded templates, hypotheses can be generated about the position and orientation of the axis with respect to these templates. The hypotheses are generated based on partial matching between the template's contour and the folded contour. Using only contour information is an important feature of the proposed method, since when it is applied to real garments it is not affected by their great variation in texture and colour. Another important feature of the proposed method is that matching is performed in both local and global scale using robust techniques that present insensitivity to deformations and articulations, respectively.

The presented experimental evaluation documented high accuracy in folding axis localization. Moreover, the correct localization rate for both virtual and real folds has been about 97%. As expected, this rate is decreased in case different garments are used as templates. Hence, using the estimated correspondences for refining the templates should be investigated. In future work, using the matching results of the proposed method for robotic planning of unfolding will also be investigated.

Acknowledgments. The authors were supported by the EC under project FP7-288553 CloPeMa.

References

1. Osawa, F., Seki, H., Kamiya, Y.: Unfolding of Massive Laundry and Classification Types. J. of Adv. Comp. Intell. and Intell. Inf. 11, 457–463 (2007)
2. Hamajima, K., Kakikura, M.: Planning strategy for task of unfolding clothes. Rob. and Aut. Syst. 32, 145–152 (2000)
3. Maitin-Shepard, J., Cusumano-Towner, M., Lei, J., Abbeel, P.: Cloth Grasp Point Detection based on Multiple-View Geometric Cues with Application to Robotic Towel Folding. In: ICRA, pp. 2308–2315 (2010)
4. Cusumano-Towner, M., Singh, A., Miller, S., O'Brien, J.F., Abbeel, P.: Bringing Clothing into Desired Configurations with Limited Perception. In: ICRA, pp. 3893–3900 (2011)
5. Willimon, B., Birchfield, S., Walker, I.D.: Model for unfolding laundry using interactive perception. In: IROS, pp. 4871–4876. IEEE Press (2011)
6. Triantafyllou, D., Aspragathos, N.A.: A Vision System for the Unfolding of Highly Non-rigid Objects on a Table by One Manipulator. In: Jeschke, S., Liu, H., Schilberg, D. (eds.) ICIRA 2011, Part I. LNCS, vol. 7101, pp. 509–519. Springer, Heidelberg (2011)
7. Hershberger, J., Snoeyink, J.: An o(nlogn) implementation of the douglas-peucker algorithm for line simplification. In: Proceedings of the 10th Annual Symposium on Computational Geometry, SCG 1994, pp. 383–384. ACM, New York (1994)
8. Ling, H., Jacobs, D.W.: Shape classification using the inner-distance. IEEE Trans. Pattern Anal. Mach. Intell. 29, 286–299 (2007)
9. Riemenschneider, H., Donoser, M., Bischof, H.: Using partial edge contour matches for efficient object category localization. In: Daniilidis, K., Maragos, P., Paragios, N. (eds.) ECCV 2010, Part V. LNCS, vol. 6315, pp. 29–42. Springer, Heidelberg (2010)

Multi-scale Image Segmentation Using MSER

Il-Seok Oh[1], Jinseon Lee[2], and Aditi Majumder[3]

[1] Division of Computer Science and Engineering/Center for Advanced Image and Information Technology, Chonbuk National University, South Korea
isoh@chonbuk.ac.kr
[2] Department of Games and Contents, Woosuk University, South Korea
jslee@woosuk.ac.kr
[3] Department of Computer Science, University of California, Irvine, CA
majumder@ics.uci.edu

Abstract. Recently several research works propose image segmentation algorithms using MSER. However they aim at segmenting out specific regions corresponding to user-defined objects. This paper proposes a novel algorithm based on MSER which segments natural images without user intervention and captures multi-scale structure. The algorithm collects MSERs and then partitions whole image plane by redrawing them in specific order. To denoise and smooth the region boundaries, hierarchical morphological operations are developed. To illustrate effectiveness of the algorithm's multi-scale structure, effects of various types of LOD control are shown for image stylization.

Keywords: Multi-scale structure, image segmentation, image stylization.

1 Introduction

Multi-scale image segmentation aims at producing a hierarchical tree-structured partitioning of image plane to analyze scene in a series of scales [1]. This output is useful for LOD (level-of-detail) control in various tasks such as image stylization and medical diagnosis. For example, DeCarlo stylized images by drawing fine details at user-specified salient regions while drawing other parts coarsely [2]. Conventional algorithms construct a multi-scale representation by applying Gaussian convolutions in well-controlled multiple levels. Then a linking process is used which finds corresponding blobs in adjacent scales [1, 3, 4].

Recently several researchers propose image segmentation algorithms inspired by MSER (maximally stable extremal region) technique that produces blobs. The blobs are highly featured regions in the sense that they are stable and salient, and have multi-scale structure [5]. When compared to the algorithms which rely on intensity extrema, MSER is more stable because it stems from stability extrema (as explained in Section 2). This stability of MSER has been shown to be superior to other techniques in performance benchmarking of local features [6].

Donoser proposed a color image segmentation algorithm which requires an user to indicate an ROI (region-of-interest) and uses it to order RGB values [7]. Gui used

R. Wilson et al. (Eds.): CAIP 2013, Part II, LNCS 8048, pp. 201–208, 2013.

MSER as initial segmentation tool for SAR (synthetic aperture radar) images and passed the results to spectral clustering process [8]. One of recent trends in text detection from natural images is to segment candidate text regions using MSER [9]. However the algorithms aim at detecting only specific object regions based on user-defined rules. Additionally they do not address using the multi-scale structure of MSER tree.

In this paper, we propose a new multi-scale image segmentation approach based on MSER. The approach can segment natural images without any user intervention. It accomplishes the segmentation by collecting MSERs and then rearranging them onto the image plane in an appropriate order that would generate desired segmentation of whole image. To denoise and smooth the region boundaries, hierarchical morphological operations and a desirable sequence of them are developed. To illustrate effectiveness of the algorithm's multi-scale structure, effects of various types of LOD control over natural images are shown for image stylization.

The contributions of this paper are as follows:

- Extending blob detection functionality of MSER to segmentation of natural images
- Presenting tree traversal algorithms for image partitioning and boundary smoothing
- Validating the effectiveness of the multi-scale structure by showing various LOD controls for image stylization

2 Algorithms

An ER (extremal region) is defined as a connected component of pixels having higher intensity values than a threshold [5]. Fig. 1 shows a 1-D version of ER at two thresholds t_i and t_j. For an ER at t_i, we can define the stability as an inverse of the ratio of the change in area $\Psi(t_i)$ in Equation (1). The MSER is an ER with local maximum stability, i.e., minimum Ψ. We call this property as *stability extremum*. For example, in Fig. 1, ER at t_i is probable to be MSER while one at t_j is not.

$$\Psi(t_i) = \frac{area_{i-\Delta} - area_{i+\Delta}}{area_i} \tag{1}$$

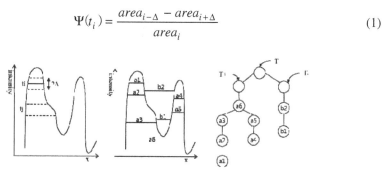

Fig. 1. 1-D illustration of MSER+ and MSER- (from left to right: ER, MSER, component tree)

The MSERs are nested and represented by a component tree shown in Fig. 1. It is usual to perform MSER detection twice, one for bright MSER+ and another one for dark MSER-, pointed by T+ and T- in the component tree, respectively. A collision between MSER+ and MSER- may happen, as exemplified by a_3 and b_2 in Fig. 1.

The nested structure provides multi-scale structure because we can choose any level of details by pruning the tree as we need. This property of MSER is the most powerful one from the perspective of our proposed image segmentation technique. A linear $O(n)$ algorithm to construct the component tree has been developed in [10] where n is the number of pixels. So image segmentation based on MSER can be expected to be very fast. We propose such a technique in the following section.

Fig. 2 shows a natural image taken from Berkeley database [11] and two segmentation results by MSER+ and MSER- trees. The white area indicates being not covered by MSERs.

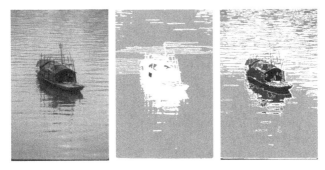

Fig. 2. Natural image and segmentation results (from left to right: original, MSER+, MSER-)

2.1   Image Segmentation Using MSER

Our method is based on post-order traversal of the component tree that partitions the image. The pseudo code is as follows.

Algorithm 1: Image segmentation by post-order traversal of component tree
1.   function postorder(t)
2.   if(t is leaf node) partition(I, t)
3.   else
4.   for(each of children, c of t) postorder(c);
5.   partition(I, t)

In order to segment using MSER+, function call, postorder(T+) is used. For MSER-, postorder(T-) is used. The function partition(I,t) labels the pixels of image I belonging to the node t. Labeling is done only when the pixel has not been labeled before so that child node has a priority over parent node. For the residual parts not covered by MSERs (white area in middle and right images of Fig. 2), assigning special label completes the image segmentation.

Inspection of the segmented images in Fig. 2 shows that MSER+ or MSER- alone cannot segment whole image. This is while MSER+ captures the regions of bright objects, MSER- captures the dark ones. Hence, both the MSER+ and MSER- component trees should be considered to get a complete image segmentation. To achieve this, we present a technique to perform postorder(T+) and postorder(T-) in the following section.

2.2   Core Node-First Traversal

For this, we first define a merger node and core node. A merger node is a node with more than or equal to two children. A *core* node is a node in the component tree that is between a leaf node and the first merger node encountered while moving upwards from the leaf node. In Fig. 1, a_6 is merger while others are core nodes. The regions of core nodes can be regarded as photometrically salient since they have distinctive intensities from surrounding regions and are called core regions. To find the core regions, we present another traversal algorithm which endows priority to the core nodes.

Algorithm 2: Image segmentation by core-first traversal
```
1.       core_first(T+)
2.       core_first(T-)
3.       postorder(T+)
4.       postorder(T-)
5.       function core_first(t)
6.          if(t is leaf node)
7.             repeat
8.                partition(I, t)
9.                prune t     // make it dead
10.               t=parent(t)
11.            until (t is not merger node)
12.         else
13.            for(each of children, c of t) core_first(c)
```

Algorithm 2 applies the function core_first() for each of two trees successively, MSER+ and MSER-. Successive applications of postorder() for two trees complete the segmentation process. The pruned dead node is excluded in the process of postorder(). Fig. 3 shows the core regions thus deciphered from MSER+ and MSER-. For this example image, no collision has occurred between them. Observation over lots of

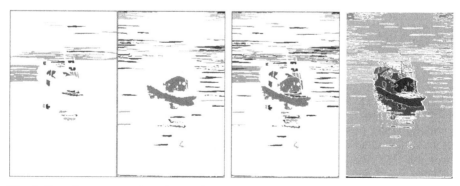

Fig. 3. Core-first segmentation (from left to right: cores from MSER+, cores from MSER-, both, results of Algorithm 2 (Colors encoding node's depth in tree, red (depth 2), green(3), blue(4), ...))

images revealed that no or only a slight collision happens. Currently occupation of the collision zones is determined arbitrarily between MSER+ and MSER- by first-come-first-occupy rule. An elaboration can be made in the future, for example by exploiting edge information as [3].

3   Hierarchical Morphology

Like any other segmentation methods, our method also needs denoising and boundary smoothing. We consider morphological operations for this purpose. However since the segmentation result is not binary but encoded in a hierarchical manner with the child-parent relationship, standard operations are not readily applicable. Hence, we propose the following hierarchical morphology algorithm:

```
Algorithm 3: Child-first dilation
1.      function postorder_dil(t)
2.          if(t is leaf node) dilation(t)
3.          else
4.              for(each of children, c of t) postorder_dil(c)
5.              dilation(t)
6.      function dilation(t)
7.          for(each pixel, p of node t)
8.              for(each pixel, q in S[p])   // S:structuring element
9.                  if(q is ancestor of p) I[q]=I[p]
```

Fig. 4. Hierarchical morphology (The label of underlined pixels should be changed into their children's label)

Fig. 4 explains the above dilation operation on a hierarchical map where node 6 is the parent of node 5 and node 7 is the parent of node 6. This example uses 3*3 structuring element. The net effect of this dilation is the expansion of children region into ancestor regions about one pixel wide.

We can easily change Algorithm 3 into a parent-first version as follows. Here the traversal is changed from post-order to pre-order.

Algorithm 4: Parent-first dilation
1.   function preorder_dil(t)
2.   if(t is leaf node) dilation1(t)
3.   else
4.   dilation1(t)
5.   for(each of children, c of t) preorder_dil(c)
6.   function dilation1(t)
7.   for(each pixel, p of node t)
8.   for(each pixel, q in S[p])
9.   if(p is ancestor of q) I[q]=I[p]

Note that in function dilation1(), the condition of if statement has been changed by reversing roles of p and q. Now we may apply various combinations of C (Child-first) and P (Parent-first) such as C, CC, CP, CPC. Fig. 5 shows effects of CPC scheme. Experiments with many natural images showed that CPC scheme produced good results. So in the remainder of this paper, we will use CPC scheme.

Fig. 5. Results before (left) and after (right) hierarchical morphology

4   Image Tooning Using Multi-scale Structure

The multi-scale structure embedded in the component tree can be used in a variety of purposes. In this section, we use this to present effects of image tooning [12] that uses a simple technique of assigning a region its average color. We illustrate this in Figure 6. The leftmost image is the original image from Berkeley database. Pruning nodes of surfer's body resulted in second image from left in which details disappeared. Right two images were produced by pruning nodes for sky and big waves.

Fig. 6. Styling using multi-scale structures (left: original, the remainings: stylized)

Fig. 7 illustrates the use of the multi-scale structure for a stylization in which core regions and non-core regions are treated differently. Three right images of Fig. 7 are ones where boundaries are emphasized by black lines. The fourth from left was generated by decreasing intensities of non-core regions by multiplying by 0.8 while increasing the intensities of cores by multiplying by 1.2. To accomplish this RGB is first converted into CIELab color space and the multiplication is done for L (luminance) component. Then the image is converted back to RGB. The effect is contrast enhancement between core and non-core. Rightmost is of reverse effect by increasing intensities of non-core regions while decreasing the intensities of cores.

Fig. 7. Contrast enhancing of core regions (from left to right: original, core regions (non-core in white), core 1.0 and non-core 1.0, core 1.2 and non-core 0.8, core 0.8 and non-core 1.2)

5   Concluding Remarks

The paper described an approach to extend MSER's blob detection functionality to the image segmentation. Appropriate traversal algorithms of component trees were presented and evaluated. The results revealed both the possibilities and limitations. We validated the effectiveness of multi-scale structure by showing various LOD control for image tooning. The paper emphasized that this was achieved without multi-level Gaussian smoothing.

In spite of good properties of MSER, some limitations still exist. We summarize them along with important future directions.

- The proposed algorithm has no process for optimizing boundary localization accuracy and smoothness and no use of color information. New formulation of MSER extraction by embedding edge-guided boundary tuning [3], smoothness prior, use of color [13], and contrast enhancement [14] would make MSER to be utilized very successfully as a true image segmentor. The revision should be done in the realm of retaining MSER's nature of seeking stability extrema and multi-scale structure.

- The proposed algorithm is expected to be advantageous in video segmentation due to its nested structure and stability. Constructing and segmenting 3-D volumes $((x,y)$ for position and t for time) using MSERs is an important future work. For this purpose, faster and more robust MSER tracking algorithm proposed in [15] can be used.

Acknowledgement. This research was supported by Basic Science Research Program through the National Research Foundation of Korea(NRF) funded by the Ministry of Education, Science and Technology(2010-0010737).

References

1. Koenderink, J.J.: The structure of images. Biological Cybernetics 50, 363–370 (1984)
2. DeCarlo, D., Santella, A.: Stylization and abstraction of photographs. SIGGRAPH, 769–776 (2002)
3. Chen, J., et al.: Edge-guided multiscale segmentation of satellite multispectral imagery. IEEE Tr. Geoscience and Remote Sensing 50(11), 4513–4520 (2012)
4. Petrovic, A., et al.: Multiresolution segmentation of natural images: from linear to nonlinear scale-space representations. IEEE Tr. Image Processing 13(8), 1104–1114 (2004)
5. Matas, J., et al.: Robust wide baseline stereo from maximally stable extremal regions. In: British Machine Vision Conference, pp. 384–396 (2002)
6. Mikolajczyk, K., et al.: A comparison of affine region detectors. International Journal of Computer Vision 65(1/2), 43–72 (2005)
7. Donoser, M., Bischof, H., Wiltsche, M.: Color blob segmentation by MSER analysis. In: IEEE International Conference on Image Processing, pp. 757–760 (2006)
8. Gui, Y., Zhang, X., Shang, Y.: SAR image segmentation using MSER and improved spectral clustering. EURASIP Journal on Advances in Signal Processing (2012)
9. Shi, C., et al.: Scene text detection using graph model built upon maximally stable extremal regions. Pattern Recognition Letters 34, 107–116 (2013)
10. Nistér, D., Stewénius, H.: Linear time maximally stable extremal regions. In: Forsyth, D., Torr, P., Zisserman, A. (eds.) ECCV 2008, Part II. LNCS, vol. 5303, pp. 183–196. Springer, Heidelberg (2008)
11. Martin, D., et al.: A database of human segmented natural images and its application to evaluating segmentation algorithms and measuring ecological statistics. In: ICCV (2001)
12. Kyprianidis, J.E., et al.: State of the art: a taxonomy of artistic stylization techniques for images and video. IEEE Tr. Visualization and Computer Graphics (2012)
13. Murphy-Chutorian, E., Trivedi, M.: N-tree disjoint-set forests for maximally stable extremal regions. In: British Machine Vision Conference, pp. 739–748 (2006)
14. Majumder, A., Irani, S.: Perception-based contrast enhancement of images. ACM Tr. On Applied Perception 4(3), 1–22 (2007)
15. Donoser, M., Bischof, H.: Efficient maximally stable extremal region (MSER) tracking. In: IEEE International Conference on Computer Vision and Pattern Recognition, pp. 553–560 (2006)

Multi-spectral Material Classification in Landscape Scenes Using Commodity Hardware

Gwyneth Bradbury[1], Kenny Mitchell[2], and Tim Weyrich[1]

[1] University College London
[2] Disney Research

Abstract. We investigate the advantages of a stereo, multi-spectral acquisition system for material classification in ground-level landscape images. Our novel system allows us to acquire high-resolution, multi-spectral stereo pairs using commodity photographic equipment. Given additional spectral information we obtain better classification of vegetation classes than the standard RGB case. We test the system in two modes: splitting the visible spectrum into six bands; and extending the recorded spectrum to near infra-red. Our six-band design is more practical than standard multi-spectral techniques and foliage classification using acquired images compares favourably to using a standard camera.

Keywords: Material classification, multi-spectral imaging, foliage classification.

1 Introduction

Material classification from images is an important task across machine vision and computational photography, with applications in a wide range of domains. One established use is in the classification of foliage and other land cover in remote, multi-spectral, LandSat data. In this case, multi-spectral techniques are key to accurate classification. However, they are also slow, costly and less practical to apply to ground-level image acquisition. Importantly, no mechanism exists to capture multi-spectral images with a hand-held camera in a single shot.

Previously spectral reconstruction has been achieved with a stereo consumer compact camera [11]. Such a system is faster, more practical, and cheaper than a true multi-spectral imaging system and results in six-band, stereo image data. Output is high resolution and images can be captured at high speed or as video.

Several systems are available for multi-spectral 3D imaging spectroscopy for close-range settings [8]. Such implementations often require a laboratory setting making them impractical for use in an uncontrolled setting.

Additionally, spectral multiplexing can be achieved using triple band-pass, dichroic filters, such as those used in Dolby's more recent cinema technology [4].

We explore a novel camera design that aids classification by increasing the spectral information known about a scene. We evaluate the design on the example of foliage classification where, additional colour information is extremely

R. Wilson et al. (Eds.): CAIP 2013, Part II, LNCS 8048, pp. 209–216, 2013.

important. In such a case, multi-spectral image acquisition is expensive and impractical while standard RGB imaging lacks accuracy. We create a single-shot, six-channel, multi-spectral acquisition system. We use this system to address the problem of material classification in ground-level, landscape imagery.

Our system is built using off-the-shelf, commodity hardware: a standard SLR camera, stereo lens and selected filters. We exploit triple band-pass filters extracted from commercial 3D cinema glasses. Each spectral band passed through one of these filters falls into one of the red, green and blue camera response curves. The transmission spectra of the filters themselves are non-overlapping in the visible spectrum, with little information lost between them. This allows capture of additional spectral information in the visible range, splitting the visible spectrum into six bands (rather than the standard three, RGB).

As we demonstrate, foliage classification especially benefits from additional spectral channels due to the very distinct 'spectral footprints' shown by different plant species. Whilst these spectra are dominant in the green region of the visible spectrum (around 550nm), they become much more pronounced in the near infra-red region (upwards of 700nm). This drives us to investigate a second configuration of the system investigating the near infra-red (NIR) spectrum alongside the visible. We implement this using band-pass filters for the regions of the spectrum above and below 720nm. The system allows for reduced error rates for foliage classification in ground-level landscape scenes in both cases.

A significant advantage to our system is its portability and ease-of-use in outdoor environments. As such, we compare our multi-spectral implementation to using a normal SLR camera for image acquisition.

2   Related Work

Multi-spectral imaging typically captures several non-overlapping spectral bands. This non-overlapping property distinguishes it from standard RGB imaging. Whilst hyper-spectral techniques are mostly applied to remote sensing and require specialised equipment such as tunable band-pass filters, multi-spectral systems are both more practical and cheaper, often using exchangeable filters or multiple band-pass filters which can be combined with a standard RGB camera.

Multi-spectral imagery has applications in a number of fields, from recovering the reflectance spectrum at a given point to recording and analysing the Earth's surface vegetation. However, whilst remote sensing systems often incorporate classification methods for analysis of the images, this has been a much lesser used technique for ground-level multi-spectral systems.

2.1   Multi-spectral Image Acquisition

3D multi-spectral image capture can be broadly categorised by three main methods: dispersive elements, diffractive media (diffraction grating) or by filtering with exchangeable or tunable bandpass filters.

Habel et al. [6] present a low-budget solution for multi-spectral photography. By creating a custom lens element using off-the-shelf parts, and with careful calibration, they create a low-cost Computed Tomography Image Spectrometer (CTIS). Whilst this diffraction-grating implementation yields a high spectral resolution in a single shot, the spatial resolution is extremely limited.

Tsuchida and Tanaka [14] present a 6-band, 2-image multi-spectral system. Given the intensity spectrum of the light source, they estimate spectral reflectance using a large-format camera and interference filters. Image capture is slow, using a scanning sensor to scan the scene line by line. This necessitates a static scene and although high resolution is achieved, the system is costly and impractical for dynamic scenes.

Fyffe et al. [4] demonstrate the use of dichroic, triple-band-pass, interference filters for spectral multiplexing. By altering the light sources for a scene, they obtain dense surface normals and surface colour reflectance from a single shot. This is easily extended to dynamic scenes but is not practical for outdoor scenes where the lighting may not be modified. The use of a beam splitter means that the problem of correspondence between shots is avoided, assuming a negligible disparity.

Finally, spectral reconstruction can be achieved with a stereo consumer compact camera as shown by Shrestha et al. [11]. They present a stereo, multi-spectral configuration focusing on spectral reconstruction rather than the stereo implications of the system.

We take a similar approach, using a stereo lens with tri-band-pass interference filters, as well as investigating the visible and NIR case.

2.2   Imaging for Classification of Vegetation

In the vast majority of vegetation classification tasks, hyper-spectral images are captured remotely and processed using texture filtering across the spectral bands. As plant species have unique spectral footprints in both the green and NIR parts of the spectrum, spectral images which focus on these ranges are often used. Hernandez et al. [7], for example, find that red and short-wave infra-red bands produce the best classification results in satellite imagery.

Also in remote sensing, Yu et al. [16] attain a detailed, object-based classification of simple vegetation classes using images with a high spatial resolution. In this case, blue, green, red and NIR comprise the spectral features used for classification along with band-ratio and spectral-derivative features and other textural and topographic features.

Shading and atmospheric interference effects can be very detrimental to vegetation classification, leading to high variation of the spectral distribution within a class, which cannot be modelled linearly [16]. Hue, however, is dependent on the spectral range but independent of illumination intensity changes [10], making it an important feature for classification [16].

Tanser and Palmer [9] compute a spectral reconstruction of vegetation classes based on ten spectral bands using mean, variation and co-variance parameters, and comparing with a tri-band approach. Their results show that, although more detailed spectral information considerably improves the classification result, it is still insufficient for high quality classification. They then use texture, particularly a Moving Standard Deviation Index, to supplement the classification.

At ground level, laser scanners can be used to create 3D maps of an environment [15] (with particular application in simultaneous localisation and mapping problems) which can be used for classification. Similarly, a ground-level survey can be carried out. This can be more accurate, but is also incredibly inefficient. Other ground-level approaches involving multi-spectral cameras are often impractical because of the less-portable nature of these systems and the need to take many sequential, filtered images of a potentially moving scene.

3   System Design and Image Acquisition

We build two systems with the following hardware. Both feature a twin-aperture, stereo lens (see Figure 1), then each of the following combinations are used: complementary triple band-pass filters (Figure 1) and standard DSLR; or 730 nm IR long-pass filter and 400-720 nm band-pass filter and an IR-modified DSLR.

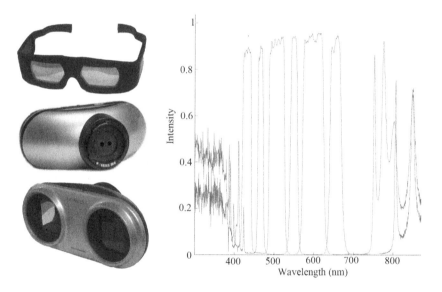

Fig. 1. Commercial stereo cinema glasses using dichroic, tri-band-pass, interference filters; twin-aperture stereo lens (left) and corresponding transmission spectra (right)

Filtering the images implies a significant proportion of the available light is lost. This means a compromise must be made between a fast shutter speed, narrow aperture and low sensor gain. Faster shutter speeds ensure that motion is frozen whilst a narrow aperture ensures that the depth of field is large enough to capture the scene. Subr et al. [12] investigate the effects that a low light budget can have on stereo reconstruction, finding that gain, exposure time and aperture restrictions lead to significant degradation of the resulting depth image but that often a compromise can be reached, determined by the type of scene.

For landscape scenes, we use a narrow aperture to obtain the greatest depth of field; however, as the filters block a significant proportion of available light, we find this is limited to f/11. We use an ISO of 1250 and a tripod to compensate for any camera shake caused by the shutter speeds required – 1/40 s to 1/60 s.

The stereo facility of the lens is both a drawback and benefit to our system. Whilst stereo matching in image pairs aquired under varying illumination is more challenging, we also gain information about the depth of points in the scene, which augments classification. We rectify and register the images based on SURF features. This then allows us to compute good disparity maps between filtered pairs of images using LibELAS [5]. In our implementation, ordinary SURF features perform equally as well as alternative approaches such as multi-spectral SIFT features [13,3].

We find disparity maps more difficult to compute in the tri-band-filtered case due to the different spectra observed by each image. This leads us to filter only one image, using a neutral density filter (ND4) for the unfiltered image to ensure appropriate exposure. The overlap between observed spectra then allows better correlation between images and so depth recovery is more successful, retaining additional spectral information.

We find that radiometric distortion is generally less of a problem for feature matching in the visible-NIR case and that good depth maps can be recovered simply using SURF features for rectification followed by LibELAS [5].

4   Supervised Classification in Six-Band, Stereo Images

The system aims to aid classification by increasing the spectral information known about a scene. Using the raw captured image pairs, we label several distinct classes in the RGB image and apply Random Forest classification [2].

We label each image with the classes: grass (two types), tree (two types), sky, and man-made, extracting colour and texture features for classification.

Previous work [1] has shown that colour, hue in particular, and entropy are the most successful features for vegetation classification in landscape images. Hence we use the 6-colour RGB bands and their transformed values in HSV space (Hue, Saturation and Value) along with local entropy. Colour features alone are not sufficient for material classification [9] and so we apply 2-dimensional discrete stationary wavelet response filters to enhance the classifier. As texture features change with the scale of the material, we also use the disparity map as a feature.

5   Results

We capture sets of 30 images for each mode of the system (tri-band and infrared filtering), under otherwise identical conditions. Images cover a park landscape in summer with varied vegetation.

We evaluate our system on the task of foliage classification first testing the classifier on monocular image data using the visible-spectrum images from each dataset. This gives us a point of comparison for the datasets we generate.

Table 1. Classification error results, showing classification error as different inputs are used with either pixel-based or super-pixel classification (right image filtered as detailed)

Classifier input data	Tri-band Pixel	Tri-band Super-pixel	Infrared Pixel	Infrared Super-pixel
Right image	**0.0233**	0.1967	0.0391	0.2786
Left image	**0.0240**	0.1977	0.0384	0.2790
Right image and disparity	**0.0212**	0.1966	0.0375	0.2789
Left image and disparity	**0.0315**	0.2228	0.0418	0.2594
Right and left images	**0.0198**	0.1988	0.0227	0.2426
Right and left images with disparity	**0.0199**	0.1941	0.0221	0.2419

In both implementations, the left stereo image always represent the visible spectrum whereas the right image is filtered. We rely on relevance detection in the random forest implementation and comparing classification error with different combinations of left and right images and disparity as input.

We also compare using a pixel classifier to a super-pixel classifier, noting that the wavelet features we use incorporate a sense of spatial extent and that the texture features may render super-pixels superfluous.

Table 1 details the error achieved against the data set used. The lowest error occurs when both images from the multi-spectral pair are used. Use of the disparity map has little influence, and using tri-band filters to split the visible spectrum results in lower error than extending the spectrum to NIR light.

6   Discussion

There are several conclusions we can draw from our results.

- Imaging with tri-band filtering performs better than imaging over the visible and NIR parts of the spectrum, despite the strong NIR reflectance of foliage. This implementation gives us only one effective additional colour channel so the information gained is lower then the tri-band case.
- Pixel-based classification performs better than super-pixel classification – probably because texture filters already contain some spatial information which makes super-pixels unnecessary.
- The most favourable results are obtained using a filtered pair of images in the visible spectrum, that is, splitting the visible spectrum into six bands rather than the standard three.

Given that vegetation has a pronounced footprint in the NIR spectrum, it is surprising that the visible-NIR test case does not out-perform the tri-band-filtered case. The most likely explanation is that the NIR images, due to the sensitivity of the image sensor, yield only one additional grey-scale channel and as such there is limited information gained in this case. In both cases, however, it is clear that additional spectral information improves the classification result.

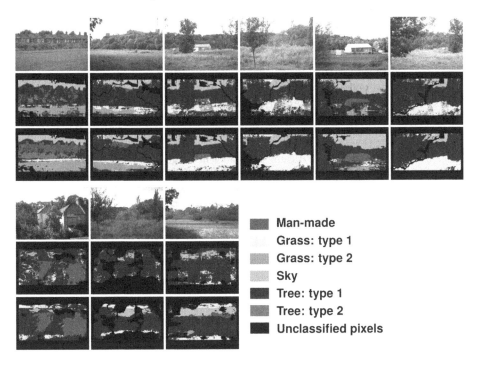

Fig. 2. Sample classification results showing visible improvement when image pairs are used for classification. Top, tri-band filtering results; bottom, visible-infrared filtering results. For each set, from top: original unfiltered image; classification using unfiltered images only; classification using both images from the pair.

Identifiable sources of error in the experiments include the following: predefined classes covered a large number of potential sub-classes such as tree species; and man-made structures such as paths and houses were grouped together. Also, data we acquire samples only a single type of landscape and so there is a possibility that the random forest is over-trained on this data-set and would not produce good results for any other environment.

7   Conclusion

We conclude that our novel, multi-spectral system leads to improved foliage recognition in ground-level landscape imagery whilst being more practical and lower cost than current alternatives, and we claim that additional spectral data improves material classification in landscapes.

Although the incorporation of depth information does marginally reduce classification error, the biggest improvement is seen when multi-spectral images are used. We suggest then, that colour features still have more of an impact than texture features in classification of different foliages classes but note that further testing would be required in order to validate this.

References

1. Bradbury, G.: Material Classification in Outdoor Scenes. MSc Computer Graphics, Vision and Imaging. University College London (2010)
2. Breiman, L.: Random Forests. Machine Lerarning 45(1), 29 (2001)
3. Brown, M., Susstrunk, S.: Multi-spectral SIFT for Scene Category Recognition. In: Computer Vision and Pattern Recognition (CVPR 2011), pp. 177–184 (2011)
4. Fyffe, G.: Single-Shot Photometric Stereo by Spectral Multiplexing. Proceedings ACM SIGGRAPH Asia Sketches, 2–7 (2010)
5. Geiger, A., Roser, M., Urtasun, R.: Efficient large-scale stereo matching. In: Kimmel, R., Klette, R., Sugimoto, A. (eds.) ACCV 2010, Part I. LNCS, vol. 6492, pp. 25–38. Springer, Heidelberg (2011)
6. Habel, R., Kudenov, M., Wimmer, M.: Practical spectral photography. Computer Graphics Forum (Proceedings EUROGRAPHICS 2012) 31(2), 449–458 (2012)
7. Hernandez-Stefanoni, L., Ponce-Hernandez, R.: Mapping the Spatial Distribution of Plant Diversity Indices in a Tropical Forest Using Multi-Spectral Satellite Image Classification and Field Measurements. Biodiversity and Conservation 13(14), 2599–2621 (2004)
8. Kim, M., Harvey, T., Kittle, D., Rushmeier, H., Dorsey, J., Prum, R., Brady, D.: 3D Imaging Spectroscopy for Measuring Hyperspectral Patterns on Solid Objects. ACM Trans. on Graphics (Proc. SIGGRAPH) 31(4), 38:1–38:11 (2012)
9. Palmer, A., Tanser, F.: Vegetation Mapping of the Great Fish River Basin, South Africa: Integrating Spatial and Multi-Spectral Remote Sensing Techniques, pp. 197–204 (2000)
10. Qi, Z.: Extraction of Spectral Reflectance Images From Multi-Spectral Images by the HIS Transformation Model. International Journal of Remote Sensing 17, 3467–3475 (1996)
11. Shrestha, R., Hardeberg, J.Y., Mansouri, A.: One-Shot Multispectral Color Imaging with a Stereo Camera. In: Digital Photography VII. Proceedings of the SPIE, vol. 7876, pp. 787609–787609–11(2011)
12. Subr, K., Bradbury, G., Kautz, J.: Binocular-Stereo Photography Under a Light-Budget. In: Proceedings of CVMP 2012, pp. 1–10 (2012)
13. Susstrunk, S., Firmenich, D., Brown, M.: Multispectral Interest Points for RGB-NIR Image Registration. In: International Conference on Image Processing (ICIP 2011), pp. 4–7 (2011)
14. Tsuchida, M., Yano, K., Tanaka, H.T.: Development of a High-Definition and Multispectral Image Capturing System for Digital Archiving of Early Modern Tapestries of Kyoto Gion Festival. In: 2010 20th International Conference on Pattern Recognition, pp. 2828–2831 (August 2010)
15. Wolf, D., Howard, A., Sukhatme, G.: Towards Geometric 3D Mapping of Outdoor Environments Using Mobile Robots. In: 2005 IEEE/RSJ International Conference on Intelligent Robots and Systems, pp. 1507–1512 (2005)
16. Yu, Q., Gong, P., Clinton, N., Biging, G., Kelly, M., Schirokauer, D.: Object-based Detailed Vegetation Classification with Airborne High Spatial Resolution Remote Sensing Imagery. Photogrammetric Engineering and Remote sensing 72(7), 799–811 (2006)

Multispectral Stereo Image Correspondence

Marcelo D. Pistarelli[1], Angel D. Sappa[2], and Ricardo Toledo[2]

[1] Departamento de Sistemas e Informática
Facultad de Cs. Exactas, Ingeniería y Agrimensura
Universidad Nacional de Rosario, Rosario, Argentina
[2] Computer Vision Center, Edifici O, Campus UAB,
08193 Bellaterra, Barcelona, Spain
mpistare@fceia.unr.edu.ar, {asappa,ricard}@cvc.uab.es

Abstract. This paper presents a novel multispectral stereo image correspondence approach. It is evaluated using a stereo rig constructed with a visible spectrum camera and a long wave infrared spectrum camera. The novelty of the proposed approach lies on the usage of Hough space as a correspondence search domain. In this way it avoids searching for correspondence in the original multispectral image domains, where information is low correlated, and a common domain is used. The proposed approach is intended to be used in outdoor urban scenarios, where images contain large amount of edges. These edges are used as distinctive characteristics for the matching in the Hough space. Experimental results are provided showing the validity of the proposed approach.

1 Introduction

Multispectral image processing has been largely studied by the remote sensing community where images from different spectral bands are generally used to extract information related with the characteristics of the materials defining the different regions of the image (e.g., vegetation, water, etc.). The stereo matching problem, although out of the main scope of remote sensing community, has been also tackled in the context of remote sensing [1].

Recent advances in multispectral imaging sensors have opened new opportunities to the research community to tackle classical computer vision problems, which are not related with the remote sensing field. Actually, nowadays multispectral applications can be found in: video surveillance (e.g., [2], [3]), driver assistance [4], energy saving [5], fire detection, etc. In most of these applications finding correspondences, or matching, between features observed in the different images is the first problem to be tackled. Feature matching is a common task in both the image registration and the stereovision problems. In both cases feature matching has been tackled for the case where the images belong to the same spectral band. In general, the approaches in the literature are based on key points detection and their corresponding description. The descriptions of such key points are later on used for finding the correspondences (e.g., [6], [7]). This kind of scheme has been recently used for finding correspondences in the

R. Wilson et al. (Eds.): CAIP 2013, Part II, LNCS 8048, pp. 217–224, 2013.

multispectral domain (e.g., [8] and [9]), but due to the nonlinear relationship between pixel intensities the matching ratio remains low and the usage of scene prior is needed (e.g., [10], [11]).

Focussing on the stereo matching problem, the current work proposes a novel approach that formulates the multispectral matching problem by representing the given image pair in a common space (Hough space). Actually, in this common space not all the image pixels are represented but just those ones corresponding to the edges extracted with the Canny algorithm [12]. The proposed approach consists of three stages. First, the edges from the multispectral images are extracted using an adaptive threshold strategy that allows to generate similar representations from the image pair. Then, the edges are represented in the common space using the classical Hough transform [13] that identifies straight lines. Finally, the most representative lines are extracted and their parameters used as descriptors to find the matchings. The proposed approach has been evaluated using a multispectral stereo rig constructed with a Long-Wave Infrared (LWIR) camera and a Visible Spectrum (VS) camera.

The manuscript is organized as follow. State of the art on multispectral stereo image correspondence problem is introduced in Section 2. The proposed approach is then presented in Section 3. Experimental results are provided in Section 4. Finally, conclusions are given in Section 5.

2   Related Work

Stereo vision problem involves different tasks, from the synchronized acquisition of a pair of images, till dense disparity maps and 3D representations. In between, tasks such as camera calibration, image rectification, correspondence search, and triangulation should be tackled. There is a large literature on all these topics (e.g., [14],[15]) when the cameras in the stereo rig work at the same spectral band. However, both the coexistence of cameras working at different spectral band and the needs to extract 3D information from such a multispectral devices require some reformulation in the pipeline of tasks mentioned above. In the current work a particular case where the cameras in the stereo rig work at the visible and infrared spectrum is considered. From the list of tasks mentioned above, we just consider the correspondence search problem assuming the multispectral stereo pair is already calibrated and rectified. Hence, epipolar lines correspond to the same rows in the different pair of images.

Finding correspondences in this multispectral scheme is a difficult task that has been solved in the literature using different strategies. For instance, the lack of overlap between VS (0.4-0.7 μm) and LWIR (9-15 μm) spectrum has been tackled in [16] through a cost function based on mutual information that is enriched with gradient information in a scale space representation. The usage of this cost function allows to obtain sparse stereo representations that are later on filled in with scene prior information generating a dense disparity map [11].

On the contrary to the previous approaches, the authors in [3] constraint the matching to those regions that contain human body silhouettes. Since their contribution is aimed at person tracking, some assumptions are applied, for example

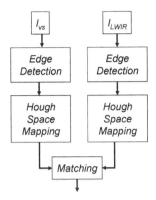

Fig. 1. Pipeline of the proposed approach (I_{VS}: visible spectum image; I_{LWIR}: long-wave infrared image)

a foreground segmentation for disclosing possible human shapes, which are corresponded by maximizing mutual information. Although, these assumptions are valid, they restrict the scope of applications to those scenarios containing pedestrians. Furthermore, it should be noted that in [3] only 3D information on those pixels defining the surface of the pedestrians body is extracted.

Inspired by the classical SIFT algorithm [6] a descriptor based on the edge histogram is proposed in [8] to find correspondences between VS and LWIR images. The proposed edge oriented histogram is then used to describe points of interest detected in a scale space representation. A scale restriction criteria is used in [9] to reduce the amount of mismatching of SIFT when it is adopted to tackle the VS and NIR correspondence case. In this particular multispectral case the spectral bands of the pair of images are nearer than in the VS-LWIR case, hence the number of right matching is considerably higher in this case.

3   Proposed Method

We propose a novel approach for finding correspondences between multispectral image pairs. Actually, only edges are considered, by representing them in a common space (Hough space). The proposed approach consists of three stages (see the pipeline in Fig. 1): *i*) edge detection; *ii*) Hough space mapping; *iii*) matching; these stages are detailed below. A case study (see Fig. 2) is used to illustrate the three stages.

3.1   Edge Detection

Since the proposed approach is intended for finding correspondences in multispectral stereo images from urban scenarios, man-made structures are the predominant features in the given images. The shape of these structures can be in part captured through an edge detector algorithm. In the current work the

Fig. 2. Multispectral stereo pair: (*left*) I_{VS} image; (*right*) I_{LWIR} image

Canny algorithm [12] is used and a scheme that automatically adapt the algorithm' thresholds is considered. This scheme allows to generate images with a similar amount of edges. Figure 3 shows the binary images $B(x, y)$ of edges extracted from a multispectral pair using the same algorithm setup in both cases. It can bee appreciated that there is a difference on the amount of extracted edges, which at the end will affect their representation in the Hough space.

Fig. 3. Edges extracted using the Canny algorithm with the same parameters in both cases: (*left*) VS image, (*right*) LWIR image

In order to diminish the difference in the amount of edges mentioned above an iterative approach is performed over one of the images in order to get a similar amount of edges in both cases. During the iterations the Canny's thresholds are updated. Finally, in order to reduce the amount of edges that do not contribute to the proposed scheme, which consist in detecting the most representative geometric features in the Hough space, edges defined by less than T_{ha} pixels are removed (in the current implementation $T_{ha} = 20$). Results from this adaptive threshold and short edge filtering are presented in Fig. 4. Although the amount of edges in this pair of images are different they look more similar than the one presented in Fig. 3.

Fig. 4. (*left*) Edges for the VS image with a user defined threshold. (*right*) Edges for the LWIR image extracted from a the Canny algorithm with an adaptive threshold

3.2   Hough Space Mapping

The Hough transform [13] for a binary image $B(x, y)$, defined as:

$$H(\theta, \rho) = \int_{-\infty}^{\infty} \int_{-\infty}^{\infty} B(x, y)\delta(\rho - x\cos\theta - y\sin\theta)dxdy \qquad (1)$$

transform every pixel from B into a sine wave $\rho = x\cos\theta - y\sin\theta$. Figure 5 shows an illustration of the mapping of two image points to the Hough space. The intersection point in the Hough space corresponds to the parameters of the straight line passing through (x, y), (u, v) in the image space.

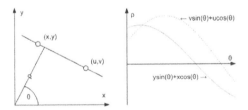

Fig. 5. Mapping of two image points to the Hough space

By applying the Hough transform to all the pixels defining the edges extracted in the previous stage we obtain a set of sine wave overlapped in the Hough space. Hence, by accumulating these mappings into a $N \times M$ matrix, the most representative ones can be easily identified just by looking at the cells with larger amounts of votes. Figure 6 depicts the Hough representations corresponding to the edges presented in Fig. 4.

3.3   Matching

The Hough representations obtained above can be understood as the feature description space that will be used for finding the matchings between the multispectral images. Essentially, this stage consists of matching points from the

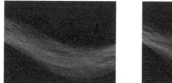 

Fig. 6. Hough representations of edges from Fig. 4 (*left*) and edges from Fig. 4 (*right*)

Hough representations that have large amount of votes and the distance between them is smaller that a user defined threshold. Additionally, a non-maximum suppression algorithm is used to avoid wrong associations. Once a matching between two points in the Hough spaces has been found (a matching is accepted when a similar orientation in a neighborhood is found, assuming a disparity value of $\pm\Delta$) the corresponding edge points in the image spaces are extracted by finding the intersections between epipolar lines and straight lines from Hough. Note that since the stereo pair is rectified, epipolar lines correspond with horizontal lines in the image pair. Figure 7 presents the matchings obtained in the multispectral pair used as a case study through the previous sections. Other more elaborated strategies for finding matchings could be used, for instance dynamic programming [17] or graph cut [18] based approaches, which would improve the results but increasing considerably the processing time.

Fig. 7. Correspondences (5163 points) obtained with the proposed approach

4   Experimental Results

The proposed approach has been evaluated with a set of rectified multispectral stereo images [8] showing the validity of the proposed approach. In all the cases the number of matchings obtained with the proposed approach are considerable larger than those presented in [8]. Note that points matched with the proposed approach lie over image edges, which is one of the difference with respect to previous approaches where key points are used for finding correspondences, instead of higher level features. Figure 8 shows two pairs of multispectral images with the points matched with the proposed approach. On average, 100 times more points are correctly matched with the proposed approach than [8] when the same data set is considered (the data set contains 100 pairs of multispectral images and is available through the following link: www.cvc.uab.es/adas/projects/simeve).

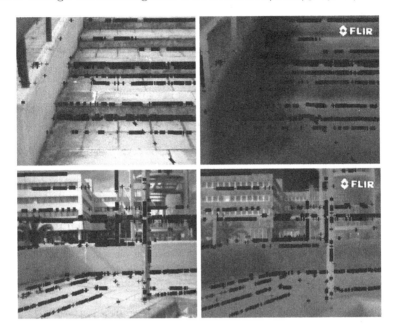

Fig. 8. Correspondences obtained with the proposed approach: (*top*) 5447 points; (*bottom*) 4512 points

5   Conclusions

This paper presents a novel approach that overcome the problem of finding feature point correspondences when images from different spectral bands are considered. The proposed solution consists in representing the given images in a common space. It is mainly intended to tackle outdoor urban scenarios, where straight lines are usually the most predominant shape characteristics. Future work will be focussed on the usage of a scale space scheme to increase the number of correct matchings as well as on the usage of the obtained correspondences towards a dense disparity map.

Acknowledgments. This work has been partially supported by the Spanish Government under Research Project TIN2011-25606.

References

1. Felicísimo, A., Cuartero, A.: Methodological proposal for multispectral stereo matching. IEEE Trans. on Geoscience and Remote Sensing 44, 2534–2538 (2006)
2. Leykin, A., Hammoud, R.: Pedestrian tracking by fusion of thermal-visible surveillance videos. Machine Vision and Applications 21, 587–595 (2010)

3. Krotosky, S., Trivedi, M.: On color-, infrared-, and multimodal-stereo approaches to pedestrian detection. IEEE Trans. on Intelligent Transportation Systems 8, 619–629 (2007)
4. Jung, S., Eledath, J., Johansson, S., Mathevon, V.: Egomotion estimation in monocular infra-red image sequence for night vision applications. In: IEEE Workshop on Applications of Computer Vision, Austin, TX, USA, February 20-21 (2007)
5. Prakash, S., Lee, P.Y., Caelli, T.: 3d mapping of surface temperature using thermal stereo. In: Int'l Conf. on Control, Automation, Robotics and Vision, pp. 1–4 (2006)
6. Lowe, D.: Object recognition from local scale-invariant features. In: IEEE Conference on Computer Vision, Kerkyra, Greece, pp. 1150–1157 (1999)
7. Bay, H., Tuytelaars, T., Van Gool, L.: SURF: Speeded up robust features. In: Leonardis, A., Bischof, H., Pinz, A. (eds.) ECCV 2006, Part I. LNCS, vol. 3951, pp. 404–417. Springer, Heidelberg (2006)
8. Aguilera, C., Barrera, F., Lumbreras, F., Sappa, A., Toledo, R.: Multispectral image feature points. Sensors 12, 12661–12672 (2012)
9. Yi, Z., Zhiguo, C., Yang, X.: Multi-spectral remote image registration based on sift. Electronics Letters 44, 107–108 (2008)
10. Barrera, F., Lumbreras, F., Sappa, A.: Multimodal stereo vision system: 3d data extraction and algorithm evaluation. IEEE Journal of Selected Topics in Signal Processing 6, 437–446 (2012)
11. Barrera, F., Lumbreras, F., Sappa, A.: Multispectral piecewise planar stereo using manhattan-world assumption. Pattern Recognition Letters 34, 52–61 (2013)
12. Canny, J.: A computational approach to edge detection. IEEE Trans. on Pattern Analysis and Machine Intelligence 8, 679–698 (1986)
13. Hough, P.: Method and means for recognizzing complex patterns. U.S. Patent 3,069,654 (1962)
14. Hartley, R., Zisserman, A.: Multiple View Geometry in Computer Vision. Cambridge University Press (2004)
15. Faugeras, O., Luong, Q.: The Geometry of Multiple Images: the Laws that Govern the Formation of Multiple Images of a scene and Some of their Applications. The MIT Press (2001)
16. Barrera, F., Lumbreras, F., Sappa, A.: Multimodal template matching based on gradient and mutual information using scale-space. In: IEEE Int'l Conf. on Image Processing, Hong Kong, pp. 2749–2752 (2010)
17. Li, Z.N.: Stereo correspondence based on line matching in Hough space using dynamic programming. IEEE Trans. on Systems, Man, and Cybernetics 24, 144–152 (1994)
18. Boykov, Y., Veksler, O., Zabih, R.: Fast approximate energy minimization via graph cuts. IEEE Trans. on Pattern Analysis and Machine Intelligence 23, 1222–1239 (2001)

NLP EAC Recognition by Component Separation in the Eye Region

Ruxandra Vrânceanu, Corneliu Florea, Laura Florea, and Constantin Vertan

The Image Processing and Analysis Laboratory (LAPI),
Politehnica University of Bucharest, Romania

Abstract. This paper investigates the recognition of the Eye Accessing Cues (EACs) used in Neuro-Linguistic Programming (NLP) and shows how computer vision techniques can be used for understanding the meaning of non-visual gaze directions. Any specific EAC is identified by the relative position of the iris within the eye bounding box, which is determined from modified versions of the classical integral projections. The eye cues are inferred via a logistic classifier from features extracted within the eye bounding box. The here proposed solution is shown to outperform in terms of detection rate other classical approaches.

Keywords: NLP, EAC, eye bounding box, eye gaze, segmentation.

1 Introduction

The recent increase of computational capabilities has led to the development of fast and complex algorithms able to exploit new human-computer interactions. In the field of computer vision most of the research done in connection to the understanding of the functioning of human mind has been aimed at interpreting facial expressions [1] and establishing their underlying emotions [2]. Yet areas of psychology, such as the Neuro-Linguistic Programming (NLP), offer unexplored opportunities for understanding the human patterns of thinking and behavior.

NLP was introduced in the 70s by Brandler and Grinder [3], as a different model for detecting, understanding and using the patterns that appear between brain, language and body. One such model is the Eye-Accessing Cue (EAC) model that uses the positions of the iris inside the eye as an indicator of the internal thinking mechanisms of a person. The direction of gaze (Fig.1), can be used to determine the internal representational system employed by a person, who may think in visual, auditory or kinesthetic terms, and the mental activity of that person, of remembering, imagining, or having an internal dialog.

In the computer vision area, extensive research has been done in the field of detecting the direction of gaze [5]. Still most of the proposed solutions use active illumination and multiple sources of light [6]. As head mounted devices may disturb one's inner thinking mechanisms, we note that the work in [7] explores the theme only from a computer vision direction. The here-proposed solution is based on free natural light and image acquisition done with a tripod-mounted camera. First, we precisely determine the eye bounding box, followed

R. Wilson et al. (Eds.): CAIP 2013, Part II, LNCS 8048, pp. 225–232, 2013.

Fig. 1. 7 Classes of EACs [4]: When eyes are not used for visual tasks, their position can indicate how people are thinking (using visual, auditory or kinesthetic terms) and the mental activity they are doing (remembering, imagining, or having an internal dialog)

by a preprocessing that enhances the separation of the iris from the brow. Once the eye region is segmented, the relative position of the weighting centers of mass for the significant eye regions are processed for the EAC recognition.

Thus, in section 2 we describe the method used for isolating the eye's bounding box; inside this bounding box various methods are employed for detecting the relative iris position and the corresponding EAC, as detailed in 3. The results achieved on a specifically constructed database are presented in section 4 and the paper ends with some conclusions.

2   Detecting the Eye Bounding Box

The proposed automatic solution starts with the standard Viola-Jones [8] face detection algorithm. All subsequent processing is then performed inside the face square, that is resized to 100×100 pixels. The eye bounding box is first initialized at a safe location for each eye, covering the middle-upper face quarter band (that is the lines from $y_1 = 25$ to $y_2 = 50$) and symmetrical vertical image quarter bands (within $x1 = 20$ and $x2 = 45$ for the left eye and from $x_1 = 55$ to $x_2 = 80$ for the right eye), as suggested by anthropometry and shown in Fig.2(I/II.a).

This bounding box is not sufficiently accurate and its location will be further refined. The literature comprises many approaches related to eye localization, many of them based on image integral projections [9]. The use of integral projections for the description of the eye region was further developed in [10] and we will take these works as a start base which will be improved by heuristics, designed to cover the specificity of the EAC testing (gaze variation). The precise eye bounding box detection is performed using the integral projections for the negative of the initial luminance eye regions I, computed as:

$$P_V(i) = \sum_{j=x_1}^{x_2} (256 - I(i,j)), \forall i = y_1, \ldots, y_2. \tag{1}$$

$$P_H(j) = \sum_{i=y_{top}}^{y_{bot}} (256 - I(i,j)), \forall j = x_1, \ldots, x_2.$$

First, the bounding box upper and lower limits (y_{top}, y_{bot}) are extracted from the vertical image projection P_V (Fig.2(I/II.b)). Then, the lateral limits are

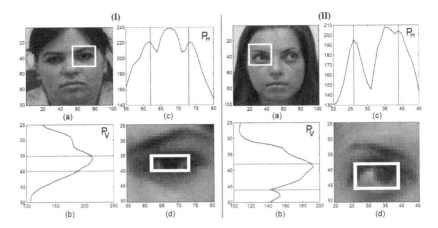

Fig. 2. Eye bounding box detections ((I)Eyes looking ahead; (II)Eyes looking sideways): a) Face square + anthropometric eye selection; b) Vertical Projection for detecting the upper/lower limits; c) Horizontal Projection for detecting the left/right limits; d) Eye Bounding Box detected inside the selection

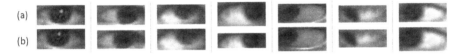

Fig. 3. Eye Bounding Box: a) Ground truth (manual markings); b) Using integral projections

extracted from the horizontal image projection P_H (Fig.2(I/II.c)). The top of the bounding box is determined at 0.98 of the maximum of P_V, while the bottom is set in the first local minimum after the maximum. If there is no such a minimum (see (Fig.2(I.b)), a standard distance of 5 pixels from the maximum is used. The lateral limits are set to the local maxima, left and right, from the maximal mode in P_H. When eyes are looking sideways such maximums might not exist and the standard distance of 5 pixels is used. Visual examples of the method's performance (compared to the ground truth) are presented in Fig.3.

3   EAC Recognition

Once the eye bounding box has been delimited, the EAC can be determined by analyzing the positions of different eye parts. The natural choice is to analyze the position of the iris, determined with an iris center localizer inside the bounding box. For improving accuracy, we segment the regions in the eye bounding box and use their relative position and average luminance as indicators of the EAC.

Pre-processing and Segmentation. The segmentation is performed inside the bounding box and we experimentally determined that the optimal number

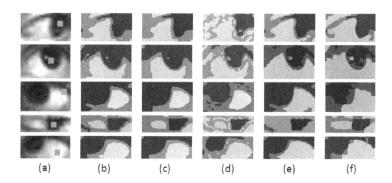

Fig. 4. Eye Features: a) Iris center using [15]; Segmentation in 3 classes using: b)K-Means; c) K-Means refined with Graph-Cuts; d) K-Means refined with pre-processing step; e) Mean Shift + region merging; f) Watershed + region merging

of classes is 3, corresponding generally to the iris, sclera and the surrounding skin area. Yet, as the iris and the brow tend to be spatially connected and have similar luminance values, before the actual segmentation, a pre-processing is required to separate the iris from the brow.

Starting from the observation that the eye iris is a large darker region of the eye [11], we look for the darkest, smooth neighborhood within the bounding box. This is found by selecting the areas that are darker than the median luminance value within the bounding box, in both the original image and a Gaussian low-pass smoothed image. The remaining of the eye bounding box is then lightened by a factor of 2, such that the segmentation will generally detect the iris as a stand alone region (Fig.4(d)).

Segmentation is a well known problem and many solutions have been proposed through the years. As we do not aim at good segmentation per se, we will require a combination of good EAC recognition in a reasonable amount of time. According to the tests performed (as visually showed in Fig.4 and numerically in section 4), the best compromise is achievable using a *K-Means* segmentation. It is possible to refine these results using *Graph Cuts* [12] (which imposes a smoothness constraint to reduce the number of disconnected regions and provide more compact classes (Fig.4(c)), yet the time overhead (508 msec in average for a portrait, compared to 22.5 msec for K-Means) is considerable when compared with the marginal accuracy improvement. Other tested segmentation methods were *Mean Shift* [13] and *Watershed* [14] (Fig.4(e), (f)). These methods, typically lead to over-segmentation. Yet, even though dynamic region merging is employed to consider light regions more similar, and separate the darker areas (the iris and the brow), the results under-perform the K-Means method.

Post-processing and Classification. To improve the region separation resulted from segmentation we rely on the same integral projections. Thus, the iris/sclera regions parts that were outside the minimum/maximum areas of the integral projections were cut.

Next the space given by the detected bounding box is normalized so it has a standard width (of 100 pixels), while preserving the aspect ratio. Also, since the height is variable, all eyes were aligned at the lower limit of the bounding box to ensure a better separation between eyes looking down, contained in narrow boxes, respectively up, with larger boxes.

The resulting eye regions' centers of mass coordinates in the normalized bounding box and average luminance were used as features describing the eye. To recognize the 7 EAC classes, given the named features, various classification methods were considered. As the number of features is small, Logistic Classification [16] gives good results.

4   Results

Database. In order to investigate the EAC detection problem we have developed a database containing all the 7 cues. 40 subjects were asked to move their eyes according to a predefined pattern and their movements were recorded. The movements between consecutive EACs were identified, the first and last frame of each move were selected and labelled with the corresponding EAC tag and eye points were manually marked. In total, the database comprises 1170 frontal face images, grouped according to the 7 directions of gaze, with a set of 5 points marked for each eye: the iris center and 4 points delimiting the bounding box.

Training and testing procedure is the standard two-fold: half of the ground truth sets were randomly chosen to train the classifier and tune the parameters used for detecting the bounding box limits and the cue of the eyes. The testing of the algorithms (and the reported results) is done on the other half of the database.

Bounding Box Detection. As an alternative to the localization of the eye bounding box limits, one may consider the information given by a facial landmarks localization solution, such as the BoRMaN algorithm described in [17]. The algorithm iteratively improves an initial facial landmark estimate by features processed with Markov Random Fields and Support Vector Regression. To construct the necessary bounding box, we have considered the four points marking the eye, returned by the BoRMaN solution. We consider this method as being the one obviously given by the state of the art and we will show that our proposed solution outperforms it.

In order to evaluate the accuracy of the bounding box localization, inspired from the standard stringent eye center localization method [18], we have normalized the absolute error with inter-ocular distance. In evaluating the bounding box limits, only the x dimension is considered for the left and the right limits, and only the y dimension for the upper and lower limits. The detection error should be below 0.05. A comparative evaluation of the proposed method to the coordinates given by the solution from [17], can be seen in Fig.5 for various errors. While being more simple, the proposed solution generally gives more accurate results and provides an acceptable error for over 85% of the database.

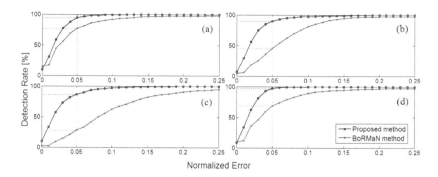

Fig. 5. Detection rate for different normalized errors (0:0.25), using BoRMaN solution (red) and the proposed solution (blue) for the bounding box limits: a) left; b) right; c)up; d)down (where the acceptable error was marked with dotted line)

Table 1. EAC Overall Recognition Rate when using: K-Means (**KM**), K-Means refined with Graph Cuts (**GC**), Mean Shift (**MS**), Watershed (**WS**)), K-Means after highlighting the darkest neighborhood (**D-KM**), and then refined with integral projections (**Prj + D-KM**), for bounding boxes obtained both manually and automatically(using integral projections)

Method	KM	GC	MS	WS	D-KM	Prj + D-KM
Manual BB	70.90	71.03	70.35	71.03	**76.68**	**84.63**
Auto BB	63.02	64.82	65.76	63.11	**67.89**	**74.30**

Segmentation. Eye regions segmentation is an important step in accurate recognition of the EAC. The results obtained with various algorithms are presented in Table 1. Although the simple methods perform similarly, the K-Means segmentation gives better results, when using the pre- and post-processing steps.

EAC Recognition. The recognition rate for each individual EAC is presented in Table 2 and the confusion matrix is shown in Fig.6(I). It can be seen that a higher confusion rate appears vertically, between eyes looking to the same side. In a NLP interpretation, this corresponds to a better separability between the internal activities and a lower one between representational systems. Visual examples of correct and false recognition are shown in Fig.6(II).

Comparison with Related Work. Given the state of the art, one intuitive way to recognize the EAC is to use the coordinates of eye fiducial points. Thus we

Table 2. Individual Recognition Rate for each EAC

VD	VR	VC	AR	AC	ID	K
88.32	76.71	75.00	61.97	57.86	63.36	76.81

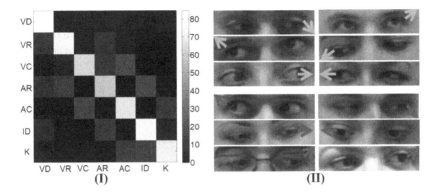

Fig. 6. (I) EAC Confusion Matrix; (II) Automatic Recognition examples: correct (green arrow) and false (red arrow)

Table 3. EAC Detection Rate for the proposed solution versus state of the art and manual markings

Method	Manual	[15] + [17]	Proposed
DR	84.63	47.82	74.30

consider as relevant the combination of the BoRMaN algorithm [17] for detecting the eye bounding box, together with the iris center, detected using the maximum isophote algorithm presented in [15]. Comparative results are presented in Table 3. As one can see, the proposed solution outperforms the state of the art, and it is close to the upper limit obtained by using the manual markings.

Although computation efficiency has not been the main focus of this paper, the proposed method is fast enough, requiring an average of 35 msec per image, with single thread Matlab implementation with binary routines.

5   Conclusions

This paper has investigated new methods for recognizing the Eye Accessing Cues model, used by NLP for better understanding the mental patterns of a person. We have proven that a good recognition rate can be obtained by the joint use of segmentation and integral projection information inside the bounding box of the eye and we have proposed a solution that while is simple and fast, it outperforms existing methods.

Future research will focus on finding more features and increasing the precision of the bounding box detection, which are critical for good EAC detection. The next step will then be the EAC tracking in order to better understand the NLP patterns. The final purpose of this research is to see to which extent the EACs can be determined and induced for a person, and how such information could be used to improve human interaction, learning, or help in overcoming psychological traumas.

Acknowledgment. This work has been co-funded by the Sectoral Operational Program Human Resources Development (SOP HRD) 2007-2013, financed from the European Social Fund and by the Romanian Government under the contract number POSDRU/107/1.5/S/76903 and POSDRU/89/1.5/S/62557.

References

1. Fasel, B., Luettin, J.: Automatic facial expression analysis: A survey. Pattern Recognition 36(1), 256–275 (1999)
2. Ekman, P.: Emotion in the Human Face. Cambridge Univ. Press (1982)
3. Bandler, R., Grinder, J.: Frogs into Princes: Neuro Linguistic Programming. Real People Press, Moab (1979)
4. Fogg, A.: Nlp representational systems and eye accessing cues (2006), http://www.golf-hypnotist.com/nlp-representational-systems-and-eye-accessing-cues/
5. Hansen, D., Qiang, J.: In the eye of the beholder: A survey of models for eyes and gaze. IEEE Trans. on PAMI 32(3), 478–500 (2010)
6. Nakazawa, A., Nitschke, C.: Point of gaze estimation through corneal surface reflection in an active illumination environment. In: Fitzgibbon, A., Lazebnik, S., Perona, P., Sato, Y., Schmid, C. (eds.) ECCV 2012, Part II. LNCS, vol. 7573, pp. 159–172. Springer, Heidelberg (2012)
7. Diamantopoulos, G.: Novel eye feature extraction and tracking for non-visual eye-movement applications. PhD thesis, Univ. of Birmingham (2010)
8. Viola, P., Jones, M.: Robust real-time face detection. IJCV 57(2), 137–154 (2004)
9. Feng, G.C., Yuen, P.C.: Variance projection function and its application to eye detection for human face recognition. Pattern Recognition Letters 19(9), 899–906 (1998)
10. Zhou, Z.: Projection functions for eye detection. Pattern Recognition 37(5), 1049–1056 (2003)
11. Wu, J., Zhou, Z.H.: Efficient face candidates selector for face detection. Pattern Recognition 36(5), 1175–1186 (2003)
12. Boykov, Y., Kolmogorov, V.: An experimental comparison of min-cut/max-flow algorithms for energy minimization in vision. IEEE Trans. on PAMI 26(9), 1124–1137 (2004)
13. Comaniciu, D., Meer, P.: Mean shift: A robust approach toward feature space analysis. IEEE Trans. on PAMI 24(5), 603–619 (2002)
14. Meyer, F.: Topographic distance and watershed lines. Signal Processing 38, 113–125 (1994)
15. Valenti, R., Gevers, T.: Accurate eye center location and tracking using isophote curvature. In: CVPR, pp. 1–8 (2008)
16. le Cessie, S., van Houwelingen, J.: Ridge estimators in logistic regression. Applied Statistics 41(1), 191–201 (1992)
17. Valstar, M., Martinez, T., Binefa, X., Pantic, M.: Facial point detection using boosted regression and graph models. In: CVPR, pp. 2729–2736 (2010)
18. Jesorsky, O., Kirchberg, K.J., Frischholz, R.W.: Robust face detection using the hausdorff distance. In: Bigun, J., Smeraldi, F. (eds.) AVBPA 2001. LNCS, vol. 2091, pp. 90–95. Springer, Heidelberg (2001)

OPF-MRF: Optimum-Path Forest and Markov Random Fields for Contextual-Based Image Classification

Rodrigo Nakamura[1], Daniel Osaku[2], Alexandre Levada[2],
Fabio Cappabianco[3], Alexandre Falcão[4], and Joao Papa[1]

[1] UNESP - Univ. Estadual Paulista, Department of Computing, Bauru-SP, Brazil
{rodrigo.mizobe,papa}@fc.unesp.br
[2] Department of Computing, Federal University of São Carlos
alexandre@dc.ufscar.br, danosaku@hotmail.com
[3] Institute of Science and Technology, Federal University of São Paulo
cappabianco@unifesp.br
[4] Institute of Computing, University of Campinas
afalcao@ic.unicamp.br

Abstract. Some machine learning methods do not exploit contextual information in the process of discovering, describing and recognizing patterns. However, spatial/temporal neighboring samples are likely to have same behavior. Here, we propose an approach which unifies a supervised learning algorithm - namely Optimum-Path Forest - together with a Markov Random Field in order to build a prior model holding a spatial smoothness assumption, which takes into account the contextual information for classification purposes. We show its robustness for brain tissue classification over some images of the well-known dataset IBSR.

Keywords: Optimum-Path Forest, Markov Random Fields, Contextual Classification.

1 Introduction

Pixel classification usually takes into account local image properties and treat pixels as independent samples in the feature space. However, adjacent pixels are more likely to come from a same class. This makes crucial to also exploit spatial and temporal contextual information for a more effective classification.

Recent works have proposed contextual versions of pattern recognition techniques for image classification, i.e., variants that consider the correlation between nearby samples. Tarabalka et al. [1] proposed a hybrid approach, called SVM-MRF, based on Support Vector Machines (SVM) and Markov Random Fields (MRF) for remote sensing image classification. The idea is to add contextual information in a second stage, which follows the traditional pixelwise SVM-based classification. In this second step, a MRF regularization is performed on the label map generated by non-contextual SVM.

R. Wilson et al. (Eds.): CAIP 2013, Part II, LNCS 8048, pp. 233–240, 2013.

Moser and Serpico [2] also proposed a similar SVM-MRF approach for contextual classification. However, their work innovates by presenting an unique formulation for both SVM and MRF, which performs contextual classification in a single step. Wu et al. [3] have also proposed a different version of the SVM-MRF classifier for mouse brain image segmentation. Therefore, the main idea behind these contextual classifiers concerns with how to model some *a priori* knowledge as a locally dependent MRF in order to hold a spatial smoothness assumption of the pixel labels [4–6].

All these works have in common a SVM classifier and a single classification iteration, being the MRF used to correct the label map. Recently, a classification technique proposed by Papa et al. [7, 8] has been successfully used for several purposes, including image analysis applications which demand retraining the classifier several rounds in interactive times [9]. The Optimum-Path Forest (OPF) classifier treats pattern recognition as an optimum graph partition problem, in which a competition among key samples from all classes generates a collection of optimum-path trees rooted at them. Its accuracy results are comparable with those obtained by SVM, but OPF training can be from hundreds to thousands times faster. This makes it attractive for pixel classification and, as far as we know, there is no previous contextual approach based on OPF.

In this work, we present a contextual classifier named OPF-MRF, which can rapidly perform several iterations of OPF classification followed by improvements on pixel description based on Markov Random Fields and contextual information from the intermediate segmentations. We demonstrate the improvements along the iterations with respect to a single OPF classification using MR-images of the brain.

The remainder of the paper is organized as follows. In Section 2, we describe the background on OPF and MRF, and present our approach and its algorithm. Section 3 discusses the experimental results for brain tissue classification, and Section 4 states conclusions.

2 Concepts and Methods

This section briefly introduces the theoretical background about the OPF classifier and Markov Random Fields. The proposed OPF-MRF approach for contextual classification is also presented.

2.1 Optimum-Path Forest

Let $\mathcal{X}$ and $\mathcal{Y}$ be a set of samples and their corresponding labels, respectively, where $\mathcal{Y} \subseteq \mathcal{M}$, being $\mathcal{M}$ the set of all possible labels. Given a labeled dataset $\mathcal{D} = (\mathcal{X}, \mathcal{Y})$, the idea behind OPF is to model $\mathcal{D}$ as a graph $\mathcal{G} = (\mathcal{V}, \mathcal{A})$ whose nodes are the samples in $\mathcal{V} = \mathcal{X}$, and the arcs are defined by an adjacency relation $\mathcal{A}$ between nodes in the feature space. The arcs are weighted by a distance function between the feature vectors of the corresponding nodes.

As a community ordered formation process, where groups of individuals are obtained based on optimum connectivity relations to their leaders, OPF employs a competition process among some key nodes (prototypes) in order to partition the graph into an optimum-path forest according to some path-cost function. By analogy, the population is divided into communities, where each individual belongs to the group which offered to it the highest reward. In addition, the dataset $\mathcal{D}$ is divided in two subsets $\mathcal{D} = \mathcal{D}_1 \cup \mathcal{D}_2$, standing for the training and test sets, respectively. Now, we have the following graphs: $\mathcal{G}_1 = (\mathcal{V}_1, \mathcal{A}_1)$ and $\mathcal{G}_2 = (\mathcal{V}_2, \mathcal{A}_2)$, $\mathcal{V}_1 \cup \mathcal{V}_2 = \mathcal{X}$, which model $\mathcal{D}_1$ and $\mathcal{D}_2$, respectively.

Now assume π_s be a path in the graph with terminus at sample $s \in \mathcal{D}_1$, and $\langle \pi_s \cdot (s,t) \rangle$ a concatenation between π_s and the arc (s,t). Let $\mathcal{S} \subset \mathcal{D}_1$ be a set of prototypes from all classes. Roughly speaking, the main idea of the Optimum-Path Forest algorithm is to minimize a cost map $\mathcal{C}(t)$ based on a path-cost function Ψ defined as:

$$\Psi(\langle s \rangle) = \begin{cases} 0 & \text{if } s \in \mathcal{S} \\ +\infty & \text{otherwise,} \end{cases}$$
$$\Psi(\pi_s \cdot \langle s,t \rangle) = \max\{\Psi(\pi_s), d(s,t)\}. \tag{1}$$

Particularly, an optimal set of prototypes $\mathcal{S}^*$ can be found by exploiting the theoretical relation between the minimum-spanning tree (MST) [10] and optimum-path tree for Ψ [11]. By computing a MST in the complete graph $\mathcal{G}_1$, we obtain a connected acyclic graph whose nodes are all samples in $\mathcal{V}_1$. In addition, every pair of samples is connected by a single path, which is optimum according to Ψ. Therefore, the optimum prototypes are defined as the nodes from distinct classes that share an arc in the MST.

In the classification phase, for any sample $t \in \mathcal{V}_2$, we consider all arcs connecting t with samples $s \in \mathcal{V}_1$, as though t were part of the graph. Considering all possible paths from $\mathcal{S}^*$ to t, we find the optimum path $\mathcal{P}^*(t)$ from $\mathcal{S}^*$ and label t with the class $\lambda(\mathcal{R}(t))$ of its most strongly connected prototype $\mathcal{R}(t) \in \mathcal{S}^*$, being $\lambda(\cdot)$ a function that returns the true label of some sample. This path can be identified by evaluating the optimum cost $\mathcal{C}(t)$ as:

$$\mathcal{C}(t) = \min\{\max\{\mathcal{C}(s), d(s,t)\}\}, \ \forall s \in \mathcal{V}_1. \tag{2}$$

Suppose the node $s^* \in \mathcal{G}_1$ is the one which satisfies (Equation 2). Given that label $\theta(s^*) = \lambda(\mathcal{R}(t))$, the classification simply assigns $\theta(s^*)$ as the class of t. Clearly, an error occurs when $\theta(s^*) \neq \lambda(t)$, where $\theta(\cdot)$ stands for the predicted label for some sample.

2.2 Markov Random Fields

Let Ω be a discrete bidimensional lattice that defines the set of possible image pixels, and l_{ij} the value of a possible occurrence of the random field $\mathcal{L}$, where $l_{ij} \in \mathcal{M}$. Let us also define a neighborhood system η_{ij} centered at pixel (i,j) as the set of elements in which the distance to this central element is less or equal to a $\sigma > 0$.

We have that $\mathcal{L} = \{l_{ij}|(i,j) \in \Omega\}$ is a MRF defined over Ω if $\mathcal{L}$ holds the following properties for the condition probability p of a pixel and the probability P of an image classification:

- $p(l_{ij}|\{l_{kz}, (k,z) \in \Omega \backslash (i,j)\}) = p(l_{ij}|\{l_{kz}, (k,z) \in \eta_{ij}\})$, $\forall (i,j) \in \Omega$; and
- $P(\mathcal{L}) > 0$, $\forall l \in \xi$, where ξ is the set of all possible realizations of $\mathcal{L}$. This means every realization of the random field can occur.

Sometimes, it is required to define a probability distribution over the images when we work with stochastical models aiming to model *a priori* knowledge of the problem. The anti-ferromagnetic Potts model is a MRF which arises from statistical physics to generalize the Ising model for multiple discrete states [12, 13], being one of the most used models for several problems.

Given a neighborhood system η_{ij}, we can define a local conditional probability as follows:

$$p(l_{ij} = m|\eta_{ij}, \beta) = \frac{\exp\{\beta \mathcal{U}_{ij}(m)\}}{\sum_{\forall k \in \mathcal{M}} \exp\{\beta \mathcal{U}_{ij}(k)\}}, \qquad (3)$$

where $\mathcal{U}_{ij}(k)$ stands for the number of pixels in η_{ij} whose label is k, β is a parameter representing the spatial dependency between neighbors, and $m \in \mathcal{M}$ means the observed label at the central pixel l_{ij}. It is worth noting that higher values of β lead to a higher spatial dependence between samples.

2.3   Proposed Algorithm

The main idea behind OPF-MRF is to exploit contextual information by means of a neighborhood lattice model. Hence, we provide a regularization schema via the maximization of a local probability (Equation 3) while searching for the optimum path according to the path-cost function. Algorithm 1 implements this idea using the Iterated Conditional Modes (ICM) algorithm, which maximizes the MRF iteratively [14]. Note that the algorithm below employs the Potts model, but any other model can be applied.

The OPF-MRF algorithm starts by training an OPF classifier (non-contextual) from $\mathcal{D}_1$ and creating a first classification map $\mathcal{Y}_2$ for $\mathcal{X}_2$ (Lines $1-2$ of Algorithm 1). The loop in Lines $3-8$ is responsible for improving the classification map as a function of the local density information provided by the Potts model (Equation 3). In other words, the classification map is then updated using ICM, which aims to maximize Equation 3 for each pixel (Line 4). After that, the original set of features for each pixel is extended with the conditional probability of each class (Lines $5-6$), given by the normalized histogram of each class over an 8-neighborhood. If we have a classification problem with c classes, for instance, the new feature vector would be composed by the old attributes together with the probability of occurrence of each one of the c classes. Further, the OPF classifier is retrained and applied in order to refine the resulting classification map generated by ICM over these new sets (Lines $7-8$). This process is repeated until the maximum number of iterations is reached.

Algorithm 1 – OPF-MRF

INPUT: A λ-labeled training set $\mathcal{D}_1 = (\mathcal{X}_1, \mathcal{Y}_1)$, a test sample set $\mathcal{X}_2$, the pair (v, d) for feature vector and distance computations, and number of iterations T.

OUTPUT: Classified test set $\mathcal{D}_2 = (\mathcal{X}_2, \mathcal{Y}_2)$.

1. *Train an OPF classifier (non-contextual) using $\mathcal{D}_1$.*
2. *Classify $\mathcal{X}_2$ generating a initial label map $\mathcal{Y}_2$.*
3. *For each iteration i ($i = 1, \ldots, T$), do*
4.   *Maximize Equation 3 using $(\mathcal{X}_2, \mathcal{Y}_2)$, a 8-neighborhood system, and ICM.*
5.   *Extend the feature vector of each pixel using the estimated probabilities*
6. $p(l_{ij} = m|\eta_{ij}, \beta)$ *for all classes.*
7.   *Train OPF using $\mathcal{D}_1$ and the new feature vector.*
8.   *Classify $\mathcal{X}_2$ to create $\mathcal{Y}_2$.*

3   Simulations and Results

In order to illustrate the improvements of OPF-MRF along the iterations, we used magnetic resonance images from the Internet Brain Segmentation Repository (IBSR)[1]. This dataset is composed by positionally normalized T1-weighted coronal brain scans (Figure 1a). A reference data is available as a result of semi-automated segmentation techniques providing a segmentation of the following regions: white matter (WM), gray matter (GM) and cerebrospinal fluid (CSF). One example of the ground truth is shown in Figure 1b. Therefore, the idea is to classify each pixel as belonging to one of these three classes.

In regard to the original feature extraction, each pixel is represented by the brightness of its 26-neighboring pixels, which we refer here as the baseline method (i.e., non-contextual information is employed in this case). In order to evaluate the robustness of OPF-MRF, we have executed experiments on four images of the IBSR. For that, each pixel is used to compose the dataset of its corresponding image, which is partitioned in training and test sets. We have used the well-known cross-validation procedure with proportion of 0.05% and 99.95% for training and test sets, respectively.

Figures 2 and 3 show the Cohen's κ [16] results for each image using three different values for the spatial constraint β (Equation 3), which controls the amount of contextual information used in the learning process. For each image, we have 10 runnings to compose a cross-validation procedure. Therefore, the value #1 in the horizontal axis for some β, for instance, stands for the mean value of OPF-MRF over 10 cross-validation runnings during the iteration #1 of the proposed algorithm (we use $T = 10$ iterations). The reader can observe that OPF-MRF have provided better results than baseline approach, i.e., OPF without contextual information. It is worth noting that removing the intra-cranial

---

[1] The description of data was provided by the Center for Morphometric Analysis at Massachusetts General Hospital, and is available at
http://www.cma.mgh.harvard.edu/ibsr/

contents and the brain steam in a given MR-image of the head (the process referred to as skull stripping) and applying techniques for inhomogeneity correction, the proposed techniques achieved better classification results (see Figure 1 (e) and (f) - with κ equals to 0.8812 and 0.8995, respectively).

The proposed approach can provide a more homogeneous solution for the classification map. It should be also observed the method is highly dependent on the initial solution. The best result has been obtained with $\beta = 0.54$, which may indicate this value is the one that best represents the trade-off between observation and a priori knowledge.

4   Concluding Remarks

We have presented a new approach for exploiting contextual information by means of Optimum-Path Forest classifier. The contextual information is treated in terms of the maximization of a conditional probability given by a Potts model over a Markov Random Field. Such model allows the use of additional information provided by the neighborhood of a given sample.

In order to illustrate an application of the proposed approach, we addressed brain tissue classification over the well-known IBSR dataset, which contains MR

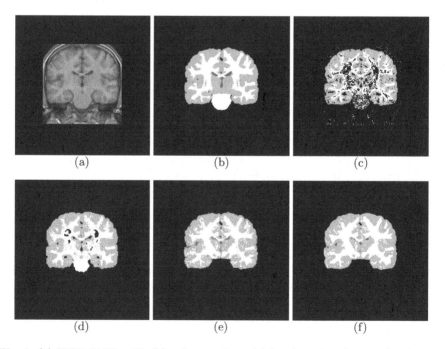

Fig. 1. (a) IBSR-01 Slice 58, (b) reference data, (c) baseline classification (traditional OPF), (d) classification with OPF-MRF, (e) Proposed approach in [15] and (f) OPF-MRF applied using the pre-processing techniques proposed in [15]

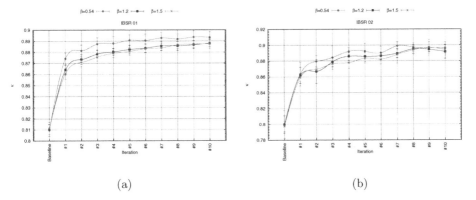

(a)   (b)

Fig. 2. Overall Cohen's κ values obtained through cross-validation for IBSR-01 and IBSR-02 datasets

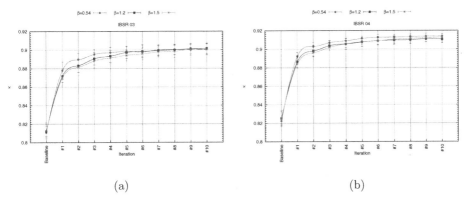

(a)   (b)

Fig. 3. Overall Cohen's κ values obtained through cross-validation for IBSR-03 and IBSR-04 datasets

images of human brains. Different spatial constraint values have been evaluated in order to find out the one which provides the best recognition rates for OPF-MRF. We have shown that OPF-MRF have obtained better results than standard OPF in all cases, which seems to be a suitable approach for contextual classification.

Acknowledgments. The authors are grateful to FAPESP grants #2009/16206-1, #2011/14058-5 and #2012/06472-9, and also CNPq grants #303182/2011-3, #475054/2011-3 and #303673/2010-9.

References

1. Tarabalka, Y., Fauvel, M., Chanussot, J., Benediktsson, J.A.: SVM- and MRF-based method for accurate classification of hyperspectral images. IEEE Geoscience and Remote Sensing Letters 7(4), 736–740 (2010)

2. Moser, G., Serpico, S.B.: Combining support vector machines and markov random fields in an integrated framework for contextual image classification. IEEE Transactions on Geoscience and Remote Sensing PP(99), 1–19 (2012)
3. Wu, T., Bae, M.H., Zhang, M., Pan, R., Badea, A.: A prior feature SVM-MRF based method for mouse brain segmentation. NeuroImage 59(3), 2298–2306 (2012)
4. Besag, E.: Spatial interaction and the statistical analysis of lattice systems. Journal of the Royal Statistical Society B36, 192–236 (1974)
5. Geman, S., Geman, D.: Stochastic relaxation, gibbs distributions, and the bayesian restoration of images. IEEE Transaction on Pattern Analysis and Machine Intelligence 6(6), 721–741 (1984)
6. Seheult, A.H., Greig, D.M., Porteous, B.T.: Exact maximum a posteriori estimation for binary images. Journal of the Royal Statistical Society 51(2), 271–279 (1989)
7. Papa, J.P., Falcão, A.X., Suzuki, C.T.N.: Supervised pattern classification based on optimum-path forest. International Journal of Imaging Systems and Technology 19(2), 120–131 (2009)
8. Papa, J.P., Falcão, A.X., Albuquerque, V.H.C., Tavares, J.M.R.S.: Efficient supervised optimum-path forest classification for large datasets. Pattern Recognition 45(1), 512–520 (2012)
9. Spina, T.V., de Miranda, P.A.V., Falcão, A.X.: Intelligent understanding of user interaction in image segmentation. Intl. Journal of Pattern Recognition and Artificial Intelligence, 26(2), 65001-1–1265001-26 (2012)
10. Cormen, T.H., Leiserson, C.E., Rivest, R.L., Stein, C.: Introduction to Algorithms, 2nd edn. The MIT Press (2001)
11. Allène, C., Audibert, J.Y., Couprie, M., Cousty, J., Keriven, R.: Some links between min-cuts, optimal spanning forests and watersheds. In: Proceedings of the International Symposium on Mathematical Morphology, pp. 253–264. MCT/INPE (2007)
12. Potts, R.B.: Some generalized order-disorder transformations. Mathematical Proceedings of the Cambridge Philosophical Society 48, 106–109 (1952)
13. Wu, F.Y.: The potts model. Reviews of Modern Physics 54, 235–268 (1982)
14. Besag, J.: On the statistical analysis of dirty pictures. Journal of the Royal Statistical Society, Series B (Methodological) 48(3), 259–302 (1986)
15. Cappabianco, F.A.M., Falcão, A.X., Yasuda, C.L., Udupa, J.K.: Brain tissue mr-image segmentation via optimum-path forest clustering. Computer Vision and Image Understanding 116(10), 1047–1059 (2012)
16. Cohen, J.: A Coefficient of Agreement for Nominal Scales. Educational and Psychological Measurement 20(1), 37 (1960)

Orthonormal Diffusion Decompositions of Images for Optical Flow Estimation

Sravan Gudivada and Adrian G. Bors

Dept. of Computer Science, University of York, York YO10 5GH, UK

Abstract. This paper proposes an ortho-diffusion decomposition of graphs for estimating motion from image sequences. Orthonormal decompositions of the adjacency matrix representations of image data are alternated with diffusions and data subsampling in order to robustly represent image features using undirected graphs. Modified Gram-Schmidt with pivoting the columns algorithm is applied recursively for the orthonormal decompositions at various scales. This processing produces a set of ortho-diffusion bases and residual diffusion wavelets at each image representation scale. The optical flow is estimated using the similarity in the ortho-diffusion bases space extracted from regions of two different image frames.

Keywords: Ortho-diffusion decomposition, optical flow estimation, diffusion wavelets.

1 Introduction

Applying kernels on undirected graphs were shown to lead to good results in various applications [1, 3, 4]. Belkin and Niyogi [1] calculate the Laplacian of a graph from the adjacency matrix of the local data and then analyze its eigenvalues The eigenvectors of the Laplacian are naturally invariant and provide a global data representation. Spectral graph properties have been used for data characterization in various applications [2, 3]. Diffusion maps [4–6] achieve dimensionality reduction by re-organizing data according to the parametrization of its underlying geometry on orthogonal sub-spaces. When the diffusion is propagated, it integrates the local data structure to reveal relational properties of the data set at various scales [5, 6]. A new analysis method on undirected graphs was proposed by Maggioni and Mahadevan in [7] using multi-scale orthogonal decompositions of graphs into sets of bases functions and residuals named diffusion wavelets for each scale of decomposition.

Image gradients in time and feature matching have been used for optical flow estimation [8–10]. Lately, various approaches have employed regularization with constraints [11] or smoothing with diffusion kernels [12]. Spectral clustering was used for motion segmentation in [2], while correlation of diffusion maps for optical flow estimation in [6]. In this study we propose an orthonormal diffusion methodology for motion estimation. The modified Gram-Schmidt algorithm with pivoting the columns, also called the $\mathcal{QR}$ algorithm, is used recursively at a set of

R. Wilson et al. (Eds.): CAIP 2013, Part II, LNCS 8048, pp. 241–249, 2013.

scales for representing the image features using orthonormal bases functions. At each iteration, non-essential bases are removed while diffusions map the graph information to a new scale. The proposed methodology is applied on blocks of pixels from image sequences, while the optical flow is estimated based on the similarity in the ortho-diffusion space between regions of the two frames from the image sequence. Graph based representation of images is outlined in Section 2. The methodology of ortho-diffusion analysis is detailed in Section 3 and its application for optical flow estimation in Section 4. In Section 5 we provide the experimental results while the conclusions are given in Section 6.

2   Graph Based Representations of Images

Let us consider as $\mathbf{X} = \{x_1, x_2, x_3...., x_n\}$ the normalized grey-level values of pixels from an image region to the interval $[0,1)$. A weight matrix $\mathbf{K}$ of size $n \times n$ is calculated as an adjacency matrix by considering the probabilities of moving from x_i to any other point assuming that each datum is the neighbour to all the others from $\mathbf{X}$:

$$K(x_i, x_k) = e^{-\frac{||x_i - x_k||^2}{\sigma^2}}, \tag{1}$$

where σ is the scale of the diffusion kernel used for normalization. Weight matrix elements will be zero when there is no edge between the corresponding nodes and in the following we consider only localized blocks of pixels from the image while neglecting the similarity of pixels from further away regions [2, 6].

For a kernel matrix $\mathbf{K}$ we consider a diagonal matrix $\mathbf{D}$ whose elements represent the degree of a node, calculated as $d(x_i) = \sum_{k=1}^{n} K(x_i, x_k)$. The degree of similarity is defined by the random walk matrix $\mathbf{P}$ for t steps on a graph as:

$$\mathbf{P}^t = (\mathbf{D}^{-1}\mathbf{K})^t \tag{2}$$

The element at a certain location from the matrix $P^t(x_i, x_k)$ represents the probability of being at node x_k at time t when starting at node x_i. The Markov matrix $\mathbf{P}$ evaluates the local similarity in the data set, while the matrix $\mathbf{P}^t$ integrates such local information for t steps leading to data representations on larger neighbourhoods. The Markov process can be analyzed by using the eigen-decomposition of its corresponding matrix. Laplacian eigenfunctions are global [1] and cannot be used to study random walks effectively at small and medium t scales.

3   Ortho-Diffusion Analysis of Images

In the following we provide a new graph decomposition which consists of data simplification and diffusion embedding into the Gram-Schmidt orthonormal decomposition of $\mathbf{P}^t$. Let us assume that an image $\mathbf{I}_p$ or a region of such a image is represented by a matrix $\mathbf{P}$ as described in the previous section. A diffusion wavelet tree is produced by the recursive orthogonal decomposition of the matrix $\mathbf{P}$ into a set of diffusion scaling functions and their orthogonal wavelet functions at each scale j, [7]. The scaling functions at the scale j span the subspace $\mathcal{V}_j$, while the wavelets span the space $\mathcal{W}_j$, representing the orthogonal complement of $\mathcal{V}_j$ into the $\mathcal{V}_{j+1}$ domain:

$$\mathcal{V}_{j+1} = \mathcal{V}_j \oplus^\perp \mathcal{W}_j \tag{3}$$

where the diffusion bases are characterized by $\mathcal{V}_{j+1} \subseteq \mathcal{V}_j$. The ortho-diffusion methodology has the following stages: orthogonalization, data compression and dilation. The ortho-diffusion bases from $\mathcal{V}_j$ represent essential image features while wavelet functions from $\mathcal{W}_j$ represent random texture and noise. A diffusion wavelet tree is produced by using dyadic powers $\mathbf{P}^{2^j}$, corresponding to dilations, which are used to create smoother and wider bumps functions to be used for data analysis on the given graph structure. By orthogonalizing and downsampling appropriately we transform sets of bumpy functions into orthonormal scaling functions by removing the non-essential information and eventually extracting only the underlying data representation.

The orthogonalization methodology consists of the recursive application of the modified Gram-Schmidt with pivoting the columns ($\mathcal{QR}$ algorithm) [7]. The $\mathcal{QR}$ algorithm decomposes a given matrix $\mathbf{P}$ into an orthogonal matrix $\mathbf{Q}$ whose columns are orthonormal bases functions and a triangular matrix $\mathbf{R}$. In the following we use the notation $[\mathbf{\Phi}_b]_{\mathbf{\Phi}_a}$ for a matrix representing the base $\mathbf{\Phi}_b$ with respect to $\mathbf{\Phi}_a$. We denote the triangular matrix by $[\mathbf{P}]_{\mathbf{\Phi}_a}^{\mathbf{\Phi}_b}$ whose column space is represented using bases $\mathbf{\Phi}_a$ at scale a, while the row space is represented using bases $\mathbf{\Phi}_b$ at scale b. The matrix $\mathbf{P}$ is represented initially at the scale $j = 0$ on the basis set $\mathbf{\Phi}_0$ as $[\mathbf{\Phi}_0]_{\mathbf{\Phi}_0}$ and let us consider its columns as the set of functions $\tilde{\mathbf{\Phi}}_0 = \{[\mathbf{\Phi}_0]_{\mathbf{\Phi}_0}\delta_k\}_k$ on the given graph, where δ_k is a set of Dirac functions. The $\mathcal{QR}$ algorithm decomposes $[\mathbf{P}]_{\mathbf{\Phi}_0}^{\mathbf{\Phi}_0}$ at the first level $j = 0$ as:

$$[\mathbf{P}]_{\mathbf{\Phi}_0}^{\mathbf{\Phi}_0} = [\mathbf{P}]_{\mathbf{\Phi}_0}^{\mathbf{\Phi}_1}[\mathbf{\Phi}_1]_{\mathbf{\Phi}_0} \tag{4}$$

where the triangular matrix $[\mathbf{P}]_{\mathbf{\Phi}_0}^{\mathbf{\Phi}_1}$ is the transformation of the matrix $\mathbf{P}$ whose columns are represented with respect to the base $\mathbf{\Phi}_1$, the rows are represented with respect to $\mathbf{\Phi}_0$ and the orthonormal matrix $[\mathbf{\Phi}_1]_{\mathbf{\Phi}_0}$ represents the base $[\mathbf{\Phi}_1]$ with respect to $[\mathbf{\Phi}_0]$.

The $\mathcal{QR}$ decomposition is applied recursively at each scale j, with base $\mathbf{\Phi}_{j+1}$ replacing $\mathbf{\Phi}_j$, starting with $j = 0$, as in equation (4). The orthonormal bases functions span $\mathbf{\Phi}_j$ representing columns in $[\mathbf{\Phi}_j]_{\mathbf{\Phi}_j}$. The $\mathcal{QR}$ decomposition is followed by the data reduction stage which removes non-essential columns and matrix' entries which do not carry significant information, thus contributing to the reduction in the required computation complexity. The columns, at a scale $j > 0$, whose norms are smaller that a given precision ϵ, are removed and only the columns representing significant vectors are further used:

$$\tilde{\mathbf{\Phi}}_j = \{\|[\mathbf{\Phi}_{j+1}]_{\mathbf{\Phi}_j}\delta_k\| > \epsilon\}_k, \tag{5}$$

where $\| \cdot \|$ represents the norm of the column extracted by the Dirac function δ_k. When eliminating a column from $[\mathbf{\Phi}_{j+1}]_{\mathbf{\Phi}_j}$, we remove its corresponding row from $[\mathbf{P}^{2^{j+1}}]_{\mathbf{\Phi}_j}^{\mathbf{\Phi}_{j+1}}$, as well. For enforcing the sparseness of the triangular matrix $[\mathbf{P}^{2^{j+1}}]_{\mathbf{\Phi}_j}^{\mathbf{\Phi}_{j+1}}$ we neglect all entries which are smaller than a threshold θ and consider them as zero. The columns representing the most significant orthonormal bases functions are pivoted among the leading columns of the matrix following pivoting.

The decomposition and data reduction stages described above are followed by data representation dilations on the graph defined as $[\mathbf{P}^{2^j}]_{\mathbf{\Phi}_j}^{\mathbf{\Phi}_{j+1}}$ for the scale j. At the scale $j+1$, we dilate the operator by squaring its corresponding matrix:

$$[\mathbf{P}^{2^{j+1}}]_{\mathbf{\Phi}_{j+1}}^{\mathbf{\Phi}_{j+1}} = ([\mathbf{P}^{2^j}]_{\mathbf{\Phi}_j}^{\mathbf{\Phi}_{j+1}}[\mathbf{\Phi}_{j+1}]_{\mathbf{\Phi}_j})^2 = [\mathbf{P}^{2^j}]_{\mathbf{\Phi}_j}^{\mathbf{\Phi}_{j+1}}([\mathbf{P}^{2^j}]_{\mathbf{\Phi}_j}^{\mathbf{\Phi}_{j+1}})^\tau. \qquad (6)$$

This corresponds to implementing a diffusion on the data representation at scale 2^j and reprojecting the given manifold data to the scale 2^{j+1}.

The extended base $[\mathbf{\Phi}_{j+1}]_{\mathbf{\Phi}_0}$ is calculated at each recursion $j+1$ with respect to the initial base $\mathbf{\Phi}_0$ as:

$$[\mathbf{\Phi}_{j+1}]_{\mathbf{\Phi}_0} = [\mathbf{\Phi}_{j+1}]_{\mathbf{\Phi}_j}[\mathbf{\Phi}_j]_{\mathbf{\Phi}_0}. \qquad (7)$$

While with each scale $j+1$, the number of bases functions decreases and the matrix $[\mathbf{\Phi}_{j+1}]_{\mathbf{\Phi}_j}$ becomes smaller, the matrix of the extended bases functions $[\mathbf{\Phi}_{j+1}]_{\mathbf{\Phi}_0}$ records only the essential image information with respect to the initial base $\mathbf{\Phi}_0$. Each basis function, representing a column of $[\mathbf{\Phi}_{j+1}]_{\mathbf{\Phi}_j}$ can be used to represent image features in a low resolution image, while its corresponding extended bases functions, representing columns of $[\mathbf{\Phi}_{j+1}]_{\mathbf{\Phi}_0}$, would map such features to the size of the original image. At the scale $j+1$, the representation of $\mathbf{P}^{2^{j+1}}$ is compressed based on the amount of the remaining underlying data assuming the desired precision ϵ and threshold θ.

4   Dense Optical Flow Estimation Using Ortho-Diffusion Vectors

Optical flow is used to determine the apparent motion from two successive frames of an image sequence. Let us consider a block of pixels $\mathcal{B}_{x,y,p}$ of size $B_x \times B_y$ pixels centered at the location $\{x, y\}$ from the frame $\mathbf{I}_p$. We consider another frame $\mathbf{I}_{p+1}$ and a search region $S_x \times S_y$ with $S_x > B_x$, $S_y > B_y$, centered at same location $\{x, y\}$. While in other approaches, such as for the initialization of the method from [12] we used either directly the greylevel in this study we use the ortho-diffusion vector representations, extracted as described in the previous section. Let us consider the extended ortho-diffusion vectors $[\mathbf{\Phi}_{x,y,p,j}]_{\mathbf{\Phi}_0}$ calculated at scale j for the block $\mathcal{B}_{x,y,p}$ and $[\mathbf{\Phi}_{k,l,p+1,j}]_{\mathbf{\Phi}_0}$ for all the blocks of identical size $B_x \times B_y$ considered from the search region $\mathcal{B}_{k,l,p+1} \in S_x \times S_y$, which could correspond to all blocks of pixels displaced by one pixel along x and y axes from the search region or which could represent a subset of such blocks. Such ortho-diffusion vectors represent robustly localized image features from the two frames $\mathbf{I}_p$ and $\mathbf{I}_{p+1}$.

In this study we propose to estimate the optical flow as the displacement of the locations where the most similar ortho-diffusion wavelets from the two frames are located. The similarity is given by the Euclidean distance between ortho-diffusion vectors:

$$(u_x, v_y) = \arg \min_{\substack{\forall \mathcal{B}_{k,l,p+1} \\ \in S_x \times S_y}} \left([\mathbf{\Phi}_{k,l,p+1,j}]_{\mathbf{\Phi}_0} - [\mathbf{\Phi}_{x,y,p,j}]_{\mathbf{\Phi}_0}\right)^T \left([\mathbf{\Phi}_{k,l,p+1,j}]_{\mathbf{\Phi}_0} - [\mathbf{\Phi}_{x,y,p,j}]_{\mathbf{\Phi}_0}\right)$$

$$(8)$$

where all available offsets $\{k, l\}$ are considered. Equation (8) is repeated for all the blocks of pixels $B_x \times B_y$ from the frame $\mathbf{I}_p$ and then for the other frames from the image sequence eventually providing a dense vector field for the image sequence.

5   Experimental Results

In the following we provide results showing how ortho-diffusion bases can be used to model images as well as the optical flow from image sequences. In all experiments the scale parameter is considered as $\sigma = 0.03$ in (1), while the precision for removing the columns in $\mathcal{QR}$ is $\epsilon = 10^{-6}$ in (5), while the matrix sparsing threshold is $\theta = 2.210^{-16}$. The recursions stop when a single ortho-diffusion vector remains from the matrix modelling the data.

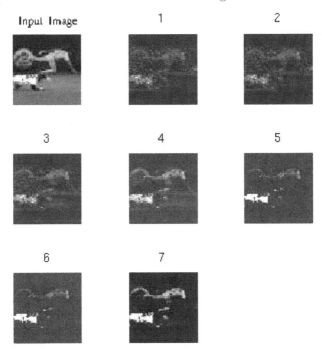

Fig. 1. Feature representations at multiple scales for an American football scene

We apply the proposed ortho-diffusion decomposition methodology for representing various images and one example is shown in Fig. 1. These images show a scene of American football play at a resolution of 50×50 pixels. We apply the proposed ortho-diffusion decomposition methodology on their Markov transition matrices and the results when reconstructing the image from its ortho-diffusion bases, according to [6], for scale j as indicated above each reconstruction are shown in Fig. 1. We can observe that the input images are reconstructed up to a certain precision for each scale, with the main features well emphasized.

In the following we present the results for dense optical flow estimation using the similarity of the ortho-diffusion bases from consecutive frames. The extended ortho-diffusion bases are calculated for each block of pixels from each frame. We define a search region in the second frame and consider all blocks of pixels from such regions as possible candidates for its displacement. The optical flow is defined by the displacement of the pairs of blocks of pixels from the two frames, whose ortho-diffusion vectors are most similar. Two frames, each of size 367×526 from the infrared Meteosat image sequence are shown in Fig. 2(a) and 2(b). The Meteosat sequence shows a storm as recorded by the satellite. We can observe a rotational motion in the center of the image combined with a divergent movement on the top right corner. We split the frames into 20×20 pixel blocks, while the offsets for the search windows are considered as $[-6, 6] \times [-6, 6]$. The estimated optical flow provided by the similarity in the ortho-diffusion vector representation for local blocks of pixels from the two frames of the Meteosat sequence is shown as a motion vector field in Fig. 2(c). The estimated optical flow models well the complex movement of the storm with few vectors of wrong directions and these could have been smoothed out as in the approach from [12].

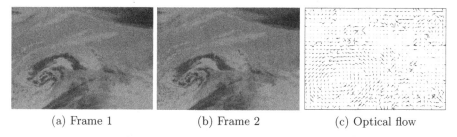

(a) Frame 1   (b) Frame 2   (c) Optical flow

Fig. 2. Estimating the optical flow in the infrared Meteosat image sequence

The standard data set for comparing optical flow estimation algorithms is the Middlebury database [11] which contains optical flow ground truth for the given image sequences. In this paper we only present the results on the Dimetrodon and Venus image sequences. A frame of size 420×380 pixels from the Venus image sequence is shown in Fig. 3(a). 20×20 pixel blocks are modelled using the proposed ortho-diffusion methodology and in Fig. 3(b) we provide the optical flow estimation, represented as a vector field. The same optical flow is shown in pseudo-color in Fig. 4(b), according to the color code from Fig. 4(a), as in [11]. The ground-truth of the optical flow is shown for comparison in Fig. 4(c). Some optical flow errors can be observed at top left, right bottom edge and in the center of the image where there are sharp disparities.

Quantitative results are defined by the average angular error (AE):

$$AE = \arccos \left(\frac{u_{gt} u_e + v_{gt} v_e + 1}{\sqrt{(u_{gt}^2 + v_{gt}^2 + 1)(u_e^2 + v_e^2 + 1)}} \right), \tag{9}$$

and the average flow error (FE):

$$FE = \sqrt{[(u_{gt} - u_e)^2 + (v_{gt} - v_e)^2]}, \tag{10}$$

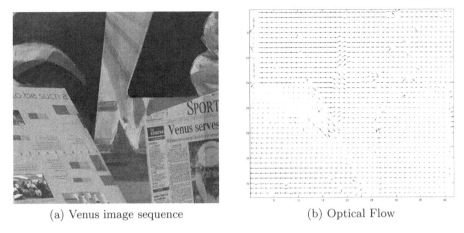

(a) Venus image sequence   (b) Optical Flow

Fig. 3. Frame from Venus image sequence and its estimated optical flow

where (u_e, v_e) and (u_{gt}, v_{gt}) are the estimated and the ground truth flows, respectively. Errors for optical flows characterized by large vectors are smaller when using the AE measure, while FE provides better error evaluation for areas characterized by low motion. The results when using minimal distances in the ortho-diffusion space are compared with those provided by Black and Anandan [8], Bruhn et al. [10], correlations of diffusion distances [6], the Media Player and Zitnick et al. [13] in Table 1 for the two sequences. While the best results are provided by the first method listed in Table 1, the proposed ortho-diffusion methodology provides similar results with the next three algorithms and better results than the last two methods.

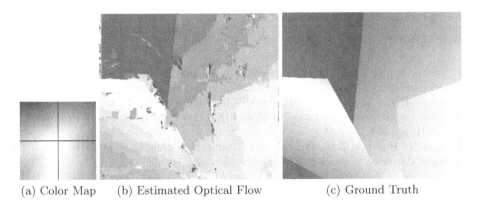

(a) Color Map   (b) Estimated Optical Flow   (c) Ground Truth

Fig. 4. Comparison with ground truth using a pseudo-code colours

Table 1. Numerical results for optical flow estimation

Methods	Average Angular Error		Average Flow Error	
	Dimetrodon	Venus	Dimetrodon	Venus
Black and Anandan [8]	9.26	7.64	0.35	0.55
Bruhn et al. [10]	10.99	8.73	0.43	0.51
Pyramid LK [9]	10.27	14.61	0.37	1.03
Diff. distance [6]	11.45	10.40	0.50	0.87
Ortho-diffusion bases	12.04	11.36	0.51	0.83
Media Player	15.82	15.48	0.94	0.85
Zitnick et al. [13]	30.10	11.42	0.55	1.08

6   Conclusion

In this paper we propose an ortho-diffusion methodology for optical flow estimation. Image data is locally represented at a succession of scales by embedding diffusions into the ortho-normal decompositions with the modified Gram-Schmidt algorithm. Data reduction by removing the non-significant bases and by sparsing the matrices involved takes place at each scale after the orthonormal decompositions, ensuring thus an appropriate representation of essential image features. The embedded diffusions are implemented as self-multiplications of the transition Markov transitions matrices at a given scale, ensuring the optimal feature projection to the next scale. The optical flow is estimated based on the similarity in the most significant ortho-diffusion vectors corresponding to blocks of pixels from consecutive frames. The methodology of ortho-diffusion representation of image features has many potential applications including feature detection, image search and retrieval, tracking, etc.

References

1. Belkin, M., Niyogi, P.: Laplacian eigenmaps for dimensionality reduction and data representation. Neural Computation 15(6), 1373–1396 (2003)
2. Robles-Kelly, A., Bors, A.G., Hancock, E.R.: Hierarchical iterative eigendecomposition for motion segmentation. In: Proc. IEEE Inter. Conf. on Image Processing, vol. II, pp. 363–366 (2001)
3. Xiao, B., Hancock, E.R., Wilson, R.C.: Graph characteristics from the heat kernel trace. Pattern Recognition 42(11), 2589–2606 (2009)
4. Coifman, R.R., Lafon, S.: Diffusion maps. Applied Comput. Harmon. Anal. 21(1), 5–30 (2006)
5. Singer, A., Coifman, R.R.: Non-linear independent component analysis with diffusion maps. Applied Comput. Harmon. Anal. 25(1), 226–239 (2008)
6. Wartak, S., Bors, A.G.: Optical Flow Estimation Using Diffusion Distances. In: Proc. Int. Conf on Pattern Recognition, pp. 189–192 (2010)
7. Magioni, M., Mahadevan, S.: Fast direct policy evaluation using multiscale analysis of Markov diffusion processes. In: Proc. Int. Conf. Machine Learn., pp. 601–608 (2005)

8. Black, M.B., Anandan, P.: The robust estimation of multiple motions: parametric and piecewise-smooth flow fields. Computer Vision and Image Understanding 63(1), 75–104 (1996)

9. Bouguet, J.: Pyramidal Implementation of the Lucas-Kanade Feature Tracker: Description of the Algorithm Technical Report TR2004-196, Intel Microprocessor Research Labs (2000)

10. Bruhn, A., Weickert, J., Schnorr, C.: Lucas/Kanade meets Horn/Schunck: Combining local and global optic flow methods. Int. Jour. of Computer Vision 61(3), 211–231 (2005)

11. Baker, S., Scharstein, D., Lewis, J.P., Roth, S., Black, M.J., Szeliski, R.: A database and evaluation methodology for optical flow. Int. Jour. of Computer Vision 92(1), 1–31 (2011)

12. Doshi, A., Bors, A.G.: Robust processing of optical flow of fluids. IEEE Trans. Image Processing 19(9), 2332–2344 (2010)

13. Zitnick, C.L., Jojic, N., Kang, S.B.: Consistent segmentation for optical flow estimation. In: Proc. IEEE Int. Conf. on Computer Vision, vol. 2, pp. 1308–1315 (2005)

Pairwise Similarity for Line Extraction from Distorted Images

Hideitsu Hino[1], Jun Fujiki[2], Shotaro Akaho[3],
Yoshihiko Mochizuki[4], and Noboru Murata[4]

[1] University of Tsukuba, 1–1–1 Tennoudai, Tsukuba, Ibaraki 305–8573, Japan
hinohide@cs.tsukuba.ac.jp
[2] Fukuoka University, 8–19–1 Nanakuma, Jonan-ku, Fukuoka, 814-0180, Japan
fujiki@fukuoka-u.ac.jp
[3] National Institute of Advanced Industrial Science and Technology,
Tsukuba, Ibaraki 305–8568, Japan
s.akaho@aist.go.jp
[4] Waseda University, 3–4–1 Ohkubo, Shinjuku-ku, Tokyo, 169–8555, Japan
motchy@aoni.waseda.jp, noboru.murata@eb.waseda.ac.jp

Abstract. Clustering a given set of data is crucial in many fields including image processing. It plays important roles in image segmentation and object detection for example. This paper proposes a framework of building a similarity matrix for a given dataset, which is then used for clustering the dataset. The similarity between two points are defined based on how other points distribute around the line connecting the two points. It can capture the degree of how the two points are placed on the same line. The similarity matrix is considered as a kernel matrix of the given dataset, and based on it, the spectral clustering is performed. Clustering with the proposed similarity matrix is shown to perform well through experiments using an artificially designed problem and a real-world problem of detecting lines from a distorted image.

Keywords: pairwise similarity, spectral clustering, line detection, distorted image.

1 Introduction

The goal of clustering is to find the intrinsic grouping in a set of unlabeled data. Clustering is one of the central topics of machine learning, statistics, data mining, and pattern recognition. A lot of methods are developed and the study of clustering is an active area of research [1,2]. Clustering methods play important roles in image processing. For example, they serve as building blocks of image segmentation [3] and object detection [4], to name a few. An important element of a clustering algorithm is the similarity measure between data points, and sometimes the Euclidean distance can be misleading.

On the other hand, detecting lines and curves in a two-dimensional image is an important problem in image processing. To detect them, the Hough transformation [5], and random sampling consensus (RANSAC) based methods [6,7]

R. Wilson et al. (Eds.): CAIP 2013, Part II, LNCS 8048, pp. 250–257, 2013.

are frequently used. Both of these approaches are based on fitting of lines or curves, and this parametric nature of these methods limits the applicability to highly-distorted and complicated line segments detection.

In this paper, a general framework of defining similarity measures between pairs of data points is proposed. The similarity matrix is then used as the kernel matrix for spectral clustering [2]. It is applied to artificial datasets and a real-world dataset of line-detection problem from an image taken by a camera with a fish-eye lens.

2   Clustering and Similarity Measure

Suppose we are given a dataset $\mathcal{D} = \{x_i\}_{i=1,\ldots,n}$, $x_i \in \mathcal{X} \subseteq \mathbb{R}^2$. The aim of clustering is to divide the given dataset $\mathcal{D}$ into subsets of data based on a certain kind of similarity defined between each pair x_i and x_j. Clustering methods with the Euclidean distance can successfully group the given dataset into clusters if the dataset is a disjoint union of clusters in $\mathcal{X}$. However, when the given dataset is not well-separable but contains certain "structure", conventional methods may fail to find reasonable cluster structures. For example, consider the case shown in Fig. 2 (a). Neither the k-means nor the spectral clustering with a Gaussian kernel, which is one of the state-of-the-art methods, can not find three intrinsic clusters. This kind of data can be successfully clustered by, for example, k-planes method [8], which fits planes for data and represent clusters by these planes instead of centroids. In this paper, we take another approach. That is, we will design a novel similarity measure between each pair of data to capture the intrinsic structure of the data like Fig. 2 (a).

2.1   Proposed Similarity Measure

In this section, we will propose a framework of defining similarity measure between x_i and x_j based on how other data are distributed around the line connecting these two points.

Given a dataset $\mathcal{D}$, we calculate the similarity S_{ij} between each pair $x_i, x_j \in \mathcal{D}$ in the following manner. We first subtract $(x_i + x_j)/2$ from all other data in $\mathcal{D}$ to obtain $\tilde{\mathcal{D}}_{[i,j]} = \{\tilde{x}_k\}_{k \neq i,j}$, $\tilde{x}_k = x_k - \frac{x_i + x_j}{2}$. We note that the re-defined data $\tilde{x}_k$ depend on x_i and x_j, and should be written as $\tilde{x}_k^{[i,j]}$, but for notational simplicity, we omit the superscript $[i,j]$. Then, we consider the coordinate system with the origin $\frac{x_i + x_j}{2}$ and axes along with the line connecting x_i and x_j and orthogonal to it. We next calculate the ℓ_1-distance $\|\tilde{x}_k\|_1 = |[\tilde{x}_k]_1| + |[\tilde{x}_k]_2| = h_k^{ij} + v_k^{ij}$ of $\tilde{x}_k$ with respect to this coordinate system. Here, h_i and v_i are the horizontal and the vertical elements of the vector $\tilde{x}_k$, and $[x]_i$ is the i-th element of a vector x. We also define $d^{ij} = \frac{\|x_j - x_i\|_2}{2}$. See Fig. 1 (Left) for an illustration of these quantities. Then, we introduce the notion of the *degree of neighborhood to the pair* (x_i, x_j) for each $\tilde{x}_k \in \tilde{\mathcal{D}}_{[i,j]}$ by $F(k|i,j; \boldsymbol{\lambda})$ with a parameter vector $\boldsymbol{\lambda}$, and define the similarity S_{ij} between x_i and x_j by the sum of this quantity for all $\tilde{x}_k \in \tilde{\mathcal{D}}_{[i,j]}$ as

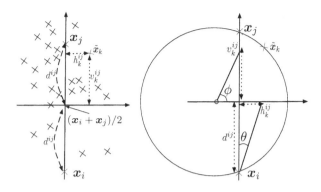

Fig. 1. Left: illustration diagram of $\tilde{\boldsymbol{x}}_k, h_k^{ij}$ and v_k^{ij}. Right: angles θ and ϕ in Eq. (3).

$$S_{ij} = \sum_{\tilde{\boldsymbol{x}}_k \in \tilde{\mathcal{D}}_{[i,j]}} F(k|i,j;\boldsymbol{\lambda}). \qquad (1)$$

The similarity S_{ij} is calculated for every pair $\boldsymbol{x}_i, \boldsymbol{x}_j \in \mathcal{D}$ to obtain the similarity matrix S, $[S]_{ij} = S_{ij}$ for the given dataset $\mathcal{D}$.

One simple candidate of the concrete form of F is

$$F(k|i,j;\boldsymbol{\lambda}=(\lambda_1,\lambda_2)) = \lambda_1 \exp\left(-\frac{\lambda_1}{d^{ij}}h_k^{ij}\right) \cdot \lambda_2 \exp\left(-\frac{\lambda_2}{d^{ij}}v_k^{ij}\right), \qquad (2)$$

that is, h_k^{ij}/d^{ij} and v_k^{ij}/d^{ij} are assumed to follow independent exponential distributions with the scale parameters $1/\lambda_1$ and $1/\lambda_2$, respectively, and the similarity S_{ij} is the sum of probability values of h_k^{ij}/d^{ij} and v_k^{ij}/d^{ij} for $k \in \{1,\dots,n\}\backslash\{i,j\}$. Another possible form of F derived from elemental geometric viewpoint is

$$F(k|i,j;\lambda) = \begin{cases} \exp\left(-\tan\theta/\lambda\right)\exp\left(-\tan\phi/\lambda\right), & h_k^{ij} < d^{ij} \\ 0, & otherwise \end{cases} \qquad (3)$$

$$= \begin{cases} \exp\left\{-\frac{1}{\lambda}\left(\frac{h_k^{ij}}{d^{ij}} + \frac{2h_k^{ij}v_k^{ij}}{(d^{ij})^2-(h_k^{ij})^2}\right)\right\}, & h_k^{ij} < d^{ij} \\ 0, & otherwise \end{cases} \qquad (4)$$

where θ and ϕ are shown in Fig. 1 (Right). When θ is large, $\tilde{\boldsymbol{x}}_k$ is considered to be far from the line connecting $\boldsymbol{x}_i$ and $\boldsymbol{x}_j$, and contribution of this point to the similarity decays exponentially. On the other hand, large ϕ implies $\tilde{\boldsymbol{x}}_k$ is far from the origin along the line, and the contribution to the similarity also decays.

In our preliminary experiments, we tried some other definition of F, and finally found the one defined in (2) and (3) are useful. Actually, two similarities (2) and (3) achieved similar experimental results, and in this paper, we show experimental results using the model (2) with $\lambda_1 = 100, \lambda_2 = 1$. There are many conceivable definitions of F, and some of these shall be explored in our future work. In our preliminary experiments, we tried some other definition of F, and finally found the one defined in (2) and (3) are useful.

2.2   Spectral Clustering with Proposed Similarity

We propose to use the similarity measure S_{ij} between x_i and x_j defined by Eqs. (1) and (2) for data clustering. In principle, we can use any clustering method with the proposed similarity measure. In this paper, we adopt the spectral clustering [2], which has been shown to be one of the state-of-the-art clustering method. There are several kinds of spectral clustering algorithms. We use the algorithm based on normalized cut [9]. In normalized cut spectral clustering, the adjacency matrix W, which represents the similarity between data, determines the clustering performance. In this paper, we propose to use the similarity matrix S defined above as an adjacency matrix for spectral clustering.

We note that the proposed method is based on "voting", and similar to recently proposed NC-spectral clustering [10]. In NC-spectral clustering, $F(k|i, j; \lambda)$ in Eq. (1) is defined by

$$F(k|i, j; \lambda) = \begin{cases} 1, & \frac{(x_i - x_k)^\top (x_j - x_k)}{\|x_i - x_k\|_2 \cdot \|x_j - x_k\|_2} \geq \lambda, \\ 0, & otherwise, \end{cases} \tag{5}$$

and the matrix S is used as the adjacency matrix in the spectral clustering.

3   Experimental Results for Artificial Data

The clustering performances are compared through a two-dimensional example. The objective dataset consists of three classes that intersect at the origin. For each class, 100 samples are generated following equations

$$x = sa_i + \epsilon, \quad i = 1, 2, 3, \tag{6}$$

where $s \sim \mathcal{N}(0, 1)$, $\epsilon \sim \mathcal{N}(0, I_2)$. The coefficient vectors of the model are $a_1 = (1, 2)^\top, a_2 = (2, 2)^\top, a_3 = (2, 1)^\top$. Here $\mathcal{N}(m, \Sigma)$ is a Gaussian distribution with mean vector m and covariance matrix Σ, and I_d is the identity matrix in $\mathbb{R}^{d \times d}$. For this dataset, five clustering methods are applied to find the three distinct clusters. For all experiments in this paper, we set the parameter $\lambda = 10$ in the proposed method. For spectral clustering with Gaussian kernel and for NC-spectral clustering, the kernel parameter and threshold parameter are tuned by trying various values and we report seemingly the best results.

We show the experimental result in Fig. 2. Points in different clusters are shown in different colors and marks. From this result, we see that the intrinsic cluster structure shown in Fig. 2 (a) can not be found by (b) the k-means method and (c) the spectral clustering method with Gaussian kernel function. On the other hand, (d) the NC-spectral clustering method, (e) the k-planes method, and (f) the proposed method successfully find the cluster structure.

4   Line Detection from Distorted Image

In this section, we apply the proposed similarity measure followed by spectral clustering for detecting line segments from a distorted image taken by a camera

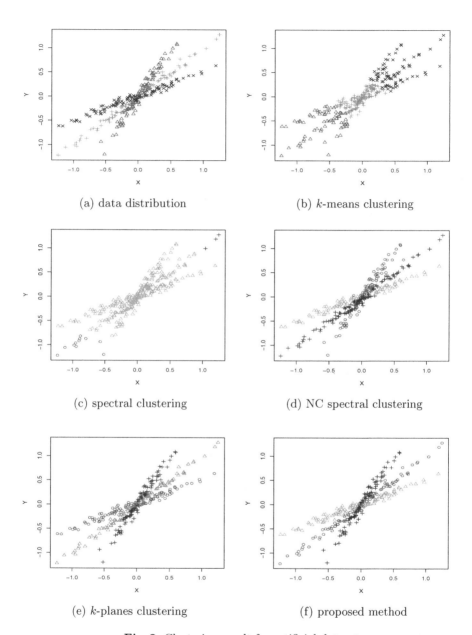

(a) data distribution

(b) k-means clustering

(c) spectral clustering

(d) NC spectral clustering

(e) k-planes clustering

(f) proposed method

Fig. 2. Clustering result for artificial dataset

with a fish-eye lens. This problem is of particular importance for calibration of radially symmetric distortion [11].

Figure 3 (a) shows a distorted checker pattern image taken by a camera with a fish-eye lens, and Fig. 3 (b) is the image after applying a Canny filter for edge detection. By thresholding operation, coordinates of the detected edges are extracted as shown in Fig. 3 (c). Since only a small number of long lines are required for calibration, we trimmed the central portion of the data as shown in Fig. 3 (d). We applied k-means, k-planes, NC-spectral clustering, and the proposed method. The number of clusters are set to fix for all of the methods. The clustering results are shown in Fig. 4.

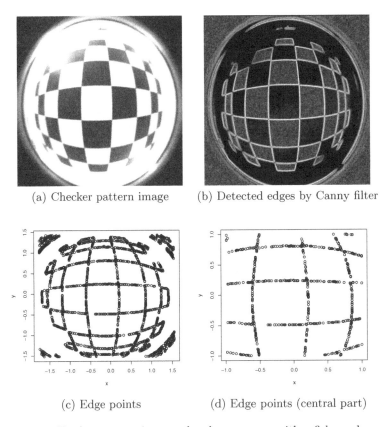

(a) Checker pattern image   (b) Detected edges by Canny filter

(c) Edge points   (d) Edge points (central part)

Fig. 3. Checker pattern image taken by a camera with a fish-eye lens

From Figs. 4 (a) and (b), we see that the k-means and k-planes algorithms can not group points on the same lines into the same clusters. Figures 4 (c) and (d) show that NC-spectral clustering can find curve-like structures, but the proposed method obtains better clustering result. We note that we applied spectral clustering with various Gaussian kernels to this line detection problem, but the performance was far from satisfiable. From these result, we can see that spectral clustering itself is not enough for our purpose, and the similarity measure equipped with the spectral clustering plays crucial role. The proposed similarity measure uses an explicit relation to line shapes in an image. However, by introducing the locality by d_{ij} in the definition of the function F, the proposed

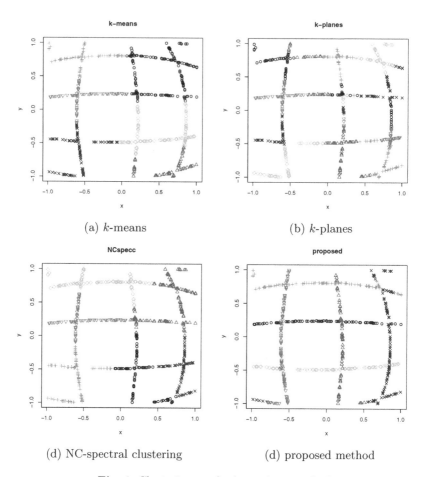

(a) k-means

(b) k-planes

(d) NC-spectral clustering

(d) proposed method

Fig. 4. Clustering results by various methods

similarity measure can capture distorted line structures unless the curvature of the distorted line is not so large.

5   Conclusion

In this paper, we proposed a framework of defining similarity measures between two points considering how other data are concentrated around the line connecting these two points. Instead of conventional similarities based on the Euclidean distance, the proposed framework aims at capturing certain kind of geometric configuration of the data, i.e., the similarity between a pair of data points is based on the confidence that these two data points constitute a curve in the input space. We experimentally showed that our proposed similarity measure can capture the intrinsic cluster structure that could not be found by conventional methods. We also our method to the problem of identifying line segments in a distorted image, and achieved a reasonable result.

Following the idea of NC-spectral clustering [10], the proposed similarity measure is used for the spectral clustering. The similarity measure is independent from the following clustering algorithm, and we can adopt any clustering method based on the similarity measure. When performing clustering, the number of clusters need to be specified in advance. Automation of this step is a very important subject of clustering study, and there are a number of studies on finding an appropriate cluster numbers [12,13]. In our future work, the suitable clustering method and the method of finding the number of clusters based on the similarity measure shall be investigated. Finally, application of the proposed method to various kind of problems to investigate the usefulness and limitation of the proposed method remain to be done.

Acknowledgement. The authors express their appreciation to reviewers for their valuable comments. Part of this work is supported by MEXT Kakenhi No.25870811.

References

1. Jain, A.K., Dubes, R.C.: Algorithms for Clustering Data. Prentice Hall (1988)
2. Ng, A.Y., Jordan, M.I., Weiss, Y.: On spectral clustering: Analysis and an algorithm. In: NIPS, pp. 849–856 (2001)
3. Coleman, G.B., Andrews, H.C.: Image segmentation by clustering. Proceedings of the IEEE 67(5), 773–785 (1979)
4. Avidan, S., Butman, M.: The power of feature clustering: An application to object detection. In: NIPS, pp. 57–64 (2004)
5. Duda, R.O., Hart, P.E.: Use of the Hough transformation to detect lines and curves in pictures. Commun. ACM 15(1), 11–15 (1972)
6. Fujiki, J., Akaho, S., Hino, H., Murata, N.: Robust hypersurface fitting based on random sampling approximations. In: Huang, T., Zeng, Z., Li, C., Leung, C.S. (eds.) ICONIP 2012, Part III. LNCS, vol. 7665, pp. 520–527. Springer, Heidelberg (2012)
7. Suetani, H., Akaho, S.: A RANSAC-based ISOMAP for filiform manifolds in nonlinear dynamical systems – an application to chaos in a dripping faucet. In: Honkela, T. (ed.) ICANN 2011, Part II. LNCS, vol. 6792, pp. 277–284. Springer, Heidelberg (2011)
8. Bradley, P.S., Mangasarian, O.L.: k-plane clustering. J. of Global Optimization 16(1), 23–32 (2000)
9. Dhillon, I.S., Guan, Y., Kulis, B.: Kernel k-means: spectral clustering and normalized cuts. In: KDD, pp. 551–556 (2004)
10. Fujiwara, K., Kano, M., Hasebe, S.: Development of correlation-based clustering method and its application to software sensing. Chemometrics and Intelligent Laboratory Systems 101(2), 130–138 (2010)
11. Hino, H., Usami, Y., Fujiki, J., Akaho, S., Murata, N.: Calibration of radially symmetric distortion by fitting principal component. In: Jiang, X., Petkov, N. (eds.) CAIP 2009. LNCS, vol. 5702, pp. 149–156. Springer, Heidelberg (2009)
12. Pelleg, D., Moore, A.W.: X-means: Extending k-means with efficient estimation of the number of clusters. In: ICML, pp. 727–734 (2000)
13. Kalogeratos, A., Likas, A.: Dip-means: an incremental clustering method for estimating the number of clusters. In: NIPS, pp. 2402–2410 (2012)

Plant Leaf Classification Using Color on a Gravitational Approach

Jarbas J. de M. Sá Junior[1], André R. Backes[2], and Paulo César Cortez[1]

[1] Departamento de Engenharia de Teleinformática - DETI
Centro de Tecnologia - UFC
Campus do Pici, S/N, Bloco 725
Caixa Postal 6007, CEP: 60.455-970, Fortaleza, Brasil
jarbas_joaci@yahoo.com.br, cortez@lesc.ufc.br
[2] Faculdade de Computação
Universidade Federal de Uberlândia
Av. João Naves de Ávila, 2121
38408-100, Uberlândia, MG, Brasil
arbackes@yahoo.com.br

Abstract. Literature describes the analysis and identification of plant leaves as a difficult task. Many features may be used to describe a plant leaf. One of them is its texture, which is also one of most important features in image analysis. This paper proposes to study the texture information of all three color channels of a plant leaf by converting it into a simplified gravitational system in collapse. We also use fractal dimension to describe the states of the gravitational collapse as they occur. This enable us to describe the texture information as a function of complexity and colapsing time. During the experiments, we compare our approach to other color texture analysis methods in a plant leaves dataset.

Keywords: Plant Leaf, Color Texture Analysis, Simplified Gravitational System, Complexity.

1 Introduction

A topic of intense research in the last years in computer vision is the identification of visual patterns, in special, the texture of a surface image. This is a very discriminative image feature and humans are able to distinguish different textures easily. However, this feature lacks of a formal definition in literature. It is usually described as a visual pattern composed by entities that have specific properties, such as size, brightness, color, etc. Nevertheless, natural textures do not fit in this definition. These textures usually present a random and persistent stochastic pattern, thus resulting in a cloud like texture appearance [1].

Literature groups texture analysis methods into four basic categories: i) signal processing methods [2,3], ii) statistical methods [4], iii) structural methods; and iv) model-based methods. More recently, literature presents some methods

R. Wilson et al. (Eds.): CAIP 2013, Part II, LNCS 8048, pp. 258–265, 2013.

that cannot be classified in these categories. These methods are based on deterministic walks [5], complex networks [6], gravitational models [7] etc. Mostly of these methods present the inconvenient of working only with gray-scale images. However, color information has been proven to be quite useful in image analysis [8,9]. This is specially true for analysis of natural textures.

In this paper, we propose we use a simplified gravitational approach together with a complexity analysis method (in this case, the Bouligand-Minkowski fractal dimension method [10]) to classify 10 plant species from the Brazilian flora. In order to achieve this goal, we analyzed color microtextures presented in the leaf surfaces. We applied the proposed approach over each color channel of the texture image, thus providing discriminative feature vectors for the plant species [3]. This work is justified due to the fact that plant leaf are often present as an information source of the plant, different from flowers and fruits, which are commonly used in the field of plant taxonomy and are not always available.

This paper starts by presenting an overview of the gravitational system and how a texture pattern can be modeled into it (Section 2). In the sequence, we describe the proposed feature vector used for image classification (Section 3). This feature vector combines both collapse and fractal dimension information computed for each color channel of the pattern under analysis. Section 4 presents an experiment proposed to evaluate the performance of our feature vector. This experiment aims to classify the color textures extracted from 10 plant species from the Brazilian flora (15 leaf samples for each species). Finally, we present the results achieved in Section 5 as also a comparison with other color texture analysis methods. Finally, Section 6 presents some remarks about the paper.

2   A Gravitational System for Texture Analysis

Recently, we have proposed a novel approach which uses gravitational system to explore a texture pattern. We starting by modeling an input texture image as a gravitational system. For this, we consider each pixel as a particle of mass m that orbits the center of the image. In the image center, we consider the existence of a massive object M. This object acts as a black hole that pulls all other particles towards it. For computational cost reasons, we do not allow particles to interact with each other, only with the object of mass M.

For the simulation of a system in gravitational collapse, we must consider two components for each pixel: its tangential speed v_{pix} and the gravitational force f_g between m and M. We compute the magnitude of the gravitational force f_g as follows

$$\|\boldsymbol{f}_g\| = \frac{G.m.M}{r^2},   (1)$$

where r is the distance between m and M. Notice that this formulation is according to the rules established by Isaac Newton [11]. The gravitational force f_g acts as a centripetal force f_c, whose magnitude is defined as

$$\|\boldsymbol{f}_c\| = m.\frac{\|\boldsymbol{v}_{pix}\|^2}{r}. \tag{2}$$

We must assure that all pixels collapse properly. We achieve this goal when we reach the highest magnitude of tangential speed v_{max}. Thus, to accomplish this, we established $f_g = f_c$, thus resulting in

$$\|\boldsymbol{v}_{max}\| = \sqrt{\frac{G.M}{r_{max}}}, \tag{3}$$

where r_{max} is the largest distance between a particle associated to a pixel and the object at the image center. In the sequence, we determine the magnitude of the tangential speed for each pixel according to the following equation

$$\|\boldsymbol{v}_{pix}\| = \left(1 + \frac{I(x,y)}{255}\right)\frac{\|\boldsymbol{v}_{max}\|}{2}, \tag{4}$$

where $I(x,y)$ is the pixel intensity and the mass of the particle.

Through the application of these rules, each pixel will have a singular spiral movement. By considering the movement of all pixels in the image, this results in new and unexplored texture configurations. By studying these configurations, we are able to obtain a more discriminative image signature. A more detailed description of the gravitational system is found in [7].

3   Gravitational Based Signature for Color Textures

In order to characterize a color texture pattern, we propose to apply our collapsing model over each color channel. In the sequence, we use a traditional texture descriptor to measure the evolution of the original pattern as it collapses. To accomplish this task, we propose to use the Bouligand-Minkowski fractal dimension method [10].

The concept of fractal dimension was originally developed by Mandelbrot to characterize the complexity of fractals, mathematical objects that do not exist in the physical world [12]. It is a measurement of complexity, which enable us to describe an object in terms of its irregularity and space occupation [13]. Later, the fractal dimension was extended for shape and texture analysis.

Among different methods to estimate fractal dimension, literature considers the Bouligand-Minkowski fractal dimension as the most accurate method due to its great sensitiveness to the structural changes [14,10]. This method uses the influence area of an object (in our case, a texture image) to compute its complexity. Consider $I(x,y)$ the intensity value associated with a pixel at a texture pattern I. We convert each pixel $I(x,y)$ into a new point in $s = (x,y,z) \in R^3$, where $z = I(x,y)$. Through the dilation of each point $s \in S$ of the resulting surface S by using a radius r, we are able to compute the influence volume $V(r)$. Then, we estimate the Bouligand-Minkowski fractal dimension D as

$$D = 3 - \lim_{r \to 0} \frac{\log V(r)}{\log r}, \tag{5}$$

with

$$V(r) = \left| \left\{ s' \in R^3 | \exists s \in S : |s - s'| \le r \right\} \right|. \tag{6}$$

Fractal dimension enables us to estimate the complexity of a texture image. However, the value that we estimate for fractal dimension depends on the dilation radius r. Thus, for a given collapsing time t, different values for fractal dimension may be estimated to compose the following feature vector

$$\psi_t = [D(r_1), D(r_2), \ldots, D(r_n)]. \tag{7}$$

We must also keep in mind that as the texture collapses, its complexity changes. This gives origin to new values for fractal dimension, D. Thus, the collapsing process and fractal dimension can be combined to provide a second feature vector that represents a texture pattern in terms of its complexity as it collapses

$$\varphi_{t_1, t_2, \ldots, t_M} = [\psi_{t_1}, \psi_{t_2}, \ldots, \psi_{t_M}] \tag{8}$$

Using this feature vector, we are able to describe a gray-scale texture pattern. Nevertheless, we can compute φ for each color channel of a color image. Then, we combine them to compose a single feature vector for that color texture, as follows:

$$\Gamma = \left[\varphi^{(R)}, \varphi^{(G)}, \varphi^{(B)} \right]. \tag{9}$$

4   Experiments

In order to evaluate our proposed approach, we propose to use a leaf database built using 10 leaves species from Brazilian flora. For each plant species, we manually collected 3 leaf samples fully developed. We washed each sample to remove impurities that could act as noise in the tests. Then, we acquired each sample by using a scanner with 1200dpi *(dots per inch)* resolution. During this stage, we oriented each leaf to have its central axis in a vertical position.

From each leaf, we extracted a total of 5 texture samples of 128×128 pixels of size. This resulted in an image dataset containing 150 texture samples grouped into 10 classes (Figure 1). The identification of plant leaves is considered a difficult task. This is mostly due to the wide pattern variation of its fundamental features, such as color and texture (Figure 2). Some os these variations depend on the maturity of the plant leaf or other factors, such as sun exposure, soil influence, fungus, diseases, climate and even environment. Thus, to avoid the extraction of texture samples that do not represent the plant, we extracted manually the texture windows.

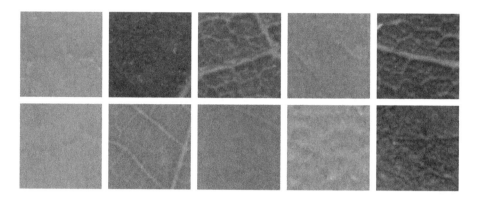

Fig. 1. Example of the texture of the 10 leaf species used in the experiment

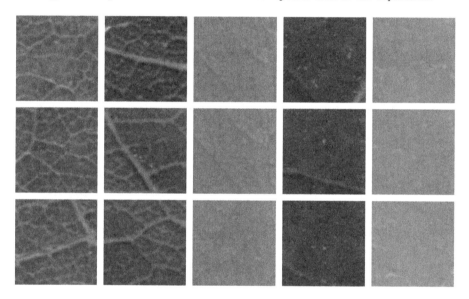

Fig. 2. Example of texture variation in a single leaf species (columns)

For the evaluation of our proposed feature vector we used Linear Discriminant Analysis (LDA) [15,16], a supervised statistical classification method. We also used *leave-one-out cross-validation* scheme to evaluate the feature vectors computed for each texture sample.

5   Results

Before we apply the gravitational approach to texture analysis, some parameters must be set: the mass M and the gravitational constant G. According to experiments previously published in [7] and the size of the texture images used in the

Table 1. Success rate (%) on the leaf database for both multiple radius values r and time steps t

	r				
Time (t)	$\{3,4\}$	$\{3,4,5\}$	$\{3,4,5,6\}$	$\{3,4,5,6,7\}$	$\{3,4,5,6,7,8\}$
$\{1,5\}$	87.33	94.00	93.33	93.33	93.33
$\{1,5,10\}$	91.33	93.33	95.33	94.67	92.67
$\{1,5,10,15\}$	92.00	93.33	94.67	96.00	93.33
$\{1,5,10,15,20\}$	91.33	96.00	94.67	94.67	87.33

Table 2. Comparison results for different texture methods

Method	Images correctly classified	Success rate (%)
Gabor EEE	139	92.67
LBP + Haralick	136	90.67
MultiLayer CCR	135	90.00
HRF	39	26.00
Proposed approach	144	96.00

experiments, the best values for these parameters are $G = 1$ and $M = 204.8$. These parameters assure a constant collapse process for the input images.

In the sequence, we evaluate the proposed feature vectors. We start by analyzing the feature vector which considers both multiple values r and different sets of time steps t in Table 1. It has been proven that the use of several r values achieves a better performance than the use of each individual r value [7]. We notice an increase in the success rate as both the sets of r values and time steps t increase. An explanation for such result lies in the fact that gravitational process helps to explore texture information by using multiple collapse stages (t values). Moreover, leaf texture are, basically, microtextures. Such textures require larger and distinct radius values for a more accurate discrimination. Notice, however, that this process is not constant. For some values of r or t, the success rate starts to decrease due to the presence of redundant information in the computed feature vector. This indicates that there is a limit in the discrimination ability of this method for this sort of texture pattern.

As an additional experiment we compared our approach with other color texture analysis methods, as shown in Table 2. We performed such experiment in order to confirm the performance of our approach. For this comparison, we considered the following methods: Gabor EEE [17,18], Histogram ratio features (HRF) [19], MultiLayer CCR [20] and LBP + Haralick method [21]. For all methods, we considered the configuration of parameters as proposed in their respective papers. For our approach we considered the parameters $t = \{1, 5, 10, 15, 20\}$ and $r = \{3, 4, 5\}$ as they lead to the maximum success rate (96.00%) and also present less descriptors than the other configuration with the same success rate ($t = \{1, 5, 10, 15\}$ and $r = \{3, 4, 5, 6, 7\}$). Results of this comparison show that our method is able to extract texture features that are more discriminative than the compared approaches as its success rate overcomes the others. This is quite impressive, especially if we consider the importance and the challenge that natural textures represent.

6   Conclusion

The characterization of leaves is a very difficult task. This is mostly due to the high similarity inter-classes and low similarity of intra-classes of plant species. In this paper we proposed to use a simplified gravitational system to characterize color leaf textures. This gravitational system enables us to explore the variations in a texture pattern as it collapses. We used the Bouligand-Minkowski fractal dimension method in order to characterize the texture in terms of its complexity, thus resulting in a feature vector which describes the variation of the complexity of each color channel during the collapsing process. In the sequence, we evaluated our approach in an experiment using linear discriminant analysis to classify a previously defined leaf texture database. We also compared our approach with traditional color texture analysis methods. Results indicate the great potential of our approach for natural texture analysis applications.

Acknowledgements. André R. Backes gratefully acknowledges the financial support of CNPq (National Council for Scientific and Technological Development, Brazil) (Grant #301558/2012-4), FAPEMIG and PROPP-UFU.

References

1. Backes, A.R., Casanova, D., Bruno, O.M.: Color texture analysis based on fractal descriptors. Pattern Recognition 45(5), 1984–1992 (2012)
2. Azencott, R., Wang, J.P., Younes, L.: Texture classification using windowed fourier filters. IEEE Trans. Pattern Anal. Mach. Intell 19(2), 148–153 (1997)
3. Casanova, D., Sá Junior, J.J.M., Bruno, O.M.: Plant leaf identification using Gabor wavelets. International Journal of Imaging Systems and Technology 19(1), 236–243 (2009)
4. Haralick, R.M.: Statistical and structural approaches to texture. Proc. IEEE 67(5), 786–804 (1979)
5. Backes, A.R., Gonçalves, W.N., Martinez, A.S., Bruno, O.M.: Texture analysis and classification using deterministic tourist walk. Pattern Recognition 43(3), 685–694 (2010)
6. da, F., Costa, L., Rodrigues, F.A., Travieso, G., Boas, P.R.V.: Characterization of complex networks: A survey of measurements. Advances in Physics 56, 167–242 (2007)
7. Sá Junior, J.J.M., Backes, A.R.: A simplified gravitational model to analyze texture roughness. Pattern Recognition 45(2), 732–741 (2012)
8. She, A.C., Huang, T.S.: Segmentation of road scenes using color and fractal-based texture classification. In: ICIP (3), pp. 1026–1030 (1994)
9. Asada, N., Matsuyama, T.: Color image analysis by varying camera aperture. In: International Conference on Pattern Recognition, vol. I, pp. 466–469 (1992)

10. Backes, A.R., Casanova, D., Bruno, O.M.: Plant leaf identification based on volumetric fractal dimension. IJPRAI 23(6), 1145–1160 (2009)
11. Newton, I.: Philosophiae Naturalis Principia Mathematica. University of California (1999) original 1687, translation guided by I.B. Cohen
12. Mandelbrot, B.: The fractal geometry of nature (2000)
13. Schroeder, M.: Fractals, Chaos, Power Laws: Minutes From an Infinite Paradise. W. H. Freeman (1996)
14. Tricot, C.: Curves and Fractal Dimension. Springer (1995)
15. Everitt, B.S., Dunn, G.: Applied Multivariate Analysis, 2nd edn. Arnold (2001)
16. Fukunaga, K.: Introduction to Statistical Pattern Recognition. 2nd edn. Academic Press (1990)
17. Hoang, M.A., Geusebroek, J.M.: Measurement of color texture. In: International Workshop on Texture Analysis and Synthesis, pp. 73–76 (2002)
18. Hoang, M.A., Geusebroek, J.M., Smeulders, A.W.M.: Color texture measurement and segmentation. Signal Processing 85(2), 265–275 (2005)
19. Paschos, G., Petrou, M.: Histogram ratio features for color texture classification. Pattern Recognition Letters 24(1-3), 309–314 (2003)
20. Bianconi, F., Fernandez, A., Gonzalez, E., Caride, D., Calvino, A.: Rotation-invariant colour texture classification through multilayer CCR. Pattern Recognition Letters 30(8), 765–773 (2009)
21. Porebski, A., Vandenbroucke, N., Macaire, L.: Haralick feature extraction from LBP images for color texture classification. In: Image Processing Theory, Tools and Applications, pp. 1–8 (2008)

Semi-automatic Image Annotation

Julia Moehrmann and Gunther Heidemann

Institute of Cognitive Science,
University of Osnabrueck, Germany
{firstname.lastname}@uni-osnabrueck.de

Abstract. High quality ground truth data is essential for the development of image recognition systems. General purpose datasets are widely used in research, but they are not suitable as training sets for specialized real-world recognition tasks. The manual annotation of custom ground truth data sets is expensive, but machine learning techniques can be applied to preprocess image data and facilitate annotation. We propose a semi-automatic image annotation process, which clusters images according to similarity in a bag-of-features (BoF) approach. Clusters of images can be efficiently annotated in one go. The system recalculates the clustering continuously, based on partial annotations provided during annotation, by weighting BoF vector elements to increase intra-cluster similarity. Visualization of top-weighted codebook elements allows users to estimate the quality of annotations and of the recalculated clustering.

Keywords: Image annotation, semi-supervised clustering, pairwise constraints.

1 Introduction

Annotation of high quality ground truth data sets is a crucial task in the development of image recognition systems. Incorrect annotations may cause a classifier to establish incorrect hypotheses and thereby degrade its recognition performance. Computer vision research has largely focused on the creation of general purpose data sets, which are useful for evaluating specific methods, but present no suitable training set for specialized, i.e., real world, recognition tasks.

We previously presented a framework for developing application specific image recognition systems (FOREST), aimed at non-expert users [1]. It allows the development of application specific image recognition systems solely through the annotation of the corresponding ground truth data. The annotation process was simplified by displaying a clustered version of the image data, allowing for efficient annotation as shown in a user study [2]. The adaption of the underlying clustering, based on partial annotations, was not possible but was desired by users to further enhance the annotation efficiency. We therefore present an extension of the annotation interface which employs a bag-of-features (BoF) approach to incorporate semi-supervised clustering based on heterogeneous feature sets and partial annotations, as shown in Figure 1. Codebook weights are adapted continuously and top-weighted BoF codebook elements are displayed in

R. Wilson et al. (Eds.): CAIP 2013, Part II, LNCS 8048, pp. 266–273, 2013.

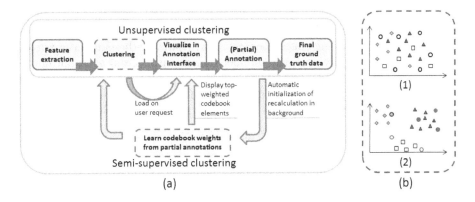

Fig. 1. a) Semi-automatic annotation process with continuous user feedback. b) shows effect of adapting weights for each category (shape indicates category, circles unlabeled elements). (1) initial distribution with uniform weights, (2) adapted data with color indicating samples assigned to same class.

the user interface (UI) to provide feedback about the clustering quality. The decision whether to reload the clustering remains with the user. For the interactive annotation process this visualization provides three huge advantages:

1. Visibility of annotation errors on degraded codebook elements in UI
2. Adaptation of manual annotation strategy for improving clustering, e.g., annotation of multiple categories or selection of images with large variety
3. Feedback about quality of recalculated clustering as basis for deciding whether to reload the semi-supervised clustering

In the following we will present the semi-supervised clustering, the annotation interface and the evaluation of the semi-supervised clustering.

2 Related Work

Human computation, i.e., using human manpower to solve large scale problems, has been employed for creating general purpose data sets. The best known applications are LabelMe [3] and the ESP game [4], with the incentive for contributing being the data itself and the joy of playing a game. Šimko et al. [5] developed a Concentration like game for annotating private photo collections. This is closer to annotating specialized data sets, but the duration for annotating data sets is unclear. While the annotation of personal photo collections serves self-interest, annotating ground truth data is a necessary burden. The integration of gaming aspects therefore bears the risk of introducing an unnecessary overhead. Acquiring external manpower for annotating specialized ground truth data is, in general, barely possible without spending money, due to the lack of external interest in the data. Completing the annotation task by oneself demands for semi-automatic support, i.e., adaption of the underlying model based on user feedback. Kumar et al. [6] presented a semi-supervised k-means clustering, using triplet constraints of the form $\{uvw|l_u = l_v \wedge l_u \neq l_w\}$, where l_u is the label of image u. Weights for each cluster are adapted using these constraints, thereby improving cluster homogeneity. However, the number of triplet constraints grows rapidly with the number of annotations and even optimized implementations take over one hour to compute [7], which is unacceptable for an interactive annotation tool. Solving this optimization in an adequate amount of time requires reduction of triplets via random sampling, but degrades the resulting clustering due to overfitting. The semi-supervised clustering in this work therefore uses partial annotations as pairwise must-link (ML) and cannot-link (CL) constraints [8] to optimize weight vectors for each available category.

Suitable features for clustering images depends on the data set. In order to create a good clustering on arbitrary data sets, it is desirable to use various features and thereby capture different image properties. Non-negative matrix factorization (NMF [9]) methods yield a set of local features and can be applied in a semi-supervised clustering process using pairwise constraints [10]. The application of NMF to arbitrary data sets with background clutter and varying viewpoints is, in general, difficult. Also, the interpretability of the resulting local features by non-expert users is questionable. Bag-of-Features (BoF) approaches [11] are successfully used in computer vision. An advantage is that they are able to cope with heterogeneous feature sets and features can be visualized by simply extracting the corresponding image patch.

3   Data Preprocessing

In this work, we extract SIFT [12], color histograms [13] and Local Binary Patterns (LBP) [14] from images around keypoints detected with the DoG (difference of Gaussian) detector [12]. There is no restriction as to adding new feature types with respect to the following BoF approach. A BoF vector $bof_{i,t}$ is calculated for every image $i \in I$ and every feature type $t \in T$, with $|T|$ being the number of different feature types, here $|T| = 3$. Codebook elements are calculated using k-means clustering on each feature type separately, resulting in BoF vectors of size $(1 \times k)$. The elements of BoF vectors are calculated using term frequency (tf) and soft weighting [15]. The final BoF vector bof_i is a concatenation, given as $bof_i = \{bof_{i,1}, bof_{i,2}, .., bof_{i,|T|}\}$. Similarity between two BoF vectors is calculated using histogram intersection [16], given in Eq. 1.

$$\widetilde{s}(u,v) = \sum_{i=1}^{k \cdot |T|} h_i(u,v) \quad h_i(u,v) = min(bof_u(i), bof_v(i)) \tag{1}$$

$$\widetilde{S} = \widetilde{s}(u,v) \quad u,v = 1,..,|I| \quad \widetilde{s}(u,u) = 0 \tag{2}$$

A hierarchical agglomerative complete linkage clustering is calculated on the images using similarity matrix $\widetilde{S}$. The clustering is determined to stop when $n = 2\sqrt{|I|}$ clusters are reached. The formula for n was chosen as it restricts the growth of the resulting clustering for very large data sets. The clusters are projected on a plane using a force directed layout [17].

4   Semi-supervised Clustering

Pairwise must-link (ML) and cannot-link (CL) constraints are given by images annotated with the same or different class labels respectively. Although pairwise constraints result in less detailed data than triplet constraints, they allow for an efficient optimization process. The idea is to adapt the weighting of codebook elements to maximize intra-class similarity of ML-constraints and minimize inter-class similarity of CL-constraints. Figure 1b) shows that weighting each labeled data sample with the weight vector associated to its category moves elements of a category closer together. For this purpose Eq. 1 is extended to calculate a weighted histogram intersection as given in Eq. 3. That is, every codebook element is associated with a weighting factor w_i. The complete weight vector $w_c = \{w_1, .., w_{k \cdot |T|}\}$ is calculated for each category c separately. The optimization of w_c according to pairwise constraints is given in Eq. 4, where $|ml_c|$ and $|cl_c|$ are the number of pairwise constraints $\{u, v\} \in ml_c$ and $\{u, v\} \in cl_c$ respectively. Without the logarithm Eq. 4 would result in a trivial solution, which is a binary vector with $\{w_i = 1$ if $ml_c(i) > cl_c(i), w_i = 0$ else$\}$.

$$s(u, v) = \sum_{i=1}^{k \cdot |T|} w_i \cdot h_i(u, v), \quad \sum_{i=1}^{k \cdot |T|} w_i = 1 \tag{3}$$

$$w_c = argmin_{w_c}(\sum_1^{|cl_c|} cl_c \cdot w_c^T - \sum_1^{|ml_c|} log(ml_c \cdot w_c^T)) \tag{4}$$

$$with \quad ml_c = \{(h_1(u, v), .., h_{k \cdot |T|}(u, v))|c = l_u = l_v\} \tag{5}$$

$$cl_c = \{(h_1(u, v), .., h_{k \cdot |T|}(u, v))|l_u = c, l_u \neq l_v\} \tag{6}$$

After calculating w_c for each category, unlabeled data samples are assigned to the best matching category, i.e., the category where the average similarity of the x best matches is the highest (here $x = 5$). Agglomerative hierarchical clustering is then performed on each category. The complete semi-supervised clustering algorithm is given in Table 1. Since the complexity of solving Eq. 4 increases with the size of the codebook, we implemented alternating optimization to solve the optimization problem for partitions of the weight vector w_c separately as proposed in [7], using the Matlab optimization toolbox.

5   Annotation Interface

The image annotation interface is displayed in Figure 2. The UI consists of several coordinated views. The main view (marked (a)) displays the clustered image data. Each cluster is represented by an image stack, whose height indicates the number of images in the cluster. The background of the main view shows a hexagonal grid. Color of hexagons encodes cluster variance information (dark/light gray values ↔ large/small intra-cluster variance). The main view provides an intuitive zooming mechanism using the mouse wheel. As the zoom is increased the cluster images grow larger until (a) displays the detailed view, i.e.,

Table 1. Semi-supervised clustering algorithm, with images I and label categories C

Given:	Bag-of-features histograms bof_i, $i \in I$
Input:	Labels l_i with $l_i = c \in C \vee l_i = \emptyset$, $|c|$ = number of elements in category c
	Unlabeled elements $U = \{u|l_u = \emptyset\}$

1.	**for each** $c \in C$
2.	Calculate w_c according to Eq. 4
3.	**end**
4.	**for each** $u \in U$
5.	**for each** $c \in C$
6.	**for** $j = 1, .., |c|$
7.	$d_u(j) = s(bof_j, bof_u)$, $l_j = c$
8.	**end**
9.	Calculate permutation π_u of d_u s.t. $d_{\pi_u(1)} \geq d_{\pi_u(2)} \geq .. \geq d_{\pi_u(|c|)}$
10.	$m_u(c) = \frac{1}{x} \sum_{r=1}^{x} (d_{\pi_u(r)})$, $x \in [1, |c|]$
11.	**end**
12.	$l_u = argmin_c(m_u)$ // *Find best matching category*
13.	**end**
14.	**for each** $c \in C$
15.	$elms = \{bof_i | l_i = c\}$
16.	$S = \widetilde{S}(elms)$ // *Calculate subset of similarity matrix $\widetilde{S}$*
17.	cluster(S) // *Perform agglomerative clustering*
18.	**end**

all images of the clusters inside the hexagon. Clusters or individual images can be selected in the main view or in the preview (e). Annotation is performed using (customizable) buttons in (c). When an image or cluster is annotated it becomes 'inactive', i.e., it is no longer selectable and is drawn semitransparent. Thereby remaining unlabeled images are better visible and accidental re-annotation is prevented. Correction of annotation errors is possible by reactivating the category. An overview of the hexagonal grid (d) highlights remaining unlabeled clusters as green hexagons and the area currently displayed in (a). Red lines on the boundary of (a) indicate the direction of remaining unlabeled images.

The optimization of w_c allows the identification of discriminative codebook elements per category. We exploit this information by displaying the ten top-weighted codebook elements. Figure 2 (b) and (f) show top-weighted codebook elements for all five categories. For (b) only one cluster per category was annotated, which explains strange codebook elements for strawberry and motorcycle, caused by the background of annotated images. For (f) several clusters per category were annotated and BoF elements represent characteristic image segments. This provides a basis for deciding whether to reload the clustering.

6   Evaluation

We evaluated the performance of the semi-supervised clustering on two data sets. Data set 1 contains 792 images taken from Caltech-101 [18] including

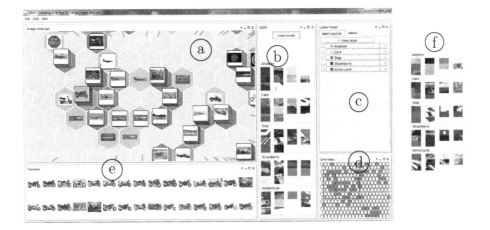

Fig. 2. Annotation interface with (a) zoomable clustered representation of image data set, (b) and (f) top-weighted codebook elements, (c) panel containing customizable label buttons, (d) overview of grid which highlights remaining unlabeled clusters (green) and the region currently displayed in (a), (e) preview of currently selected cluster

airplanes, motorcycles, cars, strawberries, stop signs. Data set 2 consists of 745 images from Graz02 [19] containing bikes and background. We used SIFT, color histograms and LBP with a codebook of $k = 100$ each and a soft-weighting value of 3. The relatively small number of codebook elements k is due to the computational costs that come along with a larger codebook. On data set 1 the semi-supervised clustering process takes about 10-15 seconds for all five categories with a total codebook size of 300. Since the recalculation process runs in a separate thread in background users do not have to wait for the calculation to finish. We found the chosen codebook size to perform well, considering efficiency and clustering performance. To investigate whether a larger codebook size might lead to more detailed codebook elements and therefore to better clustering results, we compared our setup to 1×300 codebook elements using individual feature types only. We evaluate the clustering performance on both data sets using the false positives (fp) of a clustering C as the number of annotated clusters increases. The evaluation considers remaining unlabeled elements only, since labeled elements remain labeled after the recalculation. Also, regarding annotation efficiency, the correctness of the unlabeled elements is of importance. False positives are calculated as

$$fp(C) = \sum_{cl=1}^{|C|} \sum_{i=1}^{|cl|} v(i), \quad v(i) = \begin{cases} 1 & \text{if } l_i \neq l_{cl} \\ 0 & \text{if } l_i = l_{cl} \end{cases} \tag{7}$$

where $|C|$ is the number of clusters, $|cl|$ is the number of elements in a cluster, l_i is the true category label of element i and l_{cl} is the true category label of the majority of elements in cluster cl. The baseline refers to the initial unsupervised

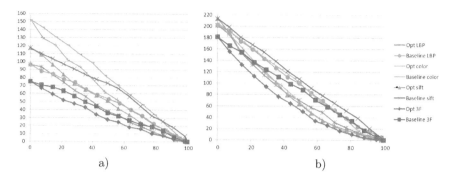

Fig. 3. Results for semi-supervised clustering using three feature types (3F) and individual feature types (averaged over 10 runs with randomly annotated clusters). Baseline indicates results for unlabeled elements on initial clustering. a) shows results on Caltech data set, b) shows results for GRAZ02 data set. Horizontal axis shows percentage of annotated clusters.

clustering and provides information about the remaining errors as the annotation is performed without recalculation. The results in Figure 3 show that the recalculation indeed improves the clustering for annotation, using heterogeneous feature sets or individual feature types. The semi-supervised clustering contains on average 10 and $20fps$ errors less for the Caltech and Graz02 data respectively. On the Caltech set, LBP features perform second best, while all individual features perform equally well on the Graz02 data. Individual feature types cannot compete with the heterogeneous BoF features on both data sets.

7   Conclusion

We presented an interactive semi-supervised image annotation process which optimizes weight vectors for each label category to increase intra-cluster similarity while minimizing inter-cluster similarity. Recalculation of the clustering using partial annotations is capable of producing a clustering with semantically more coherent cluster elements. Best matching features for top-weighted codebook elements are displayed in the UI to provide feedback about the clustering and the quality of annotations. This allows user to adapt their annotation strategy and create semantically meaningful clusters, allowing for an efficient completion of image annotation tasks. The semi-supervised learning process is also extremely well suited for visual exploration of image data sets, if annotation is not a major concern.

Future work will focus on the annotation of regions of interest within individual images to further enhance the quality of annotated ground truth data.

References

1. Moehrmann, J., Heidemann, G.: Efficient development of user-defined image recognition systems. In: Park, J.-I., Kim, J. (eds.) ACCV Workshops 2012, Part I. LNCS, vol. 7728, pp. 242–253. Springer, Heidelberg (2013)

2. Moehrmann, J., Heidemann, G.: Efficient Annotation of Image Data Sets for Computer Vision Applications. In: International Workshop on Visual Interfaces for Ground Truth Collection in Computer Vision Applications, pp. 2:1–2:6 (2012)
3. Russell, B.C., Torralba, A., Murphy, K.P., Freeman, W.T.: LabelMe: A database and web-based tool for image annotation. International Journal of Computer Vision 77(1), 157–173 (2008)
4. von Ahn, L., Dabbish, L.: Labeling images with a computer game. In: ACM CHI, pp. 319–326 (2004)
5. Šimko, J., Bieliková, M.: Personal image tagging: a game-based approach. In: Proceedings of the Intl. Conference on Semantic Systems, pp. 88–93. ACM (2012)
6. Kumar, N., Kummamuru, K.: Semi-supervised clustering with metric learning using relative comparisons. IEEE Transactions on Knowledge and Data Engineering 20(4), 496–503 (2008)
7. Cai, H., Yan, F., Mikolajczyk, K.: Learning weights for codebook in image classification and retrieval. In: IEEE CVPR, pp. 2320–2327 (2010)
8. Xing, E., Ng, A., Jordan, M., Russell, S.: Distance metric learning, with application to clustering with side-information. Advances in Neural Information Processing Systems 15, 505–512 (2002)
9. Lee, D., Seung, H.: Learning the parts of objects by non-negative matrix factorization. Nature 401(6755), 788–791 (1999)
10. Chen, Y., Rege, M., Dong, M., Hua, J.: Non-negative matrix factorization for semi-supervised data clustering. Knowledge and Information Systems 17(3), 355–379 (2008)
11. Csurka, G., Dance, C.R., Fan, L., Willamowski, J., Bray, C.: Visual categorization with bags of keypoints. In: Workshop on Statistical Learning in Computer Vision, ECCV, pp. 1–22 (2004)
12. Lowe, D.: Distinctive image features from scale-invariant keypoints. International Journal of Computer Vision 60, 91–110 (2004)
13. Manjunath, B.S., Ohm, J.-R., Vasudevan, V.V., Yamada, A.: Color and texture descriptors. IEEE Transactions on Circuits and Systems for Video Technology 11(6), 703–715 (2001)
14. Ojala, T., Pietikäinen, M., Mäenpää, T.: Multiresolution gray-scale and rotation invariant texture classification with local binary patterns. IEEE Transactions on Pattern Analysis and Machine Intelligence 24(7), 971–987 (2002)
15. Jiang, Y.-G., Yang, J., Ngo, C.-W., Hauptmann, A.G.: Representations of keypoint-based semantic concept detection: A comprehensive study. IEEE Transactions on Multimedia 12(1), 42–53 (2010)
16. Lazebnik, S., Schmid, C., Ponce, J.: Beyond bags of features: Spatial pyramid matching for recognizing natural scene categories. In: IEEE CVPR, vol. 2, pp. 2169–2178 (2006)
17. Fruchterman, T., Reingold, E.: Graph drawing by force-directed placement. Software: Practice and Experience 21(11), 1129–1164 (1991)
18. Fei-Fei, L., Fergus, R., Perona, P.: Learning generative visual models from few training examples: an incremental Bayesian approach tested on 101 object categories. In: Workshop on Generative-Model Based Vision (2004)
19. Opelt, A., Pinz, A., Fussenegger, M., Auer, P.: Generic object recognition with boosting. IEEE Transactions on Pattern Analysis and Machine Intelligence 28(3), 416–431 (2006b)

Segmentation of Skin Spectral Images Using Simulated Illuminations

Zhengzhe Wu[1], Ville Heikkinen[1], Markku Hauta-Kasari[1], and Jussi Parkkinen[2]

[1] School of Computing, University of Eastern Finland, Joensuu, Finland
firstname.lastname@uef.fi
http://www.uef.fi/spectral
[2] School of Engineering, Monash University Sunway Campus, Selangor, Malaysia
firstname@monash.edu

Abstract. Spectral imaging has been drawing attentions in skin segmentation related medical and computer vision applications. Usually spectral images contain radiance spectra or approximated reflectance spectra of objects. The reflectance spectrum is independent of illuminations, whereas the radiance spectrum is dependent on the illumination that was used during the measurement. Recently, the general illumination is using increasingly LED lights that have different spectral characteristics when compared to incandescent or fluorescent lights. In this paper, we studied effects of illuminations in unsupervised pixel-based skin segmentation with the Spectral Clustering (SC) algorithm based on two sets of skin spectral images, human hand and face. We adopted the eigengap heuristic to select the illumination in skin segmentation with the SC algorithm. Spectral radiance images under three CIE standard illuminants (A, D65, and F11), and two white LED illuminations, were respectively simulated from corresponding spectral reflectance images. The experimental results showed that CIE D65 illuminant return the highest average segmentation accuracies with 2.1% point and 3.4% point higher than the lowest results of illuminant CIE A in hand images and illuminant CIE F11 in face images, respectively. The accuracies of two LED illuminations are also high with around 1.5% point and 1.0% point decreases in average from the accuracy of illuminant CIE D65.

Keywords: skin segmentation, skin image segmentation, skin spectral image, illumination selection, CIE illuminant, LED.

1   Introduction

Skin segmentation is an important step in several medical and computer vision applications. In these applications, conventional RGB images are often used. Recently, with the development of spectral imaging devices, spectral images are becoming popular in skin segmentation related applications, such as allergic skin detection [1]. Spectral images could represent objects more accurately when compared to RGB images, since they contain spectra of objects with tens to hundreds of bands measured

R. Wilson et al. (Eds.): CAIP 2013, Part II, LNCS 8048, pp. 274–281, 2013.
© Springer-Verlag Berlin Heidelberg 2013

at different wavelengths. By utilizing the spectral information, segmentation and recognition problems can be alleviated [2] [3].

Spectral images usually contain radiance spectrum or approximated reflectance spectrum at each pixel location. Reflectance spectrum can be assumed to be independent of illumination properties [4]. Radiance spectrum is a mixture of the spectrum of the illumination and the object reflectance. Here we assume that the radiance spectrum can be simulated pixel-wise by using the element-wise product of reflectance spectrum from that pixel location and illumination spectral characteristics. Illumination has an important role in many color image processing tasks. For instance, in telemedicine, robustness of segmentation to the illumination is important. Moreover, LED illuminations are used increasingly nowadays, due to their various advantages when compared to ordinary light sources, such as high energy efficiency and long service life. However, LED illuminations have different spectral characteristics when compared to incandescent or fluorescent lights.

We studied the effect of illuminations in segmenting skin spectral images, based on two datasets that contain human hand and face images. The unsupervised pixel-based segmentation of skin images was explored with the Spectral Clustering (SC) algorithm [5] with Nyström method [6]. We also evaluated the illumination selection method that is based on the SC algorithm and the eigengap heuristic [7]. Spectral radiance images under three CIE standard illuminants (A, D65, and F11) and two white LED illuminations, were simulated by corresponding spectral reflectance images and Spectral Power Distributions (SPDs) of the illuminations. The flowchart of the segmentation is shown in Fig. 1. The experimental results showed that there are differences in segmentation accuracies of different illuminations. CIE D65 illuminant gave the highest average segmentation accuracy. There are no dramatically effects of LED illuminations on results, which are higher than those of illuminants CIE A and F11.

2   Skin Spectral Image Segmentation

In our study, all spectral radiance images were simulated from spectral reflectance images using the SPDs of three CIE illuminants (A, D65, and F11), and two white LED lights. The relative SPDs of those illuminations can be seen in Fig. 1. The spectral clustering algorithm with Nyström method was employed in pixel-based image segmentation on both normalized spectral reflectance and radiance images.

Spectrum Normalization. Simulated radiance spectrum at each pixel was normalized by their Euclidean norms in order to remove the magnitude of the illumination spectrum. We also removed the magnitude from reflectance spectrum in each pixel as a pre-processing for the segmentation.

Spectral Clustering for Pixel-Based Segmentation. We treated skin segmentation as a general unsupervised image segmentation problem which does not use any training skin pixel. The Spectral Clustering (SC) algorithm proposed in [5], which uses the symmetric normalized graph Laplacian, was used to do pixel-based image segmentation. The SC algorithm is a relaxation of the graph partitioning problem by using eigenvectors of matrices, usually the Laplacian matrix derived from the data [5]. These eigenvectors induce a new data representation that can be more easily clustered than using the original data. The SC algorithm has been successfully used in images segmentation tasks, including spectral image segmentation [8].

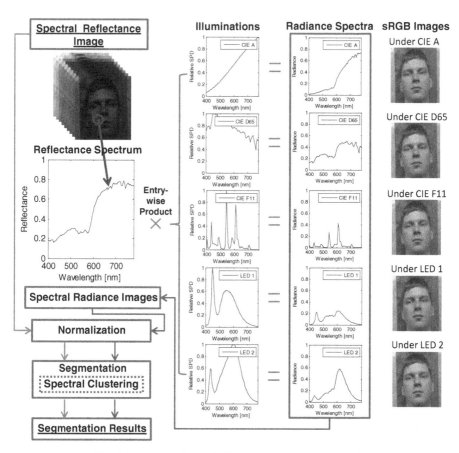

Fig. 1. Processing flow of skin spectral image segmentation

In our work, the normalized spectra were used as input data points in the SC algorithm. To calculate the similarity between each spectrum, the Gaussian similarity function was used, which can be written as $S_{ij} = \exp\left(-\|x_i - x_j\|^2 / 2\sigma^2\right)$ if $i \neq j$ and $S_{ii} = 0$, where $\|\cdot\|$ is the Euclidean norm, x_i and x_j are the normalized spectra corresponding to i^{th} and j^{th} pixels in one spectral image, and σ controls the rapidity of decay of S_{ij}. The performance of the SC algorithm is sensitive to σ and it is not trivial to select the optimal value. Therefore, the σ value was optimized to produce the maximal segmentation accuracy for each image by using large sets of initial values. Moreover, to reduce the computational demands of the SC algorithm,

Nyström method [6] was used in our work. By using Nyström method, an approximation of the eigenvectors of the Laplacian matrix could be obtained with small number of sample pixels. This approach is computationally efficiency, and usually returns segmentation results that are visually as good as those of the original SC algorithm [6]. Other methods using the sparse similarity matrix often make the homogenous segments over-segmented. Also block-wise and region based approaches usually involve the merging process that is not a trivial task.

3   Illumination Selection

We adopted the eigengap heuristic to select the illumination in skin segmentation. Eigengap is the absolute difference between adjacent eigenvalues of the Laplacian matrix in the SC algorithm. It is a measurement of the performance of the SC algorithm, and can be used as a quality criterion for the SC algorithm to automatically choose the number of clusters [7]. In our work, we assumed that the number of segments k of each image is known. For each spectral radiance image I_R, simulated from the corresponding spectral reflectance image and the SPDs of different candidate illuminations, we could compute the absolute difference d of kth and $(k+1)^{th}$ eigenvalues of the Laplacian matrix derived from I_R. Therefore, the illumination with the largest d value can be selected as the illumination for segmenting the current scene. Since the eigen-decompositon of the Laplacian matrix is one embedded step in the SC algorithm, no additional computational step is needed when using this approach.

4   Spectral Reflectance Skin Image Dataset

Two spectral reflectance skin image datasets, hand and face, from [9] were used in this study. Hand spectral images were acquired by an ImSpector V8 spectral camera with the spectral range of 380–780 nm and 5 nm sampling interval. The spatial size of these images is 160×148. There are one female and 6 males (3 East-Asians and 4 Caucasians) in this dataset. Their simulated sRGB representations under illuminant CIE D65 are shown in Fig. 2 from H#1 to H#9. Face spectral images were acquired by an ImSpector V10 (E) spectral camera with the spectral range of 400–1000 nm and 5 nm sampling interval. The spatial size of these images is 806×800. This face dataset includes 5 females and 8 males. Among these 13 persons, there are 2 East-Asians, 6 Caucasians, one Asian Indians, and 4 Africans. F#1 to F#13 in Fig. 2 give the simulated sRGB representations of face spectral images under illuminant CIE D65.

5   Experiments

5.1   Experiment Setup

Five sets of spectral radiance images were simulated by using CIE Standard illuminants A, D65, and F11, as well as two white LED light sources manufactured by

Osram. The SPDs of the LEDs were measured with a Hamamatsu PMA-11 fiber spectrometer. The first six bands of hand images were removed due to noises, so the spectral range used in experiments is 410–780 nm. For face images, only bands of visible spectral ranges from 400–780 nm were used. To increase the segmentation speed, some of the boundary parts of face images were removed, and the images were down-sampled spatially twice by simply taking a pixel by every two pixels horizontally and vertically. Hence, the down-sampling decreased the size of face images into ¼ of their original size after boundary part removing. After these processing, the new spatial size of face images is 165×150. The sRGB representations under CIE D65 of processed images F#3, F#5, and F#6, are shown in the left part of Fig. 3.

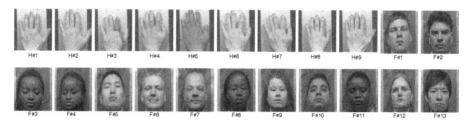

Fig. 2. Simulated sRGB representation of skin spectral image dataset of human hands and faces under illuminant CIE D65. H#1 and H#9 are from the same person, but H#1 was measured after 5 minute exercise. H#3 and H#8 are from another same person, but H#3 was acquired after the forefinger tied after 5 minutes.

Fig. 3. Examples of manually made ground truth of spectral images H#1, H#3, F#3, F#5, and F#6 shown by pseudo-colors

We performed the clustering with 1000 different σ values in the range of [0.01, 0.02, ..., 10] for each image in order to search the optimal value. One percent of total pixels were uniformly sampled from each image for Nyström method. At the last step of the SC algorithm, k-means algorithm was used to obtain the final segmentation results. As the clustering results of k-means are highly sensitive to the initial cluster centroids, we used repeated k-means algorithm (60 repetitions) with random initial centroids and 100 iterations each time. Therefore, we could somewhat obtain the best segmentation results for each test image.

The segmentation results were evaluated by the Segmentation Accuracy (SA). The SA is the percentage of corrected segmented pixels calculated based on the manually made segmentation Ground Truth (GT), defined as $SA = N_C/N_T$, where N_C is the number of correct segmented pixels against the ground truth and N_T is the number of total pixels in the image. The GTs of images H#1, H#3, F#3, F#5, and F#6, are shown in Fig. 3, where segments are represented by different pseudo-colors. The result with the highest SA for each image was chosen as the final segmentation result among segmentation results generated from 1000 different σ values in the SC algorithm.

5.2   Effects of Illuminations

Hand Images. From Table 1, we can see that spectral radiance images under illuminant CIE D65 return the highest SA of six in nine hand images. The highest SAs of the three remaining images are all from spectral reflectance images. The average SA of CIE D65 is the highest when compared to others. It is 2.1% point higher than the lowest one CIE A. The reasons may be that illuminant CIE A gives large weights in red color spectral regions, while D65 has relatively flat spectrum shape. The average SA of CIE F11 is the second lowest, since it has three big peaks and several small peaks in its SPDs that give more weights on some useless bands in segmentation. Two LEDs have similar results, whose average SAs are both higher than those of A and F11. There are two wide peaks in the SPDs of both LED illuminations. Moreover, illuminant CIE A and F11 return relatively low SAs of some images, such as H#3 for CIE A and H#8 for CIE F11 with 4.4% and 9.5% points lower than those of CIE D65.

Table 1. Segmentation accuracies of hand spectral images

Image	Number of Segments	Segmentation Accuracy (SA) (%)					
		Reflectance	A	D65	LED1	LED2	F11
H#1	3	**97.0**	96.4	96.9	96.5	96.6	96.1
H#2	3	**96.9**	96.2	96.8	96.2	96.8	96.2
H#3	5	92.5	89.2	**93.6**	92.5	92.0	92.5
H#4	3	95.9	95.3	**96.0**	95.2	95.5	94.8
H#5	3	97.1	96.3	**97.2**	96.5	96.6	96.6
H#6	3	96.8	96.1	**96.9**	96.4	96.3	96.6
H#7	3	96.5	96.0	**97.0**	96.1	96.3	96.6
H#8	4	**95.5**	87.3	95.2	88.0	88.0	85.7
H#9	3	95.9	94.5	**96.0**	95.8	95.7	95.5
Total Average SA (%)		96.0	94.1	**96.2**	94.8	94.9	94.5

Face Images. The results of face images are shown in Table 2, where we omitted the results of F#11, since it seems to be an outlier. The illuminant CIE D65 gave the highest average SA and the highest SAs of 5 in 12 images. The highest SAs of 4 in 12 images come from LED2. The CIE A, LED1, and the reflectance image gave the highest SA of one of the remaining three images, respectively. According to the total average SA, two LEDs return better results than those of CIE illuminants A and F11, the same as in hand images. CIE F11 gave the lowest average SA, which may result from the peaks in the SPD of CIE F11. Its SA is around 3.4% point lower than that of CIE D65. In addition, similar to hand images, the SAs of some images, such as F#5 for CIE A and F#9 for CIE F11, are relatively lower than those of CIE D65 with 4.9% point and 11.1% point differences.

Table 2. Segmentation accuracies of face spectral images

Image	Number of Segments	Segmentation Accuracy (SA) (%)					
		Reflectance	A	D65	LED1	LED2	F11
F#1	4	94.5	94.2	**94.8**	90.8	92.5	90.0
F#2	5	85.0	85.7	**85.9**	84.9	85.6	83.6
F#3	6	78.2	76.2	**78.9**	74.4	78.2	74.1
F#4	5	88.4	87.2	88.4	87.9	**89.2**	85.2
F#5	5	89.5	84.4	89.3	**91.1**	90.8	89.1
F#6	4	93.5	90.1	93.2	93.8	**94.2**	93.5
F#7	4	94.7	92.5	94.0	95.6	**95.9**	94.7
F#8	5	83.3	79.6	**83.5**	79.6	80.7	78.5
F#9	4	90.1	89.3	**90.2**	89.2	89.8	79.1
F#10	4	91.0	**91.4**	91.3	90.2	90.8	89.5
F#12	4	95.4	95.5	96.5	96.3	**96.9**	93.8
F#13	4	**85.1**	84.3	84.9	78.6	78.9	77.9
Total Average SA (%)		89.1	87.5	**89.2**	87.7	88.6	85.8

From the results of hand and face images, we could see that illuminant CIE D65 and reflectance data give relatively high average SAs. CIE A and F11 gave the lowest average SAs. LED illuminations do not have dramatically effects on results, whose SAs are in the middle level when compared to others. Furthermore, there is no clear difference in results between different skin tones with the change of illuminations.

5.3   Illumination Selection

We tested our illumination selection method on hand spectral images. For simplicity, we fixed the σ value to be 2 in the SC algorithm. The results are shown in Table 3. The values in bold are the best results in each row, and the underlined values are the

Table 3. Illumination selection results of hand spectral images with σ = 2 in the SC algorithm

Image	Number of Segments	Segmentation Accuracy (SA) (%)					
		Reflectance	A	D65	LED1	LED2	F11
H#1	3	**96.6**	95.7	96.5	93.0	96.3	89.8
H#2	3	**96.4**	95.2	96.3	92.6	96.1	89.7
H#3	5	**91.1**	72.4	89.1	90.8	82.4	87.4
H#4	3	**96.6**	95.1	95.7	94.4	95.2	93.1
H#5	3	**96.6**	95.9	96.5	93.2	96.3	91.9
H#6	3	**96.8**	95.5	96.7	94.8	96.1	92.4
H#7	3	**96.5**	95.5	96.4	94.9	96.2	92.3
H#8	4	84.7	83.6	83.7	83.8	**87.4**	81.8
H#9	3	95.5	94.6	**95.6**	91.3	95.4	90.7

results of the selected illumination from our method. We could see our method worked well on 6 in 9 images. However, when the number of segments in the image increases, such as H#3 and H#8, our method selected the wrong data representation. It may due to when the scene in the image becomes complex and has more objects, there are more "noisy" pixels in the image and the clusters are overlapping. Therefore, the eigengap cannot well measure the quality of the segmentation.

6   Conclusion

In this paper, we explored pixel-based skin spectral image segmentation by using the spectral clustering algorithm with Nyström method. We first studied the illumination dependence in skin spectral image segmentation for two datasets, human hand and face. Then we adopted the eigengap heuristic to select the illumination for skin image segmentation. Spectral radiance images under CIE A, D65, and F11, as well as two white LED illuminations, were simulated in the experiments based on corresponding spectral reflectance images. The experimental results showed that CIE D65 illuminant return the highest average segmentation accuracies, while illuminant CIE A in hand images and illuminant CIE F11 in face images return the lowest results, which are around 2.1% and 3.4% points lower compared to CIE D65, respectively. Especially in some cases, illuminants CIE A and F11 return relatively low accuracies when compared to CIE D65, with maximum difference of around 7.9% and 11.1% points. Both LED illuminations gave higher average results than CIE illuminants A and F11. However, the differences between the average SAs of illuminants are not very large. More representative test images may be needed to form a more solid conclusion.

References

1. Nishino, K., Fujiyama, T., Hashizume, H., Nakauchi, S.: Detection and Visualization of Intracutaneous Allergic Type-Specific Elements Using Long-Wavelength Near-Infrared Hyperspectral Imaging. Skin Research and Technology 19(1), e157–e166 (2013)
2. Wu, Z., Heikkinen, V., Parkkinen, J., Hauta-Kasari, M.: Utilization of Spectral Information in Clustering Based Color Image Segmentation. In: 6th European Conference on Colour in Graphics, Imaging, and Vision (CGIV 2012), pp. 307–313 (2012)
3. Pan, Z., Healey, G., Prasad, M., Tromberg, B.: Face Recognition in Hyperspectral Images. IEEE Trans. Pattern Anal. Mach. Intell. 25(12), 1552–1560 (2003)
4. Berns, R.S.: Billmeyer and Saltzman's Principles of Color Technology, 3rd edn. John Wiley & Sons, New York (2000)
5. Ng, A.Y., Jordan, M.I., Weiss, Y.: On Spectral Clustering: Analysis and an Algorithm. In: Advances in Neural Information Processing Systems 14, pp. 849–856 (2002)
6. Fowlkes, C., Belongie, S., Chung, F., Malik, J.: Spectral Grouping Using the Nyström Method. IEEE Trans. Pattern Anal. Mach. Intell. 26(2), 214–225 (2004)
7. Von Luxburg, U.: A Tutorial on Spectral Clustering. Statistics and Computing 17(4), 395–416 (2007)
8. Li, H., Bochko, V., Jaaskelainen, T., Parkkinen, J., Shen, I.F.: Kernel-Based Spectral Color Image Segmentation. JOSA A 25(11), 2805–2816 (2008)
9. Spectral Image Database, University of Eastern Finland, Spectral Color Research Group, https://www.uef.fi/spectral/spectral-database

Robust Visual Object Tracking via Sparse Representation and Reconstruction

Zhenjun Han, Qixiang Ye, and Jianbin Jiao

University of Chinese Academy of Sciences
{hanzhj,qxye,jiaojb}@ucas.ac.cn

Abstract. Visual object tracking plays an essential role in vision based applications. Most of the previous research has limitations due to the non-discriminated features used or the focus on simple template matching without the consideration of appearance variations. To address these challenges, this paper proposes a new approach for robust visual object tracking via sparse representation and reconstruction, where two main contributions are devoted in terms of object representation and location respectively. And the sparse representation and reconstruction (SR^2) are integrated into a Kalman filter framework to form a robust object tracker named as SR^2KF tracker. The extensive experiments show that the proposed tracker is able to tolerate the appearance variations, background clutter and image deterioration, and outperforms the existing work.

Keywords: Visual Tracking, Sparse Representation, Sparse Reconstruction.

1 Introduction

Object tracking is important to many computer vision applications ranging from visual surveillance [1], human computer interaction [2] and automatic robotics [3]. Although the state of the art has advanced significantly in the past decade [4]-[9], some challenging problems still remain open.

Tracking in complex environment requires two crucial components: discriminative object representation and effective spatial location. The object representation models the characteristics of a target, which include the shape, pose or even the reflectance properties. Appearance based representation [4] gains popularity recently because 2D images can be used straightforwardly. However, appearance variations are often caused by a number of factors in the natural environment, including shape deformation, background variation, lighting changes as well as occlusion [5]-[6]. It is imperative for a robust appearance representation to model such variations. Another goal of object tracking is to locate the target spatially. Considering the noise from the backgrounds and the object itself, it is useful for employing the probabilistic estimation framework, e.g., Kalman filter [7] or particle filter [8]. However, the template matching (the core of the estimation framework) is widely known for the drifting problem due to error accumulation over the time [10].

R. Wilson et al. (Eds.): CAIP 2013, Part II, LNCS 8048, pp. 282–289, 2013.

In this paper, we treat the representation as the classification between two-class linear regression models [5]-[6] and apply sparse signal optimization to address this problem. The rationale behind this scenario is that we compactly represent the object with discriminative features. Secondly, to facilitate the accurate location, the target object is reconstructed as a superposition of the searching candidates instead of the straightforward template matching. The reconstruction can handle the errors due to object occlusion and image corruption uniformly since the noise or errors are often sparse w.r.t. to the standard (pixel) basis. The proposed sparse representation and reconstruction (SR^2) are finally integrated into a Kalman filter to form a robust visual tracker named as SR^2KF tracker. Figure 1 shows the framework of our approach. The most related work is [9], where a robust visual tracking method is proposed by modeling the tracking as a sparse approximation problem (we refer it as SAP tracker in this paper). In SAP tracker, although the challenges of object occlusion are addressed seamlessly, the object appearance variation is not fully considered.

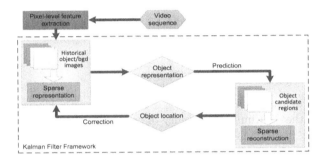

Fig. 1. The flowchart of the proposed tracking approach

The rest of the paper is organized as follows. In Section 2, we introduce the sparse representation. Section 3 presents the reconstruction strategy for object location. Section 4 describes the SR^2KF tracker. The experimental results are reported and analyzed in Section 5. Finally, we conclude the paper in Section 6.

2 Sparse Representation for Object Appearance

As the core of visual tracking, we treat the extraction of discriminative representation as a two-class (object versus background) classification problem. The existing work [11] has contended that the sparse representation selects the subset which represents the input signal most compactly and is naturally discriminative. We exploit the discriminative nature of sparsity for object appearance.

2.1 Online Construction and Update of the Training Samples

The sparse representation is obtained in an optimization framework based on the aggregation of the historical tracking results called as training samples in this paper. Let M be the number of time steps (frames) of the historical tracking. The training sample set is defined as $T = \{(\ell_j^+, \ell_j^-)\}, j = 1, ..., M$, where ℓ_j^+ and ℓ_j^- are the object (positive sample) and the corresponding background region (negative sample) obtained at the jth step, respectively. We adopt the histograms of oriented gradient and color (HOGC) [12] as the pixel-level feature for the object and background regions [12].

An update scheme is performed to keep the latest appearance information of the object and background in the training set. At each tracking step, a pair of positive and negative samples (ℓ_j^+, ℓ_j^-) are randomly selected and re-placed with the latest tracking result and the corresponding background. For only two samples in the set updated each time, the tracking stability is thus ensured and the feature drifting is avoided even when the noisy samples are updated.

2.2 Sparse Solution via an Improved $l1$-Norm Minimization

The existing work [13] has demonstrated that the sparse problem can be effectively resolved by $l1$-norm minimization. In the context of feature representation, we formulate our problem as following

$$\min \|S\|_1,$$
$$s.t. \begin{cases} S^T \ell_j^+ \geq \alpha \\ S^T \ell_j^- \leq -\alpha \end{cases}, \tag{1}$$

where $\|\cdot\|_1$ represents the $l1$-norm and $S \in R^N$ is the vector of sparse coefficients which measure the discriminative ability of each component in HOGC features. The constraints in Eq. (1) ensure that the training samples can be correctly classified and the shortest distance between two classes is 2α.

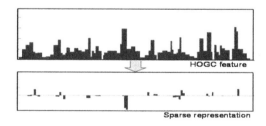

Fig. 2. Sparse representation of the object appearance via $l1$-norm minimization

Given the sparse solution S and the object O in the current step (frame), the representation is calculated as

$$F = S \otimes \text{HOGC}(O), \tag{2}$$

where $\text{HOGC}(O)$ represents the histogram features of object O and $\otimes$ denotes the dot-product operation. Figure 2 shows an example of the sparse representation given the HOGC features. The obtained sparse representation is finally used as a prior to locate the object in the successive frame.

3   Sparse Reconstruction for Object Location

The existing work [14] shows that the sparse reconstruction is robust to noise and insensitive to partial occlusion. We thus exploit it to identify the most informative candidates for accurate object location.

3.1   Instantaneous Sample Set for Reconstruction

In our approach, with the pre-identification in the instantaneous frame, all the possible candidates will be firstly selected to form a sample set, which is used for reconstruction based location. The instantaneous sample set is dynamically built up in a search window (the black rectangle region in Figure 3). A sample in the search window (the red rectangle region in Figure 3) is specified by a triplet $r = (x, y, s)$ [12], where $x \in (0, W)$ and $y \in (0, H)$ are the image coordinates and $s > 0$ is the scale of the candidate. Let K be the number of selected candidates, the instantaneous sample set is defined as $A = \{a_k\}, k = 1, ..., K$.

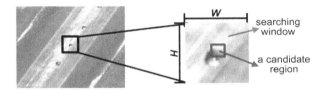

Fig. 3. The searching window for instantaneous sample set construction

3.2   Sparse Reconstruction for Object Location

The aim of the sparse reconstruction is to approximate the potential object location by a linear superposition of the instantaneous samples given the prior object representation as follows

$$A\psi = F, \tag{3}$$

where F is the given sparse representation, and $\psi = \{\varphi_k\}$, $k = 1, ..., K$ is the reconstruction vector in which φ_k is the reconstruction coefficient for the kth sample in the instantaneous set A.

Intuitively, the search window is larger than the target region with some instantaneous samples from non-object regions. Only a few samples are suitable for linear superposition. Even in the case of partial occlusion, the number of effective object samples are limited. Consequently, ψ subjects to sparse property. We can then formulate the sparse reconstruction as

$$\min ||\psi||_1, \\ s.t. A\psi = F. \tag{4}$$

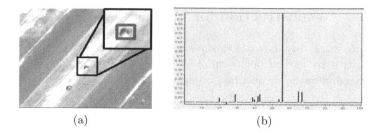

(a)   (b)

Fig. 4. Sparse reconstruction for object location. (a) The object location calculated by reconstruction strategy. (b) The coefficient vector of sparse reconstruction.

Figure 4(b) shows an example of the solution ψ. Among 100 samples, about 10 samples are enough for the approximation with the corresponding coefficients.

Essentially, the entries in the reconstruction vector are the confidences showing how the corresponding candidates are the object. Therefore, the object location with its scale $O(x, y, s)$ is finally identified as

$$O(x, y, s) = \sum_{k=1}^{K} a_k(x, y, s) \cdot \varphi_k. \tag{5}$$

Figure 4(a) shows the result of object location calculated by Eq. (5).

4   SR^2 Kalman Filter

We integrate the sparse representation and reconstruction (SR^2) into the Kalman filter (KF) and develop a robust object tracker named as SR^{2}KF tracker. The Kalman filter addresses the general problem of estimating the state X of a discrete time process that is governed by a linear stochastic difference equation as

$$X_{t+1} = MX_t + u_t, \tag{6}$$

with a measurement Z that is

$$Z_t = HX_t + v_t. \tag{7}$$

The random variables u_t and v_t represent the state and measurement noise, respectively. They are assumed to be independent and have normal distribution. In SR^{2}KF tracker, the first order Markov model is employed, *i.e.*

$$X_t = \begin{pmatrix} F_t \\ \Delta F_t \\ P_t \\ \Delta P_t \end{pmatrix}, Z_t = \begin{pmatrix} F_t \\ P_t \end{pmatrix}, \tag{8}$$

and

$$M = \begin{pmatrix} I_{N \times N} & I_{N \times N} & 0 & 0 \\ 0 & I_{N \times N} & 0 & 0 \\ 0 & 0 & I_{L \times L} & I_{L \times L} \\ 0 & 0 & 0 & I_{L \times L} \end{pmatrix}, H = \begin{pmatrix} I_{N \times N} & 0 & 0 & 0 \\ 0 & 0 & I_{L \times L} & 0 \end{pmatrix}. \tag{9}$$

where F_t is the sparse representation at time (frame) t and $\Delta F_t = F_t - F_{t-1}$, $P_t = (x_t, y_t)$ denotes the center coordinates of the object bounding box and $\Delta P_t = P_t - P_{t-1}$, $I_{N \times N}$ and $I_{L \times L}$ are the identity matrixes where N is the dimension of the sparse representation and L is 2.

5   Experimental Results

To demonstrate the effectiveness of the proposed approach, we performed comprehensive experiments on several public benchmarks. To avoid the influence from detection, the target objects were initialized manually.

Ten image sequences were selected from the public sets VIVID [15], CAVIAR [16] and SDL [17]. The selected test data consists of a variety of challenging cases in the complex environments, e.g., occlusion among objects, object scale variation and rotation, lighting changes, and clutter background. To quantitatively evaluate the performance, we adopt the displacement error rate (DER) [12] between the tracking result and the ground-truth.

5.1   Evaluation on the Appearances Variation

The average and variance of DER were used to validate the effectiveness of the sparse representation against other two representative feature representation methods: variance ratio feature shift [5] and peak difference feature shift [6].

In Figure 5(a), the sparse representation is with the average DER ranging from 0.04 to 0.1. The variance of DER for our approach is 2.62×10^{-4} which is much lower than the ones of variance ratio feature shift (value at 3.80×10^{-3}) and peak difference feature shift (value at 2.41×10^{-3}). This demonstrates that the proposed object representation is more robust to the appearance variation.

5.2   Evaluation on Partial Occlusion

Partial occlusion is another key issue for inaccurate location and unstable tracking. The Kalman filter [7] and particle filter [8] are two well-acknowledged tracking algorithms which can handle the partial occlusion to some extent. We thus conducted the evaluation on all test data and compared the proposed reconstruction strategy with the Kalman filter and particle filter based tracking algorithms.

In Figure 5(b), the performance of the reconstruction strategy is apparently better than the Kalman filter and particle filter measured by average DER. In addition, the stability measured by variance of DER also outperforms the ones of Kalman filter (5.81×10^{-3}) and particle filter (1.30×10^{-3}).

5.3   Evaluation of SR^{2}KF Tracker

We finally evaluated the performance of SR^{2}KF tracker and compared with the SAP tracker [9] against different complex situations including image deterioration, appearances variations of object and background, and partial occlusion.

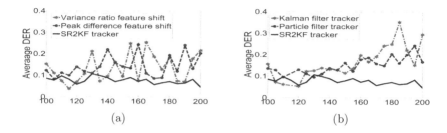

(a)   (b)

Fig. 5. Experimental results. (a) For appearance variation; and (b) partial occlusion.

The first test sequence (as shown in Fig. 6(a)) is from VIVID data set. During the tracking process, the object subjects to severe image quality deterioration (at 220th frame), which results in the degeneration of its appearance representation in pixel-level space. The sequence shown in Fig. 6(b) from SDL set is quite challenging due to the clutter backgrounds, the similarity of other objects to the tracking target in appearance, and severe occlusion. In these tracking conditions, the SAP tracker failed in tracking ultimately but SR^2KF tracker worked successfully. The experimental results demonstrated that our proposed SR^2KF tracker is effective for visual object tracking and outperforms [9].

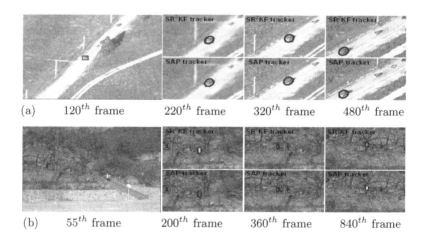

(a) 120th frame 220th frame 320th frame 480th frame

(b) 55th frame 200th frame 360th frame 840th frame

Fig. 6. Tracking results of SR^2KF tracker and the SAP tracker in [9]. The tracking result is marked with red rectangle and the ground-truth is with blue ellipse.

6   Conclusions and Future Work

Object representation and location are two primary issues in visual tracking. In this paper, we implemented a visual object tracking approach named as

SR^{2}KF tracker by integrating the sparse representation and reconstruction into a Kalman filter framework. The sparse representation is able to encode the variant appearance patterns and the reconstruction scenario is robust to object partial occlusion for location. The extensive evaluation demonstrates our approach is powerful for visual tracking problems compared with the existing work.

The future work includes 1) more pixel-level appearance and motion features will be integrated in the current approach to improve the performance, and 2) the case of complete occlusion will be addressed.

Acknowledgements. This work is supported in Part by National Basic Research Program of China (973 Program) with Nos. 2011CB706900, 2010CB731800, and National Science Foundation of China with Nos. 61039003, 61271433 and 61202323.

References

1. Stauffer, C., Grimson, W.: Adaptive background mixture models for real-time tracking. In: CVPR (1999)
2. Bradski, G.: Real time face and object tracking as a component of a perceptual user interface. In: IEEE Workshop on Applications of Computer Vision (1998)
3. Papanikolopoulos, N., Khosla, P., Kanade, T.: Visual tracking of a moving target by a camera mounted on a robot: a combination of control and vision. IEEE Trans. Robotics and Automation, 14–35 (1993)
4. Shi, J., Tomasi, C.: Good features to track. In: CVPR (1994)
5. Collins, R., Liu, Y.: On-line selection of discriminative tracking features. In: ICCV (2003)
6. Collins, R., Liu, Y., Leordeanu, M.: Online selection of discriminative tracking features. IEEE Trans. PAMI, 1631–1643 (2005)
7. Cuevas, E., Zaldivar, D., Rojas, R.: Kalman filter for vision tracking. Technical Report (2005)
8. Isard, M., Blake, A.: Condensation - conditional density propagation for visual tracking. In: IJCV, pp. 5–28 (1998)
9. Mei, X., Ling, H.: Robust Visual Tracking and Vehicle Classification via Sparse Representation. IEEE Trans. PAMI, 2259–2272 (2011)
10. Matthews, I., Ishikawa, T., Baker, S.: The template update problem. IEEE Trans. PAMI, 810–815 (2004)
11. Xu, R., Zhang, B., Ye, Q., Jiao, J.: Cascaded l1-norm minimization learning (CLML) classifier for human detection. In: CVPR (2010)
12. Han, Z., Jiao, J., Zhang, B., Ye, Q., Liu, J.: Visual object tracking via sample-based Adaptive Sparse Representation (AdaSR). Pattern Recognition, 2170–2183 (2011)
13. Donoho, D.: For most large underdetermined systems of linear equations the minimal l1-norm near solution approximates the sparsest solution. Comm. on Pure and Applied Math., 797–829 (2004)
14. Wright, J., Yang, A., Ganesh, A., Sastry, S., Ma, Y.: Robust face recognition via sparse representation. IEEE Trans. PAMI, 210–227 (2008)
15. VIVID Dataset, http://vividevaluation.ri.cmu.edu/datasets/datasets.html
16. CAVIAR Test Case Scenarios, http://homepages.inf.ed.ac.uk/rbf/CAVIAR
17. SDL Data set, http://www.ucassdl.cn/resource.asp

Sphere Detection in Kinect Point Clouds via the 3D Hough Transform

Anas Abuzaina, Mark S. Nixon, and John N. Carter

School of Electronics and Computer Science, University of Southampton, UK
{aa6g08,msn,jnc}@ecs.soton.ac.uk

Abstract. We introduce a fast, robust and accurate Hough Transform (HT) based algorithm for detecting spherical structures in 3D point clouds. To our knowledge, our algorithm is the first HT based implementation that detects spherical structures in typical in 3D point clouds generated by consumer depth sensors such as the Microsoft Kinect. Our approach has been designed to be computationally efficient; reducing an established limitation of HT based approaches. We provide experimental analysis of the achieved results, showing a robust performance against occlusion, and we show superior performance to the only other HT based algorithm for detecting spheres in point clouds available in literature.

Keywords: Evidence gathering, point clouds, 3D object detection, Hough transform, 3D vision, Kinect.

1 Introduction

Much progress has been made in the development of 3D acquisition methods and technologies, especially recently when new 3D sensing technologies became available to the public such as the Microsoft Kinect. By providing a third dimension of the spatial coordinates of their output data (point clouds), the Kinect and similar depth sensors provide practical and accurate means for overcoming traditional problems in computer vision applications. Such problems are mainly related to background and foreground segmentation, object occlusion, unknown object scaling and changing lighting conditions. In this research we are interested in detecting parametric shapes, specifically spheres, in 3D point clouds generated by the Kinect sensor. We extend the Hough Transform (HT) [1] to three dimensions and show its robust ability to detect spheres in point clouds of a real environment. To our knowledge, our research is the first HT based implementation to detect spherical structures in real point clouds acquired by depth sensors such as the Kinect. To ensure our algorithm's practicability, we have reduced computational complexity and ensured acceptable time performance by using a sparse matrix representation. We provide experimental analysis based on a number of factors, emphasising on performance against occlusion ratio, and we show superior performance to the only other HT based algorithm for detecting spheres in point clouds available in literature.

R. Wilson et al. (Eds.): CAIP 2013, Part II, LNCS 8048, pp. 290–297, 2013.

2   Parametric Shape Detection in 3D

In 3D, parametric shapes such as planes, spheres, cylinders and cones can be considered as geometric primitives that are used to explain parts of the 3D point cloud. According to [2], such geometric primitives enable the system to add surface information for parts of the object that were not covered by the sensor data. Moreover, exploiting the knowledge about the shape enables to eliminate inaccuracies caused by sensor noise as it determines the best shape fit for the sensor data.

There have been two main directions of methods for detecting parametric shapes in 3D data: approaches based on RANSAC [3] and on Hough transform (HT) [1]. RANSAC (RANdom SAmple Consensus) based approaches decompose the point cloud into a concise structure of inherent shapes and a set of remaining points using random sampling, each detected shape serves as a proxy for a set of corresponding points. These approaches have been proven to be efficient for detecting parametric 3D shapes (planes, spheres, cylinders, etc.), such as in [4]. The other direction of methods for detecting parametric shapes is to use evidence gathering techniques such as the Hough transform (HT), in which a voting procedure is carried in the parameter space from which object candidates are obtained as local maxima. Hough transform based methods have been successfully implemented to detect planes [5][6], spheres [7][8] and cylinders [9] in 3D data. HT based methods in general have faster runtime than RANSAC. Moreover HT approaches can detect multiple instances of the shape while RANSAC methods are limited to a single instance. In this research we will develop an efficient HT based approach to detect spheres. A good comparisons between RANSAC and HT approaches for detecting parametric shapes in 3D data are in [10] and in [11].

3   The 3D Hough Transform for Sphere Detection

The Hough Transform (HT) [1] is a well-known technique originally developed to extract straight lines, since then it has been extended to extract parametric shapes (such as conic sections) and non-parametric shapes in 2D images. The Hough Transform is recognized as a powerful evidence gathering tool in shape analysis that gives good results even in the presence of noise and occlusions. The implementation of Hough transform based methods defines a mapping from the image (or point cloud in case of 3D) to an accumulator space; the evidence is the votes which original image points cast in the accumulator space. In three dimensions, a sphere has a simple polar parametric representation given by the following equations:

$$
\begin{aligned}
x &= c_x + r\cos\theta\sin\varphi \\
y &= c_y + r\sin\theta\sin\varphi \\
z &= c_z + r\cos\varphi \\
(0 &\leq \theta \leq 2\pi, 0 \leq \varphi \leq \pi)
\end{aligned}
\tag{1}
$$

where x, y and z are the Cartesian coordinates of the surface points, c_x, c_y and c_z are the coordinates of the centre of the sphere, r is the radius expressed in the same units as the centre and surface points and θ and φ are the azimuthal and polar angles respectively. The implementation of the 3D HT to detect spheres is as follows: each point on the sphere surface defines a set of spheres in the accumulator space; these spheres are defined by all possible values of the radius, and they are centered at the coordinates of the point. For a given radius value, each point on the sphere defines only one sphere in the accumulator space. After gathering all evidence of the points on the sphere using the HT mapping equations (2) applied for each point in the sphere's surface, the maximum of the accumulator space corresponds to the parameters of the original sphere. Algorithm 1 describes the implementation of the 3D HT for sphere detection.

Since we are dealing with 3D point clouds, there will be four parameters to vote for (cx, cy, cz and r), hence the accumulator space is 4-dimensional .

$$c_x = x - r \cos \theta \sin \varphi$$
$$c_y = y - r \sin \theta \ sin\varphi \qquad (2)$$
$$c_z = z - r \cos \varphi$$

---

for *for every point* (x, y, z) **do**
    for $(r = r_{min}; r \leq r_{max}; r + +)$ **do**
        for $\theta = 0; \theta \leq 2\pi; \theta + +$ **do**
            for $\varphi = 0; \varphi \leq \pi; \varphi + +$ **do**
                $c_x = x - r \cos \theta \sin \varphi$
                $c_y = y - r \sin \theta \sin \varphi$
                $c_z = z - r \cos \varphi$
                Accumulator$[r][c_x][c_y][c_z] + +$
            end
        end
    end
end
Search Accumulator for peak.

Algorithm 1. 3D Hough transform for sphere detection (3DHT)

4   Implementation

To reduce memory requirements, and for fast access of elements, we use a multi-dimensional sparse matrix representation for the accumulator space. Sparse matrices store only non-zero elements, and provide direct mapping between indices and their corresponding values. The non-zero elements are stored in a hash table that grows when it is filled so that the search time is $O(1)$ in average regardless of whether element is present or not, and regardless of the size of the matrix.

We are interested in detecting spheres in real data, which is point clouds acquired from the Kinect and similar depth sensors. Point clouds generated by these sensors are 2.5D, i.e. only points on surfaces facing the sensor are acquired, which are about 50% of the total number of points on the object's surface, hence a complete geometry of the object cannot be acquired. Our algorithm is able to robustly detect "partial" spheres such those acquired by depth sensors, without this characteristic it would not be applicable on real data.

Point clouds generated by the Kinect have on average 300k points, each point cloud have been cropped to a suitable volume before applying Algorithm 1 to discard redundant points, i.e. points that are far away from the interest area of the scene. Figure 1 shows the robust performance of Algorithm 1 applied on Kinect point clouds of different scenes including a football and an orange. The left row shows original textured point clouds, the middle row shows detected spheres superimposed on original clouds and the third row shows the untextured point clouds with detected spheres. Figure 2 demonstrates the algorithm's capability to detect semi-spherical objects.

5   Analysis

Our experimental analysis on Kinect clouds shows that the *volume point density*, i.e. the number of points on a 3D surface, is ~ 25 points per cube centimetre (taken at distance of 1m). We are interested in coordinate values to the nearest centimetre, hence it is not necessary to include all points in voting process.

Taking every ith point instead of every point in the cloud, reduces the processing time significantly. However if the point step (i) is too large, false detection will occur. Based on our experimental analysis, a point step value of $(i = 20)$ is a suitable value for typical Kinect clouds. Table 1 shows the total processing time of Algorithm 1 for detecting spheres with pre-defined radius, for undefined radii, the processing time is simply multiplied by the number of the radii in the given range $[r_{min}, r_{max}]$. The computation of Algorithm 1 is divided to three processes:

1. Mapping: This is the process of transforming of points from the point cloud 3D space to the 3D Hough (parameter) space, applied by equations 2. This process is the most time consuming, it takes roughly 59.4% of the total processing time when Algorithm 1 is applied on a typical Kinect point cloud.
2. Voting: In this process, casting of votes occurs by accessing the elements of the sparse matrix and incrementing their values according to the Hough mapping. This process takes roughly 40.2% of total processing time.
3. Detection: A search algorithm is performed in this process to find the peak of the accumulator. This process is extremely fast and it is less than 0.4% of total processing time. This is due the implementation of a sparse matrix for the accumulator in which the search time is always $O(1)$.

The work of [7] is the only HT based method dedicated for detecting spheres in 3D point clouds. However in their paper their method is only demonstrated

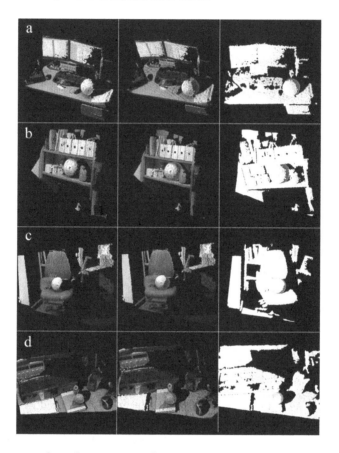

Fig. 1. Accurate sphere detection in real point clouds. Point cloud resolution: (a) 146k points, (b) 193k points, (c) 174k points and (d) 120k points

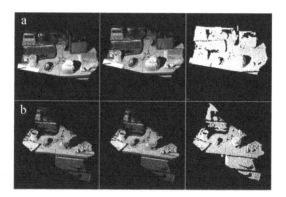

Fig. 2. Detection of semi-spherical objects. Point cloud resolution: (a) 136k points, (b) 64k points

on a high resolution point cloud of calibration object of a number of "perfect" spheres acquired by an optical shape measurement system (SMS). Their algorithm takes approximately 8 seconds in total to process a point cloud of 63K points. Additionally they only provide performance analysis based on the parameter space resolution (bin size). Even though our developed algorithm is similar to [7] in terms of spherical equations used for voting and sparse matrix use, in our research we are the first to apply HT based method to detect spheres in point clouds in real life scenarios of typical household and office environments generated by consumer depth sensors such as the Kinect. Moreover we demonstrate the capability of detecting semi-spherical objects such as apples an bowls. Additionally, we provide performance analysis against a number of different elements. Finally and most importantly, our algorithm detects spheres correctly in significantly less time.

In [7], their algorithm takes approximately 8 seconds in total to process a point cloud of 63K points. It can be seen from Table 1 that our algorithm is approximately 4 times faster than their achieved result, that is if *every* point has been taken in the voting process. However our algorithm can correctly detect spheres up to 57 times faster if the point step (i) is increased to a suitable value. We are interested in providing a performance measure in terms of accuracy of

Table 1. Total processing time of Algorithm 1 at point steps of 1,10 and 20, with angle step of 10 ° of both θ and φ and a fixed raduis (running on 2.4GHz Intel Core i7 and 4GB RAM)

Point cloud name	No. of points	Time(s), i =1	Time(s), i =10	Time(s), i =20
Deskball	146k	5.30	0.76	0.44
ShelfBall	193k	7.11	0.91	0.55
Chairball	174k	6.31	0.89	0.52
Bowl	136k	4.08	0.46	0.24
Orange	120k	3.42	0.38	0.20
Apple	64k	2.06	0.25	0.14

detection and computational time; there are a number of elements affect the algorithm's performance:

1. The number of points on the surface of the sphere which cast votes. These points should be enough to vote for the correct peak in the parameter space, if only few points are present on the sphere there will be no notable peak and hence the detection will fail. This number can be relative to the total number of points that a "complete" sphere would have, this number can be defined as the *occlusion ratio*. We have already shown our algorithm can perfectly detect partial spheres acquired by the Kinect. Figure 3 shows the Euclidean distance error for the coordinates of the spheres at increasing occlusion ratios. The ratios are quantified by dividing the number of points on the occluded sphere by the number of points on the original non-occluded sphere. The root mean square (RMS) is given by:

$$RMS\ error = \sqrt{(x_G - x)^2 + (y_G - y)^2 + (z_G - z)^2} \tag{3}$$

where (x_G, y_G, z_G) are the ground truth coordinates of the centre. The occlusion performance analysis was carried out on four point clouds of a synthetic sphere with no other objects in the cloud. These spheres had different point densities and the error values are the average from the four clouds.

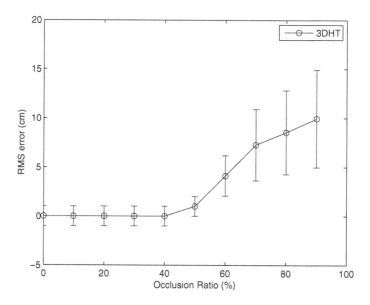

Fig. 3. RMS error metric of Algorithm 1 (3DHT) at increasing occlusion ratio

2. The step size of the azimuthal angle θ and polar angle φ. So far, in all generated figures, we have used an angle step of 10 degrees for both angles when applying Algorithm 1, which gave perfect accuracy and satisfying results in terms of processing time. Having an angle step of $10°$ means that for each point there will be (36×18) iterations in the casting process. Obviously, reducing the number of iterations leads to faster detection performance; the choice of an angle step is a trade-off between processing speed and accuracy.
3. The resolution of the accumulator space, or in other words the bins size that votes cast into. The larger the bin size is, the smaller the dimensionality of the accumulator, as multiple votes will vote in the same bin. Bin size is also a trade-off between memory storage and accuracy, and it does not have an effect processing time due to the implementation of a sparse matrix for the accumulator, in which the search time is always $O(1)$. Rounding to the nearest bin size significantly reduces memory storage requirements for the accumulator, however it comes on the expense of reduced accuracy in

detecting the location in 3D space. In all our experiments on kinect point clouds we have used a bin size of 1 cm^3, and hence all detected centres are of $1cm$ precision.

6   Conclusions

We introduced a fast and accurate Hough Transform (HT) based algorithm for detecting spherical structures in 3D point clouds. We showed its robust ability to detect spheres in Kinect point clouds of typical environments. Our approach has been designed to be computationally efficient, reducing an established limitation of HT based approaches. We provided experimental analysis based on a number of elements, emphasising on performance against occlusion ratio and we showed superior performance to the only other HT based algorithm for detecting spheres in point clouds available in literature.

References

1. Hough, P.: Method and Means for Recognizing Complex Patterns. U.S. Patent 3.069.654 (1962)
2. Rusu, R.B.: Semantic 3D Object Maps for Everyday Manipulation in Human Living Environments. PhD thesis, Computer Science department, Technische Universitat Munchen, Germany (2009)
3. Fischler, M.A., Bolles, R.C.: Random Sample Consensus: A Paradigm for Model Fitting with Applications to Image Analysis and Automated Cartography. Communications of the ACM 24(6), 381–395 (1981)
4. Schnabel, R., Wahl, R., Klein, R.: Efficient RANSAC for Point-Cloud Shape Detection. Computer Graphics Forum 26(2), 214–226 (2007)
5. Borrmann, D., Elseberg, J., Lingemann, K., Nüchter, A.: The 3D Hough Transform for plane detection in point clouds: A review and a new accumulator design. 3D Research 2(2), 1–13 (2011)
6. Ogundana, O.O., Coggrave, C.R., Burguete, R.L., Huntley, J.M.: Automated detection of planes in 3-D point clouds using fast Hough transforms. Optical Engineering 50(5), 053609–053609 (2011)
7. Ogundana, O.O., Coggrave, C.R., Burguete, R.L., Huntley, J.M.: Fast Hough transform for automated detection of spheres in three-dimensional point clouds. Optical Engineering 46(5), 051002–051002 (2007)
8. Cao, M.Y., Ye, C.H., Doessel, O., Liu, C.: Spherical parameter detection based on hierarchical Hough transform. Pattern Recognition Letters 27(9), 980–986 (2006)
9. Rabbani, T., Van Den Heuvel, F.: Efficient Hough transform for automatic detection of cylinders in point clouds. ISPRS WG III/3, III/4 3, 60–65 (2005)
10. Tarsha-Kurdi, F., Landes, T., Grussenmeyer, P.: Hough-transform and extended RANSAC algorithms for automatic detection of 3D building roof planes from lidar data. International Archives of Photogrammetry. Remote Sensing and Spatial Information Systems 36, 407–412 (2007)
11. Kotthäuser, T., Mertsching, B.: Triangulation-based plane extraction for 3D point clouds. In: Su, C.-Y., Rakheja, S., Liu, H. (eds.) ICIRA 2012, Part I. LNCS, vol. 7506, pp. 217–228. Springer, Heidelberg (2012)

Watermark Optimization of 3D Shapes for Minimal Distortion and High Robustness

Adrian G. Bors and Ming Luo

Dept. of Computer Science, University of York, York YO10 5GH, UK

Abstract. An optimization-based methodology is proposed in this paper preserving mesh surfaces in 3D watermarking. The Levenberg-Mar- quardt optimization algorithm is used for displacing the vertices according to the message to be embedded. A specific cost function is used by this method in order to ensure minimal surface distortion while the watermark would be enabled with high robustness to attacks. This cost function consists of three components representing the distance to the original surface, to the watermarked surface and the vertex displacement, respectively. The proposed methodology is statistical, blind and robust. A study of its crypto-security is provided as well in this research study.

Keywords: 3D watermarking, Levenberg-Marquardt optimization, mesh surface preservation, robust and blind watermarking.

1 Introduction

This paper describes a 3D watermarking approach for preserving object surfaces, considered as meshes. 3D watermarking embeds a message in the content of a 3D object by invisibly displacing vertices on its surface. We should be able to detect the message even after the object would be attacked such as by adding noise, smoothing, surface simplification, etc. Watermarking of graphical objects, known as 3D watermarking, started as an active field of research in late '90s. 3D watermarking methods can be categorized as deterministic [1] or statistical [2,3,4]. Statistical watermarking alters, differently for a bit of 0 or 1, the shape of histograms of localized distances for a set of vertices and distribute the distortions onto the surface of the object. From the data representation domain, watermarking approaches can be classified as being performed in spatial and in transform domains. Transform domain watermarking considers embedding a message in the mesh spectral domain [5], wavelet domain or the spheroidal harmonic coefficients. Spatial domain watermarking considers embedding changes directly in the geometry of the 3D object [1,3]. Watermarking, invariably introduces distortions in the mesh surface [1]. 3D watermarking methods which minimize the surface distortion employ vertex displacements along the geodesic front propagation lines [3] and local minimization of the Quadric Error Metric (QEM), based on geometric projections, [6].

R. Wilson et al. (Eds.): CAIP 2013, Part II, LNCS 8048, pp. 298–306, 2013.

In the proposed methodology we form normalized distributions of distances from vertices to the object center. As in [2,3] we employ two watermarking methods by changing the mean or the variance of these normalized distributions. Displacement of vertices from the object' surface is optimized using the Levenberg-Marquardt algorithm in spherical coordinates. A new surface distortion metric is proposed as the cost function for the optimization process in order to ensure minimal object distortions. Section 2 outlines the statistical embedding method, Section 3 describes the distortion criterion used, The watermark embedding approach using the Levenberg-Marquardt optimization is described in Section 4. Section 5 outlines security aspects of the watermark. Section 6 provides the experimental results, while Section 7 concludes the paper.

2   Statistical Watermarking

Let us assume that we want to embed a code of M bits into a 3D object $\mathcal{O}$. We denote the object center by O and a vertex on its surface as V_j, while their corresponding coordinates are $\mathbf{o}$ and $\mathbf{v}_j$, respectively. The vertices of the mesh object $\mathcal{O}$ are clustered into M bins such that each bin is used for embedding one bit of message B_i, $i = 1, \ldots, M$. Vertices are clustered according to their distance from $\mathbf{v}_j$ to the object center $\mathbf{o}$, which is considered as reference:

$$\mathbf{o} = \frac{\sum_{\mathbf{v}_j \in \mathcal{O}} A(\mathbf{v}_j)\mathbf{v}_j}{\sum_{\mathbf{v}_j \in \mathcal{O}} A(\mathbf{v}_j)} \tag{1}$$

where $A(\mathbf{v}_j)$ represents the area of all triangular faces containing the vertex $\mathbf{v}_j$. The object center defined in this way is more robust than by simply taking the average of all its vertices, as it was used in [2], particularly when considering the watermark robustness to various attacks such as remeshing or simplification, etc.

For a given vertex $\mathbf{v}_j \in \mathcal{O}$, let us denote its distance to the reference point given by the center, representing the vertex norm, by $\rho_j = \|\mathbf{v}_j - \mathbf{o}\|$ and consider this as a statistical variable. After ranking the distances from the center to vertices, we evaluate $\rho_{min} = \min_{\mathbf{v}_j}(\rho_j)$ and $\rho_{max} = \max_{\mathbf{v}_j}(\rho_j)$, where $\mathbf{v}_j \in \mathcal{O}$. Consequently, the vertices are grouped into M sets according to their distances to the object center, as:

$$\mathcal{B}_i = \{\mathbf{v}_j \in \mathcal{O} \mid \rho_{min} + \varepsilon(\rho_{max} - \rho_{min}) + (i - 1)\rho_b \leq \rho_j ,$$
$$\rho_j < \rho_{max} - \varepsilon(\rho_{max} - \rho_{min}) + i\rho_b\} \tag{2}$$

where $i = 1, \ldots, M$ and each of these sets contains a number of vertices located in an identical range of distances from the object center, equal to:

$$\rho_b = \frac{(1 - 2\varepsilon)(\rho_{max} - \rho_{min})}{M} \tag{3}$$

where $\varepsilon \in [0, \varepsilon_{max}]$ represents a trimming ratio, accounting mostly for characteristic object features, which should not be affected by the watermark. For the first statistical watermarking method the variables are normalized to the range $[0, 1]$:

$$\tilde{\rho}_{ij} = \frac{\rho_{ij} - \rho_{i,min}}{\rho_{i,max} - \rho_{i,min}}. \tag{4}$$

In the second method, the variable ρ_{ij} is normalized to the range $[-1, 1]$ as:

$$\tilde{\rho}_{ij} = 2\frac{\rho_{ij} - \rho_{i,min}}{\rho_{i,max} - \rho_{i,min}} - 1 \tag{5}$$

As shown in [2], the distribution of the statistical variable $\tilde{\rho}_{ij}$ is close to a uniform distribution. In this case the expected mean and variance are $1/2$ and $1/3$, respectively. The two statistical watermark embedding methods, change differently for a bit of zero and for a bit of one, the mean of the statistical variables normalized by (4) and the variance of those normalized by (5), respectively. The same histogram mapping function is used in this approach as in [2,3].

3   Watermark Distortion Metric Criterion

Let us consider that we are provided with the statistical variable $\hat{\rho}_j$, sampled from a distribution function characterizing the statistical watermark. A chosen vertex V_j is displaced to a new location $\hat{V}_j$ such that $\|O\hat{V}_j\| = \hat{\rho}_j$, where O is the center of the 3D object. In the following we consider $E(\cdot) = \mathbf{f}^T\mathbf{f}$ as a function measuring simultaneously the distortion between the watermarked and the original surface, the smoothness of the resulting watermarked surface as well as the original vertex displacement according to $\mathbf{f} = (\sqrt{k_1}\mathbf{f}_1, \sqrt{k_2}\mathbf{f}_2, \sqrt{k_3}\mathbf{f}_3)^T$ with each of the components $\mathbf{f}_1$, $\mathbf{f}_2$ and $\mathbf{f}_3$ are characterized by their weighting parameters k_1, k_2 and k_3, such that $k_1 + k_2 + k_3 = 1$.

The first error metric component $\mathbf{f}_1$ defines the distortion of the watermarked vertex with respect to the original surface:

$$\mathbf{f}_1 = \begin{pmatrix} < (\hat{\mathbf{v}}_j - \mathbf{v}_j), \ \mathbf{n}_1 > \mathbf{n}_1 \\ \vdots \\ < (\hat{\mathbf{v}}_j - \mathbf{v}_j), \ \mathbf{n}_l > \mathbf{n}_l \end{pmatrix} \tag{6}$$

where $\hat{\mathbf{v}}_j$ is the location of the watermarked vertex $\hat{V}_j$, $< \cdot, \cdot >$ is the dot product and $\mathbf{n}_l$, $l = 1, \ldots, \mathcal{N}_{V_j}$, is the normal vector of a triangle adjacent to the vertex V_j from the original surface. The vector $< (\hat{\mathbf{v}}_j - \mathbf{v}_j), \ \mathbf{n}_l > \mathbf{n}_l$ represents the projection of the vertex displacement along the orthogonal direction from $\hat{V}_j$ to the polygon $\mathbf{F}_l$, $l = 1, \ldots, \mathcal{N}_{V_j}$, which is adjacent to $\hat{V}_j$. Let us define $D(\hat{\mathbf{v}}_j, \mathbf{F}_l)$ the distance from vertex $\hat{V}_j$ to the polygon $\mathbf{F}_l$. We have:

$$\mathbf{f}_1^T\mathbf{f}_1 = \sum_{l=1}^{\mathcal{N}_{V_j}} D^2(\hat{\mathbf{v}}_j, \mathbf{F}_l). \tag{7}$$

The metric $\mathbf{f}_1^T \mathbf{f}_1$ represents the Quadric Error Metric (QEM), *i.e.* the squared distance from the watermarked vertex to the original surface following the vertex displacement due to watermark embedding [6]. It could result in twisted polygons when using only this distance as a surface error function for 3D watermarking.

The second vector function component $\mathbf{f}_2$ enforces surface smoothness and is defined for measuring the distance of the watermarked vertex to the updated surface as:

$$\mathbf{f}_2 = \begin{pmatrix} < (\hat{\mathbf{v}}_j - \mathbf{v}_j),\ \hat{\mathbf{n}}_1 > \hat{\mathbf{n}}_1 \\ \vdots \\ < (\hat{\mathbf{v}}_j - \mathbf{v}_j),\ \hat{\mathbf{n}}_l > \hat{\mathbf{n}}_l \end{pmatrix} \tag{8}$$

where $\hat{\mathbf{n}}_l$, $l = 1, \ldots, \mathcal{N}_{V_j}$ is the normal vector of the polygon contained in the modified surface, neighbouring the watermarked vertex $\hat{V}_j$ of location $\hat{\mathbf{v}}_j$.

The third error function component $\mathbf{f}_3$ represents the vertex displacement between the watermarked vertex and the original vertex locations :

$$\mathbf{f}_3 = \hat{\mathbf{v}}_j - \mathbf{v}_j. \tag{9}$$

This constraint is added in order to compensate for the surface error which is not accounted for by the previous two distortion function components $\mathbf{f}_1$ and $\mathbf{f}_2,$. When $k_2 = 0$ and $k_3 = 0$ we obtain the criterion used for watermarking in [6], while for $k_1 = 0$ and $k_2 = 0$ we have the criterion used in [2].

4   Optimal Vertex Placement

The embedding of the watermark is performed by an optimization algorithm using $E(\cdot)$ as a cost function for enforcing minimal surface distortion. The constraint that we have to enforce is $||O\hat{V}|| = \hat{\rho}_j$, *i.e.* the watermarked vertex should be on the sphere $\mathcal{S}(O, \hat{\rho}_j)$ centered in the object center O, of radius given by the statistical variable $\hat{\rho}_j$ corresponding to the bit to be embedded. Simultaneously we aim to produce minimal distortion to the object surface. The vertex location $\hat{\mathbf{v}}$ is represented in a spherical coordinate system, centered at O of coordinates bfo, as defined by (1). The spherical coordinate system is defined by the orientation angles ϕ, θ and radius $\hat{\rho}_j$. In the following we consider the vertex norm $\hat{\rho}_j$ as given by sampling the distribution corresponding to the watermak message and we update the vector $\psi = (\hat{\phi}, \hat{\theta})^T$.

Initially, the vertex V is moved along the direction of $\overrightarrow{OV}$ to $\hat{V}$ such that $||O\hat{V}|| = \hat{\rho}_j$, as in [2]. Then, we use the iterative Levenberg-Marquardt optimization in order to find the optimal vertex location minimizing the surface error $E(\cdot)$. Levenberg-Marquardt method [7] represents an iterative gradient-descend minimization approach which solves nonlinear least square problems, subject to constraints. The given nonlinear problem is initially linearized by using a Taylor expansion around the vector $\psi = (\hat{\phi}, \hat{\theta})^T$:

$$\mathbf{f}(\psi + \mathbf{h}) = \mathbf{f}(\psi) + \mathbf{J}\mathbf{h} \tag{10}$$

where $\mathbf{f}(\cdot)$ is the given surface distortion function, defined in the previous section, and $\mathbf{h} = (\Delta\phi, \Delta\theta)^T$ is the step size. $\mathbf{J}$ is the Jacobian matrix of the vector function $\mathbf{f}$ calculated as $\mathbf{J} = (\partial\mathbf{f}/\partial\hat{\phi}, \partial\mathbf{f}/\partial\hat{\theta})$.

The vector ψ_k is updated at each iteration k

$$\psi_{k+1} = \psi_k + \mathbf{h}_k, \tag{11}$$

while $\mathbf{h}_k$ is calculated from:

$$(\mathbf{J}_k^T\mathbf{J}_k + \mu_k\mathbf{I})\mathbf{h}_k = \mathbf{J}_k^T\mathbf{f}_k, \tag{12}$$

where $\mu_k > 0$ is the damping factor at iteration k, $\mathbf{f}_k$ and $\mathbf{J}_k$ represent the surface distortion metric and its Jacobian, calculated at iteration k with respect to ψ_k. The initial damping factor is chosen as $\mu_0 = 10^{-6} \ \max\{\mathrm{diag}(\mathbf{J}_0^T\mathbf{J}_0)\}$ where $\mathbf{J}_0$ corresponds to the Jacobian matrix of $\mathbf{f}$ calculated for ψ_0. When ψ_k is close to the optimal value, the convergence rate of the Levenberg-Marquardt is almost quadratic. The Levenberg-Marquardt optimization process is terminated when either the step size $\mathbf{h}_k$ becomes too small, or the error $E(\cdot)$ is too small, or when the loop exceeds a pre-set number of iterations [7]. The 3D watermarking methodology is blind and in the detection stage, the watermark message is extracted bit by bit using statistical detection as in [2,3,6].

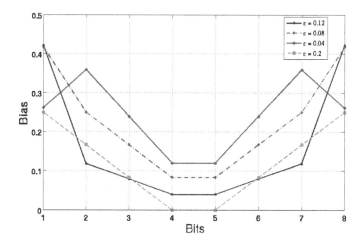

Fig. 1. The bias in the estimation of the means for each bin, corresponding to the attempts by a crypto-attacker attempting to find the embedded watermark message, when $M = 8$ alternating bits of 1 and 0, and $\varepsilon_{max} = 0.15$

5   Watermark Security

We have only one security parameter ε, representing the trimming ratio used for removing the vertices that are either too close to the object center or they are located at the other extremity, according to (2). A crypto-attacker would need to guess the value of ε by using exhaustive search, which given the nature of the watermarking process would actually be limited to a set of quantized values. The worst case scenario for an attacker would be when the watermark code consists of a sequence of consecutive bits of 1 and 0. It the statistical variable from a bin has an uniform distribution then its mean expectation is $E[\hat{\mu}] = \frac{1}{2}$. Let us assume $E[\hat{\mu}] = \frac{3}{4}$ when embedding $B_i = 1$ and $E[\hat{\mu}] = \frac{1}{4}$ for $B_i = 0$. In Figure 1 we evaluate the bias in the estimation of the mean for the statistical variables from bins estimated by an crypto-attacker attempting to break the watermark code. We consider that the watermark has $M = 8$ bits and $\varepsilon_{max} = 0.15$, while the attacker tries several values $\varepsilon \in \{0.04, 0.08, 0.12, 0.2\}$. A resulting bias of $\frac{1}{4}$ or larger, corresponds to a uniform distribution or to a bit flip and would result into a wrongly estimated bit for the crypto-attacker. It can be observed from Figure 1, that due to the symmetry of the trimming, the middle bits are more likely to be identified during a crypto-attack.

The number of trials that are required for a cryto-attack on the watermarked object to succeed, depends on how well the attacker can guess the location of half bins and the number of embedded bits M, as follows:

$$\tau = \frac{\varepsilon(\rho_{max} - \rho_{min})}{\frac{\rho_b}{2}} = \frac{2\varepsilon M}{(1 - 2\varepsilon)} \tag{13}$$

where we have used (3). This expression would result for $\varepsilon_{max} = 0.15$ into a number of 28 and 55 trials for a crypto-attacker, when assuming a number of 64 and 128 embedded bits, respectively. The number of required trials would double if considering asymmetric trimming for the range of vertex norms.

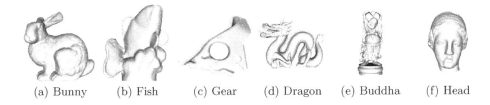

(a) Bunny   (b) Fish   (c) Gear   (d) Dragon   (e) Buddha   (f) Head

Fig. 2. 3D Models used in the experiments

Table 1. Watermarked object distortion measured by MRMS, where all the figures should be multiplied with 10^{-4}

Object	L-MMean	L-MVar	QSPMean	QSPVar	ChoMean	ChoVar
Bunny	0.40	0.21	0.43	0.25	1.18	0.62
Fish	0.12	0.06	0.15	0.07	0.48	0.24
Gear	409.59	148.16	679.46	212.11	1860.67	1023.67
Dragon	0.29	0.13	0.36	0.15	1.09	0.57
Buddha	0.29	0.16	0.27	0.16	0.91	0.47
Head	0.12	0.06	0.13	0.06	0.32	0.16

6   Experimental Results

In this following, we provide the results when hiding digital information into six 3D graphical models: Bunny, Fish, Gear, Dragon, Buddha and Head, which are shown in Figure 2. For each result we consider the embedding of one hundred different watermark codes into each graphical object and $M = 64$ bits, $\alpha = 0.1$, $\varepsilon_{max} = 0.15$. Following empirical estimations, throughout the experimental results we consider the weighting of $(k_1, k_2, k_3)=(0.49, 0.49, 0.02)$ for the surface distortion components. We compare the results provided by the watermarking method ensuring surface preservation based on the Levenberg-Marquardt optimization method, (denoted as L-M) with the methods proposed by Cho *et al.* [2], and that using quadric error metric (QSP) from [6]. All these methods rely on using the object center as the reference. For each method we employ two different statistical approaches, corresponding to modifying the mean or the variance of the histogram of distances from vertices to the object center and these are identified by appending either "Mean" or "Var" to the name of the watermarking method.

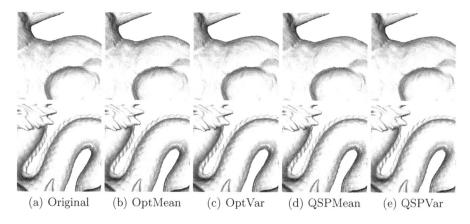

(a) Original   (b) OptMean   (c) OptVar   (d) QSPMean   (e) QSPVar

Fig. 3. Visual comparison of details of 3D watermarked Bunny and Dragon

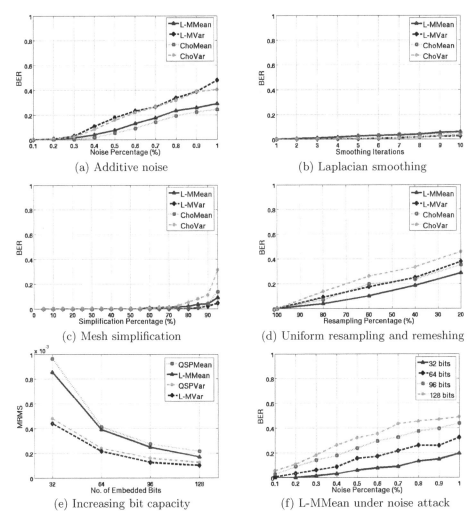

Fig. 4. Robustness against various attacks for the Dragon object in (a)-(d). Message length influence for Bunny object in (e), (f).

A very important requirement for hiding digital information into graphical objects consists of achieving a minimal surface distortion such that it is not visible. Table 2 compares the distortions introduced by the two methods proposed in this paper and the Cho's methods under the same parameter settings. We use MRMS, proposed in [8] as the numerical distortion measure for comparing various watermarking methods. As it can be observed from these results, L-MMean and L-MVar provide better surface preservation results than the other methods. Figure 3 compares close details of the distortions produced by the methods L-M and QSP for two objects with very different surface properties: Bunny and Dragon. The surface distortion minimization methods described in this paper produce much smaller distortion than Cho's method [2] which is known to introduce ripples on mesh surfaces.

The proposed methodology is robust against attacks that do not distort the graphical object surface including affine transformations, vertex reordering, etc. In the following we compare the proposed methodology against the approaches of Cho's method [2] and QSP from [6]. In the first four plots from Figure 4 we assess the robustness against additive noise, Laplacian smoothing, mesh simplification and uniform resampling for the Dragon object. Each test result represents the average of bit error ratios (BER) representing the ratio of bits lost after each attack from the total number of embedded bits. In Figure 4(e) we assess the influence of the bit capacity, while in Figure 4(f) we consider noise as well for the L-MMean method, both of these studies for the Bunny object. These experimental results prove the robustness ability of the proposed methodology while producing minimal distortion to the 3D object surface.

7   Conclusions

The proposed methodology considers a novel surface error function as an optimization cost function for 3D watermarking. The error function consists of three components measuring the distortion with respect to the original surface, the watermarked surface and the Euclidean distance from the original vertex location. The 3D object surface distortion is minimized by employing the Levenberg-Marquardt algorithm in spherical coordinates. The robustness of the proposed 3D watermarking methodology to various attacks was shown experimentally. Watermarks can be used for information hiding, copyright protection, for embedding object-specific information.

References

1. Bors, A.G.: Watermarking mesh-based representations of 3-D objects using local moments. IEEE Trans. on Image Processing 15(3), 687–701 (2006)
2. Cho, J.W., Prost, R., Jung, H.Y.: An oblivious watermarking for 3-D polygonal meshes using distribution of vertex norms. IEEE Trans. Signal Processing 55(1), 142–155 (2007)
3. Luo, M., Bors, A.G.: Surface-preserving watermarking of 3-D shapes. IEEE Trans. on Image Processing 20(10), 2813–2826 (2011)
4. Zafeiriou, S., Tefas, A., Pitas, I.: Blind robust watermarking schemes for copyright protection of 3D mesh objects. IEEE Trans. on Visualization and Computer Graphics 11(5), 496–607 (2005)
5. Liu, Y., Prabhakaran, B., Guo, X.H.: Spectral Watermarking for Parameterized Surfaces. IEEE Trans. on Information Forensics and Security 7(5), 1459–1471 (2011)
6. Luo, M., Bors, A.G.: Shape watermarking based on minimizing the quadric error metric. In: Proc. IEEE International Conference on Shape Modeling and Applications, Beijing, China, pp. 103–110 (2009)
7. Levenberg, K.: An algorithm for least-squares estimation of nonlinear parameters. The Quarterly of Applied Mathematics 2, 164–168 (1944)
8. Cignoni, P., Rocchini, C., Scopigno, R.: Metro: Measuring error on simplified surfaces. Computer Graphics Forum 17(2), 167–174 (1998)

Wavelet Network and Geometric Features Fusion Using Belief Functions for 3D Face Recognition

Mohamed Anouar Borgi, Maher El'Arbi, and Chokri Ben Amar

REGIM : REsearch Groups on Intelligent Machines,
University of Sfax, ENIS, BP 1173 Sfax 3038 Tunisia
{anoir.borgi,chokri.benamar}@ieee.org, maher.elarbi@gmail.com

Abstract. One of the challenges in pattern recognition technologies, especially face recognition, is the ability to handle scenarios where subjects are non-cooperative in terms of position (face pose) or deformation (face expression). In this paper, we propose an innovative approach for 3D face recognition that combines heterogeneous features by using evidence theory based on belief functions. The first feature is generated via wavelet network algorithm, which approximates every face, by an optimal linear combination. The second feature models each facial surface by a collection of facial curves based on geodesic distance. The fusion procedure adopt a refined model of belief function based on the Deampster-Shafer rule in the context of confusion matrix. Experimental evaluation performed on subset of the FRGC v2 database, shows that the recognition rate increases with fusion of redundant and/or independent data. Further, the technique demonstrates robustness under different facial expressions.

Keywords: 3D face recognition, wavelet network, facial curves, evidence theory , confusion matrix.

1 Introduction

One of the key challenges for face recognition is finding efficient and discriminative facial appearance descriptors that are resistant to large variations in illumination, pose, facial expression, aging, partial occlusions and other changes. Most current recognition systems use just one type of features [18]. However for complex tasks such as face recognition, it is often the case that no single feature modality is rich enough to capture all of the classification information available in the image. Finding and combining complementary feature sets has thus become an active research topic in pattern recognition [1],with successful applications in many challenging tasks including handwritten character recognition and face recognition [20] [21].

Several fusion scheme for 3-D face recognition that combine different kinds of features are proposed in the literature. Pan and Wu [2] present a method for face identification where they combine both profile and surface models. Profile experts are modulated by the use one vertical and two horizontal profile features-based

R. Wilson et al. (Eds.): CAIP 2013, Part II, LNCS 8048, pp. 307–314, 2013.
© Springer-Verlag Berlin Heidelberg 2013

extractions, while the surface expert makes use of a weighted ICP-based surface matcher. The similarity scores coming from these matchers are fused via the sum fusion rule. In [3], Gkberk et al. have briefly discussed features coming from shape such as point-cloud, surface-normal or shapes coming from profile information. In this first round of fusion experiments, they have observed that some fusion techniques outperform the classifiers taken individually. They experimented with various fusion methods such as fixed or arithmetic rules at score level, rank-based combination rule, and voting method such plurality voting. Another type of fusion rule based on shape is proposed in [4]. A different pairs region of the face from the gallery and probe images are compared or matched, and the matching scores are combined with the product fusion rule. Also a feature-level fusion scheme is presented in [5] where global shape features are concatenated with the local features.

In addition, fusion rules are used when shape and texture modalities are present in face recognition systems. A classical approach is to consider separately classifiers for each modality taken individually and then to make fusion at the score, rank, or decision level [6]. Another approach is proposed in [7]which uses a local feature analysis technique with the help of Principal Component Analysis to extract features from shape and texture information. This classifier tries to combine texture and shape information with the sum fusion rule. Mian et al. [8] propose another approach where texture and shape features are combined together in order to cope with the variations caused by expressions, illumination, pose,..,etc. The texture features are based on scale-invariant feature transform (SIFT). Tensors constructed in locally defined coordinate bases are used as 3-D descriptors. The two schemes are fused at score level with confidence-weighted sum rule. Y. Wang et al. [9]used 2-D Gabor wavelet features as local descriptors for the texture schema and local 3-D shape descriptors as point signatures and then their similarity scores are combined by weighted sum fusion rule. A different algorithm that uses feature fusion via hierarchical graph matching is presented in [10].

All the proposed approach presented above did not take into account the fact that information is by-passed by the uncertainty, the indistinctness and the ambiguity. Evidence theory is a flexible framework to model ignorance and arbitrary and offers a natural context to remedy from all those information weakness. Belief functions is the most widely used method from the evidence theory which combines different pieces of evidences into a single value that approximates the probability of an event [11]. In this paper,we addresses the problem of 3D face recognition by combining wavelet network features and geometric features on an evidence fusion theory based on belief functions. For each kind of feature, a confusion matrix is obtained then a mass belief functions are computed and finally combined using Dampster-Shafer rule.

The remainder of this paper is organized as follows: Section 2 briefly describes the proposed approach, section 3 presents experimental results. In Section 4 , we give comparison to other state of the art approaches and Section 5 concludes the paper.

2   The Proposed Algorithm

The baselines of the proposed face recognition algorithm are shown in Figure 1.

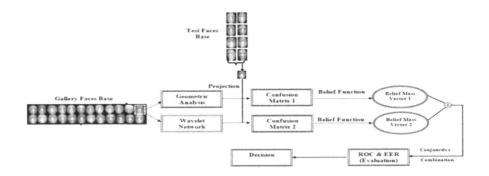

Fig. 1. Overview of the proposed algorithm

First, every gallery image will be approximated with wavelet network and geometric curves in the offline training step. Then, in the online test step, a probe image presented to make recognition will follow the same steps in the training phase. We compute, distances between wavelet weights and between face curves between trained and test features and obtain two confusion matrices. Next, two belief mass matrices are determined for each feature. Finally, we combine those matrices using conjunction fusion rule. A detailed description is provided in next subsections.

2.1   Geometric Features Extraction (GF)

The goal of this step is to represent facial surfaces as an indexed collection of closed curves named facial curves. A facial curves are obtained based on the following fact: the surface distance is defined as the length of the shortest path between a point and a fixed reference point which is assumed to be the tip of the nose, along the facial surface. We tried to make this procedure invariant with respect to changes in facial expressions [13]. Figure 2 illustrates examples of extracted curves [19].

For a given Gallery faces, the geometric features are gathered as follows : First, a Gaussian Filter is applied in order to improve the extraction performance, then, we extract pixel locations at a certain range and finally, use an interpolation between the extracted points in order to obtain closed curve.

2.2   Wavelet Network Features (WNF)

This step consist of approximating each 3D face using a wavelet network. A wavelet networks were introduced as an alternative to feed forward neural

Fig. 2. Example of face with extracted curves

networks for function approximation. This concept is born from the combination of wavelet decomposition and neural networks.

Wavelet network algorithm approximates 3D face with a linear combination of wavelets that are multiplied by corresponding weights according to:

$$\check{f} = \sum_{i=1}^{N} w_i * \psi_{n_i} \tag{1}$$

Where $\check{f}$ denote the face image approximation, w_i the weights, ψ_{n_i} the wavelet and N the number of wavelets.

The mother wavelet used in our work is the second derived of the Beta function [14]. Figure 3 illustrate an example of a reconstructed face using wavelet networks.The quality of reconstructed image increases with the number of used wavelets.

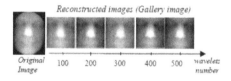

Fig. 3. Examples of 2D face and reconstructed images by beta wavelet networks

2.3   Building Confusion Matrix, Belief Masses Determination and Fusion

Once geometrical and wavelet network features are obtained, we construct confusion matrix for each kind of feature. For the geometrical features, we extract the set of curves, as in the procedure in the offline step, and then we compare two facial shapes (more details can be found in [16]). The tool used essentially nowadays for this kind of features is Riemannian analysis of shapes which try to construct geodesic paths between shapes and to use geodesic lengths. For the wavelet network features, the test face image undergoes wavelet network training and the obtained wavelet network features are projected in wavelets network features of the concurrent image and new weights specific to this image are created. We compute a similarity score by comparing weights.

First, for the geometric features, we compute the distance for each pair of surfaces and for the wavelet network features, we compute the Euclidean distance for each pair of wavelet network weights. Then, a distances matrices normalization step is performed on the generated distances from the two matches wavelet network and geometric features. In this paper, we use the Min-Max normalization. Next, a Bayesian Assignment approach [17] is adopted to conclude the belief mass functions values from the confusion matrix according to the following formula :

Let $\Omega = \{\omega_1, \omega_2, ..., \omega_n\}$ be the discernment context.

$$\forall \omega_i \in \Omega, m(\omega_i) = \frac{n_{ki}}{\sum_{j=1}^{K} n_{kj}} = \frac{n_{ki}}{n_k} \qquad (2)$$

A belief mass m is equal to the ratio of class objects ω_i that have been classified in ω_k , divided by the total number of objects classified in ω_k. Finally, the conjunctive combination rule [15] is applied according to the following formulas:

$$\forall A \subseteq \Omega, m_{GF\cap WNF}(A) = m_{GF} \cap m_{WNF}(A) = \sum_{B\cap C=A} m_{GF}(B)m_{WNF}(C) \quad (3)$$

where m_{GF} and m_{WN} denote two Belief mass functions for geometric features GF and wavelet network features WNF.

3   Experimental Results

To demonstrate the effectiveness of the proposed algorithm, MATLAB simulation results are given in this section. We used a subset of FRGC (Face Recognition Grand Challenge) v2 dataset. This database contains variations of facials expressions. In our work, we consider 250 faces :125 faces of different person for the training step and 125 faces of the same person with different facial expressions for the test step. Thus, we obtain a 125x125 term similarity matrix. The diagonal terms representing the same person are called intra-class. Whereas the off-diagonal terms representing different persons are called impostors faces or inter-class. We used the receiver operator characteristic (ROC) curves, the Equal Error Rate (EER) and the Rank-1 Recognition Rate as evaluation criteria. Figure 4 shows the obtained ROC after applying only geometric features, only wavelet network features and the fusion by belief function.

Figure 5 shows the obtained Equal Error Rate when applying only geometric feature, wavelet network feature and combined feature by belief function.

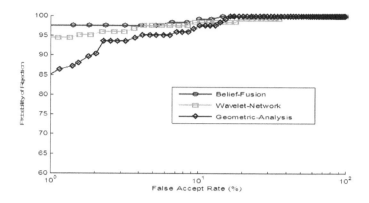

Fig. 4. ROC curves Results

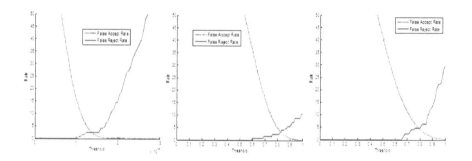

Fig. 5. EER Results

Table 1. Rank-1 Recognition Rate

Method	Geometric Feature	Wavelet Network Feature	Belief function Fusion
Rank-1 (%)	70.4	89.6	94.4

We can see clearly the important improvement made by the belief fusion in term of Rank-1 Recognition Rate which reached 94.4 % and the important value of Equal Error Rate sought to decrease.

For better confidence on the proposed fusion approach, we added Iterative Closest Point algorithm [19] to see its impact on the recognition results.

We can notice from the table above that performances of the proposed approach increases when an other feature is added in the fusion even if the features are redundant, they complete each others.

We also compared fusion based on belief function with arithmetic, voting and ranking methods. Rank-1 Recognition Rate are given in table 1.

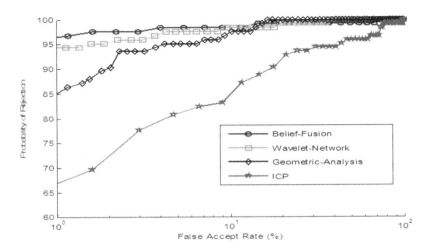

Fig. 6. ROC curve results with ICP

Table 2. Rank-1 Recognition Rate with ICP

Method	Minimum	Product	Plurality Voting	Borda Count	Belief functions
Rank-1 (%)	92	96.8	92	83.8	96.8

4   Conclusion

In this paper,we addresses the problem of 3D face recognition by combining wavelet network features and geometric features on a evidence fusion theory based on belief functions. For each kind of feature, a confusion matrix is obtained then a mass belief functions are computed and finally combined using Dampster-Shafer rule. Experimental results, in term of ROC curves, Equal Error Rate and Rank-1 Recognition Rate, have shown that our approach present an excellent recognition rate and outperform those sources of information taken individually and is very competitive with other fusion techniques such as arithmetic, voting and ranking rules.

References

1. Borgi, M.A., Said, S., Ben Amar, C.: Information Fusion for 3D Face Recognition. In: IEEE 2011 International Conference on Image Information Processing, ICIIP, November 3-5. Jaypee University of Infor-mation Technology, Waknaghat (2011)
2. Pan, G., Wu, Z.: 3D face recognition from range data. Int. J. Image Graph. 5(3), 573–593 (2005)
3. Gökberk, B., Salah, A.A., Akarun, L.: Rank-based decision fusion for 3D shape-based face recognition. In: Kanade, T., Jain, A., Ratha, N.K. (eds.) AVBPA 2005. LNCS, vol. 3546, pp. 1019–1028. Springer, Heidelberg (2005)
4. Chang, K., Bowyer, K., Flynn, P.: Adaptive rigid multi-region selection for handling expres-sion variation in 3D face recognition. In: Proc. IEEE Workshop Face Recog. Grand Challenge Experiments, p. 157 (2005)

5. Xu, C., Wang, Y., Tan, T., Quan, L.: Automatic 3D face recognition combining global geome-tric features with local shape variation information. In: Proc. Int. Conf. Autom. Face Gesture Re-cog., pp. 308–313 (2004)
6. Chang, K.I., Bowyer, K.W., Flynn, P.J.: An evaluation of multimodal 2D + 3D face biome-trics. IEEE Trans. Pattern Anal. Mach. Intell. 27(4), 619–624 (2005)
7. Ben Abdelkader, C., Griffin, P.A.: Comparing and combining depth and texture cues for face recognition. Image Vis. Comput. 23(3), 339–352 (2005)
8. Mian, A., Bennamoun, M., Owens, R.: Face recognition using 2D and 3D multimodal local features. In: Bebis, G., et al. (eds.) ISVC 2006. LNCS, vol. 4291, pp. 860–870. Springer, Heidelberg (2006)
9. Wang, Y., Chua, C.-S.: Robust face recognition from 2D and 3D images using structural Hausdorff distance. Image Vis. Comput. 24(2), 176–185 (2006)
10. Husken, M., Brauckmann, M., Gehlen, S., von der Malsburg, C.: Strategies and benefits of fu-sion of 2D and 3D face recognition. In: Proc. IEEE Workshop Face Recog. Grand Challenge Experiments, p. 174 (2005)
11. Yager, R.R., Liu, L.: Classic works of the Dempster-Shafer theory of belief functions. STUDFUZZ, vol. 219. Springer, Heidelberg (2008)
12. Said, S., Ben Amor, B., Zaied, M., Ben Amar, C., Daoudi, M.: Fast and efficient 3D face recognition using wavelet. In: IEEE International Conference on Image Processing, ICIP, Cairo Egypt, November 7-11 (2009)
13. Zaied, M., Jemai, O., Ben Amar, C.: Training of the Beta Wavelet Networks by the Frame Theory: Application to face Recognition. In: IEEE International Conference on Image Processing Theory, Tools and Applications, IPTA 2008, Sousse, Tunisia, November 23-26, pp. 165–170 (2008)
14. Ben Amar, C., Zaied, M., Alimi, M.A.: Beta Wavelets. Synthesis and application to lossy im-age compression. Journal of Advances in Engineering Software 36(7), 459–474 (2005)
15. Denoeux, T.: Conjunctive and Disjunctive Combination of Belief Functions Induced by Non Distinct Bodies of Evidence. Artificial Intelligence 172, 234–264 (2008)
16. Samir, C., Srivastava, A., Daoudi, M.: Automatic 3D Face Recognition Using Shapes of Fa-cial Curves. IEEE Transactions on Pattern Analysis and Machine Intelligence 28(11), 1858–1863 (2006)
17. Mercier, D., Cron, G., Denoeux, T., Masson, M.: Fusion of multi-level decision systems using the Transferable Belief Model. In: Proceedings of FUSION 2005, Philadelphia, PA, USA (July 2005)
18. Berretti, S., Bimbo, A.D., Pala, P.: 3d face recognition using isogeodesic stripes. IEEE Transactions on Pattern Analysis and Machine Intelligence 32(12), 2162–2177 (2010)
19. Zaied, M., Said, S., Jemai, O., Ben Amar, C.: A novel approach for face recognition based on fast learning algorithm and wavelet network theory. International Journal of Wavelets, Multiresolution and Information Processing, IJWMIP 9(6), 923–945 (2011)
20. Ben Soltana, W., Ardabilian, M., Chen, L., Ben Amar, C.: A mixture of Gated Experts Optimized using Simulated Annealing for 3D Face Recognition. In: IEEE International Conference on Image Processing, ICIP 2011, Art. N 6116304, Belgium, November 11-14, pp. 3037–3040 (2011)
21. Ben Soltana, W., Bellil, W., Ben Amar, C., Alimi, M.A.: Multi Library Wavelet Neural Networks for 3D face recognition using 3D facial shape representation. In: 17th European Signal Processing Conference EUSIPCO 2009, Glasgow Scotland, August 24-28, pp. 55–59 (2009)

A Color-Based Selective and Interactive Filter Using Weighted TV

Cédric Loosli[1], François Lecellier[2], Stéphanie Jehan-Besson[3], and Jonas Koko[1]

[1] LIMOS, Université Blaise Pascal - CNRS UMR 6158, Complexe des Cézeaux,
63173 Aubière, France
[2] XLIM-SIC, UMR CNRS 7252, Bd Marie et Pierre Curie BP 30179,
86962 Futuroscope Chasseneuil Cedex, France
[3] GREYC Laboratory, CNRS UMR 6072, Bd du Maréchal Juin, 14050 Caen, France

Abstract. In this paper we propose to introduce a new color interactive and selective filtering tool based on the minimization of a weighted vectorial total variation term (TV_g) with the L^2 norm as data term. Our goal is to filter one region of an image while preserving the other. To this end, we introduce color moments in the TV_g term. Up to now, color moments have been mainly introduced for indexation purposes. In our case, the user selects some points in the area to preserve and some other points in the area to be filtered. Reference color moments are then computed on patches around the selected points and are included in the TV_g term. Two main functions g are tested within the HSL color space leading to interesting results on both synthetic and real images. Convex optimization tools are used to solve the minimization issue and we take benefit of an augmented Lagrangian formulation and Uzawa block relaxation schemes. The proposed filtering tool may be interesting as a pre-processing step for segmentation, movie post-production or object-oriented compression.

Keywords: color filtering, moments color, total variation, convex optimization, augmented Lagrangian.

1 Introduction

In many image processing issues, a filtering step is required in order to remove noise or spurious details from the initial image. The image may then be decomposed in regions (e.g. homogeneous regions) using a segmentation algorithm, or some regions of interest may be selected using well-defined algorithms (active contours for example). The interactive color filtering tool proposed in this paper is quite different from a simple filtering step and may even be considered as a pre-segmentation algorithm. Indeed, the main idea is to filter and simplify some parts of the image while preserving some others using color properties of the regions. In order to obtain such a filtering tool, we focus on the minimization of functionals that take benefit of a color weighted total variation (TV_g) regularization term coupled with the minimization of a L^2 data term. Indeed, the total variation (TV) regularization term owns some interesting geometrical properties [19,1,7], that can be nicely used for denoising and segmentation. The TV regularization term was first proposed for denoising in [20] coupled with the minimization of the L^2

R. Wilson et al. (Eds.): CAIP 2013, Part II, LNCS 8048, pp. 315–323, 2013.

norm as a data term (the well-known ROF model). More recently, Bresson et al [1] proposed to introduce a spatially adaptive TV term using a function g inside the integral
of the TV term. The function g allows to take into account the image gradient in the
regularization term in order to preserve object boundaries during the denoising process.
Some other authors also take benefit of such a weighted TV [5,13,1,14,16,17,6].

In this paper, we propose to settle an interactive color image filtering algorithm by introducing color moments in the weighted TV regularization term. The user is expected
to draw a curve on the region to be removed and another curve on the region to be preserved. The color moments of the chosen points are then computed on small patches
and the corresponding characteristics are included in a well-adapted g function in the
TV_g term. As far as color moments are concerned, they are considered as a powerful
color descriptor. They have been introduced in [18] for image indexation and retrieval in
order to complete or replace SIFT descriptors. They appear to be more interesting than
the classical color histograms used in [9,11,15]. Indeed, color histograms are not able to
represent the spatial layout of the color repartition. In an original manner, we propose to
take advantage of such a representation for our selective color filtering tools. Concerning the optimization of the whole functional $(TV_g + L^2)$, we rely on the mathematical
framework previously introduced in [16] for grey level images and in [17] for color images. The optimization of the vectorial $TV_g + L^2$ is based on an augmented Lagrangian
approach and Uzawa block relaxation schemes. Our numerical scheme presents the advantage to be robust regarding with the choice of the penalty parameter and is efficient
in terms of computational cost. The proposed filtering tool may be very interesting as
a pre-processing step for segmentation, movie post-production or object-oriented compression.

In the rest of the paper, we first detail the main principles of our selective filtering
tool in section 2. The optimization process is detailed in section 3 and the color-based
weighted TV is introduced in section 4. Finally some experimental results on both synthetic and real images are given in section 5.

2   Selective Filtering Based on the Minimization of a Weighted TV

2.1   Geometrical Properties of TV and Weighted TV

The classical ROF (Rudin, Osher and Fatemi) model [20] aims to recover the original
image $u(x)$ given a noisy image $f(x)$ by minimizing the total variation under L^2 data
fidelity:

$$E(u) = \int_\Omega |\nabla u(x)| \, dx + \lambda \int_\Omega (u(x) - f(x))^2 \, dx, \qquad (1)$$

where $\Omega \subset \mathbb{R}^2$ is the image domain and λ a positive scale parameter.

The first integral is the classical regularization term called TV (Total Variation) term.
This term has proven its efficiency for image restoration and also presents some interesting geometrical properties. In order to better explain these properties, let us denote
the upper level sets of the image by $U^\alpha(u) = \{x, u(x) > \alpha\}$ like in [4]. From a geometrical point of view, the co-area formula [8] states that, for any function which belongs
to the space of bounded variations $BV(\Omega)$, there is a relation between the TV regularization term and the perimeter $Per(U^\alpha)$ of the set U^α. We can write $Per(U^\alpha(u)) =$

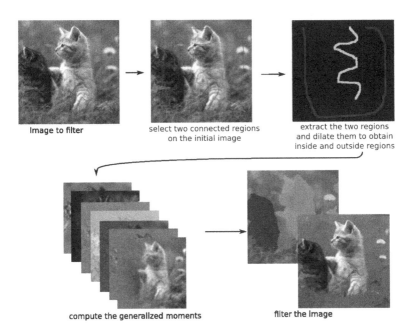

Fig. 1. Main principles of the proposed color-based interactive and selective filtering tool

$\int_{\Omega} |\nabla \chi_{U^{\alpha}(u)}| \, dx$ for all α where $\chi_{U^{\alpha}}(u)$ stands for the characteristic function of the set $U^{\alpha}(u)$. Such geometrical features may contribute to explain the properties of this regularization term. Indeed, when decreasing the weight λ of the data term, components will be removed in an order determined by their size and their geometry. For example, small components will be removed first and sharp angles will be smoothed. In [7], the authors establish a connection between this model and morphological operators such as opening and morphological granulometry.

The introduction of a g function in TV may produce different filtering results. Indeed, the TV_g term, when applied to a characteristic set is equivalent to a weighted perimeter $\int_C g(s) ds$ where C designates the boundary of the set and s its arc length. In [1], the function g is then chosen as $g(x) = 1/(1 + \beta G_{\sigma} * |\nabla f|)$ in order to introduce the image gradient directly in the regularization term (β is a positive constant and $G_{\sigma}*$ represents the convolution with a Gaussian of variance σ). This term allows to preserve object boundaries and sharp angles during the regularization process and can also be used for shape segmentation [1]. Indeed, this regularization term corresponds to the classical criterion proposed in geodesic active contours [2]. Note that such a spatially varying TV term has also been investigated by different authors with various g functions (e.g. for salt and pepper denoising) [5,13,1,14,16,17,6].

2.2   Color Selective Filter Using Weighted TV

In this paper, we propose to test the availability of the weighted TV regularization term in order to perform a kind of selective filtering of the image components. This idea is closely related to the design of geometrical filters in the framework of mathematical morphology where some shapes are removed on the basis of their geometric properties. Some examples of geometrical filtering using the TV_g term are given in [16,17]. Rather than using geometric properties, we here propose to take benefit of color moments and of a vectorial TV term in order to include some color features in the function g. In order to introduce a selective filtering scheme, we add an interactive step where two regions are manually selected (using a curve drawn on each region). The color moments of each point within each region are computed leading to a reference vector of moment for each region. The function g is then designed in order to filter one region while preserving the other one and inversely. The main principle of this scheme is summarized in Fig.1.

3   Fast Dual Minimization of $TV_g + L^2$

We define Ω as the image domain $\subset \mathbb{R}^d$, $d = 2,3$ and $\mathbf{u}(x) = (u_1(x), u_2(x), u_3(x)) \in \mathbb{R}^3$ as a vector-valued function defined on Ω that corresponds to the color intensity with the three values of each color channel. In the rest of the document, vector valued functions are denoted by bold-face letters (e.g. $\mathbf{u} = (u_1, u_2, u_3)$). Let us also note the Euclidean scalar product by $\mathbf{u} \cdot \mathbf{v} = \sum_{i=1}^{3} u_i v_i$, for $\mathbf{u}$ and $\mathbf{v}$ in $\mathbb{R}^d$. Moreover, for $\mathbf{u} \in \mathbf{R}^d$, we use the notation $|\mathbf{u}|_2 = (\mathbf{u} \cdot \mathbf{u})^{1/2}$ for the Euclidean norm.

Let g be a continuous, positive valued and bounded function defined on Ω, we consider the following weighted total variation regularization term, denoted by TV_g :

$$TV_g(\mathbf{u}) = \int_\Omega g(x) \left[|\nabla u_1|_2^2 + |\nabla u_2|_2^2 + |\nabla u_3|_2^2 \right]^{1/2} dx.$$

The considered function g is described later in section 4.

Let $\mathbf{f} = (f_1, f_2, f_3)$ be the input color image to be filtered, we propose to address the following vectorial $TV_g + L^2$ minimization problem:

$$\min_{\mathbf{u} \in \mathbf{X}} E(\mathbf{u}) = J(\mathbf{u}) + \lambda \int_\Omega |\mathbf{u}(x) - \mathbf{f}(x)|_2^2 dx. \tag{2}$$

where $\mathbf{u}$ is the unknown image to restore and $\mathbf{X}$ is a suitable functions space.

3.1   Augmented Lagrangian Methods for the $TV_g + L^2$ Model

In this section we propose to remind the convex optimization tools used in order to solve (2). This framework is issued from our previous works notably [16] where the resolution is performed for grey level images, and [17] where the vectorial $TV_g + L^\tau$ model has been solved for vectorial images with $\tau = 1$ or 2. We remind here only few elements for completeness. The convex minimization problem (2) is transformed into a suitable saddle-point problem by introducing an auxiliary unknown. An augmented Lagrangian approach is then introduced and solved using Uzawa relaxation schemes. Some details are given thereafter for the reader convenience but only briefly for space reasons.

Let us introduce the auxiliary unknown $\mathbf{p} = \mathbf{f} - \mathbf{u}$ and rewrite the functional E as

$$E(\mathbf{u},\mathbf{p}) = TV_g(\mathbf{u}) + \lambda \int_{\Omega} |\mathbf{p}(x)|_2^2 \, dx. \tag{3}$$

The minimization problem (3) becomes $\min_{(\mathbf{u},\mathbf{p}) \in K} E(\mathbf{u},\mathbf{p})$,, where the constraint set K is defined by $K = \{(\mathbf{u},\mathbf{p}) \in X \times X \mid \mathbf{u} + \mathbf{p} - \mathbf{f} = 0 \text{ in } \Omega\}$. With this constrained minimization problem, we associate the Lagrangian functional $\mathscr{L}$ defined on $\mathbf{X}^3$ by

$$\mathscr{L}(\mathbf{u},\mathbf{p};\mathbf{s}) = E(\mathbf{u},\mathbf{p}) + (\mathbf{s}, \mathbf{u} + \mathbf{p} - \mathbf{f})_{\mathbf{X}}. \tag{4}$$

In (4), $\mathbf{s}$ is the Lagrange multiplier associated with the constraint in K. We now introduce the augmented Lagrangian defined, for $r > 0$, by

$$\mathscr{L}_r(\mathbf{u},\mathbf{p};\mathbf{s}) = \mathscr{L}(\mathbf{u},\mathbf{p};\mathbf{s}) + \frac{r}{2} \, \| \mathbf{u} + \mathbf{p} - \mathbf{f} \|_{L^2}^2 \tag{5}$$

where r is the penalty parameter.

3.2 Uzawa Block Relaxation Methods

We apply an Uzawa block relaxation method by using an alternative minimization procedure (see e.g. [10,12]). Such algorithms are fast, easy to implement, and also robust to the choice of the penalty parameter which allows to choose a value of r that minimizes the number of iterations and so the computational cost [17]. Given $\mathbf{p}^{-1}$ and $\mathbf{s}^0$, we compute successively $\mathbf{u}^k$, $\mathbf{p}^k$ and $\mathbf{s}^{k+1}$ as follows:

Algorithm 1. Uzawa block relaxation algorithm

Initialization. $\mathbf{p}^{-1}$, $\mathbf{s}^0$ and $r > 0$ given.
Iteration $k \geq 0$. Compute successively $\mathbf{u}^k$, $\mathbf{p}^k$ and $\mathbf{s}^k$ as follows.

    Step 1. Set $\tilde{\mathbf{p}} = \mathbf{s}^k + r(\mathbf{p}^{k-1} - \mathbf{f})$, compute $\mathbf{v}^k$ and then $\mathbf{u}^k = \mathbf{f} - \mathbf{p}^{k-1} + \frac{1}{r}(\nabla \cdot \mathbf{v}^k - \mathbf{s}^k)$.

    We can compute $\mathbf{v}^k$ using the following semi-implicit scheme due to Chambolle [3]:

$$v_i^{\ell+1} = \frac{v_i^{\ell} + \tau \nabla (\nabla \cdot v_i^{\ell} - \tilde{p}_i)}{1 + (\tau/g) \left[\sum_{i=1}^{3} |\nabla(\nabla \cdot v_i^{\ell} - \tilde{p}_i)|_2^2 \right]^{1/2}}, \quad i = 1,2,3, \quad \text{where} \quad \tau > 0 \tag{6}$$

    Step 2. Update the Lagrange multiplier: $\mathbf{s}^{k+1/2} = \mathbf{s}^k + \frac{r}{2}(\mathbf{u}^k + \mathbf{p}^{k-1} - \mathbf{f})$.

    Step 3. Compute $\mathbf{p}^k = -(\mathbf{s}^k + r(\mathbf{u}^k - \mathbf{f}))/(r + 2\lambda)$

    Step 4. Update the Lagrange multiplier: $\mathbf{s}^{k+1} = \mathbf{s}^{k+1/2} + \frac{r}{2}(\mathbf{u}^k + \mathbf{p}^k - \mathbf{f})$.

---

4 Proposition of a Weighted TV Term Based on Color Moments

Let us now introduce the weighted TV regularization designed for our color selective filtering tool. Given a color image $\mathbf{u} = (u_1, u_2, u_3)$, we propose to take benefit of generalized color moments M_{pq}^{abc} introduced in [18]. The color moment of order $p+q$ and degree $a+b+c$ is defined as follows:

$$M_{pq}^{abc} = \int \int_D x_1^p x_2^q [u_1(x_1,x_2)]^a [u_2(x_1,x_2)]^b [u_3(x_1,x_2)]^c dx_1 dx_2 \,, \tag{7}$$

where $x = (x_1, x_2)$ is a pixel in a 2D image and a, b, c, p and q some positive integers and D the moment computation domain (it can be the whole image or a patch).

In order to use a semi-local information on color (which can be interesting when considering texture regions), we propose to compute color moments on small patches around each pixel of the considered region. We denote this small neighborhood by D_n where n represents the half size of the neighborhood. Note that the moments of degree 0 correspond simply to the classical geometric moments of D_n and so they do not provide useful information for filtering since they only encode the fixed geometry of D_n. In our application we consider 27 moments which are M_{00}^{abc}, M_{01}^{abc} and M_{10}^{abc} with $(a,b,c) \in$ $\{(1,0,0);(0,1,0);(0,0,1);(1,1,0);(1,0,1);(0,1,1);(2,0,0);(0,2,0);(0,0,2)\}$. The corresponding 27-vectors of moments are noted $\mathbf{M}(x)$ where $x \in \Omega$. In our application we consider the HSL color space which conducts in practice to better results than the RGB color space. Note that the space color can be changed easily using a simple conversion at the beginning of the process.

The semi-supervised filtering scheme has been previously described in Figure 1. In the first step, we draw two curves on the image, one for the "inside" region and the other for the "outside" region. The "outside" region Ω_{out} will be filtered and the "inside" one Ω_{in} remains without filtering. A dilatation of what we can call "the markers" is performed and the color moments for each selected region are then computed. For the dilatation step, we use a square of half size of 2 pixels as a structuring element. We present thereafter two main solutions for the design of a weighted TV term taking into account these color moments.

4.1   Definition of Weighted TV Based on the Average Moment Vector

The most straightforward method is to compute an average moment vector of the markers Ω_{in} and Ω_{out} (averaging each component of the vector). The average value for the component α is $\mu_i^\alpha = \frac{1}{|\Omega_i|} \int_{\Omega_i} M_\alpha(x_1,x_2) dx_1 dx_2$ with $\alpha \in [0,27]$ and $i = in$ or out. We then propose to select the order α^* that corresponds to the maximum distance between the two average values as follows :

$$\alpha^* = \max_{\alpha \in [0,27]} (|(\mu_{in}^\alpha - \mu_{out}^\alpha)|) \,, \tag{8}$$

We then propose to introduce the following thresholding function :

$$T(x) = \begin{cases} c_1 \text{ if } M_{\alpha^*}(x) < \mu_{\alpha^*} \\ c_2 \text{ if } M_{\alpha^*}(x) \geq \mu_{\alpha^*} \end{cases} \tag{9}$$

where μ_{α^*} corresponds to the average of the moments M_{α^*} of order α^* of the whole image Ω and is then chosen as a threshold. We choose $c_1 = 0.01$ and $c_2 = 1$ or inversely in order to uppermost smooth the pixels corresponding to the reference region r_{out} or r_{in}. A regularized continuous version of the function $T(x)$ is needed which is obtained by a Gaussian filtering: $g(x) = G_\sigma * T(x)$ ($\sigma = 0.05$).

4.2 Definition of a Weighted TV Using $1 - nn$ Selection

The previous method is not able to deal with large variations of color inside each reference region. In order to cope with this problem, we propose to consider the whole 27 vector as a descriptor. We then compute the L_2 distance between the 27 moments of pixel $\mathbf{x}$ and the 27 moments of each pixel of the inside and outside region and we select the nearest pixel in each reference region. So, for each pixel x of the image, we choose the pixel $\mathbf{x}^*$ in the reference region r_i ($i = in$ or out) such that :
$x_i^* = \arg\min_{\mathbf{y} \in r_i} \left[\sum_\alpha (M^\alpha(x) - M^\alpha(y))^2 \right]$. For each pixel x, the pixel x_i^* designates the pixel in the region r_i with the nearest moment values to x in the sense of the L^2 norm.

A thresholding function is then defined using $T(x) = c_1$ if $x_{in}^* \in r_{in}$ and c_2 if $x_{in}^* \in r_{out}$. We choose $c_1 = 0.01$ and $c_2 = 1$ in order to uppermost smooth the pixels corresponding to the reference region r_{out} while preserving r_{in}. The role of r_{in} and r_{out} can be inverted to preserve r_{out}. A regularized continuous version of the function $T(x)$ is needed which is obtained by a Gaussian filtering: $g(x) = G_\sigma * T(x)$ ($\sigma = 0.05$).

5 Experimental Results

To test our approach, we conduct tests on synthetic and natural images using the two different g functions (μ and $1 - nn$). The patch size is chosen as $n = 3$ which represents a good trade-off between precision and quantity of information (a higher patch size can be needed in order to filter texture with larger patterns or to filter images with a higher resolution). The results are depicted in Fig.2 and Fig.3. In each figure, we both display the two results obtained when choosing r_{in} or r_{out} to be preserved.

The comparison between μ and $1 - nn$ is straightforward. The $1 - nn$ method outperforms significantly the other one showing the interest of designing a well-adapted function g. This can be easily explained since μ only compares the average of the whole selection to the current moment of the pixel. The $1 - nn$ method selects interactively the nearest vector of moments inside each region and then the nearest region (inside or outside) to apply the filtering. So it delivers a more local descriptor of the selected regions.

In order to get some quantitative results on the accuracy of the object contour in the filtered image, we propose to filter an image with an available reference segmentation. We take the leaf image and the reference segmentation mask respectively displayed in Fig.4.(a) and (b). We then perform our filtering algorithm using different parameters and we perform a simple threshold on the image in order to get the object without the background. The mask obtained after filtering O is then compared to the reference mask O_{ref} using the Dice coefficient ($DC(O, O_{ref}) = \frac{2|O \cap O_{ref}|}{|O| + |O_{ref}|}$) and the number of false positive and false negative pixels. The results are displayed in Table 1 for two different resolutions of the same image and for different values of the half patch size. Of course when dealing with a higher resolution, the mask is closer to the reference segmentation mask (the value of DC is near 1). The number of FP increases with the patch size while the number of FN decreases. This can be explained by the fact that the contour is better defined with a small size patch. On the contrary, choosing a small patch size leads to less robust description of the selected region and then increases the number

(a)   (b)   (c)   (d)   (e)   (f)

Fig. 2. Experimental results on a synthetic image and on two natural images (selection and filtering of the background in (a) and of the geometric components in (b), selection and filtering of the two cats in (c) and of the background in (d), selection and filtering of the leopard in (e) and of the background in (f)) using μ approach and HSL space.

(a)   (b)   (c)   (d)   (e)   (f)

Fig. 3. Experimental results on a synthetic image and two natural images (selection and filtering of the background in (a) and of the geometric components in (b), selection and filtering of the two cats in (c) and of the background in (d), selection and filtering of the leopard in (e) and of the background in (f)) using $1 - nn$ approach and HSL space.

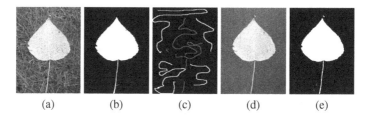

(a)   (b)   (c)   (d)   (e)

Fig. 4. The image (a) represents the initial image and (b) the reference segmentation mask. The image (c) corresponds to the selected components of the two regions after the dilatation process, the image (d) to the filtering result using $1 - nn$ approach and HSL space ($\lambda = 0.1$ and $n = 3$) and the image (e) to the mask obtained from (d) after a simple thresholding.

Table 1. Computation of the Dice Coefficient (DC), the number of false positive pixels (FP) and the number of false negative pixels (FN) according to the half patch size for two resolutions of the leaf image

Resolution: $643 * 496$				Resolution: $321 * 248$			
n	1	3	5	7	n	1	3	5	7
DC	0.989	0.990	0.989	0.988	DC	0.984	0.986	0.986	0.982
FP	770	898	1043	1348	FP	176	230	332	508
FN	811	487	376	267	FN	377	249	157	99

of FN pixels. The best trade-off seems to occur for a half patch size of 3 for the two resolutions regarding with these quantitative parameters. Since the results give a strong smoothing effect on the outside region while preserving all the details of the inside one, this method may give a way to perform an object-oriented compression. The algorithm can also be used as a pre-processing step for different applications such as segmentation or object selection or even artistic post-production of images or movies.

References

1. Bresson, X., Esedoglu, S., Vandergheynst, P., Thiran, J.P., Osher, S.: Fast global minimization of the active contour/snake model. JMIV 28, 151–167 (2007)
2. Caselles, V., Kimmel, R., Sapiro, G.: Geodesic active contours. IJCV 22, 61–79 (1997)
3. Chambolle, A.: An algorithm for total variation minimization and applications. JMIV 20(1-2), 89–97 (2004)
4. Darbon, J., Sigelle, M.: Image restoration with discrete constrained total variation part I: Fast and exact optimization. JMIV 26(3), 261–271 (2006)
5. Dong, Y., Hintermüller, M., Montserrat Rincon-Camacho, M.: A multi-scale vectorial L^τ-TV framework for color image restoration. IJCV 92, 296–307 (2011)
6. Donoser, M., Urschler, M., Hirzer, M., Bischof, H.: Saliency driven total variation segmentation. In: IEEE ICCV, pp. 817–824 (2009)
7. Duval, V., Aujol, J., Gousseau, Y.: The TV L1 model: a geometric point of view. Multiscale Model. Simul. 8, 154–251 (2009)
8. Fleming, W., Rishel, R.: An integral formula for total gradient variation. Archiv der Mathematik 11, 218–222 (1960)
9. Forsyth, D.: A novel algorithm for color constancy. Journal of Computer Vision, 5–36 (1990)
10. Fortin, M., Glowinski, R.: Augmented Lagrangian Methods: Application to the Numerical Solution of Boundary-Value Problems. North-Holland, Amsterdam (1983)
11. Funt, B., Finlayson, G.: Color constant color indexing. IEEE PAMI, 522–529 (1995)
12. Glowinski, R., Tallec, P.L.: Augmented Lagrangian and Operator-splitting Methods in Nonlinear Mechanics. SIAM, Philadelphia (1989)
13. Goldlücke, B., Cremers, D.: An approach to vectorial total variation based on geometric measure theory. In: CVPR, vol. 106, pp. 327–333 (2010)
14. Grasmair, M.: Locally adaptive total variation regularization. In: Tai, X.-C., Mørken, K., Lysaker, M., Lie, K.-A. (eds.) SSVM 2009. LNCS, vol. 5567, pp. 331–342. Springer, Heidelberg (2009)
15. Healey, G., Slater, D.: Using illumination invariant color histogram descriptors for recognition. In: Computer Vision and Pattern Recognition, pp. 355–360 (1994)
16. Koko, J., Jehan-Besson, S.: An Augmented Lagrangian Method for $TVg+L^1$-norm Minimization. JMIV 38(3), 182–196 (2010)
17. Loosli, C., Jehan-Besson, S., Koko, J.: Uzawa block relaxation methods for color image restoration. In: Fusiello, A., Murino, V., Cucchiara, R. (eds.) ECCV 2012 Ws/Demos, Part II. LNCS, vol. 7584, pp. 492–503. Springer, Heidelberg (2012)
18. Mindru, F., Tuytelaars, T., Gool, L.V., Moons, T.: Moment invariants for recognition under changing viewpoint and illumination. In: Computer Vision and Image Understanding, pp. 3–27 (2004)
19. Nikolova, M., Esedoglu, S., Chan, T.F.: Algorithms for finding global minimizers of image segmentation and denoising models. SIAM Journal of Applied Mathematics 66(5), 1632–1648 (2006)
20. Rudin, L., Osher, S., Fatemi, E.: Nonlinear total variation based noise removal algorithms. Physica D 60, 259–268 (1992)

A Composable Strategy
for Shredded Document Reconstruction

Razvan Ranca and Iain Murray

School of Informatics, University of Edinburgh,
10 Crichton Street, Edinburgh, Scotland, United Kingdom
ranca.razvan@gmail.com, i.murray@ed.ac.uk

Abstract. The reconstruction of shredded documents is of interest in domains such as forensics, investigative sciences and archaeology, and has therefore been approached in many different ways. This paper takes a step towards bridging the gap between previous, disparate, efforts by proposing a composable, probabilistic solution. The task is first divided into independent sub-problems, and novel approaches to several of these sub-problems are then presented. The theoretical properties and empirical performance of these novel approaches are shown to compare favourably to those of previously published methods.

Keywords: shredded document, strip-cut, cross-cut, unshred, deshred.

1 Introduction

The US Federal Trade Commission recommends the shredding of sensitive documents as a good protection method against becoming one of the millions of victims of identity theft[1]. However, the successfully solved DARPA Shredder challenge[2] and the appearance of commercial document reconstruction services[3], raises questions about the current security offered by the shredder. Further research in this area will benefit projects such as the ongoing effort to recover the shredded archives of the East German secret police, which consist of 16,000 bags of shredded documents. Since it took 3 dozen people 6 years to reconstruct 300 of these bags ([5]), at this rate, the project would require 11,520 person-years.

In this paper, we approach the unshredding challenge by splitting the problem into four independent sub-problems. A *pre-processing* step transforms the noisy images of scanned shreds into uniform "ideal shreds". A *scoring function* looks at the potential match between every pair of ideal shreds and indicates the viability of that match. A *search method* is then employed to find a placement of the ideal shreds in 2D space that obtains a good global score, where the global score is the sum of the local scores determined by each pair of neighbouring shreds. Finally, a *user-interaction* step can be weaved in with any of the above as to help catch errors before they have a chance to propagate.

---

[1] http://consumer.ftc.gov/features/feature-0014-identity-theft
[2] http://archive.darpa.mil/shredderchallenge/
[3] eg: http://www.unshredder.com/

R. Wilson et al. (Eds.): CAIP 2013, Part II, LNCS 8048, pp. 324–331, 2013.
© Springer-Verlag Berlin Heidelberg 2013

In Sections 3 to 5, we will present: a novel, composable and probabilistic scoring function; an original, graph-inspired, search heuristic which balances speed and accuracy while achieving modularity; and a tractable up/down orientation detection method which can be used as part of the pre-processing step.

2   Related Work

Significant effort has been made towards finding a good search function. In [9] the authors show that the search is NP hard by reduction to the Travelling Salesman Problem. Prandtstetter ([8]) attempts an Integer Linear Programming solution which yields good results but is intractable for more than 150 shreds. In [10, 11], good results are obtained by applying evolutionary algorithms to the problem.

In contrast, relatively little progress has been made in developing the score function. In [2, 8–11], the authors settled on a formulation which selects a score based on a weighted difference of the adjacent pixels on either side of the proposed join ([2] provides a formal definition of this method). Sleit, Massad and Musaddaq ([13]) refine this formulation by placing an emphasis on black pixels, thus discounting the information content of white pixels. In [7], the authors try a different approach, by employing optical character recognition techniques. Their method is however left as a proof-of-concept, since it is not integrated with a search function or evaluated against any other scoring methods.

Pre-processing can be split into several independent functions, which have been previously explored. Skeoch ([12]) shows how to extract the shreds from scanned input images via rectangle and polynomial fitting. The authors of [3] fix the skew of the extracted shreds by framing the issue as an optimisation problem and finding the best rotation angle for each shred. Up/down orientation of documents is explored in [1, 4] with good results, though the methods are only evaluated on full documents, not shreds.

Finally, user-interaction has been approached in many ways. For instance, in [3, 13], the authors allow the users to mark correct and incorrect edges between successive runs of the search method, while in [14] the scoring function is influenced by the user drawing what the neighbour of a shred might look like.

3   Probabilistic Score

We propose a novel score function formulation, which uses a probabilistic model to directly estimate the likelihood of two edges matching. Employing a probabilistic model offers several advantages, such as an increase in robustness given by the ability to train the model on the given document shreds and an ease of composability with other models, which can be achieved by simply multiplying the different predicted probabilities and re-normalising the results.

We test this idea by implementing a basic probabilistic model, which is based on the conditional probability that a pixel is white or black given a few of its neighbouring pixels. Formally, given edge *Et*, *ProbScore* returns the best match for Et and the probability of that match. ProbScore is defined as:

procedure PROBSCORE(Et)

    Initialise ps ▷ *probabilities of matches, initially all 1*

    for all $Ex \in Edges$ **do**

        for all $pixel \in Ex$ **do**

            $ps_{Ex} \leftarrow ps_{Ex} * \Pr(pixel | Neighbours_{Et}^{pixel})$

    Normalise ps ▷ *probabilities must sum up to 1*

    return $\arg\max ps, \max ps$

Empirical results show that this probabilistic score compares favourably to the most common scoring function used in literature ([2]), both on noise-less documents and on several noisy documents (see Figure 1). Additionally, in order to showcase the benefits offered by the composable nature of ProbScore, we combine it with another probabilistic model called *RowScore*. RowScore calculates the distance between rows of text in neighbouring shreds and applies a Gaussian model to this distance. Even such a simple probabilistic model gives ProbScore a small but consistent boost (see Figure 1). In a similar way, ProbScore could be composed with more complex models, such as that proposed in [7].

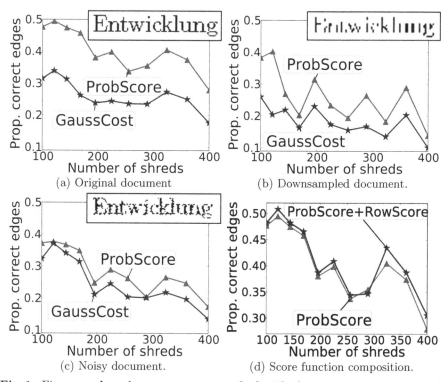

Fig. 1. Figures **a**, **b** and **c** compare our method with the most common previously used function. A sample word from each document is shown in the upper right corners. Figure **d** shows the improvement obtained, on a noiseless document, by composing our function with another, very simple, probabilistic model.

4   "Kruskal-Inspired" Heuristic Search

We present a search method inspired by the minimum spanning tree "Kruskal's algorithm" ([6]). The method greedily picks the most probable edge and tries to match the two shreds along that edge. This process creates multiple clusters of shreds which will eventually be merged into a single solution. Before performing a merge, we check if the move would result in two shreds being superimposed, in which case the merge is aborted.[4]

The Kruskal heuristic outperforms previously proposed bottom-up heuristics, but is still significantly more tractable[5] than any of the top-down optimising search functions (see Figure 2).

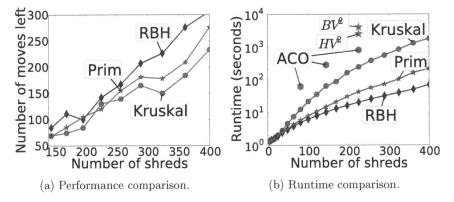

(a) Performance comparison.   (b) Runtime comparison.

Fig. 2. Figure **a** shows the performance of our method compared to that of two heuristics introduced in [10]. Here the X-axis shows how many moves would have to be performed to get from the outputted solution to the correct solution. Figure **b** shows the scalability of our approach when compared to the aforementioned heuristics and a few top down optimising searches introduced in [11] (ACO is an Ant Colony Optimisation, while HV^2 and BV^2 are genetic algorithms).

A novel aspect of the Kruskal heuristic is that, if the next move is uncertain, the execution can be stopped. The early stopping mechanism is triggered when the score of the next best move is below some threshold. Once the search has been stopped we return a partial solution, which can significantly reduce the search space of the problem. As seen in Figure 3, even the extremely conservative 99.95%

---

[4] A conceptually similar search heuristic is introduced in [13]. That formulation, however, uses a static list of scores and thus cannot be used with our probabilistic scoring function which requires the scores to be updated after every merge.

[5] The Kruskal, Prim and RBH heuristics are written in python, while the ACO, BV^2 and HV^2 optimisation methods are written in C. Additionally, the implementation of Kruskal is a non-optimised proof-of-concept. A non-naive re-implementation could bring its performance more in line to that of Prim. As such, the scalability results should be viewed as upper bounds on the performance of the heuristics.

328   R. Ranca and I. Murray

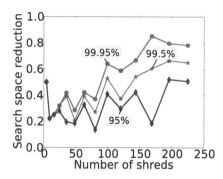

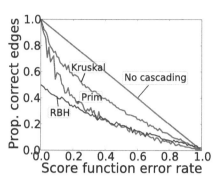

Fig. 3. The reduction in search space corresponding to 3 stopping conditions. "Search space reduction" is defined as $\frac{\text{Final no. pieces}}{\text{Initial no. pieces}}$.

Fig. 4. The effect the error in score has on the final error of the method for the 3 search heuristics. The cascading effect causes a small error in the score to be exaggerated by the search method.

stopping condition helps us reduce the search space to between 40% and 80% of its original size.[6] Since the complexity of the search function is exponential in the number of pieces, these reductions are significant and may allow previously intractable search methods to now be run on the smaller instance.

Another benefit of our Kruskal heuristic can be seen when analysing the *cascading effect*, which is an issue common to all greedy, bottom-up, heuristics. The cascading effect is caused by the inability of the heuristics to correct a wrongly placed shred. This inability means that the search will instead try to find additional pieces which match well with said, wrongly placed, shred. These pieces will therefore have a significant probability of also being wrong, thus starting a chain reaction. While cascading is a problem for all heuristics, our method proves to be more resilient than previous formulations (see Figure 4).

Finally, in Figure 5, we show some full and partial reconstructions of documents. One thing worth noticing from this example is that cross-cut documents are significantly harder to solve than strip-cut ones, even if the total number of shreds is the same. This difficulty is due to the short edges produced by cross-cutting, which are harder to model accurately. Horizontal cuts also have a significant chance of falling between two lines of text, in which case the score function has no information on how to order the lines.

5   Pre-processing – Up/Down Orientation Detection

We present a tractable method for one phase of the pre-processing step, namely the up/down orientation detection of shreds. The idea behind this method is to find the *inner* and *outer* rows of each shred, to then count the number of

---

[6] A "99.95% stopping condition" means that the algorithm continues running only while it is at least 99.95% sure of the correctness of its next move.

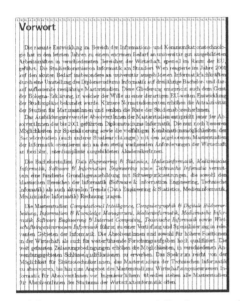

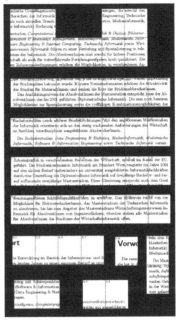

(a) Cross-cut document, full solution.

(b) Strip-cut document, full solution.   (c) Cross-cut document, partial solution.

Fig. 5. Figures **a** and **b** show full reconstructions on the cross-cut variant (64% correct) and the strip-cut variant (100%correct). Figure **c** shows a partial reconstruction (with a threshold of 99.5%) which successfully reduces the search space from 49 to 10 shreds while not introducing any errors.

black pixels in the corresponding *upper regions* and *lower regions*, and to finally predict that more black pixels will be present in the upper region (see Figure 6).

In this formulation, we define the outer rows as being delimited by those y coordinates in which a transition is made from a row of pixels that contains no black pixels to a row that contains at least 1 black pixel (or vice versa). We then filter the resulting, preliminary, outer rows such that only those taller than a minimum threshold are kept, since a row that is only 1 or 2 pixels tall is quite likely spurious. Subsequently, we select an inner row inside each outer row by searching for the two y coordinates exhibiting the greatest difference between

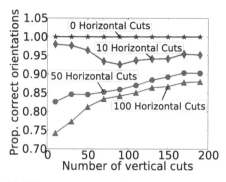

(a) The inner lines delimit the inner row, and the outer lines the outer row.

(b) For Roman script, the upper region will tend to contain more black pixels than the lower one.

(c) The proportion of correctly oriented shreds as the number of cuts grows.

Fig. 6. Figure **a** shows an example of inner and outer rows for one word and Figure **b** shows the corresponding upper and lower regions. Figure **c** shows the results obtained by using these upper and lower regions for orientation detection.

the sum of black pixels in consecutive rows of pixels. Thus, the greatest increase in number of black pixels between 2 consecutive rows is the upper limit of the inner row, and the greatest decrease is the lower limit of the inner row.

As can be seen in Figure 6, the results are perfect for strip-cut documents (i.e. 0 horizontal cuts) and steadily degrade as we introduce more horizontal cuts. This happens because horizontal cuts reduce the number of rows printed on each shred and therefore make the system more vulnerable to noise. One apparently odd thing about these results is that, for the lower two curves, the performance improves as the number of vertical cuts increases. This behaviour is caused by completely white pieces, which are declared as being always correctly oriented. For the lower two curves, increasing the number of vertical cuts increases the number of white pieces faster than the added noise can degrade the performance, so the overall proportion of correctly predicted orientations increases.

6   Conclusions and Future Work

This paper presents a modular and composable framework for the shredded document reconstruction problem and provides sample solutions for several of its components. Specifically, we propose: a probabilistic scoring function which outperforms currently used alternatives; a search heuristic which can either solve simpler reconstruction problems or reduce the search space for more complex ones; and an up/down orientation detection method which obtains good results on taller shreds while being very computationally efficient.

Future work will look at implementing more advanced score and search functions. Solving the cross-cut domain will likely require scoring functions which employ computer vision techniques and search function which solve the cascading problem by performing a partial exploration of the search tree. Additionally, the current state of the pre-processing components makes it necessary to spend a significant amount of time arranging and scanning the shreds, as to minimise noise. Further work is required to create more robust and efficient pre-processing components that will lead to an efficient unshredding pipeline. Lastly the user-interaction aspect needs to be more closely analysed. Good progress has been made by the authors of [9, 13], which have shown that a fully automatic reconstruction method can be modified to incorporate user input with relative ease. The question of how to extract the maximum amount of information from a minimum number of user interactions remains, however, open.

References

1. Aradhye, H.: A generic method for determining up/down orientation of text in roman and non-roman scripts. Pattern Recognition 38(11), 2114–2131 (2005)
2. Biesinger, B.: Enhancing an evolutionary algorithm with a solution archive to reconstruct cross cut shredded text documents. Bachelor's thesis, Vienna University of Technology, Austria (2012)
3. Butler, P., Chakraborty, P., Ramakrishan, N.: The deshredder: A visual analytic approach to reconstructing shredded documents. In: 2012 IEEE Conference on Visual Analytics Science and Technology (VAST), pp. 113–122. IEEE (2012)
4. Caprari, R.: Algorithm for text page up/down orientation determination. Pattern Recognition Letters 21(4), 311–317 (2000)
5. Heingartner, D.: Back together again. New York Times (2003)
6. Kruskal, J.: On the shortest spanning subtree of a graph and the traveling salesman problem. Proceedings of the American Mathematical Society 7(1), 48–50 (1956)
7. Perl, J., Diem, M., Kleber, F., Sablatnig, R.: Strip shredded document reconstruction using optical character recognition. In: 4th International Conference on Imaging for Crime Detection and Prevention 2011 (ICDP 2011), pp. 1–6. IET (2011)
8. Prandtstetter, M.: Two approaches for computing lower bounds on the reconstruction of strip shredded text documents. Technical Report TR1860901, Technishe Universitat Wien, Institut fur Computergraphik und Algorithmen (2009)
9. Prandtstetter, M., Raidl, G.R.: Combining forces to reconstruct strip shredded text documents. In: Blesa, M.J., Blum, C., Cotta, C., Fernández, A.J., Gallardo, J.E., Roli, A., Sampels, M. (eds.) HM 2008. LNCS, vol. 5296, pp. 175–189. Springer, Heidelberg (2008)
10. Prandtstetter, M., Raidl, G.: Meta-heuristics for reconstructing cross cut shredded text documents. In: Proceedings of the 11th Annual Conference on Genetic and Evolutionary Computation, pp. 349–356. ACM (2009)
11. Schauer, C., Prandtstetter, M., Raidl, G.R.: A memetic algorithm for reconstructing cross-cut shredded text documents. In: Blesa, M.J., Blum, C., Raidl, G., Roli, A., Sampels, M. (eds.) HM 2010. LNCS, vol. 6373, pp. 103–117. Springer, Heidelberg (2010)
12. Skeoch, A.: An investigation into automated shredded document reconstruction using heuristic search algorithms. Ph.D. thesis, University of Bath, UK (2006)
13. Sleit, A., Massad, Y., Musaddaq, M.: An alternative clustering approach for reconstructing cross cut shredded text documents. Telecommunication Systems, 1–11 (2011)
14. Zhang, H., Lai, J., Bacher, M.: Hallucination: A mixed-initiative approach for efficient document reconstruction. In: Workshops at the Twenty-Sixth AAAI Conference on Artificial Intelligence (2012)

A Global-Local Approach to Saliency Detection

Ahmed Boudissa[1], JooKooi Tan[1], Hyoungseop Kim[1], Seiji Ishikawa[1],
Takashi Shinomiya[2], and Krystian Mikolajczyk[3]

[1] Kyushu Institute of Technology, Japan
{ahmed,etheltan,kimhs,ishikawa}@ss10.cntl.kyutech.ac.jp
[2] Japan University of Economics, Japan
t.shinomiya@aa.cyberhome.ne.jp
[3] University of Surrey, United Kingdom
k.mikolajczyk@surrey.ac.uk

Abstract. In this paper, we present a novel approach to saliency detection. We define a visually salient region with the following two properties; global saliency i.e. the spatial redundancy, and local saliency i.e. the region complexity. The former is its probability of occurrence within the image, whereas the latter defines how much information is contained within the region, and it is quantified by the entropy. By combining the global spatial redundancy measure and local entropy, we can achieve a simple, yet robust saliency detector. We evaluate it quantitatively and compare to Itti et al. [6] as well as to the spectral residual approach [5] on publicly available data where it shows a significant improvement.

Keywords: Saliency, Entropy, Segmentation.

1 Introduction

Recent advances in hardware architecture and processing power gave rise to the industrial interest in computer vision applications and algorithms. More specifically, there has been a significant progress in the field of object detection, which typically consists of a number of computationally intensive stages. It is believed that the human biological visual system has the early stage of attention [2], in which the background or clutter is discarded without the need of an exhaustive analysis of the scene as illustrated in Fig. 1. This motivates many researchers to model the visual attention and propose saliency detection approaches that can provide input to the object detection approaches.

2 Related Work

This work focuses on methods for automatic salient region extraction. The goal is to detect the salient regions efficiently to produce promising candidates for subsequent stages of computationaly demanding algorithms. Limiting the search can greatly speed up the process [10] and allow for real-time applications.

R. Wilson et al. (Eds.): CAIP 2013, Part II, LNCS 8048, pp. 332–337, 2013.

Fig. 1. Illustration of saliency detection

The existing approaches can be divided into two major categories, local and global. Bottom-up or local approaches are feature based, concerned with the local appearance of images. For example, Itti et al. [6] model the biological early attention mechanism using several feature maps (color, orientation, luminance etc.), which have also shown promise in image compression applications. Within the same category, Hou and Zhang [5] propose a frequency based model using the spectral representation of images. In [8], [9], [6] and [11] saliency is defined in terms of local Shannon's information maximization principles. In [8], it is proposed to use entropy based locally salient features to estimate the global transformation between two images. Global approaches, attempt to detect image regions that exhibit certain properties e.g. Seo and Milanfar [12] use regions self-similarity based on a regression kernel. Gofermanet et al. [4] present a multi-scale salient object detector using a distance computation between different image patches to find the region of interest, which proved useful in image retargeting and image collage creation. A theoretical formulation of top-down visual saliency, related to the recognition problem, is proposed in [3].

3   Saliency Model

In this paper we propose a simple yet robust approach to detect salient regions in an image by measuring the following properties:

- spatial redundancy, probability of occurrence within an image which quantifies the uniqueness of the concerned region.
- local information content, which defines how much information is contained within the region, and it is quantified using entropy.

3.1   Spatial Redundancy

The spatial redundancy of a patch within an image is estimated by measuring how similar it is to the other patches. Typically it is assumed that a patch is salient if it is dissimilar to the nearby patches. However, in practice, due to noise, change of view point or illumination conditions, direct comparison of patches results in an inaccurate estimation. For a better estimate of the similarity between two regions R_i and R_k we model it with the Gaussian function with zero-mean and variance σ. The global saliency measure for region R_i compared to N other regions, becomes the following:

$$S_{R_i} = \frac{1}{N} \sum_{k=1}^{N} (1 - e^{\frac{-D_E(R_i, R_k)}{\sigma^2}})/D_S(R_i, R_k). \tag{1}$$

where $D_E(R_i, R_k)$ is the Euclidean distance between region attributes such as colour distribution. In addition, we incorporate the spatial distance between patches normalized by the image size (i.e. $D_S(R_i, R_k)$ in Eq. 1) in order to downweight the importance of distant patches. This allows to maintain the integrity of an object that typically consists of nearby patches. The proposed similarity measure combines the appearance and the spatial distance and it normalizes distances computed for different attributes of image patches, or in different colour spaces (Gray, RGB, L*a*b or HSV), unlike the Euclidean distance directly used in [4] [7].

3.2   Local Information Content

According to Shannon's information theory, the information content can be measured with the entropy of the signal at a certain location in time or space. Including the entropy in our saliency measure eliminates the homogeneous backgrounds and unique regions of low complexity. In Fig. 2 we show images of different complexity which is reflected by their histograms resulting in different entropy:

$$H_{R_i} = - \sum_{v=0}^{255} p_{v,R_i} \ln p_{v,R_i} \tag{2}$$

with p_{v,R_i} representing the probability of pixel intensity v within region R_i estimated with a histogram.

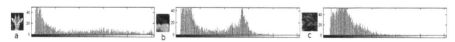

Fig. 2. Different histogram distributions resulting in different entropy for (a) high, (b) medium and (c) low complexity patches

3.3   Global-Local Saliency

In contrast to the candidate selection process from [9] we combine the local entropy of a region with the global saliency measure. The spatial redundancy and the local entropy measures expressed in equations (1) and (2) are combined into a saliency S_i which is used to generate a saliency map:

$$S_i = H_{R_i} \cdot S_{R_i} \tag{3}$$

The map is generated by computing the saliency for every region in the image implemented as a scanning window of size W. In the following section we provide a qualitative and quantitative evaluation of this saliency detection measure.

4   Experimental Results

The dataset we use to evaluate the proposed method has also been used in [7] and [5]. It consists of 62 natural images with salient and non-salient regions manually labelled by 4 different annotators. Example images are displayed in Fig. 4. Instead of selecting a specific threshold for the saliency measure as in [9] and [4], which gives a limited insight into the overall performance, we evaluate our method and compare to other approaches using precision-recall curves. Given the ground-truth segmentation maps we perform pixel-wise comparison to the thesholded saliency map and calculate precision-recall values by varying the saliency threshold.

The method proposed in this paper is parametrised by the region size as well as the size of the Gaussian in colour space for patch similarity function. By varying each parameter, we assess their mutual correlation and the optimal operating configuration. Fig. 3 shows the performance for different size of the scanning window $W = \{5, 10, 20\}$ and standard deviation $\sigma = sigma = [1, \ldots, 8]$ of the Gaussian in Eq 1. The performance is relatively independent of the size

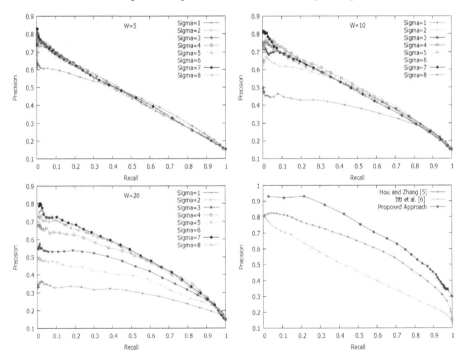

Fig. 3. Precision-recall of salient region detection w.r.t. scanning window size W and Gaussian weighting $\sigma = Sigma$ (cf. Eq. 1) in colour similarity. Comparison to Itti et al. [6] as well as Hou and Zhang [5] methods is in the bottom-right figure.

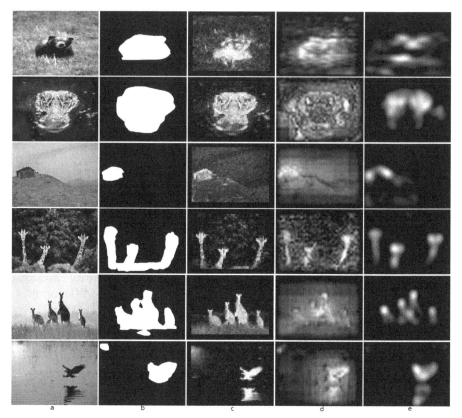

Fig. 4. Saliency maps comparison. (a) Original image, (b) ground truth, (c) our approach, (d) Itti et al. [6], (e) Hou and Zhang [5]. The use of the entropy measure creates sharper saliency maps and highlights the body of the objects in addition to the boundaries.

of selected windows, but it varies slightly depending on the size of the Gaussian. The smaller the scanning window, the faster the performance peaks, and remains stable. For large scanning window ie. $W = 20$, the complexity, thus the uniqueness of the region increases, resulting in high saliency scores for the cluttered background.

Fig. 3 (bottom-right) shows the performance comparison between the proposed method and two other popular methods: Itti et al. [6] as well as Hou and Zhang [5]. Our approach outperforms both methods due to the combination of local and global characteristics. Also, the entropy measure participates greatly in eliminating low complexity regions. The uniform areas have very compact histograms, leading to low entropy, which balances the saliency score in case of an erroneously low spatial redundancy value. In Fig. 4 we display the saliency maps generated by our method as well as by the approaches from [6] and [5]. The use of the entropy down weights the uniform areas, but the spatial redundancy preserves the object's integrity even if the entropy within the region is low.

5 Conclusion and Future Work

In this paper, we introduced a novel combined global-local saliency measure. It is based on local entropy and global redundancy of the region. We evaluate the approach on available benchmarks and compare to state-of-the-art approaches. It outperforms the classical methods, and due to its simplicity, it has the potential of improving speed and accuracy of various object detection algorithms.

As future prospects, an automatic way to select the parameters of the method should be explored as well as more efficient implementations. The challenge remains to define a robust saliency measure and collect diverse benchmark data. We also intend to evaluate the saliency algorithms as a first step in more complex computer vision applications.

Acknowledgement. This study was supported by JSPS KAKENHI under Grant-in-Aid for scientific Research (22510177) and Chist-Era EPSRC grant EP/K01904X/1.

References

1. Bruce, N., Tsotsos, J.: Saliency based on information maximization. Advances in Neural Information Processing Systems 18, 155–162 (2006)
2. Carandini, M., Demb, J., Mante, V., Tolhurst, D., Dan, Y., Olshausen, B., et al.: Do we know what the early visual system does? Journal of Neuroscience 25, 10577–10597 (2005)
3. Gao, D., Han, S., Vasconcelos, N.: Discriminant saliency, the detection of suspicious coincidences, and applications to visual recognition. IEEE Transactions Pattern Analysis and Machine Intelligence (2009)
4. Goferman, S., Zelnik-Manor, L., Tal, A.: Contextaware saliency detection. In: IEEE Conference on Computer Vision and Pattern Recognition, pp. 2376–2383 (2010)
5. Hou, X., Zhang, L.: Saliency detection: A spectral residual approach. In: IEEE Conference on Computer Vision and Pattern Recognition, pp. 1–8 (2007)
6. Itti, L., Koch, C., Niebur, E.: A Model of Saliency-basedVisual Attention for Rapid Scene Analysis. IEEE Transactions on Pattern Analysis and Machine Intelligence 20, 1254–1259 (1998)
7. Jain, A., Wong, A., Fieguth, P.: Saliency detection via statistical non-redundancy. In: IEEE International Conference on Image Processing, pp. 1073–1076 (2012)
8. Kadir, T.: Scale, Saliency and Scene Description. University of Oxford (2001)
9. Kadir, T., Brady, M.: Scale Saliency and Image Description. International Journal of Computer Vision 45, 83–105 (2001)
10. Liu, T., Yuan, Z., Sun, J., Wang, J., Zheng, N., Tang, X., Shum, H.: Learning to Detect a Salient Object. IEEE Transactions on Pattern Analysis and Machine Intelligence 33, 353–367 (2011)
11. Wang, W., Wang, Y., Huang, Q., Gao, W.: Measuring Visual Saliency by Site Entropy Rate. In: IEEE Conference on Computer Vision and Pattern Recognition (2010)
12. Seo, H.J., Milanfar, P.: Static and space-time visual saliency detection by self-resemblance. Journal of Vision, 1–27 (2009)

A Moving Average Bidirectional Texture Function Model

Michal Havlíček and Michal Haindl

Institute of Information Theory and Automation of the ASCR
Prague, Czech Republic
{haindl,havlimi2}@utia.cz

Abstract. The Bidirectional Texture Function (BTF) is the recent most advanced representation of visual properties of surface materials. It specifies their appearance due to varying spatial, illumination, and viewing conditions. Corresponding enormous BTF measurements require a mathematical representation allowing extreme compression but simultaneously preserving its high visual fidelity. We present a novel BTF model based on a set of underlying mono-spectral two-dimensional (2D) moving average factors. A mono-spectral moving average model assumes that a stochastic mono-spectral texture is produced by convolving an uncorrelated 2D random field with a 2D filter which completely characterizes the texture. The BTF model combines several multi-spectral band limited spatial factors, subsequently factorized into a set of mono-spectral moving average representations, and range map to produce the required BTF texture space. This enables very high BTF space compression ratio, unlimited texture enlargement, and reconstruction of missing unmeasured parts of the BTF space.

Keywords: BTF, texture analysis, texture synthesis, data compression, virtual reality, moving average random field.

1 Introduction

Realistic virtual reality scenes require objects covered with synthetic textures visually as close as possible to the corresponding real surface materials appearance they emulate under any required viewing conditions. Such textures have to model real non-Lambertian rugged surfaces whose reflectance is illumination and view angle dependent. Recent most advanced visual representation of such surfaces is the Bidirectional Texture Function (BTF) [1, 2] which is a 7-dimensional function describing surface appearance variations due to varying spatial position and illumination and viewing angles. Such a function is typically measured by thousands of images per material sample, each taken for a specific combination of the illumination and viewing condition. Visual textures can be either represented by digitized measured textures or textures synthesized from an appropriate mathematical model. Using digitized textures directly suffers among others with extreme memory requirements for storage of a large number of digitized cross

R. Wilson et al. (Eds.): CAIP 2013, Part II, LNCS 8048, pp. 338–345, 2013.

sectioned slices through different material samples of the measured BTF space [2]. Moreover this solution become even unmanageable for physically correctly modeled scenes with BTF surfaces representation because even a simple scene with only several materials requires to store tera bytes of textural data which is still far out of limits for any current and near-future hardware. Several so called intelligent sampling methods (for example [4–6] and some others) were proposed to reduce these extreme memory requirements. All these methods are based on some sort of original small texture sampling and the best of them produce very realistic synthetic textures. However, they still require to store thousands images for every combination of viewing and illumination angle of the original target texture sample and additionally they often produce images with undesirable visual artifacts like visible seams (except for the method presented in [7]). Some of them are very computationally demanding and none of them is able to generate previously unseen textures (i.e., BTF space reconstruction). Contrary to the sampling approaches, the synthetic textures generated from mathematical models are more flexible and extremely compressed, because only tens of parameters have to be stored only instead of the original visual measurements. They may be evaluated directly in a procedural form and can be used to fill virtually infinite texture space without visible discontinuities. On the other hand, mathematical models can only approximate real measurements, which might result in visual quality compromise. A BTF texture representation requires seven dimensional mathematical models, but it is possible to approximate this general BTF model with a set of much simpler three or two dimensional factorial models. Such a compromise obviously leads to some information loss.

The proposed underlaying moving average model suffers from inability to represent low frequencies present in natural textures. But this problem can be negotiated by utilizing a multiple resolution decomposition such as the Gaussian Laplacian pyramid. The hierarchy of different resolutions of an input image provides a transition between pixel level features and region or global features and hence such a representation simplify modelling a large variety of possible textures. Each band limited component is modeled independently. BTF moving average model represents a novel method for efficient rough texture modelling which combines an estimated range map with synthetic smooth multi-spectral texture generated by the set of multiscale mono-spectral moving average models. The texture visual appearance during changes of viewing and illumination conditions are simulated using either the bump mapping [8] or displacement mapping [9] technique. The obvious advantage of this solution is the possibility to exploit direct support for both bump and displacement mapping techniques in the contemporary graphics hardware.

2   Moving Average BTF Model

The BTF model combines an estimated enlarged material range map (section 2.1) with synthetic multiscale multi-spectral smooth texture (sections 2.2-2.6). We seek a trade-off between an extreme compression ratio and the visual quality by using several probabilistic BTF subspace dedicated models. The intrinsic

BTF space dimensionality is estimated using the eigenanalysis approach and the segmentation is done using the K-means clustering in the perceptually uniform CIE Lab color-space (see details in [2, 10]). Each modeled BTF subspace is further spectrally decorrelated (section 2.2) and decomposed into several spatial factors (section 2.3). The mono-spectral band limited parts of single BTF subspaces are modeled using the 2D moving average models (section 2.4). Finally, the overall BTF texture visual appearance during changes of viewing and illumination conditions is simulated using either the bump [8] or displacement mapping [9] techniques.

2.1   Range Map Modelling

The overall roughness of a textured surface significantly influences the BTF texture appearance. Such a surface can be specified using its range map, which can be either measured or estimated by several existing approaches such as the shape from shading [11], shape from texture [12] or photometric stereo [13]. The photometric stereo enables to acquire the normal and albedo fields from at least three intensity images obtained for different illuminations but fixed camera position while a Lambertian opaque surface is assumed. The BTF model range map estimate can benefits from tens of ideally mutually registered BTF measurements (e.g., 81 for a fixed view of the University of Bonn data [3]) and uses the overdetermined photometric stereo from mutually aligned BTF images. However, the photometric stereo method is not well suited for surfaces with highly specular reflectance, highly subsurface scattering or strong occlusion, since it breaks the Lambertain reflectance assumption. Estimated range map is enlarged into any required size using the roller method [7].

2.2   Spectral Decorrelation

Measured visual surface data can be spectrally decorrelated only approximately, therefore this step leads to certain loss of information. Spectral factorization is performed by the Karhunen-Loeve transformation (K-L). The original data space $\tilde{Y}$ is transformed into new one with coordinate axes $\bar{Y}$. New basis consists of the eigenvectors of the second-order statistical moments matrix $V = E\{\tilde{Y}_r \tilde{Y}_r^T\}$ where r denotes a multiindex $r = (r_1, r_2)$, $r \in I$, with the row and column indices, • all possible values of the corresponding index, and I is a finite discrete 2-dimensional rectangular $M \times N$ index lattice. The projection of a random vector $\tilde{Y}_r$ onto the K-L coordinate system uses transformation matrix which consists of eigenvectors of V. The total number of those eigenvectors depends on the number of spectral bands in the original data. If we assume that components of the transformed data $\bar{Y}_{r,\bullet} = T\tilde{Y}_{r,\bullet}$ are Gaussian then they are independent and thus each mono-spectral factor can be modeled independently.

2.3   Spatial Factorization

The spatial factorisation is technique that enables separate modelling of individual band limited frequency components of input image data and thus to use random field models with small compact contextual support. Each grid resolution represents a single spatial frequency band of the texture which corresponds to one layer of Gaussian-Laplacian pyramid (G-L) [2]. The input data are decomposed into a multi-resolution grid and all resolution data factors represents the Gaussian pyramid of level k which is a sequence of k images in which each one is a low-pass down-sampled version of its predecessor. An analysed data are decomposed into multiple resolutions factors using the Laplacian pyramid and the intermediary Gaussian pyramid. Each level of Laplacian pyramid generates a single spatial frequency band of the data. Laplacian pyramid contains bandpass components and provides a good approximation to the Laplacian of the Gaussian kernel. It can be computed by differencing single Gaussian pyramid layers.

2.4   2D Moving Average Texture Model

Single mono-spectral smooth texture factors are modelled using the moving average model [14] (MA^{2D}). A stochastic mono-spectral texture can be considered to be a sample from 2D random field defined on an infinite 2D lattice. Let us denote I a finite discrete 2-dimensional rectangular index lattice for some input factor Y represented by the MA^{2D} random field model, Y_r is the intensity value of a mono-spectral pixel $r \in I$ in the image space. The model assumes that each factor is the output of an underlying system which completely characterizes it in response to a 2D uncorrelated random input. This system can be represented by the impulse response of a linear 2D filter. The intensity values of the most significant pixels together with their neighbours are collected and averaged, and the resultant 2D kernel is used as an estimate of the impulse response of the underlying system. A synthetic mono-spectral factor can be generated by convolving an uncorrelated 2D random field with this estimate. Suppose a stochastic mono-spectral texture denoted by Y is the response of an underlying linear system which completely characterizes the texture in response to a 2D uncorrelated random input e_r, then Y_r is determined by the following difference equation:

$$Y_r = \sum_{s \in I_r} b_s e_{r-s} \tag{1}$$

where b_s are constant coefficients and $I_r \subset I$. Hence Y_r can be represented $Y_r = h(r) * e_r$ where the convolution filter $h(r)$ contains all parameters b_s. In this equation, the underlying system behaves as a 2D filter, where we restrict the system impulse response to have significant values only within a finite region. The geometry of I_r determines the causality or non-causality of the model. The selection of an appropriate model support region is important to obtain good results: small ones cannot capture all details of the texture and contrariwise, inclusion of the unnecessary neighbours adds to the computational burden and can potentially degrade the performance of the model as an additional source of noise.

Fig. 1. Original colorful texture and it synthesis using CAR^{2D}, $GMRF^{2D}$, and MA^{2D} models (from left to right)

2.5   Parameter Estimation

To fit the model given in equation (1) to a given image Y, the parameters of $h(r)$ have to be estimated. This may be performed by using a method [14] similar to the one-dimensional Random Decrement Technique [15]. The procedure begins by arbitrarily selecting a threshold, γ usually chosen as some percentage of the standard deviation (σ) of the intensities of the input. All results in the paper use $\gamma = 0.5\sigma$. The analysis starts from the top left corner of Y and proceeds to the bottom right corner identifying the pixels at which the intensity crosses the threshold. When a threshold crossing occurs at location r, the intensity values of the support region defined by I_r around the crossing point are saved in memory (index set Γ), if among the four adjacent pixels to r, at least one in the same row and one in the same column are less than the threshold. The same procedure is followed at the next threshold crossing point and these intensity values are added to the previously saved. The summed up segments are divided by the total number of segments for the corresponding parameter estimates, i.e.,

$$\hat{b}_s = \frac{1}{cardinality\{\Gamma\}} \sum_{\forall r \in \Gamma} Y_{r+s} \quad \forall s \in I_r \ . \tag{2}$$

Additional details can be found in [14].

2.6   Model Synthesis

The underlying MA^{2D} model is able to generate synthetic images from the model parameters. Synthetic mono-spectral factor can be generated by convolving an uncorrelated 2D random field with the estimate of $\hat{h}(r)$ according (1). It has been proved [16] that the synthesized image closely approximates the first and second order statistics of the original one when e_r is the white noise. The synthetic band limited multi-spectral factors are created by the inverse K-L transformation $\tilde{Y}_{r,\bullet} = T^{-1}\bar{Y}_{r,\bullet}$ from the corresponding monospectral factors. Fine-resolution synthetic multi-spectral smooth texture is then obtain by the G-L pyramid collapse which is inverse procedure to that described in section 2.3.

Fig. 2. Two BTF wood synthetic materials mapped on the 3D shell model under two different illumination angles

3 Results

We have tested the model on BTF colour textures from the University of Bonn BTF measurements [3] consist of several materials such as wood (Fig.2) or leather. Each BTF material sample comprised in the University of Bonn database is measured in 81 illumination and 81 viewing angles and has resolution 800×800 pixels. The resulting texture quality is approaching existing alternative BTF models based on 2D random fields: Causal Auto-Regressive model (CAR^{2D}) [17] and Gaussian Markov random field model ($GMRF^{2D}$) [18].

Table 1. Processing time for single models

model	analysis $[s]$	synthesis $[s]$
$GMRF^{2D}$	5.63	21.68
CAR^{2D}	8.49	3.62
MA^{2D}	2.32	3.66

BTF moving average model represents a simple alternative to these BTF models. Multi-spectral (both BTF or non-BTF) models based on spectral factorization (2D random field models) have problems to correctly represent spectrum of motley textures (Fig. 1-left). The MA^{2D} models spectrally outperforms (Fig. 1) both these alternative models due to its weak spatial correlations. The main advantage of the moving average model is its stability, which is a problem which has to be occasionally treated for CAR type models. The GMRF models require approximate parameters estimation and demanding texture synthesis. Another advantage of the model is its numerical efficiency, Tab.1 compares analysis and synthesis times for a 128×128 texture with 4 pyramid levels on the 2GHz Pentium 4 processor.

4   Conclusion

The presented BTF moving average model offers the possibility to describe and enlarge BTF textures and represents the simple alternative to existing 2D BTF models. The preliminary test results of the model on available BTF data are promising although they are only approximation of the original measurements. Even not so successful results can be used for the preattentive BTF textures applications. The presented BTF moving average model enables fast seamless enlargement of BTF texture to arbitrary size and very high BTF texture compression ratio which cannot be achieved by any alternative sampling based BTF texture enlargement method. This is advantageous for transmission, storing or modelling visual surface texture data. Model has low computation complexity, does not need any time consuming numerical optimisation like the usually employed Markov chain Monte Carlo method or some of their deterministic approximation, or Fourier transformation. On the other hand, the necessary spectral and spatial factorizations increase overall time and computing demands. This model may be also used to reconstruct BTF space (i.e., missing parts of the BTF measurement space) or even non existing (i.e., previously not measured) BTF textures. Due to its simplicity, the model is also potentially capable of direct implementation inside the graphical card processing unit or a multithreaded implementation.

Acknowledgements. This research was supported by the grant GAČR 102/08/0593 and partially by the project GAČR 103/11/0335.

References

1. Dana, K.J., Nayar, S.K., van Ginneken, B., Koenderink, J.J.: Reflectance and texture of real-world surfaces. In: CVPR, pp. 151–157. IEEE Computer Society (1997)
2. Haindl, M., Filip, J.: Visual Texture. Advances in Computer Vision and Pattern Recognition. Springer, London (January 2013)

3. Müller, G., Meseth, J., Sattler, M., Sarlette, R., Klein, R.: Acquisition, synthesis and rendering of bidirectional texture functions. In: Eurographics 2004, STAR - State of The Art Report, Eurographics Association, Eurographics Association, pp. 69–94 (2004)
4. Kawasaki, H., Seo, K.D., Ohsawa, Y., Furukawa, R.: Patch-based btf synthesis for real-time rendering. In: IEEE International Conference on Image Processing, ICIP, September 11-14, vol. 1, pp. 393–396. IEEE (2005)
5. Lefebvre, S., Hoppe, H.: Appearance-space texture synthesis. ACM Trans. Graph 25(3), 541–548 (2006); BTF sampling
6. Leung, C.S., Pang, W.M., Fu, C.W., Wong, T.T., Heng, P.A.: Tileable btf. IEEE Transactions on Visualization and Computer Graphics 13(5), 953–965 (2007)
7. Haindl, M., Hatka, M.: BTF Roller. In: Chantler, M., Drbohlav, O. (eds.) Proceedings of the 4th International Workshop on Texture Analysis, Texture 2005, pp. 89–94. IEEE, Los Alamitos (2005)
8. Blinn, J.: Simulation of wrinkled surfaces. SIGGRAPH 1978 12(3), 286–292 (1978)
9. Wang, L., Wang, X., Tong, X., Lin, S., Hu, S., Guo, B., Shum, H.: View-dependent displacement mapping. ACM Transactions on Graphics 22(3), 334–339 (2003)
10. Haindl, M., Filip, J.: Extreme compression and modeling of bidirectional texture function. IEEE Transactions on Pattern Analysis and Machine Intelligence 29(10), 1859–1865 (2007)
11. Frankot, R.T., Chellappa, R.: A method for enforcing integrability in shape from shading algorithms. IEEE Trans. on Pattern Analysis and Machine Intelligence 10(7), 439–451 (1988)
12. Favaro, P., Soatto, S.: 3-D shape estimation and image restoration: exploiting defocus and motion blur. Springer-Verlag New York Inc. (2007)
13. Woodham, R.: Photometric method for determining surface orientation from multiple images. Optical Engineering 19(1), 139–144 (1980)
14. Li, X., Cadzow, J., Wilkes, D., Peters, R., Bodruzzaman II, M.: An efficient two dimensional moving average model for texture analysis and synthesis. In: Proceedings IEEE Southeastcon 1992, vol. 1, pp. 392–395. IEEE (1992)
15. Cole Jr., H.A.: On-line failure detection and damping measurement of aerospace structures by random decrement signatures. Technical Report TMX-62.041, NASA (May 1973)
16. Li, X.: An efficient two-dimensional FIR model for texture synthesis. PhD thesis, Vanderbilt University (1990)
17. Haindl, M., Filip, J.: A fast probabilistic bidirectional texture function model. In: Campilho, A.C., Kamel, M.S. (eds.) ICIAR 2004. LNCS, vol. 3212, pp. 298–305. Springer, Heidelberg (2004)
18. Haindl, M., Filip, J.: Fast BTF texture modelling. In: Chantler, M. (ed.) Texture 2003. Proceedings, pp. 47–52. IEEE Press, Edinburgh (2003)

A Multiscale Blob Representation of Mammographic Parenchymal Patterns and Mammographic Risk Assessment

Zhili Chen[1,*], Liping Wang[1], Erika Denton[2], and Reyer Zwiggelaar[1]

[1] Department of Computer Science,
Aberystwyth University, Aberystwyth, SY23 3DB, UK
{zzc09,liw19,rrz}@aber.ac.uk
[2] Department of Radiology,
Norfolk and Norwich University Hospital, Norwich, NR4 7UY, UK
erika.denton@nnuh.nhs.uk

Abstract. Mammographic parenchymal patterns have been found to be a strong indicator of breast cancer risk and play an important role in mammographic risk assessment. In this paper, a novel representation of mammographic parenchymal patterns is proposed, which is based on multiscale blobs. Approximately blob-like tissue patterns are detected over a range of scales and parenchymal patterns are represented as a set of blobs. Spatial relations between blobs are considered to reduce the overlap between connected dense tissue regions. Quantitative measures of breast density are calculated from the resulting blobs and used for mammographic risk assessment. The proposed approach is evaluated using the full MIAS database and a large dataset from the DDSM database. A high agreement with expert radiologists is indicated according to the BI-RADS density classification. The classification accuracies for the MIAS and DDSM databases are up to 79.44% and 76.90%, respectively.

Keywords: mammographic parenchymal patterns, breast density, multiscale blob detection, mammographic risk assessment.

1 Introduction

It has been indicated that increased breast cancer risk is associated with mammographic parenchymal patterns showing high breast density [1]. Therefore, characterising mammographic parenchymal patterns from the aspect of breast tissue density is of great importance for mammographic risk assessment. Parenchymal patterns are formed by the spatial distribution of dense tissue. As described by Tabár's tissue model [1], mammographic tissue appearance is composed of four building blocks: nodular, linear, homogeneous, and radiolucent. Example image patches (selected by an expert radiologist) are shown in Fig. 1.

---

* Zhili Chen is also with the Faculty of Information and Control Engineering, Shenyang Jianzhu University, Shenyang, 110168, China.

R. Wilson et al. (Eds.): CAIP 2013, Part II, LNCS 8048, pp. 346–353, 2013.

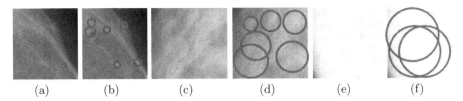

Fig. 1. Example image patches of different tissue patterns and detected blobs: (a), (b) linear tissue; (c), (d) nodular tissue; (e), (f) homogeneous tissue

A variety of methods have been developed for the characterisation of mammographic parenchymal patterns. Karssemeijer [2] extracted features from a set of greylevel histograms generated from a series of peripheral regions within the breast. Petroudi *et al.* [3] modelled mammographic parenchymal patterns with a statistical distribution of textons. Oliver *et al.* [4] extracted morphological and texture features from fatty and dense tissue regions. Bueno *et al.* [5] characterised breast parenchymal texture using statistical features derived from greylevel histograms and co-occurrence matrices. Tzikopoulos *et al.* [6] used a fractal dimension related feature and a set of statistical features. He *et al.* [7] computed features based on greylevel histograms of multi-resolution local windows.

Our proposed approach is distinct from existing approaches. Effectively, we focus on nodular and homogeneous tissue in Tabár's model. We assume that nodular and homogeneous tissue can be approximated as blob-like regions of various sizes. As such, we propose to represent parenchymal patterns as a set of multiscale blobs. We detect blob-like tissue structures over a range of scales. Detected blobs superimposed on the example image patches are shown in Fig. 1.

In addition, the proposed approach is linked to mammogram synthesis work [8], where synthetic mammograms were generated by simulating breast tissue with different sized phantom elements (shells and blobs). The formation of parenchymal patterns was modelled by the projection of these simulated tissue structures. In this paper, we aim to inverse this generation process, and decompose parenchymal patterns in mammograms into a set of blobs at different scales (inclusion of shell-like structures is seen as future work).

2   Multiscale Blob Representation

Blob-like structures can be identified by searching for scale-space extrema, and the characteristic size of each blob can be estimated by the scale level at which the extremum is detected [9,10]. We use the Laplacian of Gaussian (LoG) operator to detect blobs at ten scales. Blobs are localised by finding extrema of the normalised Laplacian with respect to both space and scale [9].

An example mammographic image can be found in Fig. 2(a). The breast region is first segmented using the approach in [11] (Fig. 2(b)). Subsequently, the mammographic image is convolved with the LoG operator at ten scales (the first scale $\sigma_1 = 8$ and the scale factor $k = \sqrt{2}$). For efficiency reasons, instead of convolving the image with an operator of increasing size, we down-sample the

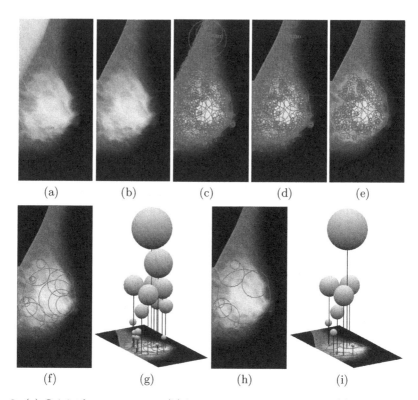

(a)   (b)   (c)   (d)   (e)

(f)   (g)   (h)   (i)

Fig. 2. (a) Original mammogram; (b) breast region segmentation; (c) initial blob detection result at ten scales; (d) false positive reduction based on spatial information; (e) false positive reduction based on average intensity thresholding; (f) blobs corresponding to global extrema over ten scales; (g) 3D view of the resulting blobs; (h) retained blobs after blob merging ($\alpha = 0.8$); and (i) 3D view of the retained blobs.

image by a factor of $1/k$ and up-sample the resulting scale-space image to the full size. In addition, to solve boundary effects, we use a deformable template for convolution, which can alter adaptively according to the current local window under convolution. Here, the tissue patterns of interest are high-intensity regions, which are detected as bright blobs (indicated by negative extrema).

To search for scale-space extrema, we first detect local extrema from each scale-space image. Each pixel in the breast region is compared with its neighbours within a local region (we use 5×5 local regions). The extrema with low contrast (less than a threshold) are discarded (the threshold can be dynamically determined according to the maximum pixel value in the image). The location of every extremum indicates the centre point of a blob, and the current scale determines the blob's radius. The initial blob detection result of the example mammographic image at ten scales is shown in Fig. 2(c). Here, we aim to detect interior blob-like tissue structures in the breast, and therefore the blobs appearing outside the breast region are ignored (Fig. 2(d)). This step can be regarded as contrast based thresholding taking spatial information into account.

In addition, it should be noted that some extrema at smaller scales might be produced by linear structures (e.g. ducts and vessels), as the LoG operator has strong responses to edges. Moreover, at larger scales, some false extrema (corresponding to non-dense tissue regions) tend to appear along the breast boundary, due to the influence of the natural profile of the breast. The reduction of such false positives is performed by setting a threshold on the average intensity within the blob area. To calculate the threshold, the fuzzy c-means algorithm is applied to partition pixels within the breast region into nine clusters based on their greylevel values in the original image. The difference between the mean intensity and the standard deviation of clusters from six to nine (corresponding to dense tissue) is chosen as the threshold. Alternative number of clusters and those selected to represent dense tissue can provide similar results. The extrema whose corresponding blobs have lower average intensity than the threshold are removed. The retained blobs after false positive reduction are shown in Fig. 2(e).

After finding extrema from 5×5 local regions at each scale, we detect global extrema over ten scales by comparing each extremum with its $5 \times 5 \times 9$ "neighbours" in the other nine scale-space images. Finally, only the global extrema of $5 \times 5 \times 10$ blocks in the whole scale space are retained. The resulting blobs are shown in Fig. 2(f), covering dense tissue regions with approximately blob-like structures. A three-dimensional view of the resulting blobs is provided in Fig. 2(g), where the mammographic image is shown in the horizontal plane, the vertical dimension corresponds to scale, and blobs are displayed as spheres.

As shown in Fig. 2(f), blob overlapping happens between connected dense tissue regions. To eliminate over-representation of dense tissue, the closely overlapping blobs are merged based on their spatial relations. For two blobs A and B (their radii are denoted by r_A and r_B and assuming $r_A \geq r_B$), we consider three types of spatial relations: external $(d \geq r_A + r_B)$, intersection $(r_A - r_B < d < r_A + r_B)$, and internal $(d \leq r_A - r_B)$. Blob merging starts from the finest scale and proceeds to coarser scales, which is based on the following criteria: the external blobs which are separately located in the breast region will be retained; the internal blobs which are contained by larger ones will be removed; when blobs A and B (their scales are denoted by σ_A and σ_B) intersect, if they are closely located $(r_A - r_B < d \leq r_A - \alpha r_B, 0 < \alpha < 1)$, the integration of the Gaussian scale-space signature over the blob area will be calculated by $\int_{(x,y) \in blob_{A,B}} g(x, y; \sigma^2_{A,B}) * I(x, y) dx dy$ and the blob with the larger value will be retained, otherwise $(r_A - \alpha r_B < d < r_A + r_B, 0 < \alpha < 1)$ both blobs will be retained. The blob merging result is shown in Fig. 2(h) and Fig. 2(i).

3   Mammographic Risk Assessment

The distribution of the detected blobs at different scales can reflect breast tissue composition, from which quantitative measures of breast density can be derived for mammographic risk assessment. The distribution of the blobs at n scales is denoted by a vector $N = (N_1, N_2, \ldots, N_n)$, where N_i $(i = 1, 2, \ldots, n)$ represents the number of blobs at scale i. We transform N into a unique number by

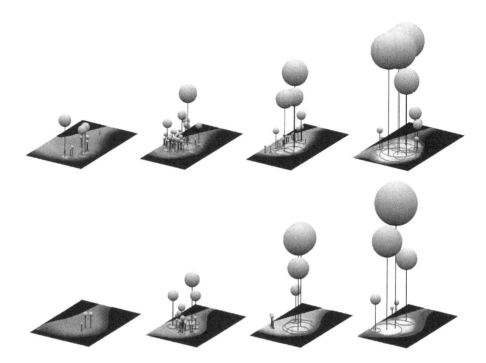

Fig. 3. 3D views of the resulting blobs for example mammograms of MIAS (top) and DDSM (bottom). From left to right, the mammograms range from BIRADS I to IV.

$BLOB = \sum_{i=1}^{n} N_i k^{2(i-1)}$ (k is the scale factor). The resulting value of $BLOB$ is defined as the measure of breast density. To avoid bias caused by the breast size, it is normalised to $BLOB_{norm} = (A_{blob}/A_{breast})BLOB$, where A_{blob} denotes the area of the blob at the finest scale, and A_{breast} represents the area of the breast. By normalising the density measure in this way, it can be deemed to be an approximation of percentage breast density, which represents the relative proportion of dense tissue in the whole breast.

4   Results and Discussion

To evaluate the proposed blob representation for mammographic risk assessment, we have used two well-known databases. One is the MIAS database [12], which contains 322 left/right MLO mammograms taken from 161 women. Three expert radiologists were involved to rate 321 valid mammograms (mdb295ll was excluded for historical reasons) into four classes based on BIRADS density classification [13]. The consensus rating was used as the classification ground truth. The second dataset was taken from the DDSM database [14], which contains 831 right MLO mammograms from 831 women. In contrast to the MIAS database, the BIRADS density rating was provided in the DDSM database.

As described in Section 2, blobs were detected at ten scales (start from 8 pixels and increase by a factor of $\sqrt{2}$). 3D views of the detected blobs for example

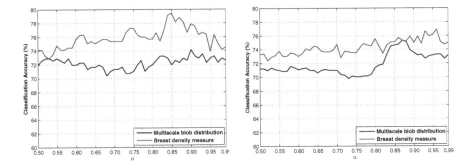

Fig. 4. The overall classification accuracy with respect to the parameter α for MIAS (left) and DDSM (right). The blue and red curves indicate the results obtained using the ten-dimensional blob distribution and the breast density measure, respectively.

mammograms of MIAS and DDSM are shown in Fig. 3 ($\alpha = 0.8$ was used for blob merging). It can been seen that the number of blobs at larger scales increases from BIRADS I to IV, indicating an increasing breast cancer risk. Specifically, for BIRADS I, the breast is almost entirely fatty, only a few small scale blobs are detected; for BIRADS II, some small and medium scale blobs are located at scattered dense tissue regions; for BIRADS III, a few relatively larger scale blobs appear in the dense tissue area; while for BIRADS IV, the breast is extremely dense and the whole breast region is mainly covered by large scale blobs.

For mammographic risk classification, the performance of the ten-dimensional blob representation of parenchymal patterns and the derived measure of breast density was tested. For the ten-dimensional blob representation, the distribution of blobs at ten scales was used as the feature vector in which element N_i was normalised by A_{blob_i}/A_{breast}, where A_{blob_i} represents the area of the blob at scale i and A_{breast} represents the area of the breast. For the breast density measure, the normalised value $BLOB_{norm}$ was used. A k-Nearest Neighbours (kNN) based classifier was used, which was initially based on a simple majority vote unless multiple classes indicated the same number of training samples among the k nearest neighbours in which case a distance weighted approach was applied. The χ^2 distance was used as the similarity measure. The leave-one-woman-out and leave-one-image-out cross validation (LOOCV) methodologies were used for the MIAS and DDSM databases, respectively.

Fig. 4 shows the overall classification accuracy (CA) with respect to different values of α varying from 0.50 to 0.99. It is shown that the breast density measure ($BLOB_{norm}$) obtained superior performance to the multiscale blob distribution. This might be explained by the fact that transforming the higher-dimensional feature vectors into a single feature value may reduce the within-class variance. For the MIAS database, the best CA was 74.14% when $\alpha = 0.9$ by using the multiscale blob distribution, and $BLOB_{norm}$ obtained the best CA of 79.44% when $\alpha = 0.85$. For the DDSM database, the best CA was 75.33% ($\alpha = 0.87$)

Table 1. Confusion matrices corresponding to the best CA for MIAS and DDSM

(a) MIAS (CA = 79.44%)

| BIRADS | Automatic | | | | |
	I	II	III	IV	CA
I	72	15	0	0	83%
II	5	88	10	0	85%
III	0	12	74	8	79%
IV	0	0	16	21	57%

(Truth)

(b) DDSM (CA = 76.90%)

| BIRADS | Automatic | | | | |
	I	II	III	IV	CA
I	83	23	0	0	78%
II	19	290	27	0	86%
III	0	53	180	22	71%
IV	0	5	43	86	64%

(Truth)

Table 2. A complete comparison of the proposed approach with related publications

Method	Feature	Classifier	Classification Scheme	Data	Evaluation	CA
[2]	greylevel statistics	kNN	four density categories	615 Nijmegen	LOOCV	67%
[3]	texton histogram	Nearest Neighbour	four BIRADS classes	132 Oxford	44/88	76%
[4]	morphological+texture	SFS+kNN+C4.5	four BIRADS classes	322 MIAS	LOOCV	86%
[4]	morphological+texture	SFS+kNN+C4.5	four BIRADS classes	831 DDSM	LOOCV	77%
[5]	statistical	PCA+LBN+SVM	four BIRADS classes	322 MIAS	10-Fold CV	75%
[6]	fractal+statistical	SVM	three density categories	322 MIAS	LOOCV	77%
[7]	greylevel statistics	kNN	four BIRADS classes	321 MIAS	LOOCV	78%
Ours	blob representation	(weighted) kNN	four BIRADS classes	321 MIAS	LOOCV	79%
Ours	blob representation	(weighted) kNN	four BIRADS classes	831 DDSM	LOOCV	77%

and 76.90% ($\alpha = 0.96$) for the multiscale blob distribution and $BLOB_{norm}$, respectively. It seems that using a large value for α in the range of [0.85, 1] tends to obtain better results, which is reasonable in the sense that only very closely located blobs are removed, which are likely to derive from the same blob-like structure in the breast. The best CA for the DDSM database was slightly lower than that for the MIAS database. This might be due to the fact that the DDSM database contains a larger number of mammograms than the MIAS database, which might introduce higher variance of breast tissue patterns.

Table 1 shows the confusion matrices corresponding to the best CA for the MIAS and DDSM databases. BIRADS IV indicated the worst performance with a large number of mammograms being misclassified into BIRADS III. This might be partly explained by the unbalanced distribution of training samples. Another reason might be that the extremely dense breasts in BIRADS IV have a more homogeneous tissue appearance all over the breast region, which possibly increases the incidence of false negatives due to the less-structured dense tissue. We compared the obtained classification results with those of related publications. Table 2 provides a summary of the comparison ([4] and [7] used the same database and the same BIRADS classification ground truth as ours allowing a direct comparison). It should be noted that [4] used a combination of two classifiers (kNN and C4.5) and the SFS algorithm for classification which tends to select a feature subset specifically for the given classifier and therefore obtain superior performance. For our method further improvement of performance is regarded as future work by employing advanced classifiers or classifier ensembles. In addition, mammographic appearance within the blob regions and topological information of the retained blobs could be investigated by incorporating greylevel/texture features and blob graph properties into the blob representation.

5   Conclusions

We have presented a blob representation of mammographic parenchymal patterns, based on the prior knowledge of anatomical structure and synthetic elements of breast tissue. We detected approximately blob-like regions and used a set of different sized blobs to represent breast tissue patterns. For mammographic risk assessment, the spatial relations between the resulting blobs and their distribution over scales were combined to generate quantitative measures of breast density. To our knowledge, the proposed approach is a first attempt to model parenchymal patterns and analyse breast density by focusing on dense tissue regions with blob-like structures. High classification accuracies were obtained for the MIAS and DDSM databases according to the four BIRADS categories.

References

1. Tabár, L., Tot, T., Dean, P.B.: Breast Cancer - the Art and Science of Early Detection with Mammography: Perception, Interpretation, Histopathologic Correlation. George Thieme Verlag (2005)
2. Karssemeijer, N.: Automated Classification of Parenchymal Patterns in Mammograms. Physics in Medicine and Biology 43, 365–378 (1998)
3. Petroudi, S., Kadir, T., Brady, M.: Automatic Classification of Mammographic Parenchymal Patterns: A Statistical Approach. In: 25th International Conference of the IEEE Engineering in Medicine and Biology Society, pp. 798–801 (2003)
4. Oliver, A., et al.: Novel Breast Tissue Density Classification Methodology. IEEE Transactions on Information Technology in Biomedicine 12(1), 55–65 (2008)
5. Bueno, G., et al.: Automatic Breast Parenchymal Density Classification Integrated into a CADe System. Int. J. Comput. Assist. Radiol. Surg. 6(3), 309–318 (2011)
6. Tzikopoulos, S.D., et al.: A fully Automated Scheme for Mammographic Segmentation and Classification Based on Breast Density and Asymmetry. Computer Methods and Programs in Biomedicine 102(1), 47–63 (2011)
7. He, W., Denton, E.R.E., Zwiggelaar, R.: Mammographic Segmentation and Risk Classification Using a Novel Binary Model Based Bayes Classifier. In: Maidment, A.D.A., Bakic, P.R., Gavenonis, S. (eds.) IWDM 2012. LNCS, vol. 7361, pp. 40–47. Springer, Heidelberg (2012)
8. Bakic, P.R., et al.: Mammogram synthesis Using a 3D Simulation. I. Breast Tissue Model and Image Acquisition Simulation. Medical Physics 29(9), 2131–2139 (2002)
9. Lindeberg, T.: Feature Detection with Automatic Scale Selection. International Journal of Computer Vision 30(2), 79–116 (1998)
10. Mikolajczyk, K., Schmid, C.: Scale & Affine Invariant Interest Point Detectors. International Journal of Computer Vision 60(1), 63–86 (2004)
11. Chen, Z., Zwiggelaar, R.: Segmentation of the Breast Region with Pectoral Muscle Removal in Mammograms. In: 14th Medical Image Understanding and Analysis, pp. 71–75 (2010)
12. Suckling, J., et al.: Mammographic Image Analysis Society Digital Mammogram Database. Excerpta Medica. International Congress Series 1069, 375–378 (1994)
13. American College of Radiology: Illustrated Breast Imaging Reporting and Data System BIRADS. 3rd ed. American College of Radiology, Philadelphia (1998)
14. Heath, M., et al.: The Digital Database for Screening Mammography. In: 5th International Workshop on Digital Mammography, pp. 212–218 (2000)

Alternating Optimization
for Lambertian Photometric Stereo Model
with Unknown Lighting Directions

Khrystyna Kyrgyzova, Lorène Allano, and Michaël Aupetit

CEA, LIST, 91191 Gif-sur-Yvette, France
{khrystyna.kyrgyzova,lorene.allano,michael.aupetit}@cea.fr

Abstract. Photometric stereo is a technique of surface reconstruction using several object images made with a fixed camera position and varying illumination directions. Reconstructed surfaces can have complex reflecting properties which are unknown a priori and often simplified by Lambertian model (reflecting light uniformly in all directions). Such simplification leads to certain inaccuracy of reconstruction but in most cases is sufficient to obtain general object relief important for further recognition. Not only surface properties but also lighting sources utilized for each image acquisition can be very complex for modeling, or even unknown. Our work demonstrates how to find surface normals from Lambertian photometric stereo model using color images made with a priori unknown lighting directions. Evaluation of model components is based on an alternating optimization approach.

Keywords: photometric stereo, Lambertian reflectance model, surface normals, alternating optimization.

1   Introduction

Photometric stereo is a method of surface reconstruction using several images (three or more) made with a fixed camera position and varying lighting directions [1], [2]. This technique permits to evaluate values of surface normal and albedo (reflecting ability) for each initial image pixel by modeling image formation process, i.e. an interaction between incident light, surface and camera.

The process of image formation can be generally presented by a bidirectional distribution function (BRDF), [3]. The simplest and the most used model of image formation is called Lambertian [1]. It assumes that incident light is reflected uniformly in all directions. A viewer (or a camera) can be located at any spatial position while appearance of the object point remains the same. This simplification makes a reflectance model independent of camera position and light emergent angle. Thus, for the Lambertian model, photometric value of an object point received by a camera depends only on the lighting direction (or incident angle) and the reflectance properties of the surface material. In the present work we supposed to have Lambertian properties in each image pixel.

R. Wilson et al. (Eds.): CAIP 2013, Part II, LNCS 8048, pp. 354–361, 2013.

In the majority of cases only images, or observations, are given and values of photometric stereo model components (albedo, surface normals, etc.) have to be found. To solve this kind of tasks, most of numerical methods need additional constraints and conditions such as lighting directions used for acquisition, [1], or reference points, [4], [5]. Our contribution consists in proposing a technique for reconstructing Lambertian surfaces without any a priori neither about reconstructed surface normals nor about lighting directions used for images acquisition. The photometric stereo model components evaluation is implemented using an alternating optimization algorithm.

2   Basic Photometric Stereo Models

The interaction between Lambertian photometric stereo model components is determined as a multiplication of albedo coefficient and cosine of the angle between lighting direction and surface point normal, [1], [2], [6]. Light is supposed to come from a single point source. If we need to find surface normals simultaneously for all image pixels or for a certain image region, a large system of linear equation which includes photometric stereo model for each image pixel can be built as follows:

$$M = A \odot (V^T N), \tag{1}$$

where '$\odot$' is the entrywise product; M is the matrix of unwrapped images made with a fixed camera position and varying illumination directions, each line of M corresponds to each image pixels intensities. Let ni corresponds to the number of images used for reconstruction; np is the number of pixels in each of the initial images. A is the matrix of albedo values. This matrix contains surface characteristics which do not depend on illumination conditions and remain the same for a pixel from one image to another. All lines of A are repeated ni times, and in each line there are albedo values for all pixels of image. V is the matrix of size $[3 \times ni]$, each column of this matrix corresponds to a single point light source position used for each image acquisition; N is the matrix of size $[3 \times np]$, each column of the matrix defines 3D normal of the object surface point (or pixel).

One needs at least three images to evaluate 3D normals of surface points. To avoid artifacts related to non-Lambertian surface properties, some authors propose to use more initial images and to implement supplementary analysis, e.g. outlier albedo values analysis,[6], [7], and knowledge or statistical estimation of reflective materials properties,[3],[8].

The basic model was extended to four-component representation in [4] as:

$$M = AN^T VL, \tag{2}$$

where matrices N and V are remained in the same form as they were presented in the basic model (Eq.1); the albedo values matrix A has the same definition as in Eq.1 but is presented as diagonal matrix of size $[np \times np]$, each line nonzero element represents pixel albedo; L is also diagonal matrix of size $[ni \times ni]$, each line nonzero element corresponds to the light source intensity which is unique for each initial image. The matrix of light sources intensities L was supplementary added to the basic model because it allows better modeling physics of image formation process taking into account different light sources used during each data acquisition.

The representation of photometric stereo model in the form of matrix multiplication permitted to look differently on the problem and to evaluate photometric stereo model components using methods of matrix factorization (decomposition into multipliers), [5],[9]. Two of these components are used to introduce lighting (V and L) and the rest ones aim to present surface properties (N and A). Matrix factorization is one of the possible efficient solutions for photometric stereo model evaluation in conditions of unknown lighting sources characteristics. But it cannot be used directly and needs supplementary prior knowledge and analysis for bas-relief ambiguity resolution [10] and system alignment to the camera-oriented coordinates direction [4]. To avoid these difficulties we exploit an alternating scheme which minimizes error between initial data and the proposed model without any other prior information and further corrections.

3   Proposed Photometric Stereo Model and Its Evaluation

The proposed structure of photometric stereo model is also four-component. Additionally it was extended to the case of color 3-channels images and presented in the form which seems to us more convenient for its further evaluation by the proposed alternating optimization procedure.

3.1   Photometric Stereo Model Description

Let us have three or more images taken with the fixed position of the camera and varying lighting direction for each acquisition. M is the matrix of unwrapped initial images, where each line corresponds to the initial images channels, e.g. first three lines of M are R, G and B channels of the first image, the second three lines are R, G, B channels of the second initial image, etc. The size of M is $[3ni \times np]$. The photometric stereo model is presented as followings:

$$M = A \odot L \odot (V^T N), \qquad (3)$$

where $\odot$' is the entrywise product; A is the matrix of albedo values; L is the matrix of light sources intensities values; V is the matrix of light sources positions used during acquisition of each initial image; N is the matrix of each surface point (pixel) normals. The presented model has the same sense as model of Eq.2, we only replaced the multiplications with the diagonal matrices by the entrywise multiplications.

In order to make a connection between the proposed model and physical properties of image formation process, some structural constraints should be applied to each model component. These physical properties cause information redundancy in components. For example, albedo is the property of surface and its values are repeated for three channels of different images. To avoid such redundancy we introduce these physical constraints using additional matrices W_A, W_L and W_V and their multiplications with appropriate informative parts A', L' and V' respectively. Matrix of albedo A should contain pixel albedo values which are different for each image channel. In order to implement this structure constraint, albedo values are presented by the means of matrix multiplication $W_A A$, where A is of the size $[3 \times np]$ and W_A is an auxiliary matrix. If I_3 is a $[3 \times 3]$ identity matrix, $W_A = [I_3 I_3 .. I_3]^T$, where I_3 element is repeated ni times.

It is assumed that each initial image was taken with a single light source, or with several light sources which can be roughly presented by a main illumination direction with three intensities (separately for R, G and B channels). Matrix of light sources positions is presented as a multiplication $W_V V^T$, where V is a $[3 \times ni]$ matrix of lighting directions and W_V is an auxiliary matrix, $W_V = [D_1 D_2 .. D_i]^T$, where D_i is $[3 \times ni]$ matrix with i^{th} column of ones and all other elements equal to zero.

The matrix L should be composed of repeated column of each channel light source intensities for all image pixels. To implement such structure light sources intensities matrix is presented as a matrix multiplication LW_L, where L is of the size $[3ni \times 1]$ and W_L is an auxiliary vector of ones with the length equal to np.

Matrix of normals N is of size $[3 \times np]$ and presents each pixel normals in 3D space.

Taking into account all previous descriptions, the photometric stereo model is transformed to the following form:

$$M = (W_A A') \odot (L'W_L) \odot ((W_V V'^{T})N), \qquad (4)$$

where the prime symbol denotes submatrices A', L' and V' of matrices A, L and V respectively.

Only the initial images intensities (matrix M) and structuring matrices (W_A, W_L and W_V) are known, and all other components (A', L', V' and N) should be evaluated. This evaluation is done using an original alternating optimization procedure.

3.2   Alternating Optimization Procedure

Alternating optimization is one of the existing heuristic procedures which consists in minimization of the objective function successively fixing all but one

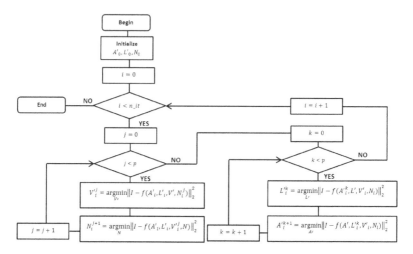

Fig. 1. Alternating optimization for the proposed photometric stereo model

variable, [11], [12]. For the first time the iterative solution for a basic Lambertian model was presented in [13]. We simplify each sub-minimization alternating stage but expand the global solution to four-component matrix representation. The quadratic loss function between the observed data (initial images) and the photometric stereo model function of all unknown components is minimized:

$$\min_{\substack{subject\ to\ A,L,V,N}} |M - f(A, L, V, N)|, \tag{5}$$

where $f(A, L, V, N) = (W_A A') \odot (L' W_L) \odot ((W_V V'^T)N)$.

In order to apply alternating optimization principle we use an algorithmic scheme, Fig.1. Alternating optimization consists in a partition of a difficult multiple-variables optimization (Eq.5) into several consecutive single-variable minimizations. Globally our system of equations is overdetermined. Alternating procedure permits to overcome this ambiguity, because on each iteration step we are able to obtain a unique optimal solution. Nevertheless, it does not provide a unique optimal solution of the global system. Moreover, in our description and experimental part the loss function is presented in the simplest form, but it can be expanded with regularization and constraining terms.

For alternating optimization initial values of each variable should be defined at the beginning of the minimization procedure. After that all variables except one are supposed to be known. The minimization subproblem is solved to find this one unknown variable. Step by step all model variables are found and the procedure is repeated. An important point, which leads to fast system convergence, is the initialization of model components. We propose to use an automatic initialization which depends only on initial images and no other prior information. In our numerical example we used the following initial values: A' was taken as a unit matrix of the appropriate sizes, L' was chosen as a column of median values of all pixel intensities for each color channel and N was defined as normals to each pixel median intensity value. Such initialization is not the only possible choice but it turned to be efficient for the evaluated examples.

For searching each model component any existing minimization algorithm can be used. In our experiments we used the least square method [14]. We do not impose any supplementary minimization constraints on the model components, the structure of each element is the most important constraint which introduces the physics of the process.

On the presented evaluation scheme (Fig.1), a predefined iteration number (itt) is used as a stopping criterion. For our experiments $itt = 10$ was enough to obtain surface of sufficient quality. On the other hand, depending on initial images and desired results, any other stopping criterion such as general model error or model component small variation from one iteration to another, can be used.

We tested different orders of components evaluation in alternating algorithm. The procedure presented in Fig.1 turned to be the most efficient. Interaction between two directions (V and N) is the core of the Lambertian surface reconstruction problem. Two rest elements (L and A) play a role of weights for $V^T N$ multiplication. Thus, in the evaluation algorithm model components are divided into two groups: the first one for the matrix multiplication model part (V and N) and the second one for the entrywise multiplication (L and A). Components of each group are evaluated separately in their own loops with p iterations ($p = 5$) for local convergence of model parameters.

4 Experiments

We present results of the photometric stereo model evaluation using publicly available images dataset from [5] and [15]. There are from 7 to 14 images in each image sequence used for photometric stereo surface reconstruction. We supposed to have only these images and no other information about lighting or reconstructed surfaces. The surface from normals reconstruction was realized as a minimization procedure described in [5].

The first used dataset (Basri, Jacobs and Kemelmacher, [5]) contains ground truth surfaces (3D scans) for all images sequences. 3D scanning was made with unknown resolution and in the presented dataset we do not have neither registration details nor object mask to numerically measure the error of reconstruction. Nevertheless, we are able to realize a visual analysis and compare the surfaces built from the evaluated normals, N, and the ground truth surfaces. The second used dataset (the MIT Intrinsic Images, [15]) comprises ground truth of the same resolution as initial images as well as object masks. This permits to visually compare obtained surfaces with ground truth easier.

Table 1 demonstrates several initial images from two used datasets, ground truth surfaces corresponding to these sequences and the obtained surface reconstruction results. For each reconstruction sequence of all available initial images (7 - 14) with fixed camera position and different illumination directions was used. Each shown experiment was realized with the same algorithm parameters ($itt = 10$, $p = 5$) and automatic initialization described in the previous section. Visual results analysis of surfaces obtained by the proposed algorithm for both databases confirm rather elevated quality and remaining of general surface aspects comparing with the ground truth.

Table 1. Example of surface reconstruction using the proposed algorithm

	Dataset 1, [5]		Dataset 2, [15]	
Image				
Ground truth				
Reconstruction				

The quality of reconstruction of the proposed algorithm also depends on the quantity of initial images. It is possible to realize the evaluation with at least three color images but the more images with different illumination directions we use and the more uniformly light sources are distributed in space for image acquisition, the better results we are able to obtain with the presented algorithmic scheme. When increasing quantity of images, we increase the quality of the obtained surface compared to the ground truth and obtain the reconstruction with more details, Table 2. Initial images for each reconstruction were chosen with approximately uniform repartition of light sources in space.

Table 2. Surface quality depending on the number of initial images used for photometric stereo reconstruction

One of initial images [15]	$ni = 3$	$ni = 5$	$ni = 10$	Ground truth

5   Conclusion

In the present work we describe the proposed Lambertian photometric stereo model and its evaluation using alternating optimization approach. The main advantage of the applied scheme is that it can be directly used to reconstruct surface from at least three initial color images in absence of any prior knowledge about lighting conditions. The proposed model includes four components.

They are surface albedo values, light sources intensities, light sources directions and surface normals. Each model element has its own structure depending on physical meaning and role in the image formation process. The presented alternating optimization provides a successive model components searching. The applicability of the proposed model was demonstrated using the publicly available photometric stereo datasets. The obtained reconstructed surfaces are visually close to the ground truth data keeping all the details of the photographed objects. Studying convergence of the presented alternating algorithm as well as a possibility of exact solution of minimization problems is in the perspectives of our work.

Acknowledgments. We would like to thank the bioMérieux Company for funding this work.

References

1. Woodham, R.J.: Photometric method for determining surface orientation from multiple images. Optical Engineering 19, 513–531 (1980)
2. Horn, B.K.P.: Robot Vision. MIT Press (1986)
3. Hertzmann, A., Seitz, S.M.: Example-based photometric stereo: shape reconstruction with general, varying BRDFs. IEEE Transactions on Pattern Analysis and Machine Intelligence 27(8), 1254–1263 (2005)
4. Hayakawa, H.: Photometric stereo under a light source with arbitrary motion. Optical Society of America 11, 3079–3088 (1994)
5. Basri, R., Jacobs, D.W., Kemelmacher, I.: Photometric stereo with general, unknown lighting. International Journal of Computer Vision 72, 239–257 (2007)
6. Coleman, E.N., Jain, R.: Obtaining 3-dimensional shape of textured and specular surfaces using four-source photometry. Computer Graphics and Image Processing 18, 309–328 (1982)
7. Barsky, S., Petrou, M.: The 4-source photometric stereo technique for three-dimensional surfaces in the presence of highlights and shadows. IEEE Transactions on Pattern Analysis and Machine Intelligence 25, 1239–1252 (2003)
8. Biswas, S., Aggarwal, G., Chellappa, R.: Robust estimation of albedo for illumination-invariant matching and shape recovery. IEEE Transactions on Pattern Analysis and Machine Intelligence 5, 884–899 (2009)
9. Miyazaki, D., Ikeuchi, K.: Photometric stereo under unknown light sources using robust SVD with missing data. In: Proceedings of the IEEE International Conference on Image Processing, pp. 4057–4060 (2010)
10. Belhumeur, P.N., Kreigman, D.J., Yuille, A.L.: The bas-relief ambiguity. International Journal of Computer Vision 35, 33–44 (1999)
11. Csiszár, I., Tusnády, G.: Information geometry and alternating minimization procedures. Statistics & Decisions (suppl. 1), 205–237 (1984)
12. Hathaway, R.J., Hu, Y., Bezdek, J.C.: Local convergence of tri-level alternating optimization. Neural, Parallel & Scientific Computation 9, 19–28 (2001)
13. Brooks, M.J., Horn, B.K.P.: Shape and source from shading. Technical report, MIT (1985)
14. Lawson, C.L., Hanson, R.J.: Solving least squares problems. Prentice-Hall (1974)
15. Grosse, R., Johnson, M.K., Adelson, E.H., Freeman, W.T.: Ground-truth dataset and baseline evaluations for intrinsic image algorithms. In: Proceedings of the International Conference on Computer Vision, pp. 2335–2342 (2009)

An Automated Visual Inspection System for the Classification of the Phases of Ti-6Al-4V Titanium Alloy

Antonino Ducato, Livan Fratini, Marco La Cascia, and Giuseppe Mazzola

DICGIM - Dipartimento di Ingegneria Chimica Gestionale Informatica e Meccanica
Università degli Studi di Palermo, Viale delle Scienze, bd 6, 90128 Palermo, Italy
{antonino.ducato,livan.fratini,marco.lacascia,
giuseppe.mazzola}@unipa.it

Abstract. Metallography is the science of studying the physical properties of metal microstructures, by means of microscopes. While traditional approaches involve the direct observation of the acquired images by human experts, Computer Vision techniques may help experts in the analysis of the inspected materials. In this paper we present an automated system to classify the phases of a Titanium alloy, Ti-6Al-4V. Our system has been tested to analyze the final products of a Friction Stir Welding process, to study the states of the microstructures of the welded material.

Keywords: Titanium, Ti-6Al-4V, Metallography, Computer Vision, Automated Visual Inspection, SVM, Texture.

1 Introduction and Previous Works

In an a industrial workflow, visual inspection and quality control of the manufacturing process, until to the end product, are traditionally performed by human experts. Even if usually the human expertise works better than a machine application, it is much slower and more expensive. Moreover, in certain applications human inspection is tedious (repetitive actions) or dangerous (e.g. underwater inspection, nuclear or chemical industry, etc.). Computer vision is an effective solution in such cases [1].

In this work we focused on a specific field of the industrial engineering: metallography, that is the study of the physical properties of metals, by optical and electron microscopy. One of the aims of metallography is to study the microstructures of an inspected metal, under certain working conditions. According to metallography, structures which are coarse enough to be discernible by the naked eye or under low magnifications are termed *macrostructures*, while those which require high magnification to be visible are termed *microstructures*. Even if useful information can often be gained by examination with the naked eye of the surface of metal objects, microscopes are required for the examination of the microstructure of the metals. Optical microscopes are used for resolutions down to roughly the wavelength of light (about half a micron) and electron microscopes are used for details below this level, down to atomic resolution. Particular features of interest are: grain size, phases content, distribution of

R. Wilson et al. (Eds.): CAIP 2013, Part II, LNCS 8048, pp. 362–369, 2013.

phases, elongated structures formed by plastic deformation. The examination of materials by optical microscopy is essential in order to understand the relationship between properties and microstructure. While the traditional approach involved the direct observation of the acquired images by human experts, resulting in a qualitative analysis of the results, with the diffusion of digital image processing techniques the analysis process became faster, simpler and more precise. Computer Vision techniques have been used in Metallography Image Analysis[2,3] to study the properties of sintered-steel and the nickel-based superalloy [4], for the automated classification of heat resistant steel structures[5], for segmenting the phases of high strength low alloy steel [6], to study the pit formation on a titanium alloy [7], and for the segmentation of a of a two-phase Ti–6Al–2Mo–2Cr–Fe titanium alloy[8]. Tejrzanowski et al. [9] presented a review of different techniques for the estimation of the size, shape and spatial distribution of structural elements of engineering materials.

In our work we proposed an automated inspection system to study the properties of a titanium alloy, and in particular of its microstructures, in order to classify the parts of the inspected material into different mechanical-physical phases. The paper is organized as follow: section 2 describes the features of the titanium alloy and one of its most important welding techniques; section 3 presents our classification system; section 4 discuss our experimental results; a conclusive section ends the paper.

2   Titanium Properties

Today, titanium alloys are common, readily available engineered metals that compete directly with stainless and specialty steels, nickel-based alloys and composites. In addition to its attractive high strength characteristics for aerospace use, titanium's exceptional corrosion resistance, derived from its protective oxide film, has encouraged extensive application in seawater, marine and industrial chemical service over the past fifty years. Today, titanium and its alloys are extensively used for: aircraft engines and airframes, spacecraft, chemical and petrochemical production, power generation, nuclear waste storage, navy ship components, automotive components, food and pharmaceutical processing, medical implants and surgical devices. An important aspect of this kind of alloy is its microstructural evolution as function of the thermo-mechanical history, depending on the applied manufacturing process. It is possible to differentiate three different kind of microstructures, called phases, having different mechanical and physical properties: Alpha, Beta, and Alpha+Beta (fig. 1). The formation and the behavior of each phase is linked to the addition of alloying elements (called stabilizers) to titanium, which enables physical-chemical effects on the creation of the single microstructural type. The most commonly used titanium alloy is Ti-6Al-4V, that is the object of study of our work. It has a chemical composition of 6% aluminum, 4% vanadium, 0.25% (maximum) iron, 0.2% (maximum) oxygen, and the remainder titanium. These alloy elements make its microstructure composed, at room temperature, of 91% of Alpha phase and 9% of Beta phase (Fig. 2). It is significantly stronger than commercially pure titanium while having similar thermal properties. Among its many advantages, it is heat treatable[11].

Fig. 1. Metallography of Alpha (light) and Beta (dark) and Alpha+Beta microstructure type*s*, on the left and on the right respectively

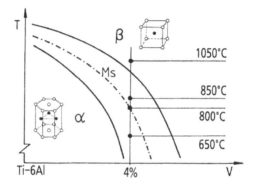

Fig. 2. Ti-6Al-4V phase diagram

2.1   Titanium Alloys Friction Stir Welded Joints

Friction Stir Welding is an important new non-fusion technique for joining sheet and plate material [12]. FSW was invented by TWI (The Welding Institute) in 1991, and is a TWI licensed technology. The tool is rotated and plunged into the material so that the shoulder works on the plate surface and the probe is buried in the workpiece. The friction between the rotating tool and the plate material generates heat, and the high normal pressure from the tool causes a plasticized zone to form around the probe. The tool is then traversed, frictionally heating and plasticizing new material as it moves along the joint line [13]. Although the majority of common titanium alloys are generally weldable by conventional means, problems with workpiece distortion, and poor weld quality, can occur. The development of FSW offers the possibility of a new method of producing high quality, low distortion, welds in Ti sheet and plates .

The parent material was found to consist of a rolled microstructure of elongated gains of alpha (light) in a matrix of alpha and beta (dark). In the deformed weld zone, the microstructure shows evidence of Alpha-to-Beta phase transformation. Significant grain growth appears to occur at this elevated temperature, producing large equiaxed beta grains in the weld center. The beta phase reverts on cooling, and the resultant weld microstructure consists of large alpha grains with a smaller amount of retained beta. The weld root zone microstructure in this case shows that only partial transformation has occurred in this region. After FSW, the preparation of a specimen to reveal the microstructure of the welded material involves the following steps: sawing the section to be examined, mounting in resins, coarse grinding, grinding on progressively finer emery paper, polishing using alumina powder or diamond paste on rotating wheel, etching in dilute acid, washing in Alcohol and drying. The specimen is then ready to be inspected by microscope.

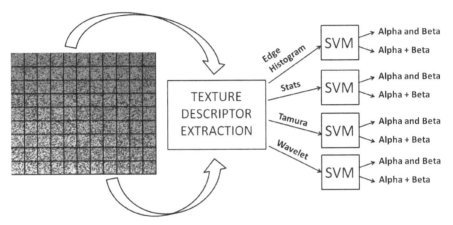

Fig. 3. Overall scheme of the proposed system

3   Proposed System

The main goal of our work is to find a compact and functional description of the image information, in order to classify all the areas of the image into the two possible classes: "Alpha and Beta" and "Alpha+Beta". In this paper we compare the results obtained with several low level features descriptors, using a common testing framework. The scheme of the overall system   is shown in fig.3:

- Images (size M×N) are first decomposed into a grid of (m×n) non overlapping subblocks of size B×B, where m=M/B and n=N/B. The value of B will be further described in the experimental section.
- Features are extracted from each sub-block and concatenated to form a BxBxNi vector, where Ni is the size of a single block descriptor vector. In our work we analyzed a set of texture descriptors, which are briefly described in the next section. Color information, in this case, is useless as the images in the dataset are, in practice, monochrome.

- Feature vectors are then used to train a Support Vector Machine used as binary classifier. SVM is the most used and the simplest solution whenever a binary classification problem has to be solved, therefore is well suited for our goals. Information about the SVM setup will be given in the experimental section. Each feature is used to train separately a classifier.
- After training, we test the classifiers to evaluate the precision of the system.

If a block is classified as "Alpha and Beta" class, it is further processed to discriminate between Alpha and Beta phases, and to assign to each pixel another label. In this case a simple adaptive threshold method is applied. For each block all the pixels whose grey values are above the average value of the block are labeled as Alpha (lightest areas), and the other ones as Beta (darkest areas). Two constraints (a minimum and maximum value) are imposed to this threshold value, to treat also the rare case in which all the pixels of a block are of the same class (i.e. all dark or all light). We preferred to use an adaptive threshold approach, rather than a global one, as it works also in case of not uniform illumination during the acquisition of the image.

3.1   Texture Descriptors

Texture is one of the most studied image features in Computer Vision, Image Processing and Computer Graphics applications. It can be considered as a measure of the perceived image surface variations. For our purpose we tested 4 different standard texture descriptors:

- Statistical: mean, standard deviation, skewness and kurtosis of the pixel grey values. Output is a 4-dimensional vector.
- Wavelet: the sub-band energy of the coefficients of a 2-level wavelet transform of the image, as described in [14]. Output is a 7-dimensional feature vector.
- Tamura [15] descriptors: Contrast, Coarseness and Directionality properties from the Tamura set of features. Output is a 3-dimensional feature vector.
- Edge Histogram [16]: in our simplified version, we filter blocks with 4 directional (vertical, horizontal, 45, 135) and a non-directional Roberts-like operators. Mean and standard deviations of the filtered blocks are considered as descriptors. Output is a 10-dimensional feature vector.

4   Experimental Results

Our dataset is composed by more than 150 images, of size 1079×816. In our experiments, for simplicity of annotation, we selected 10 examples of images representing the "pure" Alpha and Beta phase and 10 representing the "pure" Alpha+Beta phase. We divided each image into blocks of size BxB. We tried with different values of B but, at last, we decided to set B=80, as it is the nearest value to the size of a microstructure in an Alpha+Beta phase. Each image is then divided into a grid of 13×10

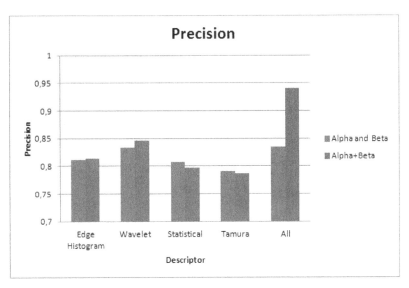

Fig. 4. Experimental results, with the single descriptors and with a combination of them

blocks, (residual pixels on the borders of the image are discarded). As a result, we had 1300 Alpha and Beta and 1300 Alpha+Beta samples. In our tests, our dataset was randomly split into training and testing images, equally. Each block is classified separately, as in the general case, Alpha and Beta and Alpha+Beta areas may be present in the same specimen. We measured the accuracy of the classifier, trained with the different descriptor vectors, in terms of precision, for both the classes. Each experiment has been repeated 100 times, and results averaged. Figure 4 shows the results obtained with the different texture descriptors Our experiments have been also repeated, using different kernels and parameters for the SVM classifier. We achieved our best results with a RBF kernel, and with C=1 and γ=1. Results are shown only for the best configuration. We have obtained around 80% precision with all descriptors, and almost 85% with the Wavelet descriptor. We furthermore concatenated the descriptors into a single vector, trained another classifier, and repeated the tests. We measured a higher value of precision ("All" bar in fig. 4), especially for the Alpha+Beta phase (almost 95%). The result is that the combination of all the texture descriptors is more effective, than the single ones, in the representing the Alpha+Beta microstructures.

A numerical evaluation of the Alpha/Beta segmentation algorithm, in case of Alpha and Beta images, is very difficult to give as, due to the resolution with which the images were acquired, there is not a precise and clear separation between Alpha and Beta pixels into the images. According to a subjective evaluation, the results are satisfactory and the values of percentage of the two phases in the Alpha and Beta specimens is consistent with the expected results. Figure 5 show a visual example of the output of our classifier, for an Alpha and Beta case.

In terms of efficiency, for the single step of descriptor extraction, we obtained similar results. Time to extract information from an input image is less than a second for all the analyzed descriptors.

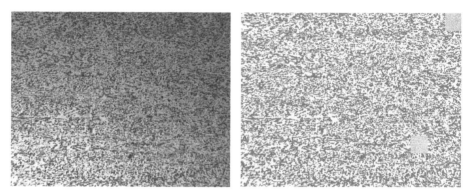

Fig. 5. A visual example. An image of Alpha and Beta input specimen (left) and the output classification (right), using the Tamura descriptor. Cyan areas have been (wrongly) classified as Alpha+Beta. Yellow pixels are classified as Alpha and purple pixels as Beta.

5   Conclusions

Nowadays the use of computer aided software allows to design a great number of manufacturing processes both from a pure mechanical and structural point of view. The actual race consists on finding a computer aided system taking into account the technological knowledge about a particular alloy in order to obtain a FEM (Finite Element Method) suite able to predict, as function of thermo-mechanical history dictated by the considered process, both the classical thermo-mechanical and the metallurgical response of the material. The state of art of the numerical codes is ready to offer several solution to improve a numerical model containing all the requested knowledge and mathematical formulation to simulate and carry-out good (after a correct calibration) results in terms of phase evolution predictions. However these types of numerical models need for a proper set-up, based on a direct comparison with the experimental data provided by the considered real process study cases, with the aim of verifying if the parameters and the used mathematical laws are correct. Unfortunately the comparison between experimental and numerical results is very difficult especially when the user have to evaluate, by observing a metallography, the phase content to obtain an accurate quantitative information. It often happens that it is not possible to obtain a direct link between the output data of the numerical code and the experimental observation of the phenomena. Therefore a computer software for image analysis is needed in order to obtain a numerical evaluation of typology of phases and their percentage content respect to the observed area. This numerical tool should be the connecting ring able to create a CAE (Computer Aided Engineering) system for the design of forming processes of the considered alloy. With this goal, we developed our classification system, that can be a very helpful and powerful instrument to support metal science experts in the analysis process. Moreover, future versions of our system would be able to detect also imperfections and defects (grooves, holes) of the welded materials.

References

1. Malamas, E.N., Petrakis, E.G.M., Zervakis, M., Petit, L., Legat, J.D.: A survey on industrial vision systems, applications and tools. Image and Vision Computing 21(2), 171–188 (2003)
2. Tan, W., Chengdong, C., Zhao, C., Li, S.: Study on key technology of metallographical image processing and recognition. In: Control and Decision Conference, CCDC 2008, pp. 1832–1837. Chinese (July 2008)
3. Gegner, J., Öchsner, A.: Digital image analysis in quantitative metallography. Pract. Metallogr. 38(9), 499–513 (2001)
4. Komenda, J.: Automatic recognition of complex microstructures using the Image Classifier. Materials Characterization 46(2-3), 87–92 (2001)
5. Topalova, I., Mihailov, A., Tzokev, A.: Automated classification of heat resistant steel structures based on neural networks. In: IEEE 25th Convention of Electrical and Electronics Engineers in Israel, IEEEI 2008, December 3-5, pp. 437–440 (2008)
6. Chatterjee, O., Das, K., Dutta, S., Datta, S., Saha, S.K.: Phase extraction and boundary removal in dual phase steel micrographs. In: 2010 Annual IEEE India Conference (INDICON), December 17-19, pp. 1–5 (2010)
7. Codaro, E.N., Nakazato, R.Z., Horovistiz, A.L., Ribeiro, L.M.F., Ribeiro, R.B., Hein, L.R.O.: An image analysis study of pit formation on Ti–6Al–4V. Materials Science and Engineering: A 341(1-2), 202–210 (2003)
8. Chrapoński, J., Szkliniarz, W.: Quantitative metallography of two-phase titanium alloys. Materials Characterization 46(2-3), 149–154 (2001)
9. Tejrzanowski, T., Spychalski, W., Rozniatowski, K.K.: Image Based Analysis of Complex Microstructures of Engineering Materials. Int. J. Appl. Math. Comput. Sci. 18(1), 33–39 (2008)
10. Sha, W., Malinov, S.: Titanium Alloy: Modelling of Microstructure, Properties and Applications. Woodhead Publishing Series in Metals and Surface Engineering, vol. 31 (April 2009)
11. Bruschi, S., Poggio, S., Quadrini, F., Tata, M.E.: Workability of Ti–6Al–4V alloy at high temperatures and strain rates. Materials Letters 58(27-28), 3622–3629 (2004)
12. Buffa, G., Ducato, A., Fratini, L.: Numerical procedure for residual stresses prediction in friction stir welding. Finite Elements in Analysis and Design 47(4), 470–476 (2011)
13. Fratini, L., Buffa, G., Shivpuri, R.: Mechanical and metallurgical effects of in process cooling during friction stir welding of AA7075-T6 butt joints. Acta Materialia 58(6), 2056–2067 (2010)
14. Serrano, N., Savakis, A., Luo, J.: Improved scene classification using efficient low-level features and semantic cues. Pattern Recognition 37, 1773–1784 (2004)
15. Tamura, H., Mori, S., Yamawaki, T.: Texture features corresponding to visual perception. IEEE Trans. Syst. Man Cybern. 8(6), 460–473 (1978)
16. Won, C.S., Park, D.K.: Efficient Use of MPEG-7 Edge Histogram Descriptor. ETRI Journal 24(1), 23–30 (2002)

Analysis of Bat Wing Beat Frequency
Using Fourier Transform

John Atanbori[1], Peter Cowling[2], John Murray[1], Belinda Colston[1],
Paul Eady[1], Dave Hughes[2], Ian Nixon[2], and Patrick Dickinson[1]

[1] University of Lincoln, Lincoln, UK
{jatanbori,jomurray,pdickinson}@lincoln.ac.uk
[2] Lincolnshire Bat Group, Lincoln, UK

Abstract. Computer vision techniques have been used extensively
to automatically monitor human activities; however, applications for
analysing animal behaviour are sparse. The analysis of bat behaviour in
particular has attracted only one or two studies. Most existing work uses
either expensive thermal imaging equipment, or bespoke sensors which
are not accessible to field researchers, ecologists, and scientists studying
behaviour. The work we present here uses spectral analysis techniques to
quantify wingbeat frequency, using a single imaging device in low-light.
We propose two modified techniques based on bounded box metrics, and
similarity matrices, for measuring periodic and cyclical motion as a 1D
time domain signal. These are transformed to the frequency domain using Short Time Fourier Transform (STFT). Finally we evaluate these
techniques against the baseline algorithm proposed by Cutler and Davis
[5], using expert-annotated ground-truth data.

Keywords: Wing beat frequency, STFT, Similarity matrices, Periodic
motion.

1 Introduction

Extensive monitoring of bat roosts is routinely conducted throughout the UK
in order to track population size and characteristics, and the impact of environ-
mental factors on these protected species. Surveys are carried out using manual
techniques, using visual inspection and high frequency audio equipment, and are
labour intensive, error-prone and expensive.

Our objective is to develop a computer vision technology which can be used to
automate bat surveying and monitoring. We wish to automatically analyse the
features of bat flight behaviour, and in particular we are interested in quantifying
wingbeat frequency using spectral analysis techniques. Physical characteristics,
such as body mass and species, are known to vary with wingbeat [4, 12], and
may potentially be used for automated classification.

The work presented here is an initial experimental investigation in which we
propose and evaluate modifications to standard analysis techniques, designed to
improve the detection and measurement of periodicity in high frame-rate videos.

R. Wilson et al. (Eds.): CAIP 2013, Part II, LNCS 8048, pp. 370–377, 2013.

We compare different similarity metrics, and investigate frequency selection criteria, for periodic flight signals which are masked by signal noise.

The paper is organised into the following sections. Section 2 analyses previous work on periodic and cyclical motion detection in human and animals. Next, we discuss low-level image processing techniques for dealing with low-light video data of bats; and present our proposed modifications for the detection of periodic motion in bat flight behaviour in Section 3. In Section 4, we describe the dataset used for our experiments, and detail our evaluation and results. Finally we summarise key conclusions and future work.

2 Related Work

Various techniques have been used in the measurement of periodic and cyclical motions, based on metrics derived from bounding boxes [7], similarity matrices [5, 10, 13], objects pose [3] and motion pattern [14], and point correspondence [9]. These are mainly based on the use of autocorrelation and Fast Fourier Transforms (FFT) to estimate the object motion period.

In the case of human activities, Ayyildiz and Conrad [1] used motion moments to classify videos, by calculating the image moments and fitting a 1D time domain function on the centriods and pixel variances. These were transformed into the frequency domain using FFT. Ren *et al.* [14], used motion templates to perform motion pattern analysis and extract periodicity information from sports videos. Laptev *et al.* [9] used point correspondence to match image sequences over a period of time, and then developed a RANSAC procedure to simultaneously estimate the period. Ghaderian *et al.* [7] detected periodicity in human activities by extracting image silhouettes and fitting bounding boxes. The distances of the targeted silhouette in four directions (top, left, right and bottom) to the bounding box sides were obtained. For the left direction, the horizontal distances from the edge of bounding boxes to the object's contour were computed and summed to form a 1D time domain functions.

Our paper derives from the work of Cutler and Davis [5], which used object similarity to detect periodicity of human and dogs in videos. The object's periodicity was estimated by extracting foreground image and resizing them to 9x15 pixels using Mitchell Filter [15]. The image similarity matrices were then formed from these images using absolute correlation. In order to account for tracking error, the similarity matrices were minimised using a local search radius to form a recurrence matrices. A Hanning filter was applied to the recurrence matrices, and each column transformed to their frequency domain using FFT. The power spectra were then averaged and Eqn. 1 applied to select the ideal frequency.

$$P(f_i) > u_p + k\sigma_p \tag{1}$$

A few researchers have focused on animals rather than humans. Plonik and Rock [13], applied the techniques used in [5] to quantify motion behaviour of jellyfish to detect their motion mode changes. However, they used the normalised sum of square differences to form the similarity matrices. Lazarevic *et al* [10], used similarity matrices based on absolute correlation to differentiate airborne targets (birds and bats). To determine periodicity they used patterns produced by the similarity matrix plots.

Some previous work has used computer vision for bat censusing. In [2, 8] thermal cameras were used to record flight data, and bats silhouettes were obtained using background subtraction. Trajectories were tracked using recursive Bayesian filtering. Fisher and Xiao [6] analysed bats' behaviour during echolocation by observing 3D position and orientation of different species of bats using a 500 frames/second stereo vision system. Recently, Breslav *et al.* [3], proposed a method of computing wingbeat of bats by comparing every shape in the input shape time signal to a prototype template shape using the shape context descriptor and the Hungarian algorithm. They scored shape poses which were used in estimation of the wingbeats.

3   Our Approach

Our techniques were derived from Cutler and Davis [5], but we propose a number of modifications. Firstly, we found that using a similarity matrix based on silhouette shape is not as effective with a target which can change orientation arbitrarily. We therefore propose that a coarser metric derived from the oriented bounding box fitted to bat's 2D object silhouette may better capture the periodicity of motion (as well as being computationally less expensive). Secondly, we find that the selection of dominant frequency proposed by Cutler and Davis is often inconclusive; we therefore propose a selection method based on correlation of the signal with individual components.

We extract the bat's image silhouette using the background Gaussian mixture model proposed by Zivkovic and Heijden [17]. To extract the connected components, we find the contours from the binary image using the contour algorithm proposed by Suzuki *et al.* [16]. We fit an oriented bounding box to the silhouette (Fig. 1), and compute a selection of metrics (height, width and hypotenuse). To solve the problem of broken silhouettes, we merge contours based on the minimum perpendicular distances from the four corner points of each minimum fitted rectangle to the boundaries of the other bounded boxes. This is repeated for all fitted rotated bounded boxes to merge broken silhouettes (Fig. 1).

Fig. 1. Foreground images of bats using improved GMM [17]

The bounding box metrics (height, width and hypotenuse) are used to form a 1D time domain function, which is transformed into the frequency domain using STFT. The 1D signal is then broken into short overlapping windows. The dominant frequencies from each window are reconstructed into synthetic signals, and used to compare with the original using the diagonal of their respective similarity matrices (Eqn. 2). The frequency which minimises this correlation is selected, and this replaces that proposed by Cutler and Davis [5] (Eqn. 1).

$$f_k = \sum_{i=1}^{n} |(t_{o_i} - t_{k_i})| \quad \{where\ k = 1, 2, 3...m\} \tag{2}$$

For comparison, the bounded box metrics are used to form self similarity matrices for the computation of STFT. The self similarity matrices in this case are computed using absolute correlation (Eqn. 3). To determine the wingbeat, each column of the similarity matrix is linearly de-trended and a Hanning filter applied. We then computed the power spectra for all columns of the self similarity matrices. For accuracy, we find the skewness of each of the fix columns of the similarity matrices and either average their spectra or estimate their median depending on the results of the skewness (Eqn. 4). The highest peak of $P(f_k)$ is then selected to represent the wingbeat frequency.

$$S_{t_1, t_2} = \sum_{i=1}^{n} |t_{1_i} - t_{2_i}| \tag{3}$$

$$P(f_k) = \begin{cases} Mean(P(f_k)) & \text{if } \left|\frac{3(mean-median)}{\sigma}\right| < 0.5 \\ Median(P(f_k)) & \text{otherwise} \end{cases} .$$

$$\tag{4}$$

4   Preliminary Results

4.1   Dataset

The data used in this research was provided by the Lincolnshire Bat Group. The bats used were rescued and being rehabilitated prior to release. The video sequences were recorded using a Casio Exilim ZR100 recording at 240 frames per second. The IR filter has been removed from the sensor of this device to facilitate IR illumination for low-light filming.

Three samples are used here, taken from a single Common Pipistrelle. The videos were taken on different days, with different recorded flight weights. The first sample used was broken into two parts. The first part had 113 frames (about 0.5 seconds of data) and the second part 96 frames (about 0.4 seconds of data). The second sample had 130 frames (about 0.6 seconds of data) and the last sample 508 frames representing about 2.2 seconds of data.

4.2   Analysis of Preliminary Results

The bounded box with diagonal selection and with self similarity techniques were evaluated against the baseline algorithm proposed by Cutler and Davis [5] and we present the preliminary results here using bats data. The sample videos were then divided into 64 frames each with an overlap of 32 frames. Three researchers were asked to manually count the number of wingbeat cycles (to the nearest quarter) in each 64-frame window. The median result was used to estimate the ground truth frequency for that video. We then used each of our algorithms to automatically estimate the frequency. For each window, we determined the algorithm giving the result closest to the ground truth, and then for each algorithm we counted the number of windows for which it was closest.

In sample 1, there were some turning, gliding and tracking errors. The bounding box with self similarity matrices achieved nearly 100% closest frequencies whiles the diagonal selection and the baseline algorithm achieved 50% (table 1). The second section of sample 1 was very irregular, so the baseline algorithm had no closest match but the two improved techniques had 50% (table 2).

Keys to all tables: (CD = Baseline Algorithm (Cutler and Davis), DS-H = Diagonal Selection - Height, DS-W = Diagonal Selection - Width, DS-HY = Diagonal Selection - Hypotenuse, SS-H = Self Similarity - Height, SS-W = Self Similarity - Width, SS-H = Self Similarity - Hypotenuse)

Table 1. Sample 1 Part 1 (Bat wingbeat frequencies in Hz). Highlights represents closest.

	C&D	DS-H	DS-W	DS-HY	SS-H	SS-W	SS-HY	GT
Window 0	3.75	3.75	3.75	11.25	11.25	7.25	11.25	11.25
Window 1	11.25	26.25	11.25	26.25	11.25	11.25	11.25	11.25
Closest	1	0	1	1	2	1	2	
%Closest	50%	0%	50%	50%	100%	50%	100%	

Table 2. Sample 1 Part 2 (Bat wingbeat frequencies in Hz). Highlights represents closest.

	C&D	DS-H	DS-W	DS-HY	SS-H	SS-W	SS-HY	GT
Window 0	-	3.75	3.75	26.25	3.75	3.75	15	12.19
Window 1	-	3.75	3.75	26.25	3.75	3.75	26.25	11.25
Closest	0	1	1	0	1	1	1	
%Closest	0%	50%	50%	0%	50%	50%	50%	

Sample 2 had more regular data with some few turning and gliding made by the bat. The baseline algorithm and improved technique based on self similarity achieved better results than the diagonal selection method. From table 3, the hypotenuse metric of the self similarity metrics (SS-HY) and baseline algorithm (C&D) had 100% closest frequencies.

Sample 3, had longer sequence, which comprises of regular and irregular data patterns with some few bat turnings and gliding. Table 4 shows both improved

Table 3. Sample 2 (Bat wingbeat frequencies in Hz). Highlights represents closest.

	C&D	DS-H	DS-W	DS-HY	SS-H	SS-W	SS-HY	GT
Window 0	11.25	26.25	26.25	26.25	3.75	11.25	11.25	13.13
Window 1	11.25	3.75	3.75	26.25	3.75	3.75	11.25	13.13
Window 2	15	15	15	15	15	3.75	15	13.13
Closest	3	1	1	1	1	1	3	
%Closest	100%	33%	33%	33%	33%	33%	100%	

techniques produced better results (about 71%) than the baseline algorithm
proposed by Cutler and Davis (36%) [5]. This may be due to bat orientation
changing frequently in the video sequence. Window 10 was ignored by baseline
algorithm because there was no ideal peak (Fig. 2) but this was detected by the
diagonal selection method.

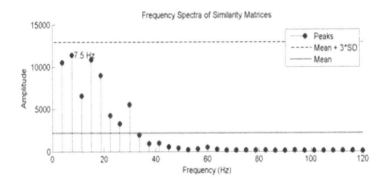

Fig. 2. Baseline Algorithm - FFT Stem plot of Window 10

4.3   Further Discussion of Results

Due to the window size and recording frequency, the algorithms were accurate
to a resolution of $240/64 = 3.75$Hz, which was coarser than the ground truth
resolution of 0.94Hz. Existing manual studies have shown that the frequencies
of different species range from 3 to 15Hz, but may vary by only around 0.3Hz
between some pairs of species [4, 12]. Hence we estimate that a resolution of
this scale should be sufficient to differentiate species. We may achieve this in a
number of ways: increasing the 1D signal length (512 frames will give 0.47Hz
or better resolution); using spectral interpolation [11]; or by keeping the bats in
the region of interest for longer. To test the result of using longer sequences, we
re-divided video sample 3 into 128 windows, and repeated our experiments. This
gave a resolution of 1.88Hz, and a smaller deviation from the ground truth. The
results appear in table 5.

Table 4. Sample 3 (Bat wingbeat frequencies in Hz). Highlights represents closest.

	C&D	DS-H	DS-W	DS-HY	SS-H	SS-W	SS-HY	GT
Window 0	15	15	15	15	11.25	15	11.25	13.13
Window 1	15	15	15	15	11.25	15	15	14.06
Window 2	3.75	15	15	15	15	15	15	15
Window 3	3.75	15	15	15	11.25	15	15	15
Window 4	11.25	3.75	26.25	11.25	15	15	11.25	15
Window 5	3.75	11.25	11.25	11.25	11.25	11.25	11.25	9.38
Window 6	-	3.75	3.75	7.5	3.75	11.25	11.25	3.75
Window 7	15	22.5	22.5	7.5	7.5	7.5	7.5	5.63
Window 8	15	7.5	3.75	3.75	7.5	3.75	15	11.25
Window 9	11.25	3.75	3.75	15	3.75	3.75	15	12.19
Window 10	-	11.25	11.25	3.75	3.75	3.75	7.5	13.13
Window 11	3.75	11.25	11.25	33.75	11.25	11.25	15	13.13
Window 12	15	18.75	18.75	3.75	3.75	3.75	15	13.13
Window 13	3.75	52.5	52.5	26.75	11.25	11.25	15	14.06
Closest	**5**	**9**	**8**	**6**	**8**	**8**	**10**	
%Closest	36%	64%	57%	43%	57%	57%	71%	

Table 5. Sample 3, 128 Window size (Bat wingbeat frequency in Hz). Highlights represents closest.

	C&D	DS-H	DS-W	DS-HY	SS-H	SS-W	SS-HY	GT
Window 0	-	1.88	15	15	28.13	7.5	7.5	13.59
Window 1	-	1.88	13.13	13.13	9.38	7.5	54.38	12.19
Window 2	1.88	1.88	1.88	13.13	9.38	7.5	48.75	9.38
Window 3	-	1.88	1.88	1.88	9.38	7.5	7.5	6.56
Window 4	-	7.5	3.75	3.75	15	15	9.38	11.72
Window 5	1.88	11.25	11.25	1.88	16.88	11.25	9.38	15
Closest	0	0	2	2	2	1	2	
%Closest	0%	0%	40%	40%	40%	20%	40%	

5   Conclusion

We have presented a preliminary investigation into the automated measurement of the wingbeat frequencies of bats using computer vision. We have proposed modifications to the baseline algorithm of Cutler and Davis [5], and shown that they provide a more accurate estimate of frequency on our sample data, as bats orientation changes. The self similarity matrix with bounding box technique was also as good as the baseline algorithm when the bat's orientation was invariant. We are investigating ways of improving the frequency resolution to enable automated classification, including increasing the 1D signal length, and spectral interpolation [11]. The use of multiple frequency components may also improve classification accuracy. We are also investigating the correlation of wingbeat frequency with body mass.

References

[1] Ayyildiz, K., Conrad, S.: Video classification by main frequencies of repeating movements. In: 12th Int'l. Workshop on Image Analysis for Multimedia Interactive Services (2011)

[2] Betke, M., Hirsh, D.E., Makris, N.C., McCracken, G.F., Procopio, M., Hristov, N.I., Tang, S., Bagchi, A., Reichard, J.D., Horn, J.W., et al.: Thermal imaging reveals significantly smaller brazilian free-tailed bat colonies than previously estimated. Journal of Mammalogy 89(1), 18–24 (2008)

[3] Breslav, M., Fuller, N.W., Betke, M.: Vision system for wing beat analysis of bats in the wild (2012)

[4] Bullen, R., McKenzie, N.: Scaling bat wingbeat frequency and amplitude. Journal of Experimental Biology 205(17), 2615–2626 (2002)

[5] Cutler, R., Davis, L.S.: Robust real-time periodic motion detection, analysis, and applications. IEEE Transactions on Pattern Analysis and Machine Intelligence 22(8), 781–796 (2000)

[6] Fisher, R., Xiao, Y.: Bat echolocation behavior from highspeed 3d video. In: Workshop on Visual Observation and Analysis of Animal and Insect Behavior, Istanbul, Turkey (2010)

[7] Ghaderian, M., Behrad, A., Kaboodi, S.A.D.: Recognition of periodic motions using one-dimensional contour based features. In: 7th Iranian Machine Vision and Image Processing, pp. 1–5. IEEE (2011)

[8] Hristov, N.I., Betke, M., Theriault, D.E., Bagchi, A., Kunz, T.H.: Seasonal variation in colony size of brazilian free-tailed bats at carlsbad cavern based on thermal imaging. Journal of Mammalogy 91(1), 183–192 (2010)

[9] Laptev, I., Belongie, S.J., Perez, P., Wills, J.: Periodic motion detection and segmentation via approximate sequence alignment. In: Tenth IEEE Int'l. Conf. on Computer Vision, ICCV, vol. 1, pp. 816–823. IEEE (2005)

[10] Lazarevic, L., Harrison, D., Southee, D., Wade, M., Osmond, J.: Wind farm and fauna interaction: detecting bird and bat wing beats through cyclic motion analysis. Int'l. Journal of Sustainable Engineering 1(1), 60–68 (2008)

[11] Lyons, R.: How to interpolate in the time-domain by zero-padding in the frequency domain (2010)

[12] Norberg, U.M.L., Norberg, R.Å.: Scaling of wingbeat frequency with body mass in bats and limits to maximum bat size. The Journal of Exp. Bio. 215(5), 711–722 (2012)

[13] Plotnik, A.M., Rock, S.M.: Quantification of cyclic motion of marine animals from computer vision. In: OCEANS MTS/IEEE, vol. 3, pp. 1575–1581. IEEE (2002)

[14] Ren, Y., Fan, B., Lin, W., Yang, X., Li, H., Li, W., Liu, D.: An efficient framework for analyzing periodical activities in sports videos. In: 4th Int'l. Congress on Image and Signal Processing, vol. 1, pp. 502–506. IEEE (2011)

[15] Schumacher, D.: General filtered image rescaling. In: Graphics Gems III, pp. 8–16. Academic Press Professional, Inc. (1992)

[16] Suzuki, S., et al.: Topological structural analysis of digitized binary images by border following. Computer Vision, Graphics, and Image Processing 30(1), 32–46 (1985)

[17] Zivkovic, Z., van der Heijden, F.: Efficient adaptive density estimation per image pixel for the task of background subtraction. Pattern Recognition Letters 27(7), 773–780 (2006)

Automated Ground-Plane Estimation
for Trajectory Rectification

Ian Hales, David Hogg, Kia Ng, and Roger Boyle

University of Leeds, Woodhouse Lane, Leeds, LS2 9JT
{i.j.hales06,d.c.hogg,k.c.ng,r.d.boyle}@leeds.ac.uk

Abstract. We present a system to determine ground-plane parameters
in densely crowded scenes where use of geometric features such as parallel lines or reliable estimates of agent dimensions are not possible. Using
feature points tracked over short intervals, together with some plausible
scene assumptions, we can estimate the parameters of the ground-plane
to a sufficient degree of accuracy to correct usefully for perspective distortion. This paper describes feasibility studies conducted on controlled,
simulated data, to establish how different levels and types of noise affect
the accuracy of the estimation, and a verification of the approach on live
data, showing the method can estimate ground-plane parameters, thus
allowing improved accuracy of trajectory analysis.

Keywords: ground-plane, trajectory, rectification, crowd-motion.

1 Introduction

In computer vision one often wishes to examine objects in terms of their size,
speed or location, accurate measurement of which is hampered by several types
of distortion that occur when the camera captures the scene. This is particularly
relevant in applications such as behaviour analysis in crowds, where such metrics
can be used to detect events or measure crowd density. By estimating the transformation undergone by the coordinate system, we can invert it to counteract
the effect of such distortions and obtain a more accurate view of the world. If
we can obtain the ground-plane orientation with respect to the camera, we can
correct for one of the most prevalent sources of error – perspective distortion.

Two broad approaches are apparent within the literature: "formal methods",
often in terms of the fundamental matrix or image homographies; and "informal
methods", providing a coarse, but still usable, impression of the scene (e.g. a scale
ratio from front to back). A common feature is the idea of "vanishing points",
which lie on the horizon line. Having obtained the equation of the horizon, it is
trivial to perform affine rectification [1]. Metric rectification can then be achieved
using knowledge of known lengths or angles, or equality of angles [2]. These
points can be determined using pairs of imaged parallel lines [1] and inclusion
of a vanishing point in a third direction allows for metric measurement [3].
The Manhattan Assumption [4] offers a viable framework to obtain additional
vanishing points from the background in man-made scenes [5]. Alternatively,

R. Wilson et al. (Eds.): CAIP 2013, Part II, LNCS 8048, pp. 378–385, 2013.
© Springer-Verlag Berlin Heidelberg 2013

known angles in the scene [6] or known reference lengths [7] can produce similar results. In pedestrian scenes, measurements (e.g. projected foot-head heights [8,9]) provide a valid reference length. Less formal methods tend to rely on the estimation of a single ground-plane. It is again common to use projected foot-head heights [10] and accuracy can be improved by tracking individuals, taking relative height measurements for each [11], which minimizes potential variations in reference length.

We base our work within the context of pedestrian crowd analysis. The methods discussed above rely on assumptions unlikely to hold in a densely crowded scene due to inter-occlusion and the inability to see geometric features in the background. Stauffer *et al.* [10] mention an alternative approach using the assumption of constant speed of moving objects, built upon by Bose and Grimson [12], who use a blob tracker to generate trajectories. They then obtain the vanishing line by assuming constant speed, before using inter-trajectory speed ratios to obtain metric rectification. However, maintained tracking was necessary to achieve metric rectification, making this approach infeasible in our domain.

We propose to use the local speed of tracked feature points as a calibration measurement, along with the assumption of constant speed, to reconstruct the ground-plane parameters. We do not require prolonged tracking of features provided we observe pedestrian motion throughout the scene. The remainder of this paper will describe our method, prove its validity on simulated data and assess its accuracy on real-world benchmark data.

2   Ground-Plane Estimation

Above, we saw that it is possible to construct the 3D scene using information from measuring objects of known real-world size at various positions within the image. In this section we show that it is equally possible to use measurements of object speed to reconstruct the plane upon which agents are moving. Throughout this work we assume that all objects move on a single, linear plane and that each observed object is moving at constant (or near-constant) speed. We do not, however, require that all objects move at the same speed.

We first track sparse features frame-by-frame for some period using the *KLT* tracker [13], until we can no longer reliably continue the trajectory. Since we deal with high density pedestrian crowds, heavy inter-occlusion is likely to result in many short trajectories. However, it only takes a few frames for us to gain valuable information from the trajectory. It is plausible that objects may have many features or no features at all assigned to them, but this is not a major concern provided we gather information from various scene positions.

We define a trajectory as a time series of points upon on a plane recorded at equally spaced time-steps. We observe these in the image-coordinate system and wish to obtain their respective points within the camera coordinate system through perspective back-projection. We define a time-series $(X_1^\tau, X_2^\tau, \ldots, X_{N_\tau}^\tau)$ as the x-coordinates of trajectory τ at times 1 to N_τ and its projection into image space as $(x_1^\tau, x_2^\tau, \ldots, x_{N_\tau}^\tau)$. We represent the orientation of the ground-plane in terms of its unit normal vector, $\underline{\mathbf{n}}$, given by equation (1). θ represents the angle of elevation (rotation in the x-axis) and ψ to represent the angle of yaw (rotation in the z-axis).

$$\mathbf{n} = \begin{pmatrix} a \\ b \\ c \end{pmatrix} = \begin{pmatrix} \sin(\psi)\sin(\theta) \\ \cos(\psi)\sin(\theta) \\ \cos(\theta) \end{pmatrix} \tag{1}$$

Given a ground-plane $\mathbf{n} \cdot \mathbf{X} = d$ for some point $\mathbf{X} = (X_t^\tau, Y_t^\tau, Z_t^\tau)^\top$ in the world and some α, equations (2) to (4) show the back-projection of a point $(x_t^\tau, y_t^\tau)^\top$ onto the point $(X_t^\tau, Y_t^\tau, Z_t^\tau)^\top$ on the ground plane at time t, where α is the negative reciprocal of the focal length f and d is the shortest distance between the camera and the ground-plane.

$$X_t^\tau = \alpha x_t^\tau Z_t^\tau \tag{2}$$

$$Y_t^\tau = \alpha y_t^\tau Z_t^\tau \tag{3}$$

$$Z_t^\tau = \frac{d}{\alpha a x_t^\tau + \alpha b y_t^\tau + c} \tag{4}$$

2.1 Speed as a Measuring Stick

An object's observed speed varies with perspective as do its other properties such as height [10]. Given a number of partial trajectories of constant speed, we show that it is possible to obtain reasonable estimates for the ground-plane parameters. Assuming a tracked object's real-world speed is constant, we can think of the trajectory as a set of piecewise linear segments, each with length given by the 3D Euclidean distance formula. We can use this distance as the "measuring-stick" from which to gain an estimation of the ground-plane.

Firstly we make some simplifying assumptions. The height of the camera with respect to the ground-plane, d, acts primarily as a scaling parameter. As we only aim to reconstruct to scale, we set this to 1 in (4), thus simplifying further calculation. We also observe that in the majority of scenes, the camera height is substantial compared to the height variations of the tracked feature points. In section 3 we offer results showing that tracked feature height variation does not significantly affect the estimate of ground-plane orientation. Finally, motion variation based on the articulation of our moving agents is negligible.

Substituting (2-4) into the distance formula, we obtain (5). This relates the known 2D projected positions of a feature point at consecutive intervals $t-1$ and t, their 3D distance in the camera plane and the plane parameters. Hereafter, we use L^τ to represent the set of distance measurements at all time-intervals for some trajectory, τ. Each element of this set is defined as follows:

$$(L_t^\tau)^2 = \alpha^2 \left(\frac{x_t^\tau}{\gamma_t^\tau} - \frac{x_{t-1}^\tau}{\gamma_{t-1}^\tau} \right)^2 + \alpha^2 \left(\frac{y_t^\tau}{\gamma_t^\tau} - \frac{y_{t-1}^\tau}{\gamma_{t-1}^\tau} \right)^2 + \left(\frac{1}{\gamma_t^\tau} - \frac{1}{\gamma_{t-1}^\tau} \right)^2 \tag{5}$$

where,

$$\gamma_t^\tau = \alpha x_t^\tau a + \alpha y_t^\tau b + c$$

For a single trajectory τ, we define a set of the distances at all time intervals:

$$\{L_t^\tau\}_{t=2}^{t=N_\tau} \tag{6}$$

We denote the mean and standard deviation of the set as $\mu(L^\tau)$ and $\sigma(L^\tau)$ for short. We now have a relationship between known image-coordinates and the unknown camera-coordinates with respect to some constant distance along points in a trajectory. We use this to measure how well a given set of parameters, θ, ψ and α fit the observed data. If a feature point is moving at constant speed and we have a good set of parameters, $\sigma(L^\tau)$ should be close to zero. Conversely, we would expect a poor parameterization to give a high spread in L^τ.

Since we do not wish to impose the constraint that all objects must move at constant speed, we normalize $\sigma(L^\tau)$ by $\mu(L^\tau)$ giving us a speed-invariant measure of correctness. We pose this correctness measure in terms of a minimization over the sum of squared errors for each trajectory as shown in equation (7).

$$E_1 = \sum_{\tau \in T} \left(\frac{\sigma(L^\tau)}{\mu(L^\tau)} \right)^2 \tag{7}$$

$$E_2 = \sigma_{\tau \in T} (\mu(L^\tau)) \tag{8}$$

As we expect tracked feature points to have originated from a set of homogeneous objects (e.g. pedestrians), we can reasonably assume that they should all move with similar (although not identical) speed. As such we include an additional term to constrain the system, E_2 in equation (8). Here we take the standard-deviation over the set of all mean speeds which penalises a high spread of speeds, thereby preventing some of the least plausible configurations.

2.2 Minimizing the Error

We solve for θ, ψ and α by minimizing the error $E = E_1 + \lambda E_2$ over all input trajectories. We experimented with non-linear optimization algorithms but due to the irregularity of the problem-space away from the vicinity of the true value, gradient descent methods tend to fall into local minima. As such we fall back to a multi-resolution global search to find the correct region. At the first level we search all combinations of α, θ and ψ, with a coarse mesh – increments of 15° in both the θ and ψ feasible ranges (0° to 90° and −45° to 45°) and for α an exponential search in the range 10^{-3} to 10^0 to find its scale.

We then take the point with minimum error from this search and produce a finer grid around it; now searching α linearly and reducing the step size for θ and ψ to 10% of their previous value. We repeat this procedure until either the lowest error point is below a given tolerance (empirically 10^{-5} is sufficient) or we reach the maximum level allowed for search. We have observed 3 levels to be sufficient for an accurate estimation on simulated data with some noise.

3 Experiments on Simulated Data

To prove the initial viability of this method we first describe a number of experiments on simulated data. This allows us to examine how various types of noise and violations of the initial premise affect the accuracy of the experiments. Core sources of error are likely to be:

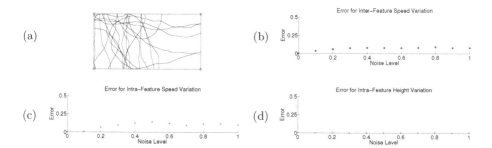

Fig. 1. An example of our simulated trajectories (a) and the results of our noise experiments (b)-(d) in terms of average angular error (dot product between ground-truth and estimated plane-normals)

1. Variation in inter-trajectory speed. That is, agents move at different speeds.
2. Variation in intra-trajectory speed; an agent varies their speed whilst moving.
3. Variation in tracked point height; i.e. some trajectories recorded on feet, some on shoulders, etc.

We generate simulated trajectories on a number of planes with parameterized noise (Fig. 1a), allowing the speed and height of trajectories to vary according to Gaussian distributions. This lets us examine the effect of the above error sources on reconstruction accuracy. We assess accuracy by rectifying the image-plane trajectories with the ground-truth parameters and our estimations, then compare the spread of normalized speeds of each. Given a perfect reconstruction, we see zero-error and all measurements are relative to a mean speed of 1.

We perform three sets of experiments on a number of different planes across the feasible range, varying the potential source of error in each in terms of the standard deviation, between 0 and 1, of a Gaussian distribution with mean 1. Examining the above issues in order, we first investigate the effect of the different agents in the scene moving at different speeds. Agents' initial speeds are chosen randomly from the distribution and remain constant throughout the simulation. From Fig. 1b we observe that even in extreme cases the average error stays low - below 10% of the mean speed. We expect the effect of intra-trajectory speed variation to be more pronounced as it is the defining metric used to recover the parameters. We take the speed of a feature at each frame from the distribution. Fig. 1c shows that although we experience more noise than with inter-trajectory speed variation, it is not so substantially pronounced as to seriously damage our result. We see that height variation has negligible affect on the accuracy of our solution – data was generated using a feasible camera height of 10m; as such the difference in point height is relatively small.

Points tracked at different heights with a low-positioned camera will be affected more strongly, but in most real-world scenes the distances between the lowest and highest tracked points are negligible with respect to the camera height. Our experiments on simulated data show that over realistic ranges, the three po-

(a)   (b)

Fig. 2. Example stills from PETS2009 (a) and students003 (b) video datasets

tential sources of error identified above have negligible detrimental effect on the accuracy of estimation. Of particular importance is the intra-trajectory speed variation, which is a violation of our assumptions and yet still does not have an especially pronounced effect on the quality of our estimation.

4   Experiments on Video Data

We gather trajectories using the tracker and split them at sharp spikes in speed, which are easily identifiable violations of the constant-speed assumption. We are typically left with considerably more trajectories than is necessary (or tractable) to process. Indeed many of these are extremely short – only 2 or 3 frames. As such we filter out trajectories shorter than 4 frames, as these provide us with no additional information towards our unknowns.

When tracking pedestrians, we observe two key differences to the trajectories produced for simulation. Firstly, we commonly track several points per person; secondly pedestrians tend to behave in a more "human" manner than in our simulated data – travelling in groups. As such we observe that many of our trajectories are extremely similar and their inclusion adds little information, but slows the processing down considerably. Therefore we first align trajectories to each other using the Hungarian algorithm [14], then cluster the trajectories based on their distance and shape similarity using Affinity Propagation [15], taking the resulting clusters as input to our ground-plane estimation system.

The majority of our results are given against the PETS2009 dataset, specifically videos taken from View001 shown in 2a and View002. Since these come with full intrinsic and extrinsic calibration, we can directly compare rotation angles. We also examine one other video dataset: "students003", Fig. 2b, from the University of Cyprus. This is only provided with an image to ground-plane homography and so does not allow for direct rotation comparison. We therefore use the homography to determine the 2D feature coordinates on the ground-plane and compare the speed ratios for each trajectory. We compare with the method in [12] (see section 1) although we exchanged the blob tracker for our KLT approach as the former provided insufficient tracks for reliable estimation when applied to our data.

Table 1. Results for plane estimation on videos from the PETS2009 dataset

Dataset	Subset	View	Time Index	θ Error (degrees)	ψ Error (degrees)
S0	Regular Flow	001	14-06	+7.2	-0.4
S1	L1	001	13-59	+1.1	+11.7
S1	L2	001	14-06	+7.5	-0.5
S1	L1	002	13-57	+0.1	-9.9
S1	L2	002	14-31	+1.9	-4.4

(a)    (b)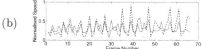

Fig. 3. Comparison of trajectory speeds rectified using the ground-truth (*black, dashed*) and estimated parameters (*red, solid*) and Bose (*green, dashed*). Examples are longest trajectories from (a) "students003" and (b) PETS2009 Regular Flow. We see that even in trajectories with some tracking error, we obtain a sensible result, generally better than Bose.

Table 1 shows the orientation error for several scenes in terms of direct difference for the two rotation components, θ and ψ. There is an area of high reflectance in View002, which interrupts tracking of most individuals, despite this, the majority of our estimates are within $10°$ of the ground-truth values – sufficient for approximate correction of trajectory speeds. Fig. 3 shows some example comparisons of normalized trajectory speeds from the "students003" and PETS Regular Flow datasets rectified using the provided homography/calibration, our estimation and that of [12]. We see that our matching is generally very close, even on trajectories with some tracking error, whereas the method of Bose and Grimson performs poorly. We put this down to the flexibility of our approach in minimising spread rather than a strict constant speed assumption.

5   Conclusions and Further Work

This paper has considered the problem of reconstructing 3D geometry from 2D observations taken from videos of pedestrian data taken using a single uncalibrated camera. Our method differs from previous techniques as it requires no knowledge of scene geometry or a fixed size object; needing only motion of individuals. We have provided evidence on simulations for the validity of our method and the assumptions held within. We have then shown results on the PETS2009 dataset which illustrate the success of the method in a number of cases and have given a qualitative comparison for another. In continuation of this work, we plan to account for variations in trajectory height to allow for tracking individuals on different parts of their bodies. We then intend to extend the method into the multi-planar domain, such that planes can be estimated and their boundaries drawn to more accurately and realistically model real-world scenes.

References

1. Liebowitz, D., Zisserman, A.: Metric rectification for perspective images of planes. In: Proceedings CVPR 1998, pp. 482–488. IEEE Comput. Soc. (1998)
2. Hartley, R., Zisserman, A.: Multiple View Geometry in Computer Vision, 2nd edn. Cambridge University Press (2004)
3. Criminisi, A., Reid, I.D., Zisserman, A.: Single view metrology. International Journal of Computer Vision 40(2), 123–148 (2000)
4. Coughlan, J.M., Yuille, A.L.: Manhattan world: Compass direction from a single image by bayesian inference. In: Proceedings ICCV 1999, pp. 941–947 (1999)
5. Pflugfelder, R., Bischof, H.: Online auto-calibration in man-made worlds. In: Proceedings DICTA 2005, pp. 519–526 (2005)
6. Zhang, Z., Li, M., Huang, K., Tan, T.: Robust automated ground plane rectification based on moving vehicles for traffic scene surveillance. In: 2008 15th IEEE ICIP, pp. 1364–1367. IEEE (2008)
7. Guo, F., Chellappa, R.: Video mensuration using a stationary camera. In: Leonardis, A., Bischof, H., Pinz, A. (eds.) ECCV 2006. LNCS, vol. 3953, pp. 164–176. Springer, Heidelberg (2006)
8. Lv, F., Zhao, T., Nevatia, R.: Self-Calibration of a Camera from Video of a Walking Human. In: Proceedings Pattern Recognition, vol. 1, pp. 562–567. IEEE Computer Society, Los Alamitos (2002)
9. Micusik, B., Pajdla, T.: Simultaneous surveillance camera calibration and foot-head homology estimation from human detections. In: CVPR 2010, pp. 1562–1569 (2010)
10. Stauffer, C., Tieu, K., Lee, L.: Robust Automated Planar Normalization of Tracking Data. In: Proceedings IEEE Workshop on VS PETS (2003)
11. Krahnstoever, N., Mendonça, P.R.S.: Autocalibration from Tracks of Walking People. In: British Machine Vision Conference, pp. 107–116 (2006)
12. Bose, B., Grimson, E.: Ground plane rectification by tracking moving objects. In: Proceedings IEEE Workshop on VS PETS (2003)
13. Shi, J., Tomasi, C.: Good features to track. In: Proceedings CVPR, pp. 593–600 (1994)
14. Kuhn, H.W.: The hungarian method for the assignment problem. Naval Research Logistics 2(1-2), 83–97 (1955)
15. Frey, B.J.J., Dueck, D.: Clustering by passing messages between data points. Science (2007)

Breast Parenchymal Pattern Analysis in Digital Mammography: Associations between Tabár and Birads Tissue Compositions

Wenda He and Reyer Zwiggelaar

Department of Computer Science, Aberystwyth University, United Kingdom
{weh,rrz}@aber.ac.uk

Abstract. We investigated the associations between Tabár based breast parenchymal patterns and Birads density parenchymal patterns in digital mammography. Breast parenchymal texture was analysed on a set of mammographc images segmented based on Tabár tissue modelling. Visual assessment indicates good and anatomically improved segmentation on tissue specific areas. At the tissue modelling stage, over and/or under training can cause tissue composition fluctuation between nodular and homogeneous tissue, whilst the percentages of radiolucent tissue are less sensitive to the algorithm's parameter configurations. The clear depiction with digital mammography allows a better segmentation on tissue specific areas, which indicates that the breast parenchymal texture may be utilised in mammographic interpretation as the new technology advances further. The average tissue compositions for the Tabár parenchymal patterns show inadequate compositions of nodular and homogeneous tissue. Stronger associates were found between Tabár tissue compositions for [nodular, homogeneous], [nodular, homogeneous, radiolucent] and Birads breast density classes I and IV.

Keywords: Tabár, Birads, breast parenchyma, mammographic segmentation.

1 Introduction

Mammographic parenchymal patterns are used as a qualitative classification of mammographic density [12]. Tabár *et al.* have proposed a mammographic modelling scheme based on mixtures of four building blocks composing the normal breast anatomy (i.e. nodular, linear, homogeneous and radiolucent). Most nodular densities correspond to Terminal Ductal Lobular Units (TDLU); linear densities correspond to either ducts, fibrous or blood vessels; homogeneous densities correspond to fibrous tissue which appears as high density (high intensities) areas in mammographic images, and may hide the underlying normal TDLU, ducts and their alterations; radiolucent areas are related to adipose fatty tissue which appears as much less/non dense (low intensities) in mammographic images [3]. Percentage density (PD) is used as a means of quantitative classification [12], to facilitate such a mammographic interpretation, the American College of Radiology's Breast Imaging Reporting and Data System (Birads) mammography lexicon [6] was developed as a quality assurance tool, covers the significant relationship between increased breast density and decreased mammographic sensitivity in detecting cancer [8]. Mammographic breast composition is categorised into four patterns:

R. Wilson et al. (Eds.): CAIP 2013, Part II, LNCS 8048, pp. 386–393, 2013.
© Springer-Verlag Berlin Heidelberg 2013

1) Birads I, the breast is almost entirely fat ($<25\%$ glandular); 2) Birads II, the breast has scattered fibroglandular densities ($25\% - 50\%$); 3) Birads III, the breast consists of heterogeneously dense breast tissue ($51\% - 75\%$); and 4) Birads IV, the breast is extremely dense ($>75\%$ glandular). Computer-aided detection (CAD) is now widely used in clinical practices to assist radiologists in interpretation of screening mammograms. To screening radiologists, accurately segmenting a given mammographic image into regions according to various parenchymal patterns is critical in order to receive second reading benefit from the CAD system; it is because segmentation accuracy can directly affect the sensitivity of a CAD system [9]. Recently advanced image acquisition using digital mammography (DM) shows improved tissue characterisation, tumour visualisation and strength in calcification localisation; leading to higher diagnostic performances and a lower recall rate for additional screening [1].

To our knowledge, one of the first and rare study in evaluation mammographic segmentation results conducted by Baker *et al.* [9] which took breast tissue density into consideration in evaluations of the accuracy of the breast region segmentation process, its accuracy has direct impact on the subsequent breast tissue parenchymal analysis results. In the study, the accuracy of segmentation in a commercially available CAD system was assessed. They concluded that out of 2020 digitised film mammographic images, 96.8% (1956) were segmented near perfect or acceptable. Unacceptable segmented breast parenthyma includes 1.2% scattered (Birads II), more than five times frequent for heterogeneous dense parenchyma (Birads III), and 1.8% extremely dense tissue (Birads IV) was missegmented; at the same time there is no unacceptable segmentation for fatty replaced tissue (Birads I). Although, there is no significant difference among breast densities, on average 25% of the breast parenchyma was excluded from the CAD analysis as results of unacceptable segmentation. One of the key hypothesis in [9] is that parenchymal texture segmentation accuracy may be improved with more advanced DM (without the need for film digitisation). Although the aforementioned study is about mammographic image background segmentation and not directly linked to mammographic parencymal segmentation within the breast region, its results and conclusions have an important implication. Segmentation process is dependent on the density of the breast parenchyma [9]. Inspired by this, our investigation is focused on finding an alternative or an add-on dependency to density parencyma (one of the major mammographic risk indicators [7]) with breast tissue characterisation improved DM. In the first instance, the association between Tabár's parenchymal patterns and Birads breast density parencyma was studied.

2   Data

The data consists of 360 'for presentation' mammographic images, which are processed for optimal visual appearance to radiologists, obtained from 90 women using Hologic's Selenia Dimensions. A total of four images were taken for each of the patients; two images in Mediolateral Oblique View (MLO) and Cranio-Caudal View (CC) were taken for the left and right breasts, respectively. In terms of breast density class distribution, the provided dataset consists a total of 56, 120, 120 and 64 images (16%, 33%, 33% and

18%) associated with Birads breast density classes I to IV, respectively. This distribution is close to mammographic screening programmes [1]. Each raw image has a resolution of either 2560 x 3328 or 3328 x 4096 pixels. Figure 1 shows example mammographic images.

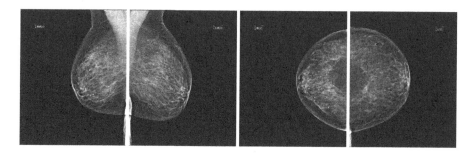

Fig. 1. Example mammographic images, from left to right showing the MLO views for the right and left breasts, and the corresponding CC views for the right and left breasts, respectively

In order to train a set of Tabár mammographic building block models, a collection of mammographic patches was obtained from the dataset. A total of 303, 70 and 255 mammographic patches in various sizes, containing examples of nodular, homogeneous and radiolucent tissue were cropped from images. Figure 2 shows example mammographic patches. Note that the linear structure tissue class from the Tabár models was not specifically included in the current experiments; instead this type of tissue was considered as part of the other tissue classes as the linear structures appear in combination with all three classes. Therefore, in the experiment only three types of Tabár tissue models (i.e. nodular, homogeneous and radiolucent), which correspond loosely to Birads tissue categories (i.e. scattered fibroglandular, heterogeneous dense and glandular), were trained and used in the segmentation process.

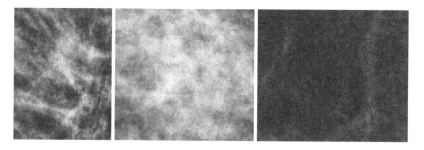

Fig. 2. From left to right, showing mammographic patches containing tissue examples for nodular, homogeneous and radiolucent tissue, respectively

3   Method

The experiment consists of four stages: 1) tissue (mammographic building blocks) modelling, 2) parameter selection, 3) training a binary model Bayes classifier, and 4) mammograhpic segmentation. We have previously developed a technique [2] to automatically segment a given mammographic image into regions, according to texture and density variations. The developed segmentation approach has shown anatomically consistent results with expert radiologist's annotations. In this study we used the same segmentation technique and updated the feature extraction process.

At the tissue modelling stage, a multiresolution grey-scale and rotation invariant local binary pattern (LBP) technique was employed [10]. It is a computational simple yet efficient approach based on 'uniform' local binary pattern, nonparametric discrimination of sample and prototype distribution. Such 'uniform' patterns are considered as fundamental breast tissue properties, which provide the vast majority of tissue specific patterns in the subsampled mammographic patches, corresponding to mammograhpic building blocks (i.e. nodular, homogeneous and radiolucent). A generalised grey-scale and rotation invariant operator $LBP_{P,R}$ was used to detect 'uniform' patterns in circular neighbourhoods of any qantisation of the angular space, at any spatial resolution [10]. A circularly symmetric neighbour set P controls the quantisation of the angular space, whereas a circle of radius R determines the spatial resolution of the operator. The operator responses are expected to be independent with respect to the multiresolution analysis. By combining the responses over different resolutions with a rotation invariant variance measure $VAR_{P,R}$ that characterises the contrast of local texture, the joint distribution $LBP_{P,R}/VAR_{P,R}$ is assumed to be able to distinguish various tissue densities and breast parenchymal patterns. This in turn incorporates both the percentage density (*e.g.* characterises contrast) [5] [11] and parenchymal texture variations (*e.g.* orientation, coarseness and thickness) [4] [3] in the derived feature vectors. The reader is referred to [10] for the methodology details.

To choose the appropriate parameters (i.e. P and R) for the LBP approach, automatic parameter selection was employed. A range of neighbourhoods (i.e. $\{7, 17, 27, 37, 47, 57, 67\}$) and corresponding radii (i.e. $\{2, 4, 7, 9, 12, 14, 18\}$) covering small to large anatomical structures were predefined. The total number of combinations ($C(n, r) = n!$ / $(r!(n-r)!)$, where n = 7, r = $\{1, 2, ..., 7\}$) for the multiresolution configuration is 127. Each LBP configuration results in a different joint distribution for a mammograhic image with respect to the feature dimension. It is expected that the joint distributions (feature vectors) are correlated; and for mammographic images associated with the same breast density classes, the distributions are close to each other in the feature space. Therefore by training a classifier using a LBP configuration, the resultant Birads density classification accuracy can be used as an indicator to determine the discriminative power of the derived feature vectors with respect to the used LBP configuration. We used a collection of 57 classifiers available in Weka [13] (*e.g.* trees (12), bayes (6), functions (5), lazy (1), meta (25), misc (1) and rules (7)); each classifier was trained using the 127 sets of feature vectors derived from 40% of randomly selected mammograhic images for each density class, and the rest of 60% of images were used for testing. It is expected that different classifiers behave differently, and the optimal LBP configuration varies from one classifier to another. The frequency of the best LBP configurations based on a total of 57 (classifiers) $\times 127 = 7239$ tests indicated that the optimal LBP configuration is $\{7, 37, 57\}$ (top three most frequently used resolutions). This optimal configuration reflects the size variations and range for the anatomical structures contained in the mammograhpic patches. The percentages of the patches used for the tissue modelling as follows: nodular 50%, homogeneous 50%, radiolucent 50%; a general clustering process was used as a means of tissue modelling, and the number of cluster centres for the nodular, homogeneous and radiolucent were 3, 9 and 5, respectively. These values were empirically defined and the reader is referred to [2] for more detailed description of the processes for tissue modelling and training a binary model Bayes classifier. With respect to the percentages of the patches used for training the classifier, the following values were used and chosen empirically: 20% of nodular patches, 50% of homogeneous patches, 25% of radiolucent patches. Note that the patches used for the tissue modelling and classifier training were mutually exclusive.

All 360 mammographic images were segmented based on Tabár tissue modelling; using the previously trained classifier, the tissue class of an unseen pixel is determined by calculating the probability of it being one of the three mammographic building blocks [2]. It is labelled to the observed tissue class where the probability is the highest. The relative proportions of the mammograpic building blocks (tissue composition) were calculated from the resultant mammographic segmentation.

4   Results and Discussion

Visual assessment indicates that the majority of the mammographic segmentation on tissue specific areas are correct anatomically. Figure 3 shows example mammograhic segmentation. Increasing or decreasing the percentages of either nodular or homogenous tissue used at the training stage can have a significant effect on the balance of tissue composition, and varying the amount of samples to be trained can lead to under or over training, which may cause missegmentation. At the same time, the percentage of radiolucent tissue remains relatively stable, as the texture appearance varies little in radiolucent across different breast density classes. The smoothness of segmentation on the borders of tissue specific areas may vary, due to the use of different maximum window sizes; a medium size windows (*e.g.*47) seem to produce better segmentation visually; lager windows seem to produce coarse segmentation. The average tissue compositions (i.e. [nodular%, homogeneous%, radiolucent%]) were derived based on all the segmentation. When comparing the standard tissue compositions for the four Tabár models, the results indicate that heterogeneous and homogeneous tissue are less presented. Empirical testing was conducted with different configuration settings, in order to assess the impact of parameter changes to the average tissue compositions. Despite the anatomically promising mammographic segmentation, the derived average tissue compositions for each Tabár risk class show discrepancies when compared to the standard Tabár parenchymal pattern models. The associations between various Tabár tissue compositions and Birads density classification (ground truth) were analysed and shown in Table 1. The results indicate that Tabár tissue compositions for [N, H] and [N, H, R] are better associated with Birads density classes; by removing percentage of radiolucent does not have signification impact on the association. However, if the association only

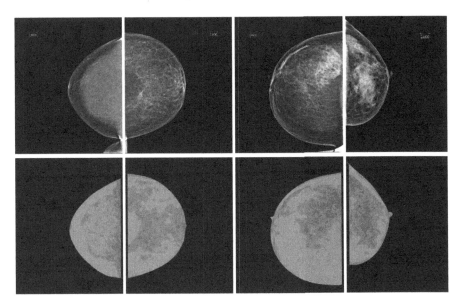

Fig. 3. The top row from left to right, showing mammographic images associated with Birads density I to IV, respectively. The corresponding segmentation are shown in the bottom row.

takes the percentages of single Tabár mammographic building block (i.e. [N] or [R]) into account, it seems to be stronger with Birads density classes I and IV; whilst tissue composition for [H] is more associated with Birads density classes II and III. Note that the percentage of radiolucent can also be considered as (100% - PD). Stronger association were found between Tabár tissue compositions for [N, H], [N, H, R] and Birads density classes I and IV. Note that the Tabár patterns are not considered to be on a continuous scale, the primary difference is Tabár I [12]. In terms of the intensity distribution, we observed that all the mammographic images appear as more 'transparent'; this makes the intensity distribution more towards the lower intensity range, and therefore there is less presence of heterogeneous (nodular) and homogeneous dense tissue.

Table 1. Associations between various Tabár tissue compositions and Birads density classes. N, H and R denote nodular, homogeneous and radiolucent, respectively. For example, Birads III - Tabár [H] reads as out of all the (360) mammographic images labelled as Birads breast density III, 61% of them are associated with Tabár IV when only percentages of homogeneous ([H]) were used as feature in Tabár scheme based classification for the mammographic images. Note that here Birads I, II, III, and IV are mapped to Tabár I, II/III, IV and V, respectively.

	Tabár [N]	[H]	[R]	[N, H]	[N, R]	[H, R]	[N, H, R]
Birads I	77%	5%	68 %	71%	70%	68%	70%
Birads II	33%	53%	25 %	35%	25%	24%	31%
Birads III	22%	61%	16%	23%	19%	23%	23%
Birads IV	55%	3%	63 %	58%	63%	64%	63%

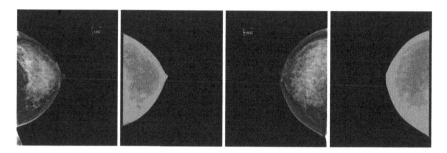

Fig. 4. Example mammographic images and the corresponding segmentation, showing anatomically correct segmentation based on visual assessment. However, the derived tissue compositions are not in agreement with standard Tabár V or Birads IV models.

Some of the discrepancies may be due to the differences in judgement as to what constitutes a dense area. Density is in the eye of the beholder [15], a more robust method may be required to determine dense tissue in relation to the analysed mammographic images. Figure 4 shows two anatomically correct segmentation but the tissue composition (Tabár scheme) or PD (Birads scheme) are not in agreement with the expected breast parenchymal tissue composition. At the same time, we can not categorically rule out that there might be mistakes in the ground truth. Also note that the established Tabár parenchymal patterns are based on traditional analogue mammography and tissue characterisation has changed significantly in more novel breast imaging systems; which may affect the perceived tissue distribution in digital mammographic images.

5 Conclusions

In this preliminary investigation, a total of 360 digital mammographic images in CC and MLO views were used. To our knowledge, this is the first study into associations between Tabár based breast parenchymal texture and Birads breast density classification in digital mammography. The results indicate that when using the optimal LBP configuration in conjunction with the segmentation method developed in [2], we can produce mammographic segmentation with significant improvement in terms of anatomical correctness; thanks to digital mammography's ability to produce images with fine tissue charaterisation. However, the average tissue compositions for the Tabár parenchymal pattern models show inadequate compositions of nodular and homogeneous tissue. Stronger associations were found between Tabár tissue compositions for [nodular, homogeneous], [nodular, homogeneous, radiolucent] and Birads breast density classes I and IV. The next stage of the investigation should incorporate a clinical evaluation [14] to verify the mammograhpic segmentation. From segmentation accuracy point of view, this study indicates that parenchymal patterns in digital mammography may be utilised with percentage densities as the technologies advance further, and improvements can be made in lesion perception, analysis in architectural distortion, and more accurate temporal analysis in changes in breast parenchymal texture. These may lead to higher cancer detection rates, a reduction in the recall rate, a higher positive predictive value for biopsy recommendation, and a decrease in the number of unnecessary biopsies.

References

1. Gillbert, F.J., Young, K.C., Astley, S.M., Whelehan, P., Gillan, M.G.C.: Digital Breast To-mosynthesis. NHSBSP Publication No 69 (September 2010) ISBN 978-1-84463-071-4
2. He, W., Denton, E.R.E., Zwiggelaar, R.: Mammographic Segmentation and Risk Classifica-tion Using a Novel Binary Model Based Bayes Classifier. In: Maidment, A.D.A., Bakic, P.R., Gavenonis, S. (eds.) IWDM 2012. LNCS, vol. 7361, pp. 40–47. Springer, Heidelberg (2012)
3. Tabár, L., Tot, T., Dean, P.B.: Breast Cancer: The Art And Science Of Early Detection With Mammography: Perception, Interpretation, Histopatholigic Correlation, 1st edn. Georg Thieme Verlag (December 2004)
4. Wolfe, J.N.: Risk for breast cancer development determined by mammographic parenchymal pattern. Cancer 37(5), 2486–2492 (1976)
5. Boyd, N.F., Byng, J.W., Jong, R.A., Fishell, E.K., Little, L.E., Miller, A.B., Lockwood, G.A., Tritchler, D.L., Yaffe, M.J.: Quantitative classification of mammographic densities and breast cancer risk: results from the Canadian national breast screening study. Journal of the National Cancer Institute 87, 670–675 (1995)
6. American College of Radiology. Breast Imaging Reporting and Data System BIRADS, 4th edn. American College of Radiology, Reston (2004)
7. Boyd, N.F., Martin, L.J., Yaffe, M.J., Minkin, S.: Mammographic density and breast cancer risk: current understanding and future prospects. Breast Cancer Research 13(6), 223–235 (2011)
8. Sickles, E.A.: Wolfe mammographic parenchymal patterns and breast cancer risk. American Journal of Roentgenology 188(2), 301–303 (2007)
9. Baker, J.A., Rosen, E.L., Crockett, M.M., Lo, J.Y.: Accuracy of segmentation of a commer-cial computer-aided detection system for mammography. Radiology 235(2), 385–390 (2005)
10. Ojala, T., Pietikainen, M., Maenpaa, T.: Multiresolution gray-scale and rotation invariant texture classification with local binary patterns. IEEE Transactions on Pattern Analysis and Machine Intelligence 24(7), 971–987 (2002)
11. Ursin, G., Astrahan, M.A., Salane, M., Parisky, Y.R., Pearce, J.G., Daniels, J.R., Pike, M.C., Spicer, D.V.: The detection of changes in mammographic densities. Cancer Epidemiol Biomarkers Prev 7, 43–47 (1998)
12. Gram, I.T., Bremnes, Y., Ursin, G., Maskarinec, G., Bjurstam, N., Lund, E.: Percentage den-sity, Wolfe's and Tabár's mammographic patterns: agreement and association with risk fac-tors for breast cancer. Breast Cancer Research 7(5), R61–R845 (2005)
13. Witten, I.H., Frank, E., Hall, M.A.: Data Mining: Practical machine learning tools and tech-niques, 3rd edn. Morgan Kaufmann, San Francisco (2011)
14. He, W., Denton, E.R.E.: Mammographic Parenchymal Pattern Segmentation: A Clinical Evaluation. In: 10th IEEE International Conference on Information Technology and Appli-cations in Biomedicine, pp. 1–4 (2010)
15. Lobbes, M.B.I., Cleutjens, J.P.M., Lima Passos, V., Frotscher, C., Lahaye, M.J., Keymeulen, K.B.M.I., Beets-Tan, R.G., Wildberger, J., Boetes, C.: Density is in the eye of the beholder: visual versus semi-automated assessment of breast density on standard mammograms. In-sights into Imaging 3(1), 91–99 (2012)

Color Transfer Based on Earth Mover's Distance and Color Categorization

Wenya Feng, Yilin Guo, Okhee Kim, Yonggan Hou, Long Liu, and Huiping Sun

School of Software and Microelectronics, Peking University, Beijing, China
{pkuwenyafeng,guoyilin1987,anniekim.pku,yghouforsec,
liul0x,hpsun}@gmail.com

Abstract. Color transfer aims at changing an original image's color theme to a target one while preserving the original image's geometric structure information. In recent studies of color transfer, there are mainly two flaws. The first one is that the original image can only transfer color with a certain type of target images. The second one is that the color transformation always brings artefacts, noises, and graininess which make the result images unnatural. In this paper, we present a novel variational-based model to solve the problems effectively. A variety of experiments and comparison with previous research have proved that this model perform perfect and robust outcome.

Keywords: Color Transfer, Variational Model, Earth Mover's Distance, Color Categorization.

1 Introduction

Color theme is a key factor to decide which category the image belongs to and it is also a significant feature used in a large number of applications in the field of image retrieval and pattern recognition etc. In addition, different color themes have different influence on observers'emotion [1]. However, manually editing the color composition of a natural image to a desired color theme may be tedious and labor-intensive, sometimes, a painful experience.

In this paper, we introduce a novel model to modify the color theme of a given image(original image) to match some desired color constraints(target image) while preserving its geometrical information as shown in Fig.1 left.

2 Related Work

Techniques in color transfer mainly include local color transfer and global color transfer.

Local color transfer is a regional color transfer between images by segmentation. Therefore these algorithms highly depend on the algorithms of image segmentation. [5][6] used an Expectation Maximization scheme and soft segments respectively; [7-9] proposed some approaches offer stroke-based controls;[10] used

R. Wilson et al. (Eds.): CAIP 2013, Part II, LNCS 8048, pp. 394–401, 2013.
© Springer-Verlag Berlin Heidelberg 2013

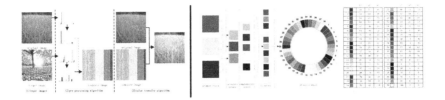

Fig. 1. Left: Overall workflow of our framework: (1) Inputs an original image and a target image; (2) performs pre-processing algorithm for each image; (3) Transfer color theme between the original image and the template image. **Right:** Color wheel and experimental results in the $L^*a^*b^*$ color space

masks to define regions. Although local color transfer methods have had lots of feasible results, they have most of the image segmentation algorithms'limitation.

In contrast, global color transfer takes into account all pixels of images instead of some pixels in corresponding regions.[11] first introduced global color transfer; [12-13] introduced some color (probability density function)pdf transfer, but they can only transfer color between similar images(the aforementioned first flaw); [14] proposed an Earth Mover's Distance method; [15] used a variational model to exchange image's chromatic composition, but they don't consider the distinct color proportion by which may lead to unnatural results when color transfer between very different type of images.

3 Pre-processing Algorithm

Colors can be divided into 3 main categories: primary colors, secondary colors and complementary colors as shown in Fig.1 right. The mixture of primary colors gets secondary colors. Complementary colors are pink, brown, black, grey and white. So, an 11-colors schema [2-3] can be generated by the 3 types of color. In addition, each hue, except white and black, has four shades. So, this generates a 38-color color wheel, a color wheel is an abstract illustrative circle of color hues. Each color of the 38 colors is obtained through experiments and we describe it in Fig.1 right. Because of the quantification of colors, each pixel can be labeled by a color number (1-38).

3.1 Definition of Color Distance and Calculating Color Proportion

Based on the $L^*a^*b^*$ color space's special properties that L component closely matches the human perception's lightness, a and b components are only related to chromatic representation[4]. So we can propose a distance to measure the disparity between colors from the point of human visual perception. For example, the distance between pixel i and pixel j in image o is formulated as follows:

$$
\begin{aligned}
D(o_i, o_j) &= \sqrt{|o_i(L) - o_j(L)| + \|o_i(a,b) - o_j(a,b)\|_2} \\
&= \sqrt{|o_i(L) - o_j(L)| + \sqrt{(o_i(a) - o_j(a))^2 + (o_i(b) - o_j(b))^2}}
\end{aligned}
\tag{1}
$$

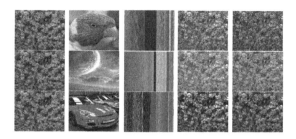

Fig. 2. The first column is the original image; the second column indicates different kind of target images; the third column is their template images; the fourth column is the result images transferred from the target images; the last column is the result images transferred from template images

The original image in the *Lab* color space define as $o : o_i = \left(o_i(L), o_i(a),\right.$ $\left.o_i(b)\right)^T$, $i, j \in \Omega \subset \mathbb{Z}^2$ denotes the spatial domain, $o_i \in \Gamma \subset \mathbb{R}^3$ denotes a discrete color image. $\|.\|_2$ is the Euclidean norm, the weight of L channel is reduced compare with a, b channels, therefore the distance between similar chromatic colors with different luminance is decreased. So similar colors are assigned to same categorization even they have different luminance.

With the above distance and the experiment results in Fig.1 right, each pixel can be assigned to a closest color label . By means of the labels, we first generate an image's 38 bins histogram and then merge it to an 11 bins histogram(Fig.1 left (2)). This results in more precise calculation of color proportion compare with directly generate an 11 bins histogram without the mergence process(Fig.3 middle). The left part of Fig.3 shows the merged 11 bins histogram can be achieved simply by summing up its corresponding bins in 38 bins histogram. It is the merged 11 bins histogram that clearly indicates the color proportion. We use a color proportion bar to show the results in Fig.3 right.

3.2 Template Image

With both of the original image and the target image's color proportion, we can design a template image (Fig.1 left (2)). The template image is used for replacing the target image to transfer color with the original image and it makes the original image transfer color with all types of images possible (Fig.2). The template image has same type of colors of the target image however with original image's proportion: First, we sort images by color frequency, then adjusting target image 's color composition according to the original image's proportion by adding or deleting its colors.

4   Color Transfer Algorithm

After the pre-processing algorithm, we get the template image. By means of it, our algorithm has ability to solve the first aforementioned flaw. First of all, we

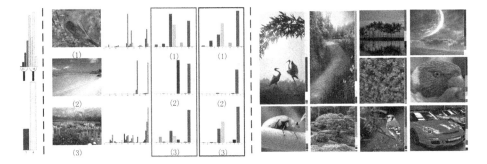

Fig. 3. Left: to merger 11 bins to 38 bins histogram. **Middle:** a comparison of merged 11 bins histogram with direct 11 bins histogram; The red rectangle and the blue rectangle represent the merged histogram and the direct histogram respectively. **Right:** each color bar on the right of the image indicates the image's color proportion.

define the original image as o, the template image as p, the intermediate image from o to p as r, the final result image as r^*. The overall variational-based model described below:

$$r^* = arg \min_{r \in \mathbb{R}^3} \{\lambda_f F(r, o) + \lambda_s E(r, p) + R(r, o)\} \tag{2}$$

Where F is a fidelity term aim to preserve image r's texture structure according to original image; E is a penalty term aim to change r's color to template image; R is a regularization term used for solve artefacts, graininess and noise problems as the second aforementioned flaw. We use the gradient descent algorithm to find the minimum of Eq(2), in the process of iteration the final result image r^* will be got.

4.1 The Fidelity Term

We use the generic Euclidean norm to devise our fidelity term, the definition and its derivative formula introduced as follows:

$$F(r, o) = \sum_i \frac{1}{2} \|r_i - o_i\|^2 \tag{3}$$

$$\frac{\partial F(r, o)}{\partial_r} = \sum_i (r_i - o_i) \tag{4}$$

4.2 The Penalty Term

Earth Mover's Distance [14] is a common measure of the distance between two probability distributions. But when we apply it to colorful image's transfer, a clear shortcoming is EMD cannot measure the distance between the 3-dimensional (e.g. R,G,B; L,a,b etc.) colorful images. In addition, most of optimization approaches

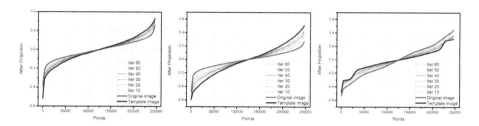

Fig. 4. These three pictures represent that in the iteration process the original image becomes closer to the template image which means the penalty term becomes smaller and smaller. The three cases(size:500x500) come from Fig.1, the first row of Fig.3 and the second row of Fig.5, totally three different color transfer cases.

are proposed for 1-dimensional statistics. So we need to project 3D image to 1D image in which EMD can be embedded. We make use of the Spherical Coordinate System to get an approximate 1D EMD of colorful image.

$$E(r,p) = \frac{1}{2|\Phi|} \sum_{\theta \in \Phi} \min_{\varphi \in \Sigma(\Omega)} \sum_{l \in \Omega} |< r_l, \theta > - < p_{\varphi_\theta(l)}, \theta >|^2 \qquad (5)$$

Where θ is a unit sphere vector from the set Φ that includes unit vectors of 14 different directions, $|\Phi|$ represents the number of vectors, $\langle ., \theta \rangle$ is the Euclidean scalar product. Eq(5) can be explained as follow: 1. Calculating scalar product of each element of image r and p by θ, after that, r and p are converted to 1D image. 2. Sorting the 1D r and p in same order. 3. Sorted r subtract sorted p, then divide 2 times the number of vectors. If θ is formulated like (x,y,z), we post classical Spherical Coordinate System as follow with a substitution $\tilde{\theta}$ in order to discriminate above θ.

$$\begin{cases} x = r \sin \tilde{\theta} \cos \phi \\ y = r \sin \tilde{\theta} \sin \phi \\ z = r \cos \tilde{\theta} \end{cases} \qquad (6)$$

when r=1; $\tilde{\theta} \in \{o, \pi\}$ with $\forall \phi$, gets 2 vectors; $\tilde{\theta} = \frac{\pi}{4}$ with $\phi \in \{\frac{\pi}{4}, \frac{3\pi}{4}, \frac{5\pi}{4}, \frac{7\pi}{4}\}$, gets 4 vectors; $\tilde{\theta} = \frac{\pi}{2}$ with $\phi \in \{0, \frac{\pi}{2}, \pi, \frac{3\pi}{2}\}$, gets 4 vectors; $\tilde{\theta} = \frac{3\pi}{4}$ with $\phi \in \{\frac{\pi}{4}, \frac{3\pi}{4}, \frac{5\pi}{4}, \frac{7\pi}{4}\}$, gets 4 vectors; totally 14 vectors available. Fig.4 shows that each curve represents an 1D image(rang from [-1,+1]) whose element is the scalar product of the spherical coordinate vector and the 3D world image; and because of the penalty term, original image gradually close to template image after iterations.

Since we use the gradient descend algorithm to calculate minimum of Eq(2), we need achieve the derivative of this penalty term with respect to r.

$$\frac{\partial E(r,p)}{\partial r_l} = \frac{1}{|\Phi|} \sum_{\theta \in \Phi} (< r_l, \theta > - < p_{\varphi_*^\theta(l)}, \theta >)\theta \qquad (7)$$

4.3   The Regularization Term

Almost all color transfer algorithms bring some level of grain, artefacts and noise etc. The regularization term is necessary for perfectly solving the second aforementioned flaw. The regularization term used to reduce the grain noise and it forces the noise level to be similar by adjusting the gradient field of the intermediate image r to match the gradient filed of the original image o. If the original image and the result image have similar gradient field, the noise should be disappear [12]. The regularization term can be shown as follow:

$$R(r, o) = \frac{1}{2} \sum_i || \nabla r_i - \nabla o_i || \tag{8}$$

The derivative of R is hard to get, we use an auxiliary variable method to deal with the problem in the gradient descent scheme below.

4.4   Gradient Descent Scheme

Because the regularization term is very hard to calculate, we need to introduce an auxiliary variable z_i with the constrain that $z_i = r_i$, then Eq(2) can be rewritten as:

$$(r^*, z^*) = arg \min_{r,z} \left\{ \lambda_f F(r, o) + \lambda_s E(r, p) + \frac{1}{2} \sum_i || \nabla z_i - \nabla o_i ||^2 \right\} \quad s.t. \ z_i = r_i \tag{9}$$

We add an additional term in order to r can be got by the alternating optimization iteration. Eq(9) is equivalent to the following equation:

$$(r^*, z^*) = arg \min_{r,z} \left\{ \lambda_f F(r, o) + \lambda_s E(r, p) + \frac{1}{2} \sum_i || \nabla z_i - \nabla o_i ||^2 \right.$$
$$\left. + \frac{\lambda_p}{2} \sum_i || z_i - r_i ||^2 \right\} \tag{10}$$

We set the iteration number $k = 0$ and $r^{(0)} = z^{(0)} = o$, then the iteration schema can be shown as follow:

$$\begin{cases} r^{(k+1)} = arg \min_r \left\{ \lambda_f F(r^{(k)}, o) + \lambda_s E(r^{(k)}, p) + \frac{\lambda_p}{2} \sum_i || z_i^{(k)} - r_i^{(k)} ||^2 \right\} \\ z^{(k+1)} = arg \min_z \left\{ \frac{1}{2} \sum_i || \nabla z_i^{(k)} - \nabla o_i || + \frac{\lambda_p}{2} \sum_i || z_i^{(k)} - r_i^{(k)} ||^2 \right\} \\ k = k + 1 \end{cases} \tag{11}$$

We make use of the gradient descent algorithm to optimize above equation. In the process of iteration, r and z can be expressed as follow:

$$\begin{cases} r^{(k+1)} = r^{(k)} - \tau \left\{ \lambda_f \frac{\partial F}{\partial r} + \lambda_s \frac{\partial E}{\partial r} - \lambda_p (r - z) \right\} \\ z^{(k+1)} = z^{(k)} - \tau \left\{ \lambda_p (z - r) \right\} \\ k = k + 1 \end{cases} \tag{12}$$

Fig. 5. Top two rows:the first column is the original images; the second column indicates target images; the third column is the results of Rabin's algorithm; the last column is ours. **Bottom seven rows:** other results of our algorithm.

τ is the gradient descent step. With the forward progress of the algorithm, we can get a series of r, z. for example, $r^{(0)}, z^{(0)}, r^{(1)}, z^{(1)}, r^{(2)}, z^{(2)}$. When $k \to +\infty$, we can get the final result image $r^*(z^*)$.

5   Results, Evaluation and Conclusion

We have carried out many experiments with different kind of original images and target images and compared with Rabin[15]'s color transfer algorithm in Fig.5. This algorithm is designed for solving two common flaws in color transfer algorithm. By means of template image, we solve the first flaw; and by means of the gradient based regularization term, the second flaw can be perfect solved. The result images show that our algorithm can transfer color between various kinds of images and effectively solve the graininess, noise problem at same time.

References

1. Ou, L.C., Luo, M.R., Woodcock, A., Wright, A.: A study of colour emotion and colour preference. Color Research and Application 29(3), 232–240 (2004)
2. Berlin, B., Kay, P.: Basic Color Terms: Their Universality and Evolution. University of California Press, Berkeley (1969)
3. Chang, Y., Uchikawa, K., Saito, S.: Example-based color stylization based on categorical perception. In: Proceedings of the 1st Symposium on Applied Perception in Graphics and Visualization, APGV 2004, pp. 91–98 (2004)
4. Aliaga, D.G., Law, A.J., Yeung, Y.H.: A virtual restoration stage for real-world objects. ACM Transactions on Graphics, TOG 27(5) (December 2008)
5. Tai, Y.-W., Tang, C.-K., Jia, J.: Local color transfer via probabilistic segmentation by expectation-maximization. In: IEEE Computer Society Conference on Computer Vision and Pattern Recognition, CVPR 2005, pp. 747–754 (2005)
6. Wang, B., Yu, Y., Wong, T.-T., Chen, C., Xu, Y.Q.: Data-driven image color theme enhancement. ACM Transactions on Graphics, TOG 29(6) (December 2010)
7. Levin, A., Lischinski, D., Weiss, Y.: Colorization using optimization. ACM Transactions on Graphics (TOG)- Proceedings of ACM SIGGRAPH 2004 23(3), 689–694 (2004)
8. Wen, C.-L., Hsieh, C.-H., Chen, B.-Y., Ouhyoung, M.: Example-based multiple local color transfer by strokes. Computer Graphics Forum 27(7), 1765–1772 (2008)
9. An, X., Pellacini, F.: User-controllable color transfer. Computer Graphics Forum 29(2), 263–271 (2010)
10. Pouli, T., Reinhard, E.: Progressive histogram reshaping for creative color transfer and tone reproduction. In: Proceeding NPAR 2010 Proceedings of the 8th International Symposium on Non-Photorealistic Animation and Rendering, pp. 81–90 (2010)
11. Reinhard, E., Adhikhmin, M., Gooch, B., Shirley, P.: Color transfer between images. IEEE Computer Graphics and Applications 21(5), 34–41 (2001)
12. Pitie, F., Kokaram, A.C., Dahyot, R.: Automated colour grading using colourdistributiontransfer. Computer Vision and Image Understanding 102(1-2), 123–137 (2007)
13. Pitie, F., Kokaram, A.C., Dahyot, R.: N-dimensional probability density function transfer and its application to color transfer. In: Tenth IEEE International Conference on Computer Vision, ICCV 2005, pp. 1434–1439 (2005)
14. Rubner, Y., Tomasi, C., Guibas, L.J.: The earth movers distance as a metric for image retrieval. International Journal of Computer Vision 40(2), 99–121 (2000)
15. Rabin, J., Peyre, G.: Wasserstein regularization of imaging problem. In: 2011 18th IEEE International Conference on Image Processing (ICIP), pp. 1541–1544 (September 2011)

Empirical Comparison of Visual Descriptors for Multiple Bleeding Spots Recognition in Wireless Capsule Endoscopy Video

Sarah Alotaibi, Sahar Qasim, Ouiem Bchir, and Mohamed Maher Ben Ismail

College of Computer and Information Sciences,
King Saud University
Saudi Arabia

Abstract. Wireless Capsule Endoscopy (WCE) is the latest technology able to screen intestinal anomalies at early stage. Although its convenience to the patient and its effectiveness to show small intestinal details, the physician diagnosis remains not straight forward and time consuming. Thus, a computer aid diagnosis would be helpful. In this paper, we focus on The Multiple Bleeding Spots (MBS) anomaly. We propose to conduct an empirical evaluation of four feature descriptors in a the challenging problem of MBS recognition on WCE video using the SVM classifier. The performance of the four descriptors is based on the assessment of the performance of the output of the SVM classifier.

Keywords: Wireless Capsule Endoscopy, Feature descriptors, SVM, Multiple Bleeding Spots.

1 Introduction

Gastro diseases is now a significant threat to millions of people. Many Gastro diseases can be treated by early detection. The conventional methods of diagnosis like CT scan, endoscopy and X-ray, have different defects such as inconvenience for patients, and invasiveness. During the last decade, wireless capsule endoscopy (WCE) has been widely used to diagnosis gastrointestinal diseases. WCE is convenient, allow seeing the small intestine without sedation, pain or air insufflations [1]. Moreover, this technique helps physicians to find the source of the unknown intestinal bleeding. The size of the capsule endoscopy is 26 mm x11 mm and it includes a micro camera, battery, source of light and a radio transmitter [1]. The patient ingests the WCE after fast for about 8 to 24 hours with a small amount of water [1]. Then, the capsule starts to capture the images during moving forward over the gastrointestinal tract. Simultaneously, the captured video is wirelessly emitted to a receiver attached to the patient. The whole process lasts up to eight hours. Thereafter, the captured video is downloaded to the computer, and the physician examines it and analyzes the state of gastrointestinal tract. WCE generates about 60,000 images per patient. It takes about two hours for an experienced physician to analyze the video [1]. This disadvantage reduce the

R. Wilson et al. (Eds.): CAIP 2013, Part II, LNCS 8048, pp. 402–407, 2013.

promotion of this newly appearing technique. As a result, WCE video analysis becomes an active filed of research. Recently, several studies have been achieved to enhance the display quality [2], identify suspicious images showing certain anomaly symptoms [3,4,5], and isolate useless frames [6,7]. Some efforts to detect red bleeding region (figure 1(b)) and ulcer region (figure 1(d)) using WCE images have been made. P. Khun et al [8] explored the performance of color and texture features in red bleeding detection. B. Li et al. [9] proposed a new method using multi-scale texture features to distinguish between red bleeding, ulcer and tumor diseases of the GI tract. In order to detect ulcer anomaly, L. Yu et al. [10] proposed an approach based on bag-of-words model and feature fusion technique. Y. Lee et al. [11] developed a method that detects bleeding spots images by using statistical features.

To the best of our knowledge there is no research or studies addressing multiple bleeding spots. Multiple bleeding spots appear in WCE as a set of small light points as shown in (figure 1 (a)). Due to the visual characteristics of these abnormally and it's similarity to the intestinal bubbles (figure 1 (e)), the recognition of the multiple bleeding spots is challenging. Moreover, the multiple bleeding spots are different from the intestinal bleeding (figure 1 (b)) which is characterized by its red color. Besides, the red bleeding has different shape and texture from the MBS anomaly. Thus, feature descriptors that are proved to recognize red bleeding may not be effective to recognize MBS.

In this paper, we propose to conduct a study that aims to find a suitable feature descriptor that can efficiently discriminate between normal WCE frames and those containing MBS anomaly. Namely, we will compare the HSV Color moment [12], the 2D wavelet descriptors [13], the Gabor filter descriptor[14], and the Edge histogram [15]. The comparison is based on the assessment of the performance of the SVM classifier [16].

2   Feature Extraction

Feature descriptors play a key role in pattern recognition. In fact, they allow a mapping from visual information (e.g the physical image) to a numerical vector in such away that it reflects the semantic content of the images (color, texture, shape etc..). Several Feature descriptors have been cited in the literature [17]. Some of them are generic, such MPEG 7 feature descriptors [15], and can be used with any data. Others are designed for a specific application. In all cases, the feature descriptor is supposed to capture the visual characteristics of the pattern to recognize. In [18], the authors presented an empirical measurement of the potential of some visual MPEG-7 descriptors for blood and ulcers detection on WCE video. Their experiments showed that the best results are obtained by the Scalable Color [15] and Homogenous Texture descriptors [15]. The paper [19] addresses the problem of tumor recognition for WCE images by using color texture feature and wavelet.

In the considered problem of MBS detection, the anomaly appears as a set of small light circles in the video frame. This is the rational behind the use of a color feature (e.g the HSV color histogram [12]), a texture feature able to

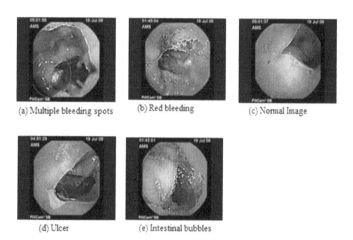

(a) Multiple bleeding spots   (b) Red bleeding   (c) Normal Image

(d) Ulcer   (e) Intestinal bubbles

Fig. 1. WCE frame snapshots. (a) frame with multiple bleeding spots anomaly, (b) Frame with red bleeding anomaly, (c) normal image, (d) frame with Ulcer anomaly, (e) frame with intestinal bubbles.

reveal small details (e.g. Discrete Wavelet Transform [13]), a frequency texture filter (e.g Gabor filter descriptor[14]), and an edge descriptor (e.g edge histogram descriptor (EHD) [15]). These features are chosen because they are judged to be promising at detecting the MBS according to this anomaly visual characteristics. In the following, we outline the previously mentioned feature descriptors that we intend to compare in this paper.

2.1   HSV Color Moment

Each region is mapped to the HSV color space [12]. The mean, standard deviation and distribution skewness of the H, S, and V components are computed. The feature subset is represented by a 9-dimensional vector.

2.2   Discrete Wavelet Transform

Discrete Wavelet Transform (DWT) [13] decomposes a digital image into four sub-bands of different frequencies. The four sub-bands are commonly referred as LL, HL, LH and HH, and they have size equal to half size of original image. DWT is applied on RGB color channels. The DWT feature descriptor is the concatenation of the HL, LH and HH components.

2.3   Gabor Filter

A 2D Gabor filter is a Gaussian kernel function modulated by a sinusoidal envelope. A set of Gabor filters with different frequencies and orientations can be used for extracting useful features from an image [14]. It consists of convolving the image with Gabor filters with different spatial frequencies and different orientations with respect to each frequency. We used 6 different orientation and 4 different frequencies on each direction resulting in a 96 feature vector.

2.4   Edge Histogram Descriptor

An MPEG-7 edge histogram descriptor (EHD) [15] is used to represent the frequency and directionality of edges within each image region. First, simple edge detector operator are used to detect edges and group into five categories: vertical, horizontal, diagonal, anti-diagonal and non edge. Then, local, global, and semi-local edge histograms are generated. The EHD feature is represented by a 150-dim vector.

3   Experiments

The purpose of this study is to find suitable feature descriptors that allow to discriminate between normal WCE video frames and those containing MBS anomaly. We conduct our experiment on a capsule endoscopic video that was collected using Imaging pillCam® SB [20]. The frames collection is generated from this video. The size of each resulting frame is 480×360. The set of frames include 230 images of MBS anomaly and 461 images of non MBS anomaly.

The feature descriptors outlined in section 2, are extracted from all frames. We use each feature independently as input to the SVM classifier [16]. In fact, we use the performance of the SVM classifier as assessment of the performance of the different features. The 5-fold cross validation method is performed with respect to each filter. The evaluation of the classification performance with respect to each feature is based on the obtained ROC curves [22] and the AUC (area under ROC curve [23]).

Table 1 shows the recognition results of multiple bleeding spots detection using the considered features descriptors. The best AUC (0.812) is obtained using the Color Moment. The DWT comes slightly behind with AUC equal to 0.788. The Gabor feature descriptor and the EHD descriptors do not perform well for MBS detection. This can be explained by the fact that these two feature descriptors take into account the spatial information while the multiple bleeding spots can appear at any location of the video frame.

Figure 2 displays the ROC curves obtained using SVM [16] with respect to each feature descriptor. It confirms the results showed in table 1. Moreover, we notice that while Color Moment performs better than DWT for false positive rate greater than 0.1, DWT performs better than Color Moment for False positive rate smaller than 0.1. However, for computer aid diagnosis systems , it is more important having high rate of true positive than having low false positive rate. This is because the physician can always discard the suggested non relevant frames. Trying to combine Color Moment and DWT does not enhance the performance of the classifier (refer to figure 2). This can be due to the high dimension of the obtained descriptor as the concatenation of DWT and Color moment descriptors. In fact, Euclidean distance measures in high dimensional space are measured across volume that increases exponentially as dimensionality increases, and points tend to become equidistant.

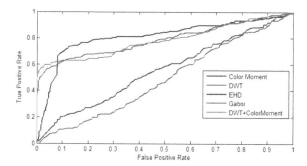

Fig. 2. ROC curves obtained using SVM with respect to each feature descriptor

Table 1. AUC measure obtained using SVM with respect to each feature descriptor

Feature descriptor	Color Moment	DWT	EHD	Gabor	DWT+Color Moment
AUC	0.812	0.788	0.557	0.490	0.7845

4   Conclusions

This paper focuses on the challenging task of MBS frame recognition on WCE video. This task is challenging because of MBS visual characteristics and the possibility to confuse them with intestinal bubble. We conducted an empirical study to compare 4 feature vectors that were judged promising for the detection of this anomaly. The experimental results showed that Color Moment is performing better than the other considered descriptors in this dataset. Trying to concatenate the Color Moment and the DWT descriptor does not enhance the result and give worse result than color moment on its own. This may be due to the curse of dimensionality. One way to overcome this limitation is to use simultaneous clustering and feature weighting [21] to summarize the large set of training samples by few representative prototypes. Each prototype would be a cluster that is identified by the clustering approach and would have its own learned feature weight. This region dependent features would be explored by the classifier to improve its accuracy.

References

1. Gerber, J., Bergwerk, A., Fleischer, D.: Gastrointestinal Endoscopy, vol. 66, pp. 1188–1195 (2007)
2. Li, B., Meng, M.-H.: Wireless capsule endoscopy images enhancement using contrast driven forward and backward anisotropic diffusion. In: IEEE International Conference on Image Processing, ICIP 2007, vol. 2, pp. II–437 (2007)
3. Miaou, S., Chang, F., Timotius, I., Huang, H.: A Multi-stage Recognition System to Detect Different Types of Abnormality in Capsule Endoscope Images. Journal of Medical and Biological Engineering 29, 114–121 (2009)

4. Mewes, P.W., Rennert, P., Juloski, A.L., Lalande, A., Angelopoulou, E., Kuth, R., Hornegger, J.: Semantic and topological classification of images in magnetically guided capsule endoscopy. In: SPIE Medical Imaging, p. 83151A (2012)
5. Kodogiannis, V., Lygouras, J.N.: Neuro-fuzzy classification system for wireless-capsule endoscopic images. Int. J. Electr. Comput. Syst. Eng. 2, 55–63 (2008)
6. Bashar, M., Kitasaka, T., Suenaga, Y., Mekada, Y., Mori, K.: Automatic Detection of Informative Frames from Wireless Capsule Endoscopy Images. In: Medical Image Analysis, vol. 14, pp. 449–470 (2010)
7. Suykens, J., Vandewalle, J.: Least Squares Support Vector Machine Classifiers. In: Neural Processing Letters, 9th edn., pp. 293–300 (1999)
8. Khun, P.C., Zhuo, Z., Yang, L.Z., Liyuan, L., Jiang, L.: Feature selection and classification for wireless capsule endoscopic frames. In: International Conference on Biomedical and Pharmaceutical Engineering, ICBPE 2009, pp. 1–6 (2009)
9. References, B., Li, M.: Capsule endoscopy images classification by color texture and support vector machine. In: 2010 IEEE International Conference on Automation and Logistics (ICAL), pp. 126–131 (2010)
10. References, L., Yu, P., Yuen, J.: Ulcer detection in wireless capsule endoscopy images. In: ICPR, pp. 45–48 (2012)
11. References, Y.-G.: Time Image Analysis of Capsule Endoscopy for Bleeding Discrimination in Embedded System Platform. International Journal of Biological and Life Sciences, World Academy of Science, Engineering and Technology 60, 1030–1034 (2011)
12. Stricker, M., Orengo, M.: Similarity of color image. In: SPIE Conference on Storage and Retrieval for Image and Video Databases III, vol. 2420, pp. 381–392 (February 1995)
13. Mallat, S.G.: A theory for multiresolution signal decomposition: the wavelet representation. IEEE Transactions on Pattern Analysis and Machine Intelligence 11(7), 674–693 (1989)
14. Jain, A.K., Ratha, N.K., Lakshmanan, S.: Object detection using Gabor filters. Pattern Recognition 30(2), 295–309 (1997)
15. Manjunath, B.S., Salembier, P., Sikora, T.: Introduction to MPEG 7: Multimedia content description language. John Wiley (2002)
16. Cortes, C., Vapnik, V.N.: Support-Vector Networks. Machine Learning 20 (1995)
17. Nixon, M.S., Aguado, A.S.: Feature Extraction and Image Processing for Computer Vision, 3rd edn (2012)
18. Coimbra, M.T., Cunha, J.P.S.: MPEG-7 Visual Descriptors—Contributions for Automated Feature Extraction in Capsule Endoscopy. Circuits and Systems for Video Technology 16, 628–637 (2006)
19. Baopu, L., Meng, M.Q.H.: Tumor Recognition in Wireless Capsule Endoscopy Images Using Textural Features and SVM-Based Feature Selection. Information Technology in Biomedicine 16, 323–329 (2012)
20. http://www.PillCam.com
21. Frigui, H., Nasraoui, O.: Unsupervised learning of prototypes and attribute weights. Pattern Recognition 37, 567–581 (2004)
22. Swets, J.A.: Signal detection theory and ROC analysis in psychology and diagnostics: collected papers. Lawrence Erlbaum Associates, Mahwah (1996)
23. Hastie, T., Tibshirani, R., Friedman, J.H.: The elements of statistical learning: data mining, inference, and prediction, 2nd edn (2009)

Exploring Interest Points and Local Descriptors for Word Spotting Application on Historical Handwriting Images

Peng Wang[1,2], Véronique Eglin[2], Christine Largeron[1],
Antony McKenna[3], and Christophe Garcia[2]

[1] Université Jean Monnet, LAHC, CNRS UMR 5516, 42023, Saint Etienne, France
[2] INSA de Lyon, LIRIS, CNRS UMR 5205, 69621, Villeurbanne, France
[3] Université Jean Monnet, IHPC, CNRS UMR 5037, 42023, Saint Etienne, France

Abstract. Recently, local features especially point descriptors have received lots of interest in the computer vision and image processing communities. SIFT and SURF descriptors have shown their powerful usefulness on natural object recognition and classification. However, the use of local descriptors such as SIFT and SURF is still not very common in handwritten document image analysis now. In this paper, we propose an investigation on the description of handwriting by applying different interest points and local descriptors on historical handwritten images in the context of a coarse-to-fine segmentation-free word spotting method. The observation and analysis based on the experimental results can help optimizing the description of handwriting according to different applications.

Keywords: word spotting, historical handwritten document, interest points, Shape Context, SIFT, SURF.

1 Introduction

As more and more libraries start to digitize their enormous amount of handwritten historical documents, the role of handwritten document image analysis becomes more and more important. Among all the applications in this domain, handwritten word spotting is one of the most popular and challenging, especially because traditional OCR techniques are unsuccessful when they are applied to handwriting offline documents, particularly historical ones.

Due to multi-source degradation, handwriting variances and large lexicons in unconstrained environments etc., word spotting on historical handwriting images faces more challenges and difficulties than normal document image analysis. To find a solution to it, many approaches have been proposed, which can be classified into two groups: one is dedicated to the detection of predefined words (associated to a training process, like the works presented in [1,2]), and the other one is retrieval-oriented with a matching scheme based on image sample comparison, which does not require any associated training process [3,4]. The investigation

R. Wilson et al. (Eds.): CAIP 2013, Part II, LNCS 8048, pp. 408–415, 2013.

on interest points and local descriptors in this paper is considered under the framework of a coarse-to-fine word spotting proposition, which belongs to the second group of methods.

Since the development of interest points and local descriptors has recently achieved a great success in the object recognition domain, people working on handwritten document images start to adapt these concepts to word spotting application. The first attempts have been made by Leydier et al. [4] and Rodríguez [5], both of whom use local gradients on dense grids as the description for handwriting characterization. Afterwards, local descriptors of a more complex version such as SIFT have been adopted in [6,7]. Even though SIFT features are still not commonly used in word spotting application, it is worth mentioning some works using related concepts for different applications. For instance, Garz and her group use SIFT features to realize layout analysis for historical manuscripts [8]. HOG features are applied by Newell et al. for robust character recognition [9]. Since the adaptation of SIFT/SURF descriptors in historical handwriting analysis is still in its early stage, until now, there is no specific statistical study on the performance of interest points and local descriptors for historical handwritten document analysis to the best of our knowledge.

In this paper[1], our dominant contribution aims at providing an experimental comparison of the efficiency and appropriateness of different interest points and local descriptors for word spotting on historical handwritten images, within a coarse-to-fine framework of segmentation-free method we developed before [10]. The rest of paper is organized as follows. Section 2 gives a brief introduction on the coarse-to-fine segmentation-free approach for word spotting. Section 3 is the discussion of the adaptation of interest points and local descriptors. The description of the dataset, the experimental protocols and the performance evaluation are presented in Section 4. Finally, the conclusion is drawn in Section 5.

2 A Coarse-to-Fine Word Spotting Solution

In this part, we present the overall scheme for a coarse-to-fine segmentation-free solution for word spotting. The selection of instances is based on the shape characterization with the definition of specific similarity measures. The workflow of the entire approach is shown in Fig.1.

Before any operation, we apply a smoothing filter on both the query and test images in order to remove noises. For test images, we segment the text into lines according to the projection profile combined with Hough transform in order to overcome the skew of text lines.

In the coarse representation step, we apply a sliding window with the same width of the query to scan each line in order to avoid the drawbacks of word segmentation. Four textural features, projection profile, upper border, lower border [3] and orientation distribution of skeleton pixels are extracted. The Dynamic Time Warping (DTW) method is used to calculate the local optimal distance for

---

[1] The research is supported by French Rhône-Alpes region program, CITERE ANR project.

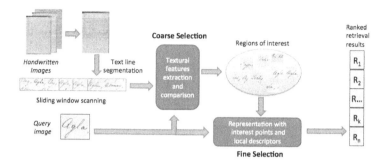

Fig. 1. A coarse-to-fine workflow for word spotting

the first three features and Chi-square for the orientation distribution. By setting an empirical threshold for the summed-up distance, regions of interest that are more similar to the query are selected for further comparison. In this way, the approach is more efficient compared to the method of directly extracting and comparing local descriptors all over the test image.

In the fine representation step, we intend to design a more concrete and specific representation model for handwriting. In [10], the entire description for handwritten text is composed of four parts: Shape Context description, loops, ascenders/descenders, and textural properties. Since the purpose of this paper is to explore interest points and local descriptors for handwriting analysis and recognition, instead of employing all components, we only focus on the description made by using different interest points and local descriptors.

3 Interest Point and Local Descriptor Investigation

To explore suitable and effective interest points and local descriptors for the information retrieval on historical handwritten document images, we apply different local descriptors for depicting the information at interest point locations. Depending on the nature of the considered descriptor, the local characterization can be restricted to a small neighborhood or based on a large amount of information in the scope of the entire shape.

3.1 Interest Points

For interest point detection, we test respectively structural points, DoG (Difference of Gaussian) [14] points and Hessian [15] points. Since DoG and Hessian detectors have been widely used, we do not describe them here. Instead, we give more explanation for structural points, which is specific to handwriting applications. Three types of points are identified as structural points. They are respectively starting/ending points, branch points and high-curved points as illustrated in Fig.2. For each skeleton pixel, we apply a 3x3 mask to check the nearest 8 neighbors of the pixel. If there is only one black pixel among the 8 neighbors, the reference pixel is considered as a starting/ending point. For branch points, we employ the Hit&Miss transformation, a basic binary morphological operation, which is generally used to detect particular patterns in a binary image. To detect high-curved points, we use the method applied in [11], which estimates the curve by using the angle between two local vectors both starting from the reference pixel, instead of calculating the curvature extreme.

It is obvious that the main difference among structural points and DoG, Hessian points is the amount. For the same sample, the number of structural points is much less than DoG and Hessian points, even after we eliminate some artificial DoG and Hessian points caused by noise. Another observation is that for different instances of the same word, the stability of structural points is higher than the other two kinds of points. The reason is that the structural point detection is completely based on the natural configuration of characters. The most variant factor for structural point detection is writing style. Otherwise, locations of points are consistent. Since DoG and Hessian points are identified upon the gradient variation, the detection is relatively random in terms of a single point. Besides, in the context of historical handwriting images, many factors can cause gradient variations, such as degraded ink trace, dirty spots and so on.

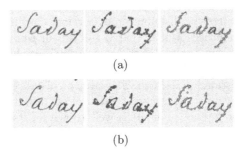

(a)

(b)

Fig. 2. (a),(b) are the interest point detection on two instances of the same word. 1st col.: structural points; 2nd col.: DoG points; 3rd col.: Hessian points.

Fig.3 presents how the point detection changes as the degradation of images increases. It can be seen that as the image becomes more degraded, the amounts of DoG points and Hessian points are sharply decreased, while the amount of structural points still keeps equivalent. The last column in Fig.3 gives an interesting result, which illustrates that structural points are actually the most stable part in DoG and Hessian points. Besides the visual observation, we also calculate the repeatability rate for each detection to have a quantitive inspection. The repeatability rate is defined as the number of points repeated between two images with respect to the total number of detected points [16]. For the case in Fig.2, the repeatabilities are $R_{structural}=80\%$, $R_{DoG}=65.71\%$ and $R_{Hessian}=72.73\%$, respectively.

Fig. 3. The point detection as the degradation increases: 1st row: structural point detection; 2nd row: DoG point detection; 3rd row: Hessian point detection. The extent of degradation increases from left to right.

3.2 Local Descriptors

For the local description part, Shape Context(SC) [12], Scale Invariant Feature Transform(SIFT) [14] and Speed Up Robust Features(SURF) [15] are selected. SC is a classic descriptor which has been widely used for document image recognition and analysis, while SIFT and SURF as popular descriptors in object recognition, have not been fully explored in handwritten document domain.

SC descriptor captures the distribution over relative positions of other shape points and thus summarizes global shape. Instead of calculating SC descriptors on the down-sampling points of the contour[12], we choose to use interest points as reference points and only use the outer contour points to calculate the descriptor. The χ^2 distance is used to calculate the distance between points.

SIFT descriptor records the gradient orientation distribution of the 16x16 neighborhood of the reference point. It is well known for its scale-invariant and rotation-invariant characteristics with the cost of expensive computation. To find matching points, Euclidean distance is used to calculate the distance between descriptors. SURF is an approximate version of SIFT. The difference is that SURF adopts integral images and calculate Harr wavelet instead of orientation histogram, which makes SURF more computationally efficient than SIFT. It also uses Euclidean distance to compare descriptors.

To study the performance of different descriptors, we use the same points with different descriptors to compare two images. Fig. 4 shows there are much more matching errors with SURF than SC and SIFT.

Similarity measure. After obtaining the local description generated by different descriptors, a process to eliminate the false correspondences of points is applied. We measure the similarity between images based on different cost functions. We consider a query image P and a test image Q respectively with m descriptors and n descriptors. The similarity cost based on the SC description is calculated in Eq.1 as in [9].

$$D_{SC}(P,Q) = \frac{1}{n} \sum_{p \in P} arg \min_{q \in Q} C(p, T(q)) + \frac{1}{m} \sum_{q \in Q} arg \min_{p \in P} C(p, T(q)) . \quad (1)$$

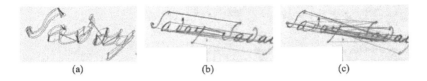

(a)   (b)   (c)

Fig. 4. Matching examples using different descriptors with structural points: (a)SC, (b)SIFT, (c)SURF

For SIFT and SURF descriptions, we sum up all the distances between corresponding points in terms of query image P as given in Eq.2.

$$D_{SIFT/SURF}(P, Q) = \sum_{p \in P} arg \min_{q \in Q} C(p, q) \ . \tag{2}$$

4   Experiments

The purpose of the experiments presented in this section is to test the performance of different combination of point detectors and local descriptors. Based on the observation and analysis of the experiment results, the discussion and conclusion are made.

We conduct the experiments on a dataset extracted from the humanity corpus containing more than 200,000 letters written by different French philosophers. Our dataset contains 4 collections of different writing styles. There are 11 pages containing approximately 2000 words. From all the word classes (a class is a set of the same word instances) in the dataset, we select a subset of 9 classes. Since the dataset consists of realistic historical letters, the number of samples per class varies from 2 to 12. Each sample in the classes is used as a query and this makes a total of 51 queries.

The evaluation protocol is the following: for each query, we rank all the regions of interest that are selected from the coarse representation. A region is classified as positive if it overlaps more than 30% with the annotated bounding box in the ground truth and negative otherwise. We combine the retrieved regions of all the documents and rerank them according to their scores. For each word class, we report the Average Precision (AP) and Average Recall (AR) for 5 ranks (rank 3, rank 5, rank 10, rank 20 and rank 30), which are standard measures in retrieval systems. Overall results (Fig.5) are evaluated by computing the mean Average Precision (mAP) and the mean Average Recall (mAR) over the 9 classes.

If we exclude the influence of interest points and only focus on the local descriptors, the results show that SC gives the best performance among three descriptors for all kinds of interest points. Compared to SIFT and SURF, SC is built on a relatively broader region, which relatively encodes the spatial information in terms of the entire image. SIFT and SURF descriptors only focus on locally spatial information (within the patch), which becomes a clear disadvantage. Marçal's work[6] has also proved the necessity of using the spatial

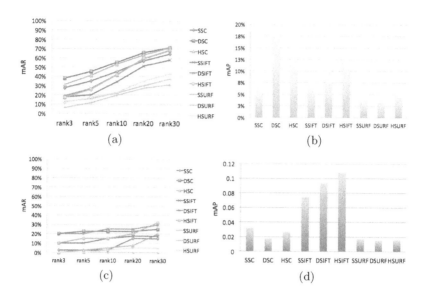

Fig. 5. (a)(b) Overall result of mAR and mAP (c)(d) results of the queries "c'est" in collection 2.(SSC(Structural points+SC), DSC(DoG points+SC), HSC(Hessian points+SC), SSIFT(Structural points+SIFT), DSIFT(DoG points+SIFT), HSIFT(Hessian points+SIFT), SSURF(Structural points+SURF), DSURFT(DoG points+SURF), HSURF(Hessian points+SURF))

distribution of features by applying SPM(Spatial Pyramid Matching) method. Overall speaking, SC is a very powerful descriptor for handwriting regardless to the selection of points. Fig.5 gives an average distribution of scores based on all word classes of different writing styles. However, the results show that the performance is quite writing-style dependent. For the compact and solid handwriting styles without any elongations, it has been observed that DOG or Hessian points associated to SIFT descriptors are more efficient. One example is given in Fig.5. In this case, contextual information carried in SC does not help much the retrieval because the distinguishability of information is sharply reduced. For the cursive handwriting style, SC based on structural points(SSC) can produce a more relevant description because a good space occupancy associated with a distinguishing shape is one necessary condition to the application of SSC. Moreover, the relevance between precision and recall for each combination shows that depending on the category of the query and the category of the writer, it is meaningful to select the method that gives individually the best performance. These results show that interest points carry very distinctive information. When the data is poor, interest points must be numerous and even redundant. On the other side, when the data is abundant, it is efficient to consider structural points that simplify the representation and the overall computation cost.

5   Conclusion

The study of historical handwritten document images is quite different and specific compared to the study of other types of images. Finding an appropriate description for handwriting characterization is very crucial for the analysis and recognition of handwriting. The results obtained from our experiments illustrate that Shape Context is a very efficient descriptor for handwriting images. Besides, interest point extraction also influences a lot the performance of the retrieval depending on the size of the query word. In the fine selection step of our proposed scheme, the mechanism for obtaining an improved recall is to select the most suitable combination of point detector and descriptor.

References

1. Andreas, F., Andreas, K., Volkmar, F., Horst, B.: HMM-Based Word Spotting in Handwritten Documents Using Subword Models. In: Proc. of the ICPR, pp. 3416–3419 (2010)
2. José, R., Florent, P.: Handwritten Word Spotting Using Hidden Markov Models and Universal Vocabularies. Pattern Recognition 42(9), 2106–2116 (2009)
3. Tony, M.R., Word Spotting, R.M.: for Historical Documents. In: Proc. of the 9th ICDAR, vol. 9(2-4), pp. 139–152 (2007)
4. Yann, L., Asma, O., Frank, L., Hubert, E.: Towards an Omnilingual Word Retrieval System for Ancient Manuscripts. Pattern Recognition 42(9), 2089–2105 (2009)
5. José, R.: Local Gradient Histogram Features for Word Spotting in Unconstrained Handwritten Documents. In: Proc. of the 11th ICFHR, pp. 7–12 (2008)
6. Marçal, R., David, A., Ricardo, T., Joseph, L.: Browsing Heterogeneous Document Collections by a Segmentation-Free Word Spotting Method. In: Proc. of the 11th ICDAR, pp. 63–67 (2011)
7. Jean, C.: Utilisation des Points d'Intérêt pour Rechercher des Mots Imprimes ou Manuscrits dans les Documents Anciens. In: Proc. of CIFED, pp. 163–178 (2012)
8. Angelika, G., Robert, S., Markus, D.: Layout Analysis for Historical Manuscripts Using SIFT Features. In: Proc. of the 11th ICDAR, pp. 508–512 (2011)
9. Andrew, J.N., Lewis, D.G.: Multiscale Histogram of Oriented Gradient Descriptors for Robust Character Recognition. In: Proc. of the 11th ICDAR, pp. 1085–1089 (2011)
10. Peng, W.: Historical Document Image Analysis and Recognition. In: Proc. of the 5th JDT du LIRIS, pp. 35–36 (2013)
11. Youssouf, C., Robert, W., Mohamed, C.: TSV-LR: Topological Signature Vector-Based Lexicon Reduction for Fast Recognition of Pre-modern Arabic Subwords. In: Proc. of the 2011 Workshop on HIP, pp. 6–13 (2011)
12. Serge, B., Jitendra, M., Jan, P.: Shape Matching and Object Recognition Using Shape Contexts. IEEE trans. on PAMI 24, 509–522 (2002)
13. Richard, G.C., Eric, L.: Strategies in Character Segmentation: A Survey. In: Proc. of the 3rd ICDAR, pp. 1028–1033 (1995)
14. David, G.L.: Distinctive Image Features From Scale-Invariant Keypoints. Intl. Journal of Computer Vision 60(2), 91–110 (2004)
15. Herbert, B., Tinne, T., Luc, V.G.: Speeded-Up Robust Features(SURF). Computer Vision and Image Understanding 110(3), 346–359 (2008)
16. Cordelia, S., Roger, M., Christian, B.: Evaluation of Interest Point Detectors. Intl. Journal of Computer Vision 37(2), 151–172 (2000)

Gravitational Based Texture Roughness for Plant Leaf Identification

Jarbas J. de M. Sá Junior[1], André R. Backes[2], and Paulo César Cortez[1]

[1] Departamento de Engenharia de Teleinformática - DETI
Centro de Tecnologia - UFC
Campus do Pici, S/N, Bloco 725
Caixa Postal 6007, CEP: 60.455-970, Fortaleza, Brasil
`jarbas_joaci@yahoo.com.br, cortez@lesc.ufc.br`
[2] Faculdade de Computação
Universidade Federal de Uberlândia
Av. João Naves de Ávila, 2121
38408-100, Uberlândia, MG, Brasil
`arbackes@yahoo.com.br`

Abstract. The analysis and identification of plant leaves is a difficult task. Among the many features available for its identification, texture pattern is one of the most important. In this work we propose to explore texture information from a plant leaf by converting it into a simplified dynamical system in gravitational collapse. We use complexity estimates, such as fractal dimension and lacunarity, to describe the states of gravitation collapse of the system and, as a consequence, the texture itself. We also compare our approach to other classical texture analysis methods in a plant leaf dataset.

Keywords: Plant Leaf, Texture Analysis, Simplified Gravitational System, Complexity.

1 Introduction

Among all the features considered in computer vision, texture is certainly one of the most important and well studied. Although it does not have a standard definition, it can be understood as a complex visual pattern, composed by entities, or sub-patterns, that have specific properties, such as slope, size, brightness etc. However, when we focus on natural textures, such definition cannot be properly applied. In this case, it is necessary to consider that these textures present a random and persistent stochastic pattern, which results in a cloud like texture appearance [1].

Basically, grayscale texture analysis methods can be grouped into four categories: signal processing methods, which are based on frequency domain, such as Fourier descriptors [2] and Gabor filters [3]; statistical methods, which explore the spatial distribution of pixels (for instance, co-occurrence matrices [4]); structural methods, which represent textures by primitives and rules; and model-based methods, which are based on fractal and stochastic models. However,

R. Wilson et al. (Eds.): CAIP 2013, Part II, LNCS 8048, pp. 416–423, 2013.
© Springer-Verlag Berlin Heidelberg 2013

over the last years, some methods that cannot be classified in these categories were presented in literature. For instance, there are methods based on deterministic walks [5], fractal dimension [1], complex networks [6], gravitational models [7] etc.

This paper proposes to apply a method based on gravitational models together with complexity descriptors (fractal dimension and lacunatity) in order to classify 10 plant species from the Brazilian flora. For this purpose, we analyzed microtextures presented in leaf surfaces, which have provided discriminative signatures for plant species [3]. Thus, this work aims to contribute to the field of plant taxonomy, whose information sources are mostly flowers and fruits (not always available), by using a powerful texture analysis method applied to an organ largely available for analysis.

Our presentation is composed as follows: Section 2 briefly describes how to convert a texture into a simplified gravitational system. Section 3 presents the Bouligand-Minkowski and gliding-box methods, which are used to obtain the complexity descriptors fractal dimension and lacunarity, respectively. Section 4 shows how to combine the gravitational model with these complexity descriptors in order to obtain a feasible signature. We describe an experiment with 10 plant species from the Brazilian flora (15 leaf samples for each species) in Section 5. Results (Section 6) show the superior performance of our proposed approach when compared with other traditional texture analysis methods. Finally, in Section 7 we present some remarks about this work.

2   Texture Analysis and the Gravitational System

In order to interpret a texture as a gravitational system, we converted each pixel into a massive particle m that orbits the image center. At this center, we located a preponderant mass M. In order to decrease the computational cost of the particle system, there is no interaction among the pixels, only between each pixel and the mass M. To simulate a process of gravitational collapse, we have to take into account two components for each pixel: a tangential speed v_{pix} and a gravitational force f_g between m and M, which acts as a centripetal force f_c.

The magnitude of the gravitational force is determined according to the rules established by Isaac Newton [8], as follows

$$\|\boldsymbol{f}_g\| = \frac{G.m.M}{r^2}, \tag{1}$$

where r is the distance between m and M.

The magnitude of the centripetal force is established according to the following equation

$$\|\boldsymbol{f}_c\| = m.\frac{\|\boldsymbol{v}_{pix}\|^2}{r}. \tag{2}$$

To obtain the highest magnitude of tangential speed v_{max} so that all the pixels can collapse properly, we established $f_g = f_c$, thus obtaining

$$\|\boldsymbol{v}_{max}\| = \sqrt{\frac{G.M}{r_{max}}}, \tag{3}$$

where r_{max} is the greatest distance between a pixel and the image center.

Next, each pixel have its magnitude of tangential speed determined according to the following equation

$$\|\boldsymbol{v}_{pix}\| = \left(1 + \frac{I(x,y)}{255}\right)\frac{\|\boldsymbol{v}_{max}\|}{2}, \tag{4}$$

where $I(x, y)$ is the pixel intensity.

These rules allow each pixel to have a singular spiral movement, resulting in new texture configurations. These configurations are unexplored texture information and, therefore, can be used to obtain an image signature. A detailed description of the gravitational system can be found in [7].

3   Complexity Analysis

3.1   Bouligand-Minkowski Fractal Dimension

Fractal dimension is a measurement of complexity that enable us to describe an object, shape or texture, in terms of its irregularity and space occupation [9]. There exist many methods to estimate fractal dimension. One of the most accurate method is the Bouligand-Minkowski fractal dimension. This is due to its great sensitiveness to the structural changes of the object [10,11]. Basically, this method computes an influence area to estimate the complexity of an object (in our case, a texture image). Let I be a texture pattern and $I(x, y)$ the intensity value associated to a pixel located at coordinates (x, y). We build a surface $S \in R^3$ by converting each pixel $I(x, y)$ into a point $s = (x, y, z) \in S$, where z is the intensity value associated to that pixel, $z = I(x, y)$. By using a radius r, we dilate each point $s \in S$ in order to compute the influence volume $V(r)$ of the whole surface. The Bouligand-Minkowski fractal dimension D is estimated as

$$D = 3 - \lim_{r \to 0} \frac{\log V(r)}{\log r}, \tag{5}$$

with

$$V(r) = \left|\left\{s' \in R^3 | \exists s \in S : |s - s'| \le r\right\}\right|. \tag{6}$$

3.2   Lacunarity

According to Mandelbrot, there exist textures with different appearances that may present the same fractal dimension. This makes fractal dimension useless to describe them, and so, lacunarity was proposed to solve this problem [9,12].

Literature presents many approaches to compute lacunarity, here included the gliding-box algorithm [12]. Initially proposed for binary images, this algorithm computes lacunarity by gliding a box of size l over the image in order to compute its distribution of gaps. Along the years, many researches have extended the method for grayscale images applications [13]. In this work, we consider the approach proposed by [13], which uses a $l \times l$ gliding-box and, for each (i, j) image coordinates used as a position of the box, it computes the relative height of the column

$$h_l(i, j) = \lceil v/l \rceil - \lceil u/l \rceil, \tag{7}$$

where u and v are the minimum and maximum pixel values inside the box, respectively. Then, the method computes the probability distribution $P(H, l)$, where H is each relative height that $h_l(i, j)$ can be assumed

$$P(H, l) = \sum_{i,j} \delta(h_l(i, j), H), \tag{8}$$

where $\delta(x, y)$ is the Kronecker's delta. Finally, we compute the probability density function

$$Q(H, l) = P(H, l) / \sum_{\forall H} P(H, l), \tag{9}$$

and lacunarity for a box size l is defined as

$$\Lambda(l) = \sum H^2 . Q(H, l) / \left(\sum H . Q(H, l) \right)^2 . \tag{10}$$

4   Gravitational Based Signature for Texture Roughness

To obtain a feature vector from a texture image, we convert the image into a gravitational model in collapse process with multiples stages, each of which corresponding to a determined time step t. Next, we explor each collapse stage by using both fractal dimension and lacunarity estimatives. As real objects do not present a constant value for fractal dimension, we apply the Bouligand-Minkowski method with different radius values r to each collapse stage in order to estimate the fractal dimensions at different scales, thus resulting in the following feature vector

$$\psi_t = [D(r_1), D(r_2), \ldots, D(r_n)] . \tag{11}$$

Alike fractal dimension, lacunarity is a scale dependent measure. Thus, it is possible to apply the gliding-box method with different window sizes l to each collapse stage, thus resulting in the following feature vector

$$\phi_t = [\Lambda(l_1), \Lambda(l_2), \ldots, \Lambda(l_n)] . \tag{12}$$

Each collapse stage represents new relations among the pixels and, therefore, new information sources to be explored. Thus, we can obtain feasible feature vectors from the concatenation of the vectors ψ and ϕ, where we compute each feature vector for a diferente time step as follows

$$\boldsymbol{\Psi}_{t_1,t_2,\ldots,t_K} = [\psi_{t_1}, \psi_{t_2}, \ldots, \psi_{t_K}], \tag{13}$$

$$\boldsymbol{\Phi}_{t_1,t_2,\ldots,t_K} = [\phi_{t_1}, \phi_{t_2}, \ldots, \phi_{t_K}]. \tag{14}$$

5   Experiments

We conducted an image classification based experiment to evaluate the performance of our proposed feature vectors. To accomplish this task, we used 10 leaf species from Brazilian flora to build a texture database. We collected 3 leaves samples from each plant species and washed them to remove impurities that could interfere in the experiments. Then, we digitalized each sample by using a scanner with 1200dpi *(dots per inch)* resolution. During the digitalization step, we aligned the central axis of each leaf to a vertical position.

After the digitalization process, we extracted 5 texture samples of 128×128 pixels from each sample, thus resulting in an image database containing 10 classes of 15 samples each (Figure 1). Plant leaves present a wide variation of its basic features, such as luminosity and texture. These variations come from different factors, such as sun exposure, soil influence, fungus, diseases, climate and even environment. Therefore, since plant leaves identification is a difficult task, we extracted manually the texture windows.

To evaluate our approach, we proposed to use Linear Discriminant Analysis (LDA), a supervised statistical classification method. The main objective of this method is to find a linear sub-space to project the data where the variance intra-classes is larger than inter-classes [14]. The method was carried out over the feature vectors using the *leave-one-out cross-validation* scheme.

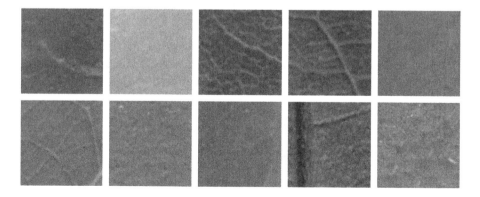

Fig. 1. Texture samples from the leaf species used in the experiment

Additionally, we performed a comparison with other texture analysis methods in order to confirm the performance of our method. The compared methods are: Fourier descriptors [2], co-occurrence matrices [4], tourist walk [5] and Gabor filters [15]. The values of parameters of Gabor filters and Tourist walk were set based on papers already established in literature. Fourier descriptors and co-occurrence matrices have their parameters set empirically.

6   Results and Discussion

Before we apply the gravitational approach to texture analysis, some considerations are necessary. These considerations refer to the values of the mass M and the gravitational constant G. According to [7], the best values for these parameters are $G = 1$ and $M = 204.8$ as they guarantee a constant collapse process for this size of images.

We start analysing the fractal dimension results obtained with the use of multiple values r and different sets of time steps t in Table 1. It is possible to notice that the success rate increases as we use increase both values r and the set of time steps t. Such behavior is due to two facts: first, as we stated before, the gravitational process makes unexplored information accessible through multiple collapse stages, each of which corresponding to a time step t; second, the leaf database consists, basically, of microtextures, which require greater radius values for a more accurate analysis.

Table 2 shows the success rate (%) obtained with multiple values of lacunarity, each one computed using a different window size l, and different sets of time steps t. We obtained the highest success rate using $l_{max} = 8$ and the set of time steps $t = \{1, 5, 10, 15\}$. These results show that lacunarity values do not present a high

Table 1. Success rate (%) on the leaf database for both multiple radius values r and time steps t

Time (t)	\multicolumn{5}{c}{r}				
	$\{3, 4\}$	$\{3, 4, 5\}$	$\{3, 4, 5, 6\}$	$\{3, 4, 5, 6, 7\}$	$\{3, 4, 5, 6, 7, 8\}$
$\{1, 5\}$	62.00	76.00	79.33	80.00	83.33
$\{1, 5, 10\}$	63.33	75.33	79.33	80.67	85.33
$\{1, 5, 10, 15\}$	66.67	75.33	79.33	80.00	86.67
$\{1, 5, 10, 15, 20\}$	68.67	78.67	78.00	80.67	86.00

Table 2. Success rate (%) on the leaf database for both multiple values of window size l and time steps t

Time (t)	\multicolumn{9}{c}{l_{max}}								
	3	4	5	6	7	8	9	10	11
$\{1, 5\}$	57.33	56.00	61.33	65.33	64.67	66.00	64.00	64.00	62.00
$\{1, 5, 10\}$	51.33	58.67	64.67	62.67	64.00	64.00	62.00	62.67	64.00
$\{1, 5, 10, 15\}$	56.00	56.67	61.33	63.33	66.67	69.33	61.33	57.33	62.67
$\{1, 5, 10, 15, 20\}$	59.33	58.00	60.67	64.00	62.67	63.33	60.00	56.67	58.00

Table 3. Success rate (%) on the leaf database for both multiple radius values r and window sizes l for the same time set $t = \{1, 5, 10, 15\}$

r	l_{max}								
	3	4	5	6	7	8	9	10	11
$\{3, 4\}$	81.33	82.67	81.33	82.00	83.33	80.67	79.33	79.33	73.33
$\{3, 4, 5\}$	85.33	83.33	83.33	84.00	84.00	84.00	84.00	81.33	82.00
$\{3, 4, 5, 6\}$	90.00	88.67	87.33	86.67	86.00	87.33	87.33	84.67	84.00
$\{3, 4, 5, 6, 7\}$	90.67	88.67	88.00	87.33	86.67	87.33	92.00	88.00	88.67
$\{3, 4, 5, 6, 7, 8\}$	90.00	88.00	88.00	88.00	87.33	90.00	89.33	86.67	86.67

Table 4. Comparison results for different texture methods

Method	Images correctly classified	Success rate (%)
Co-occurrence matrices	130	86.67
Fourier descriptors	94	62.67
Gabor filters	114	76.00
Tourist walk	107	71.33
Proposed approach	138	92.00

discriminative capacity in comparison to fractal dimension. This suggests that the gliding-box method is not so discriminative for microtexture textures and it should not be applied alone for leaf identification.

Table 3 shows the results obtained with multiple values r and l combined into a single feature vector using the same time step set $t = \{1, 5, 10, 15\}$. We chose this set as it provides the highest success rate in both previous tests, Table 1 (86.67%) and Table 2 (69.33%). For the leaf database studied, these results demonstrate that the synergism obtained from the concatenation of both fractal dimension and lacunarity performs better than each of these estimates applied alone. Moreover, it is possible to notice that, even though the low success rates present in Table 2, lacunarity represents a new texture information that contributes significantly with dimension fractal, allowing our proposed method to obtain a success rate of 92.00%.

Finally, Table 4 presents a comparison with other texture analysis methods. For this comparison, we used the highest success rate present in Table 3. Results demonstrate that our approach can extract high discriminative feature vectors from an important and challenging natural texture database, once it overcomes all the compared methods. Moreover, it is important to stress that it is superior to the second best method (co-occurrence matrices) in 5.33%, a relevant difference that emphasizes the performance of our method.

7   Conclusion

In this paper we address the problem of leaf textures classification. By using a simplified gravitational system, we are able to explore the variations in a texture pattern as it collapses. We used both fractal dimension and lacunarity to estimate the complexity of the texture, thus resulting in a feature vector describing the variation of the complexity of the texture pattern as it collapses. In addition, we evaluated our approach in an experiment using a statistical classifier, the linear discriminant analysis. For this experiment, we collected and build a leaf texture database. To improve our analysis, we also compared our approach with other texture analysis methods found in literature. The high similarity inter-classes and low similarity of intra-classes of plant species makes the identification of leaves a very difficult task. In this sense, results indicate that our approach holds great potential for natural texture analysis applications.

Acknowledgements. André R. Backes gratefully acknowledges the financial support of CNPq (National Council for Scientific and Technological Development, Brazil) (Grant #301558/2012-4), FAPEMIG and PROPP-UFU.

References

1. Backes, A.R., Casanova, D., Bruno, O.M.: Color texture analysis based on fractal descriptors. Pattern Recognition 45(5), 1984–1992 (2012)
2. Azencott, R., Wang, J.-P., Younes, L.: Texture classification using windowed fourier filters. IEEE Trans. Pattern Anal. Mach. Intell 19(2), 148–153 (1997)
3. Casanova, D., Sá Junior, J.J.M., Bruno, O.M.: Plant leaf identification using Gabor wavelets. International Journal of Imaging Systems and Technology 19(1), 236–243 (2009)
4. Haralick, R.M.: Statistical and structural approaches to texture. Proc. IEEE 67(5), 786–804 (1979)
5. Backes, A.R., Gonçalves, W.N., Martinez, A.S., Bruno, O.M.: Texture analysis and classification using deterministic tourist walk. Pattern Recognition 43(3), 685–694 (2010)
6. da Costa, L.F., Rodrigues, F.A., Travieso, G., Boas, P.R.V.: Characterization of complex networks: A survey of measurements. Advances in Physics 56, 167–242 (2007)
7. Sá Junior, J.J.M., Backes, A.R.: A simplified gravitational model to analyze texture roughness. Pattern Recognition 45(2), 732–741 (2012)
8. Newton, I.: Philosophiae Naturalis Principia Mathematica. University of California (1999), original 1687, translation guided by I.B. Cohen.
9. Mandelbrot, B.: The fractal geometry of nature. Freeman & Co.(2000)
10. Tricot, C.: Curves and Fractal Dimension. Springer (1995)
11. Backes, A.R., Casanova, D., Bruno, O.M.: Plant leaf identification based on volumetric fractal dimension. IJPRAI 23(6), 1145–1160 (2009)
12. Allain, C., Cloitre, M.: Characterizing the lacunarity of random and deterministic fractal sets. Physical Review A 44(6), 3552–3558 (1991)
13. Du, G., Yeo, T.S.: A novel lacunarity estimation method applied to SAR image segmentation. IEEE Trans. Geoscience and Remote Sensing 40(12), 2687–2691 (2002)
14. Everitt, B.S., Dunn, G.: Applied Multivariate Analysis, 2nd edn. Arnold (2001)
15. Manjunath, B.S., Ma, W.-Y.: Texture features for browsing and retrieval of image data. IEEE Trans. Pattern Anal. Mach. Intell 18(8), 837–842 (1996)

Heterogeneity Index for Directed Graphs

Cheng Ye, Richard C. Wilson, and Edwin R. Hancock*

Department of Computer Science, University of York,
York, YO10 5GH, UK
{cy666,richard.wilson,edwin.hancock}@york.ac.uk

Abstract. Although there are a number of existing measures for quantifying the structural properties of undirected graphs, there are relatively few corresponding measures for directed graphs. To fill this gap in the literature, in this paper, we explore how to extend Estrada's heterogeneity index from undirected to directed graphs and define an analogous heterogeneity measure for directed graphs. From the perspective of object recognition, this measure opens up the possibility of using directed graphs (such as nearest neighbour graphs) to represent the arrangement of object features. This type of representation is potentially more discriminating than an undirected graph. We show how our new heterogeneity measure can be used to characterize k-nearest neighbour graphs representing the arrangement of object features extracted from objects in the COIL-20 database. We compare the performance of this measure with the original Estrada's heterogeneity index. Finally we achieve the conclusion that our measure gives a better characterization performance.

Keywords: directed graph, heterogeneity index, object recognition.

1 Introduction

Recently there has been considerable interest in analyzing the properties of complex networks since they can provide convenient models in modelling large-scale systems in biology, physics and the social sciences. To render such models tractable, it is essential to have to hand methods for characterizing their salient properties. Structural complexity is perhaps the most important property of a complex network. In order to analyze such property it is imperative that computationally efficient measures are to hand that can be used to represent and quantify the structural complexity.

In this context graph theoretic methods are often used since they provide effective tools for characterizing network structure together with the intrinsic complexity. This approach has lead to the design of several practical methods for characterizing the global and local structure of undirected networks. However, there is relatively little work aimed at characterizing directed network structure. One of the reasons for this is that the graph theory underpinning directed networks is less developed than that for undirected networks.

---

* Edwin R. Hancock is supported by a Royal Society Wolfson Research Merit Award.

R. Wilson et al. (Eds.): CAIP 2013, Part II, LNCS 8048, pp. 424–431, 2013.

The aim in this paper is to explore whether the heterogeneity index developed for undirected graphs can be extended to the domain of directed graphs as an effective graph characterization.

1.1   Related Literature

It is known that the spectrum of the Laplacians can be used as an elegant means to characterize the topological structure of undirected graphs. For example, Luo et al. [6] have used the leading eigenvectors of the graph adjacency matrix to establish pattern spaces for graphs. Wilson et al. [9] have used the spectral decomposition of the Laplacians and showed how the coefficients of permutation invariant polynomials, which come from the elements of the spectral matrix for the Laplacians, can be used as graph features that capture the metric structure of graphs. Moreover, Ren et al. [8] have developed a novel method to characterize unweighted graphs by using the polynomial coefficients determined by the Ihara zeta function. To do this, they construct a pattern vector of Ihara coefficients, and successfully use this to cluster unweighted graphs.

Working in the domain of structural pattern recognition, Xiao et al. [10] have explored how the heat kernel trace can be used as a means to characterize the structural complexity of graphs. To do this, they first consider the zeta function associated with the Laplacian eigenvalues and use the derivative of zeta function at origin as a characterization for distinguishing different types of graphs. Escolano et al. [2] have used the concept of thermodynamic depth to measure the complexity of networks. They first define the polytopal complexity of a graph and then introduce a phase-transition principle which links this complexity to the heat flow, and thus obtain a complexity measure referred as flow complexity. Recently, Han et al. [5] have developed simplified expressions of von Neumann entropy on undirected graphs. To do this, they replace the Shannon entropy by its quadratic counterpart, investigate how to simplify and approximate the calculation of von Neumann entropy. They also explore the relationship among the heterogeneity index, commute time and the von Neumann entropy, and introduce a graph complexity measure based on thermodynamic depth.

Here we build on the work of Estrada [4], who has proposed an index that can be used to quantify the heterogeneous characteristics of undirected graphs. This index depends on vertex degree statistics and graph size. The lower bound of this quantity is zero, which occurs for a regular graph (i.e. all the vertices have the same degree). The upper bound is equal to one, which is obtained for a star graph (i.e. there exists a central vertex and all other vertices connect and only connect to it).

The above provides a brief survey of recent work on the topological structure together with the intrinsic complexity of undirected graphs. However, in the real world, directed graphs are also common as many networks can be modelled with them. For instance, the World Wide Web is a directed network in which vertices represent web pages while edges are the hyperlinks between pages. Turning our attention to directed graphs, Berwanger et al. [1] have proposed a new parameter for the complexity of infinite directed graphs by measuring to what extent the cycles in graphs are intertwined. This index is defined according to the definitions of tree width, directed tree width and hypertree width and a similar 'robber-and-cops' game. Recently Escolano et al. [3] have extended the concept of heat diffusion thermodynamic depth for undirected networks to directed networks and thus obtain a measure to quantify the complexity of structural patterns encoded by directed graphs.

1.2 Paper Outline

One natural way of capturing the structure of directed networks is to use statistics that capture the balance of in-degree and out-degree at vertices. In this paper we show how to extend the heterogeneity index from undirected to directed graphs. Following Estrada's idea, we first establish a local index to measure the irregularity of in-degrees and out-degrees of nodes connected by a single edge. Then we sum up all the edge irregularity and normalized the summation, thus we obtain the heterogeneity index for directed graphs.

The use of structural information in object recognition has been shown to give an important source of information concerning feature arrangement. However, in most cases the structural representation used is based on an undirected graph, in other words the relations between features are represented by undirected edges. However, directed edges can provide powerful additional constraints upon feature arrangement which can potentially improve and disambiguate recognition performance. For instance, they arise when a k-nearest neighbour graph is used to represent spatial adjacency. Unfortunately, whereas there is abundant methodology for characterizing undirected graphs, there are relatively few methods for directed graphs. The secondary aim in this paper is therefore to explore whether the new directed heterogeneity measure can be used for simple object recognition experiments.

The outline of this paper is as follows. In Sect.2, we develop the directed version of the heterogeneity index. In Sect.3, we test both undirected and directed forms of heterogeneity index on real-world data and compare their behaviours. Finally, we conclude this paper with an evaluation of our contribution and the suggestions for future work.

2 Heterogeneity Index of Directed Graphs

In this section, we present an index which quantifies the heterogeneous properties of directed graphs by developing and extending Estrada's work. We take our analysis further by showing how this index is related to the graph size and node in-degree and out-degree.

Suppose $G(V, E)$ is a graph with vertex set V and edge set $E \subseteq V \times V$, then according to Estrada [4], the normalized heterogeneity index for undirected graphs has the following form

$$\tilde{\rho}^U(G) = \frac{1}{|V| - 2\sqrt{|V| - 1}} \sum_{(i,j) \in E} \left\{ \frac{1}{d_i} + \frac{1}{d_j} - \frac{2}{\sqrt{d_i d_j}} \right\}. \tag{1}$$

Following this work, in order to establish a corresponding heterogeneity index for directed graphs, we first require a local index to measure the irregularity associated with a single edge $(i, j) \in E$. Estrada [4] uses the following quantity to measure the variation in node degrees in undirected graphs

$$\sigma_{ij}^U = [f(d_i) - f(d_j)]^2 \qquad (2)$$

where $f(d)$ is a function of the vertex degree. To extend this measure to directed graphs, we measure the difference in out-degree and in-degree and write

$$\sigma_{ij}^D = [f(d_i^{out}) - f(d_j^{in})]^2. \qquad (3)$$

This local heterogeneity measure takes on a value zero when the out-degree of the starting vertex is the same as the in-degree of the end vertex. On the other hand, the index should become larger when the difference of both degrees increases, thus we can select $f(d) = d^{-1/2}$.

Therefore the local heterogeneity index associated with the irregularity of the edge $(i, j) \in E$ in a directed graph is given by

$$\sigma_{ij}^D = \left(\frac{1}{\sqrt{d_i^{out}}} - \frac{1}{\sqrt{d_j^{in}}} \right)^2. \qquad (4)$$

To compute the global heterogeneity index of a directed graph we sum the local measure over all edges in the graph to obtain

$$\rho^D(G) = \sum_{(i,j) \in E} \left\{ \frac{1}{\sqrt{d_i^{out}}} - \frac{1}{\sqrt{d_j^{in}}} \right\}^2 = \sum_{(i,j) \in E} \left\{ \frac{1}{d_i^{out}} + \frac{1}{d_j^{in}} \right\} - 2 \sum_{(i,j) \in E} \frac{1}{\sqrt{d_i^{out} d_j^{in}}}. \qquad (5)$$

The heterogeneity index should take on a minimal value when the graph is regular, i.e. all the vertices have the same in-degree and out-degree. It is maximal when the graph is a star graph, i.e. there exists a central vertex such that all the other vertices connect and only connect to it. We calculate the lower and upper bounds of $\rho^D(G)$ according to these constraints.

For a regular directed graph, suppose all the vertices have the same in-degree and out-degree d_0, then $\rho^D(G) = \sum_{(i,j) \in E} \left\{ \frac{1}{d_0} + \frac{1}{d_0} \right\} - 2 \sum_{(i,j) \in E} \frac{1}{d_0} = 0.$

On the other hand, for a star graph, suppose that the central vertex has out-degree (in-degree) $|V| - 1$ and all the other vertices have in-degree (out-degree) 1. Then, $\rho^D(G) = \sum_{i=1}^{|V|} (\frac{1}{|V| - 1} + 1) - 2 \sum_{i=1}^{|V|} \frac{1}{\sqrt{|V| - 1}} = \frac{|V|(|V| - 2\sqrt{|V| - 1})}{|V| - 1} \approx |V| - 2\sqrt{|V| - 1}.$

We hence have the following lower and upper bounds for the heterogeneity index

$$0 \leq \rho^D(G) = \sum_{(i,j)\in E} \left\{ \frac{1}{d_i^{out}} + \frac{1}{d_j^{in}} - \frac{2}{\sqrt{d_i^{out} d_j^{in}}} \right\} \leq |V| - 2\sqrt{|V|-1}. \quad (6)$$

Therefore we can define the normalized heterogeneity index of directed graphs as

$$\tilde{\rho}^D(G) = \frac{1}{|V| - 2\sqrt{|V|-1}} \sum_{(i,j)\in E} \left\{ \frac{1}{d_i^{out}} + \frac{1}{d_j^{in}} - \frac{2}{\sqrt{d_i^{out} d_j^{in}}} \right\} \quad (7)$$

This index is zero for regular directed graphs, one for star graphs, i.e. $0 \leq \tilde{\rho}^D(G) \leq 1$. Clearly, this index depends on two terms, the first one is the graph size while the second one is based on the statistics of node in-degree and out-degree.

3   Experiments and Evaluations

We have suggested a novel version of Estrada's heterogeneity index to measure the heterogeneous characteristics of directed graphs quantitatively. In this section we aim to evaluate it on real-world data and give empirical analysis of its properties. To this end we gauge the difference between the undirected and directed versions of the heterogeneity index, and compare their behaviours by using them as graph features to characterize undirected and directed graphs respectively.

3.1   The Dataset

For our experiments we utilize the COIL-20 object recognition dataset collected by Nene et al. [7], in which each 3D object contains 72 images collected from equally spaced changes in viewing direction over 360 degrees. Previous attempts to construct graph based representations of this data have extracted feature points using the SIFT detector, and then represented the arrangement of feature points using their Delaunay triangulation, and example of which is shown in Fig.1(a). This yields an undirected representation of adjacency relations. Here on the other hand we wish to explore the use of directed graphs, so we establish a k-nearest neighbour (kNN) graph on the extracted feature points. This is performed as follows: For each detected feature point i we use the coordinates to select the k nodes which are nearest neighbours by comparing the Euclidean distances between node i and the other nodes in the graph. Fig.1(b) shows the k-nearest neighbour graph constructed using this algorithm on the feature points shown in Fig.1(a), here we let k=3, so every node has out-degree 3. However, these directed graphs might have lost some information of the original image as a number of edges have been abandoned from the undirected graphs. In order to reduce the effects of such problem, we create the symmetrized version of directed graphs by changing all the directed edges to bidirectional ones, which is shown in Fig.1(c).

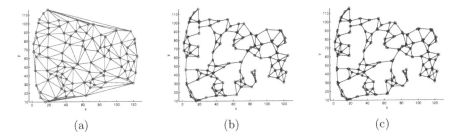

(a)   (b)   (c)

Fig. 1. Example of undirected and directed graphs in the dataset

3.2 Undirected and Directed Heterogeneity Index

Equations (1) and (7) give the heterogeneity index for undirected and directed graphs respectively. We aim to use them as characterizations to distinguish different types of graphs and also to compare their properties. To do this, we select 4 similar objects from the COIL-20 dataset which are shown in Fig.2. As described, there are 72 views for each object with view number 1 to 72, and for each view there are a k-nearest neighbour graph and a corresponding bidirectional graph.

Fig. 2. Objects selected from COIL-20 dataset

We calculate the heterogeneity index for both directed and undirected graphs extracted from the object images. Fig.3 shows the plot of heterogeneity index against the view number. Here the different objects are represented by 4 curves of different colours. In order to better visualize we plot the quantity J, which is the unnormalized heterogeneity index as it has a wider range than that of the normalized form. In particular, for undirected graphs,

$$J^U = \sum_{(i,j)\in E} \left\{ \frac{1}{d_i} + \frac{1}{d_j} - \frac{2}{\sqrt{d_i d_j}} \right\},$$

for directed graphs,

$$J^D = \sum_{(i,j)\in E} \left\{ \frac{1}{d_i^{out}} + \frac{1}{d_j^{in}} - \frac{2}{\sqrt{d_i^{out} d_j^{in}}} \right\}.$$

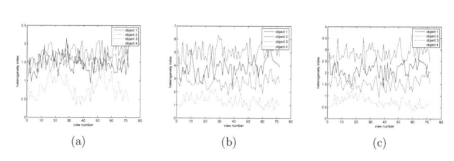

(a)   (b)   (c)

Fig. 3. Object recognition using undirected/directed Heterogeneity Index

Fig.3(a) shows the behaviour of the undirected heterogeneity index. It is clear that only the lower curve can be separated for all view numbers. The remaining 3 curves overlap in the central part of the plot and the corresponding objects cannot be distinguished. The other two plots, Fig.3(b) and Fig.3(c) are similar, they show the behaviours of the directed heterogeneity index for the k-nearest neighbour graphs and bidirectional graphs respectively. Although the 4 curves fluctuate significantly, they are well separated apart from some slight overlap. In other words, the directed version of heterogeneity index gives better object separation.

We investigate this different performance in more depth. Fig.4(a) shows superimposed histograms of J^U for the undirected graphs of each object. The main feature to note is that only the red histograms (object 4) can be well separated from the remaining three object, which are severely overlapped. In Fig.4(b) and Fig.4(c), we show the histograms for the directed heterogeneity measure J^D for both k-nearest neighbour and bidirectional graphs. From these plots it is clear that the 4 different-colour histograms are well separated, although the magenta

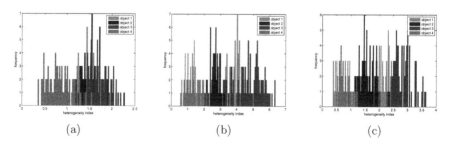

(a)   (b)   (c)

Fig. 4. Object recognition using undirected/directed Heterogeneity Index

(object 1) and the blue (object 3) histograms overlap slightly. This confirms that the directed heterogeneity index gives better performance than undirected version. This result is not unexpected, since the directed version of heterogeneity index quantifies the imbalance of node in-degrees and out-degrees, and the pattern of in-degrees and out-degrees can be used to distinguish nodes.

4   Conclusion

In this paper, motivated by the aim of developing novel and effective methods for quantifying the structural complexity of directed graphs, we have followed Estrada's idea and constructed a directed version of heterogeneity index that can be used to measure the heterogeneous properties of directed graphs. Then in order to evaluate this index and analyze its properties, we have undertaken experiments on a real-world image dataset and the experimental outcomes have demonstrated the effectiveness of our measure. In the future, our work can be extended by undertaking more experiments on different real-world datasets and developing more novel means to measure the topological structure together with the intrinsic complexity of directed graphs.

References

1. Berwanger, D., Gradel, E., Kaiser, L., Rabinovich, R.: Entanglement and the Complexity of Directed Graphs. Theoretical Computer Science 463, 2–25 (2012)
2. Escolano, F., Hancock, E.R., Lozano, M.A.: Heat Diffusion: Thermodynamic Depth Complexity of Networks. Physical Review E 85, 036206 (2012)
3. Escolano, F., Bonev, B., Hancock, E.R.: Heat Flow-Thermodynamic Depth Complexity in Directed Networks. Structural, Syntactic, and Statistical Pattern Recognition, 190–198 (2012)
4. Estrada, E.: Quantifying Network Heterogeneity. Physical Review E 82, 066102 (2010)
5. Han, L., Escolano, F., Hancock, E.R., Wilson, R.C.: Graph Characterizations from Von Neumann Entropy. Pattern Recognition Letters 33, 1958–1967 (2012)
6. Luo, B., Wilson, R.C., Hancock, E.R.: Spectral embedding of graphs. Pattern Recognition 36, 2213–2230 (2003)
7. Nene, A.K., Nayar, S.K., Murase, H.: Columbia Object Image Library (COIL-20). Technical Report CUCS-005-96 (February 1996)
8. Ren, P., Wilson, R.C., Hancock, E.R.: Graph Characterization via Ihara Coefficients. IEEE Transactions on Neural Networks 22, 233–245 (2011)
9. Wilson, R.C., Hancock, E.R., Luo, B.: Pattern Vectors from Algebraic Graph Theory. IEEE Transactions on Pattern Analysis and Machine Intelligence 27, 1112–1124 (2005)
10. Xiao, B., Hancock, E.R., Wilson, R.C.: Graph Characteristics from the Heat Kernel Trace. Pattern Recognition 42, 2589–2606 (2009)

High-Precision Lens Distortion Correction Using Smoothed Thin Plate Splines

Sönke Schmid[1,2,3], Xiaoyi Jiang[1,2,3], and Klaus Schäfers[2,3]

[1] Dept. of Mathematics and Computer Science, University of Münster, Germany
[2] European Institute for Molecular Imaging, University of Münster, Germany
[3] Cluster of Excellence EXC 1003, Cells in Motion, CiM, Münster, Germany

Abstract. Lens distortion and its modelling is an important factor for the calibration of optical cameras. Most calibration algorithms include a distortion model to cope with the discrepancy to a pinhole camera model induced by the camera lenses. However, for high-precision calibration sophisticated distortion models have to be used and their often numerous parameters have to be determined during calibration. In this work we present a simple, nonparametric method based on smoothed thin plate splines for correcting the lens distortion with a very high precision.

Keywords: optical camera, calibration, lens distortion.

1 Introduction

Data acquisition with optical cameras is the prerequisition for many tasks in computer vision. In addition to the pure image data additional information about the camera, its internal parameters, position, and orientation are required for many tasks like stereometry and 3D tracking. Traditionally, cameras are modeled as pinhole camera using a linear function to map points from the 3D scene onto the image plane. However, in practice the pinhole model is not totally correct due to image distortion caused by an optical lense of the camera. Especially when using special lenses, like wide angle lenses or fish eye lenses, the discrepancy to the pinhole camera model cannot be ignored. There exists a wide variety of calibration algorithms, most incorporating some kind of distortion model, like a low grade polynomial model, to treat the lens distortion with a sufficient accuracy. However, for tasks requiring very high precision more sophisticated models have to be used. In general the more complex a model is, the more parameters have to be determined during calibration.

In this work we present a nonparametric approach using smoothed thin plate splines (STPS), that can be performed very easily and does provide a very high precision. For motivating our work, we describe in the following section our project of tracking small animals with high accuracy under special circumstances and requirements to the tracking hardware. In section 3 we shortly overview state of the art methods for lens distortion correction. In section 4 we present our method based on smoothed thin plate splines and its practical realization. Finally, we evaluate our method in section 5 and 6 comparing it to state of the art high-precision methods and discuss its advantages and application areas.

R. Wilson et al. (Eds.): CAIP 2013, Part II, LNCS 8048, pp. 432–439, 2013.

2   Motivation

There are many situations where high-precision lens distortion correction (undistortion) is needed, for instance in systems towards high-precision measurement. One such situation is the following project we are working on: We aim to track freely moving small animals with high precision inside a positron emission tomograph (PET). Normally, the animals have to be anesthetized during 15-60 minutes of data acquisition to avoid motion artifacts. However, anesthesia influence the metabolism which is measured by PET. To avoid this, the aim of our project is to track awake and freely moving animals during the scan and use the information to correct the acquired PET data for motion. For this task a small animal chamber of $20 \times 10 \times 9$ cm was build (Fig. 4) with a pair of stereo cameras positioned on both small sides of the chamber.

For this application a very high tracking accuracy below 0.5 mm is required. The small tube and required base distance for sufficient depth accuracy enforce the usage of very small cameras. We are using ACa640-100gm cameras from "Basler" providing a resolution of 659×494 pixels at 100 fps combined with wide angle lenses BM2420 from "Lensation" with field of view of 87° horizontal and 67° in vertical angle. Simulatons showed that a tracking error of more than one pixel in the camera images results in a triangulation error exceeding the required precision. First tests using a simple polynomial model for lens undistortion lead to deviations from a pinhole camera model of up to 5 pixels.

3   Lens Distortion Models and Related Works

Optical lenses induce a deviation from the pinhole camera model. Due to their form the main component of the distortion is of radial symmetric nature. In addition to the radial components, there exist less significant tangential or non-symmetrical components in typical lens distortion induced by lens imperfections and imprecise assembly of the camera, namely decentering distortion and thin prism distortion. Typically, a simple, low grade polynomial model is used to compensate for most of the radial distortion [2,14]

$$r'(r) = br + cr^2 + dr^3 + \dots \qquad (1)$$

extended by mixed terms for approximating tangential components of the distortion [14].

$$\begin{pmatrix} \delta x(x,y) \\ \delta y(x,y) \end{pmatrix} = \begin{pmatrix} 2k_1 xy + k_2(r^2 + 2x^2) \\ k_1(r^2 + 2y^2) + 2k_2 xy \end{pmatrix} \qquad (2)$$

Although the polynomial model can theoretically be used to approximate any radial distortion function it was found that a too high polynomial order may cause numerical instability limiting the approximation accuracy [8]. Selecting a more appropriate distortion model (e.g. division model, rational model, field of view model) can improve undistortion [4] for most tasks to a sufficient accuracy. However, these models can hardly compete with dedicated high-accuracy lens undistortion methods.

3.1   Nonparametric Undistortion

Instead of choosing a distinctive and therefore limited distortion model the undistortion of a camera image can be seen as a homography between two images. This is discussed in detail by Gioi [5]. The only requirement on such a homography is to map the camera image onto an undistorted image complying with a pinhole camera. This requirement can be reduced to "straight lines have to be straight", meaning that any straight line occuring in the 3D scene has to be straight in the undistorted camera image [2]. Clearly, a homography fullfilling this requirement is unique except an affine transformation in the image space. The undistorted images are the images of a virtual pinhole camera whose internal and some of the external parameters can differ from the original camera. However, the camera center remains at the same location. Any affine transformation in the homography will be accounted for in the calibration of the virtual camera.

There exists a number of methods using a nonparametric approach for lens undistortion. For example, Goshtasby [7] describes the possibility to place a regular grid in front of the camera and morph it onto a regular grid by interpolating between the control points using Bezier patches. Gioi [5] uses SIFT control points of a very dense and complex pattern, segments the image into small triangles defined by the control points and maps each triangle with an affine transformation onto an undistorted pattern.

3.2   High-Accuracy Distortion Correction

Many feature detection algorithms can achieve subpixel accuracy, e.g. line detection [1] or checkerboard corner detection [10]. Therefore, lens undistortion algorithms with subpixel accuracy are highly desireable to achieve combined with the above mentioned methods high-precision stereo measurements.

For the validation of the undistortion accuracy the reprojection error of the whole camera system was a widely used measurement. However, [5] questions the validity of this validation due to the fact that, amongst other effects, calibration of the optical camera compensates some of the error in the lense undistortion underrating it significantly. They propose to measure the undistortion accuracy by determining the straightness of lines using the root mean square error (RMSE) of the distance of the edge points to a straight line. In addition they present the high-accuracy lens undistortion method mentioned above and reported an RMSE below 0.1px outperforming conventional methods. The same group also presented another undistortion method [6] based on several images of a harp of wire and used the massive amount of edge points to determine the parameters of a 11th grade polynomial distortion function dropping the RMSE below 0.06px.

Both presented high-accuracy methods require a very accuratly manufactured calibration pattern. To reach this precision with our hardware setup a calibration pattern of the size of appr. 30×20 cm with an accuracy below $10\mu m$ is required. Additionally, the pattern calls for a planarity with deviations below 50μ. Stronger deviations in planarity lead to detectable displacements in the images and are corrected as if induced by the lens distortion.

4   Lens Undistortion Using Smoothed Thin Plate Splines

We propose to use a planar checkerboard pattern to provide very accuratly detectable feature points even under distortion [9,10] as a calibration pattern. Additionally, a method is needed to determine the mapping between the control points. Local affine transformations do not provide in a globally smooth mapping function and therefore are not the best choice. For this task the popular method (smoothed) thin plate splines proposes itself. Additionally, we tested moving least squares [11] that performed worse than STPS for this purpose.

4.1   Smoothed Thin Plate Splines

Thin plate splines (TPS), developed by Duchon [3] and motivated by the physical deformation behavior of thin metal plates, is one of the most popular methods for nonrigid registration [12]. For 2D it provides a smooth mapping function $f(x, y)$ that maps a number of given points p_i onto new locations q_i. In between the smoothness is assured by the minimization of a smoothness energy functional:

$$E_{tps}(f) = \int \int \left(\frac{d^2 f}{dx^2} \right)^2 + \left(\frac{d^2 f}{dx \, dy} \right)^2 + \left(\frac{d^2 f}{dy^2} \right)^2 dx \, dy \qquad (3)$$

It was found that STPS extending traditional TPS performs even better for the current task (see Sec. 5). STPS allows for small deviations in the mapping from the given point correspondences, if this deviation improves the overall smoothness. The mapping function is given by the minimization of the energy functional

$$E_{stps}(f) = \sum_{i=1}^{n} \|f(p_i) - q_i\|^2 + \lambda \int \int \left(\frac{d^2 f}{dx^2} \right)^2 + \left(\frac{d^2 f}{dx \, dy} \right)^2 + \left(\frac{d^2 f}{dy^2} \right)^2 dx \, dy, \qquad (4)$$

where n is the number of given point correspondences and λ is a constant to configure the tradeoff between the accuracy of the mapping of the control points and the smoothness of the mapping function. It was proven that this energy functional has a unique minimizer and there exists a closed-form solution [13]:

$$f(x, y) = A \cdot \begin{pmatrix} x \\ y \\ 1 \end{pmatrix} + \sum_{i=1}^{n} \beta_i \cdot \phi \left(\left\| \begin{pmatrix} x \\ y \\ 1 \end{pmatrix} - p_i \right\| \right) \qquad (5)$$

with $\phi(r) = r^2 \log(r)$, $A \in \mathbb{R}^{3 \times 3}$ an affine transformation, and $B = [\beta_1 \ldots \beta_n]^t \in \mathbb{R}^{n \times 3}$. A, B are given as the solution of following linear system:

$$\begin{pmatrix} M & P \\ P^T & 0 \end{pmatrix} \cdot \begin{pmatrix} B \\ A \end{pmatrix} = \begin{pmatrix} Q \\ 0 \end{pmatrix} \qquad (6)$$

with P, Q containing the given points p_i, q_i and $M_{i,j;i \neq j} = \phi(\|p_i - q_i\|)$, $M_{i,i} = \lambda$. For better performance in case of $\lambda > 0$ we calculate the affine transformation A as a prestep and solve for B using the above formular replacing p_i by Ap_i.

(a) distorted calibration image   (b) distortion corrected image

Fig. 1. (a) Distorted calibration image of a checkerboard pattern. (b) Calibration image after undistortion with detected corners mapped onto a regular grid using STPS.

4.2   Determining the Undistortion Function

For the lense undistortion using STPS a set of control points has to be acquired in a calibration image and for each detected point a target position has to be assigned. The quality of the undistortion depends on the density of control points and their detection accuracy. As stated above, a regular checkerboard pattern is used and the smallest edge length possible is chosen that does not hinder the corner point detection. The detected corners can easily be sorted and assigned to points of a regular grid (Figure 1(a)). The stepsize of the undistorted grid can be chosen arbitrarily. However, it is reasonable to choose the stepsize as the size of the most central least distorted checkerboard field.

To manufacture a calibration pattern with the very high accuracy discussed in section 3.2 a typical desktop printer with a sufficient printing resolution of 600 dpi was used. To provide the required planarity the pattern was printed on self-adhesive etikette paper and attached to a granite plate (Fig. 4(b)) which has a confirmed planarity below $10\mu m$ and is very cheap to acquire.

5   Validation on Synthetic Data

Our method was validated using synthetic and real image data. For synthetic validation a grid of control points (Fig. 2) was distorted using the polynomial, radial distortion function $r'(r) = 0.7 * r + 0.00036r^2 + 0.0000012r^3$ which approximates our cameras. The undistortion function based on STPS was determined using the control points and their positions after distortion (Fig. 2 left). Figure 2 (center) shows gary-coded the Euclidian error between its original position and its position after distortion and correction. As can be seen, STPS does correct extraordinary well for the distortion. However, at the very border of the image, STPS does not extrapolate the distortion function outside the control point region. This fact reduces the effective camera resolution and field of view slightly but can be easily taken into account during hardware setup. Aside the image boundary there are two erroneus regions in the undistortion. One is at the very corner and less significantly near the border of the grid due to the low number of effective control points for this region. The other region is in the very center resulting from the fact that (S)TPS does not continue the radial distortion to the very singularity of the distortion center but fades to a rigid transformation. However, these errors can be easliy improved with a more dense grid and are rather insignificant compared to

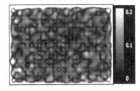

Fig. 2. Left: Grid of control points after application of synthetic lens distortion. Center: Gray-coded undistortion error of STPS ($\lambda = 10$). Right: Undistortion error of STPS ($\lambda = 10$) with a simulated detection inaccuracy of the control points.

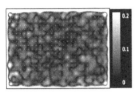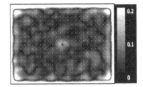

Fig. 3. Behaviour of STPS with increasing smoothness $\lambda = \{100, 1000, 10000\}$

(a) camera setup of our project   (b) camera test setup

Fig. 4. (a) Construction model of the animal chamber and the manufactured chamber halfway inserted into the quad-HIDAC PET-scanner (16 cm in diameter). (b) Setup for the acquisition of calibration images for lens undistortion and for validation.

the errors resulting from inaccuratly detected control points (Fig. 2). To simulate this, the distorted control points were additionally displaced by a Gaussian random value with mean zero and standard deviation of 0.08 pixels. As can be seen, the highest undistortion error arises at the position of the control points and is diminuished in between. Therefore, the final undistortion accuracy with STPS is strongly dependent on the detection accuracy of the control points.

Fig. 3 shows the influence of the smoothness parameter of STPS. With an increasing smoothness parameter λ the undistortion error caused by a very badly detected calibration point can be diminished (Fig. 3 center), justifying STPS compared to TPS. However, a too high smoothness parameter lets the mapping function fade to a rigid transformation (Fig. 3 right). The optimal value for the smoothness parameter is dependent on the type and strength of the lens distortion and the density of the calibraton grid. For our setup we found a value in range of $\lambda \in [500, 1500]$ to be optimal.

6   Validation on Real Data

In addition to validation on synthetic data, our method was validated on real images measuring the straightness of straight lines after undistortion. For this

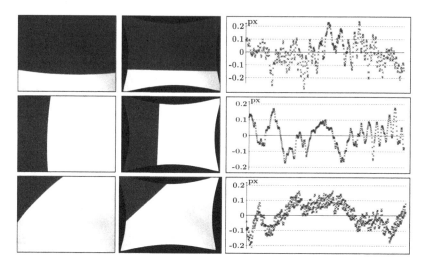

Fig. 5. Left: Images of a distorted straight egde; Center: Undisorted images; Right: Signed distance of undistorted edge positions to the line of best fit. The root mean squre errors are form top to bottom: 0.097px, 0.078px, and 0.077px.

purpose the undistortion function was determined as described in Section 4.2. Then images were taken of a straight edge (Fig. 4(b)). Some of the acquired images can be seen in Fig. 5 in the left column. The images were undistorted (Fig. 5 center column) and for each pixel on the edge, the edge position was determined with subpixel accuracy [1] ignoring the outer 20 pixel boundary of the image. A straight line was fitted through the detected edge pixels and the orthogonal distance of the detected edge positions to the fitted line calculated (Fig. 5 right column). Since the undistortion function is very smooth, the bumpy plot very probably results from the accuracy of the edge detection. Alltogether this experiment was performed with all four cameras of our experimental setup and for each camera 20 validation images were acquired with the edge positioned in different directions and positions. The RMS errors are in a range of $[0.0583; 0.1126]$px with a mean RMSE of 0.084 px. Comparing the absolute values to the works on high-precision lens undistortion our method performes better than the method based on SIFT features [5] but is inferior to the lens undistortion using a calibration harp [6]. However, these values cannot be compared directly due to different lenses used for validation. Furthermore, for the presented precision of lens undistortion the accuracy of the edge detection [1] used for validation does have a significant influence. It can be said that the fabrication of our calibration pattern is easier than that of a high precision wire harp.

7   Conclusion and Future Work

We presented an efficient and easy to apply method for high-precision lens undistortion based on STPS. It performes very well except for a small margin at the image borders which can be accounted for in experimental setups. Our method is comparable to the currently best methods in literature and the realization is very easy. For our project we achieved a mean triangulation accuracy of 0.125mm combining this lens undistortion with sophisticated calibration methods.

In future we plan to evaluate the potential of a locally adapted smoothness parameter, an in-depth analysis of the impact of the grid density, and test more dense patterns. Additionally, further mapping functions will be evaluated.

Acknowledgments. This work was supported by the Deutsche Forschungsgemeinschaft, DFG EXC 1003 Cells in Motion – Cluster of Excellence, Münster, Germany.

This study was partly supported by the project DA 1064/3-1 (Positron emission tomography of non-anesthetized freely-moving mice) of the Deutsche Forschungsgemeinschaft (DFG).

References

1. Devernay, F.: A Non-Maxima Suppression Method for Edge Detection with Sub-Pixel Accuracy. INRIA Research Rep. 2724 (1995)
2. Devernay, F., Faugeras, O.: Straight lines have to be straight: automatic calibration and removal of distortion from scenes of structured enviroments. Mach. Vision Appl., 14–24 (2001)
3. Duchon, J.: Splines minimizing rotation-invariant semi-norms in Sobolev spaces. Lecture Notes in Mathematics, vol. 571, pp. 85–100 (1977)
4. Claus, D., Fitzgibbon, A.-W.: A Rational Function Lens Distortion Model for General Cameras. In: Proc. IEEE Conf. on Comp. Vis. and Pattern Rec., pp. 213–219 (2005)
5. Grompone von Gioi, R., Monasse, P., Morel, J.-M., Tang, Z.: Towards high-precision lens distortion correction. In: 17th IEEE Int. Conf. on Im. Proc., pp. 4237–4240 (2010)
6. Grompone von Gioi, R., Monasse, P., Morel, J.-M., Tang, Z.: Lens distortion correction with a calibration harp. In: Proc. 18th Int. Conf. on Im. Proc., pp. 617–620 (2011)
7. Goshtasby, A.: Correction of image deformation from lens distortion using bezier patches. Comput. Vision Graph. Image Process. 47, 385–399 (1989)
8. Ma, L., Chen, Y.Q., Moore, K.L.: Analytical piecewise radial distortion model for precision camera calibration. Proc. on Vis., Im. and Sign. 153, 468–474 (2006)
9. Mallon, J., Whelan, P.F.: Which pattern? Biasing aspects of planar calibration patterns and detection methods. Pattern Recognition Letters 28, 921–930 (2007)
10. Mühlich, M., Aach, T.: High accuracy feature detection for camera calibration: a multi-steerable approach. In: Proc. of 29th DAGM conf. on Pattern rec., pp. 284–293 (2007)
11. Schaefer, S., McPhail, T., Warren, J.: Image deformation using moving least squares. ACM Trans. Graph. 25, 533–540 (2006)
12. Sun, W., Zhou, W., Yang, M.: Non-rigid registration of medical images with scale-space corner detection and thin-plate spline. Biomed. Sign. Proc. 7, 599–605 (2012)
13. Wahba, G.: Spline models for observational data. In: Soc. for Ind. and App. Math. CBMS-NSF Reg. Conf. Series in App. Math (SIAM), vol. 59 (1990)
14. Zhang, Z.: A Flexible New Technique for Camera Calibration. IEEE Trans. Pattern Anal. Mach. Intell. 22, 1330–1334 (2000)

Identification Using Encrypted Biometrics

Mohammad Haghighat, Saman Zonouz, and Mohamed Abdel-Mottaleb

Department of Electrical and Computer Engineering, University of Miami
haghighat@umiami.edu, {s.zonouz,mottaleb}@miami.edu

Abstract. Biometric identification is a challenging subject among computer vision scientists. The idea of substituting biometrics for passwords has become more attractive after powerful identification algorithms have emerged. However, in this regard, the confidentiality of the biometric data becomes of a serious concern. Biometric data needs to be securely stored and processed to guarantee that the user privacy and confidentiality is preserved. In this paper, a method for biometric identification using encrypted biometrics is presented, where a method of search over encrypted data is applied to manage the identification. Our experiments of facial identification demonstrate the effective performance of the system with a proven zero information leakage.

Keywords: face recognition, encrypted biometrics, search over encrypted data.

1 Introduction

In recent years, there has been a significant attention to substitute biometrics for passwords in authentication systems [7]. Biometric identifiers are distinctive, measurable characteristics used to label and describe individuals [6]. The well-known biometrics used for human identification are the fingerprints, face, iris, voice and DNA. Some of the advantages of biometrics over passwords are their precise identification, highest level of security, mobility, difficulty to forge, not being transferable, and user friendliness.

Besides the above-mentioned advantages, there are challenges that biometric systems face. One of the challenges is the changes in the biometric data over time. Biometric data of a person changes over time. For instance, facial features change due to the changes in illumination, head pose, facial expression, cosmetics, aging, and occlusions because of beard or glasses. Therefore, biometric systems usually identify subjects based on the nearest matches, rather than exact matches. Biometric-based identification is provided through a matching process between the biometric information of the querying subject and of the whole subjects available. The closest match will usually identify the subject. Therefore, these security systems have to store biometric information of all subjects in a database to be utilized at the time of query.

Another challenge faced in biometric systems relates to the possibility of identity theft. What if an attacker gains access to this database and steals the biometric information of an individual? The biometric information is unique and irrevocable, and unlike passwords you can never ask the users to change their biometrics. So, the system must guarantee the users' preservation of privacy, and the biometric information database has to be encrypted. However, the varying characteristic of biometrics brings about a serious

R. Wilson et al. (Eds.): CAIP 2013, Part II, LNCS 8048, pp. 440–448, 2013.

problem in encrypted domain since a little change in the plaintext results in big differences in the ciphertext. This difference misleads the classifier in the recognition process.

The problem of searching over encrypted biometrics has been considered for the first time by Bringer *et al.* in [3]. They have introduced an error tolerant searchable encryption system that makes it easy for the system to cope with the variations of the biometric data. In this method, the iris code system proposed in [4] is employed for biometric representation. This algorithm makes use of a locality sensitive hashing function that gives identical or very similar hash results to the biometric data that are close to each other. Using the locality sensitive hashing function, the (potentially malicious) database provider can cluster the data into groups based on the pattern that the data is being searched/processed for every received query. Therefore, he may eventually be able to sort the data records that could lead to a potential breach in the confidentiality of the data. To address the above-mentioned vulnerability, our proposed algorithm employs query over encrypted data with proven zero information leakage.

In this paper, we present a method for privacy-preserving identification using encrypted biometrics. The proposed algorithm applies a security approach to a face recognition system with a proven zero data disclosure possibility. While all the feature vectors are encrypted, it performs the classification using an effective method of search over encrypted data that can also consider the variations of the biometrics.

This paper is organized as follows. Section 2 demonstrates the structure of a typical pattern recognition system modified to be utilized in an encrypted domain and how the biometric data is stored in the database in an encrypted form. The structure of the search over encrypted data algorithm is presented in Section 3. Section 4 gives some experimental results to evaluate the performance of the system; and finally, Section 5 concludes the paper.

2   Populating the Biometric Database

Although this work can be applied to any biometric data, we have used face images as the biometric identifiers. In order to evaluate our algorithm, the Facial Recognition Technology (FERET) database is used in our approach [10]. We selected six hundred frontal face images for 200 subjects, where all the subjects have three different images. In FERET database, these images are letter coded as *ba*, *bj*, and *bk*. For preprocessing, Viola and Jones face detection algorithm [12] was applied to the images and the detected facial images were resized to 120×120 pixels. Fig. 1(a) illustrates some samples of the database after this preprocessing.

We can divide the feature vector generation into two major steps: feature extraction and dimensionality reduction. However, since we need to encrypt the feature vectors, there is also an additional quantization stage. Note that, feature vectors consist of real numbers; however, encryption algorithms are applied on integer values. Therefore, there is a need to consider an effective quantization method.

2.1   Feature Extraction

The frequency and orientation representations of Gabor wavelets (filters) are similar to those of the human visual system and they have been found to be particularly

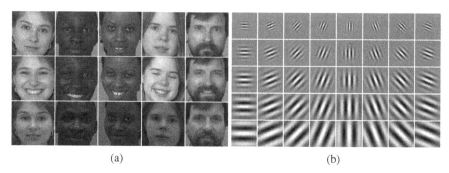

(a)   (b)

Fig. 1. (a) Face samples from FERET database after face detection. First row: *ba*. Second row: *bj*. Third row: *bk*. (b) Gabor wavelets in five scales and eight orientations.

appropriate for texture representation and discrimination [11]. Gabor filters have been widely used in pattern analysis applications [8,9,11]. The most important advantage of Gabor filters is their invariance to illumination, rotation, scale, and translation. Furthermore, they can withstand photometric disturbances, such as illumination changes and image noise.

In the spatial domain, a two-dimensional Gabor filter is a Gaussian kernel function modulated by a complex sinusoidal plane wave, defined as:

$$G(x,y) = \frac{f^2}{\pi\gamma\eta} exp\left(-\frac{x'^2 + \gamma^2 y'^2}{2\sigma^2}\right) exp\left(j2\pi f x' + \phi\right)$$
$$x' = xcos\theta + ysin\theta$$
$$y' = -xsin\theta + ycos\theta$$

(1)

where f is the frequency of the sinusoidal factor, θ represents the orientation of the normal to the parallel stripes of a Gabor function, ϕ is the phase offset, σ is the standard deviation of the Gaussian envelope and γ is the spatial aspect ratio which specifies the ellipticity of the support of the Gabor function.

Our proposed algorithm, employs forty Gabor filters in five scales and eight orientations as shown in Fig. 1(b). Fig. 2 illustrates the face detection step along with the real parts of the result images after applying Gabor filters on the face image. Given the fact that the adjacent pixels in the image are highly correlated, we can remove the information redundancy by downsampling the feature images resulting from Gabor filters [8, 11].

Gabor filters are extrac the variations in different frequencies and orientations in the face. Here the size of the output feature vector is the size of the image (120×120) multiplied by the number of scales and orientations (5×8) divided by the row and column downsampling factors (4×4) which is $120 \times 120 \times 5 \times 8/(4 \times 4) = 36000$ in total. The feature vector is still very large even after downsampling. Therefore, we will need to use dimensionality reduction methods [5].

For dimensionality reduction, we use general discriminant analysis (GDA). The basic idea is close to the support vector machines (SVM) in a way that the GDA method provides a mapping of the input vectors into high-dimensional feature space. In the transformed space, linear properties make it easy to extend and generalize the classical

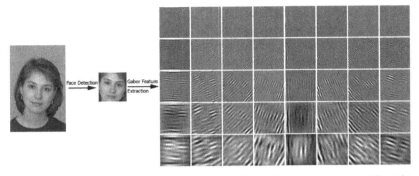

Fig. 2. Face detection and feature extraction, results of applying filters shown in Fig. 1(b) on a face image

linear discriminant analysis (LDA) to non-linear cases. More details for this approach are presented in [1, 11].

Note that the number of features in a LDA-based method (like Fisherfaces or GDA) depends on the number of classes in the classification problem and can be at most $C-1$, where C is the number of classes. Here, the maximum size of the projected vectors is 199 which has a significant reduction in comparison with 36000.

2.2 Feature Quantization

The proposed method combines the feature quantization and classification in range queries over a few parallel k-d trees. The feature vectors are fed into a k-d tree which partitions the feature space along each feature using hyperplanes. These boundary lines are treated as the quantization thresholds. A k-d tree of the depth L that can quantize $L-1$ features has $2^{L-1}-1$ nodes and 2^{L-1} leaves, therefore, it needs 2^L-1 samples to be built. The maximum number of quantized features can be calculated using the equation below. In our experiments, since the number of classes (C) is 200, the number of quantized features is restricted to seven. In order to make use of more features, we employ several k-d trees in parallel using different sets of features.

$$L_{max} = \lceil \log_2 (C+1) \rceil - 1 \tag{2}$$

GDA sorts the features according to their discriminative power. Therefore, it is important to select the first features of the GDA to construct the k-d trees. On the other hand, the deeper you go towards the leaves of the tree, the number of boundary lines (i.e., 2^L) increases. In order to have a reasonable quantization we are just using the four deepest levels of each tree for quantization. For this reason, it is also better to use the most discriminative feature in a higher level of the tree where the boundary lines are more dense. Therefore, the features will be used in reverse order, i.e., the least discriminative feature for the root and the most discriminative feature for the leaves.

In our experiments, we make use of 77 features to construct 11 k-d trees. Each of the first 11 features of the GDA, i.e., the most discriminative ones, are used for the leaves of a tree where we have the highest number of boundary lines. Consequently, the last 11 features (67 to 77) are used for the roots where there is only one boundary line defined.

Then, the first three levels of each tree, which have the coarsest quantizations, are disregarded such that each tree is quantizes four features. Therefore, using 11 trees quantizes the first 44 features of the GDA output. Note that in real systems the number of subjects will be higher, which, based on equation (2), increases the number of features used in each tree.

2.3 Biometric Record Encryption

Most of the security systems maintain a single biometrics database that their agents can have access to. Increasing the number of subjects makes the database huge such that storing all these records locally is often not feasible. Therefore, we assume that the database is stored in a public cloud. Face features as the biometric key attribute are encrypted to prevent attackers from unauthorized access to these confidentiality-sensitive records.

Let us assume that the trusted gateway intends to encrypt and send a user's biometric data record to the database and that the encryption should be such that it preserves the capability to be searchable by specific queries. Our solution makes use of search-aware encryption [2] and delicately applies it on a biometric identification system. C_i denotes the encrypted feature vectors of the i-th person. In the first step, all the cryptographic parameters, i.e., public keys, P, and private (secret) keys, S, are generated:

$$P \leftarrow (P_1, P_2, \cdots, P_t), \tag{3}$$

$$S \leftarrow (S_1, S_2, \cdots, S_t), \tag{4}$$

where t denotes the possible number of predicates (queries) that the customer can ask for in the future. t directly depends on the number of features and quantization boundary lines. The Encryption is carried as using the following assignments for $0 < j < t+1$

$$C_j \leftarrow \begin{cases} \text{Encrypt}(P_j, M) & \textit{if Predicate}_j(F) = 1, \\ \text{Encrypt}(P_j, \perp) & \text{Otherwise.} \end{cases} \tag{5}$$

where F is the feature vector of the subject's biometric and M is his/her ID or any relevant data. M is encrypted using the public key corresponding to the predicate which is only true by his biometric. Once completed, this step will give us a ciphertext vector

$$C \leftarrow (C_1, C_2, \cdots, C_t), \tag{6}$$

whose length is the number of possible predicates t. Note that, only one of the ciphertexts includes the data of the subject. The encryption will be completed locally by the trusted gateways so that the (untrusted) cloud provider will only have access to ciphertexts, and not the encryption keys.

3 Query over Encrypted Biometrics

After storing the biometric samples of the individuals in the database, the system is ready to respond to queries. The query over encrypted biometrics approach is briefly

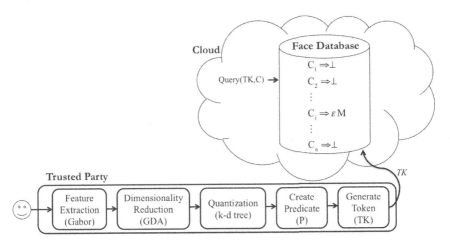

Fig. 3. Framework of the system

described in this section. Different components of the proposed system and their inter-connection are illustrated in Fig. 3. At the time of the query, a face image of the client is fed into the system. Features of the face image are extracted and quantized using the k-d tree method described in Section 2. Because of the changing characteristic of biometrics, an upper boundary and a lower boundary are derived from the query feature vector to be compared to the existing feature vectors stored in database. The query is answered by records whose feature vectors fall in between these two boundaries. Therefore, a conjunctive predicate is created for the comparison query.

$$\mathbf{P} = \begin{bmatrix} l_1 < p_1 < u_1 \\ l_2 < p_2 < u_2 \\ \vdots \\ l_n < p_n < u_n \end{bmatrix} \tag{7}$$

Conjunctive query over encrypted data makes it possible to utilize a number of queries altogether with minimum amount of information leakage. For example, in the above predicate, $2n$ comparisons must be verified conjunctively $((l_1 < p_1 \wedge p_1 < u_1) \wedge (l_2 < p_2 \wedge p_2 < u_2) \wedge \ldots \wedge (l_n < p_n \wedge p_n < u_n))$. In order to guarantee the privacy-preserving ability of the system, such a query should carry no more information than the truth value of the conjunctive predicate. That is, if all the comparisons are true, then the query result is εM; however, if any of the comparisons is false, then the query not only will give no output, but even the cloud provider will be unable to identify which comparison is false. For example, if a conjunction $(P_1 \wedge P_2)$ is false, an eavesdropper should not be able to identify which one of the P_1 or P_2 or both were false.

3.1   Cryptographic Token Generation

As mentioned in the last section, for any query, we will have an accepted range. The range is defined by a lower and upper boundary where the features of the query fall in between these two boundaries. Using the range query predicate, our algorithm defines a token including the encrypted private key corresponding to that query predicate[1]. The comparisons are applied in a conjunctive manner such that the ciphertext can be decrypted only if the result of all the propositions are true in union.

3.2 Biometric Database Query

The final step of the searchable encryption scheme is processing the received query on the encrypted biometric records using the single private key that the trusted gateway has sent. It is easy to follow that the system will retrieve (correctly decrypt) only the records which match the received query, and will get $\perp$ as the result of all other decryptions (see equation (5)). The retrieved records are then sent back to the trusted gateway. It is worthy of mention that for absolute data disclosure prevention, the trusted party should encrypt the records using a symmetric key such that M is already encrypted (εM) and the database provider is not allowed to see the actual record.

4 Experimental Results and Evaluations

Accuracy of a biometric recognition system depends on different factors in the system, e.g., the informativity of features, number of features, and classifier performance. There is a huge variety of face recognition systems in the literature. Depending of what features and which dimensionality reduction method they use and the applied classifier, these methods have different recognition accuracies.

As mentioned before, our test face recognition algorithm utilizes Gabor features and general discriminant analysis dimensionality reduction. Fig. 4(a) demonstrates the performance of this approach using a simple nearest neighborhood classifier. Note that a leave-one-out cross-validation is considered in our experiments with three samples for each subject. The previous methods mentioned in Section 1 have not evaluated the biometric recognition rate or false positive rate after applying their security algorithms. Table 4(b) illustrates the recognition rate and false positive rate of the proposed security algorithm using different number of trees and features.

Note that we accept a subject as a potential match whenever more than half of the trees gives a true response for its predicate. As it can be seen in Table 4(b), with an increase in the number of features, the recognition rate increases and we have better results that prove the discriminative power of our employed features. On the other hand, using more trees makes the classifier more accurate. Note that since we are using conjunctive query, more features bring about more probability to have a negative response which on the other hand leads to a reduction in false positive rate.

As mentioned before, we apply a range query over the encrypted database. Here, the recognition rate is directly related to the width of the accepted region. As the number of quantization levels increases exponentially with the level of the tree ($2^{L-1} + 1$), the intervals get smaller. Therefore, in order to have a consistent range in all levels, the number of accepted intervals should also increase. In the above experiment we have

---

[1] Recall from equation 4 that S includes a private key for each possible predicate (query).

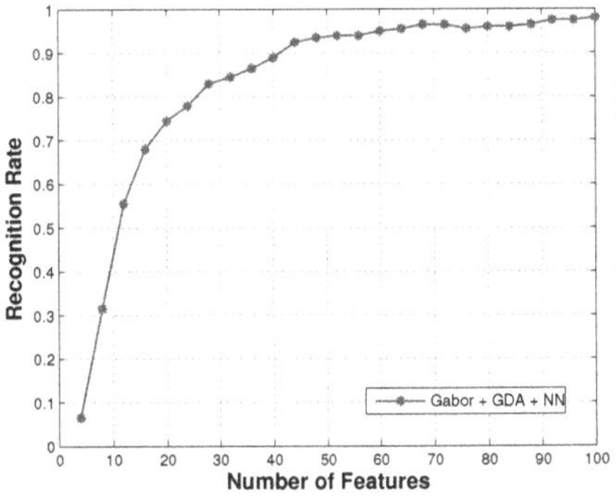

No. of Trees	No. of Features	Recognition Rate	False Positive Rate
1	4	77.50	24.62
3	12	82.50	15.58
5	20	83.00	10.93
7	28	87.50	8.38
9	36	91.50	5.38
11	44	93.50	3.32

(a)   (b)

Fig. 4. (a) Accuracy of the face recognition using Gabor features, GDA dimensionality reduction, and nearest neighborhood classifier. (b) Accuracy of the secure face recognition system.

chosen the width of the acceptance region to be $2^{L-2} + 2$. In addition to the number of features, the accepted region width will also be another degree of freedom for the designer to consider a trade-off between the recognition rate and false positive rate.

5   Conclusions and Future Work

In this paper, we presented a privacy-preserving biometric identification solution that stores and processes individual biometric records while they are encrypted. The proposed algorithm applies a security approach to a face recognition system with a proven zero data disclosure possibility. Applying a secure approach will allow the users of biometric-based systems to store their information in public clouds which will give them the opportunity of having more effective storage along with the computational power of the cloud infrastructures as well as the controlled and flexible data accessibility by multiple agents. A working prototype of the proposed system is implemented and evaluated using a real-world biometric database. The experimental results show that proposed system can be used in practice for trustworthy storage of sensitive records as well as precise identification of clients with proven zero data disclosure possibility.

References

1. Baudat, G., Anouar, F.: Generalized discriminant analysis using a kernel approach. Neural Computation 12(10), 2385–2404 (2000)
2. Boneh, D., Waters, B.: Conjunctive, subset, and range queries on encrypted data. In: Vadhan, S.P. (ed.) TCC 2007. LNCS, vol. 4392, pp. 535–554. Springer, Heidelberg (2007)
3. Bringer, J., Chabanne, H., Kindarji, B.: Error-tolerant searchable encryption. In: IEEE International Conference on Communications, ICC 2009, pp. 1–6 (2009)
4. Daugman, J.G.: High confidence visual recognition of persons by a test of statistical independence. IEEE Transactions on Pattern Analysis and Machine Intelligence 15(11), 1148–1161 (1993)

5. Haghighat, M.B.A., Namjoo, E.: Evaluating the informativity of features in dimensionality reduction methods. In: 2011 5th International Conference on Application of Information and Communication Technologies, AICT, pp. 1–5 (October 2011)
6. Jain, A., Hong, L., Pankanti, S.: Biometric identification. Communications of the ACM 43(2), 90–98 (2000)
7. Jain, A., Ross, A., Pankanti, S.: Biometrics: a tool for information security. IEEE Transactions on Information Forensics and Security 1(2), 125–143 (2006)
8. Liu, C., Wechsler, H.: Gabor feature based classification using the enhanced fisher linear discriminant model for face recognition. IEEE Transactions on Image Processing 11, 467–476 (2002)
9. Meshgini, S., Aghagolzadeh, A., Seyedarabi, H.: Face recognition using gabor-based direct linear discriminant analysis and support vector machine. Computers & Electrical Engineering 39(3), 727–745 (2013)
10. Phillips, P.J., Moon, H., Rizvi, S.A., Rauss, P.J.: The FERET evaluation methodology for face-recognition algorithms. IEEE Transactions on Pattern Analysis and Machine Intelligence 22(10), 1090–1104 (2000)
11. Shen, L.L., Bai, L., Fairhurst, M.: Gabor wavelets and general discriminant analysis for face identification and verification. Image and Vision Computing 25(5), 553–563 (2007)
12. Viola, P., Jones, M.J.: Robust real-time face detection. International Journal of Computer Vision 57(2), 137–154 (2004)

Illumination Effects
in Quantitative Virtual Microscopy

Doreen Altinay and Andrew P. Bradley

School of Information Technology and Electrical Engineering,
The University of Queensland, Australia
{daltinay,bradley}@itee.uq.edu.au

Abstract. For quantitative virtual microscopy to be accepted into clinical practice, a virtual image has to be a 'glass faithful' representation of the underlying cellular objects, unaffected by artefacts such as illumination or optical distortion. In this paper we present experimental results from systematic measurements of features from calibration slides at different locations in the field-of-view. Our results show that measurements differ slightly from the expected values. However the values in the different locations are similar confirming the efficacy of virtual microscopy as objects can be measured independent of their location.

Keywords: Illumination effects, Quantitative virtual microscopy, Calibration.

1 Introduction

Traditionally, conventional quantitative microscopy has taken the field-of-view (FOV) approach, where each and every cell is centered in the FOV and measured quantitatively. While this guarantees that each object is acquired with optimal illumination and focus it is time consuming. In addition, long exposure times result in fading of microscopic specimens [7] and the context is easily lost by observing/measuring cells in isolation. A cell might belong to a clump of cells which could give vital clues as to whether a sample contains malignant cells or not. Virtual microscopy (VM), in contrast, creates a digital image of the whole specimen on the computer that has the look-and-feel of a real microscope. Here, microscopic FOV images are captured of the entire glass slide and assembled to create a single virtual slide [3]. Therefore, VM is preferable as the specimen is acquired rapidly and only once, hence minimizing fading. However, for quantitative VM to be accepted, the virtual image has to be demonstrated to be a 'glass faithful' representation of the underlying cellular objects. Virtual slides have to be unaffected by artefacts due to the illumination or optics of the acquisition system, especially since virtual images contain objects imaged both in the centre and periphery of each FOV.

The most commonly compared features to distinguish between normal, benign and malignant cells are nuclei size, nuclei shape, nuclei/cytoplasm ratio, optical density and chromatin structure [10]. However, before these features can be

R. Wilson et al. (Eds.): CAIP 2013, Part II, LNCS 8048, pp. 449–456, 2013.

measured accurately, the microscope system has to be calibrated [2]. While cells
of varying size and shape are unsuitable for calibration, circles from a calibration
slide have known properties and are therefore ideal for this purpose.

Due to the narrow light path of the microscope, issues related to lighting as
well as optical effects (e.g. lens distortion) have to be measured and compensated
for. Uneven illumination and a poor choice of illumination intensity can nega-
tively impact results. There are several ways to correct for uneven illumination,
either while images are acquired (a-priori) or after acquisition (a-posteriori). Another issue is ambient lighting which is caused by stray light entering the light
path of the microscope leading to shadows on the acquired objects. This can be
prevented by eliminating any light source other than the microscope's (halogen)
lamp, e.g. by enclosing the microscope in a light-tight box. Lastly, different illumination intensities may lead to different measurements which should be taken
into account when measuring cells quantitatively. Good contrast is achieved by
a histogram of equal distribution in the shadows, midtones and highlights [5].

A common way to eliminate optical artifacts, such as lens distortion, is by
determining the extrinsic and intrinsic parameters of the microscope which then
result in distortion parameters and can be corrected for by back-projection. In
a previous experiment [1] we have compared several algorithms that are used in
the literature by applying them to a calibration grid and estimating the distortion parameters. Although the results differed considerably, they indicated, that
the distortion is less than one pixel and therefore potentially insignificant [1].
However, the true lens distortion is not known and illumination effects still can
cause problems. In the presence of lens distortion and illumination gradients,
circles in the periphery of the field-of-view are slightly larger and oval-shaped
compared to those in the centre. Therefore, it is necessary to perform a well controlled calibration that measures objects in the centre and periphery to ensure
that their size and shape are not dependent on their location in the FOV.

In this paper we present experimental results obtained by measuring important features of objects at different locations in the FOV of a microscope. Along
the way we address the necessary calibration and compensation of any systemic
inhomogeneity and/or distortion. To the best of our knowledge, such an extensive experiment showing problems that arise due to illumination effects and
distortion has not been done yet, but is vital to demonstrate that a VM system
is 'glass faithful'.

2 Materials and Methods

A Zeiss Axio Imager.M1 was used to acquire the images for this experiment. Its
light source is a 12V, 100W halogen lamp and the microscope provides a range
of voltage settings to vary the illumination intensity. The CCD camera module
attached to the microscope is a peltier cooled Spot Pursuit camera (100% fill
factor) with an image resolution of 2048 by 2048 pixels and CCD cell size of 7.4
by 7.4 μm. The calibration slide used contains an 11 by 11 grid of circles with
a diameter of 250 μm. Images were acquired on the 10× and 20× magnification

objectives with an N.A. of 0.29 and 0.5 respectively. Each dataset (10× and 20× magnification) has a total of 1089 FOV images, 121 circles in the centre and 968 circles in the periphery (121 for each location – N, E, S, W, NE, NW, SE, SW). The circle images were acquired during the night with no room lights to minimize ambient illumination effects. Two circle images, for 10× and 20× magnification, are displayed in Figure 1.

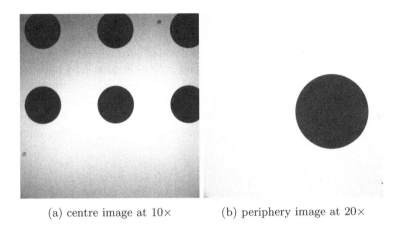

(a) centre image at 10×   (b) periphery image at 20×

Fig. 1. Examples of centre and periphery images at 10× and 20× magnification

The experiments are separated into individual sections as follows:

1. **Uneven background correction** — 1089 images were acquired without ambient lighting using the 10× magnification objective.
2. **Ambient lighting** — 1089 images each where acquired with and without ambient illumination with the 10× magnification objective
3. **Illumination intensity** — 1089 images each at 7 illumination intensities were acquired without ambient lighting using the 10× magnification objective
4. **Comparison expected values vs. measured values** — 1089 images were acquired without ambient lighting using the 10× magnification objective, and 40 additional grey scale images which were generated containing synthetic anti-aliased circles for comparison. Both image dimensions and circle radii are identical to the ones acquired.
5. **Measured features: centre vs. periphery 10× & 20×** — 1089 images were acquired without ambient lighting using the 10× and 20× magnification objectives

For all images a focus value was chosen after acquiring images at several depths of focus, calculating their variance and using the focal depth where the variance was the highest. This was done at different circles within the circle grid including the outer-most corners. The expected values of all features could be determined by calculating the relationship between resolution in pixels per μm using images acquired from a calibration slide.

To segment the circles, Otsu's thresholding [9] and Canny's edge detection algorithm [4] are the natural choice since circles are clearly distinguishable from the background [8] and uneven background illumination has already been corrected for during acquisition. Note: We did not use active contours as they are optimized and have constraints to find circles.

In this experiment we have chosen to measure parameters encompassed by the Minkowski functionals (i.e. area and perimeter for 2D binarized objects) because they are invariant to rotation and translation [6]. The roundness and eccentricity measurements have been added as additional parameters with eccentricity being more accurate as it does not depend solely on area and perimeter. All measurements, i.e. area, perimeter, eccentricity and roundness, were computed using functions from the OpenCV toolkit (homepage: `http://opencv.org`). The microscopy platform to acquire the images is written in Python (homepage: `http://python.org`) which uses functions provided by the Zeiss microscope software development kit.

3   Results

Uneven Background Correction — The spread of grey values of the original images was 164. After correcting for uneven background the spread dropped to 7 grey values, which is still slightly larger than the observed image noise. Therefore, images acquired for the remaining experiments were background corrected during acquisition.

Ambient Lighting — Table 1 shows the difference in measured area for images acquired with and without ambient illumination. While the minimum value is similar, the range is about 3 times larger for images acquired with ambient light, therefore the remaining results are without ambient illumination. Since both segmentation algorithms yielded similar results, only the results obtained using Otsu's methods will be discussed in the following.

Table 1. Area of centre circles segmented with Otsu and Canny when acquired with and without ambient illumination

method	ambient light	minimum	maximum	range
Otsu	with	137634.0	138444.5	810.5
	without	137625.0	137885.5	260.5
Canny	with	136794.5	138752.0	1957.5
	without	136768.0	137390.0	622.0

Illumination Intensity — Figure 2 depicts the roundness of centre and periphery circles, including their STD bars, at different illumination intensities. There is a steady increase in the roundness up to a setting of 8V (75%), before it plateaus.

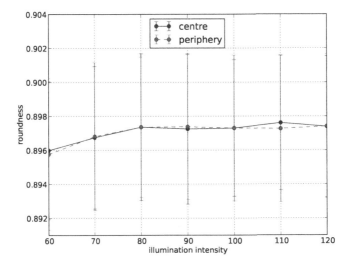

Fig. 2. Roundness of circles at different intensities

Comparison Expected Values vs. Measured Values — Table 2 shows the area values and radii between the acquired circles (column 5) and the simulated circles (column 3 & 4). For the simulated circles the table shows both the black pixel count and the measured value. Column 5 & 6 shows that the area of the simulated circles is smaller than the area of the acquired circles. The expected value is smaller than both measurements.

Table 2. Area values and radii from simulated (S) and acquired circles (A) as well as their expected values (E)

	expected value	simulated circles		acquired circles	differences	
		black pixel count	measured value		S - E	A - E
area	135196.63	135261	135848	137729	651.37	2532.37
radius	207.5	207.55	207.99	209.4	0.49	1.9

Measured Features: Centre vs. Periphery 10× and 20× — Tables 3 and 4 show the area, perimeter, eccentricity and roundness values for circles acquired in the centre and periphery with the 10× and 20× magnification objectives, respectively. The radius is also calculated from the measured area and perimeter. For the 10× objective the area values differ by up to about 300 pixels between centre and periphery which translates to a radius difference of about 0.3 of a pixel. Although the area difference for the 20× objective is about 800 pixels it also translates to a radius difference of about 0.3 of a pixel.

The mean area in the periphery is slightly larger than the mean area in the centre for both magnification objectives. Because the test set contains 7 times more periphery images than centre images, the area of the periphery images has a larger spread than the area of the centre images. The eccentricity and roundness values are very close to 0.0 and 0.9, respectively.

The p-value of the Wilcoxon rank-sum is stated as well where the null hypothesis states that the mean of the two independent distributions centre and periphery is the same for all four parameters:

$$H_0 : centre_{parameter} = periphery_{parameter}.$$

The null hypothesis H_0 for the parameters area and perimeter are rejected. The null hypothesis H_0 for both the eccentricity and roundness can not be rejected for images acquired with the 10× magnification objective and the 20× magnification objective.

Table 3. Minimum, maximum and expected values of centre (c) and periphery (p) circles captured at 10× magnification at a fixed illumination intensity and the p-value of the Wilcoxon rank-sum

parameter	location	min	mean	max	exp value	p-value
area	c	137625	137729	137885	135265.6 (207.0)	$p < 0.005$
	(radius)	209.4	209.4	209.5		
	p	137544	137836	138149		
	(radius)	209.3	209.5	209.7		
perimeter	c	1386	1388	1419	1303.7 (207.6)	$p < 0.005$
	(radius)	220.8	221.0	226.0		
	p	1386	1389	1420		
	(radius)	220.7	221.2	226.1		
eccentricity	c	-2.9×10^{-8}	1.3×10^{-6}	9.2×10^{-6}	0.0	$p > 0.05$
	p	-1.4×10^{-6}	1.4×10^{-6}	1.7×10^{-5}		
roundness	c	0.860	0.897	0.900	1.0	$p > 0.05$
	p	0.859	0.897	0.901		

Table 4. Minimum, mean, maximum and expected values of centre (c) and periphery (p) circles acquired at 20× magnification and segmented with Otsu at a fixed illumination intensity and the p-value of the Wilcoxon rank-sum

parameter	location	min	mean	max	exp value	p-value
area	c	544208.5	544598.6	545029.5	537806 (413.7)	$p < 0.005$
	(radius)	416.2	416.4	416.5		
	p	543404.5	544257.7	545226.0		
	(radius)	415.9	416.2	416.6		
perimeter	c	2758.3	2762.1	2827.4	2599.4 (413.7)	$p < 0.005$
	(radius)	438.9	439.6	449.9		
	p	2756.0	2761.5	2844.5		
	(radius)	438.6	439.5	452.7		
eccentricity	c	-3.5×10^{-7}	9.6×10^{-8}	2.5×10^{-6}	0.0	$p > 0.05$
	p	-4.3×10^{-6}	-6.9×10^{-8}	6.7×10^{-6}		
roundness	c	0.856	0.897	0.899	1.0	$p > 0.05$
	p	0.847	0.897	0.900		

4   Discussion

Uneven Background Illumination — Although the grey value spread dropped dramatically from 164 to 7 grey values from the uncorrected to the illumination corrected image, a slight grey value spread is still visible. This shows that the a-priori illumination correction method does not completely remove the illumination gradient.

Ambient Lighting — Although the minimum area for images acquired with and without ambient illumination is the same, the spread is 3 times larger with ambient illumination. This shows that ambient lighting increases the measured area due to shadows. It is therefore important to eliminate any external light sources to take precise measurements.

Illumination Intensity — Figure 2 makes clear that it is important to choose the correct illumination intensity as it has a significant influence on the measurements.

Comparison Expected Values vs. Measured Values — Table 2 compares the counted vs. measured values of simulated circles as well as measured values between simulated circles and acquired circles. When simply counting the black pixels on simulated circles to determine the area (column 3), it can be seen that the area is closer to the expected value (column 2) but slightly larger. The measured area of both the simulated circles (column 4) and the acquired circles (column 5) is larger than the black pixel count due to the fact that digital circles are approximated by pixels. The area of the acquired circles is larger compared to the simulated circles. This can be explained by the thresholding step applied to the acquired circles which are grey scale images and thus do not have a steep gradient.

Measured Features: Centre vs. Periphery 10× and 20× — Although the area results between centre and periphery look quite different, the radii differ by less than one pixel. The circles in the centre and periphery have similar measurements. The roundness value is 0.9 for all circles. This value will never be 1.0 because circles in digital images are approximated in a square grid, resulting in jagged edges, which in turn result in a longer perimeter. The results in Table 2 clearly show that the measured value can only approximate the expected value. This is due to the fact that the expected value is calculated assuming a perfectly round circle which can never be exactly obtained in a sampled image.

Both eccentricity and roundness show similar values in the centre and periphery. In the presence of lens distortion, objects in the centre are rounder and smaller while objects in the periphery tend to be more oval shaped and larger. The shape difference, however, is not the case here. Therefore, there either is no distortion or it is insignificant and not visible in our experimental set up.

5   Conclusion

A good illumination correction algorithm and the elimination of external light sources clearly decrease the variability of the measurements of features in objects and are thus very important pre-processing steps. Although the area of measured objects differs slightly with our employed illumination correction, the radii are almost identical in the centre and periphery of FOV images. Interestingly, statistical analysis suggests that the means of the area and perimeter are likely to be different between centre and periphery, while the eccentricity and roundness are indistinguishable in our test set. While these results do not give a clear answer to the question of 'glass faithfulness' of VM systems they do indicate that these differences are more likely caused by uneven background illumination rather than optical distortion.

References

1. Altinay, D., Bradley, A.P., Mehnert, A.: On the estimation of extrinsic and intrinsic parameters for optical microscope calibration. In: Digital Image Computing: Techniques and Applications (DICTA 2010), pp. 190–195 (2010)
2. Bengtsson, E.: Computerized cell image analysis: Past, present, and future. In: Scandinavian Conference on Image Analysis, pp. 395–407 (2003)
3. Bradley, A.P., Wildermoth, M., Mills, P.: Virtual microscopy with extended depth of field. In: Proceedings of the Digital Imaging Computing: Techniques and Applications, DICTA 2005, vol. 2005, pp. 235–242. Inst. of Elec. and Elec. Eng. Computer Society, Cairns (2005)
4. Canny, J.: A computational approach to edge detection. IEEE Trans. Pattern Analysis and Machine Intelligence 8(6), 676–698 (1986)
5. Gonzales, R.C., Woods, R.E.: Digital Image Processing, 3rd edn. Addison-Wesley Pub. (March 1992)
6. Legland, D., Kieu, K., Devaux, M.-F.: Computation of minkowski measures on 2d and 3d binary images. Image Anal. Stereol 26, 83–92 (2007)
7. Leong, F.J., McDee, J.O.: Automated complete slide digitization: a medium for simultaneous viewing by multiple pathologists. Journal of Pathology 195(4), 508–514 (2001)
8. Meijering, E.: Cell segmenation: 50 years down the road (life sciences). IEEE Signal Processing Magazine 29(5), 140–145 (2012)
9. Otsu, N.: A threshold selection method from gray-level histograms. IEEE Transactions on Systems, Man and Cy. 9, 62–66 (1979)
10. Rahmadwati, Naghdy, G., Ross, M., Todd, C., Norachmawati, E.: Classification cervical cancer using histology images. In: 2010 Second International Conference on Computer Engineering and Applications, pp. 515–519 (2010)

Improving the Correspondence Establishment Based on Interactive Homography Estimation*

Xavier Cortés, Carlos Moreno, and Francesc Serratosa

Universitat Rovira i Virgili, Departament d'Enginyeria Informàtica i Matemàtiques, Spain
{xavier.cortes,francesc.serratosa}@urv.cat,
carlosfrancisco.moreno@estudiants.urv.cat

Abstract. We present a method to find the correspondences between salient points of images in which an oracle can interact and influence on the final correspondences between points. The oracle looks up the current point correspondences and imposes new mappings or modifies some of them. This interaction influences on two aspects. On one hand, a new homography is computed such that the Least Square Error is minimized on the imposed correspondences. On the other hand, the Similarity Matrix between the set of points is modified and so, the interaction influences on the output of the Correspondence Algorithm. The method is independent of the algorithm to compute the homography and the correspondences. Practical evaluation shows that in few interactions of the oracle, the optimal correspondence is achieved.

Keywords: Homography Estimation, Iterative Closest Point, Interactive Correspondence, Hungarian Algorithm.

1   Introduction

In recent years, interaction between robots and humans has increased rapidly. Applications of this field are very diverse, ranging from developing automatic exploration sites [1] to using robot formations to transport and evacuate people in emergency situations [2]. Within the area of social and cooperative robots, the nature of interactions between a group of people and a set of accompanying robots has become a primary point of interest [3].

One of the low level tasks that these systems have to face is the automatic recognition of scenes and objects the robot visualises. Usually, the interpretation of scenes is performed trough two steps. Firstly, detecting salient points of the image and secondly, searching for the correspondences of these points and the salient points in the previously learned images [4]. Salient points (that play the role of parts of the image to be matched) are image locations that can be robustly detected among different instances of the same scene with varying imaging conditions. These points can be corners (intersection of two edges) [5], maximum curvature points [6] or isolated points of maximum or minimum local intensity [7]. There is an evaluation of

---

* This research is supported by the CICYT project DPI 2010-17112.

R. Wilson et al. (Eds.): CAIP 2013, Part II, LNCS 8048, pp. 457–465, 2013.

the most competent approaches in [8]. When salient points have been detected, several correspondence methods can be applied that obtain the homography that maps one image into the other [9], discards outlier points [10] or characterises the image into an attributed graph [11], [12].

Humans are very good at finding the correspondences between local parts of an image regardless of the intrinsic or extrinsic characteristics of the point of view. Current automatic methods to extract parts of images and their correspondences in non-controlled environments are far away of having the performance of a human. For this reason, in this paper, we propose a semi-automatic method in which humans can interact into the system when it is considered the quality of the automatically found correspondence is not good enough and then they impose a partial or total correspondence between some local parts of two scenes.

We advocate for a cooperative model in which robots have cameras and they have to identify objects and scenes in a cooperative manner with the aim of detecting specific objects or performing Simultaneous Localisation And Mapping (SLAM). We assume there is a master system that receives images from robots and finds the correspondences between images of these robots. These images may have been taken from different scenes or from the same scene but with completely different points of view, illuminations and so on. When scenes or objects from scenes have been localized, the master system sends new orders to the robots such as specific movements, grasping objects and so on. When a robot is not able to recognize the scene, then it stops and asks to the master system to localize it or send it the information of the scene. The master obtains the whole information through the correspondence between the current and past images of all the robots. Due to the environment (for instance, rescue inside buildings), we assume it is not possible to localise the robots through GPS, 3D triangulation or sensors on the wheels.

Figure 1 is a screen shot of the master system. We can visualize the cameras of robot 1 and 2 and the salient points automatically extracted. Blue lines represent the automatically extracted correspondences and the orange line represents the correspondence imposed by the human since he or she has realized one of the correspondences was wrong. This interaction influences over the obtained homography and also over the rest of the correspondences.

A similar interaction method was presented in [13]. In that case, there is only one robot and the human decides if a selected part of the image is a face and in the case that it is, imposes the name of the person.

Figure 2 shows a schematic view of our Interactive Correspondence Method (ICM). The user has access to the original images, both set of salient points and the

Fig. 1. Screen shot of the interactive system with robot 1 and robot 2 images

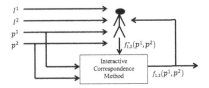

Fig. 2. Basic scheme of our Interactive Correspondence Method (ICM)

current correspondence $f_{1,2}$ between them. Then, the user imposes some point mappings $f_{1,2}^*$ and the output of the module is a correspondence in which the oracle has influenced. This process is repeated until the user considers the correspondence is good enough.

The rest of the paper is organized as follows. The next section summarizes the method to estimate a homography given some correspondence points. Section 3 schematically explains the main steps to find the correspondences of salient points of two images. Section 4 presents our interactive method to estimate the correspondences and section 5 shows the practical evaluation. Section 6 concludes the paper.

2   Homography Estimation Given a Correspondence

Given two images I_1, I_2 and a set of pairs corresponding points on these images $\{\{(x_1, y_1), (x_1', y_1')\}, ..., \{\{(x_n, y_n), (x_n', y_n')\}\}$ it is possible to obtain a transformation matrix F that projects each of the points in I_1 into the points in I_2 with a minimal error. Then $[x_i', y_i', 1]^T = F \cdot [x_i, y_i, 1]^T$, where $(x_i', y_i') \in I_2$ and $(x_i, y_i) \in I_1$.

If we suppose that the mean error has a normal distribution, then the least-square estimation is optimal [14]. Moreover, if we assume an affine transformation, then the transformation matrix is defined as

$$F = \begin{bmatrix} a & -b & c \\ b & a & d \\ 0 & 0 & 1 \end{bmatrix}$$

Where $a = S \cdot cos(\alpha)$, $b = S \cdot sin(\alpha)$, $S = scale$, $c = $ translation in x and $d = $ translation in y.

In this case the error function is usually estimated as follows:

$$E(a, b, c, d) = \sum_{i=1}^{n} [[ax_i - by_i + c - x_i']^2 + [bx_i + ay_i + d - y_i']^2]$$

We find the minimum through deriving the function; $\frac{\delta E}{\delta a} = 0$, $\frac{\delta E}{\delta b} = 0$, $\frac{\delta E}{\delta c} = 0$ and $\frac{\delta E}{\delta d} = 0$. We arrive to the following linear problem, A $(a, b, c, d)^T + B = 0$. Where

$$A = \begin{bmatrix} \sum_i(x_i^2 + y_i^2) & 0 & \sum_i x_i & \sum_i y_i \\ 0 & \sum_i(x_i^2 + y_i^2) & \sum_i -y_i & \sum_i x_i \\ \sum_i x_i & \sum_i -y_i & n & 0 \\ \sum_i y_i & \sum_i x_i & 0 & n \end{bmatrix}, \text{ and } B = \begin{bmatrix} \sum_i(x_i x_i' - y_i y_i') \\ \sum_i(x_i' y_i - x_i y_i') \\ \sum_i -x_i' \\ \sum_i -y_i' \end{bmatrix}$$

We solve this linear system using LU factorization [15].

3   Automatic Correspondence Estimation

This section provides the explanation of an automatic correspondence selection based on homography estimation between two set of points.

Figure 3 shows the main steps of the automatic correspondence estimation. Any interest point extraction algorithm like, Harris [16], DoG [17] or LoG [18][19] (or manual detection) can be used to obtain the salient points P_1 and P_2, given images I_1 and I_2. While theses salient points are obtained, we proceed to obtain the homography $H_{1,2}$ between them, for instance using the Iterative Closest Point Algorithm [20]. Then, we project P_1, and obtain P_1' where $P_1' = H_{1,2} \cdot P_1$, to get the most similar possible correlative position of corresponding points from P_1' to P_2. Finally, we compute the similarity matrix $M_{1,2}$ between P_1' to P_2, given the Euclidean Distance between the points (the similarity is computed as the inverse of the distance). The last step is to solve the assignation problem (for instance, the Hungarian algorithm [21]), to get the correspondences $f_{1,2}$ from P_1 to P_2. Note that the correspondences function between P_1' and P_1 is the identity by construction.

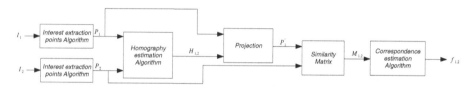

Fig. 3. Scheme of an Automatic Correspondence Estimation model

4   Interactive Correspondence Estimation

Figure 4 presents the main scheme of interactive correspondence estimation. It is based on the correspondence estimation model shown in section 3 but the oracle interaction is considered in two steps (interactive correspondence estimation and interactive similarity restrictions). Dashed lines in the scheme show the interactive part of the model.

Both images I_1 and I_2 and their sets of points P_1 and P_2 are presented to the oracle, together with the current correspondences $f_{1,2}$ and the oracle decides and imposes some correspondences between points $f_{1,2}^*$. Note that $f_{1,2}^*$ can represent a partial labelling between points. So, the oracle is asked to impose only some correspondences. In our experiment section, we suppose the oracle only imposes one correspondence each interaction. The iterative algorithm appends the new points mapping to the ones imposed in the previous iterations and stops when the oracle decides the current correspondences are good enough. The oracles feedback is used to estimate a homography between P_1 and P_2 and also to modify the similarity matrix.

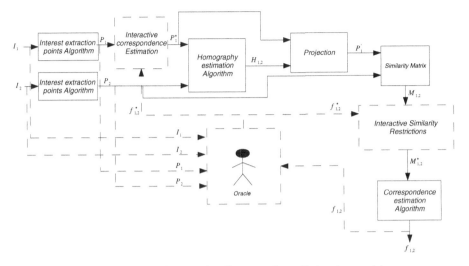

Fig. 4. Scheme of Interactive Correspondence Estimation model

In the first case (figure 5), the scheme of the interactive homography estimation is composed of two steps. In the first one, a homography $H^*_{1,2}$ is deducted (section 2) and in the second step, the set of points P_1 are projected obtaining the new set of points $P^*_1 = H^*_{1,2} \cdot P_1$.

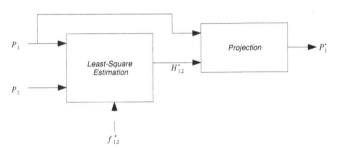

Fig. 5. Scheme of Interactive Homography Estimation

In the second case, the oracle intervenes over the similarity matrix before solving the assignation problem. The above algorithm we use is inspired in the algorithm presented in [22] although in that case, the interactive algorithm modified a cost matrix instead of a similarity matrix. The main idea is that if the oracle considers a pair of points has to be labelled, then, independently of their original similarity, the method imposes their similarity to be the maximum. Moreover, to force the correspondence to be a bijection, the model imposes a zero similarity to the other combinations of correspondences that the pair of points are involved.

Algorithm *Interactive Similarity Restrictions*
   Input: *Similarity Matrix* $M_{1,2}$, *Oracle's correspondences* $f^*_{1,2}$
   Output: *Similarity Matrix with Restrictions* $M^*_{1,2}$

Forall $c_j^i \in f_{1,2}^*$; c_j^i is an oracle's correspondence from i to j
   $M_{1,2}(i, j) = \infty$;
   $M_{1,2}(i, b) = 0$; $\forall b \neq j$
   $M_{1,2}(a, j) = 0$; $\forall j \neq j$
End forall

We force a rigid transformation between images but non-rigid transformations appear in a real application. For this reason, if the interactive actions only influences on the homography estimation, the model may not achieve the correspondences imposed by the oracle. That is, although the oracle has imposed the matching between all points, it may happen that $f_{1,2} \neq f_{1,2}^*$. We show this effect in the practical evaluation.

5   Practical Evaluation

To experimentally validate our method, we have used four image databases.

APARTMENTS database [23]: It consists of ten images of an apartments building taken from different perspectives. Twelve salient points have been manually extracted from each image (figure 1). Each point represents the same part of the scene through the whole images, presenting a combination of rigid and non-rigid relations between them. The first 11 points represent parts of the building and the 12th point is the highest part of a lamppost.

HOTEL [24], **HOUSE** [24] and **FACES** [25]: They are composed of a set of reference points associated with different frames. Each test has T elements $\{P^t, P'^t, O^t\}, 1 \leq t \leq T$. Each element has a pair of sets of points P^t and P'^t and an oracle matching O^t. Each set of points P^t are the original points in the database. T is the number of sets of points of these datasets. Sets of points P'^t have been randomly generated through distorting P^t to make the automatic correspondence establishment more difficult for the automatic method (similar to [26]). First, we added a global artificial transformation for all points (rotation noise with a uniform probability distribution around $360°$ and translation noise with a normal distribution respect to initial position). And second, we added an individual noise for each point following a normal distribution. This noise simulates different viewpoints highly separated between them and makes the oracles interaction useful to find a good solution since the transformation between the original frame and the artificial one is non-rigid. Both sets of points P^t and P'^t have the same number of points. The oracle correspondences O^t has been computed together with the generation of the distorted sets of points P'^t. Nevertheless, by construction, we do not guarantee this correspondence to obtain the minimum cost.

The aim of this method is to minimize the distance between the automatically extracted correspondence and an ideal one. We suppose the ideal correspondence is the one that the oracle would impose when he had interacted on all the points. In these databases, these correspondences relate the same parts of the building in different scenes or the same parts of different faces. The metric used to evaluate the goodness of the method is the hamming distance between the ideal and the current correspondence at each iteration.

In the APARTMENTS dataset, each value of the results below is the average of the hamming distance obtained while executing the method for all combinations of pairs of the 10 images. In the HOTEL, HOUSE and FACES datasets, each result value is the average of the hamming distance while executing the method for each image and its corresponding set of points created artificially.

Figures 6 and 7 show the average hamming distance respect the number of iterations in the four different databases. In interaction 0, the correspondences are automatically computed (figure 3). In the interaction 1, the Interaction Homography Estimation module is not used due to two matchings are needed to deduct a unique affine homography. Nevertheless, the imposition on the similarity matrix is performed with the first oracles feedback. The interaction 2 is the first one that the whole model is applied. We show three different curves that represent: 1) the case in which the whole method is used ⎯⎯⎯ ; 2) the case in which the interactive similarity restrictions are not imposed ⎯⎯⎯ ; 3) the case in which the interactive correspondence estimation is not imposed ⎯•⎯ (see figure 4).

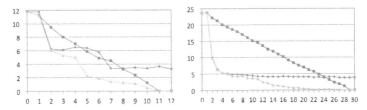

Fig. 6. Hamming distance respect iterations. **a)** APARTMENTS **b)** HOUSE

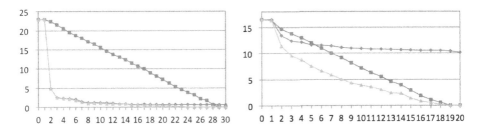

Fig. 7. Hamming distance respect iterations. **a)** HOTEL **b)** FACES

While using (⎯⎯⎯), the model establishes an initial homography at second interaction, for this reason the hamming distance presents a steep descent. Throughout the other iterations, the model slightly updates the homography and imposes the restrictions and so the hamming distance decreases until arriving to zero. When restrictions are not imposed (⎯⎯⎯), the hamming distance does not arrive to zero. This is because, in a real application, a rigid homography does not exist, which would allow to deduct the ideal correspondence applying only this transformation. Finally, in the case that only the restrictions are imposed but a homography is not estimated using the oracles information (⎯•⎯), the hamming distances arrives to zero but more slowly than using the whole method. Through these experiments we show the need of using the whole method since one of the most important qualities that an interactive method needs to have is the ability to react in few oracles interaction.

6   Conclusions and Future Work

When a team of robots needs to have consistent shared information of its environment based on its computer vision systems, usually the completely automatic methods fail to find a good enough correspondence between the different parts of the scene. In these cases, an interactive method can improve the correspondence establishment and so increase the consistency of the shared information.

We have presented an interactive method that, given two images taken from different robots, the oracle imposes some correspondences between their local parts to estimate a homography and to restrict the point correspondences.

Results show that in the firsts iterations, there is an important increase on the quality of the correspondences. This result is important since it means it is not necessary a long-term dependence on the oracle but the initial knowledge of the oracle is crucial.

Nowadays, we are modelling the interaction on several sets of points simultaneously with the aim of obtaining a coherent set of homographies between different scenes. Moreover, we are also studding models for non-rigid homographies. Finally, we want to apply active query strategies at it was done in [26] and [27] to suggest the points to be imposed by the oracle.

Finally, this method is going to be expanded with a tracking method based on probabilities [28] and an automatic method to recognise written symbols, such as, "exit" or "elevator", which is going to be based on a matching graph technique [29].

References

1. Trevai, C., Fukazawa, Y., Ota, J., Yuasa, H., Arai, T.: Cooperative exploration of mobile robots using reaction-diffusion equation on a graph. In: IEEE International Conference on Robotics and Automation, vol. 2 (2003)
2. Casper, J., Murphy, R.R.: Human–robot interactions during the robot-assisted urban search and rescue response at the world trade centre. IEEE Transactions on Systems, Man, and Cybernetics, Part B 33, 367–385 (2003)
3. Garrell, A., Sanfeliu, A.: Cooperative social robots to accompany groups of people. International Journal of Robotics Research 31(13), 1675–1701 (2012)
4. Xu, M., Petrou, M.: 3D Scene interpretation by combining probability theory and logic: The tower of knowledge. Computer Vision and Image Understanding 115(11), 1581–1596 (2011)
5. Tomasi, C., Kanade, T.: Detection and tracking of point features., Tech. Rep. CMUCS-91-132, Carnegie Mellon University (1991)
6. Han, W., Brady, M.: Real-time corner detection algorithm for motion estimation. In: Image and Vision Computing, pp. 695–703 (2005)
7. Rosten, E., Drummond, T.W.: Machine learning for high-speed corner detection. In: Leonardis, A., Bischof, H., Pinz, A. (eds.) ECCV 2006, Part I. LNCS, vol. 3951, pp. 430–443. Springer, Heidelberg (2006)
8. Mikolajczyk, K., Schmid, C.: A performance evaluation of local descriptors. IEEE Trans. Pattern Anal. Mach. Intell. 27(10), 1615–1630 (2005)

9. Zhang, Z.: Iterative point matching for registration of free-form curves and surfaces. Int. J. Comput. Vision 13(2), 119–152 (1994)
10. Fischler, M.A., Bolles, R.C.: Random sample consensus: a paradigm for model fitting with applications to image analysis and automated cartography. Commun. ACM 24(6), 381–395 (1981)
11. Sanromà, G., Alquézar, R., Serratosa, F., Herrera, B.: Smooth Point-set Registration using Neighbouring Constraints. Pattern Recognition Letters 33, 2029–2037 (2012)
12. Sanromà, G., Alquézar, R., Serratosa, F.: A New Graph Matching Method for Point-Set Correspondence using the EM Algorithm and Softassign. Computer Vision and Image Understanding 116(2), 292–304 (2012)
13. Villamizar, M., Andrade-Cetto, J., Sanfeliu, A., Moreno-Noguer, F.: Bootstrapping Boosted Random Ferns for discriminative and efficient object classification. Pattern Recognition 45(9), 3141–3153 (2012)
14. Pedhazur, E.J.: Multiple regression in behavioral research: Explanation and prediction, 2nd edn. Holt, Rinehart and Winston, New York (1982) ISBN 0-03-041760-0
15. Bunch, J.R., Hopcroft, J.: Triangular factorization and inversion by fast matrix multiplication. Mathematics of Computation 28, 231–236 (1974)
16. Harris, C., Stephens, M.: A combined corner and edge detector. In: Proceedings of the 4th Alvey Vision Conference, pp. 147–151 (1988)
17. Lowe, D.: Distinctive Image Features from Scale-Invariant Keypoints. International Journal of Computer Vision 60(2), 91 (2004)
18. Lindeberg, T.: Feature detection with automatic scale selection. International Journal of Computer Vision 30(2) (1998)
19. Mikolajczyk, K., Schmid, C.: Scale and affine invariant interest point detectors (PDF). International Journal of Computer Vision 60(1), 63–86 (2004)
20. Zhang, Z.: Iterative point matching for registration of free-form curves and surfaces, pp. 119–152 (1992)
21. Kuhn, H.W.: The Hungarian method for the assignment problem Export. Naval Research Logistics Quarterly 2(1-2), 83–97 (1955)
22. Serratosa, F., Cortés, X., Solé-Ribalta, A.: Interactive graph matching by means of imposing the pairwise costs. In: ICPR 2012, pp. 1298–1301 (2012)
23. http://deim.urv.cat/~francesc.serratosa/databases/
24. Caetano, T.S., Caelli, T., Schuurmans, D., Barone, D.A.C.: Graphical Models and Point Pattern Matching. IEEE Trans. on PAMI 28(10), 1646–1663 (2006)
25. Jesorsky, O., Kirchberg, K.J., Frischholz, R.W.: Robust Face Detection Using the Hausdorff Distance. In: Bigun, J., Smeraldi, F. (eds.) AVBPA 2001. LNCS, vol. 2091, pp. 90–95. Springer, Heidelberg (2001)
26. Cortés, X., Serratosa, F.: Active-Learning Query Strategies applied to select a Graph Node given a Graph Labelling. In: GbR 2013, Austria, Vienna, pp. 61–70 (2013)
27. Cortés, X., Serratosa, F., Solé, A.: Active Graph Matching based on Pairwise Probabilities between nodes. In: SSPR 2012, Hiroshima, Japan, pp. 98–106 (2012)
28. Serratosa, F., Alquézar, R., Amézquita, N.: A Probabilistic Integrated Object Recognition and Tracking Framework. Expert Systems With Applications 39, 7302–7318 (2012)
29. Serratosa, F., Cortés, X., Solé, A.: Component Retrieval based on a Database of Graphs for Hand-Written Electronic-Scheme Digitalisation, ESWA 40, pp. 2493–2502 (2013)

Interactive Segmentation of Media-Adventitia Border in IVUS

Jonathan-Lee Jones[1], Ehab Essa[1], Xianghua Xie[1,*], and Dave Smith[2]

[1] Department of Computer Science, Swansea University, UK
[2] ABM-UHT Morriston Hospital, Swansea, UK
http://csvision.swan.ac.uk/

Abstract. In this paper, we present an approach for user assisted segmentation of media-adventitia border in IVUS images. This interactive segmentation is performed by a combination of point based soft constraint on object boundary and stroke based regional constraint. The edge based boundary constraint is imposed through searching the shortest path in a three-dimensional graph, derived from a multi-layer image representation. The user points act as attraction points and are treated as soft constraints, rather than hard constraints that the segmented boundary has to pass through the user specified points. User can also use strokes to specify foreground (region of interest). The probabilities of region of interest for each pixel are then calculated and their discontinuity is used to indicate object boundary. This combined approach is formulated as an energy minimization problem that is solved using a shortest path search algorithm. We show that this combined approach allows efficient and effective interactive segmentation, which is demonstrated through identifying media-adventitia border in IVUS images where image artifact, such as acoustic shadow and calcification, are common place. Both qualitative and quantitative analysis are provided based on manual labeled datasets.

Keywords: Image segmentation, graph segmentation, Dijkstra shortest path, IVUS segmentation, media-adventitia border.

1 Introduction

The Intra-Vascular UltraSound (IVUS) imaging technique is a common-place catheter based technology, frequently used in cardiology diagnosis. This catheter based approach is widely used to assess the severity of any stenosis present and to categorize their morphology. It also allows for the measurement of vessel diameter the location of any lesions, as well as many other clinical and therapeutic studies [1]. In most IVUS images, a cross-section of the arterial wall is proceeded, with three regions: the lumen, the vessel (made up of the intima and media layers), and the adventitia surrounding the vessel wall. The media-adventitia border is the dividing layer representing the outer arterial wall. In IVUS images, the media

---

* Corresponding Author.

R. Wilson et al. (Eds.): CAIP 2013, Part II, LNCS 8048, pp. 466–474, 2013.

can be seen as a dark band, with no other distinct features. It is encapsulated by the adventitia, which is a wide layer of fibrous connective tissue. Figure 1 provides an example of IVUS images.

There have been many different approaches to the problem of segmenting IVUS images, e.g. [1–6]. These can be broadly categorized into fully automatic methods, or methods that allow user interactions. In [2] the authors used contour detection and tracing with smoothness constraint and circular dynamic programming optimization to segment lumen border. It assumes homogeneity of the lumen region and high contrast between lumen and artery wall. Katouzian et al. [3] applied complex brushlet transform and constructed magnitudes-phase histograms of coefficients that contain distinct peaks corresponding to lumen and non-lumen regions. The lumen region is then segmented based on K-means classification and a parametric deformable model. Homogeneity of the lumen region is critical to the success of the method. Methods based on region growing, e.g. [6], also suffers from such limitations, since artifacts and irregularities are very common in IVUS images. Particularly for media-adventitia border, the region inside the border is non-uniform as seen in Fig. 1. Calcification in arterial wall leads to acoustic shadowing and high reflectance, as well as catheter and guid wire occlusion and artifacts. Stent placed against internal wall also produces strong features and acoustic shadows that break homogeneity. Incorporating user prior knowledge into segmentation hence is often necessary and has been shown to be an effective approach. For instance, in [4] Ehab et al. incorporated a shape prior into graph cut construction to regularize segmentation of media-adventitia border. However, these approaches generally require significant amount of training data and model re-training is often necessary in order to adapt to new dataset. User initialization is an alternative approach to transfer expert knowledge into segmentation, e.g. [7–13]. However, most user interactions are limited to either boundary based landmark placement or strokes indicating foreground and background regions. in this work, we propose an approach to combine these two different types of user interactions, i.e. boudary based and region based, to segment media-adventitia border in IVUS. The user points, however, are treated as soft constraint, instead of hard constraint in most interactive segmentation methods. We show that this soft user constraint allows effective combination of boundary and region based features. The method is evaluated on an IVUS dataset with manually labelled "ground-truth" and compared against state-of-the-art techniques.

2   Proposed Method

The proposed method involves the user selecting a series of points on the image. These represent the start and the end point for the segmentation, and the user selected points act as the attraction points in the shortest path search which results in the segmentation. In order to enhance the image segmentation, the user can also select areas for foreground using strokes. An energy functional is then formulated based on the combination of the attraction force that is computed using distance transform and the discontinuity in foreground probability.

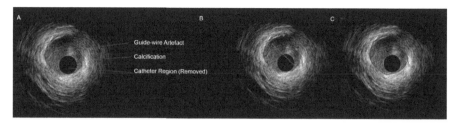

Fig. 1. (a) Original IVUS image. (b) User input (stroke to indicate region of interest and points to indicate boundary). (c) Segmentation result.

By assuming the user points are in a sequential order, we construct a multi-layer graph with each layer encapsulating a single individual user point. The segmentation problem is then transformed into searching the shortest path in this layered graph. This layered approach allows the segmentation to be carried out in polynomial time, instead of an NP-hard optimization problem, at the same time achieving global minima.

2.1   User Input

The proposed method allows two different types of user input: attraction points to indicate media-adventitia border and strokes to indicate region of interest. Fig. 1 provides an example of segmentation using the proposed method. Conventionally, user input to segmentation is focused on foreground and background specification [7–10]. For example, in [8], the user interaction consists of dragging a rectangle around the object of interest and in doing so the user specifies a region of background that is modeled in separating the foreground object. Several other methods require user to specify points on the object boundaries instead [11–13]. However, more often than not, these boundary based user points are treated as anchor points and the segmentation path has to go through them. This kind of hard constraint is not always desirable. It does not allow imprecise user input, and it can lead to difficulties in combining region based and boundary based approaches as discrepancy between different object descriptions is generally expected. Notably, in [13] the authors introduced soft constraint user point by embedding the user constraint in distance functions. The segmentation result is considered to be the shortest path to loosely connect the user points. However, it is known to be a NP-hard problem. Hence, it is assumed that the user points are placed in sequential order and such a constraint reduced the computational complexity to polynomial time. This user input constraint is generally acceptable in identifying IVUS media-adventitia borders. In this work, we follow this approach to treat boundary based user points. However, we also allow user to place region based strokes. These strokes are used to model foreground probability, and the discontinuity in foreground probability indicates the presence of object boundary. We combine these two types user input with image features in an energy functional which is then optimized using graph partitioning through finding the shortest path from the first to last user points.

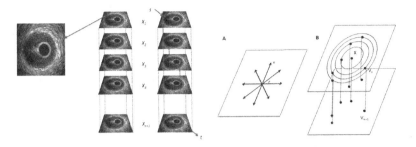

Fig. 2. Layered Graph Construction. The stack of images in the middle and right show how the graph is constructed out of a number of layers corresponding to the number of user points n. The diagrams on the right illustrate the internal layer edges (A) and the edges between neighboring layers (B).

2.2 Layered Graph Construction

In order to impose soft constraint for user point, we follow the approach proposed in [13] to construct a layered graph so that given a set of attraction points we fit a curve to follow the edges in the image and pass through the vicinity of the given points. The user points are assumed to be placed in a sequential order, which is acceptable in our application. The computational complexity, however, is reduced to polynomial time.

For each user point, $X_i, i \in \{1, 2, ..., n\}$, we create a layer of directed graph. In that way we have a series of layers equal to the number of user points n, plus an additional layer to ensure a closed curve, as shown in Fig. 2. This results in a multi-layer directed graph, $G = (V, E)$. For each pixel p, there exits an edge e to each of its neighboring 8 pixels on the same layer. Therefore, a pair of neighboring pixels $(p, q) \in N$ with a corresponding edge $e = (v_p, v_q)$ also have an edge to the corresponding point on the superseding layer $e = (v_{p_n}, v_{p_{n+1}})$. For each edge, we assign a weight w to build a weighted graph (G, w). These weights are calculated based on whether the edge is internal to a layer (w_i) or trans-layer (w_x). By creating the graph in this way, an order is established with the user points. Edges of zero weight are added from the start node r to each pixel in the first layer, and from the terminal node t to the last layer $n + 1$. If P is the set of pixels in the image, we can define the set of nodes V as $V = \{s, t\} \cup \{p \in P \wedge 1 \leq i \leq n + 1\}$ and thusly the set of edges as,

$$E = \{(s, v_p)|p \in P\} \cup \{(v_p, n + 1h, t)|p \in P\}$$
$$\cup \{(v_{p_i}, v_{-q_i})|(p, q) \in N \wedge 1 \leq i \leq n + 1\} \qquad (1)$$
$$\cup \{(v_{p_i}, v_{p_{i+1}})|p \in P \wedge 1 \leq i \leq n + 1\}$$

The segmentation is thus to find the shortest path from the start point r to the end point t, see Fig. 2.

2.3   Edge Weights and Energy Minimization

The edges on the directed layered graph are categorized as internal edges w_i within individual layers and interlayer edges w_x. The weighting for these two types edges is assigned differently.

The internal edges are assigned with two types of weights, i.e. boundary based edge weights and region based edge weights. The boundary based edge weights are calculated based on the magnitude of image gradients, i.e. using an edge detection function $g = 1/(1 + \nabla I)$ where I denotes the image or its smoothed version using, for instance, Gaussian. Hence, for any given edge between neighboring pixels (v_p, v_q) we assign a weight (w_e) according to $w_e((v_p, v_q)) := 1/2\|p - q\|(g(p) + g(q))$. The region based edge weights are computed from foreground probabilities. The user strokes placed in the foreground provide an estimation for foreground intensity distribution, which is then used to evaluate each pixel in the image. The discontinuity in this generated probability map is then used to compute the region based edge weight in the similar fashion to image intensity, i.e. $w_f((v_p, v_q)) := 1/2\|p - q\|(g_f(p) + g_f(q))$ where g_f is the edge detection function based on probability values. The internal edge weight is thus the linear combination of the boundary based weight and region based weight: $w_i = w_e + w_f$.

The attraction force imposed by user points is materialized through the interlayer edge weights w_x. We apply distance transform to the user points in each layer of the graph, and the interlayer edge weight is assigned as $w_x = d(v_{pi}, v_{pj})$ where d denotes the distance transform function. This distance weighting produces isolinear bands of weight around the user point, with increasing weight to go through to the next layer as the distance from the user point increases.

Therefore, the energy function for any curve C in our method is a combination of three terms, i.e.

$$\mathcal{E}(C, s_1, ..., s_n) = \alpha \sum_{i=1}^{n} \|C(s_i) - X_i\| + \beta \int_0^{L(C)} g(C(s)) ds$$

$$+ \int_0^{L(C)} g_f(C(s)) ds, \qquad s.t. s_i < s_j, \forall i < j. \tag{2}$$

The first term is used to enforce the soft constraint by the user points, and it penalizes the path further away from the user points. The second term is the boundary based data term that prefers the path passing through strong edges, whileas the last term is the region based data term which prefers path traveling through abrupt changes in foreground probability. By using the layered graph construction, the minimization of the energy functional is achieved by finding the shortest path from the start point r to the end point t. The Dijkstra's algorithm is used to calculate the shortest path in the layered directed graph. Note, the interlayer edges are unidirectional so that the path can not travel back to previously visited layers.

A smoothing constraint may be added to the energy functional to reduce oscillations of the segmented media-adventitia border. However, for simplicity we use radial basis function (RBF) interpolation to obtain the final smoothed segmentation. The images are transformed from Cartesian coordinates to Polar coordinates so that the RBF interpolation is reduced to a 1D problem which is efficient to solve.

Table 1. Quantitative comparison. HD: Hausdorff Distance (pixels); AOR: Area Overlap Ratio (%); Spec: Specificity (%); Sens: Sensitivity (%), Acc: Accuracy (%).

Method		HD	AOR	Spec	Sens	Acc
Star Graph-cut	Mean	60.57	81.22	89.22	89.86	89.29
	STD	15.64	1.00	12.00	1.00	6.52
Star Graph-cut with F/B labeling	Mean	43.81	86.05	90.39	93.99	92.17
	STD	23.89	9.00	9.00	5.00	5.65
Proposed method w/o F/B labeling	Mean	46.28	69.34	84.92	89.43	88.12
	STD	9.73	9.24	5.82	10.53	8.76
Proposed method with F/B labeling	Mean	33.57	89.93	94.21	93.14	94.41
	STD	5.35	9.16	3.88	5.37	7.67

3   Experimental Results

The proposed method was evaluated on an IVUS dataset containing 248 manually labeled images from 7 different patients and was compared against the recent star graph-cut method [10] which utilizes user input and a generic shape prior as a constraint. This star shape constraint requires the object boundary does not occlude itself from the center of the object, star point, which is very appropriate for IVUS segmentation. It also allows varies degree of user input, i.e. a single user point (star point) and additional foreground and background labeling. We also show performance of the proposed method with user points alone, i.e. without user strokes.

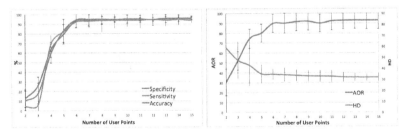

Fig. 3. Initialization dependency test.

The quantitative comparison is based on a number of metrics, including Hausdorff distance, area overlap ratio, specificity, sensitivity and accuracy. Table 1 shows the quantitative results. The star graph-cut method performed reasonably well. However, with foreground and background labeling, the performance clearly

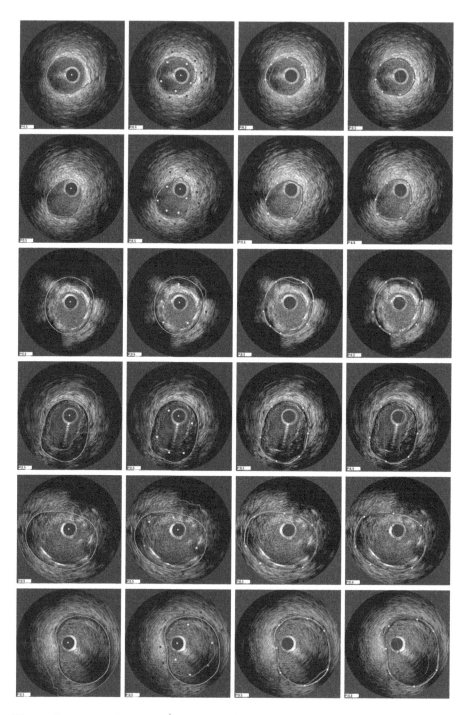

Fig. 4. Comparison between groundtruth (green) and (from left to right) Star Graph Cut [10], Seeded Star Graph Cut, Single Method [13], Proposed Method (red).

improved. The implicit shape prior in star graph construction proved useful in segmenting media-adventitia border which conforms very well to this shape constraint. Comparable performance was achieved for the proposed method without regional support. However, the full proposed method outperformed the rest. Several typical segmentation results are shown in Fig. 4.

To study the robustness of the proposed method, we carried out an initialization dependency test. We tested our method with 15 user points as initialization. We then randomly remove one user point each time for testing until we only have 2 points left for initialization. The overall results using 5 different metrics are shown in Fig. 3. The proposed method achieved good performance with just six user points. Considering in actual application where user input is far experienced than this random process, even less points may be needed.

4   Conclusion

We presented an interactive segmentation technique which combines boundary based and region based object representations. We adopted layered graph representation to simplify computation. The proposed method was compared against a very recent graph cut technique that uses both implicit shape prior and user initialization. Both qualitative and quantitative comparisons on a manually labeled IVUS dataset showed promising performance of the proposed method.

References

1. Katouzian, A., Angelini, E.D., Carlier, S.G., Suri, J.S., Navab, N., Laine, A.F.: A state-of-the-art review on segmentation algorithms in intravascular ultrasound (IVUS) images. IEEE Trans. Info. Tech. in Biomed. 16(5), 823–834 (2012)
2. Luo, Z., Wang, Y., Wang, W.: Estimating coronary artery lumen area with optimization-based contour detection. T-MI 22(4), 564–566 (2003)
3. Katouzian, A., Angelini, E.D., Sturm, B., Laine, A.F.: Automatic detection of luminal borders in ivus images by magnitude-phase histograms of complex brushlet coefficients. In: EMBC, pp. 3072–3076 (2010)
4. Essa, E., Xie, X., Sazonov, I., Nithiarasu, P., Smith, D.: Shape prior model for media-adventitia border segmentation in IVUS using graph cut. In: Menze, B.H., Langs, G., Lu, L., Montillo, A., Tu, Z., Criminisi, A. (eds.) MCV 2012. LNCS, vol. 7766, pp. 114–123. Springer, Heidelberg (2013)
5. Sonka, M., Zhang, X., Siebes, M., Bissing, M.S., DeJong, S.C., Collins, S.M., McKay, C.R.: Segmentation of intravascular ultrasound images: A knowledge-based approach. T-MI 14(4), 719–732 (1995)
6. Brathwaite, P.A., Chandran, K.B., McPherson, D.D., Dove, E.L.: Lumen detection in human IVUS images using region-growing. In: Computers in Cardiology, pp. 37–40 (1996)
7. Boykov, Y., Jolly, M.-P.: Interactive organ segmentation using graph cuts. In: Delp, S.L., DiGoia, A.M., Jaramaz, B. (eds.) MICCAI 2000. LNCS, vol. 1935, pp. 276–286. Springer, Heidelberg (2000)
8. Rother, C., Kolmogorov, V., Blake, A.: Grabcut: interactive foreground extraction using iterated graph cuts. ACM Transactions on Graphics 23(3), 309–314 (2004)

9. Sinop, A.K., Grady, L.: A seeded image segmentation framework unifying graph cuts and random walker which yields a new algorithm. In: ICCV, pp. 1–8 (2007)
10. Veksler, O.: Star shape prior for graph-cut image segmentation. In: Forsyth, D., Torr, P., Zisserman, A. (eds.) ECCV 2008, Part III. LNCS, vol. 5304, pp. 454–467. Springer, Heidelberg (2008)
11. Cohen, L., Kimmel, R.: Global minimum for active contour models: A minimal path approach. IJCV 24(1), 57–78 (1997)
12. Falcáo, A.X., Udupa, J.K., Samarasekera, S., Sharma, S., Hirsch, B.E., de, A., Lotufo, R.: User-steered image segmentation paradigms: Live wire and live lane. Graphical Models and Image Processing 60(4), 233–260 (1998)
13. Windheuser, T., Schoenemann, T., Cremers, D.: Beyond connecting the dots: A polynomial-time algorithm for segmentation and boundary estimation with imprecise user input. In: ICCV, pp. 717–722 (2009)

Kernel Maximum Mean Discrepancy for Region Merging Approach

Alya Slimene and Ezzeddine Zagrouba

Team of research SIIVA, RIADI Laboratory, University of Manouba
Institut supérieur d'informatique (ISI), Université de Tunis El Manar
2 rue abou rayhane bayrouni, 2080, Ariana, Tunisia
`alya.slimene@gmail.com`,
`ezzeddine.zagrouba@fsm.rnu.tn`

Abstract. Kernel methods are becoming increasingly challenging for use in a wide variety of computer vision applications. This paper introduces the use of Kernel Maximum Mean Discrepancy (KMMD) for region merging process. KMMD is a recent unsupervised kernel-based method commonly used in analysing and comparing distributions. We propose a region merging approach based on the KMMD framework which aims at improving the quality of an initial segmentation result. The performance of the proposed method has been compared with four states of the art region merging methods over a test of Berkeley image segmentation data set by means of the probabilistic rand index and variation of information errors. Experiments show that our approach succeeds in achieving a segmentation quality equal to or greater than the referenced methods.

Keywords: Kernel methods, image segmentation, clustering, region merging; MMD.

1 Introduction

Image segmentation is an important low level computer vision task. It aims at partitioning an input image into different and homogenous regions which should be the most semantically meaningful in order to be easily analyzed and efficiently applied in further high level image processing tasks. Different methods have been used in this context which can be classified into three meaningful groups involving clustering methods, region based methods and edge methods. However, clustering methods seems to be an intuitive strategy to deal with image segmentation task[1], discarding the spatial information represent the main drawback of such methods [2]. Different methods have been approached to deal with this issue. The most widely and intuitively used solution to incorporate spatial coherence within clustering method consists in applying a connected component labeling on the classification result[3]. Despite this strategy of spatial information integration can be efficiently applied in non textured image, its adoption in textured ones can lead to inaccurate results. In fact and since, it operates by splitting one cluster into several non overlapping regions grouping all adjacent

R. Wilson et al. (Eds.): CAIP 2013, Part II, LNCS 8048, pp. 475–482, 2013.

pixels that were assigned to the considered cluster, several isolated regions with singular pixels can hence be generated. An other approach that has been proposed to incorporate spatial information consists in adopting a region merging strategy[2]. The outline of this paper is structured as follows: Section 2 gives a review of the basic literature of kernel methods. In section 3 we introduce the proposed unsupervised region merging approach. Section 4 discusses the different proposed methods by analyzing the experimental results obtained by using real data. Finally, the conclusion drawn from this study are summarized in Section 6.

2   Related Work

2.1   Kernel Methods

Kernel methods represent a category of machine learning algorithms recently used for pattern analysis. They have gained popularity among supervised learning algorithms with Support Vector Machine (SVM) since they have been exhibiting excellent performance. Those methods derive their name from the use of kernel functions concept. Those functions consist in defining, on an input domain $\mathcal{X}$, a similarity measure k expressed as follows

$$k : \mathcal{X} \times \mathcal{X} \mapsto \mathbb{R}$$
$$(x_i, x_j) \mapsto k(x_i, x_j) \tag{1}$$

The function k needs to be symmetric, in other words, for all $x_i, x_j \in \mathcal{X}$, $k(x_i, x_j) = k(x_j, x_i)$. Indeed, it requires to be positive semi definite, such that, for any finite set of points $\{x_i\}_{i=1}^m$ in $\mathcal{X}$, and real numbers $\{\alpha_i\}_{i=1}^m$ we have, $\sum_{i,j=1}^m \alpha_i \alpha_j k(x_i, x_j) \geq 0$. Those conditions state for the Mercer's theorem. Furthermore, Kernel function can be regarded as a generalization of dot products, which are gererally considered as a straightforward way to measure similarity among patterns. Such generalization can be reached through mapping the data from the original input space into a higher dimension (feature space) by means of an implicit mapping function ϕ. So, for any two points $x_i, x_j \in \mathcal{X}$ we have $k(x_i, x_j) = \langle \phi(x_i), \phi(x_j) \rangle$. This defines the kernel trick concept. The Gaussian kernel function is the most widely used one which is expressed as follows

$$k(x_i, x_j) = \exp\left(\frac{\|x_i - x_j\|^2}{\sigma}\right) \tag{2}$$

2.2   Previous Work on Kernel Methods Based Region Merging Approach

KM or kernel graph cut [4] method consists in finding the labeling which minimizes, in a kernel-induced space, the segmentation energy functional $\mathcal{F}$, roughly solved by graph cut optimization [5]. The mapping to kernel-induced space is performed by integrating the kernelizing metric into the data term of the energy function $\mathcal{F}$. The kernelizing metric can be explained as follows: for a given

x_i, $x_j \in \mathcal{X}$, the squared norm $\|x_i - x_j\|^2$ is transformed to the one between images of these points which can be expressed as $\|\phi(x_i) - \phi(x_j)\|^2$ and computed as follows

$$\|\phi(x_i) - \phi(x_j)\|^2 = \phi(x_i)^T \phi(x_i) - 2\phi(x_i)^T \phi(x_j) + \phi(x_j)^T \phi(x_j)$$
$$= k(x_i, x_j) - 2k(x_i, x_j) + k(x_j, x_j). \tag{3}$$

Besides, as noted in [5] the Boycov energy function is defined as follows

$$\mathcal{F}_K(\{\mu_l\}, \lambda) = \sum_{l \in \mathcal{L}} \sum_{p \in R_l} (\mu_l - I_p)^2 + \alpha \sum_{\{p,q\} \in \mathcal{N}} r(\lambda(p), \lambda(q)) \tag{4}$$

where $\mathcal{L}$ is a set of finite labels expressed as $\{l_i\}_{i=}^{N_{reg}}$ and N_{reg} represents the number of region. λ stands for an indexing function which assigns a region label to each pixel p of an image Ω. μ_i represents the mean vector modelling the region R_l with label l. $\mathcal{N}$ denotes the neighborhood adjacency, such as a 4-connected neighborhood system. Therefore, integrating equation (3) into (4), the energy function is rewritten as

$$\mathcal{F}_K(\{\mu_l\}, \lambda) = \sum_{l \in \mathcal{L}} \sum_{p \in R_l} k(I_p, I_p) - 2k(I_p, \mu_l) + k(\mu_l, \mu_l) + \alpha \sum_{\{p,q\} \in \mathcal{N}} r(\lambda(p), \lambda(q))$$
$$\tag{5}$$

In the sequel, the KM algorithm can be summarized in the following steps:

1. Construct an initial segmentation of the image through using K-means algorithm.
2. Update the region parameter and compute the derivative of $\mathcal{F}_K$ with respect to μ_l.
3. Form the final segmentation map given region parameters (provided by the previous step) by employing a graph-partitioning algorithm based on the graph cut iterations.
4. Repeat step 2 and step 3 until convergence.

3   Proposed Approach

In this section we present our unsupervised region merging approach which aims at improving an initial segmentation result gotten from a clustering algorithm and that may exhibit an over-segmentation scheme. There are two essential properties in a region merging algorithm: the merging predicate and the merging order. The basic idea behind the merging predicate issue is to use a logic test to decide about the merging possibility of two adjacent regions. Two crucial issues must be taken into account: a similarity measure and a preset threshold. Selecting the optimal threshold value is a difficult task since a big value will lead to an incomplete merging or an under-merging, whereas a small one can result in an over-merging [6]. Actually and to overcome this difficulty, some works suggest to use an interactive scheme to achieve a region merging task [7]. The merging order issue stands for the sequence followed to consider regions for the merging task. It is an important step to be considered, because the merging results can be quite different according to the merging order even with the same merging predicate. The proposed approach relies on using a local entropy based region model and testing the pairs of regions according to an increasing order of area size. Indeed, it provides an automatic region merging technique that doesn't require any step of user selection for object markers. Since it's based on the use of kernel methods it's called KM2DRM for kernel maximum mean discrepancy for region merging approach.

Algorithm 1. KM2DRM

Input : An initial segmentation S_0 containing a set of regions $\mathbf{R} = \{R_1, \ldots, R_N\}$
Output : Region merging result

1. Pairwise regions ordering
2. Sampling data from the pairs i of regions.
3. Evaluating the consistency of the merging test for regions R_k and R_l depicted from the pairs i. Merge R_k and R_l if test true.
4. Go back to step 2, until no pairs of regions can be considered.
5. Go back to step 1, until no merging of adjacent regions can be occurred.
6. Return the segmentation results.

3.1 Merging Test

The Maximum Mean discrepancy (MMD) is a measure of distance between probability distributions.It's based on approximating the divergence between two distributions by means of the maximum divergence between mean function values defined on samples drawn from each of those distributions. Let $\mathcal{F}$ be a class of functions $f : \mathcal{X} \rightarrow \mathbb{R}$, let x and y be random variables defined on the space $\mathcal{X}$ with respective probability distribution p and q, then for a given two observations sets $X = \{x_i, \cdots, x_m\}$ and $Y = \{y_i, \cdots, y_n\}$ drawn respectively from p and q, the MMD is defined as follows

$$MMD\left[\mathcal{F}, p, q\right] = \sup_{f \in \mathcal{F}} \left(\mathbf{E}_x\left[f\left(x\right)\right] - \mathbf{E}_y\left[f\left(y\right)\right]\right). \qquad (6)$$

where $\mathbf{E}_x\left[f\left(x\right)\right]$ (respectively $\mathbf{E}_y\left[f\left(y\right)\right]$) is a shorthand notation of $\mathbf{E}_{x \sim p}\left[f\left(x\right)\right]$ (respectively $\mathbf{E}_{y \sim q}\left[f\left(y\right)\right]$) which denotes expectation with respect to p where $x \sim p$ indicates that x has distribution p. An empirical estimate of the MMD is expressed as

$$MMD\left[\mathcal{F}, X, Y\right] = \sup_{f \in \mathcal{F}} \left(\frac{1}{m}\sum_{i=1}^{m} f\left(x_i\right) - \frac{1}{n}\sum_{i=1}^{n} f\left(y_i\right)\right). \qquad (7)$$

As explained in [8] the ideal class of function $\mathcal{F}$ is represented by the unit ball in a reproducing kernel Hilbert space (RKHS) $\mathcal{H}$. In this space, the function f

can be expressed as an inner product such that $f(x) = \langle f, \phi(x) \rangle_{\mathcal{H}}$. Where $\phi(x)$ represent a feature mapping from $\mathcal{X}$ to $\mathbb{R}$ which can be rewritten by virtue of kernel function as $k(x, .)$. Denoting by $\mu_p = \mathbf{E}_p[\phi(x)]$ the expectation of in feature space. The squared MMD can be then expressed in RKHS (KMMD) as $\| \mu_p - \mu_q \|_{\mathcal{H}}^2$

$$MMD^2[\mathcal{F}, p, q] = \mathbf{E}_{x,x'}[k(x, x')] - 2\mathbf{E}_{x,y}[k(x, y)] + \mathbf{E}_{y,y'}[k(y, y')] \qquad (8)$$

where x'(resp. y') is an independent copy of x (resp. y) with the same distribution. An unbiased empirical estimate of the KMMD is expressed as

$$MMD^2[\mathcal{F}, X, Y] = \frac{1}{m(m-1)} \sum_{i=1}^{m} \sum_{j \neq i}^{m} k(x_i, x_j) + \frac{1}{n(n-1)} \sum_{i=1}^{n} \sum_{j \neq i}^{n} k(y_i, y_j)$$

$$- \frac{2}{mn} \sum_{i=1}^{m} \sum_{j=1}^{n} k(x_i, y_j) \qquad (9)$$

The objective is to use the KMMD in a statistical hypothesis testing to decide, for two i.i.d samples $X \sim p$ and $Y \sim q$, if the null hypothesis $\mathcal{H}_0 : p = q$ or the alternative hypothesis $\mathcal{H}_A : p \neq q$ is occurred. To be done, the empirical estimate of the KMMD is compared to a threshold: if the threshold is exceeded then the null hypothesis is rejected. The value of this threshold define the range of the acceptance region. When working with statistical test, two errors can be encountered: type I error and type II error. A Type I error is the incorrect rejection of a true null hypothesis. A Type II error consists in the acceptance of a false null hypothesis. Generally, probabilities of those errors are bounded. In fact, the level α of a test is an upper bound on the probability of a type I error. This parameter is involved in tuning up the value of the threshold. In [9], two bounds on the KMMD are suggested to be used. The first relies on using the Hoeffding bound [10] for an unbiased statistics. The second is based on estimating the acceptance region $(1 - \alpha$ quantile of the null distribution) through using a bootstrap technique on the aggregated data[11].

3.2 Sampling Strategy

In this section we present how we have applied the KMMD based merging predicate in the merging task. For this issue, we have adopted a windowing strategy to sample pixels from two considered regions R_i and R_j. Let R_i be the region with the smallest area and with label i. To decide if R_i can be merged into R_j, we choose from the smallest region a seed point sp where its location is far away from the boundary. Then from this point, we extract the set of pixels of label i that's lying on the window $\mathcal{W}_{sp}$ of size ω that's centered on sp. Next, to extract points from the region R_j we use an other window $\mathcal{W}_{exp}$ expansion of $\mathcal{W}_{sp}$ by factor of 0.5ω. From the four corners of $\mathcal{W}_{exp}$, four windows of size ω are used. The one selected is the one which has the biggest number of labeled pixels in R_j.

4   Experimentation

In order to show the effectiveness of our approach, experiments have been carried out on natural images of the Berkeley data set [12]. KM [4] was used to provide a basis of comparison for the proposed approach. As input for the KM2DRM approach, the set of initial image segmentation results is obtained from the PSO-SVDD kernel clustering method presented in [13]. The proposed method was implemented in Matlab. For both methods, the gaussian kernel is used where the value of sigma was fixed for all images in the data set, such as to provide optimal performance on the training set. It was set to 0.5 for KM and 0.3 for KM2DRM. As an objective evaluation of the proposed method, we make use of the probabilistic rand index (PRI) [14] and the variation of information (VOI)[15] measures. A quantitative comparison of the proposed methods against

Table 1. Average Performance

Algorithms	humans	PSO-SVDD	Mean-shift	CTM	KM	KM2DRM
PRI	0.8754	0.7532	0.7550	0.7627	0.7650	0.7884
VOI	1.1040	3.4573	2.4770	2.2035	2.4091	2.3356

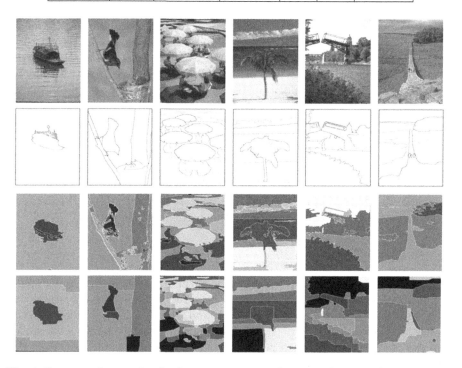

Fig. 1. Segmentation result: the first row represent the original image, the second row shows the ground truth, the third row shows the segmentation result with the proposed method and the fourth represents the segmentation result with the KM method.

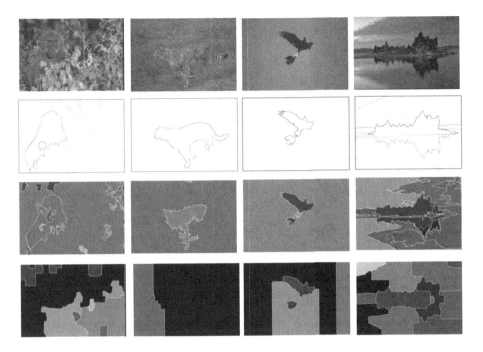

Fig. 2. Other Segmentation results.

four state-of-the-art methods is illustrated in table 1. PRI ranges from 0 to 1, higher is better. VOI ranges between $[0, \infty[$, lower is better. However, KM2DRM outperforms Mean-Shift, CTM, and KM in terms of PRI indice, the CTM has the lowest value of VOI and this due to its optimization of an information theoretic criterion. Moreover, those results assert the ability of the proposed approach to enhance the segmentation quality of the PSO-SVDD.

In Figure 1 and 2, we illustrate the segmentation results obtained by the KM [4] (fourth line) and the KM2DRM methods (third line). We can observe that the segmentation results obtained with the proposed method has been able to exhibit natural boundaries and in comparison has been able to achieve a good segmentation when applied to image of cheetah and monkey where the skin tones are highly correlated to the backgound.

5   Conclusion

In this paper, we have presented and tested a novel kernel based approach for region merging. The main idea underlying the proposed method was to investigate a new approach using the kernel two sample test within a region merging approach. The aim of such strategy consists in improving an initial segmentation result obtained through using a clustering method and further application of connected component labeling. The fundamental quality of the proposed technique is that it is able to find the value of the statistical test threshold automatically. Experiments on natural images show the efficiency of the proposed approach.

References

1. Lee, J., Wang, J., Zhang, C.: Color image segmentation: Kernel do the feature space. In: Lavrač, N., Gamberger, D., Todorovski, L., Blockeel, H. (eds.) ECML 2003. LNCS (LNAI), vol. 2837, pp. 253–264. Springer, Heidelberg (2003)
2. Matas, J., Kittler, J.: Spatial and feature space clustering: Applications in image analysis. In: Computer Analysis of Images and Patterns, pp. 162–173 (1995)
3. Lefèvre, S.: A new approach for unsupervised classification in image segmentation. In: Guillet, F., Ritschard, G., Zighed, D.A., Briand, H. (eds.) Advances in Knowledge Discovery and Management. SCI, vol. 292, pp. 113–131. Springer, Heidelberg (2010)
4. Salah, M.B., Mitiche, A., Ayed, I.B.: Multiregion image segmentation by parametric kernel graph cuts. IEEE Transactions on Image Processing 20(2), 545–557 (2011)
5. Boykov, Y., Veksler, O., Zabih, R.: Fast approximate energy minimization via graph cuts. IEEE Transactions on Pattern Analysis and Machine Intelligence 23(11), 1222–1239 (2001)
6. Ning, J., Zhang, L., Zhang, D., Wu, C.: Interactive image segmentation by maximal similarity based region merging. Pattern Recogn. 43(2), 445–456 (2010)
7. Felzenszwalb, P.F., Huttenlocher, D.P.: Efficient graph-based image segmentation. Int. J. Comput. Vision 59(2), 167–181 (2004)
8. Borgwardt, K.M., Gretton, A., Rasch, M.J., Kriegel, H.-P., Schölkopf, B., Smola, A.J.: Integrating structured biological data by kernel maximum mean discrepancy. Bioinformatics 22(14), e49–e57 (2006)
9. Gretton, A., Borgwardt, K.M., Rasch, M.J., Schölkopf, B., Smola, A.: A kernel two-sample test. J. Mach. Learn. Res. 13, 723–773 (2012)
10. Hoeffding, W.: Probability inequalities for sums of bounded random variables (1962)
11. Arcones, M.A., Gine, E.: On the boostrap of u and v statistics. Annals of Statistics 20(2), 655–674 (1992)
12. Martin, D., Fowlkes, C., Tal, D., Malik, J.: A database of human segmented natural images and its application to evaluating segmentation algorithms and measuring ecological statistics. In: Proc. 8th Int'l Conf. Computer Vision, vol. 2, pp. 416–423 (2001)
13. Slimene, A., Zagrouba, E.: A new pso based kernel clustering method for image segmentation. In: Seventh International Conference on Signal Image Technology and Internet-Based Systems, pp. 350–357 (2011)
14. Unnikrishnan, R., Hebert, M.: Measures of similarity. In: Application of Computer Vision, vol. 1, pp. 394–400 (2005)
15. Meila, M.: Comparing clusterings: an axiomatic view. In: Proceedings of the 22nd International Conference on Machine Learning, pp. 577–584 (2005)
16. Liu, X., Wang, D.: A spectral histogram model for textons and texture discrimination. Vision Research 42(23), 2617–2634 (2002)

Laplacian Derivative Based Regularization for Optical Flow Estimation in Driving Scenario

Naveen Onkarappa and Angel D. Sappa

Computer Vision Center, Edifici O, Campus UAB,
08193 Bellaterra, Barcelona, Spain
{naveen,asappa}@cvc.uab.es

Abstract. Existing state of the art optical flow approaches, which are evaluated on standard datasets such as Middlebury, not necessarily have a similar performance when evaluated on driving scenarios. This drop on performance is due to several challenges arising on real scenarios during driving. Towards this direction, in this paper, we propose a modification to the regularization term in a variational optical flow formulation, that notably improves the results, specially in driving scenarios. The proposed modification consists on using the Laplacian derivatives of flow components in the regularization term instead of gradients of flow components. We show the improvements in results on a standard real image sequences dataset (KITTI).

Keywords: Optical Flow, Regularization, Driver Assistance Systems, Performance Evaluation.

1 Introduction

Computer vision has got applications in innumerable ways to our lives. Recently the idea of using computer vision for driving assistance has opened new research opportunities. The need of the safety has steered driver assistance applications getting interest from both academia and major corporations as well. Having vision sensors such as cameras mounted on automotives, acquiring information from such sensors and using it to alert the driver and/or control the vehicle is the basic structure of advanced driver assistance systems (ADAS). Optical flow techniques for the motion estimation are the very necessary and important ingredients in making several ADAS applications such as egomotion estimation, moving object detection, collision avoidance, automated control a reality. Optical flow field is the motion vector field indicating the displacement of pixels between consecutive images in a sequence.

Optical flow techniques, which give dense flow fields, are formulated as variational energy minimization problems. These methods are referred to as global methods. On the other hand, the methods that produce sparse flow fields for some detected feature points on an image are referred to as local methods. The first local method has been proposed by Lucas and Kanade [1] in 1981. The variational formulation is also proposed in 1981 by Horn and Schunck [2]. There have been huge number of contributions in these three decades to improve the

R. Wilson et al. (Eds.): CAIP 2013, Part II, LNCS 8048, pp. 483–490, 2013.

accuracy of estimated flow field. We can coarsely group such developments into: formulation of robust and higher order data terms, improving edge preserving regularizations, adding more features/information to the energy model and to the minimization techniques of the energy functions. The thesis [3] gives a detailed survey on the improvements in data term and regularization terms proposed through the last years looking for accurate results. Also an attempt to evaluate performance of several optical flow techniques is made in [4]. In recent years, the research on optical flow is getting a lot of interests [5]. Most of the research concentrates on variational methods [2], [6], [7], which produce dense flow fields. Some of the works deal with preserving flow edges (e.g., [8], [9], [10]) and formulating sophisticated data terms [11]. A recent work [12] discusses the concepts such as pre-processing, coarse-to-fine warping, graduated non-convexity, interpolation, derivatives, robustness of penalty functions, median filtering and proposes a method considering the best of the variants of discussed concepts.

All the contributions mentioned above are targeted, performed and evaluated on few standard datasets. One of the most well known optical flow benchmark dataset is Middlebury [13], which contains limited scenarios and image pairs have small displacements. This dataset do not involve much realistic characteristics. A big challenge when real dataset with realistic scenarios need to be obtained lies on the difficulty in obtaining ground-truth optical flow. Recently, Geiger et. al [14] have proposed a new real dataset of driving scenarios containing large displacements, specularity, shadows and different illuminations. They have also provided sparse ground-truth flow field. This dataset is referred to as KITTI [15]. One can think that the state of the art methods that give the best results on Middlebury dataset can also perform similarly on KITTI dataset. However, by analyzing the KITTI flow evalation we can appriciate that such a statement is wrong due to the difficulties of this particular dataset. There are few attempts those tried to adapt the existing methods to the driving scenario using epipolar geometry and rigid body motion information. The approach in [16] estimates both optical flow and fundamental matrix together. The accuracy of this method reduces when there is a dynamic scene as one can expect that the driving scenario is always dynamic.

Driving scenarios vary very largely by environment, weather conditions and day-light conditions. The driving environment itself involves the situations such as urban, highway, countryside with different geometry of scenes and textures. Apart from these the vehicle speed [17] and turning in road also matters causing very large displacement. So developing an optical flow technique that withstands all such difficult scenarios is a challenging research topic. Actually there is a lack of specialized methods for driving scenarios where occurs a variety of difficulties. In the current work, we propose an improvement over an existing state of the art method [12]. In this work, we specifically deal with the importance of regularization. We propose a modication to the derivative operator in the regularization that deals with large variations in speed and rotations that exist in KITTI dataset. The performance analysis done on the KITTI dataset shows that the proposed modification improves the results.

The paper is organized as follows. Section 2 gives an overview of the basic optical flow formulation and the proposed modification. Experimental results are provided in section 3 followed by the conclusions in section 4.

2   Optical Flow Overview and Proposed Modification

In this section, we first give an overview of basic variational formulation of optical flow estimation. In general, variational energy models involve a data term and a regularization term. The data term formulates the assumption of some matching characteristics typically the intensity of the pixel and it is also called brightness constancy assumption (BCA). The classical variational method of Horn and Schunck [2] assumes the constancy of brightness, which is also called optical flow constraint (OFC). The OFC can be formulated as: $I_1(x + u) - I_0(x) = 0$, where I_0 and I_1 are two images, $x = (x_1, x_2)$ is the pixel location within the image space $\Omega \subseteq \mathbf{R}^2$; $u = (u_1(x), u_2(x))$ is the two-dimensional flow vector. Linearizing the above equation using first-order Taylor expansion we get OFC as: $(I_{x_1} u_1 + I_{x_2} u_2 + I_t)^2 = 0$, where subscripts denote the partial derivatives. Using only OFCs do not provide enough information to infer meaningful flow fields, making the problem ill-posed. Particularly, optical flow computation suffers from two issues: first, no information is available in non-textured regions. Second, one can only compute the normal flow, i.e., the motion perpendicular to the edges. This problem is generally known as the aperture problem. In order to solve this problem it is clear that some kind of regularization is needed. The Horn and Schunk [2] method overcomes this by assuming the resulting flow field globally smooth all over the image, that can be realized as penalizing large flow gradients ∇u_1 and ∇u_2. Combining OFC and homogeneous regularization in a single variational framework and squaring both constraints yields the following energy function:

$$E(u) = \int_\Omega \{ \underbrace{(I_{x_1} u_1 + I_{x_2} u_2 + I_t)^2}_{Data\ Term} \tag{1}$$
$$+ \alpha \underbrace{(|\nabla u_1|^2 + |\nabla u_2|^2)}_{Regularization} \} \, dx,$$

where α is the regularization weight. This energy function is minimized for flow vectors using corresponding Euler-Lagrange equations. Another alternative way to solve this is by using dual formulation [18].

Based on the above basic formulation, the authors in [12] proposed a formulation using median filtering in addition to the other improvements proposed in previous literature and explored by them. It is known that median filtering at every iteration of flow computation improves the results. The work in [12] incorporates this filtering heuristics into the objective function. This improved non-local median filtering based method is called C+NL. In most of the methods in literature authors try to penalize the gradient of the estimated flow vectors

using different and combinations of robust penalizing functions. In a driving sequence, there occurs large variations in magnitude and orientations due to change
in speed of the vehicle, turn of the vehicle, specularity, and scene dynamics. In
general, driving scenarios are very dynamic with large variations. Hence, in the
current work we propose to penalize the Laplacian of flow components instead of
their gradients. With the basic formulation notation, the equation (1) becomes:

$$E(\boldsymbol{u}) = \int_{\Omega} \{ \underbrace{(I_{x_1} u_1 + I_{x_2} u_2 + I_t)^2}_{Data\ Term} \tag{2}$$
$$+ \alpha \underbrace{(|\triangle u_1|^2 + |\triangle u_2|^2)}_{Regularization} \} \, d\boldsymbol{x}.$$

In summary, we propose to modify the derivative of flow components in the regularization to second derivative as shown in equation (2) in the approach presented
in [12]. We will refer to this method as C+NL-M. With second derivative regularization, it allows more variations in flow components. Hence, as shown in
the next section the proposed modification results in more accurate optical flow
estimations.

3   Experimental Results

The proposed modification has been evaluated with respect to the state of the
art method C+NL, which is one of the best approach on Middlebury dataset.

Fig. 1. Results for a pair of images; (*top*) 1st image of the pair; (*middle*) error map;
and (*bottom*) computed flow field.

The analysis of performance is carried out on the standard dataset KITTI [14]. This dataset contains image pairs of real driving scenarios with varied real characteristics that make optical flow computation a real challenge in such scenarios. This dataset consists of 194 training image pairs and 195 test image pairs. The results on few of the testing pairs from KITTI are shown in Figures 1, 2 and 3. In these figures, the (*top*) is the 1st image of individual pairs, (*middle*) is the error map, and the (*bottom*) is the computed flow field. The red area in the (*middle*) indicates the occluded pixels falling outside image boundary.

Table 1. Error values for the image pairs shown in Fig. 1 by C+NL

Error	Out-Noc	Out-All	Avg-Noc	Avg-All
2 pixels	32.68 %	42.11 %	11.1 px	17.5 px
3 pixels	30.74 %	40.00 %	11.1 px	17.5 px
4 pixels	29.56 %	38.48 %	11.1 px	17.5 px
5 pixels	28.56 %	37.13 %	11.1 px	17.5 px

Fig. 2. Results for a pair of images; (*top*) 1st image of the pair; (*middle*) error map; and (*bottom*) computed flow field.

Table 2. Error values for the image pairs shown in Fig. 1 by C+NL-M

Error	Out-Noc	Out-All	Avg-Noc	Avg-All
2 pixels	25.27 %	32.90 %	9.1 px	16.1 px
3 pixels	22.43 %	30.04 %	9.1 px	16.1 px
4 pixels	21.14 %	28.73 %	9.1 px	16.1 px
5 pixels	20.19 %	27.75 %	9.1 px	16.1 px

Fig. 3. Results for a pair of images; (*top*) 1st image of the pair; (*middle*) error map; and (*bottom*) computed flow field.

The evaluation performed by the KITTI server computes the average number of bad pixels for non-occluded or all pixels for available ground-truth. This evaluation is performed over the optical flow computed on testing set with our modified approach that has been uploaded to the KITTI server. Table 1 shows the errors for the image pair shown in Fig. 1 for the approach C+NL, whereas Table 2 shows the errors for the same pair for the proposed approach C+NL-M. It can be appreciated that C+NL-M gives better results and as presented below C+NL-M is ranked higher than the C+NL by the KITTI evaluation procedure. It should be noted that both C+NL and C+NL-M in this work use fast version of their implementations.

The evaluation table ranks all methods according to the number of non-occluded erroneous pixels at the specified end-point error threshold. At the time of submission (on 5th April 2013), our proposed method ranks 8th, whereas C+NL ranks 16th for 2 pixel threshold. The ranking table from the KITTI web service is shown in Fig. 4. For 3 pixel threshold our method ranks at 9th as shown in Fig. 5. This shows that changing the regularization to Laplacian notably improves the results, specifically in the sequences of driving scenarios. At the time of acceptance of this publication, the previous entry of C+NL in [15] has been replaced by a modified version by the original authors. Note that our proposed modified method better performs compared to the original approach in [12].

Rank	Method	Setting	Out-Noc	Out-All	Avg-Noc	Avg-All	Density	Runtime	Environment	Compare
1	PCBP-Flow	ms	6.33 %	11.59 %	0.9 px	2.2 px	100.00 %	3 min	4 cores @ 2.5 Ghz (Matlab + C/C++)	
	Koichiro Yamaguchi, David McAllester and Raquel Urtasun. Robust Monocular Epipolar Flow Estimation, CVPR 2013										
2	MotionSLIC	ms	6.72 %	14.06 %	1.0 px	2.7 px	100.00 %	11 s	1 core @ 3.0 Ghz (C/C++)	
	Koichiro Yamaguchi, David McAllester and Raquel Urtasun. Robust Monocular Epipolar Flow Estimation, CVPR 2013										
3	PR-Sceneflow		6.91 %	12.39 %	1.3 px	3.3 px	100.00 %	150 sec	4 core @ 3.0 Ghz (Matlab + C/C++)	
	Anonymous submission										
4	TGV2ADCSIFT		8.86 %	18.47 %	1.6 px	4.5 px	100.00 %	8s	GPU @ 1.5 Ghz (C/C++)	
	Anonymous submission										
5	Data-Flow		10.86 %	19.00 %	2.3 px	5.7 px	100.00 %	3 min	2 cores @ 2.5 Ghz (Matlab + C/C++)	
	Anonymous submission										
6	TGV2CENSUS		13.33 %	21.11 %	2.9 px	6.6 px	100.00 %	4 s	GPU+CPU @ 3.0 Ghz (Matlab + C/C++)	
	Manuel Werlberger. Convex Approaches for High Performance Video Processing, 2011										
	Rene Ranftl, Stefan Gehrig, Thomas Pock and Horst Bischof. Pushing the Limits of Stereo Using Variational Stereo Estimation, IEEE Intelligent Vehicles Symposium 2012										
7	fSGM		14.56 %	25.94 %	3.2 px	12.2 px	100.00 %	60 s	1 core @ 2.4 Ghz (C/C++)	
	Simon Hermann and Reinhard Klette. Hierarchical Scan Line Dynamic Programming for Optical Flow using Semi-Global Matching, Intelligent Mobile Vision, ACCV-Workshop 2012										
8	C+NL-M		21.13 %	28.37 %	7.4 px	14.5 px	100.00 %	5 min	2 cores @ 2.5 Ghz (Matlab)	
	Anonymous submission										
9	eFolki		22.01 %	31.50 %	5.2 px	10.8 px	100.00 %	0.026 s	GPU @ 700 Mhz (C/C++)	
	Anonymous submission										
10	HS		22.02 %	31.18 %	5.8 px	11.7 px	100.00 %	1 min	1 core @ 2.5 Ghz (Matlab + C/C++)	
	Berthold K. P. Horn and Brian G. Schunck. Determining optical flow. A Retrospective, AI 1993										
11	RSRS-Flow		22.68 %	31.81 %	6.2 px	12.1 px	100.00 %	4 min	1 core @ 2.5 Ghz (Matlab)	
	Hrayim Ghom and B.S. Manjunath. Robust Simultaneous Registration and Segmentation with Sparse Error Reconstruction, IEEE Transactions on Pattern Analysis and Machine Intelligence 2012										
12	GC-BM-Bino	ms	23.07 %	33.10 %	5.0 px	12.0 px	83.73 %	1.3 s	2 cores @ 2.5 Ghz (C/C++)	
	Bernd Kitt and Henning Lategahn. Trinocular Optical Flow Estimation for Intelligent Vehicle Applications, Proceedings of the IEEE International Conference on Intelligent Transportation Systems 2012										
13	ALD		24.28 %	33.63 %	10.9 px	16.0 px	100.00 %	110 s	1 core @ 2.5 Ghz (C/C++)	
	M. Tesol, S. Vost and A. Bruhn. Adaptive Integration of Feature Matches into Variational Optical Motion Estimation, ACCV 2012										
14	LDOF		24.43 %	33.87 %	5.5 px	12.4 px	100.00 %	1 min	1 core @ 2.5 Ghz (C/C++)	
	T. Brox and J. Malik. Large Displacement Optical Flow, Descriptor Matching in Variational Motion Estimation, PAMI 2011										
15	GC-BM-Mono	ms	24.79 %	34.59 %	5.0 px	12.1 px	84.33 %	1.3 s	2 cores @ 2.5 Ghz (C/C++)	
	Bernd Kitt and Henning Lategahn. Trinocular Optical Flow Estimation for Intelligent Vehicle Applications, Proceedings of the IEEE International Conference on Intelligent Transportation Systems 2012										
16	C+NL		26.42 %	35.28 %	9.0 px	16.4 px	100.00 %	3 min	1 core @ 2.5 Ghz (C/C++)	

Fig. 4. Evaluation table for 2 pixel error threshold (data from [15])

Rank	Method	Setting	Out-Noc	Out-All	Avg-Noc	Avg-All	Density	Runtime	Environment	Compare
9	C+NL-M		19.17 %	26.35 %	7.4 px	14.5 px	100.00 %	5 min	2 cores @ 2.5 Ghz (Matlab)	
16	C+NL		24.64 %	33.35 %	9.0 px	16.4 px	100.00 %	3 min	1 core @ 2.5 Ghz (C/C++)	

Fig. 5. Evaluation table for 3 pixel error threshold (data from [15])

4   Conclusions

We explore and realized that the state of the art optical flow methods does not necessarily perform well for driving scenarios. Towards this, in this paper we propose a modification of the regularization term in a state of the art method. The derivative of flow components are changed to Laplacian from gradient. The experimental results are performed on a standard benchmark data set (KITTI) that contains real image pairs of a driving scenario with challenging characteristics. The evaluation shows that the proposed modification performs better. We envisage that the KITTI dataset will lead research to the development of new approaches that can perform in very complex scenarios and our future work concentrates on this line.

Acknowledgments. This work has been partially supported by the Spanish Government under Research Project TIN2011-25606. Naveen Onkarappa is supported by FI grant of AGAUR, Catalan Government.

References

1. Lucas, B.D., Kanade, T.: An iterative image registration technique with an application to stereo vision (DARPA). In: DARPA Image Understanding Workshop, pp. 121–130 (April 1981)
2. Horn, B.K.P., Schunk, B.G.: Determining optical flow. Artificial Intelligence 17, 185–203 (1981)
3. Bruhn, A.: Variational Optic Flow Computation: Accurate Modelling and Efficient Numerics. PhD thesis, Department of Mathematics and Computer Science, Saarland University, Saarbrücken (2006)
4. Barron, J.L., Fleet, D.J., Beauchemin, S.S.: Performance of optical flow techniques. International Journal of Computer Vision 12(1), 43–77 (1994)
5. http://vision.middlebury.edu/flow/
6. Brox, T., Bruhn, A., Papenberg, N., Weickert, J.: High accuracy optical flow estimation based on a theory for warping. In: Pajdla, T., Matas, J(G.) (eds.) ECCV 2004. LNCS, vol. 3024, pp. 25–36. Springer, Heidelberg (2004)
7. Wedel, A., Pock, T., Zach, C., Cremers, D., Bischof, H.: An improved algorithm for TV-L1 optical flow. In: Dagstuhl Motion Workshop, Dagstuhl Castle, Germany, pp. 23–45 (September 2008)
8. Weickert, J., Schnörr, C.: A theoretical framework for convex regularizers in pde-based computation of image motion. Internal Journal of Computer Vision 45(3), 245–264 (2001)
9. Wedel, A., Cremers, D., Pock, T., Bischof, H.: Structure- and motion-adaptive regularization for high accuracy optic flow. In: IEEE International Conference of Computer Vision, Kyoto, Japan, pp. 1663–1668 (2009)
10. Zimmer, H., Bruhn, A., Weickert, J.: Optic flow in harmony. Internal Journal of Computer Vision 93(3), 368–388 (2011)
11. Steinbruecker, F., Pock, T., Cremers, D.: Advanced data terms for variational optic flow estimation. In: Vision, Modeling, and Visualization Workshop, Braunschweig, Germany, pp. 155–164 (2009)
12. Sun, D., Roth, S., Black, M.J.: Secrets of optical flow estimation and their principles. In: IEEE Conference of Computer Vision and Pattern Recognition, San Francisco, CA, USA, pp. 2432–2439 (June 2010)
13. Baker, S., Scharstein, D., Lewis, J.P., Roth, S., Black, M.J., Szeliski, R.: A database and evaluation methodology for optical flow. In: IEEE International Conference of Computer Vision, pp. 1–8 (October 2007)
14. Geiger, A., Lenz, P., Urtasun, R.: Are we ready for autonomous driving? the KITTI vision benchmark suite. In: Computer Vision and Pattern Recognition (CVPR), Providence, USA (June 2012)
15. http://www.cvlibs.net/datasets/kitti/eval_stereo_flow.php?benchmark=flow
16. Valgaerts, L., Bruhn, A., Weickert, J.: A variational model for the joint recovery of the fundamental matrix and the optical flow. In: Rigoll, G. (ed.) DAGM 2008. LNCS, vol. 5096, pp. 314–324. Springer, Heidelberg (2008)
17. Onkarappa, N., Sappa, A.D.: An empirical study on optical flow accuracy depending on vehicle speed. In: IEEE Intelligent Vehicles Symposium, pp. 1138–1143 (June 2012)
18. Zach, C., Pock, T., Bischof, H.: A duality based approach for realtime TV-L^1 optical flow. In: DAGM Symposium, Heidelberg, Germany, pp. 214–223 (September 2007)

Local and Global Statistics-Based Explicit Active Contour for Weld Defect Extraction in Radiographic Inspection

Aicha Baya Goumeidane[1], Nafaa Nacereddine[1], and Mohammed Khamadja[2]

[1] Centre de recherche Scientifique et Technique en Soudage et Controle,
(CSC), Cheraga, 16002 Alger, Algeria
ab_goumeidane@yahoo.fr, nafaa.nacereddine@enp.edu.dz
[2] SP_Lab, Electronic Dept., University Constantine 1,
Ain El Bey Road, 25000 Constantine, Algeria
m_khamadja@yahoo.fr

Abstract. Welding is a process of utmost importance in the metal industry. With the advances in computer science and artificial intelligence techniques, the opportunity to develop computer aided technique for radiographic inspection in Non Destructive Testing arose. This paper deals with the weld defects detection in radiographic films. A greedy active contour model is used exploiting global and local statistics to drive the model to the boundaries. Moreover, and to decrease the computation cost, the local statistics computation is done only for pixels in a selected band. Results seem to be promising ones.

Keywords: Radiographic inspection, Weld defects, Active contours.

1 Introduction

Welding is a process of utmost importance in the metal industry. The quality of a welded joint determines whether the weld is suitable for subsequent manufacturing processes, or if the joint must be re-welded. Flaws that may result from welding operation are determining for the following operations. Nondestructive testing (NDT) are examination techniques of industrial materials and assemblies using methods that do not alter their structure in any way, permitting further utilization [1]. Radiography is recognized to be one of the oldest and still effective examination tool in NDT. X-rays penetrate welded target and produce a "shadow picture" of the internal structure of the target. Therefore, the radiographic weld joint interpretation is a complex problem requiring expert knowledge but is, unfortunately, a time consuming operation and results could be subjective and biased. Many efforts have been done to automate the inspection process to get more objective interpretations to the radiographs. This has been done by employing image processing and analysis techniques that can give more consistency to the interpretation Segmentation with deformable models or active contours seems to be quite suitable for radiographic images to extract defects

R. Wilson et al. (Eds.): CAIP 2013, Part II, LNCS 8048, pp. 491–498, 2013.

because of many reasons. The most important one is the fact that the active contours are sophisticated approach to contour extraction that incorporate global view of edge detection by assessing continuity and curvature combined with the local edge strength [2]. Hence, the broken edges are bridged; the blurred and the weak ones are delineated, and the overall defect shape to be extracted is recovered by the mean of one smooth curve located as close as possible to the real boundary. The obtained structure is a defect shape description that can be readily used by the subsequent analysis stages. Deformable models originally introduced by Kass et al. [3], are curves that evolve under the influence of internal and external forces. These curves are able to expand or contract over time within an image to match desired image features. From the model representation point of view, active contours can be categorized into two groups: parametric active contours (also called snakes), where the curve model is represented explicitly by the mean of an ordered collection of discrete points named snaxels (snake pixels) or nodes; and geometric active contours proposed by Osher and Sethian [4], who provide an implicit formulation of the active contour in a level set framework, the curve being the level 0 of a surface. The expression of the explicit form is easy to implement, accelerate the computation and therefore allows real time application [5, 6]. Unfortunately, these models cannot handle topological changes without empiric solutions [7]. From the used image information point of view, active contours can be also categorized into edge based approaches and region based ones. The edge-based approaches are called so because the information used to drawn the curves to the edges is strictly along the boundary. Hence, a strong edge must be detected in order to drive the snake. This obviously causes poor performance of the snake in weak gradient fields. That is, these approaches fail in the presence of noise. Several improvements have been proposed to overcome these limitations but still they fail in numerous cases. The region-based approaches, used at first by Cohen et al. [8] and Ronfard [9], are interested by both regions delimited by the contour. Thus, to guide the curve progression, the pixels characteristics of the inner and the outer region defined by this curve are considered. These approaches are well adapted to situations for which it is difficult to extract boundaries of the target [10–16, 18]. However, one can note that such methods are computationally intensive since the computations are made over a region [10]. Some attempts have been made to detect defects with region based active contours where background and defect were considered as homogeneous regions. However this is rarely the case because of the nature of industrial radiographic images, with, among other characteristics, high luminance variability particularly for the background. This paper deals with the defects detection in radiographic films, and uses the works presented in [12, 13] as a baseline to a new region-based greedy explicit active contour which exploits an association of local and global statistical formulation and an adaptive active contour nodes representation. Section 2 details the mathematical formulation of the method. Section 3 is devoted to the implementation of the model progression. Results are shows in Section 4. We draw the main conclusions in section 5.

2   Local and Global Statistics Association for Bayesian Active Contour Formulation

Let $c = \{c_0, c_1, ..., c_{N-1}\}$ be the boundary of a connected image region R_1 of the image plane I and R_2 the points that do not belong to R_1. Let z_x be the gray-level value observed at the pixel x, $Z = \{z_x\}$ the set of the image gray-levels, and $p(z_x)$ the gray-level density . The purpose of this work is the estimation of the contour c of the region R_1. Then, according to Bayes rule:

$$p(c|Z) = p(c) \times p(Z|c)/p(Z) \tag{1}$$

Since we want to do no assumption about the shape of c, therefore, all shapes are equally possible. Thus, $p(c)$ is removed from the above equation. Moreover, $p(Z)$ is the a priori probability density function (pdf) of gray values Z which is independent of the choice of the region then $p(c/Z)$ can be written as:

$$p(c|Z) = p(Z|c) \tag{2}$$

And, by using the MAP estimation, we have

$$\hat{c} = \arg\max_c p(Z|c) \tag{3}$$

Under the assumption of conditional independence, i.e. given a region, all the region pixels grey values are independent. Thus

$$p(Z|c) = \prod_{x \in R_1} p(z_x) \times \prod_{x \in R_2} p(z_x) \tag{4}$$

hence:

$$\log p(Z|c) = \sum_{x \in R_1} \log p(z_x) + \sum_{x \in R_2} \log p(z_x) \tag{5}$$

There are various approaches to model the probability density $p(Z)$. Most of them assume a global probability density for each region which means that the gray-values distribution depends on the region where all pixels gray-values have in common the same distribution parameters. Therefore, intensity variations inside a region are ignored. These approaches are spatially homogenous regions methods. They have many advantages and perform better than edge-based models in handling the noise and weak boundaries. However, they cannot deal with the intensity inhomogeneities, which are almost unavoidable. However, to deal with region inhomogeneity, one has to take into consideration gray level values variations that can occur inside each region. Each pixel gray value will have its own pdf depending on its position in the region. As the radiographic images are well described by Gaussian distribution [11], we consider, in this work the locally homogeneous modeling with local Gaussian distributions. That is why, the Gaussian parameters, which are spatially varying, are computed locally. As proposed by [12], let w be the window in which the local *pdf*'s computations are done. Thus, for the pixel x, the associated *pdf* is computed as follows:

$$p_w(z_x) = \frac{1}{\sqrt{2\pi}\sigma_w} \exp -\frac{(z_x - \mu_w)^2}{2\sigma_w^2} \tag{6}$$

where μ_w and σ_w are the local intensity mean and standard deviation respectively computed over the window centered at the pixel s. To the window w is associated a weighting function $w_{s,d}$ which depends on the distance, noted $dist(s, x)$, between the current pixel x and the window's center s, and subjected to the following constraints:

- $\sum_{x \in w} w_{s,d}(x) = 1$,

-if $dist(s, x) > d, w_{s,d}(x) = 0$, where d is a fixed distance related to the window size

Furthermore, it is recommended to choose a weighting function that gives bigger weights for the closer pixels to the window center s. These local parameters are computed as follows [14]:

$$\mu_w = \frac{\sum_{x \in w} w_{s,d}(x) z_x}{\sum_{x \in w} w_{s,d}(x)} \qquad \sigma_w^2 = \frac{\sum_{x \in w} w_{s,d}(x)(z_x - \mu_w)^2}{\sum_{x \in w} w_{s,d}(x)} \tag{7}$$

By introducing the above weighting function, the expression of the window-based log likelihood function for the entire image, denoted by $L_{\mathbf{Z}|\mathbf{c}}$ is given below:

$$L_{\mathbf{Z}|\mathbf{c}} = \sum_{s \in I} [\sum_{x \in w | (x,s \in R_1)} w_{s,d}(x) \log p_w(z_x, \mu_w, \sigma_w) + \sum_{x \in w | (x,s \in R_2)} w_{s,d}(x) \log p_w(z_x, \mu_w, \sigma_w)] \tag{8}$$

Nevertheless, local region-based segmentation models are found to be more sensitive to noise than global ones. Such models may also be more sensitive to initialization if the local scale is not appropriate [15]. That is why and in view of extracting defects from radiographic images, characterized by inhomogeneous background and piece-wise homogeneous region objects (defects), we have used local modeling for the non-uniform radiographic background while global modeling is applied to the defect region which is quite homogeneous. If μ and σ are the normal distribution parameters of the defect region (R_1) then the new formulation of $L_{\mathbf{Z}|\mathbf{c}}$ adapted for this case is

$$L_{\mathbf{Z}|\mathbf{c}}^{New} = \sum_{x \in R_1} \log p(z_x, \mu, \sigma) + \sum_{s \in I} \sum_{x \in w | (x,s \in R_2)} w_{s,d}(x) \log p_w(z_x, \mu_w, \sigma_w) \tag{9}$$

Since the first part of the equation is no more concerned with the windowing operation then the first summation over the whole image is reduced to a summation over the R_2 pixels. This yields to:

$$\hat{c} = \arg \max_{c} L_{\mathbf{Z}|\mathbf{c}}^{New} \tag{10}$$

We expect that this formulation will not only reduce the undesirable effect of local modeling as mentioned above, but also reduce the computation cost of the overall maximization formulation of (8). Furthermore, and to reduce much more the computation load, on the background (R_2) the processing will be done only on a band defined by c and c_p, an external parallel contour to the model c as illustrated by Fig.1. Nevertheless, pixels in the external neighborhood of c_p have to be taken into consideration to compute local means and standard deviations inside this band.

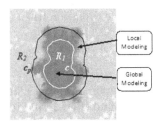

Fig. 1. The various image regions involved in the statistics computation

On the other hand, the weighting function $w_{s,d}$ plays a key role in the proposed segmentation model. In fact, it cannot be too large, leading to prohibitive time cost and inaccuracy, neither be too small, causing sensitivity to noise and evolution instability [16] and should be properly chosen. We have chosen a circular window with a truncated Gaussian kernel as a weighting function [13], then $w_{s,d}(x) = \frac{1}{a} \exp \frac{|dist(s,x)|^2}{2\sigma_d^2}$ if $dist(x,s) \leq d$ and $w_{s,d}(x) = 0$ otherwise.

where a is a scalar and σ_d the standard deviation of the gaussian kernel which can be seen as a scale parameters and should be chosen carefully [12](must not exceeds $\frac{1}{2}d$)

3   Implementation

The pseudo-code for the proposed model can be outlined as follows:

> ***Step 0*** Initialize c
> ***Step 1*** Construct c_p
> ***Step 2*** Compute the local means and standard deviation inside the band (c, c_p) using (7).
> ***Step 3*** Compute the sample mean μ and standard deviation σ for the region inside c
> ***Step 4*** Update the contour c according to (9) and (10)
> ***Step 5*** Go to ***step 1*** if the convergence criteria is not reached

The proposed model is an explicit point-based snake, that uses the greedy evolution strategy, which evolves the snake points in an iterative manner by local neighborhood search around these points, and this, to select new ones which maximize

$L_{\mathbf{Z}|\mathbf{c}}{}^{New}$. The search is done only in the orthogonal directions to the contour at the snake points. This choice is justified by the fact that for the active contour external and internal energies, it can be shown that if the optimal deformation is small, then it needs be only normal to the template [17]. In addition, with this configuration, the space search compared to the 8-neighbors is reduced from 1 to $1/4$. Furthermore, as the model requires an intensive computation and to reduce much more the computation cost, an adaptive snake representation is used as proposed in [18]. This representation allows the first iterations to be carried out just with few snake points which accelerates considerably the evolution. Other snake points will be added if needed to launch the evolution when it stops.

4   Results

The snake we propose, is tested first on a synthetic image consisting of an object in a non-uniform intensity background (Fig. 2) and its results are compared with global statistics-based model presented in [18]. In the present model, the weighting function parameters d and σ_d are chosen equal to 6 and 3 respectively. Empirically, the width of the band $(\mathbf{c}, \mathbf{c}_p)$ is chosen to be equal to d. This choice seems to be sufficient for our images. The proposed snake behaves correctly to its final

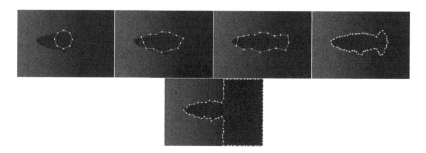

Fig. 2. Above: Our model evolution: initial contour, two intermediate contours and the final contour. Below the global statistics-based model final contour.

contour in few iterations while the global statistics model diverges. Furthermore, the model is tested on weld defect radiographic images containing one defect in Fig.3. The region inside the model is modeled with a global normal distribution and while the background is modeled with local gaussian one. The same comparison with the global statistics-based model is done on radiographic images. For a same initialization our model converges to the right contour and the other model diverges. This is mainly due to the very uniform background. Moreover, other test was carried out, among them the next figure (Fig. 4) which shows the behavior of our model on two other defects. The initial contours are sets of eight model points describing circles crossing the defect in each image, the final ones match perfectly the defects boundaries. This model can be useful when a computer aided detection is needed for recovering a defect shape from

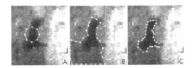

Fig. 3. A: Initialization, B: Global statistics-based model final contour, C: Our model final contour

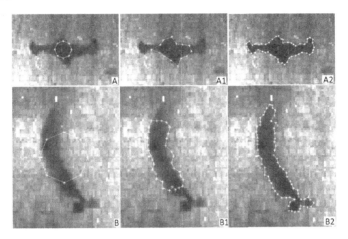

Fig. 4. The proposed model evolution on radiographic images: A and B: Initial contours, A1 and B1: Intermediate contours, A2 and B2: Final contours

the entire weld joint radiographic image which is consisting of many objects and which, unfortunately, makes the radiographic background varying, non-uniform one and inhomogeneous. Furthermore, the strategy of selecting a band outside the snake model where the local statistics computation will be carried out, has considerably decreased the computation load. Moreover, we have no more the need of selecting a region of interest as done in several papers dedicated to weld defect detection, to process the radiographic image, the proposed model exclude all pixels in the image that are not concerned with the statistics computation.

5   Conclusion

We have described a new approach of boundary extraction of weld defects in radiographic images. This approach is based on statistical formulation of contour estimation improved with a combination of local and global modeling. Experiments, on synthetic and radiographic images, show the ability of the proposed technique to give a good estimation of the contours by fitting almost boundaries.

References

1. Halmshaw, R.: The Grid: Introduction to the Non-Destructive Testing in Welded Joints. Woodhead Publishing, Cambridge (1996)
2. Fl Gunn, S., Nixon, M.S.: A robust snake implementation: A dual active contour. IEEE Trans. Pattern Analysis and Machine Intelligence 19, 63–68 (1997)
3. Kass, M., Witkin, A., Terzopoulos, D.: Snakes: Active Contour Models. International Journal of Computer Vision, 321–331 (1988)
4. Osher, S., Sethian, J.: Fronts Propagating with curvature-dependent speed: algorithms based on Hamilton-Jacobi formulations. J. Comp. Phys. 79, 12–49 (1998)
5. Srikrishnan, V., Chaudhuri, S.: Stabilization of parametric active contours using a tangential redistribution term. IEEE Trans. Image Processing 18, 1859–1872 (2009)
6. Ma, Z., Tavares, J.M.R.S., Jorge, R.M.N.J.: A review of the current Segmentation Algorithms for medical images. IMAGAPP, 135–140 (2009)
7. McInerney, D.T.: T-snakes: topology adaptive snakes. Medical Image Anal. 4(2), 73–91 (2000)
8. Cohen, L., Bardinet, E., Ayache, N.: Surface reconstruction using active contour models. In: SPIE Conf. on Geometric Methods in Computer Vision, San Diego, CA (1993)
9. Ronfard, R.: Region-based strategies for active contour models. Int. Journal of Computer Vision 13(2), 229–251 (1994)
10. Chesnaud, C., Réfregier, P., Boulet, V.: Statistical Region Snake-Based Segmentation Adapted to Different Physical Noise Models. IEEE Transaction on PAMI 21(11), 1145–1157 (1999)
11. Nacereddine, N., Hamami, L., Ziou, D., Goumeidane, A.B.: Adaptive B-Spline Model Based Probabilistic Active Contour for Weld Defect Detection in Radiographic Imagin. Image processing and challenges AISC 84(2), 289–297 (2010)
12. Li, C., Kao, C., Gore, J., Ding, Z.: Minimization of region-scalable fitting energy for image segmentation. IEEE Transactions on Image Processing 17, 1940–1949 (2008)
13. Wang, L., He, L., Mishra, A., Li, C.: Active contours driven by local gaussian distribution fitting energy. Signal Processing 89(12), 2435–2447 (2009)
14. Brox, T., Cremers, D.: On Local Region Models and a Statistical Interpretation of the Piecewise Smooth Mumford-Shah Functional. Int. J. Comput. Vis (2009)
15. Yang, Q., Boukerroui, D.: Ultrasound image segmentation using local statistics with an adaptive scale selection, pp. 1096–1099 (2012) ISBI 1096-1099
16. Zhu, S., Yuille, A.: Region competition: unifying snakes, region growing, and Bayes/MDL for multiband image segmentation. IEEE Trans. Pattern Anal. Mach. Intell. 18(9), 884–900 (1996)
17. Tagare, H.: Deformable 2-D template matching using orthogonal curves. IEEE Trans. on Medical Imaging 16(1), 108–117 (1997)
18. Goumeidane, A.B., Khamadja, M., Nacereddine, N.: Adaptive and Statistical Polygonal Curve for Multiple Weld Defects Detection in Radiographic Images. In: DICTAP, Part I, CCIS, vol. 166, pp. 184–198 (2011)

Minimum Entropy Models
for Laser Line Extraction

Wei Yang, Liguo Zhang, Wei Ke, Ce Li, and Jianbin Jiao

School of Electronics, Electrical and Communication Engineering,
University of Chinese Academy of Sciences
Yuquan 19A, Beijing, China
jiaojb@ucas.ac.cn

Abstract. Minimum entropy model can find the optimal gray space
for laser line extraction. A global model named Minimum Entropy Deconvolution is established to search for the peaks which constitute the
laser line. Not only does it reach a high accuracy, but also it retains
the line smoothness, which the previous work often paid little attention
to. Besides, this work could extract several laser lines. Experimental results show that the robust models and fast algorithms outperform the
compared.

Keywords: Gray space, Minimum entropy blind deconvolution, Laser
line extraction.

1   Introduction

Laser line extraction is a decisive step that determines the accuracy of 3D reconstruction. Most researches focus on the peaks detection, then the laser line
is composed of these peaks after further processing.

Fisher et al. [1] gave a comparison of the most common approaches and concluded that all of them displayed performance within the same range. Haug et
al. [2] indicated that the center of mass produced the best results. Strobl et al. [3]
presented a laser line extraction algorithm based on this approach by means of
a color Look-Up table. In [4], proper observation and transition probability for
HMM were defined while detecting laser stripes.

Normally, since the laser light is red, these aforementioned researches used the
red component of image as a gray-level image to process. However, it may not
show the distinct features of laser, and sometimes it is inappropriate to extract
the laser line. For instance, it is difficult to distinguish the laser light from the
white one in the background by using only red component. Some work reduced
these interferences by using a color absorber to obtain the gray-level image.
Although they illuminated good results, the requirement for optical filtering
implies a line extraction algorithm was not robust [5–7]. H. Ta et al. [8] tried to
extract the laser line in YCbCr and HSI spaces in light of past experience. The
crucial point is that little research focused on how to select the most appropriate
gray space to extract the laser line. And H. Ta et al. extracted laser line only

R. Wilson et al. (Eds.): CAIP 2013, Part II, LNCS 8048, pp. 499–506, 2013.

in low-level noises, as other work used local information and assumed the cross section of the laser line was a Gaussian distribution [1–3, 5, 9, 10]. Thus they needed not too many overexposed pixels, and they were only applied if the difference between the light intensity of laser and background was significant. Some approaches took advantage of global information for extraction to solve the problem [4, 7]. Both methods are less sensitive to local interferences and robust to blurry images.

In this paper, a model based on minimum entropy is firstly built to find the optimal gray-level space for extraction. Then a minimum entropy deconvolution model is solved to reset the peaks to the center of laser stripe. At last, all the peaks that are selected along each row or column in the image constitute the laser line. The method uses global information for extraction and allows line gaps and strong noises. Although other work also searches for the peaks, they pay more emphasis on the accuracy, and this paper can obtain a robust and smooth result as well as high accuracy, especially in high noise level scenes.

2   Methodology

2.1   Gray Space

Because linear transformation is continuous and does not cause gaps [11], this paper uses a linear transformation to obtain a gray-level image from original image. In a discrete color image f_{ij} (with a size of $M \times N$), color of a pixel is given as corresponding tristimulus R_{ij} (red), G_{ij} (green), and B_{ij} (blue). Hence, the linear transformation defines as equation (1):

$$F_{ij} = \omega_r R_{ij} + \omega_g G_{ij} + \omega_b B_{ij} \tag{1}$$

where F_{ij} is the desired gray-level image, $i = 1, 2, \ldots, M$, $j = 1, 2, \ldots, N$, ω_r, ω_g and $\omega_b \in R$. In order to extract the laser line conveniently, the gray-level image determined by the transformation coefficients should highlight the characteristics of laser. Now an objective function need to be defined to search the optimal ω_r, ω_g and ω_b.

Owing to the tight focusing and strong brightness of beam, one of the most remarkable features of laser is that energy concentration is remarkably high, which makes the stripe show its waveform with a few spikes and distinguish it from the background in the image (Fig. 1, an example of laser profiles, which is obtained through showing all the image row vectors). In other words, the contrast between the laser and background is high. The objective function should retain and enhance this feature so that the laser line extraction will become much easier after transformation. Thus, the contrast can be used as the objective function. In Fig. 1, gray values of the pixels within the laser stripe are near to their averages. In these areas, the greater energy concentration is, the more striking contrast will be, and also a higher Kurtosis. They are equivalent to contrast and Kurtosis. Therefore, it is reasonable to define contrast as Kurtosis:

$$V = \frac{\mu_4}{\sigma^4} - 3 \tag{2}$$

where Kurtosis V is defined as the fourth moment around the mean μ_4 divided by the square of the variance σ^4 of the probability distribution minus 3.

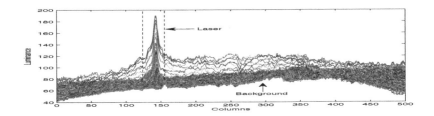

Fig. 1. Example of laser profiles

The transform result of the laser stripe is expected to be of very high Kurtosis while competing signals the background is of very low Kurtosis. A signal with high Kurtosis is great order, and vice versa. In the context of communication systems, disorder is synonymous to the concept of entropy. It is also declared that the greater the disorder of a signal is, the greater its entropy gets. Wiggins [12] originally presented the minimum entropy deconvolution technique (MED) based on this reason. He proposed to maximize a Varimax Norm function, which is equivalent to maximizing Kurtosis with assumed zero-mean. For this reason, the transformation model can be named as minimum entropy model. However, minimizing instead of maximizing equation (2) is appropriate for the signal with a kurtosis less than zero. Thereupon, an alternative choice of objective function which is differentiable everywhere can be defined as the square of Kurtosis. If the image is thought to process as a Multi-channel signal (with N segments and M elements per segment), the objective function can be written as

$$V = \left(\sum_{j=1}^{N} \frac{\sum_{i=1}^{M} (F_{ij} - \mu_j)^4}{\left(\sum_{i=1}^{M} (F_{ij} - \mu_j)^2 \right)^2} - 3 \right)^2 \tag{3}$$

where μ_j is the mean of column j in the transform image F_{ij}.

The solution of maximizing equation (3) is corresponding to equation (4)

$$\frac{\partial V}{\partial \omega_r} = 0, \frac{\partial V}{\partial \omega_g} = 0, \frac{\partial V}{\partial \omega_b} = 0 \tag{4}$$

Although it is difficult to solve equation (4), it could be approximately calculated the maxima value of referring to in [13]. An infinite set of color feature space is determined by the in continuous coefficients in equation (1). For convenience to obtain ω_r, ω_g and ω_b, they are discretized as integer and values range are limited from -2 and 2. It is feasible because the linear combinations sample the set of 1D color feature subspaces of 3D RGB space uniformly, and some common features are covered, such as R+G+B, R-B, and so on. Furthermore, it is also efficient to compute. Considering that the laser is red and R component of original image has higher energy, narrow $\omega_r \geq 0$. That is $\omega_r \in \{0, 1, 2\}$, $\omega_g, \omega_b \in \{-2, -1, 0, 1, 2\}$. Absolutely, it is not allowed if $(\omega_r, \omega_g, \omega_b) = (0, 0, 0)$. The optimal parameters can be computed by the traversal method.

In Fig. 2, the optimal coefficient vector of a typical image is $(\omega_r, \omega_g, \omega_b) = (1, -1, 0)$, and the gray-level space is R-G. A cross laser is used here. It also makes comparisons with R. Two advantages of R-G are obvious. On the one hand, it distinguishes the laser from the background. On the other hand, it has much smaller amount of data than raw image.

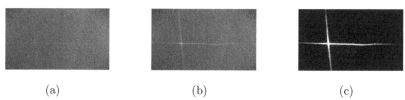

(a)   (b)   (c)

Fig. 2. The color feature transport result: (a) raw image, (b) the gray-level image of R, (c) the gray-level image of R-G.

Ideally, the horizontal component and the vertical component of a cross laser are comparatively independent, and their intensity is subject to Gaussian distribution. All the intensity maxima are right in the center of the stripes and the laser lines can be extracted precisely just by taking the peaks out.

However, it becomes not feasible in practical environments for the block speckle noise, energy diffusion, light saturation, light saturation crosstalk, natural light, and other factors [11]. These noise sources combine together, make the constructive and destructive interferences within the laser stripes, lead to the laser intensity no longer obey Gaussian distribution and some peaks are no longer in the center of stripes.

Some measures should be taken to focus energy on the center of laser stripes and reset the peaks back to the center. The image signal entropy will decrease with the energy focusing. At last, the signal with the minimum entropy will be composed of a series of narrowband pulses. From the point of view of signal processing, this process can be described as a problem of minimum entropy deconvolution.

2.2   Minimum Entropy Deconvolution

Taking the input image as a Multi-channel signal in columns (with N segments and M elements per segment) or in rows (with M segments and N elements per segment). In the former case, the horizontal component of the laser stripe is largely restored, and the vertical component information is suppressed synchronously, and vice versa. Then the whole recovered information of the laser stripes can be obtained by executing the two operations separately. The model in columns to extract the horizontal laser line can be formulated as

$$B_{ij} = \sum_{k=1}^{L} W_k F_{i-k+1,j} \tag{5}$$

where μ_{Bj} is the mean of column j of B_{ij}, $k = 1, \ldots, L$, L is the order of the filter, which has significant impact on the MED outputs. Experience shows that an efficiency and reliable length is 5% of the number of elements per segment. The objective function can be written as equation (3) with replacing F_{ij} as B_{ij}.

The MED searches for an optimum set of filter coefficients that recover the output signal with the maximum value of Kurtosis. For convenient, the causal filter is normalized. Differentiating V with respect to the W_k and equating to zero yields, an iteratively converging local-maximum solution can be derived as

$$\sum_{l=1}^{L} W_l \sum_{j=1}^{N} V_j U_j^{-1} \sum_{i=1}^{M} F_{i-l,j} F_{i-k,j} = \sum_{j=1}^{N} U_j^{-2} \sum_{i=1}^{M} (B_{ij} - \mu_{Bj})^3 F_{i-k,j} \qquad (6)$$

where $U_j = \sum_{i=1}^{M} (B_{ij} - \mu_{Bj})^2$, $V_j = \dfrac{\sum_{i=1}^{M} (B_{ij} - \mu_{Bj})^4}{\left(\sum_{i=1}^{M} (B_{ij} - \mu_{Bj})^2\right)^2}$, and W_k is iteratively

selected. The general procedure is as follows in Algorithm 1. Fig. 3 shows the comparison of energy concentration between input signal and signal is filtered by MED.

Algorithm 1. The general procedure of MED

1. Assume the initial value of W. Here setting $W = [11 \ldots 1 \ldots 11]^T / \sqrt{L}$.
2. Compute the output signal B_{ij} through Eq.(5).
3. Compute new filter coefficients by solving for W in Eq.(6).
4. Repeat from step 2 and 3 for a specified number of iterations or until the change in V between iterations is below a specified small value.

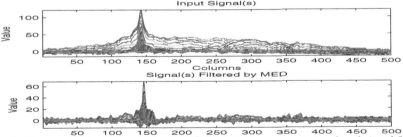

Fig. 3. The comparison of energy concentration between input signal and signal filtered by MED

2.3   Laser Line Extraction

Extraction of the laser line can be completed by extracting the peaks of every column or every row, respectively. Furthermore, a group delay in rows compared with the ideal curve has to be taken into account. This phase shift $\Delta i = -P_W$ can be computed from 2D convolution theorem and equation (5), where P_w is the phase of W_k.

The model to extraction of the vertical laser line in rows has the same formula form and processing.

2.4   Smoothness

This paper gives a definition of smoothness. A kind of understanding of smoothness is the measure of similarity between the extracted and true line. Consequently the smoothness should be the function about the error between the two data. The error is defined as $\{e_i\}$. Obviously, S should satisfy: 1) $\forall i$, $e_i = C(C$ is a constant), the extracted line has the same form with the true line, the line is the most smooth, and S should be its minimum value, i.e. $S = 0$; 2) the more even the distribution of $\{e_i\}$ is, the smoother is the line, the letter S is, and vice versa. For example, the waveform of $\{e_i\}$ is quickly waved, this line is very rough, and S is large, though the values of $\{e_i\}$ may be very small. Therefore S is a function has the symmetrical form with 1D entropy (Fig. 4). It can be computed as

$$S = H + \log(num) \tag{7}$$

where $H(p) = -\sum_{j=1}^{num} (n_j/num)\log_2 (n_j/num)$ is the entropy of array $\{e_i\}$, num is quantization orders, n_j is the number of e_j after quantization.

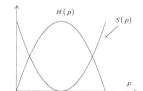

Fig. 4. The form of the smoothness function

3   Experimental Results

To evaluate the effectiveness of models, some experiments have been carried out to compare the performance with the proposed approaches [3, 6] which are known as Centre of Mass (CM), Linear Approximation (LA), Quadratic Approximation (QA), and Akima splines Approximation (AA) in different gray spaces (R & R-G, the gray-level images obtained by CCD using optical filters also are treated as R components). For comparing the better gray space further, the comparison experiments of MED are also used in R and R-G.

These experiments are concerned with a set of test images in outdoor scenes. This paper presents typical one with the size of 500×375 pixels (Core 3.40 GHz CPU and a 4.0 GB RAM).

Table 1. Experimental result

Laser line	Color space	Method Index	CM	LA	QA	AA	MED
Horizontal laser line	R	Time (ms)	18.3	320.2	168.1	130.3	22.3
		Smoothness	5.2667	8.2495	7.9673	8.1243	1.4858
	R-G	Time (ms)	17.9	310.4	167.6	196.6	20.9
		Smoothness	5.1600	8.0299	7.9336	8.0243	1.4439
Vertical laser line	R	Time (ms)	18.8	∞	∞	∞	20.6
		Smoothness	5.7304	5.8531	5.8531	5.8531	5.9231
	R-G	Time (ms)	17.6	120.2	147.2	166.6	19.9
		Smoothness	5.7282	7.6794	7.7102	7.6047	1.5669
The whole	R	Total time (ms)	35.6	∞	∞	∞	41.1
Line	R-G	Total time (ms)	33.8	406.5	302.5	355.4	38.7

"∞" means that the time is too long to afford in practice, $num = 500$.

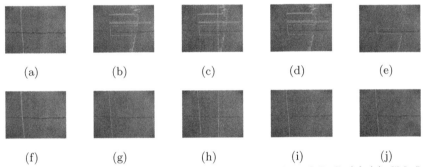

(a)   (b)   (c)   (d)   (e)

(f)   (g)   (h)   (i)   (j)

Fig. 5. The extraction result of the above methods in R and R-G: (a)-(e) CM, LA, QA, AA and MED in R, respectively, (f)-(j) CM, LA, QA, AA and MED in R-G, respectively.

The extraction quality of the method in this paper shows similar results for all tested images (Table 1 and Fig. 5). As a whole, it is easy to see two points: on the one hand, the component R-G is better than R in all methods, and on the other hand, the laser line extraction model based MED is more valid, accurate, and smooth than other approaches or models.

It is worth noting that the data vertical laser line obtained in R is so tough that its consumed time is too long to afford in practice. Taking into account this factor, it no longer fits the data using LA, QA, AA and MED. Nonetheless, the error of MED overall is smaller than the former. And they are smoother than the fitting data obtained by LA, QA and AA in R-G. This phenomenon is determined by the more even distribution of the former error, although most of its elements are larger and they have similar offsets relative to the true data. It also suggests that the definition of smoothness is appropriate.

All the calculations are based on the full image. It can be seen that the speed of MED is fast enough to use to the reality. If the region of interest is selected, the speed will rise tenfold.

4   Conclusion

The paper proposes a fast, accurate and robust method to extract the laser line in high noise level environments. And it ensures smoothness of the extracted line, which others paid little attention to. Experimental results demonstrate that the models are promising. In the future, they are planned to apply in 3D reconstruction.

Acknowledgement. This work is supported in Part by National Basic Research Program of China (973 Program) with Nos. 2011CB706900,2010CB731800, and National Science Foundation of China with Nos. 61039003,61271433 and 61202323.

References

1. Fisher, R.B., Naidu, D.K.: A Comparison of Algorithms for Subpixel Peak Detection. In: Image Technology, Advances in Image Processing, Multimedia and Machine Vision, pp. 385–404 (1996)
2. Haug, K., Pritschow, G.: Robust laser-stripe sensor for automated weld-seam-tracking in the shipbuilding industry. In: Proc. IECON, pp. 1236–1241 (1998)
3. Strobl, K., et al.: The DLR multisensory hand-guided device: the laser stripe profiler. In: ICRA, pp. 1927–1932 (2004)
4. Zhang, L., et al.: Robust weld line detection with cross structured light and Hidden Markov Model. In: ICMA, pp. 1411–1416 (2012)
5. Li, Y., et al.: Measurement and defect detection of the weld bead based on online vision inspection. IEEE Trans. Instrum. Meas. 59, 1841–1849 (2010)
6. Molleda, J., et al.: Shape Measurement of Steel Strips Using a Laser-Based Three-Dimensional Reconstruction Technique. IEEE Transactions on Industry Applications 47, 1536–1544 (2011)
7. Schnee, J., Futterlieb, J.: Laser Line Extraction with Dynamic Line Models. In: Proc. CAIP, pp. 126–134 (2011)
8. Ta, H., et al.: A novel laser line detection algorithm for robot application. In: ICCAS, pp. 361–365 (2011)
9. Forest Collado, J.: New Methods for Triangulation-based Shape Acquisition using Laser Scanners. Ph.D. thesis, Universitat de Girona (2004)
10. Forest, J., et al.: Laser stripe peak detector for 3d scanners. a fir filter approach. In: Proc. ICPR, pp. 646–649 (2004)
11. Kender, J.: Saturation, Hue and Normalized Color: Calculation, Digitization Effects and Use, Technical Report, Department of Computer Science, Carnegie-Mellon University (1976)
12. Wiggins, R.A.: Minimum entropy deconvolution. Geoexplorafion 16, 21–35 (1978)
13. Collins, R.T., et al.: On-line selection of discriminative tracking features. In: Proceedings Ninth IEEE International Conference on Computer Vision, pp. 346–352 (2003)

A Convenient and Fast Method of Endoscope Calibration under Surgical Environment

Meiqing Liu[1], Dayuan Yan[2], Xiaoming Hu[3], Ya Zhou[4], and Zhaoguo Wu[5]

[1] School of Optoelectronics, Beijing Institute of Technology, Beijing, China
meiqingfly1@126.com
[2] School of Software, Beijing Institute of Technology, Beijing, China
ydyuan@bit.edu.cn
[3] School of Life Science, Beijing Institute of Technology, Beijing, China
bithxm@bit.edu.cn
[4] School of Optoelectronics, Beijing Institute of Technology, Beijing, China
zhouya@bit.edu.cn

Abstract. How to get the calibration parameters of an endoscopic camera online is one of the most important steps in the three-dimensional reconstruction and draws great attention from researchers. One of general approach requires two persons and one accurate pre-printed checkerboard, which is not desirable in actual use. In this paper, a convenient endoscope calibration method is presented. Instead of preparing a checkerboard in advance, computer display screen is used as a flexible calibrating-board to display checkerboards with different sizes to fill the endoscopic view. Instead of holding the checkerboard with different posture, the user could hold the endoscopic camera in front of the screen-displayed calibrating-board in various orientations. The whole calibration process can be implemented by just one person, which is of practical significance in real operating room. The experimental results show that such method is time-saving without additional manual intervention. The precision of calibration can be achieved at sub-pixel.

Keywords: endoscope calibration, image processing, computer display screen, sub-pixel.

1 Introduction

Nowadays Endoscope-assisted minimal invasive surgery is widely used in clinical operation. However the surgeons are guided by the monocular video which can only provide a distorted two-dimensional (2-D) image of the surgical site, where valuable information such as the lateral size and the depth of the imaged object is lost. To make the endoscopic diagnosis more objective and reproducible, a three-dimensional reconstruction of pathological structures is in great need.

Because of its small aperture and relatively large field of view, the endoscope image exists large radial distortion which will influence the precision of the reconstruction and make 3D reconstruction from it to be a challenge. Several aspects of performing endoscope calibration have been largely studied in the literature.

R. Wilson et al. (Eds.): CAIP 2013, Part II, LNCS 8048, pp. 507–514, 2013.

The endoscope calibration is classified with self-automatic calibration and traditional with checkerboard calibration. Different models are constructed to implement these two calibrations. The model of automatic calibration is presented in reference[1]. Many papers proposed complicate methods aiming at solving the calibrating problem of oblique viewing endoscope[2][3] which is useful in inspecting narrow cavities. But the accuracy is not the key point to be pursed in these papers. Although the traditional calibration method can work well for the forward viewing endoscopes in which the optical axis is aligned with the cylindrical probe, the calibration process is labor-intensive to some extent and not desirable for the practical users: doctors and surgeons. The purpose of this paper is to find a convenient way to implement the calibration of the forward viewing endoscope which is the most widely used in the real medical environment. The procedure of calibration is robust and automatic and a non-expert user can execute it quickly. The key point is the precision of the calibration proposed in this article is in the range of sub-pixel.

Zhang's method[4] is popular in camera calibration and also applied to endoscope calibration in many literatures. This calibration requires at least three images of a standard sign board captured by the camera from different orientations to calculate the parameters and distortion coefficients. Though Bouguet's toolbox[5] is a kind of popular software that implements Zhang's method for calibrating a generic camera from a minimum of three images of a checkerboard, it requires more human intervention to complete whole calibration so it does not meet the requirements of endoscopic calibration under surgical environment.

There are four steps to complete a general camera calibration as follows: 1. Prepare a sign board; 2. Capture images; 3. Process images to extract mark points; 4. Calculate the intrinsic and extrinsic parameters and distortion coefficients. In the first step, the black and white checkerboard is convenient to be used to extract the corners, and then these corners are used in endoscope calibration. But the range of ordinary endoscope view field is substantially about 15 mm, to make the checkerboard of production under endoscopic vision imaging clearly, it requires the size of checkerboard is between 10-12 mm (70%-80% field of view), which is too small that the checkerboard corners lack of precision (a corner point will occupy four pixels) under the endoscopic vision if using an ordinary checkerboard printed on a paper. Therefore, transparencies printing are generally used. In the second step, one person holds a hard board at several postures and another person captures the corresponding images at the same time. These two steps are time-consuming and labor-intensive for surgeons to complete a pre-process endoscope calibration.

The robustness of automatic calibration is worse than traditional calibration and the higher complexity of time add the burden to subsequent research. The method of calibration proposed in this article has potential advantages: 1. The whole process of calibration is convenient and non-human intervention. 2. The time is saved by automatic detect mark points and calculate the parameters. 3. Non-expert user can execute it easily. It can quickly accepted by doctors without extensive preoperative training, which is of practical significance in an operating room.

2   Calibration Principle

2.1   Camera Model

The checkerboard in computer screen is defined as the world coordinate system and the imaging plane of CCD sensor is defined as the image coordinate system. The points in the world coordinate system are composed of matrix M and points in the image coordinate system are composed of matrix m. Without loss of generality, the computer screen plane is assumed on $Z = 0$ of the world coordinate system. A camera is modeled by the usual pinhole: the relationship between a 3D point and its image projection is connected by homography H:

$$s\tilde{m} = H\tilde{M} . \tag{1}$$

Where s is an arbitrary scale factor, $\tilde{m}$ and $\tilde{M}$ are denoted as the augmented vector by adding 1 at the last element.

The algorithm of singular value decomposition (SVD)[6] is proposed to disintegrate H so that the intrinsic and extrinsic parameters are calculated.

2.2   Calibration Methods

In the above section, the intrinsic and extrinsic parameters of the camera model are solved by linear methods. Then maximum likelihood estimation method is proposed in this section to optimize parameters. Assuming a total of n pieces of the screen checkerboard of the image have been obtained, and m mark points on each image have been extracted, the maximum likelihood estimation of parameters can be estimated by calculating the minimum value of equation (7).

$$\sum_{i=1}^{n} \sum_{j=1}^{m} \|m_{ij} - \hat{m}(K, R_i, t_i, M_j)\|^2 . \tag{2}$$

Where $\hat{m}(K, R_i, t_i, M_j)$ is the projection of point M_j in image i. K is an internal matrix and rotation R is parameterized by a vector of three parameters and T is translation matrix. Minimizing is a nonlinear minimization problem, which is solved with the Levenberg-Marquardt algorithm[7]. The value solved by SVD decomposition method could regard as the initial value of the maximum likelihood estimate.

3   Methodology

3.1   Automatically Generated Checkerboard

Now most computers are equipped with liquid crystal displays (LCD) where each pixel is constituted with red, green, and blue filters in front of them. The light via different cells can be displayed on the screen in different colors. LCD has very high geometric accuracy and pure planarityso the calibration accuracy can be improved. The calibration parameters are calculated based on Zhang's calibration. In order to calculate homography matrix the size of each grid in checkerboard of computer screen must be known, so it is necessary to control the output of the checkerboard full-screen display on the LCD screen. Screen resolution and LCD pixel pitch can be checked in the reference data from plant. A LCD screen resolution of 1280 x 1024 pixels with dot pitch of 0.264 mm is used in our experiment.

As the introduction was mentioned, the precision that using an ordinary checkerboard printed on a paper can hardly reach the realistic requirement. Exchanging the paper printing to transparencies printing would reduce the error of extracting corner, one corner point usually occupy two pixels. If the LCD screen was used to control generate checkerboard the precision would achieve one pixel. This is very significant for endoscopic calibration.

3.2   Analysis of Endoscopic Image

One of the endoscopic images is shown in Fig.1 (a), where each pixel mixed with three colors in the white area, this can be obviously seen from Fig.1 (b) .The mixed colors in each pixel makes low contrast with the black areas, which increasing the difficulty of extracting the corners. Fig.1 (b) is the zoomed view of Fig.1 (a), which contains a small piece of 4 x 4 pixels, and each pixel value has three channels (RGB). The intersection (yellow dots) in the small yellow circle is the corner to be extracted.

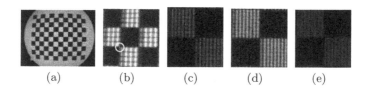

(a)   (b)   (c)   (d)   (e)

Fig. 1. Captured images of different checkerboard using an endoscopy. (a) is one of the captured images when the computer is display the checkerboard and (b) is the partial enlarged version of (a). (c) (d) (e) represent red-black, green-black and blue-black checkerboard image that are captured from computer screen.

The precision of one pixel would be achieved if we extract the corners as seen from Fig.1 (b). The requirement of higher decision brings us to control the output RGB single-channel image. The one of third pixel is displayed in computer screen and the corners are extracted under sub-pixel precision. Red-black, green-black and blue-black checkerboard image are shown in Fig.1 (c) (d) (e). In these three photographs, mark points area is obvious contrast with the background area. The algorithm is presented following to extract these mark points.

3.3   Algorithm of Corner Detection

Harris[8] corner detection method is commonly used in the calibration of the endoscope but it appears false detection and inaccurate extraction under visible noise and larger distortion.

An extraction method under general experimental conditions to quickly and automatically extract mark points is presented in this paper. Two gradient feature calculations and some simple determination processing are required in the method to get position of mark points.

The process of extraction algorithm in this paper is described as follows: 1. Images smoothing. The noise of image caused by sensor or other reasons is required to be reduced by Gaussian filter. 2. Calculate the gradient feature of image. By testing a local maxim of the gradient response to identify a number of possible mark points, which contains all the mark points and part of mistakenly extracted. Subsequently, eliminate false extraction according to central symmetry gradient feature of mark points. 3. The mark points should be first corresponded to screen checkerboard corner points in order to facilitate the calculation of the camera parameters and distortion parameters. The sequence of each corner point of screen checkerboard is constant, the mark points from extraction should be sorted and tagged, so that these can correspond to the corners in the world coordinate system. This is convenient to calculate single mapping matrix between two coordinate systems until now.

The idea of sorting is that the extracted mark points are traversed from left to right, top to bottom. The traversal points of each row are firstly sorted in order to reduce the computational complexity, then releasing the first row traversal points and continuing to sort the second row until the last row. The whole idea of sorting as follows: 1. Coordinate of this image is given as x-y coordinates, x represents the horizontal coordinate, y represents the vertical coordinate, the first point is defined as the minimum value of point in y coordinate. 2. Search the three neighborhood points, wherein the two point's coordinate values have the minimum difference compared with the first point at the same time. The two points are defined as the same row with the first point, then comparing the difference between the values of the x coordinate with the first point, the smaller is the second point and larger is the third point. 3. The third point is regarded as the next starting point and continues to search the neighborhood of three points, and so on. This search is the point of a row in the same direction, if the starting point is located in the middle of a line, after this sort the point of the other side will be missed. So the first point must be marked. 4. The corner points to be extracted are analyzed whether reaching assumption value after finishing the first row in one direction. If the condition does not reach the assumption, the second point in the third step is set as a starting point to continue to search until reaching an initial value (the x-axis is set to 11 and the y-axis is 9 in later experiment). 5. The points from the second row to the last row are sorted as the above four steps.

4   Experimental Results

A dual-screen display is needed in this experiment, one is used to display the checkerboard, the other monitor is used to show the endoscopic images. A 10 x 12 size cells, each cell including 8 x 8 pixels are used in this paper. The accuracy of the extracted points is the key point for subsequent calibration. According to the above description of mark points extraction algorithm, the experiment is realised under endoscopic environment and the results are shown in Fig. 2 (a) (b) (c).

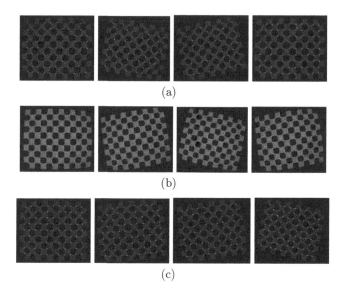

Fig. 2. The result of corners extraction.(a) is the result of red-black corners extraction, (b) is green-black and (c) is blue-black.

The result of extraction in Fig.2 (b) is the best and no mistaking or missing points in it when compared with Fig.2 (a) and Fig.2 (c). This is because that the CCD sensor is the simulation of the human perception of color. Comparing with the response of red and blue, CCD camera has a greater one in green. The higher contrast of green and background makes the better extraction. The corners to be extracted have sub-pixel precision so that we can use the green and black checkerboard corners as the mark points to calculate the intrinsic and extrinsic parameters.

The contrast of intrinsic parameters calculated by two sets of image is shown in Table 1, the first set from capturing computer screen as this paper mentioned and the image is shown in Fig.3 (a) and the second set from ordinary image collection as shown in Fig.3 (b). It is worth emphasizing that two sets of image are from the same endoscopy.

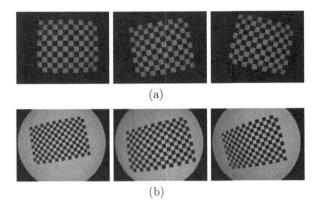

Fig. 3. Two sets of endoscopic images. (a) is from capturing computer screen and (b) is from ordinary image collection.

Table 1. Contrast of intrinsic parameters

	f_{c1}	f_{c2}	$alpha\_a$	u_0	v_0
1	773.2450	783.2848	-1.6273	234.4932	259.2315
2	774.1251	784.3678	-1.6321	235.3414	260.1826

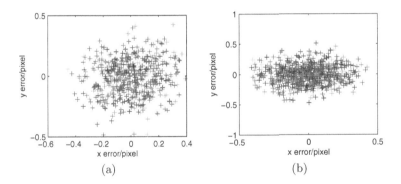

Fig. 4. Result of back-projection error. (a) represents the error of first set from capturing computer screen and (b) represents the error of second set from ordinary image collection.

The difference between these two sets of data is less than one pixel as seen from Table 1, it demonstrates that the method of using screen and the algorithm of corner extracting could meet actual application The order of points in the image coordinate is correspond with the order of points in the world coordinate. According to Zhang's calibration method the parameters of intrinsic and extrinsic can be calculated, then LM algorithm is introduced to optimize the parameters. The errors of back projection points can be calculated after parameter optimization and the contrast of back-projection error of the above two sets of images are shown in Fig.4.

The result of back-projection error demonstrates that the precision is achieved sub-pixel, the back-projection error can meet the requirements.

5   Conclusion

The article proposes a convenient method for the endoscopic calibration. The experiment result demonstrates that this method could meet the surgery real environment. Algorithm to quickly extract accurate mark points is proposed. The way of improving the precision of calibration is presented.

Computer screen display is used to substitute the pre-print checkerboard. Labor and material resources are eliminated. The image collection process is simplified with one person to operate. The preparation and calibration process becomes concise.

LCD has very high geometric accuracy and pure planarity so the calibration accuracy is improved to sub-pixel by controlling the RGB single-channel image to be output.

References

1. Barreto, J., Roquette, J., Sturm, P., Fonseca, F.: Automatic camera calibration applied to medical endoscopy. In: Proc. British Machine Vision Conf (BMVC), London, U.K, September 7-10 (2009)
2. Melo, R., Barreto, J.P., Falcao, G.: A New Solution for Camera Calibration and Real-Time Image Distortion Correction in Medical Endoscopy CInitial Technical Evaluation. IEEE Transactions on Biomedical Engineering 59(3) (March 2012)
3. Fukuda, N., Nakamoto, M., Okada, T., Chen, Y.-W.: Comparison of accuracy on camera calibration method with distortion correction for oblique-viewing endoscope for computer assisted endoscopic surgery. IEICE Tech. Rep., vol. 109, no. 407, MI 2009-91, pp. 87-92 (January 2010)
4. Zhang, Z.: Flexible camera calibration by viewing a plane from unknown orientations. In: Proc. ICCV, pp. 666–673 (1999)
5. Camera Calibration Toolbox for Matlab,
   http://www.vision.caltech.edu/bouguetj/calib_doc/index.html
6. Zhang, Z.: A Flexible New Technique for Camera Calibration. IEEE Transactions on Pattern Analysis and Machine Intelligence 22(11), 1330–1334 (2000)
7. Mor, J.J.: The Levenberg-Marquardt algorithm: implementation and theory. In: Proceedings of the Biennial Conference on Numerical Analysis, pp. 105–116. Springer, Berlin (1978)
8. Harris, C., Stephens, M.: A Combined Conner and Edge Detector. In: Proceedings of the 4th Alvey Vision Conference, pp. 147–151. The University of Sheffield Printing Unit, Manchester (1988)

SAMSLAM:
Simulated Annealing Monocular SLAM

Marco Fanfani, Fabio Bellavia, Fabio Pazzaglia, and Carlo Colombo

Computational Vision Group, University of Florence
Via Santa Marta, 3, 50139, Florence, Italy
{marco.fanfani,carlo.colombo}@unifi.it,
{bellavia.fabio,fabio.pazzaglia}@gmail.com

Abstract. This paper proposes a novel monocular SLAM approach. For a triplet of successive keyframes, the approach inteleaves the registration of the three 3D maps associated to each image pair in the triplet and the refinement of the corresponding poses, by progressively limiting the allowable reprojection error according to a simulated annealing scheme. This approach computes only local overlapping maps of almost constant size, thus avoiding problems of 3D map growth. It does not require global optimization, loop closure and back-correction of the poses.

Keywords: SLAM, Structure from Motion, RANSAC, Feature Matching, Disparity, Simulated Annealing, 3D Registration, Pose Estimation.

1 Introduction

Simultaneous Localization and Mapping (SLAM) approaches are designed to estimate both the camera positions and the 3D map of the environment in real-time. Early SLAM implementations were based on the Extendend Kalman Filter [1]. Alternative approaches inspired by Structure from Motion (SfM) techniques were proposed recently [2], and proved to outperform the former [3].

Single camera [1, 2], stereo or multiple camera [4] SLAM systems have appeared. While stereo or multiple camera configurations provide more reliable solutions, monocular SLAM leads to a more general and simple operative environment.

Different feature description and matching strategies [1,2,5,6] have been used to detect and track keypoints across the image frames: Robust to high degrees of blur [6], with hierarchical pose refinement [7], or exploiting the high computational power offered by modern GPUs through a dense approach [5].

SfM-based approaches typically exploit iterative non-linear optimization refinement schemes (such as Bundle Adjustment [8]) over sub-sequences of relevant frames (keyframes). While beneficial for accuracy improvement, such global optimization schemes require a good inizialization and are not tolerant to outliers. Moreover, optimization of long sub-sequences requires a large memory space, and refined estimates are obtained with some delay with respect to the current

R. Wilson et al. (Eds.): CAIP 2013, Part II, LNCS 8048, pp. 515–522, 2013.

camera position. Loop closure detection [9], enforcing pose constraints on already visited scenes, which obviously requires looping paths, is also frequently employed to reduce error accumulation over long tracks.

This paper proposes a novel monocular SLAM system, where a local, robust simulated annealing scheme replaces the global, SfM optimized approach for the purpose of obtaining both the 3D map and the camera pose. The proposed approach works locally on triplets of successive overlapping keyframes, thus guaranteeing scale and 3D structure consistency. Each update step uses RANSAC and alternates between the registration of the three 3D maps associated to each image pair in the triplet and the refinement of the corresponding poses, by progressively limiting the allowable reprojection error. Since the proposed method does not require neither global optimization nor loop closure, it doesn't perform any back-correction of the poses and does not suffer of 3D map growth. In addition, the method can be implemented in an efficient way through a multi-thread scheme.

The paper is organized as follows. Section 2 introduces the proposed SLAM system and the novel approach to the computation of the camera pose and the registration of the 3D points based on the simulated annealing process, while the experimental evaluation of the system is described in Sect. 3. Conclusions and final discussions are given in Sect. 4.

2   The SAMSLAM Approach

2.1   Overview

Given a calibrated image sequence $S = \{I_t\}$, with radial distortion corrected, our SLAM approach proceeds by detecting successive triplets $T_i = \{I_{k_{i-1}}, I_{k_i}, I_{k_{i+1}}\}$ of image *keyframes* $\{I_{k_i}\} \subseteq S$, $k_0 = 0, k_i < k_{i+1}$ — see Fig. 1.

A local 3D map $\mathcal{M}_i$ is built upon the current keyframe triplet T_i using the simulated annealing scheme described in Sect. 2.2, which also recovers the relative poses between keyframe pairs, P_{k_{i-1},k_i} and $P_{k_{i-1},k_{i+1}}$. As the keyframe triplet is updated from T_i to T_{i+1}, the first keyframe is dropped and a new one is queued, so that the 3D maps $\mathcal{M}_i$ and $\mathcal{M}_{i+1}$ overlap and the consistency of scale and 3D structure is guaranteed.

Image alignment for the generic pair (I_{t_1}, I_{t_2}) is based on keypoint matching. For each image, keypoints are extracted using the HarrisZ detector [10]. The sGLOH descriptor [11] with Nearest Neighbour matching is then used to obtain the candidate correspondences. These are then refined on a temporal constraint basis as follows. Let $\mathbf{x}_t = [x_t, y_t]^T \in I_t$ be a generic keypoint of image I_t, a *match* $(\mathbf{x}_{t_1}, \mathbf{x}_{t_2})$ must satisfy the flow motion restriction $\| \mathbf{x}_{t_1} - \mathbf{x}_{t_2} \| < \delta_r$, where δ_r is the maximal flow displacement. Moreover, for a triplet T_i, after a further match refinement by normalized RANSAC [12], only matches which form a *loop chain*

$$\mathcal{C}_i = \left\{ (\mathbf{x}_{k_{i-1}}, \mathbf{x}_{k_i}), (\mathbf{x}_{k_i}, \mathbf{x}_{k_{i+1}}), (\mathbf{x}_{k_{i+1}}, \mathbf{x}_{k_{i-1}}) \right\}$$

through the corresponding keyframes are retained. The chain matches are used to estimate the 3D map $\mathcal{M}_i$ and the relative keyframe poses P_{k_{i-1},k_i} and $P_{k_{i-1},k_{i+1}}$.

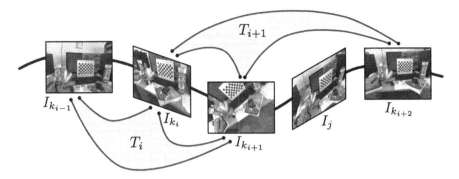

Fig. 1. Overview of the SAMSLAM approach. Keyframe triplets T_i and T_{i+1} are used to estimate successive overlapping local 3D point maps, which are then employed to retrieve the pose of a generic image frame I_j.

Note that, since outliers are dropped out by the simulated annealing scheme, only a fraction of the loop chain matches contribute to 3D points in the map $\mathcal{M}_i$.

The relative pose $P_{k_{i-1},j}$ for a generic image I_j, $k_{i+1} < j$, is estimated according to the 3D map $\mathcal{M}_i$ by employing a robust version of ePnP [13]. In order for I_j to become the next keyframe $I_{k_{i+2}}$, a significant 2D motion with respect to $I_{k_{i+1}}$ has to be detected, in which case the current keyframe triplet T_i is updated to T_{i+1}.

2.2 Simulated Annealing 3D Map and Pose Estimation

The keyframe triplet T_i is related to the matches $(\mathbf{x}_{k_{i+v}}, \mathbf{x}_{k_{i+w}}) \in \mathcal{C}_i$, with $v, w \in \{-1, 0, 1\}$ and $v < w$. The simulated annealing approach starts by associating to each pair $(I_{k_{i+v}}, I_{k_{i+w}})$ an initial 3D map $\mathcal{M}_i^{v,w}$, obtained by triangulation on the matches $(\mathbf{x}_{k_{i+v}}, \mathbf{x}_{k_{i+w}})$. The relative pose $P_{k_{i+v},k_{i+w}}$ is extracted from the essential matrix for the first triplet T_1, while for all triplets T_i, $i > 1$ relative poses are initialized with the estimates obtained at triplet time $i - 1$. After this initialization, the method registers the 3D maps $\mathcal{M}_i^{v,w}$ and refines the poses $P_{k_{i+v},k_{i+w}}$ at each iteration q (in all experiments, a maximum of 8 iterations were run). A block diagram of the proposed method is illustrated in Fig. 2.

3D map registration is done by the Horn method [14], fixing a 3D reference map $\mathcal{M}_i^{\mathrm{ref}}$ from one of the maps $\mathcal{M}_i^{v,w}$ for all iterations. Inconsistent 3D points with negative depths in any of the three associated stereo configurations $(I_{k_{i+v}}, I_{k_{i+w}})$ are removed as well as points far from any of the corresponding camera centres, since the uncertainty in point localization increases with distance. The proportion p of points discarded by this latter constraint linearly decreases with the iteration q since a more refined model is obtained as the iterations go on. In our experiments p is made to decrease from 30% to 1%. Remaining points in the resulting submap $\widetilde{\mathcal{M}}_i^{v,w}$ are registered to the reference submap $\widetilde{\mathcal{M}}_i^{\mathrm{ref}}$ through the Horn method, made robust to outliers by RANSAC. Reference 3D points of $\widetilde{\mathcal{M}}_i^{\mathrm{ref}}$ are mapped to $\widetilde{\mathcal{M}}_i^{v,w}$ according to the transformation $H_i^{v,w}$

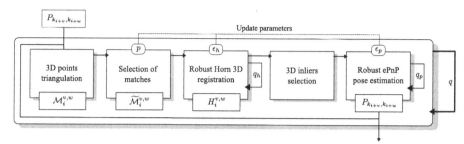

Fig. 2. Diagram of the simulated annealing 3D map and pose estimation executed for each keyframe triplet T_i

estimated by the Horn method and back-projected to the corresponding images I_v and I_w. The distances between the back-projected points and the effective matches $\mathbf{x}_v$ and $\mathbf{x}_w$ are used to define inliers. The inlier threshold value ϵ_h linearly decreases with the iteration q, from 20 to 4 pixels in our experiments. At each RANSAC iteration q_h the transformation $H_i^{v,w}$ is refined. The sampling set is a subset of the whole validation set and contains only the 25% of points in $\widetilde{\mathcal{M}}_i^{v,w}$ with maximal flow displacement. This is beneficial to map accuracy, since high disparity matches are characterized by a better localization in 3D space.

The pose refinement step also works on the reference 3D map $\widetilde{\mathcal{M}}_i^{\mathrm{ref}}$. The ePnP with RANSAC is applied to points associated to the common inliers found in the Horn registration step between the maps $\widetilde{\mathcal{M}}_i^{v,w}$. The reprojection error threshold ϵ_p used to define inliers linearly decreases with the iteration q, from 5 to 3 pixels in the experiments. Similarly to 3D map registration, a constraint on the sampling set depending on the RANSAC iteration q_p is used. The refined poses $P_{k_{i+v},k_{i+w}}$ replace the previous ones for the next iteration q.

Figure 3(a) shows an example of the simulated annealing scheme on the first keyframe triplet T_1 of the *Monk* video sequence (see Sect. 3). Fig. 4 shows the corresponding 3D maps $\widetilde{\mathcal{M}}_i^{v,w}$ for different iterations q. The average reprojection error gradually decreases for each image pair $(I_{k_{i+v}}, I_{k_{i+w}})$ to less than 2 pixels, while the number of 3D point inliers increases and the 3D registration improves. Note that the first iteration $q = 1$ of the first keyframe triplet T_1 is the most time consuming in terms of RANSAC iterations with $q_h, q_p \simeq 500$, while in the other cases $q_h, q_p \simeq 50$ since only refinements are required. The RANSAC-based design can be useful to define efficient parallel and multi-threaded implementations of the simulated annealing scheme.

3   Results

In order to evaluate the performance of our monocular SLAM approach, two different experiments have been carried out: A quantitative direct measure of the odometry accuracy, and an indirect evaluation of the 3D reconstruction quality of an object acquired using a structured-light framework.

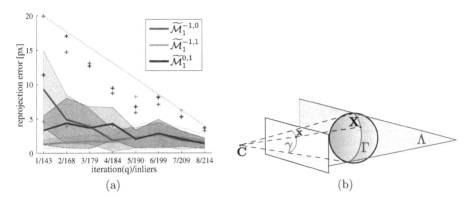

Fig. 3. (a) The reprojection errors as the iterations proceed for the first keyframe triplet T_1 of the *Monk* video sequence. The reference map is $\widetilde{\mathcal{M}}_1^{\text{ref}} = \widetilde{\mathcal{M}}_1^{-1,1}$. Solid lines indicate the average reprojection errors, while bands show the behaviour of the standard deviation. Marks represents the maximal values and the dashed gray line is the RANSAC linear threshold bound ϵ_h. (b) The laser scanner configuration for the evaluation of the *Monk* sequence. (Best viewed in color)

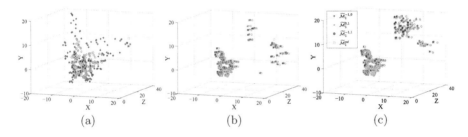

Fig. 4. The 3D maps $\widetilde{\mathcal{M}}_i^{v,w}$ and the reference map $\widetilde{\mathcal{M}}_1^{\text{ref}}$ at iterations $q = 1, 5, 8$ for the keyframe triplet T_1 of the *Monk* video sequence. (Best viewed in color)

Three different indoor video sequences with a resolution of 640×480 pixels and about 800 frames have been used in the former case — see Table 1(a). The first two sequences (*Desk1* and *Desk2*) explore the same desktop environment as the camera undergoes two different motions, while the last sequence (*Monk*) contains an object scanned by a laser fan projector. This last sequence is also used for the indirect evaluation through 3D reconstruction. A known planar pattern is included in the background of all test sequences to recover accurate ground-truth poses using the approach described in [15].

Table 1(a) shows the Euclidean distance error of the camera centres normalized to the ground-truth path length, while corresponding tracks are shown in Fig. 5. Since the scale information is lost, the camera centres have been registered to the known ground-truth metric scale using the Horn method. SAMSLAM error is about 1% on average, i.e. less than 1 cm for a track length of 100 cm, and tracks are well aligned.

Table 1. (a) Distance error of the camera centres with respect to the ground-truth length. (b) 3D reconstruction error for the *Monk* sequence.

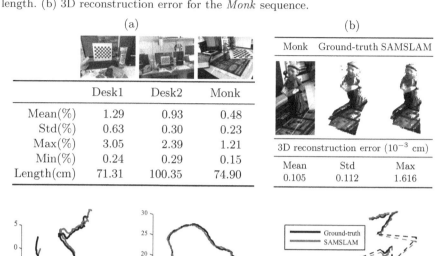

(a)

	Desk1	Desk2	Monk
Mean(%)	1.29	0.93	0.48
Std(%)	0.63	0.30	0.23
Max(%)	3.05	2.39	1.21
Min(%)	0.24	0.29	0.15
Length(cm)	71.31	100.35	74.90

(b)

Monk	Ground-truth	SAMSLAM

3D reconstruction error (10^{-3} cm)

Mean	Std	Max
0.105	0.112	1.616

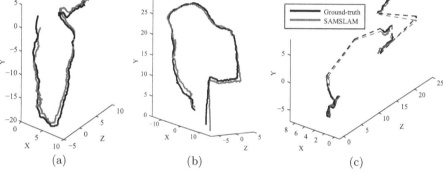

(a)   (b)   (c)

Fig. 5. Track comparison for the video sequences *Desk1* (a), *Desk2* (b) and *Monk* (c). Dashed lines for the *Monk* sequence indicate that no ground-truth has been provided. (Best viewed in color)

For the 3D laser-scanned reconstruction test on the *Monk* sequence, a device equipped with a camera and a laser fan projector kept in fixed relative position is used in order to get an accurate 3D model. As depicted in Fig. 3(b), C is the camera centre, Λ the laser fan plane, Γ the 3D laser trace and γ the 2D laser image.

In basic projection geometry of laser profile Γ onto the image, each point $\mathbf{x}$ of the imaged laser profile γ can be backprojected onto the laser plane Λ, obtaining its pre-image $\mathbf{X} \in \Gamma$. The backprojection equation can be expressed as $\mathbf{X} = \alpha K^{-1}\mathbf{x}$, where $\alpha = d[\mathbf{n}^\top K^{-1}\mathbf{x}]^{-1}$, $\mathbf{n}^\top \mathbf{X} - d = 0$ is the equation of the laser plane Λ in inhomogeneous camera-centred coordinates, $\mathbf{x}$ is a homogeneous 3-vector, and K is the camera calibration matrix. A 3D profile is obtained in the camera framework for each frame moving the scanning device. Knowing the estimated motion, it is possible to collate all the 3D profiles in a unique model.

Table 1(b) shows the 3D Euclidean reconstruction errors with respect to the ground-truth obtained with the estimated motion and the reconstructed model. Even in this case the error is low while the 3D reconstruction is almost identical to the ground-truth.

4   Conclusions

This paper presents a mono SLAM approach, relying on a local keyframe optimization, based on simulated annealing, which iteratively refines both the motion estimates and the 3D structure. Direct evaluation of track error and indirect validation through structured-light 3D reconstruction show good performance of the approach, that does not require neither global optimization nor loop closure techniques.

Future work will include solutions for a better 3D registration and pose handling in the case of noisy correspondences, due for example to motion blur, and to enforce the system for long tracks, also adaptively correcting the reference 3D map in the case of faults. Furthermore, efficient and optimized implementation of the system will be developed.

Acknowledgements. This work has been carried out during the THESAURUS project, founded by Regione Toscana (Italy) in the framework of the "FAS" program 2007-2013 under Deliberation CIPE (Italian government) 166/2007.

References

1. Davison, A.: Real-time simultaneous localization and mapping with a single camera. In: Proc. 9th IEEE International Conference on Computer Vision, pp. 1403–1410 (2003)
2. Klein, G., Murray, D.: Parallel tracking and mapping for small AR workspaces. In: Proc. IEEE/ACM International Symposium on Mixed and Augmented Reality, pp. 225–234 (2007)
3. Strasdat, H., Montiel, J., Davison, A.: Visual SLAM: Why filter? Image and Vision Computing 30, 65–77 (2012)
4. Mei, C., Sibley, G., Cummins, M., Newman, P., Reid, I.: RSLAM: A system for large-scale mapping in constant-time using stereo. International Journal of Computer Vision 94, 198–214 (2011)
5. Newcombe, R., Lovegrove, S., Davison, A.: DTAM: Dense Tracking and Mapping in Real-Time. In: Proc. 13th International Conference on Computer Vision (2011)
6. Pretto, A., Menegatti, E., Bennewitz, M., Burgard, W.: A visual odometry framework robust to motion blur. In: Proc. IEEE International Conference on Robotics and Automation (2009)
7. Strasdat, H., Davison, A.J., Montiel, J.M.M., Konolige, K.: Double window optimisation for constant time visual SLAM. In: Proc. of the International Conference on Computer Vision, pp. 2352–2359 (2011)
8. Triggs, B., McLauchlan, P., Hartley, R., Fitzgibbon, A.: Bundle adjustment - a modern synthesis. In: Proc. of the International Workshop on Vision Algorithms: Theory and Practice, pp. 298–372 (2000)

9. Ho, K., Newman, P.: Detecting loop closure with scene sequences. International Journal Computer Vision 74(3), 261–286 (2007)
10. Bellavia, F., Tegolo, D., Valenti, C.: Improving Harris corner selection strategy. IET Computer Vision 5(2) (2011)
11. Bellavia, F., Tegolo, D., Trucco, E.: Improving SIFT-based descriptors stability to rotations. In: Proc. of International Conference on Pattern Recognition (2010)
12. Bellavia, F., Tegolo, D.: noRANSAC for fundamental matrix estimation. In: Proc. of he British Machine Vision Conference, pp. 1–98 (2011)
13. Moreno-Noguer, F., Lepetit, V., Fua, P.: Accurate Non-Iterative O(n) Solution to the PnP Problem. In: Proc. of IEEE International Conference on Computer Vision (2007)
14. Horn, B.K.P.: Closed-form solution of absolute orientation using unit quaternions. Journal of the Optical Society of America A 4(4), 629–642 (1987)
15. Fanfani, M., Colombo, C.: LaserGun: A tool for hybrid 3D reconstruction. In: Chen, M., Leibe, B., Neumann, B. (eds.) ICVS 2013. LNCS, vol. 7963, pp. 274–283. Springer, Heidelberg (2013)

Spatial Patch Blending for Artefact Reduction
in Pattern-Based Inpainting Techniques

Maxime Daisy, David Tschumperlé, and Olivier Lézoray

GREYC Laboratory (CNRS UMR 6072), Image Team, 6 Bd Marechal Juin, 14050 Caen/France
{maxime.daisy,david.tschumperle,olivier.lezoray}@ensicaen.fr

Abstract. Patch-based (or "pattern-based") inpainting, is a popular processing technique aiming at reconstructing missing regions in images, by iteratively duplicating blocks of known image data (patches) inside the area to fill in. This kind of method is particularly effective to process wide image areas, thanks to its ability to reconstruct textured data. Nevertheless, "pathological" geometric configurations often happen, leading to visible reconstruction artefacts on inpainted images, whatever the chosen pattern-based inpainting algorithm. In this paper we focus on these problematic cases and propose a generic *spatial-blending technique* that can be adapted to any type of patch-based inpainting methods in order to reduce theses problematic artefacts.

Keywords: inpainting, pattern, patch, blending.

  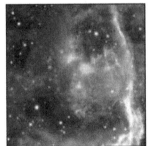

(a) Masked colored image. (b) Inpainting obtained with the algorithm from [1]. (c) Inpainting result + patch blending (proposed algorithm).

Fig. 1. Illustration of our contribution (portions on the region of interest of a larger picture)

1   Context and Current Issues

Image inpainting is the technique that is used to reconstruct the missing parts in an image while keeping the geometrical consistency in the reconstructed portion as much as possible. A good review of inpainting methods can be found in [2] where two main kinds of techniques are described:

- "Geometry-based" methods [3,4,5,6], introduced by Masnou and Morel [3] in their seminal work on area disocclusion by level-line completion, solve the inpainting

R. Wilson et al. (Eds.): CAIP 2013, Part II, LNCS 8048, pp. 523–530, 2013.

problem by applying partial derivative equations and finding a function that minimizes an energy that expresses the inpainting problem. These methods allow to locally extend the geometry of the image structures at the boundaries of the inpainting domain. Nevertheless, no texture regeneration is possible with these techniques, and image flattening effects may appear between known parts and reconstructed ones, especially for real images.

- "Pattern-oriented" methods [1,2,7,8,9,10,11,12], introduced by Efros and Leung [12] in their work on texture extrapolation, are based on copy and paste of patches from known parts of the image into the area to be recovered. These algorithms generate a kind of patchwork of image pieces by iteratively choosing the most similar patches to those living on the boundaries of the inpainting domain. Results given by these methods are particularly interesting for wide and textured area reconstructed.

Some variations intend to mix these two approaches to either create hybrid methods [10,13,6], or to average several patches [1,14] for computing the final patch used for the reconstruction. In any case, there are always local configurations that do not satisfy the selected similarity criteria. Copying and pasting, or averaging such kind of patches may produce visual artefacts appearing as block effects or strong discontinuities in the image. These configurations are actually not so uncommon: an inpainting mask often covers regions where transitions in texture or luminosity occur and there are no ways a single patch taken around can fit perfectly for the reconstruction.

In this paper we introduce an original approach based on *spatial patch blending*, to reduce these kinds of artefacts. The advantages of our proposed algorithm are twofold: First, it can be added to any type of pattern-based inpainting algorithms, and second, it is able to reconstruct patches that are *smart combinations* of those located in the known area of the image. Moreover, we propose a way to perform this patch blending only on locations where inpainting artefacts occur by automatically detecting the most visible artefact points. The simultaneous application of these two contributions (spatial patch blending and inpainting artefacts detection) is illustrated by several inpainting results where the visual artefacts are clearly reduced compared to a classical patch-based inpainting approach.

This paper is organized as follows. Second section exposes the principle of our patch blending technique for patch-based image inpainting post processing. Third section shows how artefacts are detected from patch-based image inpainting results. Last section concludes with some commented results.

2   A Patch Blending Algorithm for Inpainting

This section shows how a classical patch-based inpainting algorithm can be modified to add our spatial patch blending feature.

Let $I : \Gamma \mapsto \mathbb{R}^3_+$ be a color image of which the missing pixels are defined over a domain $\Omega \subset \Gamma$ (inpainting mask). Let ψ_p denote a square-sized ($N \times N$ with N odd) image patch centered at $p \in \Gamma$. The ith color component of a patch ψ_p will be denoted by $\psi_p^i \in \mathbb{R}^{N \times N}$. Most of the pattern-oriented inpainting algorithms are based on these two steps:

1. The lookup, for each $p \in \Omega$, of the "best" patch ψ_q (with $\psi_q \subset \Gamma \setminus \Omega$),
2. The copy of the patch ψ_q on $\psi_p \cap \Omega$ inside the image I to be reconstructed.

Based on this copy/paste principle, the content of Ω is filled in an iterative and mostly concentric way (however, some points of interest can be processed in priority).

Our technique consists in modifying this kind of inpainting algorithm to be able to post-process the inpainting result with a patch blending method in order to visually improve the quality of the rendered image I. This modification requires to save both the map $\mathcal{U} : \Gamma \mapsto \Gamma$ of the locations of the original patch centers, and the map $\mathcal{S} : \Omega \mapsto \mathbb{R}^2$ of the offsets between the reconstructed points and the centers of the partially copied patches. The connected component labelization $\mathcal{L}$ of $\mathcal{U}$ defines the partition of the patches pieces in the known parts of the image that were stuck back in Ω. Using the following data sets : $I, \mathcal{U}, \mathcal{S}$ and $\mathcal{L}$, we are then able to generate an image $J : \Gamma \mapsto \mathbb{R}^3_+$ of which the patches of I, used to fill Ω, spatially blend one to another. In practice, for each point $p \in \Omega$, this blending is realized with a set Ψ_p of patches $\{\psi_{p_1}, \ldots, \psi_{p_n}\}$, obtained from a neighborhood $\mathcal{V}(p)$ around p, and that contains p. This set is built from a full search of all the centers of the different patches that were copied in $\mathcal{V}(p)$. Then, the blending is computed for the pixel p by the spatial merging of all the patches contained in Ψ_p as follows for each color component i:

$$J^i(p) = \frac{\sum\limits_{\psi_q \in \Psi_p} w(q,p)\, \psi_q^i(p-q)}{\varepsilon + \sum\limits_{\psi_q \in \Psi_p} w(q,p)} \tag{1}$$

with $\varepsilon \in \mathbb{R}$ close to 0 used to stabilize the equation. The quantity $\psi_q^i(p-q)$ represents the pixel value at the coordinates $((N/2, N/2)^T + (p-q))$ in ψ_q^i. The Gaussian weights $w(q,p) = e^{-\frac{d(q,p)^2}{\sigma^2}}$ give more importance in the blending computation to the patches of Ψ_p, that are the spatially closest to the point p. The variance σ is the key parameter, related to the amplitude of the spatial blending. The function $d(p,q)$ defines the minimal spatial distance between the point p and the sub-domain of the patch that was used for the reconstruction of q.

$$d(q,\, p) = \min_{q' \in \mathcal{V}(p)} \|q' - p\| \quad \text{where} \quad \mathcal{L}(q') = \mathcal{L}(q) \tag{2}$$

The usage of the distance $d(p,q)$ allows to generate a spatial blending orthogonally oriented according to the boundaries of the patches in the neighborhood of p. Fig. 2 illustrates a synthetic situation where we want to apply this blending technique. In the latter figure, p is the point where the blending has to be computed, and $\{\psi_0, \ldots, \psi_3\}$ are the patches contained in Ψ_p. The x and y component of the vectors of $\mathcal{S}$ are respectively represented by the red and green components in the first figure. The point c_0 is the center of the patch ψ_0 and one has $\mathcal{S}(p) = c_0 - p$. In Fig. 2(b), the arrows represent the minimal distances from p to each neighbor patch. The weights w related to ψ_1, ψ_2, ψ_3 are respectively represented by the lighting intensities in the red, green and blue channels (with $w(p,q) = 0$ for $q \in \psi_0$). Algorithm. 1. summarizes the main steps of our patch blending process.

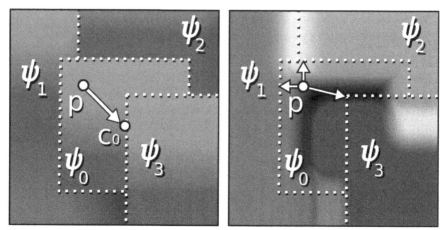

(a) Representation of the map S of the offsets (b) Representation of the weights w used to
with the patch centers.   compute (1) for every point of ψ_0.

Fig. 2. Illustration of both S and w quantities computed for the patch blending

Our spatial patch blending technique uses all the patches from which a point $p \in \Omega$ could have been reconstructed during the inpainting process if the filling order had been different from those really used. Intuitively this comes to keep a list of candidate patches (rather than the only one of the basic copy/paste process) for each $p \in \Omega$ reconstructed during a patch-based inpainting. It is very different from an inpainting process that would average the K best patches (like in [1]) to reconstruct each point p since here the blending uses the geometry of the piece of patch copied at p and also the spatial configuration of the neighbour patches.

Here, one can notice that the blending is computed with a constant amplitude σ. Actually, all the areas of the inpainted image do not contain reconstruction artefacts of the same strength, so it would be naturally desirable to be able to locally vary σ. Hence, the third section explains our second contribution, the adaptation of σ to the local artefacts strength.

Algorithm 1. Spatial patch blending for inpainting

---

1 **for** $p \in \Omega$ **do**
2   **var** centers = list($\varnothing$);
3   **var** distances = list($\varnothing$);
4   **for** $q \in \mathcal{V}(p)$ **do**
5   **var** c = q + $S(q)$;
6   **if** $(c \notin centers) \wedge (p \in \psi_c)$ **then**
7   insert(centers, c) ;
8   insert(distances, $d(c, p)$) ;   // see (2)
9   J(p) = blend(p, centers, distances) ;   // see (1)

---

3 Automatic Detection of Inpainting Artefacts

Here, we explain a method to automatically detect artefacts produced by patch-based inpainting algorithms. This method uses the additional $\mathcal{U}$ data provided by modifying patch-based inpainting methods as described in the previous section.

Most of the visual artefacts due to a reconstruction mainly appear when two patches with not enough similarity were copied close to each other inside Ω. In practice, the point $p \in \Omega$ where artefacts appear are inside areas verifying these two conditions :

1. $\|\nabla I(p)\|$ is high, and so indicates strong spatial discontinuities in the image values.
2. Patches pasted inside the neighborhood of p come from different and far locations producing discontinuities inside $\mathcal{U}$.

Therefore, our proposition is to track down the set $\mathcal{E}$ of these artefact points (also named *break points*) as the set of points verifying the condition $\mathcal{R}(p) > \tau$ where :

$$\forall p \in \Omega, \quad \mathcal{R}(p) = \frac{\|\nabla I(p)\| \cdot |\operatorname{div}(\mathcal{U})(p)|}{\alpha} \tag{3}$$

and $\alpha = (\max_{q \in I} \|\nabla I(q)\|) \times (\max_{q \in I} |\operatorname{div}(\mathcal{U}(q))|)$ is a normalization factor allowing the user parameter τ, related to the detected break points density, to be chosen within $[0, 1]$. $\mathcal{R}(p)$ is used to locally estimate the strength of the geometrical break due to the reconstruction since $|\operatorname{div}(\mathcal{U})|$ determines whether two patches stuck next to each other come from close locations (low $|\operatorname{div}(\mathcal{U})|$), or far locations (high $|\operatorname{div}(\mathcal{U})|$). Consequently, if $\mathcal{R}(p)$ is high, the point p fulfills both 1. and 2. and is more likely to locate an artefact inside the image I.

By associating to each point $p \in \mathcal{E}$ a Gaussian function the variance of which depends on $\mathcal{R}(p)$, a spatial map $\sigma : \Gamma \mapsto \mathbb{R}_+$ of the local blending amplitude can be defined as follows:

$$\forall p \in \Gamma, \quad \sigma(p) = \rho \times \frac{\sum\limits_{r \in \mathcal{E}} w_b(p, r)}{\max\limits_{q \in \Gamma} \sum\limits_{r \in \mathcal{E}} w_b(q, r)} \tag{4}$$

where $w_b(p, r) = e^{-\frac{\|p-r\|^2}{(3\rho \mathcal{R}(r))^2}}$ and ρ is a user parameter defining the maximal width of the spatial patch blending inside J. Using $\sigma = \sigma(p)$ in the patch blending equation (1), we are able to locally change the blending amplitude according to the presence (also the strength) or not of the artefacts. For the sake of performance, the blending is made only inside a subset $\Omega' \subset \Gamma$ where $\sigma(p)$ is high enough. It should be noted that in the case of strongly textured areas, it may happen that 1. and 2. are simultaneously verified for some points where no visual artefact exist. The experiments we made suggest that using spatial patch blending in these areas does generally not damage the quality of the reconstruction.

4 Results and Conclusions

Fig. 3, 4 and 5 illustrate different results of "blended inpainting" on synthetic and real color images, as well as comparisons with other classical inpainting algorithms presented in [1,4,8,7,11]. The images of Fig.4 has been post-processed with a contrast

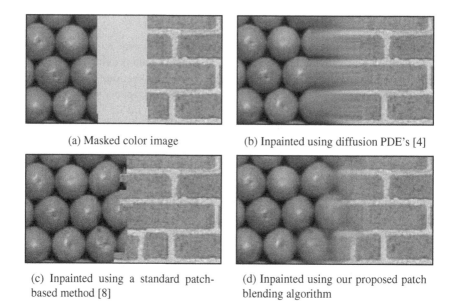

(a) Masked color image   (b) Inpainted using diffusion PDE's [4]

(c) Inpainted using a standard patch-   (d) Inpainted using our proposed patch
based method [8]   blending algorithm

Fig. 3. Illustrating the advantage of patch blending on a synthetic case

(a) Masked colored image.   (b) Inpainting result from [11]. (c) Inpainting result + patch
                                                              blending (proposed algorithm).

Fig. 4. Comparison with the patchwork algorithm [11]

enhancement filter for printing quality purpose. Through these examples, it is particularly interesting to see that our proposed blending method creates results which have
all the good properties of other approaches at the same time, something between pure
diffusion techniques (Fig.3b) where colors are smoothly interpolated but without reconstructed textures, and pure patch-based techniques (Fig.3c) where repetitive patterns are
fully reconstructed. This way, the visual artefacts due to incoherent patch collage are
strongly reduced, while the computation time overhead is negligible. The effect is close
to the results of [10,15], but our blending formula is explicit and straightforward to compute (no Poisson Equation to solve) and allows more flexibility in the choice of the local

(a) Masked colored image (used in [1]).

(b) Inpainting result from [1].

(c) Inpainting result + patch blending (proposed algorithm).

(d) Masked colored image.

(e) Inpainting result with [8].

(f) Inpainting result + patch blending (proposed algorithm).

(g) Masked image.

(h) Inpainting obtained with [7].

(i) Inpainting obtained with [8].

(j) Inpainting result + patch blending (proposed algorithm).

Fig. 5. Comparison of the patch blending results with the state of the art inpainting methods [1,8,7]

blending amplitude. Moreover, our approach only requires to set two additional parameters τ (threshold for the artefacts detection) and ρ (maximum blending amplitude) which are quite intuitive and easy to adjust. This makes our contribution very generic, easy to implement, and relevant for the improvement of any kind of patch-based inpainting algorithms.

References

1. Meur, O.L., Gautier, J., Guillemot, C.: Examplar-based inpainting based on local geometry. In: ICIP, Brussel, Belgium, pp. 3401–3404 (2011)
2. Caselles, V.: Examplar-based image inpainting and applications. SIAM News 44(10) (December 2011)
3. Masnou, S., Morel, J.-M.: Level lines based disocclusion. In: ICIP, vol. 3, pp. 259–263 (1998)
4. Tschumperlé, D., Deriche, R.: Vector-valued image regularization with pdes: A common framework for different applications. IEEE Trans. PAMI 27(4), 506–517 (2005)
5. Bertalmio, M., Sapiro, G., Caselles, V., Ballester, C.: Image inpainting. In: Proc. of the 27th Annual SIGGRAPH Conference, SIGGRAPH 2000, New York, NY, USA, pp. 417–424 (2000)
6. Sun, J., Yuan, L., Jia, J., Shum, H.-Y.: Image completion with structure propagation. ACM Trans. Graph. 24(3), 861–868 (2005)
7. Harrison, P.: Image Texture Tools. PhD thesis, Monash University (2005)
8. Criminisi, A., Pérez, P., Toyama, K.: Region filling and object removal by exemplar-based image inpainting. IEEE Trans. Im. Proc. 13(9), 1200–1212 (2004)
9. Wexler, Y., Shechtman, E., Irani, M.: Space-time completion of video. IEEE Trans. Pattern Anal. Mach. Intell. 29(3), 463–476 (2007)
10. Arias, P., Facciolo, G., Caselles, V., Sapiro, G.: A variational framework for exemplar-based image inpainting. Int. J. Comput. Vision 93(3), 319–347 (2011)
11. Pérez, P., Gangnet, M., Blake, A.: Patchworks: Example-based region tiling for image editing. Technical report, Microsoft Research, MSR-TR-2004-04 (2004)
12. Efros, A.A., Leung, T.K.: Texture synthesis by non-parametric sampling. In: Proc. of ICCV1999, pp. 1033–1038. IEEE Computer Society Press, Washington, DC (1999)
13. Kawai, N., Sato, T., Yokoya, N.: Image inpainting considering brightness change and spatial locality of textures and its evaluation. In: Wada, T., Huang, F., Lin, S. (eds.) PSIVT 2009. LNCS, vol. 5414, pp. 271–282. Springer, Heidelberg (2009)
14. Türkan, M., Guillemot, C.: Image prediction based on neighbor-embedding methods. IEEE Trans. Im. Proc. 21(4), 1885–1898 (2012)
15. Pérez, P., Gangnet, M., Blake, A.: Poisson image editing. ACM Transactions on Graphics (SIGGRAPH 2003) 22(3), 313–318 (2003)

Spatio-temporal Support for Range Flow Based Ego-Motion Estimators

Graeme A. Jones[1] and Gordon Hunter[2]

[1] Digital Imaging Research Centre, School of Computing and Information Systems,
Kingston University
g.jones@kingston.ac.uk
[2] School of Mathematics, Kingston University
g.hunter@kingston.ac.uk

Abstract. A real-time *range flow* based ego-motion estimator for a moving depth sensor is presented. The estimator recovers the translation and rotation components of a sensor's motion and integrates these temporally. To ensure accurate inter-frame motion estimates, an iterative form of the estimator is developed. To minimise drift in the pose, additional temporal constraint is provided through the use of *anchor frames*. The algorithm is evaluated on the recently published TUB RGB-D Benchmark. Performance is commensurate with alternative methodologies such as SLAM but at a fraction of the computational cost.

1 Introduction

Recovering the ego-motion of a moving camera within a static scene supports many applications in robotics and computer vision. The presented work is motivated by *pre-vis* applications in the film industry; specifically the ability to render digital assets into the scene during production in real-time. A low-cost commodity depth camera can be easily mounted on and calibrated to high quality production cameras and used to extract changes in sensor pose from the induced motion of the rigid scene. This work explores the effectiveness of the computationally efficient *range flow* technique to generate this real time pose information directly from the depth stream of a Kinect sensor.

A number of challenges within the approach are addressed. An iterative version of the *small rotations* motion estimator is developed to ensure the most accurate inter-frame estimates. The considerable problem of *drift* is addressed - the accumulated error between true and estimated sensor pose. *Anchor frames* which enjoy significant overlap with subsequent frames are stored and used to provide additional temporal range flow constraint within the estimation process. Where there are loops in the data sequence, it is advantageous to select anchors from previously seen parts of the scene. The evaluation of new algorithms which exploit the depth modality requires depth datasets with associated ground truth. Our work is validated using the recently published TUB RGB-D Benchmark which in addition to its extensive set of sequences, also provides an evaluation framework of metrics and tools.

R. Wilson et al. (Eds.): CAIP 2013, Part II, LNCS 8048, pp. 531–538, 2013.

2   Related Work

There have been a variety of approaches developed to recover the motion of an image sensor moving within a scene. These include the matching of depth features [12,13], *iterated closest point* (ICP) [4,10], *simultaneous location and mapping* (SLAM) [5,11] and *range flow* [8,9]. Impressive real-time results have been achieved particularly by SLAM. Viable depth sensors have been available for over two decades whether using laser range finders or stereo vision systems. It was realized that the *optical flow* mechanism could be easily extended to depth images [9,14]. The recent availability of commodity frame-rate depth sensors has given rise to renewed interest in recovering motion from depth data[7,10].

Analogous to optical flow, *range flow* is a per-pixel constraint on the 3D displacement of an imaged 3D point given its local spatio-temporal depth derivatives. These must be combined across a region or an image to provide sufficient constraint to extract 3D motion. Where the goal is to recover a 3D displacement field given a possibly moving scene with independently moving objects, this per-pixel constraint can be embedded in a global energy functional which penalises pixel motions which do not satisfy the local range flow constraints and which are not locally smooth [3,7] - an approach essentially equivalent to regularisation in optical flow[2]. Alternatively if some motion model is used which is valid for the rigid scene, then a large number of pixel constraints can be used to over constrain very few motion parameters. In the case of optical flow, such models include affine motion, zoom and the *small rotation* approximation of the 3D rotation and translation of the camera[1].

3   Range Flow Motion Estimator

Analogous to the *constant brightness equation* used to generate the *optical flow* constraint, the following depth constraint relates how a 3D point is captured in temporally separated depth images. A 3D point $\mathbf{X} = (X, Y, Z)^T$ (measured in the depth camera's coordinate system) is captured at pixel position $\mathbf{x} = (x, y)^T$ in the depth map Z_t. This point undergoes a 3D motion $\Delta\mathbf{X} = (\Delta X, \Delta Y, \Delta Z)^T$ which results in an image motion $\Delta\mathbf{x}$ between frames t and τ. Given that the depth of the 3D point will have moved by ΔZ, the depth value captured at this new image location $\mathbf{x} + \Delta\mathbf{x}$ will have consequently changed by this amount i.e.

$$Z_\tau(\mathbf{x} + \Delta\mathbf{x}) = Z_t(\mathbf{x}) + \Delta Z \qquad (1)$$

Taking the first-order Taylor expansion of the term $Z_\tau(\mathbf{x} + \Delta\mathbf{x})$ in the above equation generates a pixel-based constraint relating the gradient of the depth image ∇Z_τ and the temporal depth difference to the unknown pixel motion and the change of depth as follows

$$\{\nabla Z_\tau(\mathbf{x}), -1\} \begin{pmatrix} \Delta\mathbf{x} \\ \Delta Z \end{pmatrix} = Z_t(\mathbf{x}) - Z_\tau(\mathbf{x}) \qquad (2)$$

However, any small 2D displacement $\Delta\mathbf{x}$ can be related directly to the 3D displacement $\Delta\mathbf{X}$ which gave rise to it by differentiating the perspective projection equations $x = x_0 + X f_x / Z$ and $y = y_0 + Y f_y / Z$ with respect to the components of the 3D position $\mathbf{X}$.

$$\frac{\partial \mathbf{x}}{\partial \mathbf{X}} = P(\mathbf{x}) = \begin{bmatrix} f_x/Z & 0 & -X f_x/Z^2 \\ 0 & f_y/Z & -Y f_y/Z^2 \end{bmatrix} \qquad (3)$$

Since $\Delta \mathbf{x} \approx \frac{\partial \mathbf{x}(\mathbf{X})}{\partial \mathbf{X}} \Delta \mathbf{X}$ equation 2 can be rewritten as a linear constraint equation of three unknowns relating the motion $\Delta \mathbf{X}$ of a 3D point imaged at pixel $\mathbf{x}$ to the gradient of the depth image ∇Z_τ and the temporal depth difference i.e.

$$\Phi(\mathbf{x}) \Delta \mathbf{X} = Z_t(\mathbf{x}) - Z_\tau(\mathbf{x}) \qquad (4)$$

where

$$\Phi(\mathbf{x}) = \{\nabla Z_\tau(\mathbf{x}), -1\} Q(\mathbf{x}), \quad Q(\mathbf{x}) = \begin{bmatrix} P(\mathbf{x}) & \\ 0 \quad 0 & 1 \end{bmatrix}$$

As the scene displacement is induced by the motion of the camera, the rotation $\boldsymbol{\omega}$ and translation $\mathbf{t}$ parameters of the scene can be recovered by substituting $\Delta \mathbf{X}$ with a function of $\boldsymbol{\omega}$ and $\mathbf{t}$. When the rotation parameters are small between consecutive frames, then $\Delta \mathbf{X} = \boldsymbol{\omega} \times \mathbf{X} + \mathbf{t}$

$$\Delta \mathbf{X} = \begin{bmatrix} Z\omega_y - Y\omega_z + t_x \\ X\omega_z - Z\omega_x + t_y \\ Y\omega_x - X\omega_y + t_z \end{bmatrix} = M(\mathbf{x})\mathbf{a} \qquad (5)$$

where $\mathbf{a}$ is the concatenated scene motion parameters $\mathbf{a} = (\boldsymbol{\omega}, \mathbf{t})^T$ and

$$M(\mathbf{x}) = \begin{bmatrix} 0 & Z & -Y & 1 & 0 & 0 \\ -Z & 0 & X & 0 & 1 & 0 \\ Y & -X & 0 & 0 & 0 & 1 \end{bmatrix} \qquad (6)$$

Thus the constraint on the motion $\mathbf{a}$ from a pixel $\mathbf{x}$ between the current frame Z_t and a target frame Z_τ is defined as

$$\Psi(\mathbf{x})\mathbf{a} = Z_t(\mathbf{x}) - Z_\tau(\mathbf{x}) \qquad (7)$$

where since $\Psi(\mathbf{x}) = \{\nabla Z_\tau(\mathbf{x}), -1\} Q(\mathbf{x}) M(\mathbf{x})$ then

$$\Psi(\mathbf{x}) = \big[-Y - Z_y f_y - Z_x XY f_x / Z^2 - Z_y Y^2 f_y / Z^2,$$
$$X + Z_x f_x + Z_x X^2 f_x / Z^2 + Z_y XY f_y / Z^2, -Z_x Y f_x / Z + Z_y X f_y / Z,$$
$$Z_x f_x / Z, Z_y f_y / Z, -1 - Z_x X f_x / Z^2 - Z_y Y f_y / Z^2 \big]$$

and $\nabla Z_\tau(\mathbf{x}) = (Z_x, Z_y)$ are the spatial derivatives of $Z_\tau(\mathbf{x})$. Combining this simple constraint function for pixels across the image generates an estimator for $\mathbf{a}$. In practice such estimators do not recover an accurate estimate of pixel motion in a single iteration. The following is an iterative form of the above constraint function which recovers an update $\Delta \mathbf{a}$ based on the current motion estimate $\mathbf{a}$ and is derived fully in Appendix A.

$$\Psi(\mathbf{x})\Delta \mathbf{a} = \{Z_t(\mathbf{x}) - Z_\tau(\mathbf{x} + \Delta \mathbf{x}(\mathbf{x}, \mathbf{a}))\} + \Delta Z(\mathbf{x}, \mathbf{a}) \qquad (8)$$

The goal is to derive an estimator for recovering the rotational and translational motion of a rigid moving scene between successive frames. This parameter estimation problem will be posed as the optimisation of an error functional.
If an error term is defined as $e(\mathbf{x}, \Delta\mathbf{a}) = \Lambda(\mathbf{x}, \mathbf{a}) - \Psi(\mathbf{x})\Delta\mathbf{a}$ where $\Lambda(\mathbf{x}, \mathbf{a}) = Z_t(\mathbf{x}) - Z_\tau(\mathbf{x} + \Delta\mathbf{x}(\mathbf{x}, \mathbf{a})) + \Delta Z(\mathbf{x}, \mathbf{a})$, then combining such error terms from
multiple pixels across the depth image $p \in \mathcal{I}$ generates the following pseudo-
inverse estimator.

$$\Delta\mathbf{a} = \left[\sum_{p \in \mathcal{I}} w_E \Psi(\mathbf{x}_p)^T \Psi(\mathbf{x}_p) \right]^{-1} \sum_{p \in \mathcal{I}} w_E \Psi(\mathbf{x}_p)^T \Lambda(\mathbf{x}_p, \mathbf{a}) \tag{9}$$

4   Minimising Drift Using Anchor Frames

Simply integrating between-frame motion estimates over time will inevitably
result in *drift* - the accumulated error between true and estimated sensor pose.
To illustrate this, figure 1 compares over time the three estimated translation
components of the camera position with the ground truth for the *Freiburg 1 Room*
sequence from the publicly available RGB-D SLAM Dataset and Benchmark[15].
The error plot (Euclidean distance between estimated and ground truth position)
clearly increases over time reaching a discrepancy of over 75cm.

To minimise this drift, additional temporal constraint can be included. Specifically we introduce the concept of an *anchor frame* which is a preceding frame
which retains significant overlap with each new frame. Once the amount of overlap falls below a threshold, the last frame is promoted as the next anchor. Updates to the motion are now computed from two sources of range flow constraint

$$\Psi(\mathbf{x})\Delta\mathbf{a} = \{Z_t(\mathbf{x}) - Z_{t-1}(\mathbf{x} + \Delta\mathbf{x}(\mathbf{x}, \mathbf{a}_{t,t-1}))\} + \Delta Z(\mathbf{x}, \mathbf{a}_{t,t-1}) \tag{10}$$

$$\Psi(\mathbf{x})\Delta\mathbf{a} = \{Z_t(\mathbf{x}) - Z_{\mathcal{A}_t}(\mathbf{x} + \Delta\mathbf{x}(\mathbf{x}, \mathbf{a}_{t,\mathcal{A}_t}))\} + \Delta Z(\mathbf{x}, \mathbf{a}_{t,\mathcal{A}_t}) \tag{11}$$

where $\mathbf{a}_{t,\tau}$ refers to the motion from frame t to frame τ, and $\mathcal{A}_t$ refers to the index
of the anchor frame at time t. The initial motion estimate $\mathbf{a}_{t,\mathcal{A}_t}^{(0)}$ is computed from
the pose of the camera at time $\mathbf{a}_{1,\mathcal{A}_t}$ and the initial estimate $\mathbf{a}_{1,t}^{(0)}$ of the pose at
time t i.e. $T(\mathbf{a}_{t,\mathcal{A}_t}^{(0)}) = T(\mathbf{a}_{1,t}^{(0)})[T(\mathbf{a}_{1,\mathcal{A}_t})]^{-1}$. To exploit this additional constraint,
the estimator of equation 9 must be modified as follows

$$\Delta\mathbf{a} = \left[\sum_{\tau \in \{t-1, \mathcal{A}_t\}} \sum_{p \in \mathcal{I}} w_p \Psi(\mathbf{x}_p)^T \Psi(\mathbf{x}_p) \right]^{-1} \sum_{\tau \in \{t-1, \mathcal{A}_t\}} \sum_{p \in \mathcal{I}} w_p \Psi(\mathbf{x}_p)^T \Lambda(\mathbf{x}_p, \mathbf{a}_{t,\tau})$$

$$\tag{12}$$

Where there are loops in the sequence, it would be advantageous to select anchors
from previously seen data rather than using the last frame. Such constraint from
early frames makes a significant impact on the degree of drift. To this end, a list
of all anchor frames is maintained. When a new anchor is required, this list is
searched for the earliest anchor overlapping the current frame.

For this new estimator, Figure 2 compares the three estimated translation
components of the camera position with the ground truth for the *Freiburg 1 Room*

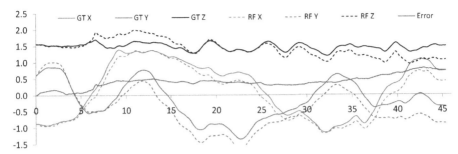

Fig. 1. Comparing Range Flow (RF) and Ground Truth (GT) positions (solid *ground truth*, dotted *estimated*)

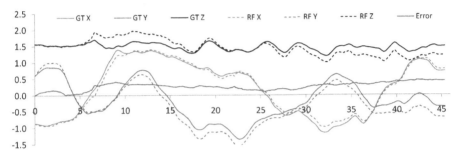

Fig. 2. Comparing Range Flow (RF) and Ground Truth (GT) positions (solid *ground truth*, dotted *estimated*)

sequence. In comparison to Figure 1, the error plot clearly shows the impact of exploiting additional temporal constraint from the anchor frames. However, a consequence of this approach, is the linear growth in storage requirements for these anchors and in the computational cost of searching through these anchors as the length of the video sequence grows.

5   Evaluation

The RGB-D Benchmark [15] is used to evaluate the above range flow based estimator. This benchmark provides Kinect depth and RGB sequences with synchronized ground truth. It also provides an evaluation tool (downloadable or online) that computes the root mean square error (RSME) between an estimated trajectory and the associated ground truth. As in the case of Endres *et al* (2012)[6], the nine Freiburg1 (FR1) sequences are used in which the Kinect sensor is moved within a typical indoor environment.

For each of the sequences, Table 1 reports the recommended RGB-D Benchmark metrics for the computed sensor trajectories. Column 3 gives some insight into the type of motion. Columns 4 and 5 list the translation and rotation RMSE measures, T-RMSE and R-RMSE respectively. These *relative pose error* metrics capture the drift in the trajectory. In column 6, the maximum value of the *absolute trajectory error* (MATE) identifies the maximum sensor positional error anywhere along the estimated trajectory (once the trajectories have been aligned[15]). Finally, column 7 reports the run time per frame.

Not surprisingly, the simple *xyz* sequence generates the most accurate results with a translation accuracy of 3.2 cm and a rotational accuracy of 2°. The maximum trajectory discrepancy is 6.55 cm. For the more challenging sequences the accuracy drops markedly. Over the seven sequences for which results were available, the average translational and rotational accuracy is 8.9 cm and 4.6° respectively. These results are very similar to those reported for the RGB-D SLAM System[6]. Nonetheless, these small drift errors can mask a more significant absolute error in sensor pose. These typically reached 40cm at some point in trajectory. For two sequences, the range flow estimator failed completely: *desk* and *floor*. In both cases, the frames and their immediate temporal neighbours were mostly occupied by a single plane resulting in a lack of motion constraint In such circumstances, the matrix in equation 9 becomes singular.

Table 1. Evaluation on TUB Freiburg 1 Dataset[15]

Sequence	Length	T-RMSE	R-RMSE	MATE	Frame time
FR1 xyz	798	3.20 cm	1.99°	6.55 cm	47.5 msec
FR1 room	1360	6.53 cm	3.16°	40.1 cm	50.2 msec
FR1 rpy	722	7.15 cm	4.89°	21.2 cm	49.1 msec
FR1 360	755	9.26 cm	6.69°	39.8 cm	49.7 msec
FR1 teddy	1418	9.73 cm	4.18°	34.1 cm	54.8 msec
FR1 desk	595	Insufficient constraint around depth frame 300			
FR1 desk2	639	12.6 cm	7.29°	41.3 cm	52.4 msec
FR1 plant	1139	13.7 cm	4.22°	43.6 cm	54.4 msec
FR1 floor	1245	Insufficient constraint from depth frame 0			

6   Discussion

A real-time *range flow*-based estimator has been developed and evaluated on the TUB RGB-D Benchmark. The estimator recovers the translation and rotation components of a sensor's motion and integrates these temporally. To minimise drift in the pose, additional temporal constraint is provided through the use of *anchor frames*. Compared to traditional SLAM approaches, range flow estimators enjoy significant advantages. No computationally expensive recovery of complex image features is required. In fact no RGB data is used at all. Motion is computed simply from a sparse grid of depth pixels and their local spatio-temporal derivatives. Using the TUB RGB-D Benchmark, pose accuracy can be judged as commensurate with SLAM approaches (as represented by the RGB-D SLAM system[6]) but available at a fraction of the computational cost. Indeed a real-time implementation is running on an old Samsung P460 Notebook. Given the low computational cost of generating reasonably accurate pose estimates, the presented approach could usefully bootstrap more computationally expensive techniques. A notable failure mode of the approach arises where there is insufficient constraint to perform the matrix inversion in the estimator e.g. where there is only a single plane in the view volume. Future work will explore the integration of complementary information such as inertial sensors or optical flow applied to the parallel RGB stream.

References

1. Anandan, P., Bergen, J.R., Hanna, K.J., Hingorani, R.: Hierarchical Model-Based Motion Estimation, pp. 1–22. Kluwer Academic Publishers, Boston (1993)
2. Baker, S., Scharstein, D., Lewis, J.P., Roth, S., Black, M.J., Szeliski, R.: A Database and Evaluation Methodology for Optical Flow. International Journal of Computer Vision 92(1), 1–31 (2011)
3. Barron, J.L., Spies, H.: The Fusion of Image and Range Flow. In: Proceedings of the 10th International Workshop on Theoretical Foundations of Computer Vision: Multi-Image Analysis, London, UK, pp. 171–189 (2001)
4. Besl, P.J., McKay, N.D.: A Method for Registration of 3-D Shapes. IEEE Transactions on Pattern Analysis and Machine Intelligence 14(2), 239–256 (1992)
5. Davison, A.J., Reid, I.D., Molton, N.D., Stasse, O.: MonoSLAM: Real-time Single Camera SLAM. IEEE Transactions Pattern Analysis Machine Intelligence 29(6), 1052–1067 (2007)
6. Endres, F., Hess, J., Engelhard, N., Sturm, J., Cremers, D., Burgard, W.: An Evaluation of the RGB-D SLAM System. In: Proc. of the IEEE Int. Conf. on Robotics and Automation (ICRA), St. Paul, MA, USA (May 2012)
7. Gottfried, J.-M., Fehr, J., Garbe, C.S.: Computing Range Flow from Multi-modal *Kinect* Data. In: Bebis, G. (ed.) ISVC 2011, Part I. LNCS, vol. 6938, pp. 758–767. Springer, Heidelberg (2011)
8. Harville, M., Rahimi, A., Darrell, T., Gordon, G., Woodfill, J.: 3D Pose Tracking with Linear Depth and Brightness Constraints. In: International Conference on Computer Vision, pp. 206–213 (1999)
9. Horn, B.K.P., Harris, J.: Rigid Body Motion from Range Image Sequences. CVGIP: Image Understanding 3(1), 1–13 (1991)
10. Newcombe, R., Izadi, S., Hilliges, O., Molyneaux, D., Kim, D., Davison, A.J., Kohli, P., Shotton, J., Hodges, S., Fitzgibbon, A.: Kinectfusion: Real-time dense surface mapping and tracking. In: IEEE International Symposium on Mixed and Augmented Reality (2011)
11. Holmes, S.A., Klein, G., Murray, D.W.: An $O(N^2)$ Square Root Unscented Kalman filter for Visual Simultaneous Localization and Mapping. IEEE Transactions Pattern Analysis Machine Intelligence 31(7), 1251–1253 (2009)
12. Sabata, B., Aggarwal, J.K.: Estimation of Motion from a Pair of Range Images: A review. CVGIP 54(3), 309–324 (1991)
13. Salvi, J., Matabosch, C., Fofi, D., Forest, J.: A Review of Recent Range Image Registration Methods with Accuracy Evaluation. Image and Vision Computing 25(5), 578–596 (2007)
14. Spies, H., Jahne, B., Barron, J.L.: Range Flow Estimation. Computer Vision and Image Understanding 85, 209–231 (2002)
15. Sturm, J., Engelhard, N., Endres, F., Burgard, W., Cremers, D.: A Benchmark for the Evaluation of RGB-D SLAM Systems. In: International Conference on Intelligent Robot Systems (October 2012)

A   An Iterative Form of the Depth Constraint

In practice estimators based on the pixel constraint of equation 7 do not recover an accurate estimate of pixel motion in a single iteration. Instead an iterative version needs to be developed which recovers an update $\Delta\mathbf{a}$ based on the current motion estimate $\mathbf{a}$. To achieve this, the depth constraint of equation 1 must be reformulated as follows

$$Z_\tau\left(\mathbf{x}+\Delta\mathbf{x}(\mathbf{x},\mathbf{a}+\Delta\mathbf{a})\right) = Z_t(\mathbf{x}) + \Delta Z(\mathbf{x},\mathbf{a}+\Delta\mathbf{a}) \tag{13}$$

The image $Z_\tau(\mathbf{x}+\Delta\mathbf{x}(\mathbf{x},\cdot))$ is a version of $Z_\tau(\mathbf{x})$ warped by the displacement field $\Delta\mathbf{x}(\mathbf{x},\cdot)$. This 2D displacement field $\Delta\mathbf{x}(\mathbf{x},\mathbf{a}+\Delta\mathbf{a})$ arises from the scene undergoing some 3D motion $\Delta\mathbf{X}(\mathbf{x},\mathbf{a}+\Delta\mathbf{a})$. As discussed in section 3, these are approximately linearly related as follows

$$\Delta\mathbf{x}(\mathbf{x},\mathbf{a}+\Delta\mathbf{a}) = P(\mathbf{x})\Delta\mathbf{X}(\mathbf{x},\mathbf{a}+\Delta\mathbf{a}) \tag{14}$$

where $P(\mathbf{x})$ is defined in equation 3. Using the small angle approximation, the 3D displacement $\Delta\mathbf{X}(\mathbf{a}+\Delta\mathbf{a})$ can be related to the current estimate $\Delta\mathbf{X}(\mathbf{a})$

$$\Delta\mathbf{X}(\mathbf{a}+\Delta\mathbf{a}) = \Delta\mathbf{X}(\mathbf{a}) + M(\mathbf{x})\Delta\mathbf{a} \tag{15}$$

where $M(\mathbf{x})$ was defined in equation 6. Thus the displacement field associated with the updated model $\mathbf{a}+\Delta\mathbf{a}$ can be related to the current estimate $\mathbf{a}$

$$\Delta\mathbf{x}(\mathbf{x},\mathbf{a}+\Delta\mathbf{a}) = \Delta\mathbf{x}(\mathbf{x},\mathbf{a}) + P(\mathbf{x})M(\mathbf{x})\Delta\mathbf{a} \tag{16}$$

From the first-order Taylors Expansion $f(\mathbf{x}+\Delta\mathbf{x}) = f(\mathbf{x})+\nabla f(\mathbf{x})\Delta\mathbf{x}$, the LHS of the depth constraint of equation 13 can now be approximated as

$$Z_\tau(\mathbf{x}+\Delta\mathbf{x}(\mathbf{x},\mathbf{a}+\Delta\mathbf{a})) = Z_\tau\left(\mathbf{x}+\Delta\mathbf{x}(\mathbf{x},\mathbf{a})\right)+\nabla Z_\tau\left(\mathbf{x}+\Delta\mathbf{x}(\mathbf{x},\mathbf{a})\right)P(\mathbf{x})M(\mathbf{x})\Delta\mathbf{a}$$

Computing the image gradients $\nabla Z_\tau\left(\mathbf{x}+\Delta\mathbf{x}(\mathbf{x},\mathbf{a})\right)$ of the warped image is problematic for two reasons. First, these gradients would require recomputing with each iteration. Second, the gradient calculation enhances the noise introduced by any interpolation process used in the warping. However as $\mathbf{a}+\Delta\mathbf{a} \to \mathbf{a}^*$, the true motion, $Z_\tau\left(\mathbf{x}+\Delta\mathbf{x}(\mathbf{x},\mathbf{a})\right) \to Z_t\left(\mathbf{x}\right)$. Therefore, we exploit the approximation $\nabla Z_\tau\left(\mathbf{x}+\Delta\mathbf{x}(\mathbf{x},\mathbf{a})\right) \approx \nabla Z_t(\mathbf{x})$. (However in the first iteration of the first frame in a sequence, where $\mathbf{a}=0$, the gradient image $\nabla Z_\tau(\mathbf{x})$ is used.) Thus the full depth constraint of equation 13 can be rewritten as

$$\nabla Z_t\left(\mathbf{x}\right)P(\mathbf{x})M(\mathbf{x})\Delta\mathbf{a} - \Delta Z(\mathbf{x},\mathbf{a}+\Delta\mathbf{a}) = \{Z_t\left(\mathbf{x}\right) - Z_\tau\left(\mathbf{x}+\Delta\mathbf{x}(\mathbf{x},\mathbf{a})\right)\}$$

The second term on the LHS of the above equation, $\Delta Z(\mathbf{x},\mathbf{a}+\Delta\mathbf{a})$, may also be expanded using equation 5 to isolate $\Delta\mathbf{a}$.

$$\Delta Z(\mathbf{x},\mathbf{a}+\Delta\mathbf{a}) = \Delta Z(\mathbf{x},\mathbf{a}) + M_3(\mathbf{x})\Delta\mathbf{a} \tag{17}$$

where M_3 is the third row of the matrix M defined in equation 6. Thus after some algebraic manipulation, the constraint of equation 13 can be defined as

$$\Psi(\mathbf{x})\Delta\mathbf{a} = \{Z_t\left(\mathbf{x}\right) - Z_\tau\left(\mathbf{x}+\Delta\mathbf{x}(\mathbf{x},\mathbf{a})\right)\} + \Delta Z(\mathbf{x},\mathbf{a}) \tag{18}$$

where the 6×1 vector $\Psi(\mathbf{x})$ is defined in equation 8.

Tracking for Quantifying Social Network of Drosophila Melanogaster

Tanmay Nath[1,3], Guangda Liu[2,4], Barbara Weyn[3], Bassem Hassan[2],
Ariane Ramaekers[2], Steve De Backer[3], and Paul Scheunders[1]

[1] Vision Lab, University of Antwerp, Belgium
{tanmay.nath,paul.scheunders}@ua.ac.be
[2] VIB, KU Leuven, Belgium
{guangda.liu,Bassem.Hassan,ariane.ramaekers}@cme.vib-kuleuven.be
[3] DCILabs, Belgium
{steve.debacker,barbara.weyn}@dcilabs.com
[4] Peira Scientific Instruments, Belgium

Abstract. We introduce a simple, high performance and fast computer vision algorithm (Flytracker) for quantifying the social network of Drosophila Melanogaster. FlyTracker is fully automated software for detecting and tracking multiple flies simultaneous using low resolution video footage. These videos were acquired using Flyworld, a dedicated imaging platform. The developed algorithm segments and tracks the flies over time. From the obtained tracks, features for each fly are derived, allowing quantitative analysis of fly behavior. These features include location, orientation and time of interaction, and allow the quantification of fly-interactions. These social interactions, when computed in a group, form a social network, from which we can infer transient social interactions. To test FlyTracker, it is compared to current state of the art software for fly tracking. Results show that FlyTracker is able to track the flies in low resolution with better accuracy and thus providing an aid in quantifying their social network.

Keywords: Machine vision, Drosophila Melanogaster, Tracking, Social Network.

1 Introduction

Behavioral scientists often do not have advanced technology to quantify the behavior of organisms. They rely on manually annotating and quantifying the organism's behavior, which is painstaking and may take several days.

Using computer vision algorithms, we can come up with solutions for automating the detection and tracking of flies and quantifying their social network. A social network is a perfect means by which to represent heterogeneous relationships in a drosophila population. The strength of network analysis is that many types of interactions (courtship, aggressive behavior, etc.) can be treated within the same conceptual framework, using the same visual and analytical tools [1].

R. Wilson et al. (Eds.): CAIP 2013, Part II, LNCS 8048, pp. 539–545, 2013.

Also, recent studies reveal that individual flies have the ability to recognize others [2] and regulate their behavior according to group membership [3], thereby regulating their social network. From this arises the need to study the social network formed by the interacting flies. It is yet to be quantified if these fly-fly interactions are stochastic or structured [4].

Machine Vision applications have been successfully used for insect's movement detection, such as houseflies [5], ants [6], bees [7] and single Drosophila in 3D environment [8]. Current state of art analysis software is Ctrax (The Caltech Multiple Fly Tracker) [9] which has been designed for automatically quantifying the individual and social behavior of the fruit fly, Drosophila Melanogaster in a closed environment.

We use our imaging platform, Flyworld, to acquire video footage of an arena containing larger numbers of flies (≥ 10). We recorded the video at 300 frames per second, in order to capture every transient behavior of unrestrained flies, which might not be possible at lower frame rates. These frames are acquired at rather low resolution and limited contrast. This resulted in Ctrax to produce spurious detection; detecting false blobs or missing real blobs. These spurious detections result in death or birth of tracks, leading to multiple tracks for a particular fly. It is impossible to construct the social network for a larger number of flies using this result. To create a social network a fixed number of detected flies at all times is required, resulting in just one track per fly. The solution to this problem, which we incorporated in the existing Ctrax algorithm, is to improve the segmentation results by utilizing the prior knowledge on the number of flies present in the chamber. Using this information we can constrain the segmentation algorithm to this number, thereby minimizing the number of spurious detections. Since the videos are recorded at low resolution, we cannot infer high level features such as wing angle, wing vibration frequency etc. Therefore, the main application of FlyTracker is to quantify the obscured social networks of Drosophila.

The rest of the paper is structured in the following manner: Section 2 describes the hardware of the imaging platform. In section 3, we will explain the entire algorithm. Section 4 discusses the experimental results and highlights the comparison with Ctrax. Section 5 discusses the application of social network construction and Section 6 summarizes the conclusion.

2   FlyWorld: Imaging Platform

Flyworld was designed to track free moving flies under certain stimulations. It is composed of several independent systems: an illumination system, a fly chamber, and various possiblities to provide stimuli. It has a high speed (300 frame per second), low resolution infrared camera to capture all movements of flies, combined with infrared backlit LEDs, to reduce light effects when monitoring flies. The videos are recorded at variable frame rate to record rapid transient motion and at the same time saving disk space when flies do not move. Unlike other studies [9], we do not clip the wings of drosophila. Clipping wings restrain fly movement and they may lose their ability to jump, thus allowing researchers to record videos at lower frame rate. But, by recording video at high frame rates, we can allow flies with unclipped wings and be able to capture and track these jumps. Flyworld is equipped with a UV light illumination as well as white light illumination, which can illuminate fly-field uniformly to simulate natural environment. There are two LCD screens on both sides of the fly chamber that can display various static images or

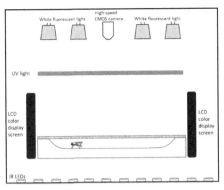

Fig. 1. FlyWorld:Imaging setup

dynamic movies to stimulate flies according to the research purpose. The fly chamber used is designed to limit all flies in a monolayer so that they can only walk on the finely cut surface, on which flies cannot feel the slope of the ground [10]. In this case, flies tend to stay less on the edge of the chamber, so that flies have more activity in the center field of the chamber to interact. If needed, a gas system can be added to introduce odor stimulation. Figure 1 shows the pictorial representation of the imaging platform.

3   Algorithm

The goal is to determine the path of each individual fly. For this, the algorithm first segments the individual flies, followed by a temporal linking step for tracking. The segmentation effectiveness is increased by using prior knowledge on the number of flies present in the chamber. This knowledge is useful for separating the touching flies. From the imaging setup described above, each fly is modeled as a single ellipsoidal dot moving in a constant background. The following subsections describe the algorithmic steps:

3.1   Background Modeling and Subtraction

The common method to segment a moving object in an image sequence is *background subtraction*. The first step in background subtraction is to model the background image. The imaging setup allows the videos to be recorded with constant background. In our setup, flies appear as dark dots on a light background. The background is modeled by selecting the frames at a reduced sampling rate (Δ) and taking the pixel wise maximum over all selected frames.

$$I_B = \max_{(t=0,\Delta,2\Delta,...,T)} I_t \qquad (1)$$

where I_t is the video frame at time t, T is the number of frames in the video and Δ is the interval between sampled frames. The flies are segmented from the background by subtracting each frame with the background image [11] and applying a threshold.

3.2   Splitting the Blobs

The splitting of the blobs is needed when flies touch each other. We can detect such an event when the number of blobs found drop below the maximum number of flies present in the chamber, n_{max}. In this case, the area of the blob will grow larger than the area of a blob containing a single fly. In such an event, we use the previous frame to estimate the maximum area of a blob containing one fly, A_{max}. All blobs in the current frame with an area larger than A_{max} are candidate blobs containing multiple flies. These blobs are then split using an *expectation-maximization algorithm* [12]. The number of mixing components, K is estimated by formulating the association problem in a graph-theoretic framework [13].

Figure 2a shows a bipartite graph with vertices at the left representing the blobs containing individual flies in the previous frame P, while vertices on the right represent the candidate blobs containing multiple flies in the current frame C. The arrows connecting the left and right vertices indicate the possibility of vertices in the previous frame to connect to vertices in the current frame.

Figure 2b shows the model for estimating the number of mixing components K. If $n_{current}$ represents the number of blobs in the current frame then the number of missing blobs is $n_{miss} = n_{max} - n_{current}$. All the vertices representing candidate blobs with multiple flies are duplicated n_{miss} times and appended to the list of vertices containing blobs in the current frame. The arrows connecting the left and the right vertices are weighted according to the distance between them. A minimum weighted matching problem is then obtained and can be solved as an assignment problem using the Hungarian algorithm.

Figure 2c shows the result of the Hungarian algorithm, where the number of connections to vertices on the right represents the corresponding mixing component K.

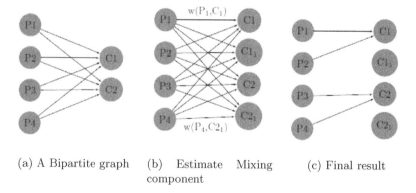

(a) A Bipartite graph   (b)   Estimate   Mixing   (c) Final result
component

Fig. 2. Algorithm for estimating the mixing component for large connected blobs. The vertices P1,..,P4 represent the individual flies in previous frame, while C1 and C2 represent the candidate blobs with multiple flies. $C1_1$, $C2_1$ are the newly appended vertices. The minimum weighted graph shows that the vertex P1 and P2 merge in C1 while P3 and P4 merge in C2,thereby the corresponding mixing component, K is 2.

3.3   Tracking

In the tracking step we link the flies found in the previous frame with the observed fly positions of the current frame [9]. The Euclidean distance between the fly positions is calculated for each pair in successive frames. This distance matrix defines the cost of assigning a found fly position to a track. This results in an assignment problem where we look for a one-to-one matching [9] of fly positions from one frame to the next frame, minimizing the assignment cost. To solve this assignment problem, we use the Hungarian algorithm.

4   Experimental Result

Videos were analyzed using FlyTracker and Ctrax[9]. Video sequences were recorded with the maximum frame rate of 300 frames per second, at a resolution of 2.4 pixel/mm. The result of the tests show that FlyTracker is able to track the flies in low resolution, and gives the correct number of flies present in the chamber which is crucial for constructing social networks. Also, other videos were acquired and analyzed with increasing number of flies and it was found that FlyTracker could track up to 49 flies without any issues. Figure 3a shows the track of one of the 10 interacting flies.

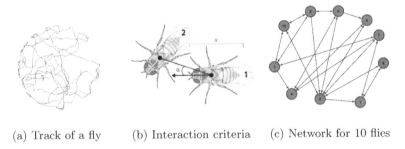

(a) Track of a fly   (b) Interaction criteria   (c) Network for 10 flies

Fig. 3. Figure showing the track of a fly, criteria of interaction and an example network constructed using FlyTracker

Table 1. Performance of FlyTracker and Ctrax

Videos	Frames analyzed	Flies Present	Tracks Detected by FlyTracker	Tracks detected by Ctrax
1	28480	10	10	31
2	31829	15	15	47
3	29105	49	49	850

5   Application

The main goal of FlyTracker is to reveal and quantify the social networks of Drosophila. After all tracks are obtained, the following features are extracted: fly position, fly orientation, distance between each fly and total time of interaction. These features are used for quantifying the transient social interactions in the group. In [4], the criteria for interaction between two flies are defined as *(i)* the angle(α) subtended by the long axis of fly 1 and the line segment connecting fly 1's center of area to that of fly 2 is less than or equal to 90 deg (see Figure 3b), *(ii)* the length of that line segment is less than or equal to two body lengths of the initiator fly *(x)*, and *(iii)* these two conditions are maintained for at least 1.5 seconds. Based on these criteria a social interaction network (SIN) is formed using the features computed from FlyTracker. SIN is evaluated based on social network analysis which measures the social relationship in terms of network theory. Figure 3c shows an example network formed by the interaction of 10 flies. Each node in the network is represented by a number, which denotes a fly. An arrow between nodes represents an interaction between two flies. Within two nodes, a node with incoming arrow represents the fly as a *interactee* [4] while a node with outgoing arrow represents the fly as a *principal interactor* [4].

6   Conclusion

In this work, we adapted an existing tracking algorithm for the purpose of building social networks. The main contribution is to improve the segmentation results by utilizing the prior information of the number of flies in the chamber and construct social network in high frame rate and low resolution imaging setups. The results of this approach are encouraging, and can be utilized to successfully quantify the social network of flies in a group. The algorithm computes the position and orientation of each individual flie, and the interacting time between flies. We plan to use these features to quantify the obscured social networks for the Drosophila Melanogaster.

Acknowledgement. The authors would like to thank the European Commission FP7-PEOPLE-2011-ITN project FliACT (289941) for funding this project.

References

1. Jens, K., David, L., Richard, J.: Animal social network:an introduction. Behavior Ecology Sociobiology 63, 967–973 (2009)
2. Yurkovic, A., Wang, O., Basu, A.C., Kravitz, E.A.: Learning and memory associated with aggression in drosophila meanogaster. Proceedings of the National Academy of Sciences 103, 17519–17524 (2006)
3. Krupp, J.J.: Social experience modifies pheromone expression and mating behavior in male drosophila melanogaster. Current Biology 18, 1373–1383 (2008)
4. Schneider, J., Dickinson, M., Levine, J.D.: Social structures depend on innate determinants and chemosensory processing in drosophila. In: Proceedings of the National Academy of Sciences (2012)
5. Wehrahahn, C., Poggio, T., Bulthoff, H.: Tracking and chasing in houseflies (Musca). Biol. Cybern. 45, 123–131 (1982)

6. Khan, Z., Balch, T., Dellaert, F.: Mcmc-based particlee filtering for tracking a variable number of interacting targets. IEEE Trans.Pattern Anal. Mach. Intell. 27, 1805–1819 (2005)
7. Veeraraghavan, A., Chellappa, R., Srinivasan, M.: Shape and behavior encoded tracking of bee dances. IEEE Trans. Pattern Anal. Mach. Intell. 30, 463–476 (2008)
8. Fry, S.N., Rohrseitz, N., Straw, A.D., Dickinson, M.H.: Trackfly:virtual reality for a behavioral system analysis in free-flying fruit flies. Journal of Neuroscience Methods 171, 110–117 (2008)
9. Branson, K., Robie, A.A., Bender, J., Perona, P., Dickinson, M.: High-throughput ethiomics in large groups of drosophila. Nature Methods 4, 3099–3104 (2009)
10. Jasper, C.S., Dickinson, M.H.: A new chamber for studying the behavior of drosophila. Plos One 36, 1389–1401 (2010)
11. Piccardi, M.: Background subtraction techniques: A review. Proceedings of the IEEE International Conference on Systems, Man and Cybernetics 4, 3099–3104 (2004)
12. Hastie, T., Tibshirani, R., Friedman, J.: The elements of statistical learning. Springer Series in Statistics, vol. 4, pp. 3099–3104. Springer, Basel (2001)
13. Padfield, D., Rittscher, J., Roysam, B.: Coupled minimum-cot flow cell tracking for high-throughput quantitative analysis. Medical Image Analysis 15, 650–668 (2011)

Virtual Top View: Towards Real-Time Agregation of Videos to Monitor Large Areas

Hagen Borstell, Saira Saleem Pathan, Michael Soffner, and Klaus Richter

Fraunhofer Institute for Factory Operation and Automation IFF
{Hagen.Borstell,Saira_Saleem.Pathan,Michael.Soffner,
klaus.richter}@iff.fraunhofer.de

Abstract. Currently, large areas are continuously monitored by camera networks, whereas an overall situation assessment within a reasonable time is a crucial requirement. In this paper, we propose our Virtual Top View (VTV) approach that provides a clear, concise and direct interpretation of on-field activities in real-time preserving the spatial relationship and, technically, employs planar homography to aggregate the Virtual Top View out of multiple, individual video streams. With an increasing number of cameras or size of the monitored area, the aggregation process slows down. Therefore, we develop acceleration methods (auto-generated warp maps) to achieve a real-time aggregation within large camera networks. Finally, we evaluate the performance and demonstrate our approach in an intra-logistics environment.

Keywords: Virtual Top View, Image Aggregation, Spatial Relationship.

1 Introduction

A monitoring of all on-field operational activities requires too much time and attention from users because projected visualizations provide too much information. In literature, various methodologies are proposed to display inputs of video streams obtained from camera networks to users in a manageable manner. We categorize these methods as: 1) sequential projections of video streams on single display interfaces, 2) projections of multiple video streams onto single video walls, and 3) projections video streams based on video analytics. The first approach contains a high volume of information which requires too much time and attention from users for monitoring on-field scene operation activities due to a lack of spatio-temporal information. The second approach provides a single visual interface to observe all possible videos linked temporally, but users need to establish spatial relationships between the images to assess the overall scene. Finally, the third approach is based on projecting the videos based on pre-defined events but users are unable to see these on-field events.

In contrast to above methodologies, in our proposed VTV approach, we aim to build a single aggregated view from multiple images by employing concepts of homography to preserve the spatial relationship of on-field components and their

R. Wilson et al. (Eds.): CAIP 2013, Part II, LNCS 8048, pp. 546–554, 2013.

operability. The proposed VTV approach is scalable in terms of number of cameras and the scene size because of our acceleration method using pre-calculated warp maps to achieve real-time functionality in larger camera networks.

The proposed VTV approach incorporates the application of homographies describing two images of the same plane in a projective space [3]. Many researchers used homographies for cross-camera object tracking, building panorama images, and image analysis. For example, Iwase and Saito [4] developed a system using homographies to transform camera-specific positions of soccer players into virtual ground image coordinates. Similarly, Park and Trivedi [7] use homographies to analyze the activities of peoples and vehicles in crowded scenes. In a similar context, Kim et al. [5] introduced Augmented Aerial Earth Maps (AEMs) containing an aerial map with additional dynamic information such as semantics of videos or videos itself. Our proposed approach is motivated by the idea of AEMs [5] with the following key contributions: (1) VTV is a spatial relationship sustaining, large projection view based on an aggregation of multiple cameras with a provision of analyzing task-specific on-field operation activities and (2) VTV is capable of integrating a large number of cameras that are distributed over a large area without compromising efficiency (real-time generation) by using warp maps. However, the VTV can easily be integrated into virtual reality environments [5], [2] as textures.

2 Proposed Approach

The VTV generation process includes three main steps: (1) registration, (2) precomposing, and (3) composing as shown in Fig. 1. In the *Registration* step, a spatial relationship between individual images and an overall view is established by incorporating the effect that any planar object in a 3D space is related to its projection by a planar homography $\mathbf{H} \in \mathbb{R}^{3\times3}$ [1]. In the *Pre-Composing* step, warp maps are created which contain pre-calculated mapping information that leads to a significant acceleration of the composing step. In the *Composing* step, VTV images are actually rendered. Registration and Pre-Composing are performed offline once, whereas the Composing process is performed online. As a result, we get an aggregated view of the overall scene such as one looking directly down onto the scene.

2.1 Characteristics of Efficient Multi Image Aggregation

Monitoring the operational activities of on-field tasks requires real-time feedback from the users and is an essential requirement particularly in large camera networks (i.e., from 6 to 16 cameras [6] or even more [5]). We consider real-time update rates as between 2 to 20 Hz, depending on the application scenario. We define the characteristics with the following three efficiency measures:

1. *Scene access efficiency*: all scene pixels (complete scene) are accessed exactly once (runtime optimal) for every source contributing information to the overall scene.

2. *Source access efficiency*: only source pixels are accessed that are actually used for composing (runtime optimal).
3. *Mapping efficiency*: planar homographies are calculated only if corresponding spatial relationships have been changed.

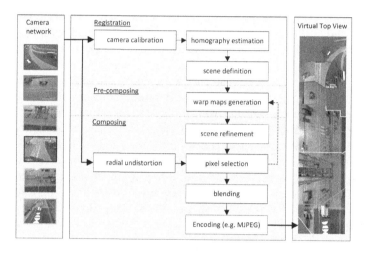

Fig. 1. VTV generation process based on multiple images from a camera network

2.2 Registration

In the registration process, we define mappings that relate source image pixels $i \in \mathcal{I}$ to scene image pixels $s \in \mathcal{S}$. Therefore, we define $\mathcal{I} = M \times N$ as a set of pixel coordinates of a source image, where $M = \{0, ..., m-1\}$ is a set of rows and $N = \{0, ..., n-1\}$ a set of columns of a source image. Furthermore, let $\mathcal{S} = P \times Q$ be a set of pixel coordinates of a scene image, where $P = \{0, ..., p-1\}$ is a set of rows and $Q = \{0, ..., q-1\}$ a set of columns of the scene image.

In image registration, an important issue is radial distortion when cameras are set up to a large field of view. In the *camera calibration*, radial distortion parameters are estimated. After that, we establish the relationship between source image pixels $i \in \mathcal{I}$ and world coordinates $w \in \mathbb{R}^2$ via homography $\mathbf{H}$. To *estimate homography*(i.e., using RANSAC algorithm), it is sufficient to use a minimum of four point correspondences [1] which are selected manually and assigned world coordinates to them. Finally, we compute scene coordinates from world coordinates via a similarity transformation:

$$s = \sigma \cdot (\mathbf{R} \cdot w) + t \tag{1}$$

where $s \in \mathcal{S}$ is a scene coordinate, $w \in \mathbb{R}^2$ is a world coordinate, $\mathbf{R} \in \mathbb{R}^{2 \times 2}$ is a 2D-rotation matrix, $t \in \mathbb{R}^2$ is a translation vector, and σ is a scaling factor. These parameters are manually determined within the *scene definition*.

2.3 Pre-composing

The Pre-Composing step refers to the question how the defined mappings should be processed to fit the stated characteristics in Section 2.1. A straightforward approach is a direct mapping $f : \mathfrak{I} \to \mathcal{S}$ which transforms source coordinates to scene coordinates and contains, among others, the homography $\mathbf{H}$ of the registration step. But, a direct mapping prevents a direct influence of scene pixels because scene coordinates are the co-domain of mapping f. As a consequence, an efficient access of scene pixels can not be ensured, e.g., pixels may be accessed multiple times (i.e., oversampling) or remain unattended (i.e., undersampling).

To overcome this shortcoming, an inverse mapping $g : \mathcal{S} \to \mathfrak{I}$ is used based on an inverse homography $\mathbf{H}^{-1}$. The inverse mapping enables a direct influence of scene coordinates and allows an efficient access by iterating through the entire scene (i.e., direct scene pixel access). Subsequently, a directly accessed scene pixels is mapped to a corresponding source pixel. As a result, the *scene access efficiency* is met in a sustainable manner. The issue with inverse mappings $g : \mathcal{S} \to \mathfrak{I}$ is that such mappings take scene pixels into account that exceed the source image boundaries ($i \notin \mathfrak{I}$). Evidently, these false mappings have a negative impact on runtime behavior. Therefore, we introduce the efficiency quality measure ε_f:

$$\varepsilon_f = |g\left(\mathcal{S}\right) \setminus \mathfrak{I}| \tag{2}$$

Since we consider camera networks, we extent our concept from one to one mapping to multi-camera mappings. Therefore, we define a set $G = \{g_0, ..., g_{c-1}\}$ of inverse mappings $g_k \in G : \mathcal{S}_k \to \mathfrak{I}_k$, where c is the number of cameras, $\mathfrak{I}_k \subseteq M_k \times N_k$ is a subset of coordinates of the k-th source image that are targeted by g_k; $\mathcal{S}_k \subseteq \mathcal{S}$ is a subset of coordinates of the scene image that are mapped by g_k. $M_k = \{0, ..., m_k - 1\}$ is a set of rows and $N_k = \{0, ..., n_k - 1\}$ a set of columns of a k-th source image. The inverse mappings may cause "false mapping" due to the violation of source image boundaries ($i_k \notin \mathfrak{I}_k$). Moreover, a set of mappings based on multiple cameras include source pixels that don't contribute to the scene, even though they are valid. Such a redundant mapping occurs when several valid source coordinates of different sources are linked to same scene coordinate. Therefore, we introduce the efficiency quality measure E_d to determine the *source access efficiency* as:

$$E_f = \sum_{k=0}^{c-1} |g_k\left(\mathcal{S}_k\right) \setminus \mathfrak{I}_k| \tag{3}$$

$$E_d = \sum_{k=0}^{c-2} \sum_{j=k+1}^{c-1} \left|\mathcal{S}_k^{-1} \cap \mathcal{S}_j^{-1}\right| \tag{4}$$

with $\mathcal{S}_k^{-1} = g_k^{-1}\left(g_k\left(\mathcal{S}_k\right) \cap \mathfrak{I}_k\right)$ and $\mathcal{S}_j^{-1} = g_j^{-1}\left(g_j\left(\mathcal{S}_j\right) \cap \mathfrak{I}_j\right)$.

While E_f represents the inefficiency caused by mappings to source locations outside the image boundaries, E_d represents the inefficiency caused by scene coordinates $s \in \mathcal{S}$ that are mapped to several source locations $i_k \in \mathfrak{I}_k$ and thus probably lead to inefficient overwriting operations. Furthermore, a problem arises because of the continuous calculation of the homographies which limits real-time ability of entire method in large camera networks. To describe this inefficiency, we consider the count of performed homographies E_m. The efficiency quality measures E_f, E_d and E_m are used to evaluate the following mapping variants which differ in their application of $g_k \in G$ to generate a complete scene $\mathcal{S}$:

- *Entire Mapping (EM)*: Iterate through $\mathcal{S}$ and apply every $g_k : \mathcal{S}_k \rightarrow \mathcal{I}_k$ at each $s \in \mathcal{S}_k$ $(\forall_k : \mathcal{S}_k = \mathcal{S})$
- *Patch Mapping (PM)*: Iterate through $\mathcal{S}$ and apply a certain $g_k : \mathcal{S}_k \rightarrow \mathcal{I}_k$ at every $s \in \mathcal{S}_k$
- *Accelerated Patch Mapping (APM)*: Iterate through $\mathcal{S}$ and assign a pre-calculated $i \in \mathcal{I}_k$ to every $s \in \mathcal{S}$

Fig. 2(left) shows the *Entire Mapping* which sequentially applies each g_k on every scene coordinate $s \in \mathcal{S}$, since $\forall_k : \mathcal{S}_k = \mathcal{S}$. As we iterate through all scene pixels and apply every mapping $g_k : \mathcal{S}_k \rightarrow \mathcal{I}_k$, this mapping type results in a maximal number of homography $E_m = p \cdot q \cdot c$. Furthermore, all pixel values of all sources are accessed and thus can be used by subsequent, sophisticated composing methods. The EM is particularly inefficient, if there is a large quantity of mapping operations that lead to pixel coordinates outside the corresponding image (E_f), because these pixels are definitely not used for composing the scene. In addition, the quality measure E_d can also become large, if views overlap significantly. The Pre-Composing step of an Entire Mapping simply provides all mappings g_k to the Composing step.

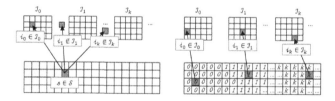

Fig. 2. Schematic illustration of the Entire Mapping (left) and Patch Mapping (right)

To increase the efficiency, we conduct a patch-wise construction of the scene named as *Patch Mapping* in Fig Fig. 2(right). Basically, we perform a patch-wise construction of a scene by assigning an appropriate inverse mapping g_k, at index k, to each scene coordinate $s \in \mathcal{S}$. Furthermore, we generate a map, i.e., these assignments are stored in a map layout and placed in memory for fast access. This approach reduces of E_f and E_d along with a pixel precise patch definition with no inefficiency arising when generating VTV sub parts $(\mathcal{S}_{sub} \subset \mathcal{S})$. In case of a run-time optimal configuration, each scene coordinate is attached to exactly one g_k (see Fig. 2) and we reach an acceleration by a factor of c compared to the Entire Mapping $(E_m = p \cdot q)$. As a consequence, the efficiency quality measures are $E_f = E_d = 0$, i.e., a more efficient mapping is achieved.

Assuming that cameras are fixed, homographies and thus mapping functions $g_k : S_k \to J_k$ are constant over time. Based on that assumption, a further acceleration is achieved by pre-measured homographies for each $s \in S$ i.e., we determine image coordinates $i_k \in J_k$ by applying g_k for each scene pixel in advance. Under optimal conditions, each scene coordinate is attached to exactly one image coordinate $i_k \in J_k$. The Pre-Composing step of a *Accelerated Patch Mapping* provides a warp map (i.e., with image coordinates as elements) to the Composing step. As a consequence, the efficiency quality measures are $E_f = E_d = E_m = 0$, i.e., the most efficient mapping is achieved.

2.4   Composing

In the composing, the VTV image is actually rendered and it comprises five steps: 1) scene refinement, 2) radial undistortion, 3) pixel selection, 4) blending and 5) encoding. In the *scene refinement*, the scene definition is adjusted according to current needs of the user. The refinement involves selecting a scene region (offset t_p, width w_p, height h_p) and step size σ_p, which allows a downscale. As a result, VTV sub parts ($S_{sub} \subset S$) can be created (Fig. 3(a)) fast and flexible.

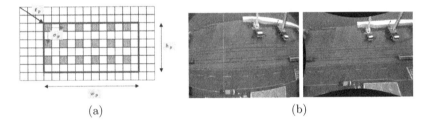

(a)   (b)

Fig. 3. a) Scene redefinition: VTV sub parts (green rectangle) defined online, b) Example of radial undistortion. (left) Radial distorted and (right) undistorted image.

Prior to pixel selection, radial distortion is corrected as shown in Fig.3(b). Afterwards, the pixel selection is conducted iteratively through the scene part with the step size σ_p and applying one of the following selection variants:

- *Entire Pixel Selection (EPS)*: Every corresponding source pixel is selected for blending.
- *Nearest Cam Pixel Selection (NCPS)*: If a scene pixel has several corresponding source pixels, then only the pixel from that source image contributes to the scene, which is closest to the scene pixel world coordinates.
- *Manual Pixel Selection (MPS)*: If a scene pixel has several corresponding source pixels, then only that pixel contributes to the scene, which was manually assigned by the user.

In the *blending*, the scene pixel values are determined based on the corresponding pixel values $\mathbf{i}_k$ of each selected $i_k \in J_k$. A brute force method is used which simply overwrites the last assigned pixel location contributing to the scene. A more sophisticated method is the pixel weighting in which each source pixel contributes to the scene with a certain weight-factor in Fig. 4. These blending methods are not optimal for VTV. On one hand there are overrides of interesting areas and on the other hand, pixel weighting leads to blurring effects that make the scene difficult to understand. However, we use fast blending methods based on NCPS and MPS selecting methods. As in these two pixel selection methods, only one pixel is selected to draw, the blending only consist of drawing this pixel. These two variants perfectly fit into the pre-composing approach, because for both variants acceleration maps can be applied. The acceleration map for the NCPS selection only has to be generated once, whereas the acceleration map for the MPS selection has to be updated every time the user adjusts the selection.

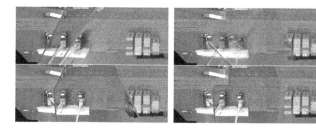

Fig. 4. Results of composing variants. Left to right: Simple overwriting (EPS), mean weighting (EPS), blending (NCPS), blending based on manual selection (MPS)

3   Experimental Results

In this section, we evaluate our approach according to the introduced efficiency measures in Section 2. The input images of our experiments are generated by a video-based monitoring system that is installed in the Hanseterminal Magdeburg, a part of Magdeburg's inland port [8]. It is equipped with 6 cameras with a resolution of 1424 x 1168 pixel that are distributed over an area of around 400 to 100 meters. Fig.5 presents inputs from the network of cameras and the corresponding generated VTV.

3.1   Efficiency Evaluation

We evaluate the efficiency of the pre-composing methods by determining the introduced efficiency measures and VTV generation time. Generally, each pre-composing method is analyzed for four scenes (i.e., denoted as scene 1 to 4) in Table 2. Scene 1 represents the configuration of the installation in Hanseterminal Magdeburg [8]. As the goal of the analysis is to show how the algorithms scales when the number of cameras are increased. The sizes of the resulting VTV output images start from 3.8M pixels based on 6 cameras up to 15.2M pixels based on 24 cameras. Our experiments are based on the following hardware setup: Intel Core I7 CPU, Q740@1.73GHz with 4GByte RAM. Currently, we use only one core for generating the VTV.

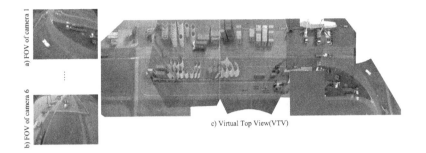

Fig. 5. Examples of input and output images of VTV patch mapping process

Table 1. Memory usage of acceleration maps

ID	Memory Usage PM (MB)	Memory Usage AMP (MB)
1	7.6	22.8
2	15.2	45.6
3	22.8	68.4
4	30.4	91.2

Table 2. Scene definitions

ID	No. of Cameras	No. of Camera pixels (M)	No. of Scene pixels (M)
1	6	9.9	3.8
2	12	19.9	7.6
3	18	29.9	11.4
4	24	39.9	15.2

Table 3. Comparison of pre-composing methods performance in different scenes

Scene ID	pre	E_m	E_f	E_d	runtime [ms]
1	EM	22,800,000	14,600,433	4,469,771	704 ± 25
1	PM	3,800,000	0	0	189 ± 24
1	APM	0	0	0	61 ± 3
2	EM	91,200,000	63,049,700	20,623,245	2,652 ± 117
2	PM	7,600,000	0	0	331 ± 21
2	APM	0	0	0	111 ± 6
3	EM	205,200,000	151,207,744	42,665,201	6,008 ± 187
3	PM	11,400,000	0	0	499 ± 28
3	APM	0	0	0	163 ± 10
4	EM	364,800,000	281,780,756	67,892,189	10,319 ± 256
4	PM	15,200,000	0	0	663 ± 35
4	APM	0	0	0	206 ± 12

As shown in Table 3, we achieve real-time composing of large scenes by applying PM and APM mapping. Only for smaller scenes (scene 1), EM mapping can be applied under real-time conditions. PM mapping accelerates the generation of the VTV depending on the size of the scene and number of the cameras. In our case we achieve an acceleration of a factor between 3 and 15. The acceleration factor further grows with the number of cameras used. Upon PM mapping, APM furthermore speeds up the generation of the VTV by a constant factor of approximately 3 (i.e., constant with respect to the number of cameras and scene size). As a result, APM mapping should be preferably used. We achieve generation times of 206ms for scenes of 15.2M, which enables a online composing rate of nearly 5 Hz of such large scenes. However, a disadvantage of the APM variant might be the higher memory requirements in Table 1. As we encode the corresponding camera and the pixel coordinates in the acceleration maps with 2 Bytes (unsigned short), we need a memory size of 2 Bytes in PM variant and of 6 Bytes in APM for every scene pixel. Within APM we currently need a continuous memory of up to 91.2 MB (scene 4), which was not a problem. The usage of PM and APM mapping limits the selection to NCPS and MPS method. However, as we focus on real-time don't use sophisticated blending methods, PM and APM fit into our VTV concept.

4   Conclusion

This paper presents the idea of VTV, an aggregated view of images obtained from the network of cameras. We have achieved the real-time processing by introducing the pre-computed warp maps allowing user to aggregate any number of cameras with large resolution. The results demonstrate the applicability of VTV and performance on various scenarios. However, the VTV does not integrate the images captured from the camera installed in tilted view.

Acknowledgments. The authors are partially funded by the Federal Ministry of Education and Research (BMBF) within the project ViERforES (No. 01IM08003C).

References

1. Agarwal, A., Jawahar, C.V., Narayanan, P.J.: A survey of planar homography estimation techniques. Technical report, Centre for Visual Information Technology International Institute of Information Technology (2005)
2. Gebert, B., Borstell, H., Nykolaychuk, M., Richter, K.: Prozessvisualisierung auf basis eines hybriden sensorsystems. In: Go-3D 2012, Computergraphik für die Praxis. Tagungsband zur Konferenz (2012)
3. Hartley, R., Zisserman, A.: Multiple View Geometry in Computer Vision, 2nd edn. Cambridge University Press (2004)
4. Iwase, S., Saito, H.: Parallel tracking of all soccer players by integrating detected positions in multiple view images. In: 17th International Conference on Pattern Recognition, pp. 751–754. IEEE Computer Society Press (2004)
5. Kim, K., Oh, S., Lee, J., Essa, I.A.: Augmenting aerial earth maps with dynamic information from videos. Virtual Reality 15(2-3), 185–200 (2011)
6. Kirch, M., Borstell, H., Poenicke, O., Richter, K.: Ortung und identifikation - konzepte und lösungen für eine sichere intralogistik. ISIS-AutoID, RFID special 1, 163–165 (2011)
7. Park, S., Trivedi, M.M.: Homography-based analysis of people and vehicle activities in crowded scenes. In: WACV 2007, pp. 51–56 (2007)
8. Richter, K., Poenicke, O.: Developing Future Logistics Applications with the Saxony-Anhalt Galileo Test Bed. In: Uckelmann, D., Scholz-Reiter, B., Rügge, I., Hong, B., Rizzi, A. (eds.) ImViReLL 2012. CCIS, vol. 282, pp. 73–80. Springer, Heidelberg (2012)

Writer Identification in Old Music Manuscripts Using Contour-Hinge Feature and Dimensionality Reduction with an Autoencoder

Masahiro Niitsuma[1], Lambert Schomaker[2],
Jean-Paul van Oosten[2], and Yo Tomita[1]

[1] School of Music and Sonic Arts, Queen's University of Belfast
mniitsuma01@qub.ac.uk
[2] Department of Articial Intelligence, University of Groningen
l.schomaker@ai.rug.nl

Abstract. Although most of the previous studies in writer identification in music scores assumed successful prior staff-line removal, this assumption does not hold when the music scores suffer from a certain level of degradation or deformation. The impact of staff-line removal on the result of writer identification in such documents is rather vague. In this study, we propose a novel writer identification method that requires no staff-line removal and no segmentation. Staff-line removal is virtually achieved without image processing, by dimensionality reduction with an autoencoder in Contour-Hinge feature space. The experimental result with a wide range of music manuscripts shows the proposed method can achieve favourable results without prior staff-line removal.

1 Introduction

Recent interest in digitisation of historical documents has doubled a number of available document in a format convenient for computational analysis. This situation has provoked a number of research in computational analysis using such historical data. Among a variety of such analyses, handwriting analysis has been of particular interest as it provides sound evidence for authentication.

One of the most significant differences between normal handwriting and musical scores is the existence of staff-lines. There have been a number of discussions on the necessity of staff-line removal in optical music recognition (OMR) research, the issue which the majority of research has considered essential. Staff-lines on scores—which are used to give meaning to certain symbols such as note-heads—prevent the segmentation of musical symbols. As text line localisation is an essential part of the OCR process, staff-line detection is one of the most important, yet difficult, aspects of OMR. The volume of research dealing with staff-line detection and removal [1–7] indicates the difficulty inherent in this process. Especially when original manuscripts have been subject to aging degradation, the result is far from satisfactory; some lines are visible and symbols can appear broken (Fig. 1).

R. Wilson et al. (Eds.): CAIP 2013, Part II, LNCS 8048, pp. 555–562, 2013.

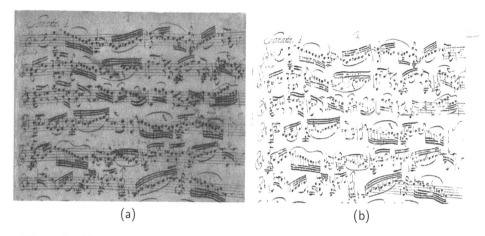

(a)   (b)

Fig. 1. Staff-line removal by Dalitz's method: (a) Original manuscript with relatively minor degradation; (b) Result image of staff-line removal obtained from (a)

In terms of writer identification, staff-lines should be regarded as background and should be removed. Most of the previous studies of writer identification in musical notation have made this assumption. In [8, 9], for instance, all the staff-lines were completely removed before feature extraction. So far, however, comparatively little empirical information has emerged on the actual effect of prior staff-line removal on the writer identification rate.

This paper has two aims: (1) To propose a method that does not require the removal of staff-lines to identify the writer of musical scores; (2) To compare writer identification rate by the presence or absence of staff-lines in more degraded and homogeneous music handwriting.

2   Methodology

2.1   Contour-Hinge Probability Distribution Function

Recently, Schomaker and Bulacu [10] proposed novel Contour-Hinge features which capture not only slant but also curvature information which is caused by the differential phase modulation for the wrist and the finger system. They reported that an accuracy of 84% has been reached using the Contour-Hinge feature for 250 writers. Moreover, the feature extraction does not involve segmentation. This makes the Contour-Hinge feature the most suitable method for writer identification from poor quality scans.

Imagine a hinge laid on the surface of the image, and place its junction on top of every contour pixel, then open the hinge and align its legs along the contour. Consider the angles ϕ_1 and ϕ_2 that the legs make with the horizontal and count the found instances in a two-dimensional array of bins indexed by ϕ_1 and ϕ_2. The final normalised histogram gives the joint probability distribution function $p(\phi_1, \phi_2)$ quantifying the chance of finding in the image two hinged contour fragments oriented at the angles ϕ_1 and ϕ_2, respectively.

2.2   Staff-Line Removal by an Autoencoder

The presence of staff-lines generate dominant angle probabilities in Hinge feature space, which are not writer invariant. Dimensionality reduction can discard those irrelevant information, thereby achieving staff-line removal not in the pixel level but in feature space. We propose the use of an autoencoder to attempt staff-line removal in feature space.

An autoencoder is a diabolo shaped neural networks, where the number of input layers and that of output layers is the same, and that of hidden layers is significantly smaller than that of input and output layers. An autoencoder minimise the difference between the input and the output of the network, whereby a low-dimensional data is produced in the narrow hidden layer. This hidden layer can be interpreted as principal component of input layers. In fact, it is well known that an autoencoder with linear neurons leads to the results strongly related to principle component analysis.

In the context of Hinge feature, the residual—obtained by subtracting the input layers from the output layers—is assumed to have no angle information stemming from general attributes such as bar lines and staff-lines. In the residual, some dimensions have lower vector-element values (suppressed) whereas other dimensions have higher values. In the context of a feature vector, which consists of a probability distribution of Hinges, this implies that the virtual presence of a Hinge with $p(\phi_1, \phi_2)$ in the image is reduced, or enhanced.

No smoothing or optimisation has been performed to present the polar plot as shown in Fig. 2, yet the predominance of (almost) horizontal angles clearly indicates that the autoencoder was able to detect the redundant information in the horizontal staff-lines. Please note that staff lines are often slightly curved and scans may be slightly rotated. Such factors introduce a natural spread around the horizontal.

Fig. 3 shows the pixels with the most prominent Hinge shape $p(\phi_1, \phi_2)$ estimated by an autoencoder from the image shown in Fig. 1 (a). The result confirms the expectation that the horizontal staff-lines originally dominated the variance in the input vector. It is understood that most of the staff-lines are suppressed by the proposed method. It should be noted that this pseudo staff-line removal is achieved not by image processing, but by the dimensionality reduction in the Contour-Hinge feature space—which encodes the horizontality. The effect is widespread and sometimes reaches beyond the staff-lines; while some pixels are left even within staff-lines. Experimentation is necessary to ensure that the Hinges (curvatures) essential for writer/scribe identification survive the suppression.

3   Experiment

There is a well-organised dataset from Fornés, Dutta, Gordo, and Lladós [11], accompanied by the staff-line removed version and writer information. However, it seems to consist mainly of modern handwriting scores, which has fewer calligraphic features than those found in early music manuscripts. Our focus is on

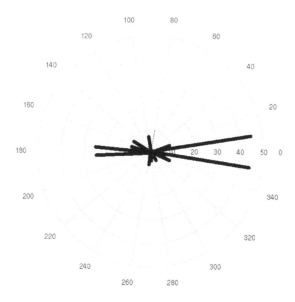

Fig. 2. Demonstration of the most suppressed Hinges; the radius shows how many times that angle (ϕ) appears in the top 3 list in the hidden layers of an autoencoder trained by Bach's autograph manuscript P967 of 6 Violin Sonatas and Partitas. It is understood that they are concentrated around 0 and 180 degrees—which are suppressed the most.

Fig. 3. Staff-line removal by an autoencoder; The 200 most suppressed dimensions are illustrated. The pixels were extracted only if they have the dominant angle probabilities detected by an autoencoder. They mostly coincide with staff-lines. The original image is shown in Fig. 1 (a).

the evaluation of the applicability to musicological problems—as the most demand for writer identification in music scores comes from musicologists whose study is concerned with determining if a certain composer is the writer of given original manuscripts.

To emulate the practical situation in musicology, it is important to use a dataset containing more degraded and homogeneous handwriting. In this study, a wide range of manuscripts were gathered from online archives. Unlike printed or modern music scores, they suffer from degradation and deformation, which prevent successful staff-line removal by image processing. It includes music manuscripts by 44 different composers from the 16th to the 20th century. The effort was made to collect as many homogeneous handwriting as possible. For instance, we included the handwriting of both Johann Sebastian Bach (JSB) and his wife Anna Magdalena Bach (AMB) (as shown in Fig.4 (a)(d)). This kind of calibration is important not only to enhance the classifiers but also to evaluate the real applicability in the domain, and yet it has not been attempted before. In order to have comparable experimental conditions, the dataset was made to contain four pages per writer (176 pages in total).

The initial images (mostly in a RGB pixel format) were binarised using Otsu's method [12]. For comparative purposes, four different versions were distinguished according to how they are processed before classification: the original dataset *Scan*, one processed by an autoencoder *Scan-R*, one processed by staff-line removal by image processing *Scan-S*, and one processed by both an autoencoder and staff-line removal by image processing *Scan-RS*. Staff-lines were removed by Dalitz's method [3] from each binarised image. 718-dimensional Hinge features were calculated and an autoencoder was applied using the top 200 hidden units.

To compare the performance of the classification method, a battery of classifiers were adopted. Classification was evaluated by 10-fold cross validation with 100 times repetition. We used the implementation included in Weka package for the following classifiers.[1] Normalised poly kernel was used as the kernel function of SVM. The number of trees was set to 100 for RF. The number of repetition for Bagging was set to 100. Euclidian distance was used as a metric for KNN and k was set to 1. These parameters were decided on the basis of the results of the preliminary experiment using the different data from those used for the experiment.

- Support Vector Machine (SVM)
- Random Forest (RF)
- Bagging
- k-Nearest Neighbour (KNN)
- Naive Bayes (NBayes)

4 Discussion

Table 1 shows the result of the experiment. For all methods, with the exception of SVM and NBayes, the residual calculation without staff-line removal (-R) performed best. It is understood that essential information for writer identification was retained by the residual calculation. KNN performed well despite its simplicity. Its performance is not far behind the result of SVM despite the significantly

---

[1] See http://www.cs.waikato.ac.nz/ml/weka for more information about Weka.

Table 1. Recognition rate for each classifier; -R denotes residual; -S denotes staff-line removal

Dataset	SVM	RF	Bagging	KNN	NBayes
Scan	**86.90**±7.16	77.16±8.03 •	68.30± 9.78 •	82.57±7.69 •	35.98±11.23 •
Scan-R	86.20±6.84	**82.22**±7.84 •	**71.88**± 8.96 •	**83.86**±7.23 •	45.57±10.77 •
Scan-S	86.06±7.45	76.71±8.71 •	63.22±10.16 •	82.11±8.96 •	31.08±10.60 •
Scan-RS	85.04±8.15	76.02±9.74 •	65.68±10.59 •	80.82±8.61 •	**48.07**±12.31 •
Average	86.05	78.04	67.27	82.34	40.17

• statistically significant degradation compared to SVM.

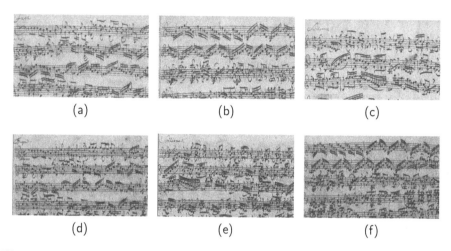

(a)　　　　　　　　(b)　　　　　　　　(c)

(d)　　　　　　　　(e)　　　　　　　　(f)

Fig. 4. Successful writer identification search and top 5 hit list: (a) query image: (AMB); (b) rank 1 (AMB, dist=116.00); (c) rank 2 (AMB, dist=116.00); (d) rank 3 (JSB, dist=176.91); (e) rank 4 (JSB, dist=243.35); (f) rank 5 (JSB, dist=260.96). The original distance is 10^4 smaller than the value shown.

shorter execution time required compared to that of SVM. This implies that the Hinge feature effectively encodes the character of each writer, and its distance directly reflects the actual distance of handwriting. On the other hand, the performance of Bagging and NBayes seems poor. This was significantly improved by an autoencoder both with and without staff-line removal. In contrast, for SVM, and KNN, the accuracy is degraded by the residual calculation when staff-line removal is attempted beforehand (-RS). This implies that SVM, and KNN managed to capture subtle features discarded by further suppression after staff-line removal. This seems to be also the reason why SVM achieved the highest accuracy rate with its high generalisation ability, using no staff-line removal and no residual calculation. As dimensionality reduction such as neural networks, does not necessarily sustain the information that can be used for classification, it seems desirable if SVM can handle the raw data without any dimensionality reduction. However, as the execution time for SVM is much longer than that of other classification methods, it seems preferable to use other classifiers such as KNN with the residual calculation from the perspective of applications.

Another advantage of the residual calculation is that we can ensure that classifiers work on writer invariant features, and not on others (e.g. staff-lines); otherwise, even if an accuracy rate is high with the current dataset, its generalisation ability may be restricted. Although more investigation is needed on the effect of staff-line removal on writer identification rate, prior staff-line removal seems to be effectively substituted by dimensionality reduction in Contour-Hinge feature space.

Fig. 4 shows a query image and top five images with the five smallest distance with the query image where the Manhattan distance is used as metrics. Homogeneous handwriting is found throughout all the images. It is notable that the distance between (a) and (b) is smaller than that between (a) and (d). Because (d) is the copy of (a) by AMB and musical content of (d) is identical to that of (a). This shows the stability of the Hinge feature within the writer's work.

5   Conclusion

Results of this study indicate that writer identification accuracy can be achieved more effectively by using Contour-Hinge feature with an autoencoder than by that with prior staff-line removal. This corresponds with the fact that humans can identify writers by investigating musical scores even with staff-lines. The proposed method is powerful and extensive, especially in the case of degraded musical scores, requiring no staff-line removal and no segmentation. Moreover, it has the advantage of avoiding subjective influence caused by manual measurement or any these human intervention, thereby improving reproducibility.

The same validation should be done using larger dataset containing a wide variety of music handwriting to investigate the degree to which these results generalise. In particular, more realistic dataset reflects the reality of application domains should be considered. It is hoped that the result of this study may accelerate the "deeper" analysis of historical documents to the extent domain experts could be benefited.

References

1. Dutta, A., Pal, U., Fornés, A., Lladós, J.: An Efficient Staff Removal Approach from Printed Musical Documents. In: Proceedings of 20th International Conference on Pattern Recognition, pp. 1965–1968. IEEE (August 2010)
2. dos Cardoso, J.S., Capela, A., Rebelo, A., Guedes, C., da Costa, J.P.: Staff detection with stable paths. IEEE Transactions on Pattern Analysis and Machine Intelligence 31(6), 1134–1139 (2009)
3. Dalitz, C., Droettboom, M., Pranzas, B., Fujinaga, I.: A comparative study of staff removal algorithms. IEEE Transactions on Pattern Analysis and Machine Intelligence 30(5), 753–766 (2008)
4. Rebelo, A., Capela, A., da Costa, J., Guedes, C., Carrapatoso, E., Cardoso, J.: A Shortest Path Approach for Staff Line Detection. In: Proceedings of AXMEDIS 2007, Third International Conference on Automated Production of Cross Media Content for Multi-Channel Distribution, pp. 79–85 (2007)

5. Rossant, F., Bloch, I.: Robust and adaptive omr system including fuzzy modeling, fusion of musical rules, and possible error detection. EURASIP Journal on Applied Signal Processing 2007(1), 160 (2007)
6. Fornés, A., Lladós, J., Sánchez, G.: Primitive segmentation in old handwritten music scores. In: Liu, W., Lladós, J. (eds.) GREC 2005. LNCS, vol. 3926, pp. 279–290. Springer, Heidelberg (2006)
7. Fujinaga, I.: Staff detection and removal. In Visual Perception of Music Notation: On-Line and Off-Line Recognition. In: George, S.E. (ed.) Visual Perception of Music Notation, pp. 1–39. IGI Publishing (2004)
8. Fornés, A., Lladós, J.: A symbol-dependent writer identification approach in old handwritten music scores. In: Proceedings of 12th International Conference on Frontiers in Handwriting Recognition, pp. 634–639. IEEE Comput. Soc. (November 2010)
9. Fornés, A., Lladós, J., Sánchez, G., Bunke, H.: On the use of textural features for writer identification in old handwritten music scores. In: Proceedings of 10th International Conference on Document Analysis and Recognition, pp. 996–1000. IEEE (2009)
10. Schomaker, L., Bulacu, M.: Automatic writer identification using connected-component contours and edge-based features of uppercase Western script. IEEE Transactions on Pattern Analysis and Machine Intelligence 26(6), 787–798 (2004)
11. Fornés, A., Dutta, A., Gordo, A., Lladós, J.: The ICDAR 2011 music scores competition: staff removal and writer identification. In: Proceedings of 2011 International Conference on Document Analysis and Recognition, pp. 1511–1515. IEEE (September 2011)
12. Otsu, N.: A threshold selection method from gray-level histograms. IEEE Transactions on Systems, Man, and Cybernetics 11(1), 285–296 (1975)

Human Action Recognition Using Temporal Segmentation and Accordion Representation

Manel Sekma, Mahmoud Mejdoub, and Chokri Ben Amar

REGIM: Research Group on Intelligent Machines Engineering
National School of Sfax (ENIS), 3038 Sfax, Tunisia
{manel_sekma,mah.mejdoub,chokri.benamar}@ieee.org

Abstract. In this paper, we propose a novel motion descriptor Seg-SIFT-ACC for human action recognition. The proposed descriptor is based both on the accordion representation of the video and its temporal segmentation into elementary motion segments. The accordion representation aims to put in space adjacency the columns of the video frames having a high temporal correlation. For complex videos containing many different elementary actions, the accordion representation may put in spatial adjacency temporally correlated pixels that belong to different elementary actions. To surmount this problem, we divide the video into elementary motions segments and we apply the accordion representation on each one separately.

Keywords: Human Action Recognition, Accordion Image, Motion Segment, Motion Descriptor.

1 Introduction

Recognizing human actions in realistic uncontrolled video is an important and challenging topic in computer vision. However, in recent years, many different space-time feature detectors (Harris3D [1], Cuboids [2] and Hessian [3]) and descriptors (HOG (Histogram of Oriented Gradients)/HOF (Histogram of Optical Flow) [4], Cuboids [2] and Extended SURF [3]) have been proposed in the state-of-the art. Feature detectors usually select the most salient Spatio-Temporal locations. Feature descriptors detect shape and motion information in the neighborhoods of selected points using usually spatial and temporal image gradients as well as optical flow. The motion descriptors are well suited to describe the human actions [5]. HOF descriptors characterize local motions. They are computed by dividing the space time neigborhood of the Harris3D interest points into small space-time regions and accumulating a local 1-D histogram of optic flow over the pixels of each sub-region. Dalal et al.[6] proposed the motion boundary histograms (MBH) descriptor for human detection. The MBH descriptor describes the relative motion between pixels by computing the gradient of the optical flow. In [5], MBH is used as motion descriptor for dense trajectories.

Recently there was a growing trend of using temporal video segmentation as preprocessing for action recognition [7,8]. It was hoped that segmentation

R. Wilson et al. (Eds.): CAIP 2013, Part II, LNCS 8048, pp. 563–570, 2013.

methods could partition videos into coherent constituent parts, and recognition could then be simply carried out based on the obtained segments. Carlos and al [7] propose a modelling temporal structure of decomposable motion segments for activity classification. They use a discriminative model that encodes a temporal decomposition of video sequences, and appearance models for each motion segment. In [8] Qiang and Gang propose a new representation of local spatio-temporal cuboids based on atomic actions that represent the basic units of human actions.

In our previous work [9], we presented a motion descriptor based on the accordion representation of the video frames. The descriptor was computed around moving points extracted with the KLT tracker. Experiments were carried out on the Weizman dataset in which each video contains only one simple action. The accordion representation transforms the video in an image that allows to put pixels which have a temporal adjacency in spatial neighbourhood. But for complex videos containing many different elementary actions, the accordion representation risk to put in spatial adjacency temporally adjacent pixels that belong to two semantically different motion segments. To surmount this problem, we propose in this work to split the video into elementary motion segments using the EHD [10,11] histogram comparison between successive frames in the video. Afterwards, the accordion representation is applied separately on each elementary motion segment. To describe the motion information, Harris3D interest points are detected on the frames of the motion segment and projected onto the image accordion relative to this segment. After that, SIFT [12] descriptor is computed around the projected Harris3D interest point. Experiments are carried out into two action recognitions datasets (hollywood2 and Olympic sports) formed by complex videos that contain different elementary actions. This paper is organized as follows: in Section 2 an overall description of the proposed motion descriptor is given. The experimental validation and results are given in section 3 and section 4. Finally, concluding remarks are presented.

2   Description of the Proposed Motion Descriptor

The graphical description of our motion descriptor (Seg-SIFT-ACC) computation is illustrated by Figure 1. Firstly, we decompose the video sequence into motion segments. After that, we create an Accordion image for every motion segment. For each motion segment, we proceed by the detection of Harris3D interest points in the video frames. Harris 3D interest points detected on a motion segment are projected onto the I_ACC relative to this motion segment. Then, for each I_ACC, we compute SIFT descriptors around Harris 3D interest points. Afterwards, we employ the bag-of-features model [13,14,15,16] on the Seg-SIFT-ACC descriptors in order to obtain a histogram of visual word occurrences for each video sequence. For classification, we use the supervised learning algorithm SVM (Support Vector Machines) [17]. The Accordion representation is presented in section 2.1. The temporal segmentation method is described in section 2.2. In section 2.3, we present the computation steps of the proposed motion descriptor.

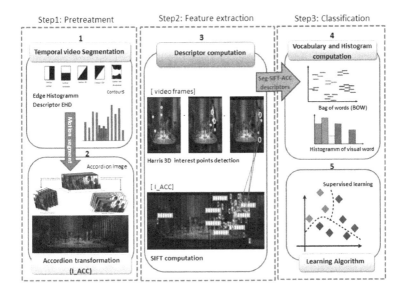

Fig. 1. Description of the proposed framework

2.1 Accordion Representation

The accordion representation [9] aims to put in spatial adjacency the pixels having a high temporal correlation. It is built by carrying out the temporal decomposition of the signal video. In a first stage, the video is transformed into temporal frames (Figure 2a). Each one represents a 2D image that collects the video pixels having the same column rank in all video frames. In a second stage (Figure 2b), the temporal frames are successively projected onto a plane called the Accodrion Image (I_ACC) througout this work. Hence, Accordion transformation tends to transform temporal correlation in the original video source into a spatial correlation in the resulting 2D image (I_ACC). The dimension($H\_acc \times W\_acc$) of I_ACC is:

$$\begin{pmatrix} H\_acc = & H \\ W\_acc = W * NbF \end{pmatrix} \tag{1}$$

where H_acc (height) and W_acc (width) are the frame sizes; NbF is the number of video frames. Each point position (x, y) on every video frame i is projected onto the I_ACC using the Equation 2 that calculates the I_ACC coordinates (x_ACC, y_ACC) of the projected point. (x_ACC, y_ACC) is obtained such as x_ACC is equal to x and y_ACC is equal to the position given to the frame column y in the I_ACC.

$$Projection : \begin{vmatrix} video & \to & \text{I\_ACC} \\ (x, y, i) & \mapsto & (x\_ACC = x, y\_ACC = i + NbF * (y - 1)) \end{vmatrix} \tag{2}$$

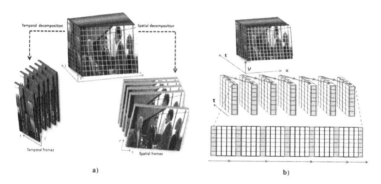

a)   b)

Fig. 2. The method of accordion representation: a) Video decomposition b) Video transformation into an Accordion image

2.2   Temporal Segmentaion

Video Segmentation Method. For complex videos containing different elementary actions, the accordion representation risk to put in spatial adjacency temporal adjacent columns that belongs to two adjacent elementary actions. To surmount this problem, we segmented the video into elementary segments. Then, an I_ACC is created for each segment separately (Figure 3). To segment the video, we compute the difference between the histogram of successive frames [18]. If the distance is above a threshold T, a cut is declared. This cut specifies start and end frames of actions in the video sequence (Figure 3). To compute the histogram, we use the Edge Histogram Descriptor (EHD) [10,11] since it can be efficiently utilized for image matching. The EHD descriptor represents the local edge distribution in the image.

As described in section 2.1, the size of the I_ACC is given by $W\_ACC = NbF \times W$, the I_ACC construction needs a high memory consumption especialley for large videos. Splitting the video into elementary units also provides a memory usage reduction.

2.3   Descriptor Computation

The Seg-SIFT-ACC descriptor is based on the computation of the histogram of gradient orientations in every local patch of the I_ACC. It reflects the motion variation along the temporal axis of the video. In a first step, we transform each motion segment into an I_ACC. After that, we project the detected Harris 3D interest points into the I_ACC (Figure 3). Afterwards, we define 16×16 patches in the I_ACC on the spatial neighbourhood of the projected Harris3D interest points. To capture the motion information from the I_ACC, SIFT descriptors are computed from the 16×16 patchs. For that, every patch is sub-divided into 4×4 sub-regions. From each sub-region, an orientation histogram with 8 bins is computed, where each bin covers 45 degrees. Each sample in the sub-region is added to the histogram bin and weighted by its gradient magnitude. The 16

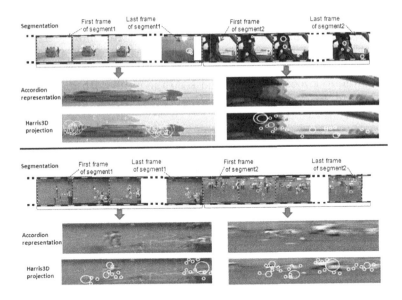

Fig. 3. Projection of the Harris3D interest points on the *I_ACC*s of the motion segments for two video examples

resulting orientation histograms are transformed into $128d$ vector. Finally, the vector is normalized to unit length to achieve the invariance against illumination changes. Thus we obtain our proposed Seg-SIFT-ACC descriptor.

3   Experimental Validation

3.1   Action Recognition Datasets

Hollywood2 Dataset: The Hollywood2 dataset [19] has been collected from 69 different Hollywood movies. There are 12 action classes. In total, there are 1707 action samples divided into a training set and a test set. The performance is evaluated by computing the average precision (AP) for each of the action classes and reporting the mean AP over all classes (mAP) as suggested in [19].

Olympic Sports Dataset: The Olumpic sport dataset [7] consists of athletes practicing different sports. There are 16 sports actions represented by a total of 783 video sequences, divided into a training set and a test set. Mean average precision over all classes is reported.

3.2   Implementation Details

The threshold T used to segment the video into motion segments is computed applying the cross validation method on the training set. We obtain the best recognition accuracy with value of T equal to 200, 120 respectively for the Hollywood2 and Olympic sports. To implement the bag of features model, we use an identical pipeline as described in [20]. For that, we cluster a subset of 100, 000 randomly selected training features with the k-means algorithm. We fix the number of visual words per descriptor to 4000 which has shown [20] to empirically give good results for a wide range of datasets and descriptors. To increase precision, we initialize k-means 8 times and keep the result with the lowest error. For classification, we use a non-linear support vector machine (SVM) with a multi-channel χ^2 kernel [17].

4   Results

In table 1, we present our result per class of Hollywood2 action and we compare our descriptor to SIFT-ACC (obtained with the same method but without segmentation) and the state-of-the-art methods. Heng and al.[5] have achieved 55.1% using the Motion Boundary Histograms (MBH) to describe the video with a dense trajectory information. Qiang and Gang in [8] propose to use a spatio-temporal cuboid based on atomic actions. where atomic actions are basic units of humain actions. They obtain mAP equal to 49.4%. Gilbert et al. propose a hierarchical approach for constructing and selecting discriminative compound features of 2D Harris corners which gives a mAP equal to 50.9%. In [21], Quoc et al present a human action recognition method that learns features from Spatio-Temporal data using independent subspace analysis. This method gives 53.3%. An extension to the standard BoW approach is presented in [22] by locally applying BoW on regions that are spatially and temporally segmented. The method gives a mAP equal to 55.7%. Our descriptor (mAP=55.9%) outperforms the approaches proposed in [8,21,23] and gives comparable results with [22,5]. A

Table 1. Comparison with the state-of-the-art: Hollywood2 dataset

Action	MBH[5]	[8]	[23]	[21]	[22]	SIFT-ACC	Seg-SIFT-ACC
AnswerPhone	-	-	40.20	-	26.30	28.1	29.9
DriveCar	-	-	75	-	86.50	87.2	88.2
Eat	-	-	51.50	-	59.20	66.8	67.1
FightPerson	-	-	77.10	-	76.20	71.9	75.4
GetOutCar	-	-	45.6	-	45.7	42.3	45.6
HandShake	-	-	28.90	-	49.7	29.7	32.9
HugPerson	-	-	49.4	-	45.40	41.8	45.8
Kiss	-	-	56.6	-	59.7	49.2	52.9
Run	-	-	47.50	-	72	75.5	77.2
SitDown	-	-	62	-	62.40	57.8	60.8
SitUp	-	-	26.80	-	27.50	33.4	35.4
StandUp	-	-	50.7	-	58.8	56.8	59.7
mAP	55.1	49.4	50.9	53.3	55.7	53.3	55.9

comparaison of our descriptor with other approaches in the state-of-the-art on the Olympic Sports dataset is shown in table 2. The HOG-HOF descriptor proposed by Laptev et al.in [4] gives a mAP equal to 62.0%. Heng and al. [5] obtain mAP equal to 71.6%. with the MBH descriptors. Carlos and al [7] propose to use a modelling temporal structure of decomposable motion segments for activity classification. This method gives 72.1%. The atomic actions approach [8] give a mAP equal to 71.0%. Our descriptor (mAP=72.5%) achieve gives a significantly better performance than [4,5,8] and it is comparable to the modelling temporal structure of decomposable motion segments reported in [7].

Table 2. Comparison with the state-of-the-art: Olympic sports dataset

Action	MBH[5]	[4]	[7]	[8]	SIFT-ACC	Seg-SIFT-ACC
mAP	71.6	62.0	72.1	71.0	70.1	72.5

Impact of the Threshold Value. We vary the threshold value and we report in table 3 the recognition accuracy on the test set. We remark that, as found by cross validation, the best threshold value used for the Hollywood2 dataset is equal to 200 and greater than the best threshold value used for the olympic sports dataset that is equal to 120. This can be explained by the fact that the gradual transitions between segments occur more frequently in Olympic sports than in Hollywood2.

Table 3. MAP of Seg-ACC-SIFT descriptor with different thresholds on the olympic sports and Hollywood2 datasets

	$T=100$	$T=120$	$T=150$	$T=200$	$T=250$	$T=350$
Olympic Sports	71.1	**72.5**	72.01	71.8	71.4	71
Hollywood2	53	54.9	55.2	**55.9**	55.1	55

5   Conclusion

In this paper, we propose a novel motion descriptor Seg-SIFT-ACC for human action recognition. Our descriptor is focused both on the accordion representation of the video and its temporal segmentation. The Accordion representation is applied on every elementary motion segment. It transforms the temporal correlation between pixels into a spatial one. The motion information is extracted by computing SIFT descriptor around Harris3D interest points projected onto the accordion representation of each motion segment. The proposed descriptor shows better and comparable performances with the state-of-the-art methods.

References

1. Laptev, I., Lindeberg, T.: Space-time interest points. In: ICCV (2003)
2. Dollar, P., Rabaud, V., Cottrell, G., Belongie, S.: Behavior recognition via sparse Spatio-Temporal features. In: VS-PETS (2005)
3. Willems, G., Tuytelaars, T., Van Gool, L.: An efficient dense and scale-invariant spatio-temporal interest point detector. In: Forsyth, D., Torr, P., Zisserman, A. (eds.) ECCV 2008, Part II. LNCS, vol. 5303, pp. 650–663. Springer, Heidelberg (2008)

4. Laptev, I., Marsza, M., Schmid, C., Rozenfeld, B.: Learning realistic human actions from movies. In: CVPR, pp. 3265–3271 (2008)
5. Heng, W., Alexander, K., Cordelia, S., Cheng-Lin, L.: Dense trajectories and motion boundary descriptors for action recognition. International Journal of Computer Vision (2013)
6. Dalal, N., Triggs, B., Schmid, C.: Human detection using oriented histograms of flow and appearance. In: Leonardis, A., Bischof, H., Pinz, A. (eds.) ECCV 2006. LNCS, vol. 3952, pp. 428–441. Springer, Heidelberg (2006)
7. Niebles, J.C., Chen, C.-W., Fei-Fei, L.: Modeling temporal structure of decomposable motion segments for activity classification. In: Daniilidis, K., Maragos, P., Paragios, N. (eds.) ECCV 2010, Part II. LNCS, vol. 6312, pp. 392–405. Springer, Heidelberg (2010)
8. Zhou, Q., Wang, G.: Atomic Action Features: A New Feature for Action Recognition. In: Fusiello, A., Murino, V., Cucchiara, R. (eds.) ECCV 2012 Ws/Demos, Part I. LNCS, vol. 7583, pp. 291–300. Springer, Heidelberg (2012)
9. Ahmed, O.B., Mejdoub, M., Amar, C.B.: SIFT Accordion: A space-time descriptor applied to human action recognition. In: ICMVIPPA 2011, Venice, Italy (2011)
10. Kwon Park, D., Seok Jeon, Y., Sun Won, C.: Efficient use of local edge histogram descriptor. ACM Multimedia Conference-MM, 51–54 (2000)
11. Sekma, M., Ben Abdelali, A., Mtibaa, A.: Application d'un descripteur MPEG7 de texture pour la segmentation temporelle de la vidéo. Sciences of Electronics of Information and Telecommunications (2012)
12. Mejdoub, M., Fonteles, L., BenAmar, C., Antonini, M.: Embedded lattices tree: An efficient indexing scheme for content based retrieval on image databases. Journal of Visual Communication and Image Representation 20(2), 145–156 (2009)
13. Lazebnik, S., Schmid, C., Ponce, J.: Beyond bags of features: Spatial pyramid matching for recognizing natural scene categories. In: Proc. of CVPR (2006)
14. Mejdoub, M., Ben Amar, C.: Classification improvement of local feature vectors over the KNN algorithm. Multimedia Tools Appl. 64(1), 197–218 (2013)
15. Dammak, M., Mejdoub, M., Zaied, M., Ben Amar, C.: Feature Vector Approximation based on Wavelet Network. ICAART (1), 394–399 (2012)
16. Mejdoub, M., Fonteles, L., Ben Amar, C., Antonini, M.: Fast indexing method for image retrieval using tree-structured lattices. CBMI, pp. 365–372 (2008)
17. Chang, C., Lin, C.: LIBSVM: a library for support vector machines (2001)
18. Petersohn, C.: Temporal video segmentation. Berlin Institute of Technology, pp. 1–272 (2010) ISBN 978-3-938860-39-7
19. Marszalek, M., Laptev, I., Schmid, C.: Actions in context. In: CVPR (2009)
20. Wang, H., Ullah, M., Klaser, A., Laptev, I., Schmid, C.: Evaluation of local Spatio-Temporal features for action recognition. In: BMVC (2010)
21. Le, Q., Zou, W., Yeung, S., Ng, A.: Learning hierarchical invariant Spatio-Temporal features for action recognition with independent subspace analysis. In: Proceedings of the IEEE Conference on Computer Vision and Pattern Recognition (CVPR 2011), pp. 3361–3368 (2011)
22. Ullah, M., Parizi, S., Laptev, I.: Improving bag-of-features action recognition with non-local cues. In: Proceedings of the British Machine Vision Conference (BMVC 2010), pp. 1–11 (2010)
23. Gilbert, A., Illingworth, J., Bowden, R.: Action Recognition using Mined Hierarchical Compound Features. IEEE Transactions on Pattern Analysis and Machine Intelligence, 883–897 (2011)

Effective Diversification for Ambiguous Queries in Social Image Retrieval

Amel Ksibi, Ghada Feki, Anis Ben Ammar, and Chokri Ben Amar

REGIM: REsearch Group on Intelligent Machines,
University of Sfax, ENIS, BP W, 3038, Sfax, Tunisia
{amel.ksibi,ghada.feki,anis.benammar,chokri.benamar}@ieee.org

Abstract. Recent years have witnessed a great popularity of social photos sharing websites, which host a tremendous volume of digital images accompanied by their associated tags. Thus, extensive research efforts have been dedicated to tag-based social image search which enables users to formulate their queries using tags. However, tag queries are often ambiguous and typically short. Search results diversification approach is the common solution which aims to increase the number of satisfied users using only a single results set that cover the maximum of query aspects. However, not all queries are uniformly ambiguous and hence different diversification strategies might be suggested. In such context, we propose a new ranking process which dynamically predicts an effective trade-off between the relevance and diversity based results ranking according to the ambiguity level of a given query. Thorough experiments using 12 ambiguous queries over the NUS-WIDE dataset show the effectiveness of our approach over classical uniform diversification approaches.

Keywords: social image retrieval, ambiguity, diversity, diversity-precision trade-off.

1 Introduction

Recent years have witnessed a great popularity of social photos sharing websites, which host a tremendous volume of digital images associated with their users' generated tags. Thus, extensive research efforts have been dedicated to tag-based social image search which enables users to formulate their queries using tags. However, tag queries are often ambiguous and typically short. The ambiguity issue occurs for two reasons. In one hand, tag queries can be interpreted with several meanings other than user's expectation. In the other hand, the rich nature of the image content can be hard for users to be described using the limited expressiveness of tags. Due to such ambiguities, images search engine generally suffer from an inability to understand the context in question. To tackle this problem, an intuitive approach is to diversify search results that covers various aspects of the query. However, promoting diversity in the search results has an impact in decreasing the precision. Thus, we need to define a parameter that controls the degree of diversification. So, a key challenge is how

R. Wilson et al. (Eds.): CAIP 2013, Part II, LNCS 8048, pp. 571–578, 2013.

to define a dynamic parameter that predicts the trade-off between the relevance and diversity based ranking.

In this paper, we propose to harness the semantic and visual similarity inter-images to ensure two-view based diversity scores estimation. In addition, we define a dynamic parameter, called 'AmbIDC indicator', that quantifies the query ambiguity level. This parameter will predict the trade-off between relevance and diversity based results ranking.

This paper is organized as follow: In section 2, we explore different orientations for diversifying search results. In section 3, we describe our proposed Adaptive social image retrieval system (ASIR) which automatically controls the degree of diversification. In section 4, we discuss experimental results.

2   Query Ambiguity Challenge in Social Image Retrieval

Query ambiguity has long been recognized as a hard issue in document retrieval. A common method to handle query ambiguity is to diversify results by displaying a good variety of results covering different meanings of the query[1]. Diversifying search results can be stated as a NP-Hard optimization problem [2] where the objective is to retrieve a ranking of documents R(q) with maximum relevance with respect to a given query q and minimum redundancy with respect to its coverage of all possible aspects underlying q.

In literature, various post-processing techniques have been proposed to deal with diversity challenge. These techniques can be categorized in two classes: search results clustering (SRC) and search results diversification(SRD). While SRC aims to gather similar results in the same cluster, SRD considers the pairwise similarity inter-documents to iteratively select the document that is not only relevant to the query but also dissimilar to the previously selected documents.

Search Results Clustering: SRC techniques have shown promise results in promoting effective diversity ranking thanks to their discriminative power[1][3]. For instance, in [1], authors created a visually diverse ranking of the image search results, through clustering of the images based on their visual characteristics. However, such approach is inefficient for practical use since on-line visual clustering is a highly time-consuming process. As alternative, textual clustering algorithms have been applied such as in IGroup[3], an image search engine, which presents the results in semantic clusters. In Google Image Swirl[4], image search results are clustered into groups and sub-groups, based on their visual and semantic similarity, to reach results diversity.

Search Results Diversification: Most of existing SRD techniques retrieve a set of documents based on only their relevance scores, and then re-rank these documents to be diverse, based on a greedy approximation[5]. For instance, Wang [6] proposed a diverse relevance ranking (DRR) scheme for social image search by estimating the relevance scores and the semantic similarities of social images based on their tags. The ranking list was generated by a greedy ordering algorithm which optimizes average diverse precision. However, there are two limits for this approach. First, the relevance scores closely rely on semantic similarity obtained from tags which can, probably, harm the searching performance.Second, the diversity score evaluated between images neglect the visual diversity.

3 Adaptive Social Image Retrieval Process

The proposed retrieval process is detailed in this section. Given a set of N predefined concepts, we model a query q and each image in the collection by a vector containing concepts weights. We present the query q by a vector $\{c_1^q, c_2^q, .., c_N^q\}$, we denote by $D_q = \{x_1^q, x_2^q, .., x_{|D_q|}^q\}$ The set of vectors corresponding to images that are associated with the set of query concepts C_q. This collection, which is a part of the large set $D = \{x_1, x_2, .., x_{|D|}\}$ is obtained by the inverted file generation[7]. Giving an image x_i, we denote by $\{c_1^i, c_2^i, .., c_N^i\}$ its corresponding index vector containing concepts' weights using our annotation approach described in [8].

3.1 Query-Image Matching

Several measures are employed, in literature, to evaluate the similarity between the user request and a given image. In [10] , experimental studies have argued that cosine similarity performs the best for our context. Given a query vector and an image vector, the semantic similarity between the sets of concepts for query q and sets of concepts for image x_i is defined using cosine similarity measure as follow:

$$S_s(q, x_i) = \frac{\sum_{t=1}^{N} c_t^q * c_t^i}{\sqrt{\sum_{t=1}^{N} c_t^{q^2}} * \sqrt{\sum_{t=1}^{N} c_t^{i^2}}} \tag{1}$$

This semantic similarity is computed between the query concept set and each concept sets of images that belong to the sub-collection D_q relative to this query. Images are, finally, ranked according to associated relevance values.

3.2 Results Re-ranking

In this section, we describe, with additionally details, the proposed re-ranking process. Two modules are investigated:off-line module to estimate inter-images similarities and on-line module to re-rank retrieved images to be relevant and diverse.

Relevance Scores Estimation. A large proportion of initial retrieved results may not be related to the query causing noisy results. To surmount such problem, we apply a relevance re-ranking model using random walk with restart process [7] by exploring contextual correlation inter-images, assuming that visually and semantically similar images to top ranked images should be upward. For this purpose, we define a similarity measure between images x_i and x_j, by fusing both their semantic and visual similarities, called hybrid similarity, as follows:

$$S_h(x_i, x_j) = \max(S_s(x_i, x_j), S_v(x_i, x_j)) \tag{2}$$

S_s referring to semantic similarity is also estimated using cosine measure. The visual similarity S_v is calculated based on Gaussian kernel function with a radius parameter σ as follows :

$$S_v(x_i, x_j) = \exp(-\frac{\|V_i - V_j\|^2}{\sigma^2}) \tag{3}$$

where V_i and V_j are respectively the weighted bag of visual features of images x_i and x_j. The value of the parameter σ is empirically computed as the average of all the pair-wise Euclidean distances between images. We denote by W the context matrix whose element W_{ij} indicates the hybrid similarity between images x_i and x_j. Elements on the diagonal of W are null.

Implementing random walk with restart process (RWS) needs two important inputs: the importance of nodes which are the relevance scores of images and the probability transition matrix $\tilde{W}$ which is the normalized matrix of W using the normalized Lapalician graph, as follows:

$$\tilde{W} = D^{-1/2} * W * D^{-1/2} \tag{4}$$

where

$$D_{ii} = \sum_{j=1}^{|D|} \tilde{W}_{ij} \tag{5}$$

$\tilde{W}_{ij}$ indicates the probability of the transition from node i to node j. We denote by $r_k(x_i)$ the relevance score of image x_i with respect to the set of query concepts C_q at iteration k. The process of RWS is formulated as follows:

$$r_k(j) = c * \sum_{i}^{N} r_{k-1}(i) * \tilde{W}_{ij} + (1 - c) * r_0(j) \tag{6}$$

where $c \in [0, 1]$ is a weight parameter to be determined. The initial value of the relevance score vector r_0 is v containing the initial relevance scores of images. In the process of re-ranking,random walk proceeds until convergence.

Diversity Scores Estimation. Intuitively, a convinced diversity scores estimation should contain both semantic diversity and visual diversity. First, we define the semantic diversity score of the image x_i as follows:

$$D_s(x_i) = \frac{1}{rank(x_i) - 1} * \sum_{x_j > x_i} (1 - S_s(x_i, x_j)) \tag{7}$$

In fact, we consider that semantic diverse results should include at least one representative image from each query subtopic. If an image is, in average, semantically dissimilar to the other images ranked higher than it, it will have an important diversity score.

Second, to define the visual diversity score of an image, we search its minimal difference with the images appearing before it for a given query. To be diverse, an image must be visually different to all images ranked before it.

$$D_v(x_i) = \min_{x_j}(1 - \max_{x_j > x_i}(S_v(x_i, x_j))) \qquad (8)$$

These two proposed measures are the ones we adopt in our system but it is worth mentioning that we can also adopt other diversity score measures.

Finally, to balance between visual and semantic diversity values, we employ a trade-off parameter λ as follows:

$$D_f(x_i) = \lambda * D_s(x_i) + (1 - \lambda) * D_v(x_i) \qquad (9)$$

Balancing Diversity and Relevance Scores. Studying the trade-off between diversity and precision is, strongly, required in order to estimate how much diversification is beneficial. Typically, this trade-off is uniformly optimized by maximizing the average diversification performance on a set of training queries. However, not all queries are similarly ambiguous. Thus, different queries might benefit from different trade-offs since any uniform choice would be suboptimal. In such context, our contribution is to fuse relevance-based ranking and diversity-based ranking for each query unevenly according to the level of query's ambiguity. To this end, we suggest the AmbIDC indicator that quantify this level. Thus, the final ranking $r_{dr}(x_i)$ of a retrieved image x_i is generated by the following formula:

$$r_{dr}(x_i) = (1 - AmbIDC) * r(x_i) + AmbIDC * d_f(x_i) \qquad (10)$$

As such, our goal is to fulfil the diversification objective by setting AmbIDC sufficiently high to capture the broad range of query aspects, but not so high as to have a significant adverse affect on the precision. To achieve this objective, the quantification of ambiguity level is estimated proportionally to the number of obtained clusters related to the corresponding query. These clusters are captured, as a social tag disambiguation process, using Flickr.tag.GetClusters service. The more is the number of clusters, the more is the tag ambiguous, the more is the need to diversify results. Therefore, The AmbIDC indicator is estimated using the following formula:

$$AmbIDC(t) = 1 - (\frac{1}{|clusters(t)|}) \qquad (11)$$

where t is an ambiguous query tag, $|clusters(t)|$ defines the number of clusters deduced by Flickr service.

4   Experiments and Results

4.1   Experiments Setup

To validate our proposed ranking process, our experiments are conducted on the challenging real-word NUS-WIDE dataset. It is one of the largest social media datasets which contains 269,648 Flickr images accompanied by their associated tags and their visual features (500 Bag of visual words). Each image is also indexed by 81 concepts. All the images are employed as the database images for retrieval, and all the 81 concepts are used for query analysis. In addition, we select a set of 12 common ambiguous tag-queries, including Apple, Jaguar, Dove, Pear, Jordan, Eagle... For performance evaluation, we use Average diverse precision (ADP)[6], Subtopic Recall at rank n (S-Rec@n)[11] and Diversity at rank n (Div@n).

4.2 Diversity Evaluation

Trade-off between Visual Diversity and Semantic Diversity Evaluation. In this experiment, we aim to study the sensitivity of our ranking process with respect to the parameter λ. This parameter is a trade-off between visual diversity and semantic diversity. We vary λ for two ambiguous queries and we measure the coverage capability of all query aspects in the top-n results using S-Rec@n. Four values of λ are tested as illustrated in figure 1.

- $\lambda=0$: corresponds to semantic diversity (S-Div)
- $\lambda=1$: corresponds to visual diversity (V-Div)
- $\lambda=0.3$: corresponds to give more importance to the semantic diversity than the visual diversity (0.3V+0.7S)
- $\lambda=0.7$:corresponds to give more importance to the visual diversity than the semantic diversity(0.3S+0.7V)

The obtained results show that the optimal value of λ is 0.7. This reveals that the semantic diversity and the visual diversity are unequally harmonized, which confirms the influence of each modality in diversity ranking.

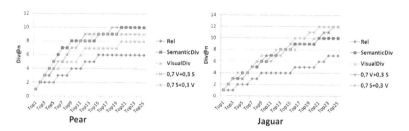

Fig. 1. Evolution curve of S-Rec@n with different values of λ for query "Pear" and "jaguar"

The Trade-off between Diversity and Relevance. In this experiment, we aim to study, mainly, whether applying adaptive trade-off for queries having different level of ambiguity in improving performance. To investigate this, we compare our approach with different existent approaches:

- relevance-based ranking[6] (RR)
- Diverse Relevance ranking [6] (DRR)
- Adaptive Diverse Relevance Ranking(ADRR)
- Flickr (relevance)

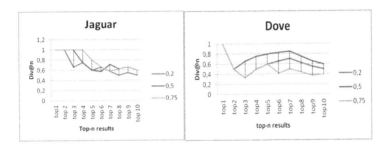

Fig. 2. Evolution curve of Div@n with different values of diversity tuning parameter for high level ambiguous queries 'Jaguar'(AmbIDC=0.75) and 'dove'(AmbIDC=0.5)

	ADRR	DRR	RR	Flickr (relevance)
ADP	0.671	0.615	0.269	0.219

Fig. 3. ADP measurements of 12 queries for different approaches

The comparison of ADP measurements between these different approaches is shown in figure 3. From this figure, a conclusion can be drawn that the proposed ranking scheme using relevance and diversity criteria outperforms those using only relevance criteria. Furthermore, the experimental results indicate that the performance of our ranking process using ambiguity indicator is superior to that using a fixed ambiguity indicator. In order to better evaluate our approach, we select two queries with different levels of ambiguity and we search for each one the best diversity tuning parameter value to balance diversity and relevance scores, then we compare it with our AmbIDC indicator value associated to each query. The obtained results are illustrated in figure 2. For a high ambiguous query such as 'Jaguar', we find that the best value of Div@n is at 0.75 which corresponds to the value of AmbIDC. In contrast, for a low ambiguous query such as 'Dove', we find that the best value of Div@n is at 0.5 which is the value of AmbIDC. As a conclusion, we can deduce the effectiveness of our approach by automatically balancing diversity and relevance ranking according to the level of ambiguity for a given query.

5 Conclusion

In this paper, we addressed the problem of result diversification in social photo retrieval and proposed a re-ranking approach that builds around the trade-off between relevance and diversity. To this end, we introduced a weighting factor, denoted AmbIDC, which regulates the contribution of relevance and diversity in the final ranking. AmbIDC was computed based on the number of clusters provided by Flickr API for a certain tag. Experimental validation was carried out on a standard data set, namely the NUSWIDE dataset. The obtained results demonstrated the effectiveness of our approach.

References

1. van Leuken, R.H., Garcia, L., Olivares, X., van Zwol, R.: Visual diversification of image search results. In: WWW 2009, pp. 341–350. ACM, New York (2009)
2. Radlinski, F., Bennett, P.N., Carterette, B., Joachims, T.: Redundancy, diversity and interdependent document relevance. SIGIR 43(2), 46–52 (2009)
3. Wang, S., Jing, F., He, J., Du, Q., Zhang, L.: Igroup: presenting web image search results in semantic clusters. In: CHI 2007, pp. 587–596. ACM, New York (2007)
4. Jing, Y., Rowley, H.A., Wang, J., Tsai, D., Rosenberg, C., Covell, M.: Google image swirl: a large-scale content-based image visualization system. In: WWW 2012, pp. 539–540. ACM (2012)
5. Carbonell, J., Goldstein, J.: The use of mmr, diversity-based reranking for reordering documents and producing summaries. In: SIGIR 1998, pp. 335–336 (1998)
6. Yang, K., Wang, M., Hua, X.-S., Zhang, H.-J.: Social image search with diverse relevance ranking. In: Boll, S., Tian, Q., Zhang, L., Zhang, Z., Chen, Y.-P.P. (eds.) MMM 2010. LNCS, vol. 5916, pp. 174–184. Springer, Heidelberg (2010)
7. Feki, G., Ksibi, A., Ammar, A.B., Amar, C.B.: Regimvid at imageclef2012: Improving diversity in personal photo ranking using fuzzy logic. In: Image CLEF 2012 (2012)
8. Ksibi, A., Ammar, A.B., Amar, C.B.: Effective concept detection using second order co-occurence flickr context similarity measure socfcs. In: CBMI, pp. 1–6 (2012)
9. Ksibi, A., Dammak, M., Ammar, A.B., Mejdoub, M., Amar, C.B.: Flickr-based semantic context to refine automatic photo annotation. In: Image Processing Theory, Tools and Applications (IPTA), pp. 377–382 (2012)
10. Feki, G., Ksibi, A., Ammar, A.B., Amar, C.B.: Improving image search effectiveness by integrating contextual information. In: CBMI (in press, 2013)
11. Zhai, C.X., Cohen, W.W., Lafferty, J.: Beyond independent relevance: methods and evaluation metrics for subtopic retrieval. In: SIGIR 2003, pp. 10–17. ACM, New York (2003)

Author Index